60-71

THE YEAR'S WORK
IN ENGLISH STUDIES—1967

The Year's Work in English Studies

VOLUME 48

1967

Edited by

GEOFFREY HARLOW, M.A., B.Litt.

and

JAMES REDMOND, M.A., B.Litt.

(Assistant Editor)

Published for

THE ENGLISH ASSOCIATION

by

JOHN MURRAY   ALBEMARLE STREET   LONDON

Printed in Great Britain by Cox and Wyman Ltd.
London, Fakenham and Reading
SBN: 7195 1936 5

Preface

For eleven years from 1958–68 Professor Dorsch, the last editor, cheerfully carried a large and increasing share of the responsibility for editing *The Year's Work in English Studies*, as well as himself contributing two of the more exacting chapters for most of the time. During that period the volume has grown in size by more than half as much again, a growth that reflects both the swelling flood of English Studies and the widening scope of the volume. No reader will be surprised to learn that pressure of other work has compelled Professor Dorsch to give up the editorship. Exactly how much this annual volume owed to his industry and care, his successor is coming increasingly, and painfully, to realize. Fortunately it is not necessary yet to say more of the debt that the English Association owes to him, since he has agreed to continue contributing the invaluable survey of general works in Chapter I.

The Association and the editor are grateful to Mr. James Redmond, whose name will already be familiar from his contributions to Chapter XIV, for accepting the position of assistant editor.

We say farewell regretfully this year to Mr. B. D. Greenslade, from whose sound scholarship the volume has benefited for a number of years, and we welcome Mr. P. Malekin in his place. We welcome also Miss Susan Brown, who has taken over the arduous task of indexing the volume.

The Year's Work does not aim at completeness. The sheer bulk of annual contributions to English studies enforces a degree of selectivity, but every effort is made to ensure that nothing of value to students of English is omitted.

We are grateful to the many authors and publishers who have sent review copies and offprints of their works, in particular those from abroad which are not available in this country (collections of essays and commemorative volumes are especially difficult to obtain). Such material should be sent to The Secretary, The English Association, 8 Cromwell Place, London, S.W.7.

C. G. H.

Abbreviations

ABC	*American Book Collector*
AKML	*Abhandlung zur Kunst-, Musik-, und Literaturwissenschaft*
AL	*American Literature*
A Ling	*Archivum Linguisticum*
AM	*Atlantic Monthly*
Ang	*Anglia*
An M	*Annuale Medievale*
ANQ	*American Notes and Queries*
AP	*Aryan Path*
AQ	*American Quarterly*
AR	*Antioch Review*
Archiv	*Archiv für das Studium der Neueren Sprachen*
Ar Q	*Arizona Quarterly*
A.R.S.	*Augustan Reprint Society*
AS	*American Speech*
A Sch	*American Scholar*
ATR	*Anglican Theological Review*
AUMLA	*Journal of Australasian Universities Modern Language Association*
AWR	*The Anglo-Welsh Review*
BA	*Books Abroad*
BAASB	*British Association for American Studies Bulletin*
BB	*Bulletin of Bibliography*
BBSIA	*Bulletin bibliographique de la Société Internationale Arthurienne*
BC	*The Book Collector*
BDEC	*Bulletin of the Department of English* (Calcutta)
BJA	*British Journal of Aesthetics*
BJRL	*Bulletin of the John Rylands Library*
B.M.	British Museum
BMQ	*British Museum Quarterly*
BN	*Burke's Newsletter*
BNYPL	*Bulletin of the New York Public Library*
BSL	*Bulletin de la Société Linguistique*
BSUF	*Ball State University Forum*
Bu R	*Bucknell Review*
BUSE	*Boston University Studies in English*
C	*Critique*
Carrell	*The Carrell Journal of the Friends of the Univ. of Miami Library*
C.B.E.L.	*Cambridge Bibliography of English Literature*
CE	*College English*
CentR	*Centennial Review*
Chau R	*Chaucer Review*
Chi R	*Chicago Review*
CJ	*Classical Journal*
CL	*Comparative Literature*
CLA	*College Language Association Journal*
CLQ	*Colby Library Quarterly*
CLS	*Comparative Literature Studies*
Col Q	*Colorado Quarterly*

ABBREVIATIONS

ComD	*Comparative Drama*
Comm	*Commonweal*
CP	*Classical Philology*
CQ	*Critical Quarterly*
CR	*Critical Review* (Melbourne)
CS	*Critical Survey*
Crit	*Critique: Studies in Modern Fiction*
Crit Q	*Critical Quarterly*
D	*Dickensian*
D.A.	*Dictionary of Americanisms*
D.A.E.	*Dictionary of American English*
DM	*The Dublin Magazine*
D.N.B.	*Dictionary of National Biography*
DR	*Dalhousie Review*
Dram S	*Drama Survey* (Minneapolis)
DS	*Dickens Studies*
DUJ	*Durham University Journal*
DVLG	*Deutsche Vierteljahrschrift für Literaturwissenschaft und Geistesgeschichte*
Ea	*Études anglaises*
EC	*Essays in Criticism*
ECS	*Eighteenth Century Studies*
EDH	*Essays by Divers Hands*
E.E.T.S.	Early English Text Society
EFT	*English Fiction in Transition*
EG	*English and Germanic Studies*
EHR	*English Historical Review*
EIC	*Essays in Criticism*
EJ	*English Journal*
ELH	*Journal of English Literary History*
ELIT	*English Literature in Transition*
ELN	*English Language Notes*
ELT	*English Language Teaching*
EM	*English Miscellany*
E.P.N.S.	English Place-Name Society
EPS	*English Philological Studies*
E & S	*Essays and Studies*
ES	*English Studies*
ESA	*English Studies in Africa*
ESQ	*Emerson Society Quarterly*
ETJ	*Educational Theatre Journal*
EWN	*Evelyn Waugh Newsletter*
Ex	*Explicator*
FH	*Frankfurte Hefte*
F Lang	*Foundations of Language*
FMLS	*Forum for Modern Language Studies*
Ga R	*Georgia Review*
HAB	*Humanities Association Bulletin*
HJ	*Hibbert Journal*
HLB	*Harvard Library Bulletin*
HLQ	*Huntington Library Quarterly*
HR	*Hudson Review*
HTR	*Harvard Theological Review*
JA	*Jahrbuch für Amerikastudien*
JAmS	*Journal of American Studies*
JEGP	*Journal of English and Germanic Philology*

ABBREVIATIONS

JGE	*Journal of General Education*
JHI	*Journal of the History of Ideas*
JJQ	*James Joyce Quarterly*
JL	*Journal of Linguistics*
JWCI	*Journal of the Warburg and Courtauld Institutes*
KR	*Kenyon Review*
KSJ	*Keats–Shelley Journal*
KSMB	*Keats–Shelley Memorial Bulletin* (Rome)
L	*Language*
Lib	*The Library*
LLM	*Les Langues Modernes*
LM	*London Magazine*
L & P	*Literature and Psychology*
LS	*Language and Speech*
MÆ	*Medium Ævum*
MCR	*Melbourne Critical Review*
MD	*Modern Drama*
M.E.D.	*Middle English Dictionary*
MFS	*Modern Fiction Studies*
M & H	*Medievalia et Humanistica*
Minn R	*Minnesota Review*
Miss Q	*Mississippi Quarterly*
MLJ	*Modern Language Journal*
MLN	*Modern Language Notes*
MLQ	*Modern Language Quarterly*
MLR	*Modern Language Review*
MNL	*Milton News Letter*
MP	*Modern Philology*
MQ	*Midwest Quarterly*
MR	*Massachusetts Review*
MS	*Mediaeval Studies*
MSE	*Massachusetts Studies in English*
N	*Neophilologus*
NCF	*Nineteenth Century Fiction*
NEQ	*New England Quarterly*
NFS	*Nottingham French Studies*
NLB	*Newberry Library Bulletin*
NM	*Neuphilologische Mitteilungen*
NMS	*Nottingham Medieval Studies*
NQ	*Notes and Queries*
NS	*Die Neueren Sprachen*
O.E.D.	*Oxford English Dictionary*
OL	*Orbis Litterarum*
PAAS	*Proceedings of the American Antiquarian Society*
PBA	*Proceedings of the British Academy*
PBSA	*Papers of the Bibliographical Society of America*
Person	*Personalist*
PLL	*Papers on Language and Literature*
PMASAL	*Papers of the Michigan Academy of Science, Arts and Letters*
PMLA	*Publications of the Modern Language Association of America*
Pol R	*Polish Review* (New York)
PP	*Philologica Pragensia*
PQ	*Philological Quarterly*
PR	*Partisan Review*
P.R.O.	Public Record Office
PULC	*Princeton University Library Chronicle*

ABBREVIATIONS

QJS	*Quarterly Journal of Speech*
QQ	*Queen's Quarterly*
QR	*Quarterly Review*
RECTR	*Restoration and 18th Century Theatre Research*
REL	*Review of English Literature* (Leeds)
Ren	*Renascence*
Ren D	*Renaissance Drama*
RenP	*Renaissance Papers*
RES	*Review of English Studies*
RI	*Rice Institute Pamphlets*
RLC	*Revue de Littérature Comparée*
RLV	*Revue des langues vivantes*
RMS	*Renaissance and Modern Studies*
RN	*Renaissance News*
RORD	*Research Opportunities in Renaissance Drama*
RP	*Renaissance Papers*
R Pol	*Review of Politics*
RQ	*Riverside Quarterly* (Saskatchewan University)
RRestDS	*Regents Restoration Drama Series*
RS	*Research Studies* (Washington State University)
R.S.L.	Royal Society of Literature
S	*Speculum*
SAB	*South Atlantic Bulletin*
SAQ	*South Atlantic Quarterly*
Sat R	*Saturday Review*
SB	*Studies in Bibliography*
SCN	*Seventeenth Century News*
SDR	*South Dakota Review*
SEL	*Studies in English Literature* (Rice University)
SELJ	*Studies in English Literature* (Japan)
SELL	*Studies in English Language and Literature*
Sew	*Sewanee Review*
Sh J	*Shakespeare Jahrbuch*
Sh Q	*Shakespeare Quarterly*
SHR	*Southern Humanities Review*
Sh S	*Shakespeare Survey*
Sh St	*Shakespeare Studies*
SIR	*Studies in Romanticism* (Boston University)
SJW	*Shakespeare–Jahrbuch* (Weimar)
SL	*Studia Linguistica*
SN	*Studia Neophilologica*
SNL	*Shakespeare Newsletter*
So Q	*Southern Quarterly*
So R	*Southern Review*
SP	*Studies in Philology*
SR	*Southern Review*
S Ren	*Studies in the Renaissance*
SSF	*Studies in Short Fiction*
SSL	*Studies in Scottish Literature*
S.T.C.	*Short Title Catalogue*
SWR	*Southwest Review*
T	*Traditio*
TCBS	*Transactions of the Cambridge Bibliographical Society*
TCF	*Twentieth Century Fiction*
TCL	*Twentieth Century Literature*
TDR	*Tulane Drama Review*

ABBREVIATIONS

ThR	*Theatre Research*
TLS	*Times Literary Supplement*
TN	*Theatre Notebook*
TP	*Terzo Programma*
TPS	*Transactions of the Philological Society*
TQ	*Texas Quarterly*
Tri-Q	*Tri-Quarterly* (Evanston, Ill.)
TS	*Theatre Survey*
TSE	*Tulane Studies in English*
TSL	*Tennessee Studies in Literature*
TSLL	*Texas Studies in Language and Literature*
UDQ	*University of Denver Quarterly*
UMSE	*University of Mississippi Studies in English*
UR	*University Review*
UTQ	*University of Toronto Quarterly*
UTSE	*University of Texas Studies in English*
UWR	*University of Windsor Review*
VN	*Victorian Newsletter*
VP	*Victorian Poetry*
VQR	*Virginia Quarterly Review*
VS	*Victorian Studies*
WAL	*Western American Literature*
WCR	*West Coast Review*
WHR	*Western Humanities Review*
WSCL	*Wisconsin Studies in Contemporary Literature*
WVB	*West Virginia Bulletin*
WWR	*Walt Whitman Review*
XUS	*Xavier University Studies*
YDS	*Transactions of the Yorkshire Dialect Society*
YR	*Yale Review*
YW	*The Year's Work in English Studies*
ZAA	*Zeitschrift für Anglistik und Amerikanistik*
ZSP	*Zeitschrift für slavische Philologie*

COLLECTIONS OF ESSAYS

Dostert Papers v. chap. II, footnote 9.
The Hidden Harmony v. chap. VII, footnote 29.
Jakobson Essays v. chap. II, footnote 1.
MacMillan Essays v. chap XI, footnote 15.
Monk Studies v. chap. XI, footnote 12.
Nordica v. chap. III, footnote 7.
Old English Poetry v. chap. III, footnote 13.
Starnes Studies v. chap. VII, footnote 26.

Contents

CONTENTS

I

Literary History and Criticism: General Works

T. S. DORSCH

1. REFERENCE WORKS

Two of the Oxford Companions have appeared in new and enlarged editions. Sir Paul Harvey's *Oxford Companion to English Literature*[1] has been revised by Dorothy Eagle. Entries relating to the twentieth century have been greatly increased in number, and old ones have been brought up to date. There has also been revision of material on earlier periods—on Old English and Shakespearian studies, for example—in the light of recent scholarship, and bibliographical notes have, where necessary, been modified.

With the help of an augmented team of contributors, Phyllis Hartnoll has thoroughly overhauled her *Oxford Companion to the Theatre*.[2] Again there are many new articles, and old entries have been brought up to date. Sixteen pages of interesting new plates have been added, and the original bibliography has been replaced by a select list of theatre books to June 1966. The new volume will be warmly welcomed by all who are interested in drama and the theatre.

First published in 1948, under the general editorship of Albert C.

Baugh, *A Literary History of England*[3] now appears in an enlarged edition which will be generally welcomed. Comparatively few changes have been made in the body of the work, but much new material has been added in the form of bibliographical supplements to the several volumes which list, and sometimes comment on, the most helpful critical studies of the last twenty years. These four solid paperbacked volumes make an extremely useful work of reference. In their 1600 pages they provide an unusually full and detailed history of English literature, finding room for numerous minor figures and movements necessarily passed over in shorter works of this nature. The eight contributors are all recognized authorities in the periods they treat, and where they can allow themselves to expand a little in their special fields of interest they augment reliable information with some admirable criticism.

English Literature: A Bibliographical

---

[1] *The Oxford Companion to English Literature*, compiled and ed. by Sir Paul Harvey, Fourth edn. revised by Dorothy Eagle. O.U.P. pp. x+961. 50s.

[2] *The Oxford Companion to the Theatre*, ed. by Phyllis Hartnoll. Third edn. revised. O.U.P. pp. xv+1088+176 plates. 84s.

[3] *A Literary History of England*, ed. by Albert C. Baugh. Second edition. New York: Appleton-Century-Crofts. Four Volumes. Vol. I: *The Middle Ages*, by Kemp Malone and Albert C. Baugh, pp. ix+1–312; Vol. II: *The Renaissance*, by Tucker Brooke and Matthias A. Shaaber, pp. x+313–696; Vol. III: *The Restoration and the Eighteenth Century*, by George Sherburn and Donald F. Bond, pp. ix+697–1108; Vol. IV: *The Nineteenth Century and After*, by Samuel C. Chew and Richard D. Altick, pp. x+1109–1605. Each vol. has bibliographical supplements and indexes.

Survey,[4] by Alex Preminger, is an extremely useful critical account of the publications which regularly produce bibliographies of English literature, whether as annual volumes like *YW* or as bibliographical numbers of journals which appear more frequently; it covers also the standard larger works such as the *Cambridge Bibliography of English Literature* and Donald F. Bond's *Reference Guide to English Studies*. The booklet is conveniently divided into a general section, followed by period sections, so that it is easy to trace bibliographies that are relevant to special fields of study.

2. COLLECTIONS OF ESSAYS

Many of the contributions to this year's *Essays and Studies*,[5] edited by Martin Holmes, are noticed in other chapters, and the volume may be treated briefly here. In 'Literature and the Transmutation of Experience' A. E. Dyson sets out to show some of the reasons why 'none of the rich emotions aroused in us by literature or drama exactly resembles the appropriate emotion in our own lives'. As he demonstrates, 'the emotions in art are always subtly transmuted, not necessarily towards greater complexity, but towards complexities of a distinctive kind'. Martin Holmes brings out some of the diverse kinds of interest to be found in Edward Hall's *Chronicle*, and some of the ways in which it influenced Shakespeare, who, he suggests, may have read it in childhood before Holinshed's better-known chronicle was published. L. G. Salingar discusses 'Farce and Fashion in *The Silent*

Woman', which he shows to be a thoroughly topical play, but turned into something more than a historical document or a passing joke by 'Jonson's intense response to the conditions of living in the present'. In 'May a Man be Caught with Faces?' Klaus Peter Steiger considers the use, in Fletcher's and Rowley's *The Maid of the Mill*, of one of the Renaissance conventions employed to express the difference between appearance and reality—'the contrast of "heart" (or, more rarely, "breast") and "face" (or "tongue" or "lip")'. J. T. Christie writes in praise of Scott's *Chronicles on the Canongate*, observing that they reveal a Scott who is 'more reflective, more tolerant, and more tender-hearted' than he is elsewhere. Edgar Jones's subject is 'Francis Adams, 1862–1893: A Forgotten Child of his Age'. Jones discusses some of Adams's poetry, but is chiefly concerned to revive interest in his novel *A Child of the Age*, which is a 'pure distillation' of the 1890s, without any of 'the often exasperating affectations' which mark so much writing of the period. J. C. Trewin, in 'Kipling and the Theatre', considers Kipling's few attempts to write plays, and reflects on the possible reasons why so dramatic a writer never succeeded as a playwright.

In a Festschrift entitled *Lebende Antike*[6] some forty scholars pay tribute to Professor Rudolf Sühnel of Heidelberg, whose main interest has long lain in classical influences on the modern European literatures, especially on English literature. Several of the papers are of relevance to English studies. In 'Sir Thomas Mores Fortuna-Verse' Hubertus Schulte Herbruggen relates More's

[4] *English Literature: A Bibliographical Survey*, by Alex Preminger. Illinois U.P. pp. 28.

[5] *Essays and Studies 1967*. N.S. Vol. XX. Collected for the English Association by Martin Holmes. John Murray. pp. v+117. 18s.

[6] *Lebende Antike: Symposion für Rudolf Sühnel*, herausgegeben von Horst Meller und Hans-Joachim Zimmermann. Berlin: Erich Schmidt Verlag. pp. 568. DM 84.

lines on Fortune to other Renaissance treatments of the theme, and dates them in 1503. Dmitrij Tschiżewskij finds some interesting parallels between passages of Shakespeare and of early Russian writings, and Robert Weimann between Shakespeare's comic techniques and those of the ancient mimes. In '"A Parodie! A Parodie!"' Thomas Gardner suggests that Daniel's masque *Tethys' Festival* of 1610 incorporated satire of Ben Jonson, with whom Daniel was carrying on a feud on both literary and personal grounds. Fritz W. Schulze brings out the influence of medieval Latin verse on Richard Brathwaite's *Barnabae Itinerarium*. In 'John Drydens "nimble spaniel": Zur Schnelligkeit der *inventio* und *imaginatio*' Karl Joseph Höltgen discusses the implications of Hobbes's and Dryden's likening the imagination to a spaniel. Ulrich Broich writes interestingly on the appearance of the *Batrachomyomachia* and the *Margites* as a 'topos' of English literary criticism from the sixteenth to the eighteenth century. Bernhard Fabian illustrates the popularity in the eighteenth century of burlesque didactic poems modelled on such classical exemplars as Virgil's *Georgics* and Horace's *Ars Poetica*. In 'Ulysses, Diomed, and Dolon: Pope and the Predecessors' William Frost offers 'a short anthology with comments' to show what Pope's *Iliad* owes, especially in Book X, to the earlier translations of Ogilby, Hobbes, and Broome. Hans Joachim Zimmermann considers the use that Pope made of Homer's simile of the flies, and discusses passages relating to flies in other English authors. In 'Der böse Adler und die gute Schlange' Helmut Viebrock shows how Shelley modified the traditional view of classical and Renaissance writers of the eagle as a noble and the serpent as an evil

creature. Erwin Wolff brings out differences in technique between Scott's *Waverley* and Thackeray's *Henry Esmond*. In 'Veteris Vestigia Flammae' Dieter Riesner shows how deeply Thomas Hardy was influenced by his classical reading. Theodor Wolpers compares Conrad with Joyce, Lawrence, and Faulkner as a myth-maker. Arno Esch studies the correspondences between Homer's *Odyssey* and Joyce's *Ulysses*, and Wolfgang Iser makes a discerning analysis of the style of the 'Oxen of the Sun' chapter in *Ulysses*. Horst Meller comments on Aldous Huxley's use of the Tithonus legend in *After Many a Summer*. Karl Heinz Göller's subject is 'King Arthur and the Grail in the Poetry of Charles Williams'; Göller commends the individuality and originality with which Williams employs the Arthurian myth as 'a poetic referent for human existence, social relations and metaphysical aspirations'. Hanz-Joachim Lang considers Thornton Wilder's treatment of the Alcestis theme in his *Alcestiad*, and Rudolf Haas writes on the use of Greek mythology in the modern novel, with special reference to John Updike's *The Centaur*. Finally, Edgar Lohner brings out the Aristotelian basis of the Chicago New Criticism.

The papers brought together from English Institute conferences of 1966, under the title *Literary Criticism and Historical Understanding*,[7] deal with the problems of applying historical understanding to the purposes of literary criticism. In the opening paper Robert Marsh lays down the aims and functions of historical interpretation—'the attempt to understand, in its own terms, something written by a particular author at a

[7] *Literary Criticism and Historical Understanding: Selected Papers from the English Institute*, ed. by Phillip Damon. Columbia U.P. pp. ix+190. $5.50. 50s.

particular time'. In 'History and Idea in 'Renaissance Criticism' Phillip Damon discusses Tasso's *Aminta* against the background of the dramatic criticism of Castelvetro and Ficino. Edward Alexander's subject is 'Roles of the Victorian Critic', with special reference to Arnold and Ruskin. Peter Elbow considers the function of irony in two speeches in *Troilus and Criseyde* (IV. 958–1082 and III. 813–40) in which Chaucer is using philosophical ideas derived from Boethius. Rudolf Gottfried examines the relationship of autobiography and art in Elizabethan literature, especially in Thomas Whythorne, George Gascoigne, Sidney, and Spenser. Francis Noel Lees shows what a historical interpretation contributes to the understanding and appreciation of one of Rossetti's sonnets. Finally, James E. Breslin sets out to demonstrate that William Carlos Williams belongs to the Whitman tradition.

The Idea of the Humanities[8] is a substantial collection of papers by R. S. Crane many of which have not been previously published, and some of which, though they have appeared in print, are no longer easily available. Parts of this volume are noticed in other chapters, and all that is required here is a general survey. Crane has a wide range of learning in English literature, and seems to be at home in many periods. In an opening section of some 150 pages, he traces, century by century, the changing definitions and evaluations of the humanities from the early Renaissance to the present day, noting, among other things, the varying strains of humanism in the sixteenth century, and discussing such matters as the later quarrel between adherents of the

ancients and of the moderns, educational theory in the eighteenth century, and the nineteenth-century rejection, and subsequent defence, of the humanities. The second half of Volume I deals with the history of ideas in the seventeenth and eighteenth centuries, and contains, in addition to some general essays, studies of such figures as John Edwards, Edmund Law, Gibbon, Adam Smith, and Burke. Volume II is more specifically devoted to literary history and criticism. Here again there are general papers, on such topics as 'History versus Criticism in the Study of Literature' and 'Critical and Historical Principles of Literary History'; there are also penetrating analyses of individual works, including *Gulliver's Travels*, *Persuasion*, and novels by Hemingway. Everywhere Crane writes concretely, with continual reference to the practice of writers; himself in complete command of his material, he never leads the reader out of his depth.

3. PARTICULAR GENRES

George R. Kernodle's *Invitation to the Theatre*[9] is much more than the 'introductory textbook' that he calls it—it is a comprehensive and at times detailed study of theatrical art which embraces all major forms of drama, whether spoken, sung, or danced. The first and most substantial section considers the various classes of drama under such headings as 'The Theatre of Realism', 'The Theatre of Romance', 'The Theatre of Exaltation', 'The Theatre of Laughter', and 'The Theatre of Disruption', analysing examples of each, with copious quotation. In the second section Kernodle takes us through all the steps in the planning and mounting

---

[8] *The Idea of the Humanities and other Essays Critical and Historical*, by R. S. Crane. Chicago U.P. Two vols.: pp. xxii + 311; viii + 332. $15. £6 15s.

[9] *Invitation to the Theatre*, by George R. Kernodle. New York: Harcourt, Brace & World. pp. viii + 677.

of a production; and in the third he discusses the techniques of the mass media, such as the cinema and television, again with detailed reference to specific examples of the genres. A final section is devoted to the methods and responsibilities of the dramatic critic. The work is lavishly illustrated with photographs and diagrams.

The World of Melodrama,[10] by Frank Rahill, is a work of considerable interest. As a dramatic form, melodrama has not received as much serious critical attention as it deserves, and Rahill's descriptive and historical study is welcome, not only as a useful contribution to theatre history, but also for what it adds to the social history of the nineteenth century. Rahill confines himself to the development of the genre in France, England, and America, tracing its origins in a number of earlier writings and movements and emphasizing the influence of 'the father of the form', the Frenchman Guilbert de Pixerécourt (1773–1844), who amalgamated his reading, gloomily moral as well as sensational, and his terrifying experiences as an aristocrat in the French Revolution, to produce the first true melodramas. Rahill is equally thorough in his treatment of the backgrounds in England and America, and in his account of the various subspecies of the form, in which he classifies the plays according to the types of hero or heroine they represent —highwaymen, the British tar, the stage Irishman, the girl who took the wrong turn, the cowboy, and the rest. Much detailed study of the melodrama remains to be done; Rahill's book has laid down many of the main lines to be followed by future workers in the field.

The Primal Curse,[11] by Honor Matthews, is a study of the part that has been played in drama, mainly English drama, by the myth of Cain and Abel. The story is first dramatized in the medieval Miracle Plays, where, for the most part, it is presented simply and vigorously as a means of teaching the Bible story. The main points of the story are a secret murder supernaturally revealed; a divinely ordained punishment which is at the same time the natural consequence of the crime; and the exile of the killer which causes him indescribable agony. The medieval drama familiarized men with the types and symbols of the story which, whether or not they were associated with the names of Cain and Abel, passed into the secular drama. They form an essential element in *Macbeth*, for example, and indeed in other plays of Shakespeare. In the seventeenth century, as belief in the Christian framework of society weakened, they reflect, in many of the tragedies of blood, a world 'in which the faith in a moral order was reduced to a faith in the destructive quality of evil'. Miss Matthews traces the myth in later periods of the drama down to the present day, when she finds it operating powerfully in the work of such playwrights as Beckett, Camus, and Pinter. She has written a perceptive book which throws light on an important dramatic theme.

Rodney Delasanta's aim, in *The Epic Voice*,[12] is to demonstrate that the epic technique of plunging *in medias res* significantly affects, not only the structure of the work, but also its method of narration. The omniscient narrator, who as a matter

[10] *The World of Melodrama*, by Frank Rahill. Pennsylvania State U.P. pp. xvii + 334. $7.50. 56s.

[11] *The Primal Curse: The Myth of Cain and Abel in the Theatre*, by Honor Matthews. Chatto & Windus. pp. 221. 30s.

[12] *The Epic Voice*, by Rodney Delasanta. The Hague: Mouton. pp. 140. Dutch Guilders 20.

B

of course would narrate events, *ab ovo*, in the order in which they occurred, gives place to the 'restricted narrator', or *nuntius*, who adds new narrative dimensions to his tale by means of oblique characterization, by exploiting the potentialities of suspense both prospectively and retrospectively, by differentiating the styles of the episodes and the main action, and by the 'foreshadowing (simply or ironically) of episodes to the main action'. As Delasanta shows, the advantages that the poet gains from the *in medias* structure are most fully and impressively exemplified in *The Odyssey*. Delasanta also analyses the revised *Arcadia, The Faerie Queene*, and *Paradise Lost* in the light of his thesis. Sidney shows remarkable skill in adapting his work to the requirements of the *in medias* strategy, but the demands of his allegory militated against Spenser's successful employment of the technique. Milton alone fully grasped and exploited its possibilities, and produced an epic that is surpassed only by the Homeric poems. Delasanta is at times rather too elaborate in his exposition, but his book adds something to our understanding of epic structures.

The 'shaping powers' referred to in the title of Rudolf Stamm's *The Shaping Powers at Work*[13] are 'the imagination and the critical faculty of the creative writers whose ways of transforming a given material, or form, or tradition' are investigated in the fifteen essays that make up the volume. Stamm covers a fairly wide range of authors. He shows, for example, how Shakespeare improved on some of Kyd's techniques, and adapted the material and effects of his sources; how Defoe transformed

Puritan literary forms; how Yeats revised one of his own poems, and how in *O.B.E.V.* he aimed at raising the poetic stature of Oscar Wilde by his careful choice of stanzas from *The Ballad of Reading Gaol*; how Bernard Shaw proposed to 'improve' *Cymbeline* by judicious cutting; how O'Neill, Eliot, and Sartre adapted the Orestes theme to their own dramatic purposes. These perceptive studies convincingly demonstrate the force of what Stamm declares to be the unifying theme of the volume, 'that transmutation in all of its many forms is a peculiarly rewarding subject for the literary student because it concentrates his attention on the texts and can yield a subtle and precise kind of evidence leading to an intimate knowledge of a writer's artistic purpose and achievement'.

G. Wilson Knight's *Poets of Action*[14] is a 'reorganization' of *The Burning Oracle*, which has long been out of print; in place of the essays on Shakespeare and Pope, Knight has included a shortened version of *Chariot of Wrath*, his wartime book on Milton as a national prophet, and his Byron Foundation lecture on Byron's dramatic prose, in this way supplementing the papers on the poetry of Milton and Byron from the original collection. Also retained from the collection are 'The Spenserian Fluidity' and 'Swift'. All these writings have been noticed in past issues of *YW*, and all that need be said is that the new combination of papers makes a better balanced, and perhaps less controversial, volume than *The Burning Oracle*.

In *Forms of Discovery*[15] Yvor

---

[13] *The Shaping Powers at Work: Fifteen Essays on Poetic Transmutation*, by Rudolf Stamm. Heidelberg: Winter. pp. 320. Paper DM 26, cloth DM 32.

[14] *Poets of Action, incorporating essays from 'The Burning Oracle'*, by G. Wilson Knight. Methuen. pp. xvii+302. 50s.

[15] *Forms of Discovery: Critical & Historical Essays on the Forms of the Short Poem in English*, by Yvor Winters. Chicago: Alan Swallow. pp. xxii+377. $8.95.

Winters brings together a number of essays, many of which have been previously published, and which as a series deal with what he believes to be 'the most important stages of our poetry considered as an art'. An opening section of 120 pages is made up of papers on 'Aspects of the Short Poem in the English Renaissance'. This is followed by a substantial essay on Charles Churchill, by sections on 'The Sentimental-Romantic Decadence of the 18th and 19th Centuries' and on turn-of-the-century poets such as Swinburne, Hardy, Bridges, Yeats, and T. Sturge Moore, and by a couple of chapters on post-Symbolist and more recent poets. The volume is, in effect, a history of the short poem in English. No more here than in his earlier volumes of criticism are Winter's larger judgements, perceptive as his detailed comments sometimes are, likely to win general acceptance. Himself a poet, he appears to find little merit in poetic methods that differ markedly from his own. There are exceptions; he approved of Fulke Greville, Charles Churchill, and a handful of other poets earlier than the twentieth century. However, he damns Shakespeare for his servility and for the general ineptitude of the Sonnets, Milton for the platitude and pomposity of his early poems, and the Romantics and Victorians for poetic deficiencies of various kinds. Only in the twentieth century, above all in America, does he find much poetry that successfully 'unifies the diverse fields of human experience and employs all the varied aspects of language'. It is a decidedly eccentric book.

Die Moderne Englische Lyrik,[16] edited by Horst Oppel, contains inter-

pretations of about thirty modern English poems, contributed by leading German scholars of English literature. The practical criticism of poetry has long been carried on more intensively in German than in English universities, and this volume as a whole exemplifies a high order of critical sensibility. Oppel himself writes on poems by R. S. Thomas, Ted Hughes, Thom Gunn, Dylan Thomas, D. H. Lawrence, Diana Witherby, Austin Clarke, and F. W. Harvey. Arno Esch and Wolfgang Iser discuss poems by Yeats and Rupert Brooke with feeling and good sense. Kurt Otten offers discerning analyses of poems by Empson and Auden, and Gerhard Müller-Schwefe writes perceptively about Hopkins's 'Spelt from Sybil's Leaves'. These are only some of the more illuminating studies in a volume which ranges widely over the field of modern verse.

From Egon Werlich comes *Poetry Analysis*,[17] another volume devoted to criticism of this kind. Werlich, however, spreads his net more widely, including, for example, sonnets by Shakespeare, Milton, and Wordsworth, and devoting only four sections to modern poems—Wilfred Owen's 'Futility', Yeats's 'Sailing to Byzantium', Eliot's 'Journey of the Magi', and Auden's 'Musée des Beaux Arts'. In an opening chapter he writes clearly and sensibly about the techniques of critical analysis, and his own interpretations show considerable insight.

The Folk-Carol of England,[18] by Douglas Brice, is chiefly concerned with folk-songs which relate to the Christmas story and the life of Christ. Brice perhaps comes as close as

---

[16] *Die Moderne Englische Lyrik: Interpretationen*, herausgegeben von Horst Oppel. Berlin: Erich Schmidt Verlag. pp. 342, DM 29.

[17] *Poetry Analysis: Great English Poems Interpreted*, by Egon Werlich. Dortmund: Verlag Lambert Lensing. pp. 238. DM 10.80.

[18] *The Folk-Carol of England*, by Douglas Brice. Herbert Jenkins. pp. xviii+174. 30s.

anyone else to a definition of the carol in his discussion of its 'extravert and uninhibited approach to the worship of God' and of its characteristic types of language and imagery, especially its picturesque references to such 'inessentials' as the beasts of the manger, the stars, the shepherds, and the angels. He also usefully differentiates the carol and related forms like the hymn and the ballad; but while the hymn is outside his province in this book, he devotes a fairly substantial chapter to ballads on the Christmas story, since they are a form of folk-poetry. Brice's book, as he is well aware, is far from being an exhaustive treatment of its subject, but it will be of interest both to folklorists and to non-specialist readers—to anyone, indeed, who is fond of carols. It is copiously illustrated with quotations and musical settings.

Also of great interest in a not unrelated field is K. M. Briggs's more considerable study, *The Fairies in Tradition and Literature*,[19] a sequel to her earlier *The Anatomy of Puck* (1959), which dealt so admirably with the fairy lore of Shakespeare and his contemporaries. In the present volume Miss Briggs opens with a historical survey of her subject, and goes on to describe the various types of being which qualify for inclusion in her study—tutelary and nature spirits, hobgoblins and imps, giants and hags and monsters, and fairy beasts and plants—enriching her descriptions, as she does throughout the book, with many anecdotes gleaned from a great variety of sources. The second section, 'Traffic with the Fairies', deals with such topics as the curiosities of fairy morality, changelings and midwives, fairy wives and lovers, and fairy encounters. Finally Miss Briggs turns

to the literary treatment of fairy lore from the eighteenth century to the present day—in the writings of, among others, Thomas Tickell, Pope, Blake, Scott, Hogg, and Yeats. It is a very lucid book, and makes enjoyable reading.

In *Approaches to the Novel*[20] John Colmer brings together the papers on the novel which were read at a seminar, 'On the Study of the Novel', in the University of Adelaide in August 1965. In the opening paper Colmer himself discusses a problem that is central to the technique of the novel—how to give an illusion of real life while at the same time giving the work the unity, pattern, and harmony that art demands. Michael J. Tolley and Rosemary Sweetapple show, with reference to *Vanity Fair* and *What Maisie Knew*, how intricate the relationship between the novelist and his story may be. Fred Langman explores the technique of multiple narration in *Wuthering Heights*, and Philip Waldron considers the effects that Jane Austen achieves in *Emma* by means of delicate nuances of style. Burwell Dodd and Robert V. Johnson offer studies of Joseph Heller's *Catch 22* and of the early novels of Evelyn Waugh to demonstrate how novelists may serve the ends of social commentary by the use of narrative techniques. Manfred Mackenzie analyses Patrick White's *The Tree of Man* in order to emphasize the importance of recognizing 'the dominant genre or mode' of a novel. Bryn Davies reminds us that the chief function of the novel is to give pleasure. And finally, in 'The Dilemma of the Contemporary Novelist', Angus Wilson considers some of the trends in modern life which militate against the art of the novelist, and the steps which some novelists have taken to solve

---

[19] *The Fairies in Tradition and Literature*, by K. M. Briggs. Routledge & Kegan Paul. pp. x+261. 42*s*.

[20] *Approaches to the Novel*, ed. by John Colmer. Oliver & Boyd. pp. xi+136. 30*s*.

their problems. The volume contains some perceptive criticism, and will encourage its readers to think about the techniques of the novel.

Like some of the contributors to Colmer's volume, Louis D. Rubin, Jr., is interested in the role of the novelist in a novel. His book, *The Teller in the Tale*,[21] is 'an attempt . . . to put the novelist back into the novel'. The reader, as he expresses it, knows that he is 'being told a story, not being given a counterfeit demonstration of real life', and the way the story is told is essential to the way in which he responds to it. It is important, therefore, to pay attention to 'the way in which the . . . authorial personality telling the story figures in the meaning of the book'. Rubin elaborates this approach by fairly detailed study of the work of Cervantes, Stendhal, Mark Twain, Henry James, Proust, Joyce, and Mauriac, touching more lightly on Herman Melville, Ellen Glasgow, Thomas Wolfe, and Robert Penn Warren. Although there is little in the way of new insights in his book, he does not make the mistake of confusing biography with literary criticism, and his studies of some of the individual novelists will help to stimulate interest in them.

The History Makers[22] is, in the words of its author, Kenneth E. Olson, 'the history of the press of the twenty-four nations of Europe, east and west, the part it has played in the political, economic, and cultural development of their peoples, and also the story of the men who have made this press'. As a survey it has some interest, but the individual chapters are too sketchy to have much value. The longest, that on Germany, which has the oldest press in Europe, is only thirty-five pages; England is covered, from the seventeenth century onwards, in twenty-seven pages, and Russia in thirty-two. Although the reactions of the newspapers to political events and their influence on these events are discussed in varying degrees of detail, their impact on economic and cultural developments is very scantily treated. It would perhaps have been better not to try to cover so much ground in a book of this length.

The Troublesome Helpmate,[23] by Katherine M. Rogers, is a historical study of misogyny in literature. Misogyny has figured extensively in literature from very early times, and Miss Rogers sets out to describe, and as far as possible to explain, 'the perennial themes and lasting conventions, the historical variations in the intensity of misogyny and the ways it is expressed, and the distinctive or extreme misogyny of certain writers'. From medieval times onwards the attitude of men to women and its representation in literature have been to a fairly large degree governed by biblical and classical attitudes and representations, and in a long introductory chapter Miss Rogers discusses these two influences in so far as they fostered misogyny. Later chapters are devoted to the middle ages, the Renaissance, the Puritan period in England, and the subsequent centuries. Many dozens of English authors are treated—Chaucer, Milton, Swift, Pope, and D. H. Lawrence at some length, but not, of course, in the same way, since their expression

[21] *The Teller in the Tale*, by Louis D. Rubin, Jr. Washington U.P. pp. xi+228. $5.95. 56s. 6d.

[22] *The History Makers: The Press of Europe from its Beginnings through 1965*, by Kenneth E. Olson. Louisiana State U.P., 1966, pp. xiii+471. $10.

[23] *The Troublesome Helpmate: A History of Misogyny in Literature*, by Katherine M. Rogers. Washington U.P. pp. xvii+288. Paperback. $2.95. 25s.

of misogynistic sentiments has different forms, different reasons, and different purposes. Reading the book, one wonders at times whether the subject justifies such a long and serious study, but it is not uninteresting, and is often illuminating, especially on the earlier periods that it covers.

4. BIBLIOGRAPHICAL STUDIES

Studies in Bibliography[24] has reached its twentieth year, and in a foreword Sir Frank Francis, Director of the British Museum, and Edgar F. Shannon, Jr., President of the University of Virginia, pay well-deserved tributes to Fredson Bowers, its editor since its foundation, and to the scholarly activities of the society of which it is the organ, the Bibliographical Society of the University of Virginia. Since many of its articles are noticed in other chapters, all that is required here is a brief general account of its contents. In 'Tudor Roses from John Tate' Allan Stevenson offers an interesting study of the paper-mark (variously described by earlier scholars as a flower or star or wheel) of John Tate the younger, who set up the first English paper-mill in the late fifteenth century. By means of a close analysis of the second section of the volume, Robert K. Turner, Jr., adds to the information that has been amassed about 'The Printers and the Beaumont and Fletcher Folio of 1647'. T. C. Duncan Eaves and Ben D. Kimpel consider 'Richardson's Revisions of *Pamela*' in successive editions of the novel, and conclude that the 1801 text 'best represents Richardson's final intention', although the text of the first

edition of 1741 should be the one reprinted, since it is 'closer to the Pamela whom Richardson actually imagined, whereas all succeeding texts try to approach the Pamela he thought he should have imagined'. In 'William Strahan's Ledgers: Standard Charges for Printing, 1738–1785' Patricia Hernlund provides much information 'not only about the thousands of books Strahan printed but about the production of the other books printed in London in the eighteenth century'. Joan Stevens contributes '"Woodcuts dropped into the Text": The Illustrations in *The Old Curiosity Shop* and *Barnaby Rudge*'; she shows that the woodcut insets 'function significantly in narrative, characterization and theme, . . and that subsequent publishing failure to honour Dickens's intentions has disastrously obliterated the pointed textual relevance which his illustrations were planned to have'. In 'Two "New" Texts of Thomas Hardy's *The Woodlanders*' Dale Kramer finds fresh evidence in two early American editions of the novel that Hardy was 'an inveterate reviser', given to making numerous small as well as significant changes in the successive printings of his novels. In 'Harriet Weaver's Letters to James Joyce, 1915–1920' John Firth publishes, with annotations, a number of letters to Joyce from Harriet Shaw Weaver, who published *A Portrait of the Artist* serially in her journal *The Egoist*. Emily K. Izsak provides a study of 'The Manuscript of *The Sound and the Fury*: the Revisions in the First Section'. G. Thomas Tanselle offers 'A System of Color Identification for Bibliographical Description'. These full-length articles are followed by a number of shorter notes: 'The Influence of Justification on Spelling in Jaggard's Compositor B', by William S. Kable; 'New

---

[24] *Studies in Bibliography: Papers of the Bibliographical Society of the University of Virginia*, ed. by Fredson Bowers. Assoc. Ed., L. A. Beaurline. Vol. XX. Virginia U.P. pp. vi + 298. $10.

Evidence on the Provenance of the Padua Prompt Books of Shakespeare's *Macbeth, Measure for Measure*, and *Winter's Tale*' by G. Blakemore Evans; 'The Library of Lady Southwell and Captain Sibthorpe', by Sister Jean Carmel Cavanaugh, S.L.; 'Coleridge's *Lines to Thelwall*: A corrected Text, and a First Version', by C. G. Martin; 'Notes on the Destruction of *The Scarlet Letter* Manuscript', by Matthew J. Bruccoli; 'Washington Irving: An Unrecorded Periodical Publication', by Daniel R. Barnes; 'A Speech by W. D. Howells', by George Monteiro; 'Some New Stephen Crane Items', by George W. Hallam; and 'An Unpublished Review by Henry James', by James Kraft. The volume ends with 'A Selective Check List of Bibliographical Scholarship for 1965', compiled by Derek A. Clarke and Howell J. Heaney.

Stanley Morison's *First Principles of Typography*[25] was first printed in 1930 and, after appearing in a number of forms, was adopted as one of the Cambridge Authors' and Printers' Guides in 1951. It has long been a standard work in its field. It is now reissued with a six-page postscript in which Morison surveys recent developments in typography.

The splendid folio entitled *Printing and the Mind of Man*[26] is a descriptive catalogue of the display of books mounted for the eleventh International Printing Machinery and Allied Trades Exhibition held in London in July 1963. The original

catalogue prepared for the exhibition was interesting enough, but this is much more so for the considerably fuller accounts it gives of the books, and as a piece of book production alone it is a pleasure to handle and read. It lists 424 books, ranging in time from the Gutenberg Bible of about 1455 to Sir Winston Churchill's most memorable war speech, printed in 1940. They were not chosen for their bibliographical interest, although many of them are in fact bibliographical showpieces, but for the impact they have made upon the thought and life of the Western world—'a carefully considered list of landmarks, furnished with annotations sufficient to explain why we had chosen them'. The 'annotations', sometimes running to a full folio page or more, account for the importance of the books and the influence they have had on the advancement of civilization, and are set out in such a way that they may be consulted with ease and read with pleasure and profit. The volume contains many excellent reproductions of title-pages and illustrations. It is fully indexed, but reference would have been made easier by the inclusion of a table of contents.

From the Modern Language Association of America comes a small pamphlet, entitled *The Publication of Academic Writing*,[27] which gives advice to young scholars who aim at the publication of their research whether in the form of books or of articles. The sections on the preparation and revision of the typescript are rather elementary, but there are more helpful sections on the nature of the publishing world, and on the

[25] *First Principals of Typograhy*, by Stanley Morison. (Cambridge Authors' and Printers' Guides.) C.U.P. pp. 24. 5s.

[26] *Printing and the Mind of Man: A Descriptive Catalogue Illustrating the Impact of Print on the Evolution of Western Civilization during Five Centuries*, compiled and edited by John Carter and Percy H. Muir, assisted by Nicolas Barker, H. A. Feisenberger, Howard Nixon, and S. H. Steinberg. Cassell. pp. xxxv+280. £7 7s.

[27] *The Publication of Academic Writing*, by Oscar Cargill, William Charvat and Donald D. Walsh. Menasha, Wisconsin: George Banta, for the Modern Language Association of America. pp. 24. 50 cents.

negotiations that must be entered upon before the author secures a contract. As a guide to beginners the work will have some value.

5. ANTHOLOGIES AND TRANSLATIONS

Perhaps most people's idea, and knowledge, of lyrical poetry is derived from their reading in such well-tried 'standard' anthologies as *The Golden Treasury* and *The Oxford Book of English Verse*, and there is nothing to quarrel about in that. But there are many hundreds of excellent poems for which Q and Palgrave could not provide room, and in *A New Canon of English Poetry*[28] James Reeves and Martin Seymour-Smith have printed a delightful collection of such poems, including none that appear in 'Oxgrave', and few that are to be found in other anthologies. Of the sixteen or seventeen anonymous medieval lyrics, probably the only ones that are very well known are 'Foweles in the frith' and 'I have a gentil cook'; one of the more agreeable rarities is 'The Cutty Wren' ('O where are you going? says Milder to Malder'—which has a not unfamiliar ring). The Elizabethan and Jacobean songbooks are very well represented, and add plenty of gems to the new canon ('Thanks, gentle Moone, for thy obscured light', and a number of 'Bonny-boots' songs, for example). Most of the Oxgrave poets appear, for no anthology could do without them; even when they fall below their very best, they can still provide much that will give delight. Among the poets who are most generously represented are Fulke Greville, Swift, Clare, Hartley Coleridge, Emily Dickinson, and the too-long-neglected Trumbull Stickney.

Poet's Choice[29] is an agreeably wide selection of poems brought together by two poets, Patric Dickinson and Sheila Shannon. It contains much that we should expect to find in any good anthology, but here and there is more adventurous than the common run of such collections—in its fairly wide representation of George Wither, for example, or the inclusion of poems by Tennyson and Arnold which do not often find their way into anthologies. What gives the volume an unusual interest is the comments by which the several period sections and a great many of the poems individually are prefaced, drawing attention to particular merits or unusual treatments, for instance, or to parallels in the work of other poets. This anthology may be warmly recommended.

T. R. Barnes's *English Verse*[30] may appropriately be noticed here, although it is as much a work of criticism as an anthology. Barnes's aim is to help the reader to 'listen' to poetry, so that he may 'hear some of the different tunes that English poets make', and at the same time 'to give him some idea of the ways these tunes established themselves and how they changed as time went on'. He therefore analyses a great many poems and passages of verse written in the last four and a half centuries—from Wyatt to the present day—paying especially close attention to word music and verse patterns as they characterize the poetry both of individual poets and of particular periods. He is thus able to offer interesting criticism of the techniques of a large number

[28] *A New Canon of English Poetry*, chosen and ed. by James Reeves and Martin Seymour-Smith. Heinemann. pp. xviii+326. 45s.

[29] *Poet's Choice: An Anthology of English Poetry from Spenser to the Present Day*, compiled by Patric Dickinson and Sheila Shannon. Evans Brothers. pp. viii+466. 35s.

[30] *English Verse: Voice and Movement from Wyatt to Yeats*, by T. R. Barnes. C.U.P. ix+324. 35s. $6.50.

of poets, and at the same time to trace the development of a number of verse forms, such as the rhymed couplet and blank verse. His book may read as a specialized history of English poetry from the Renaissance onwards, and the selection of passages that he studies makes an unusual and attractive anthology.

James Gibson's four-volume anthology, *Poetry and Song*,[31] is designed primarily for use in schools, and to this end the contents of the several volumes are to some extent graduated according to the difficulty they might present to young readers. However, the work as a whole offers much that will be to the taste of older and more experienced readers of verse. As his title suggests, Gibson wants to emphasize the essential kinship between poetry and song; he has therefore largely confined himself to lyrical poetry, with a generous admixture of folk-songs, carols, shanties, and other 'popular' types of verse. He has cast his net wide, and included translations, and he has sought out much that is unusual in English poetry. The gramophone recordings that have been made to accompany this anthology are noticed in a later section of this chapter (see footnote 39).

Parlour Poetry[32] is a splendid anthology of the improving verse so dearly loved by our grandparents. It offers most of the gems recited in Victorian and Edwardian drawing-rooms by well-scrubbed boys and girls drilled by their teachers of elocution in all the appropriate gestures, facial contortions, and voice-inflexions—'Casabianca', 'Tell me not in mournful numbers', 'Love, Sweet Love', 'Home, Sweet Home', 'The Village Blacksmith', 'The Old Arm-chair', 'Excelsior', 'Bishop Hatto', 'Curfew must not ring tonight', 'The lips that touch liquor shall never touch mine', 'The Inchcape Rock', 'In the Workhouse: Christmas Day', 'Woodman, spare that tree', and a host of others voicing equally elevating sentiments. All the great names of Victorian popular verse are here: Felicia Hemans, Longfellow, Ann Taylor, Thomas Haynes Bayly, Ella Wheeler Wilcox, Eliza Cook, Jean Ingelow, George R. Sims, and the rest. The volume is embellished with appropriate engravings, and its binding and format are in period.

Douglass Parker is an experienced translator of Aristophanes. His latest contribution to William Arrowsmith's complete Greek Comedy series is a translation of the *Ecclesiazusae* to which he gives the title *The Congresswomen*.[33] This play, with its burlesque and satire of many political institutions and catchwords with which we are all too familiar today, and some social ones as well, should have a particular interest for modern readers or audiences. Parker's version misses none of the comedy—and none of the obscenity. Except in the choral sections, it employs a loose five-beat line in which it is possible to convey almost all the shades of feeling of the original. It reads as if it would be very lively on the stage. Leo and Diane Dillon provide some amusing sketches in the 'ancient Greek' style.

Betty Radice completes her Penguin translation of the plays of

---

[31] *Poetry & Song: An Anthology*, chosen by James Gibson. Macmillan. Four volumes. Book I, pp. xiv+162. 8s. 6d. Book 2, pp. xiv+154. 8s. 6d. Book 3, pp. xviii+181. 9s. 6d. Book 4, pp. xviii+225. 11s. 6d.

[32] *Parlour Poetry: A Hundred and One Improving Gems*, selected and introduced by Michael R. Turner. Michael Joseph. pp. 264. 30s.

[33] *Aristophanes. 'The Congresswomen'*, translated by Douglass Parker. Michigan U.P. pp. vii+101. $4.50.

Terence in *'Phormio' and Other Plays*.[34] The 'other plays' are *The Girl from Andros (Andria)* and *The Self-Tormentor (Heauton Timorumenos)*. Something of Terence is of course lost in a prose version, but Mrs. Radice has perhaps come as close as any other translator to capturing the spirit of the plays and reproducing the felicities of Terence's language. Her two volumes are to be warmly recommended.

Catullus lends himself to imitation or adaptation in English, as has been delightfully demonstrated by so many of our poets from Skelton to Tennyson, but it is questionable whether he can be worthily translated. C. H. Sisson is the latest of several recent translators,[35] and it cannot be said that he captures the grace and elegance, or indeed any of the 'feel', of the poems. 'You ask me, Lesbia, how many kisses / Make enough kisses for me to take from you'—presumably an attempt at something like the original hendecasyllables; 'I have and I love. You may well ask, why I do so./I do not know, but I feel it and suffer'—twenty-two dull words for the original fourteen. Wherever one turns, the *venustus* Catullus is turned into this kind of flatness. Nor is the unsavoury Catullus rendered more successfully. Sisson's volume confirms one's feeling that Catullus must be left to those who can read him in the original—which is yet another of the sad deprivations that must be suffered by those who have not been properly educated.

6. GRAMOPHONE RECORDS

The *English Poets* spoken anthology

has made further progress with the addition this year of a record devoted to the verse of Arnold, Clough, and FitzGerald, and two records devoted to that of Thomas Hardy.[36] The readers for the former are Marius Goring, Ian Holm, and Derek Jacobi. This is a disappointing record. Marius Goring reads most of the Arnold. Goring has shown on other occasions that he can read verse with understanding and feeling, that of George Herbert, for example, but he makes little of Arnold. He delivers the meditative elegiac passages of *The Scholar Gipsy* in an inflated declamatory manner that at times almost robs them of meaning, and he shows little more feeling for the shorter poems, such as *Dover Beach*. Ian Holm also tends to over-dramatize the verse of these poets that has been entrusted to him. Derek Jacobi is rather more successful, but even he sometimes spoils the effect of a poem, Clough's *The Latest Decalogue*, for example, by ignoring the lineation. It is helpful to be able to hear the Victorian poets as well as read them, but it could have been wished that they had been read more sympathetically.

In view of Thomas Hardy's considerable, though perhaps somewhat inflated, recent popularity as a poet, the two Hardy records are likely to be given a warm welcome. And, indeed, he reads aloud very well. He is represented by some seventy poems, mostly from the shorter lyrics, but with a handful of the 'lyrical ballads', such as *The Choirmaster's Burial* and *A Trampwoman's Tragedy*. These two

[34] Terence. *'Phormio' and Other Plays*, translated by Betty Radice. Penguin Books. pp. 204.
[35] *Catullus*, translated by C. H. Sisson. MacGibbon & Kee. pp. 94. 25s.
[36] The English Poets. *Arnold, Clough, Fitz-Gerald*, read by Marius Goring, Ian Holm and Derek Jacobi. One twelve-inch record, RG 521. *Thomas Hardy*, read by Ian Holm, Barbara Jefford, David King, and Richard Pasco. Two twelve-inch records, RG 581-2. Directed by George Rylands, in association with the British Council and O.U.P. Argo Record Co. Ltd. Each record 37s. 6d.

poems, read by Richard Pasco and Barbara Jefford respectively, are perhaps the most successful among these recordings; for again the readers tend to be too dramatic, to impose their own—not always very satisfactory—interpretations on the poems, and that matters less in poems of this type than in the lyrics. It is unfortunate that actors and 'professional' readers seldom show themselves to be the best readers of poetry. Poets reading their own verse almost invariably speak in a comparatively neutral voice, and allow the words and rhythms to make their own effects, as is admirably demonstrated in the record from the series *The Poet Speaks* noticed below; the *English Poets* readers have increasingly taken to 'acting' the poems, which often results in a falsification, or at best distortion, of the poet's intention. This said, it must be added that the present recordings in the series can still give a good deal of pleasure.

A selection from the writings of Wilfred Owen[37] can be much more warmly commended. Richard Johnson as the poet, Tony Church as his brother Harold, and Frank Duncan as Siegfried Sassoon read a number of Wilfred's poems and letters, interspersed with passages from Harold Owen's *Journey from Obscurity* and Sassoon's *Siegfried's Journey*. This combination provides an extremely moving portrait of Owen, and substantiates the high claims that are made for him as a poet; the poetic maturity is seen no less clearly in the letters than in the poems.

The tenth record of the series entitled

The Poet Speaks[38] presents the voices of twelve living poets reading their own verse. These poets are listed in the footnote; most of them are represented by two or three poems apiece, but George Barker is allowed ten poems, and perhaps it may be granted that he deserves this special prominence. The poems are for the most part familiar from their appearance in anthologies of recent verse. This collection derives its particular value from the fact that we hear the poems spoken by the poets themselves, and hence as the poets would presumably wish them to be spoken; as has already been suggested, the poems are very largely allowed to speak for themselves, and the hearer's personal response is rightly the most important factor in their interpretation.

Six of the fourteen records which are planned to accompany James Gibson's anthology *Poetry and Song* (see note 31) have appeared.[39] A couple of dozen readers and singers, together with the choir of St. John's College, Cambridge, have collaborated in the production of these records. What has already been said of the printed anthology may be repeated here—that, although the work is intended for schoolchildren, it will certainly appeal also to older people, for it is not the practice nowadays to 'write down' or 'read down' to schoolchildren. The hundreds of poems and songs recorded represent almost every level of maturity. This is a series which will give much pleasure.

[37] *Wilfred Owen*, in poetry and letters ed. by Frederick Woods. Wilfred Owen read by Richard Johnson, Harold Owen by Tony Church, Siegfried Sassoon by Frank Duncan. Directed by Harley J. Usill. One twelve-inch record, RG 593. Argo Record Co. Ltd. 37s. 6d.

[38] *The Poet Speaks*, Record Ten. Edmund Blunden, Andrew Young, Edwin Muir, Geoffrey Grigson, John Wain, Dannie Abse, George Barker, W. S. Graham, Christopher Logue, Edward Lucie-Smith, Edward Brathwaite, B. S. Johnson. Directed by Peter Orr, and recorded in association with the British Council and the Poetry Room in the Lamont Library of Harvard University. One twelve inch record, RG 583. Argo Record Co. Ltd. 37s. 6d.

[39] *Poetry and Song*, ed. by James Gibson, and recorded in association with Macmillan and Co. Ltd. Directed by Harley Usill. Six twelve-inch records, DA 50–55. Argo Record Co. Ltd. Each record 37s. 6d.

II

English Language

R. M. WILSON

An impressive tribute to one of the most influential of modern linguists consists of three large volumes, with over 200 articles in some 2500 pages, and a list of 374 books and papers and 101 items of miscellanea published at various times by Roman Jakobson.[1] The articles included here vary in length and quality. Most of them are in English, and deal with many aspects of linguistic and literary studies. Those concerned with general linguistics or with English language will be noticed in the appropriate place, but it should be emphasized that these by no means exhaust the interest to be found in the three volumes. G. Wilson[2] reprints thirty-six essays on various aspects of linguistics, mainly by experts on the subject, and primarily intended for students. They are arranged under six headings: the student and the language; correctness; linguists and their critics; grammar; related matters; and the science of language. Long introductions to the sections and to each essay sometimes give a partial explanation of what follows, sometimes provide a historical context. The collection includes work by many important American scholars, and contains much of interest and value, though the reasons for reprinting some of the

articles are not very evident. *Classics in Linguistics*[3] begins with extracts from Aristotle and Castiglione, and continues with passages from standard works by such authors as Leonard, Pedersen, Boas, Saussure, etc. In addition, the famous 'Third Anniversary Discourse' by Sir William Jones is reprinted, along with articles by Bloomfield, Sapir, Trnka, and Chomsky. Most of these are certainly classics in linguistics, but they are easy enough of access elsewhere. The four articles and two extracts from books in *The Structure of Language*[4] represent four schools of linguistic thought: structural, behavioural, tagmemic, and transformational. They are in chronological order, and according to that aspect of the language which they emphasize, beginning with the sound, and proceeding beyond the sentence. The final essay, by N. Chomsky, gives a critical summary of major research during the last decade, and attempts to define the general area of future work. C. F. Hockett[5] has revised and enlarged his *Four Lectures on Theoretical Linguistics* in an attempt to provide an introduction to mathematics for the linguist, though it is

---

[1] *To Honor Roman Jakobson. Essays on the Occasion of his Seventieth Birthday*. The Hague: Mouton & Co. 3 vols. pp. xxxiii+1–832; xii+833–1668; ix+1669–2464. 450 Guilders. Abbreviated as *Jakobson Essays*.

[2] *A Linguistics Reader*, ed. G. Wilson. New York: Harper & Row. pp. xxxii+341. 40s.

[3] *Classics in Linguistics*, by D. E. Hayden, E. P. Alworth and G. Tate. New York: Philosophical Library. pp. vii+373. $10.

[4] *The Structure of Language*, by O. Thomas. New York: Bobbs-Merrill. pp. 64. $1.

[5] *Language, Mathematics and Linguistics*, by C. F. Hockett. The Hague: Mouton & Co. pp. 243. 21 Guilders.

also a criticism of the current preoccupation with algebraic grammar. Consequently the first part deals with various mathematical points, whilst the remaining chapters constitute an examination of various types of grammars. D. Bolinger[6] writes on modern linguistics for the average reader, and deals at varying length with a number of subjects: descriptive and historical linguistics, types of semantic change, dialectology, modern tendencies in linguistics, etc. European developments tend to get ignored, the historical part is not always free from error, and the explanations are not always as clear as they might be. But the book contains much useful information, the use of technical terms is kept to a minimum, and the author usually succeeds in keeping a reasonable balance between information and readability.

Most of the thirty-five articles on the psychology of language, reprinted by L. A. Jakobovits and M. S. Miron,[7] were originally published during the last ten years, but some important earlier works are also included. In the first part is traced the theoretical development of the subject, the second discusses the significance of linguistic theories in the study of grammar and syntax, whilst the third is concerned with psychological theories of meaning. The result shows some of the ways in which psychologists and linguists have combined to contribute to the increase of knowledge in this field. J. Lyons and R. J. Wales present five papers given at the Psycholinguis-

tic Conference held in Edinburgh in 1966.[8] Those of most general interest are perhaps the ones dealing with the language of children by N. McNeill and by E. S. Klima and Ursula Bellugi. In addition, J. P. Thorne writes 'On Hearing Sentences', R. J. Wales and J. C. Marshall on 'The Organization of Linguistic Performance', and J. Fodor and M. Garrett provide 'Some Reflections on Competence and Performance'. Each paper is followed by a prepared commentary and an edited version of the general discussion that followed. In the main one is left with the impression that there is little agreement between linguists and psychologists, and that even scholars in the same subject have difficulty in grasping what the speaker is trying to say. On the same subject is Edith C. Trager's 'Linguistics and the Design of Psycholinguistic Experiments'.[9]

R. H. Robins[10] describes in turn the contributions made to our knowledge of language by Greece, Rome, the Middle Ages, and the Renaissance, and goes on to deal with the nineteenth century. Most readers will be particularly interested in the final chapter on linguistics in the present century, and here, in some forty excellently organized pages, Robins brings out clearly the achievements of the Bloomfield school, and the revolutionary impact of Chomsky, at the same time demonstrating their debt to other scholars. Altogether an excellent book, at once interesting and authoritative. *The Main Trends*

[6] *Aspects of Language*, by D. Bolinger. New York: Harcourt, Brace & World. pp. viii+326. $3.95.
[7] *Readings in the Psychology of Language*, ed. L. A. Jakobovits and M. S. Miron. Englewood Cliffs, N. J.: Prentice-Hall. pp. xi+636. 93s.
[8] *Psycholinguistic Papers*, ed. J. Lyons and R. J. Wales. Edinburgh U.P. pp. v+243. 42s.
[9] In *Papers in Linguistics in Honor of Léon Dostert*, ed. W. M. Austin. The Hague: Mouton & Co. pp. 177. 34 Guilders. Abbreviated as *Dostert Papers*.
[10] *A Short History of Linguistics*, by R. H. Robins. London: Longmans. Bloomington: Indiana U.P. pp. viii+248. 25s.

in Modern Linguistics[11] is the translation of a French work first published in 1963. Approximately a quarter of it is devoted to the formation of linguistic method in the nineteenth century, with ten pages for Saussure, and eighty for modern linguists. The twentieth century is dealt with under such headings as 'The Geneva School', 'Phonology', 'Structuralism', etc., and the result is a clear and concise account of some of the developments now taking place. But there are omissions: there is no section on syntax; Chomsky is mentioned only within the context of statistical linguistics; and, throughout, the view is narrowly continental and European, with very little mention of the influential contribution by American linguists. A. A. Hill emphasizes that 'The Current Relevance of Bloch's "Postulates"' (*L*) lies in the fact that they point to the basis of the minimal-pair identification test, the most powerful tool in phonological analysis, and also emphasize the basic necessity of sound-discrimination in the development of human language. V. V. Belyi points out 'Some Facts about Weiss's Influence on Bloomfield' (*ZAA*), which show that to some extent the methodological and epistemological views of the former determined the views of the latter on subject-matter, and also on the main task of linguistics as a science of language.

L. G. Heller and J. Macris[12] define a linguistic parameter as any variable which differentiates any two categories in a language, either on the functional or on the signalling plane. By making use of such parameters, they hope to reveal the dynamics of the system and the causes of different kinds of change and reaction. W. L. Chafe, 'Language as Symbolization' (*L*), views language as a system in which semiological structures are symbolized as phonological structures manifested in sound, and questions the place of separate semantic and syntactic components within such a system, and F. C. Southworth provides 'A Model of Semantic Structure' (*L*). In 'Distinctive Features and Phonetic Features' (*Jakobson Essays*) F. W. Householder examines Jakobson's 'distinctive features', emphasizing that these are not to be described as 'universal phonetic features' since, whatever else they may be, distinctive features must be terms of binary opposition. New features must perhaps be added to Jakobson's list, but these are to be sought in the oppositions of natural languages, not in the phonetic specifications with which we might ultimately be able to correlate them. H. Kučera, 'Distinctive Features, Simplicity, and Descriptive Adequacy' (*Jakobson Essays*), examines some of the assumptions which underlie the structure of the phonological component in generative transformational grammar, while B. Malmberg gives some 'Réflexions sur les traits distinctifs et le classement des phonèmes' (*Jakobson Essays*). In another collection,[13] J. C. Street deals with 'Methodology in Immediate Constituent Analysis', and M. Joos writes on 'The Completion of Descriptive Linguistics'. W. M. Austin, 'Logicalism and Formalism in Linguistics' (*Dostert Papers*), criticizes some of the basic assumptions of transformational grammar, suggesting a new schema, that of the directed graph, which is then exempli-

[11] *The Main Trends in Modern Linguistics*, by M. Leroy, Oxford: Blackwell. Berkeley: California U.P. pp. xi + 155. 25s.

[12] *Parametric Linguistics*, by L. G. Heller and J. Macris. The Hague: Mouton & Co. pp. 79. 10 Guilders.

[13] *Approaches in Linguistic Methodology*, ed. Irmengard Rauch and C. T. Scott. Wisconsin U.P. pp. x + 157. 57s.

fied. 'Some Critical Remarks on the Treatment of Morphological Structure in Transformational Generative Grammar' (*Lingua*), by S. C. Dik, examines the place accorded to the description of morphological structure in the theory of transformational generative grammar, while E. Stankiewicz's 'Opposition and Hierarchy in Morphophonemic Alternations' (*Jakobson Essays*) attempts to provide a, structural and explanatory interpretation of the morphophonemic phenomena of language. H. L. Smith would define 'The Concept of the Morphophone' (*L*) as a structural unit between phoneme and morpheme. It is seen as the basic unit of the morpheme, and is itself composed of dialectally different phonemic variants, which are non-contrasting in the same lexical items. I. B. Khlebnikova, 'Notes on Grammatical Category' (*PP*), argues that the notion of grammatical category has not been uniformly defined by linguists, and that only the functional approach can yield a solution to the problems involved. Grammatical categories must be established separately for every language, and such categories can apply only to the plane of meaning. A. Schaff deals with the 'Specific Features of the Verbal Sign' (*Jakobson Essays*), and decides that it has its place in the general definition of the sign, provided this is broad enough, such a conception being supported by both theoretical and practical considerations. S. Żółkiewski makes a 'Contribution au Problème de l'Analyse Structurale' (*Jakobson Essays*), while Y. Malkiel's 'Linguistics as a Genetic Science' (*L*) illustrates some problems in the causation of language change, and R. D. King, in 'Functional Load and Sound Change' (*L*), investigates the theory that the former of these plays a significant part in the latter, concluding that, if

indeed it is a factor, it is one of the least significant. In 'Notes on One Aspect of the Internal Structuration of the Phonological System' (*Jakobson Essays*) J. Vachek considers the relation between the vocalic and consonantal zones; N. Chomsky presents 'Some General Properties of Phonological Rules' (*L*) as they have emerged within the framework of generative grammar; S. K. Šaumjan, 'Phonology and Generative Grammars' (*Jakobson Essays*), comments on the status of phonology as a linguistic science in the light of generative grammar, and of phonology within the framework of the transformational model; and R. Stanley discusses 'Redundancy Rules in Phonology' (*L*), and the role they play in the phonological component of a generative grammar. Z. Vendler[14] deals with the transformations of nominalizations under conjunctions and relative clauses, and with adjectives, while Tatiana Slama-Cazacu writes 'Sur la Formation du Système Phonématique chez l'enfant' (*Jakobson Essays*), and R. I. McDavid, in 'Language, Linguistics and the Three Cultures' (*Dostert Papers*), pleads for co-operation between the humanities, the physical sciences, and the social sciences, complaining that most of the obstacles to it come from the humanities.

From R. Barthes[15] comes a concise scientific definition of Saussurean linguistics, and P. Lamb attempts to make available to the teacher the methods and theories of modern linguistics.[16] He deals in turn with the contribution of linguistics to the

[14] *Adjectives and Nominalizations*, by Z. Vendler. The Hague: Mouton & Co. pp. 134. 18 Guilders.
[15] *Elements of Semiology*, by R. Barthes. Cape. pp. 111. 7s. 6d.
[16] *Linguistics in Proper Perspective*, by P. Lamb. Columbus, Ohio: Merrill. pp. xi + 147. $3.95.

knowledge of language, and to the teaching of reading, spelling, and grammar. At the end of each chapter a select list of books provides guidance for more advanced work, and a useful glossary of linguistic terms is also included. On the whole the attempt is reasonably successful, but the author tries to cover too much ground, with the result that some aspects of the subject are dealt with so briefly as to be misleading. From C. F. and F. M. Voegelin comes a long and interesting article on 'Anthropological Linguistics and Translation' (*Dostert Papers*). P. L. Garvin, 'The Automation of Discovery Procedures in Linguistics' (*L*), discusses the theoretical significance of a proposed computer program for the automation of discovery procedures, and presents an outline of a type of heuristic computer program which would be suitable for the automation of the procedures employed in the initial phases of field-work. The same author writes on 'The Georgetown-IBM Experiment of 1954: An Evaluation in Retrospect' (*Dostert Papers*), and on 'Heuristic Syntax in Russian-English Machine Translation' (*Jakobson Essays*). On the same subject is B. Henisz-Dostert, 'Experimental Machine Translation' (*Dostert Papers*).

Glossaries of linguistic terms come from D. J. Steible and M. Pei.[17] In the first, the definitions are sometimes too brief, but illustrative quotations are given, and there are numerous cross-references. The second contains the technical terminology of descriptive, historical, and geolinguistics, with the definitions so far as possible in the words of those who gave them

currency. Synonyms, near-synonyms, and opposites also appear, while cross-references allow the user to follow a topic through its various ramifications. The beginner and the more advanced student alike will find both books useful. In 'The Linguistic Usage of "palatal" with its Derivatives' (*The Canadian Journal of Linguistics*) R. C. De Armond gives a careful definition of that term, and also of *palatalize* and *palatalization* as they are used by modern linguists.

R. F. S. Hamer's concise account of Old English sound changes[18] manages to be reasonably straightforward without becoming misleading. He begins with a brief phonetic summary, and goes on to trace the changes in pronunciation from Germanic to West Saxon, with a brief section on the major variations in other dialects. R. Howren describes 'The Generation of Old English Weak Verbs' (*L*), predicated on a constituent-structure analysis, which differs in some respects from that implied in traditional grammars of Old English. A. Joly, 'Gepréfixe lexical en vieil anglais' (*The Canadian Journal of Linguistics*), shows that its prime function is to indicate that the sense of the simple word to which it is prefixed is transcended, that the idea represented by the word is not only covered, but surpassed. Later it tended to become a grammatical verbal prefix, and was then lost because of important supervening changes in the lexical and verbal system of Old English. M. Rissanen shows that 'Old English *pæt an* "Only"' (*NM*) was accepted as the translation of the Latin exclusive adverbs, and consequently came to be used, side by side with the appositive *an*, even in contexts in which exclusiveness was indicated

---

[17] *Concise Handbook of Linguistics*, by D. J. Steible. New York: Philosophical Library. pp. 146. $6.

Glossary of Linguistic Terminology, by M. Pei. Columbia U.P. pp. xviii+299. $6.50. 48s.

[18] *Old English Sound Changes for Beginners*, by R. F. S. Hamer. Oxford: Blackwell. pp. 35. 5s.

with regard to nouns or pronouns. The preference for the phrase *þæt an* as compared with *þæt an þæt* in these contexts was perhaps due to the fact that the formation of a subordinate clause was here often more awkward than in contexts in which exclusiveness was indicated with regard to verbal action. P. W. Pillsbury[19] makes use of modern techniques to describe the inflexional characteristics and syntactic behaviour of nouns in dialogue passages of eleventh-century Old English prose texts. He deals in turn with substantive types, noun case, the morphotactics of the nouns, noun suffixes, and the noun inflexional series. The general aims of the investigation are to show that a descriptive approach to historical stages of the English language is both methodically feasible and descriptively rewarding. The author succeeds in demonstrating the first of these, but so far as the second is concerned little if anything new seems to emerge. According to R. A. Peters, in 'Morphemic Classification of Old English Adverb Subsets' (*The Canadian Journal of Linguistics*), whereas verbs, adjectives, pronouns, and nouns are identified as sets marked by morphemes of case, number, tense, etc., adverbs are identified as a set marked by function. Since this is inconsistent, an analysis of the adverbs on a morphemic basis is provided, as well as a morphemic identification of characteristic subsets of them. A. Bammesberger, 'Old English *brecþa* and *-brecþ*' (*L*), shows that the first of these, occurring at *Beowulf* 171, is a masculine *n*-stem, not a feminine *o*-stem as it is sometimes taken to be. The second occurs only in compounds and is a different formation. In 'A Romance Congener

of O.E. *symbel*' (*ES*) P. A. Erades argues that the word is a Germanic one and not a Latin loan, while P. F. O'Dwyer points out that 'Old English *Unwitweorc*: A Ghost Word' (*ELN*), occurring only in the *Blickling Homilies*, is really a misreading of *inwitweorc*. H. A. Roe, 'A Note on Loanwords from Old Norse' (*ES*), suggests that *-ht-* in such words merely indicates that Old English speakers identified preaspirated Old Norse *-tt-* with Old English *-ht-* rather than with *-tt-*. Consequently this group of loanwords cannot be used to date either the earliest Norse contacts or the Scandinavian assimilation of *-ht-* with *-tt-*. In 'The Functional Motivation of Linguistic Change' (*ES*) C. Jones describes the grammatical sub-system of gender as it appears in the *Lindisfarne Gospels* and the *Durham Ritual*. This sub-system was limited in duration and in dialectal provenance, the change to an almost complete loss of the grammatical category of gender in Southern texts apparently taking place without the intermediate development of a system of the type described here. A later article by the same author, 'The Grammatical Category of Gender in Early Middle English' (*ES*), examines the system in some early Middle English texts, more particularly in the *Peterborough Chronicle*, Laȝamon's *Brut*, and the *Southern Legendary*.

M. Rissanen[20] investigates the different uses of the numeral *one* in Old and early Middle English. After an introductory chapter on the etymology, forms, and phonological development of the word, the discussion is divided into chapters on the basis of its principal functions or

---

[19] *Descriptive Analysis of Discourse in Late West Saxon Texts*, by P. W. Pillsbury. The Hague: Mouton & Co. pp. 91. 18 Guilders.

[20] *The Uses of One in Old and Early Middle English*, by M. Rissanen. Mémoires de la Société Néophilologique de Helsinki XXXI. pp. xxx+325. $6.

shades of meaning, the syntactic uses being considered within the framework of this division. Most of the present functions of *one* can be found as early as the Old English period; the pronominal uses develop during the thirteenth and fourteenth centuries; the roots of the intensifying expressions are traceable in Old English; the formal distinction between *one* and *a* is fairly well established by the end of the fourteenth century; before cardinal numbers both come to imply approximation; while the use of *sum* as the indefinite article becomes obsolete in early Middle English. Phonological and morphological differences between the dialects appear in both Old and Middle English, but there is little dialectal variation in syntactic use and shades of meaning, nor did foreign languages play any significant part in the development. H. Fujiwara, 'On the Word Order in the Phrase of the *to*-Infinitive during the Transitional Period from OE. to ME.' (*The Annual Collection of Critical Studies, Gakushuin University, Tokyo*), shows that in late Old English the modifier of the *to*-infinitive was already beginning to move towards the end of the infinitival phrase, and this tendency becomes even more predominant in early Middle English.

S. Suzuki[21] describes in detail the phonology, accidence, and syntax of the Corpus manuscript of the *Ancrene Wisse*. The Old English vowels and diphthongs are taken in turn, and their developments classified under nouns, adjectives, verbs, and adverbs. In the consonants the orthographical changes are listed, and the various sound-changes that have taken place are exemplified. The examination has been carried out carefully and syste-matically, but exceptional forms are not always specifically noted, and, when they are, the suggested explanations are sometimes unconvincing. On the other hand, the description of accidence and the useful notes on syntax are particularly valuable, the latter adding a good deal to our knowledge of an unduly neglected subject. Much of the material appears also in the same author's 'Linguistic Features in *Ancrene Wisse*' (*Anglica*). G. Kristensson[22] investigates the dialects of the six northern counties and Lincolnshire between 1290 and 1350, making use of personal names in the Lay Subsidy Rolls which can be taken as reflecting the actual spoken dialect. Since these sources are not available for Durham and Cheshire, less satisfactory documents had to be used for these counties. Forms are given to illustrate the development of the Old English vowels and diphthongs, the consonants as usual being treated in rather less detail. In general the evidence suggests some corrections to the Moore, Meech, and Whitehall map, more particularly in the developments of OE. $\bar{a}$, $æ$, $\bar{æ}^2$, $\bar{o}$, y, and a/o before nasals. Thirty-three distribution maps are given, and since the territory covered matches that of the first volume of the Survey of English Dialects, the investigation provides valuable evidence for the earlier history of the northern dialects. In addition, H. M. Logan, 'The Computer and Middle English Dialectology' (*The Canadian Journal of Linguistics*), notes some possible applications of the former to various problems of the latter, but emphasizes that the computer does not

---

[21] *The Language of the Ancrene Wisse*, by S. Suzuki. Tokyo: Metropolitan U.P. pp. viii+147.

[22] *A Survey of Middle English Dialects 1290–1350. The Six Northern Counties and Lincolnshire*, by G. Kristensson. Lund Studies in English 35. Lund: Gleerup. pp. xxii+299. Sw. Cr. 45.

eliminate the need for knowledge, though it does ease the inevitable drudgery.

In 'Dramatic Use of the Second-Person Singular Pronoun in *Sir Gawain and the Green Knight*' (*SN*) W. W. Evans shows that the author follows carefully the usual distinctions, with the result that his use of *thou* indicates clearly the implied attitudes of one character to another, as well as various intentions or attitudes not otherwise expressed. P. Haworth takes '"Warthe" in "Sir Gawain and the Green Knight"' (*NQ*) as a variant of *wath* 'ford', and H. M. Smyser, in 'Chaucer's Use of *Gin* and *Do*' (*S*), suggests that whereas the *gan*-periphrasis is used merely for convenience of rhyme and metre, *do* almost always has a causative meaning, though it too may sometimes serve metrical and rhyming convenience. Margaret Schlauch examines the 'Stylistic Attributes of John Lydgate's Prose' (*Jakobson Essays*) as they appear in his political tract, *The Serpent of Division*. The heightened style used here is to be associated with the propaganda aim of the treatise, being distinct from the straightforward style of the chroniclers and biographers of the period. Nor is Lydgate's writing mannered to the same degree in all his writings; while some of his traits are shared by other prose writers of the time, some seem to be idiosyncrasies of his own. In 'The Syllabic Value of Final "-es" in English Versification about 1500' (*NQ*) P. J. Frankis concludes from a pattern-poem by Hawes that, whilst the *-es* plural ending was counted as a syllable, final *-e* was not. N. Davis, 'Style and Stereotype in Early English Letters' (*Leeds Studies in English*), points out the use of widespread epistolary conventions in the opening and closing formulas of the *Paston Letters*, and notes other aspects of

the style which would seem to have been developed in written use. Previous critics have emphasized the colloquial elements in the letters, but it is quite clear that many of these are not really colloquial, and that the conventional and unspontaneous elements have in general been underrated. Vivian Salmon's 'Elizabethan Colloquial English in the Falstaff Plays' (*Leeds Studies in English*) is an attempt to get as close as possible to the spoken language of the period. Spoken language evolves within a given situation, involves at least two participants, and because the linguistic symbols in use are spoken they are ephemeral, to some extent dependent on the physical ability of the speaker to produce them, and open to influence by stress, rhythm, and intonation. These characteristics of speech determine linguistic form, and the author goes on to illustrate them from the prose portions of the Falstaff plays. The result shows a good many contrasts between Elizabethan and current speech, while at the same time illustrating similarities between Elizabethan usage and that of some modern European languages more particularly in the use of certain ritual formulas, of formal modes of address, and of the retention of the second person singular pronoun. In the same way Joan Mulholland examines the use of '"Thou" and "You" in Shakespeare: A Study in the Second Person Pronoun' (*ES*).

K. J. Kohler, in 'Aspects of Middle Scots Phonemics and Graphemics: The Phonological Implications of the Sign ⟨I⟩' (*TPS*), makes use of material from modern Scottish dialects to test the theory that in Middle Scots the diphthongs *ai, ei, oi, ui*, were monophthongized to the corresponding long vowels. In most dialects the continuations of early Scottish /a:/ and /ai/ are still distinct, and even in those areas where this is not the case today, it can be demonstrated that the convergence occurred after the Middle Scots period. Moreover, the descendants of early Scots /ǫ:/ and /oi/ are differentiated in all the modern dialects. The promiscuous use of the graphemes *a, e, o, u*, by the side of *ai, ei, oi, ui*, was a scribal practice, which originated under special cultural and linguistic conditions, different for each of the four pairs. The Scottish scribes, taking advantage of the fluctuation in the spelling of certain words, developed a regular system of vowel representation, the principle of which is to add *i, y*, to the simple vowel symbols *a, e, o, u*, whenever it was felt necessary to make the meaning of these graphemes unambiguous and where no other sign indicated length. C. T. Scott, 'On the Dating of NE *ee* and *ea* Spellings from ME *ē* and *ę̄*' (*Approaches in Linguistic Methodology*, see footnote 13), proposes a methodological approach to the dating of spelling conventions, making use of it to date as closely as possible the fixing of the *ee* and *ea* spellings for ME *ē* and *ę̄*. Words deriving from these were still phonemically distinct in the latter part of the sixteenth century, and their eventual coalescence in sound was probably not accomplished until as late as the eighteenth century. In 'Swift and the English Language: A study in Principles and Practice' (*Jakobson Essays*) Barbara Strang points out that, linguistically, Swift was facing a situation that was new in certain ways, and that he faced it in a highly conservative manner. Except in special circumstances, he normally contents himself with a minimal kind of innovation, the development of potential by forming familiar elements into new complex words, or into nonce-words not intended to take a place in the lasting word-stock of the language. He is fond of exploiting the potential of familiar patterns of word-formation for satirical purposes, but, for all that, his self-discipline in restricting lexical innovations is the more remarkable since we know him to have been a man of exceptional linguistic inventiveness. Susie I. Tucker has written a fascinating book on eighteenth-century vocabulary and usage.[23] In the first part she describes the century's own views of the subject; what was felt to need explanation, what was complained about or apologized for, and what new words were thought to be needed. In the second part the emphasis shifts to our own views, and we discover what difficulties the use of certain words involves us in, either because they have since been lost or have later changed their meanings. The author has a wide and detailed knowledge of the literature of the century, and especially of the periodicals, and the result is an exceptionally interesting and valuable book on the subject. Particularly significant is the number of words and senses that have been noted for which *O.E.D.* gives either no entry at all or only a much later one.

The only part of the *Middle English Dictionary* to appear completes the entries for *H*.[24] It contains long and important articles on *hongen* and *hous*, and its virtues and rare shortcomings remain much as before. What perhaps comes out more particularly in this part is the unsatisfactory use of surnames and place-names to illustrate the different words and senses; some of them are almost certainly wrongly identified, and

[23] *Protean Shape. A Study in Eighteenth-Century Vocabulary and Usage*, by Susie I. Tucker. Athlone Press. pp. xi+322. 55*s*.

[24] *Middle English Dictionary. Part H.5*, by S. M. Kuhn and J. Reidy. Michigan U.P. pp. 897–1053. 21*s*.

others probably so. The second volume of Klein's etymological dictionary[25] has the merits and defects of the first: the definitions are sometimes too brief, even for an etymological dictionary; many of the words included have never really been part of the vocabulary; and new words tend to be omitted. On the other hand, the dictionary contains much accurate and detailed information on the sources of a large number of words, making good, but critical, use of the latest information. Words are traced as far back as possible, with numerous cognates from other languages, and with bases given for Indo-European words. The work will be found particularly useful since it sometimes supplements the information in *The Oxford Dictionary of English Etymology*, especially in words ultimately derived from Semitic. Of the two American dictionaries,[26] the first is twenty years old but has been skilfully brought up to date, while the second is based on the recent *Random House Dictionary of the English Language*. Both are full, easy to consult, with clear definitions helped by numerous line drawings, and good and accurate etymologies. Each is as up to date as could reasonably be expected, including a good deal of general encyclopaedic information and numerous idiomatic expressions; both are good in their definitions of technical scientific terms. Their systems of indicating pronunciation are very similar, though the slight changes in the

second are on the whole improvements. The second of them is rather more comprehensive, a little more up to date, and the illustrations clearer and more enlightening. Both have a good deal of additional information: lists of colleges and universities in the United States, lists of common signs and symbols, and a guide to usage. The second also has a brief history of the English language, a note on dialect, and a list of English given names. Both are excellent value for the money, and, if the second is the more expensive, its greater comprehensiveness makes it worth it. Another good dictionary comes from Canada.[27] It too has clear definitions, helped by the use of illustrations and by sentences exemplifying the use of the word. Variant spellings are given, and maps are used whenever possible to indicate the location and extent of the items that can be territorially defined. The level of usage is given, and restrictive phrases show limitations of meaning, while synonyms not used in the definition are shown at the end of the entry. Many recent words are included, but the particular interest of this dictionary lies in the large number of distinctively Canadian words, spellings, and pronunciations that appear in it. R. R. Lodwig and E. F. Barrett[28] give a brief general account of dictionaries, describing the different types of them, the problems connected with their compilation, and their use. They then deal with types of word-formation, words and their meanings, and change of meaning. On the whole the book is well done, it reads interestingly, and the authors have managed to

[25] *Klein's Comprehensive Etymological Dictionary of the English Language. Vol. II, L-Z*, ed. E. Klein. Elsevier. pp. iii+855–1776. £9.

[26] *The American College Dictionary*, ed. C. L. Barnhart and J. Stern. New York: Random House. pp. xxviii+1444. $6.95.

The Random House Dictionary of the English Language. College Edition, ed. L. Urdang and S. B. Flexner. New York: Random House. pp. xxxi+1568.

[27] *Dictionary of Canadian English. The Senior Dictionary*, ed. W. S. Avis, P. D. Drysdale, R. J. Gregg, and M. H. Scargill. Toronto: Gage. pp. xxvii+1284. $7.75.

[28] *The Dictionary and the Language*, by R. R. Lodwig and E. F. Barrett. New York: Hayden. pp. x+181. $4.45.

find many new and relevant examples. Janet M. Bately, 'Ray, Worlidge, and Kersey's Revision of *The New World of English Words*' (*Ang*), shows the inadequacy of Starnes and Noyes's account of Kersey's sources for 'country words'. Kersey used a number of other works besides Worlidge's *Dictionarium* and he made no use at all of Ray. J. H. Friend[29] has made a detailed study of the history of American lexicography between 1798 and 1864. He deals briefly with the earliest American dictionaries, and more fully with Webster's 1806 one. The 1828 dictionary is compared with that of Johnson, and an examination made of Webster's spelling preferences, his treatment of Americanisms, and his handling of etymology. The following chapter describes the work of Worcester, compares it with that of Webster, and gives an interesting account of the war of the dictionaries. It is clear that Worcester considerably influenced the production of later dictionaries, and he deserves much of the credit that has been monopolized by Webster. The history of American lexicography between 1798 and 1864 is a record of extraordinarily rapid progress, and by the end of the Civil War the dictionaries that went under the names of Worcester and Webster were superior to any of those produced on this side of the Atlantic. But these American dictionaries rested on an English tradition which, by 1860, had already begun the ferment that was to produce the *O.E.D.*, the greatest of all dictionaries of the English language. F. G. Cassidy, in 'A Descriptive Approach to the Lexicon' (*Approaches in Linguistic Methodology*, see footnote 13), suggests that an ideal lexicon comprising a full inventory of the morphs and morph combinations of a language, arranged and studied structurally, is now possible, while H. Kučera and W. N. Francis[30] have obtained lexical and statistical information from the analysis of a corpus of American English consisting of over a million words. Five hundred samples of approximately equal length were taken, distributed among fifteen categories representing a full range of subject-matter and prose styles. Much of the book is taken up with two lists which give the order of frequency. Other tables and graphs analyse the distribution in the corpus of the occurrences of frequent words, word length, and sentence length. The results will be of particular value to lexicographers, linguists, and textbook writers. H. H. Josselson, 'Lexicography and the Computer' (*Jakobson Essays*), describes the part played in lexicography by computers and related electronic data-processing equipment at the present time, and the much larger role they are destined to play in the future, while A. H. Marckwardt traces the 'Lexical Redistribution in Modern English *say* and *tell*' (*Dostert Papers*).

The first of the following books[31]

[29] *The Development of American Lexicography 1798–1864*, by J. H. Friend. The Hague: Mouton & Co. pp. 129. 29 Guilders.

[30] *Computational Analysis of Present-Day American English*, by H. Kučera and W. N. Francis. Brown U.P. pp. xxv+424. $15.

[31] *Patterns of Language. Papers in General, Descriptive and Applied Linguistics*, by A. McIntosh and M. A. K. Halliday. Longmans. pp. xi+199. 27s. 6d.

Word and Symbol. Studies in English Language, by C. L. Wrenn. Longmans. pp. xiii+197. 27s. 6d.

The Many Hues of English, by M. Pei. New York: Random House. pp. viii+214. $4.95.

Anniversary Papers by Colleagues and Pupils of George Lyman Kittredge. New York: Russell & Russell. pp. vii+462. $11.

The English Language in the School Program, ed. R. F. Hogan. Champaign, Illinois: National Council of Teachers of English. pp. x+280. $2.50.

A Short History of Literary English, by W. F. Bolton. Arnold. pp. x+86. 15s.

contains six papers by A. McIntosh and five by M. A. K. Halliday, only four of which have not previously been published. Of these, two by McIntosh, 'Linguistics and English Studies', and 'Some Thoughts on Style', deal with the contributions of linguistics to the study of style, while a third, 'A Four-Letter Word in "Lady Chatterley's Lover"', is concerned with formulating the necessary rules by means of which a computer could distinguish between the different senses of *know*. The only previously unpublished paper by Halliday, 'Typology and the Exotic', deals with the classification of languages. C. L. Wrenn reprints ten articles, the first of which, 'Word and Symbol', surveys modern developments in the study of language, emphasizing the close interdependence of language and literature. The author's wide and humane learning comes out well in these stimulating essays, and if those on the language of Spenser, Milton, and Eliot most clearly illustrate the value of a knowledge of the history of the language for the literary critic, any reader will find here much else of interest. The book by M. Pei contains a series of short articles, many of which originally appeared as reviews of various books on the English language. They read interestingly, and are reasonably accurate, but rarely go very deeply into the particular subject. Also of note is a reprint of the series of essays presented to G. L. Kittredge. The next volume contains twenty-two papers, most of which were given before the National Council of Teachers of English in 1963 and 1964. Some of them are by such professional linguists as N. Chomsky, W. N. Francis, H. Kurath, R. I. McDavid, and others by those engaged in the teaching of English. As a rule the speakers have kept the particular audience in mind, and the

result is much useful information on modern tendencies in linguistics, and their possible applications in the classroom. W. F. Bolton gives a brief sketch of the history of the English language, of which the first part deals in some thirty pages with changes in sound, vocabulary, and grammar from Old English to the present day. The second part is concerned with opinions about language at various periods, but the whole subject is treated so briefly that there are some distortions and inevitable omissions.

Of the books on modern English grammar,[32] that by H. V. King makes good use of modern theories on the subject. It is divided into three parts: syntax; phonetics, including stress and intonation; and morphology and word-formation. The introductions to the various sections are well done, with clear explanations, and there are numerous carefully constructed exercises. Similarly, M. Finder uses the methods and results of structural linguistics. He comments on the nature of language, gives a simple structural description of English, and describes the methods of inquiry used by modern linguists. In addition, there are chapters on the relation

[32] *Guide and Workbook in the Structure of English*, by H. V. King. Englewood Cliffs, N. J.: Prentice-Hall. pp. xiii+126. 37s.
A Structural View of English, by M. Finder. Boston: Ginn. pp. iv+108. $1.56.
A Description of English, by A. E. Darbyshire. Arnold. pp. ix+182. 14s.
A Transformational Syntax, by B. Hathaway. New York: Ronald Press. pp. x+315. $6.
Modern Grammar, by P. Roberts. New York: Harcourt, Brace & World. pp. viii+439. $5.95.
The Elements of English, by W. Brandford. Routledge. pp. ix+198. 25s.
Essays on the Teaching of English in Honor of Charles Swain Thomas, ed. R. M. Gay. New York: Russell & Russell. pp. xxi+286. $9.
The Five Clocks, by M. Joos. New York: Harcourt, Brace & World. pp. xvi+108. $1.45.

between the written and spoken languages, and sections on the phonemes of English. The explanations are clear and straightforward, and technical language is avoided as much as possible. A. E. Darbyshire sets out to give an objective insight into the problems of what happens when language is being used. An attempt is made to harmonize the Bloomfield and Firth traditions, and to bring into contact with them the knowledge derived from communications engineering. The author deals in turn with language in general, with the various techniques of description, and with phonology, grammar, and lexis, while an appendix gives a useful brief description of transformational-generative grammar. B. Hathaway provides a grammar of modern American English which employs the techniques of transformational grammar. He deals in turn with various grammatical concepts, the parts of speech, the different sentence patterns, and word-formation. Numerous exercises are included, along with a necessary glossary of technical terms. P. Roberts makes use of the same techniques, and although mainly concerned with syntax, many of the chapters have short sections on semantics, phonology, morphology, and the history of the language. W. Brandford's description of the patterns of English contains a good deal of information on language in general, and so makes a good introduction to general linguistics. Though intended for a first year University course, it will also be found useful by those concerned with the teaching of English to non-native speakers. A collection of essays in honour of C. S. Thomas is the reprint of a book originally published in 1940. Most of them are on the teaching of English, and deal with such subjects as the use of linguistics, the curriculum, creative writing, etc., but there is also an interesting view of the English public schools. Many are by practising teachers, and as such they have much of value and interest to all concerned with the subject. In addition, M. Joos's influential work on the different registers of English, with an interesting introduction by A. H. Marckwardt, is now available as a paperback, whilst E. M. Uhlenbeck's 'Language in Action' (*Jakobson Essays*) analyses a rather pompous example of newspaper English.

The first of the following books[33] contains a series of essays on the teaching of foreign languages, and many of them will have relevance for those engaged in the teaching of English to non-native speakers. The selections move from the discussions of theories of language and of language teaching to the practical aspects of the classroom and the qualifications of language teachers. L. A. Hill reprints seventeen articles originally published between 1958 and 1963, along with a previously unpublished one dating from 1956. The author has had considerable experience in the teaching of English as a foreign language, and there is much of interest in these essays which range from a description of English noun classes to the best use of the tape-recorder or the film. J. D. O'Connor provides a systematic introduction to the pronunciation of English, beginning with a discussion of general problems and going on to describe the speech organs. Consonants,

---

[33] *Foreign Language Teaching. An Anthology*, ed. J. Michel. New York: Macmillan. pp. x+404. 63s.

Selected Articles on the Teaching of English as a Foreign Language, by L. A. Hill. O.U.P. pp. vii+142. 8s. 6d.

Better English Pronunciation, by J. D. O'Connor. C.U.P. pp. viii+179. 21s.

English Stress Patterns, by E. L. Tibbitts. Cambridge: Heffer. pp. 77. 8s. 6d.

vowels, and diphthongs are treated in detail, followed by sections on words in combination, on rhythm patterns, and on intonation. Remedial exercises are given, and an appendix summarizes the main pronunciation difficulties of Arabic, Cantonese, Hindi, French, German, and Spanish speakers. E. L. Tibbits provides a series of exercises for non-native speakers on English patterns of stress and rhythm. The examples are arranged in groups, beginning with a single stressed syllable and going up to twelve, with a phonetic transcription on the opposite page.

P. S. Rosenbaum[34] is concerned with sentences embedded in noun and verb phrases. These phrases, called complementations, are examined in the light of two proposed sets of rules: phrase structure rewriting rules which generate underlying sentence structure, and transformational rules which map the underlying structure on to a new derived surface structure. An analysis and defence of the phrase structure is offered, and the transformational rules justified with respect to noun-phrase and verb-phrase complementation. The author then applies his theories to complementation in adjectival predicate constructions, and finally presents a survey of earlier research. The main conclusions of this study are to be found in the same author's 'Phrase Structure Principles of English Complex Sentence Formation' (*JL*). In 'A transformational Re-Examination of English Questions' (*L*) J. L. Malone makes a semantic analysis of interrogation and declaration in modern English, with a transformational presentation of the results. D. L. Olmsted, 'On Some Axioms about Sentence Length'

(*L*), concludes that the assumption of infinite sentence length is not only not factual, it is also counter-intuitive, while A. J. Compton, in 'Aural Perception of Different Syntactic Structures and Lengths' (*LS*), shows that perception of sentences is affected by their syntactic structure, and varies according to the grammatical complexity of the statements. Y. Mōri, 'The Speaker and the Sentence-Subject' (*The English Literary Society of Japan*), deals in turn with the genesis of belief-context, form versus meaning in basic sentences, the sentence-subject of higher order, sense and reference, and modalities, concluding that success in speech largely depends on how well the speaker reflects himself in the sentences of his making. W. F. Klatte, 'Sentence Morphemes in English' (*The Canadian Journal of Linguistics*), attempts to define a form class of English represented by the vocalic nasals and nasalized central vowels, e.g. *hmm*, *hunh*; by the *yes-* and *no-*forms, e.g. *unh-hunh*; by the various vocalic nuclei, *oh*, *ah*, *er*, *ooh*; by forms such as *well*, *so*, *why*; exclamations such as *gosh*, *wow*, *gee*; vocatives such as *John*; and sentence adverbs such as *certainly*. Each of these is discussed in some detail, and it is decided that such sentence morphemes should be incorporated into the normal linguistic system of English. S. Hattori investigates 'The Sense of Sentence and the Meaning of Utterance' (*Jakobson Essays*), and Vera Vouk makes use of a 100-hour sample of spoken English, as recorded in Hansard, for a 'Comparison of Speech Forms used in Utterances and References to Utterances' (*ES*). H. A. Koefoed, in 'Structure and Usage as Applied to Word-Order' (*Årbok for Universitetet i Bergen. Humanistisk Serie*), explains the concept of Danish sentence structure developed by Diderichsen,

---

[34] *The Grammar of English Predicate Complement Constructions*, by P. S. Rosenbaum. M.I.T. Press. pp. xii+128. 47s.

and shows how this can be applied not only to other Scandinavian languages but to German and English as well. Eirian C. Davies, 'Some Notes on English Clause Types' (*TPS*), by the application of transformational type tests, shows that there are differences in the underlying deep grammar of clauses, according to the sub-type of clause comment adjunct which they are found to contain. Moreover, the different sub-types of clause comment adjunct can be correlated with differences in the origin of the comment, and in what the comment is about. R. A. Hudson discusses 'Constituency in a Systemic Description of the English Clause' (*Lingua*), while L. G. Jones examines the 'Grammatical Patterns in English and Russian Verse' (*Jakobson Essays*) in an attempt to illustrate the possibilities of a mathematical poetics, and R. Abernathy, 'Rhymes, Non-rhymes, and Antirhyme' (*Jakobson Essays*), points out various notions about verse structure in terms of rhyme that have corollaries which tend to be overlooked, either because a proper logical perspective is lacking, or because of the bulk of material needed for their empirical investigation.

F. Behre[35] examines the use of such phrases as *a good deal, a lot, much*, in Agatha Christie's writings. It is found that the various structural groups do not always present uniform types, but the author's frequent use of qualifiers and intensifiers in familiar patterns is not, as it is sometimes said to be, a criterion of careless writing. On the contrary, it demands considerable skill to make this kind of writing 'live' in the talk of her characters and the narrative of her story-

[35] *Studies in Agatha Christie's Writings*, by F. Behre. Gothenburg Studies in English 19. Stockholm: Almqvist & Wiksell. pp. 203. Sw. Cr. 28.

tellers. The distribution of the various patterns is then investigated in some detail. D. Bolinger, 'Adjectives in English: Attribution and Predication' (*Lingua*), claims that traditional relative clause transformation fails to explain many instances of attributive adjectives, and he offers two solutions to account for the restrictions in their use. P. C. Doherty deals with 'The Syntax of the Compared Adjective in English' (*L*), and according to Y. Birenbaum, in the classification of 'English Compound Adjectives Consisting of a Noun Stem plus an Adjective Stem' (*ZAA*), semantic analysis should be supported by taking into account their transformational potentialities. By this is meant finding corresponding word-groups with identical relations between the components. In this way various types are distinguished, and a classification proposed which embraces almost all adjectives of the pattern under discussion. G. L. Trager makes 'A Componential Morphemic Analysis of English Personal Pronouns' (*L*) in which they are morphemically segmented into three components: a prefix indicating person, a bound base that is the pronominal base, and a final component that is either a case suffix or a postfix of gender. J. R. Ross, 'On the Cyclic Nature of English Pronominalization' (*Jakobson Essays*), believes that certain facts about anaphoric pronouns can be accounted for if the rule which introduces them is an obligatory cyclically-ordered transformation, while R. Arnold's '"Them" als demonstratives Adjektiv' (*ZAA*) shows that this use is first recorded in colloquial English in the second half of the seventeenth century, and that thereafter its popularity quickly increased. In 'The Lag of Relative "Who"' (*N*) H. H. Meier attempts an explanation of the fact that *who* was the last to establish itself as a simple relative. It was for long used only in the oblique cases, not in the nominative, and an examination of its rise shows clearly the various forces that helped or hindered it. On the whole it is noticeable that the delaying factors are structural, unintentional, and native, whereas the helping factors are normative, intentional, and foreign. This inner contrast goes far to explain the time-lag in the development of *who* as a relative in comparison with *that* and *which*. N. E. Osselton shows that in current English 'Introductory *this*' (*ES*) has an individualizing function which it shares with the indefinite article, and R. Huddleston, in 'More on the English Comparative' (*JL*), deals with the morphology of the compared adjective or adverb. A. Joly[36] derives *than* from OE *þonne*, the instrumental *þon* plus the negative particle *ne*. Formerly *than* was not the only comparative conjunction, and all the other particles used in comparative sentences were in some way related to negation. Consequently, from a historical viewpoint, it is legitimate to include *than* among these negative words. In modern English, except in dialects, it is now the only comparative particle in the language, but the negative value is still there though no longer felt.

C. A. Hidalgo analyses studies of 'English Verb Inflection' (*Lingua*) by A. A. Hill, C. F. Hockett, and B. Bloch, and offers his own proposed transformational treatment of it. W. H. Hirtle[37] describes the uses in English of the simple and progressive forms, and discusses the question whether the latter is to be regarded as a tense, a mood, an aspect, or as something else. An event in the progressive is represented as having already started, and therefore beyond the control of the subject. In the case of the simple form, the whole event is attributed to the subject, and is then seen as wholly subservient to it, the subject conditioning the event but not being conditioned by it as with the progressive. Basically the relationship underlying both is that between subject and verb, a relationship that involves not only a temporal link but also the closely connected one of conditioner and conditionee. In general the simple and progressive forms appear to express two possibilities, the active voice and the middle voice respectively. 'A Grammatical Description of the Accusative with Infinitive and Related Structures in English' (*ES*) by J. A. van Ek begins with a brief introduction to generative - transformational grammar, and goes on to describe the constructions in terms of this technique. E. Bach proposes a re-analysis of '*Have* and *be* in English Syntax' (*L*) in which the two forms in their use as main verbs are eliminated from the base and reintroduced by transformational rules. These rules are shown to be minor additions to those required on independent grounds, and it is further suggested that the use of these forms as auxiliaries can be explained in the same way. J. S. Gruber speculates on the syntactic and semantic nature of the verbs '*Look* and *See*' (*L*) in an attempt to find out the syntactic structures underlying the sentences in which these verbs are overtly manifested, and in 'Auxiliaries and the Criterion of Simplicity' (*L*) Erica C. García makes use of such words as *keep*, *begin*, *continue* as a test of the criterion, deciding that so long as the basic concept of 'descriptive

[36] *Negation and the Comparative Particle in English*, by A. Joly. Quebec: Laval U.P. pp. 44. $2.95.

[37] *The Simple and Progressive Forms. An Analytical Approach*, by W. H. Hirtle. Quebec: Laval U.P. pp. x + 115. $4.

adequacy' remains undefined, reliance on the derived criterion of simplicity must be illusory. D. Bolinger examines the problems posed for generative grammar by 'The Imperative in English' (*Jakobson Essays*), while T. Kisbye, 'On the So-Called Imperative with Preposed Pronominal Subject (1489–1695)' (*Archiv*), points out that the type 'You go to the king' does not occur in printed English between these dates. He distinguishes between a hortatory and a suggested indicative, of which the second survives in Johnson and is responsible for the re-establishment of the first which had disappeared because of its precarious word order and formal unmarkedness following primarily upon the *thou* becoming *you* shift. M. A. K. Halliday's 'Notes on Transitivity and Theme in English' (*JL*) includes two parts of a proposed three-part treatment of the subject. The first contains a number of observations concerning transitivity, while the second deals with 'theme', used here as a general term for all those choices involving the distribution of information in the clause. In 'English Colloquial Metaphor and the Syntax' (*PP*) J. Nosek considers intransitive, transitive, and independent verbs, along with adverbial modifiers, under the aspect of the metaphor-syntax relationship. Using four sets of criteria, one may say that a verb derives its metaphorhood not only from its nominal but also from its adverbial complementations. In colloquial style, however, a syntactically unmodified verb may also be inherently metaphorical. K. Hasegawa, 'The Passive Construction in English' (*SELJ*), points out the difficulties in Chomsky's version of passive transformation, and offers a more adequate alternative to the treatment of English passives. In 'Passive and Pseudo-passive Verbal Groups in English'

(*ES*) Ljiljana Mihailovič notes the possible ambiguity of the construction *be* plus past participle. The verb *be* is an auxiliary verb in the periphrastic passive verbal group, and it is a verb of incomplete predication in the predicates of equational type. The past participle is also an ambiguous construction, since it can be homonymous with a predicative adjective. Therefore the criteria for classifying a *be* plus past participle group must be found outside the group itself, and depend on its contextualization.

D. Abercrombie[38] has written a good general introduction to phonetics in which English is used as the source for most of the illustrative material. The first chapter provides a general background to the subject and places it within the field of linguistic studies. Following chapters deal with the nature of the vocal organs and their use in the production of speech; the analysis of speech into suitable units for description; the division of the units into vowels and consonants; the ways in which particular languages organize these into language-bearing patterns; and the roles in speech of such features as voice quality, rhythm, and intonation. The different kinds of phonetic notation and their particular purposes are then described, while other subjects discussed include types of assimilation, the different kinds of consonants, and the theory and application of the cardinal vowel diagram. The book is intended primarily for students of such subjects as linguistics, speech therapy, and communications engineering, and since no previous knowledge is assumed, the presentation is made as simple as possible, with the minimum use of diagrams

[38] *Elements of General Phonetics*, by D. Abercrombie. Edinburgh U.P. Chicago: Aldine. pp. iv+203. 30s.

and exotic symbols. Ilse Lehiste[39] reprints thirty-two articles by different authors on various aspects of acoustic phonetics. Those articles have been chosen which are recognized as pioneering works on the subject, and the result is a collection which will be of particular value to those who come to the field with a background of general linguistics and articulatory phonetics. P. Ladefoged[40] reprints the results of a number of experiments on the mechanisms by which speech is produced and perceived, a subject recently extended and modified by research in the fields of physiological and acoustic phonetics and in perception psychology. The book makes valuable contributions to our knowledge of stress and respiratory activity, the nature of vowel quality, and units in the perception and production of speech. W. N. Francis proposes 'A Modified System of Phonemic Transcription for one Idiolect of English' (*Dostert Papers*). The idiolect is in fact his own, and he replaces the more troublesome features of the Trager-Smith system in a way that may make it easier to learn for those who are not primarily linguists, and whose use of phonemic transcription is practical rather than theoretical. J. Krámský, 'Some Remarks on the Problem of the Phoneme' (*Jakobson Essays*), decides that the crucial test of the validity of this linguistic unit lies above all in its usefulness in methodology. The concept has expanded the horizons of language studies to such an extent that modern linguistics is unthinkable without it. E. Fischer-Jørgensen deals with the 'Perceptual Dimensions of Vowels' (*Jakobson*

Essays), while L. Lisker and A. S. Abramson, in 'Some Effects of Context on Voice Onset Time in English Stops' (*LS*), suggest reasons for the less sharp separation between voiceless and voiced consonants which appears in ordinary speech. C. F. Hockett, 'Where the Tongue Slips, There Slip I' (*Jakobson Essays*), examines various types of slips of the tongue, and considers the phonetic factors that produce them, while the investigation by Elaine P. Hannah and L. Engler of 'Juncture Phenomena and the Segmentation of a Linguistic Corpus' (*LS*) is intended to check the usefulness of the terminal juncture as a means of segmenting a linguistic corpus.

P. Lieberman[41] attempts to determine how people actually produce and perceive intonation, and to differentiate between the linguistic and emotional aspects of intonation and stress. He shows that intonation is a central feature and innate characteristic, based on universal constants of human psychology, and goes on to analyse the articulatory, acoustic, perceptual, phonetic, and syntactic dimensions of intonation for American English and for various related and unrelated languages. The resulting description is based on the breath-group which can span and delimit any constituent of the derived phrase marker, most often the primary constituents such as the sentence. Physiologic, acoustic, and perceptual criteria are dealt with, intonation in infant speech, the phonemic phrase, and prominence, stress, and emphasis in American English. The last two chapters are concerned with the perception and production of speech, and with a review of various studies

---

[39] *Readings in Acoustic Phonetics*, ed. Ilse Lehiste. M.I.T. Press. pp. ix+358. 93s.

[40] *Three Areas of Experimental Phonetics*, by P. Ladefoged. O.U.P. pp. vii+180. 15s.

[41] *Intonation, Perception, and Language*, by P. Lieberman. M.I.T. Press. pp. xiii+210. 60s.

of intonation from Sweet to Stetson and later. M. A. K. Halliday[42] reprints, with slight changes, previously published papers on 'The Tones of English' and 'Intonation in English Grammar'. To these have been added a short text of natural conversation transcribed and marked for intonation and rhythm, some additional tables, and a bibliography. Maria Schubiger has 'A Note on Two Notional Functions of the Low-Falling Nuclear Tone in English' (*ES*), K. L. Pike proposes a theory of 'Suprasegmentals in Reference to Phonemes of Item, of Process, and of Relation', and F. Daneš deals with the 'Order of Elements and Sentence Intonation' (both in *Jakobson Essays*).

C. E. Osgood, G. J. Suci, and P. H. Tannenbaum[43] discuss the nature and theory of meaning, and present an objective method for its measurement which they call the semantic differential. This is not a specific test, but rather a general technique of measurement that can be adapted to a wide variety of problems. Most of the book is taken up with a description of the method, and of its far-reaching implications for empirical research. B. Trnka, 'Words, Semantemes, and Sememes' (*Jakobson Essays*), offers a discussion of the fundamental notions of structural semantics which suggests some directions for its further development. In 'The Syncategorematic in Poetry: From Semantics to Syntactics' (*Jakobson Essays*) M. W. Bloomfield takes the distinction between the metaphoric and metonymic or the symbolic and contiguous dichotomy in the linguistic process, and tries to show the usefulness of this distinction in

the study of literature. Irena Bellert advocates 'A Semantic Approach to Grammar Construction' (*Jakobson Essays*), claiming that a grammar based on a purely semantic approach will necessarily give a closer approximation to the adequacy of descriptions of natural languages, and L. Zawadowski draws up 'A Classification of Signs and Semantic Systems' (*Jakobson Essays*). R. A. Waldron's[44] book on sense and sense-development is divided into two parts. In the first he attempts to define meaning in linguistic terms, and summarizes the contributions to the subject by various scholars from Saussure to Ullmann and later. In the second he distinguishes three main types of semantic change: shift, metaphoric transfer, and metonymic transfer, dealing with each of these in considerable detail. The author has succeeded in finding numerous new and enlightening illustrative examples, and useful notes give a good deal of additional information. The only thing missing from this otherwise excellent book is an index of the words used as examples. From H. Koziol[45] comes an interesting and scholarly work, though on more traditional lines. But there is plenty of originality in the treatment of specific questions, and these owe much to previous articles by the author. Particularly useful is the large number of apposite examples drawn from the entire history of the language. The provision of a subject index and bibliography would have been useful, though so far as the latter is concerned there are numerous references in the notes following the various subsections. In general, within its own self-imposed

[42] *Intonation and Grammar in British English*, by M. A. K. Halliday. The Hague: Mouton & Co. pp. 62. 18 Guilders.

[43] *The Measurement of Meaning*, by C. E. Osgood, G. J. Suci, and P.H. Tannenbaum. Illinois U.P. pp. iii+346. 29s. 6d.

[44] *Sense and Sense Development*, by R. A. Waldron. Deutsch. pp. 224. 30s.

[45] *Grundzüge der englischen Semantik*, by H. Koziol. Wiener Beiträge zur englischen Philologie LXX. Wien-Stuttgart: Braumüller. pp. xv+279.

limitations, this is a particularly informative and readable book. In the second edition of C. S. Lewis's *Studies in Words*[46] are additional chapters on *world*, *life*, and the phrase *I dare say*. These are dealt with in some detail, and provide further interesting and significant examples of change of meaning. G. G. Pocheptsov, 'Syntaktische Wortvarianten. Zur Frage der Typen der Wortvariierung' (*ZAA*), points out that some lexicological variants may be called syntactical, since the meaning is conditioned by the structural particularities of the surroundings. According to the character of the relationship between the lexical content of the word variants and their syntactic particulars, a further distinction between syntactical and lexical-syntactical variations can be made. In 'Some Recent Developments in the Use of Nouns as Premodifiers in English' (*ZAA*) C. Mutt shows the increasing use of plural attributives, of compound words and various nonce-formations, and of nouns in apposition.

Ivor Brown[47] comments on a number of words which are of interest in various ways. The articles vary in length from brief notes to short essays, and read as well as the author's previous similar books. E. G. Fichtner's 'The Etymology of *goliard*' (*N*) connects the word with Primitive Germanic **galan*, **gōl* 'sing'. It probably originated in the medieval German dialects of the Rhine as a derogatory term for wandering clerics, the suggested connexions with L *gula* and with the biblical *Golias* resulting from medieval attempts to establish a suitable etymology for the word. H. Meier and Gertrud de Pena,

'"Tanzen". Über Ursprung und Geschichte eines europäischen Wortes' (*Archiv*), derive English *dance* from L *rotare*, *rotundare*, either via Anglo-Norman or via French, while K. Malone, 'On the Etymology of *scarf*' (*Dostert Papers*), proposes derivation from ON *skarfr*, and Margaret Stobie shows that in Canadian English 'A Bluff is a Grove of Trees' (*ELN*). According to J. K. Crellin the *O.E.D.* definition of 'Possets' (*NQ*) fails to distinguish between the posset whey and the thick curdled preparation. Other corrections to *O.E.D.* from *NQ* include B. Sanders, '"Point"': "Canon's Yeoman's Tale"'; G. A. Starr, 'Antedatings from Nicholas Udall's Translation of Erasmus's "Apophthegmas"'; J. C. Maxwell, '"Unavoided"'; R. Q. Tentilove, '"Commend" (used reflexively)'; C. Hart, 'Early English Kites and an Antedating of O.E.D.'; R. Hall, 'O.E.D. Antedatings in Philosophy'; Susie I. Tucker, 'Some Addenda to O.E.D.' and 'Notes on Sheridan's Vocabulary'; J. C. Maxwell, '"Academician"'; P. G. Scott, 'An Early Use of "Aesthetic"'; J. C. Maxwell, 'The Connotation of "Saga"'.

In 'Some Place Names of the West Riding' (*YDS*) A. H. Smith comments on general problems of meaning and interpretation in place-names, and goes on to deal with some of the types current in that area. K. I. Sandred, 'Notes on English Compound Place-Names in -*hamstede*' (*Namn och Bygd*), shows that although phonetic reduction has taken place in several such names, the same explanation hardly seems possible for all of them, though definite evidence one way or the other is lacking. In any case no conclusion is possible in the case of such English names until the operation of reduction in English place-names has been properly

---

[46] *Studies in Words*, by C. S. Lewis. 2nd ed. C.U.P. pp. vii+343. £2. Paper 13*s*. 6*d*.
[47] *A Ring of Words*, by I. Brown. Bodley Head. pp. 157. 18*s*.

studied, especially since investigations of related elements and of continental Germanic material are lacking. The same author notes that names with 'The Derivative Suffix *-et, -ett(e)*' (*Namn och Bygd*) are especially characteristic of the south-east, and he makes use of the Kentish Tithe Awards to show that such formations must go back to the Old English period, and are closely related to similar names on the continent. It seems likely that further investigation of them may throw a good deal of light on problems of typography, distribution, stratification, and early settlement history. J. McN. Dodgson, 'Hodge and Dodge' (*NQ*), suggests that in Cheshire place-names the first of these probably represents a dialect form of *hog*, analogous with the form *dodge* for *dog*.

A. B. Cottle[48] has produced an excellent dictionary of surnames containing over 8,000 English, Scottish, Welsh, and Irish family names. A lively introduction describes the four classes into which they fall, gives a brief account of the history of the study of surnames, and shows something of their interest and importance, especially as a reflex of social history. In the entries themselves, the name is assigned to its class, the meaning given, derivation, location if from a place-name, some indication of its frequency, and any restriction of it to a particular area. In addition, much miscellaneous information appears which, if not always strictly relevant, is invariably interesting. Altogether this is a particularly good book. Accurate without being dogmatic, learned but never dull, it manages to pack much information into a comparatively small space. From P. H.

Reaney[49] comes an authoritative book on surnames which deals with all aspects of the subject, ranging from misleading modern spellings, through the uses in names of obsolete words and meanings, to their classification, dialectal variation, distribution, etc. The different types are dealt with in detail, and special attention is paid to the identification of the places from which French surnames are taken. Chapters are included on the development of hereditary names, and on the homes of family names. Numerous illustrative examples are given from medieval records, printed and unprinted, and the development and origin of various names is clearly demonstrated by a succession of forms. The book deals with so many names that it becomes not only an interpretation of the author's standard *Dictionary of British Surnames*, but an extension to it, including a good deal of new material. The frequent lists may not make for easy reading, but the full indexes of subjects and names make the book easy to use for reference, and as such it will certainly prove indispensable. W. O. Hassall[50] defines the surname, and gives some indication of the sources for our knowledge of them, and of the available reference books. The different types of surname are dealt with in turn, while additional chapters deal with Christian names from surnames and with surnames which have become ordinary words. A large number of names are treated in the book, but so much of it consists of lists that it will be more useful for reference than for general reading, and not all the numerous illustrations are particularly relevant. The book by P.

[48] *The Penguin Dictionary of Surnames*, by A. B. Cottle. Penguin Books. pp. 334. 6*s*.

[49] *The Origin of English Surnames*, by P. H. Reaney. Routledge. pp. xix+415. 50*s*.

[50] *History through Surnames*, by W. O. Hassall. Oxford: Pergamon Press. pp. xv+224. 25*s*.

Hughes[51] gives a much more elementary account of the subject which, though reasonably well done, is too brief to go very far into it, nor are the etymologies always accurate.

Two further volumes of the *Survey of English Dialects*[52] contain the responses from seventy-five localities in the ten southern counties to Books I–VI of the Dieth-Orton questionnaire. The arrangement of the material follows the pattern of the volumes dealing with the northern counties, but the map of the southern network and the list of localities are transferred to a fold-out section at the front of the book. Tape recordings have been secured from all localities, and these were checked by the editors with the fieldworkers' transcriptions and the latter to some extent standardized. Obviously much of value has been learned by the editors from the production of the earlier volumes, with the result that these are easier to use, and perhaps rather more reliable. As the survey proceeds we are getting a good view of those rural dialects which still survive, and these volumes will certainly provide material for future detailed work on the subject. B. Hedevind[53] gives a detailed description of a modern dialect which could well serve as a model for future similar surveys. Dentdale is still comparatively isolated, and good informants were found more easily than is often the case. All the necessary information is given here: maps, the historical and geographical background, names

and details of informants, and an account of previous work on the subject. The phonemes of the present dialect are described in detail, and their development traced from late Northern Middle English. More than twenty transcriptions of tape recordings are included, and these also give good illustrations of the life of the area. The author evidently knows the area well, and has a full command of the most recent techniques in both descriptive and historical linguistics. M. Barry points out that, of the 104 known sets of 'Yorkshire Sheep-Scoring Numerals' (*YDS*), not one was obtained at first-hand from a shepherd. They are found mainly in the Yorkshire dales, none is recorded earlier than 1745, and they have been obsolete since the last quarter of the nineteenth century. It seems clear that they are ultimately Welsh, and it is usually assumed that they were imported from Wales during medieval times or a little later, but there is not much direct evidence to support this.

Dimensions of Dialect[54] contains a number of articles, most of which are concerned with the social dialects of the United States. They include R. I. McDavid, 'A Checklist of Significant Features for Discriminating Social Dialects'; F. Elizabeth Metz, 'Poverty, Early Language Deprivation, and Learning Ability'; E. Dale, 'Vocabulary Deprivation of the Underprivileged Child'; and K. S. Goodman, 'Dialect Barriers to Reading Comprehension'. In addition, the following articles appear in the *Publication of the American Dialect Society*:[55] N. A. Heap, 'A

[51] *Your Book of Surnames*, by P. Hughes. Faber. pp. 59. 12*s.* 6*d.*

[52] *Survey of English Dialects. Vol. IV. The Basic Material: The Southern Counties. Parts I and II*, by H. Orton and M. F. Wakelin. Leeds: Arnold. pp. 384; 385–782. £7 7*s.* each.

[53] *The Dialect of Dentdale in the West Riding of Yorkshire*, by B. Hedevind. Studia Anglistica Upsaliensia 5. Stockholm: Almqvist & Wicksell. pp. xviii+351. Sw. Cr. 60.

[54] *Dimensions of Dialect*, ed. Eldonna L. Evertts. Champaign, Illinois: National Council of Teachers of English. pp. vi+76. $1.25.

[55] *Publication of the American Dialect Society, Numbers 45 and 46*. Alabama U.P. pp. 39; 39. 1966.

Burley Tobacco Word List from Lexington, Kentucky'; A. L. Hench, 'Use by the *DAE* and the *DA* of Schele de Vere's Manuscript Notes'; B. G. Skillman, 'A Cleburne County, Arkansas, Word List'.

A Dictionary of Canadianisms[56] follows the tradition established by the *O.E.D.*, even though this has meant the exclusion of terms for which only oral evidence is available. A Canadianism is defined as a word, expression, or meaning which is native to Canada or distinctively characteristic of Canadian usage. The editors have confined themselves to source materials by persons native to or resident in Canada, or by visitors commenting on their experiences in the country. Some non-Canadian entries have been included. These are intended to clarify terms lending themselves freely to the formation of new Canadian compounds or to extensions of meaning; to serve as reference points for synonyms which are themselves Canadian; and to call attention to terms having special interest in various areas of Canadian activity. In the dictionary itself, the entry word is followed by the pronunciation, part of speech, etymology where relevant, and an indication of its usage. Then come the illustrative quotations, while, in addition, many of the entries include short notes offering additional information. The editors have succeeded in combining economy with the maximum of help to the reader; the dictionary is easy to use, gives all the information one could wish for, and shows clearly the contribution of Canadian English to various areas of activity. An excellent historical, descriptive, and etymological *Dic-*

tionary of Jamaican English[57] deals with the forms of English in use in Jamaica between 1655 and 1962. It includes all words and senses recorded in books about Jamaica, and in addition makes use of such oral sources as tape recordings and direct interviews, from which have been obtained dialect words for which a written form is unknown. For each entry the pronunciation is given when it differs from that of standard English, sense, part of speech, level of usage, spelling variants, etymology, and dated quotations. The introduction describes the sources used, the methods employed, and contains also a historical phonology of Jamaican English. The dictionary itself contains over 15,000 entries, and is followed by a seven-page supplement of additional words. D. DeCamp, 'African Day-Names in Jamaica' (*L*), shows that a system of day-names, indicating the sex and the day of the week on which a child was born, was carried from Africa to Jamaica in the seventeenth and eighteenth centuries. As personal names they are now almost extinct, but survive as pejorative common nouns. R. Hill, in 'Prospects of the Study of Early Australian Pronunciation' (*ES*), notes some possible sources of information, and indicates the kind of results to be expected from a study of them.

From H. Aarslef[58] comes an important description of the study of language during a period which saw the clash between the philosophical and the philological approaches to language. The opening chapter deals with the doctrines of language in the eighteenth century, with particular emphasis on Condillac's extension of

[56] *A Dictionary of Canadianisms on Historical Principles*, ed. W. S. Avis, C. Crate, P. Drysdale, D. Leechman, and M. H. Scargill. Toronto: Gage. pp. xxiii+927. $25.

[57] *Dictionary of Jamaican English*, ed. F. G. Cassidy and R. B. Le Page. C.U.P. pp. lxxi+489. £5.

[58] *The Study of Language in England 1780–1860*, by H. Aarslef. Princeton U. P. pp. vii+279. $7.50.

Locke. The next two are concerned with Horne Tooke's *Diversions of Purley*, tracing its long-continued, and mostly unfortunate, influence on the subject. The foundations of modern linguistics begin with Sir William Jones, and there is an excellent account of the 'Anniversary Discourses' which shows clearly that Schlegel was much more heavily indebted to Jones than has been generally allowed. The last two chapters describe the growth of the new philology in England. The interest in it was largely due to a desire to counter the materialistic philosophy of the Utilitarians, and it is this renewed interest in language that leads to the foundation of the Philological Society and to the projected publication of *A New English Dictionary*.

III

Old English Literature

R. M. WILSON

R. Arnold's interesting *Social history of England from 55* B.C. *to* A.D. *1215* devotes considerable space to the Anglo-Saxon period.[1] The author is mainly concerned to show how society was organized, how justice was done, the forms of government, and the relationships between the different classes. Good use is made of all types of available evidence, and occasional slips are of minor importance, e.g. Ecgbeorht of Northumbria was killed by the Picts, not the Mercians (p. 152), and it was Edric, not Eric the Wild who rebelled against the Conqueror (p. 268). Nearly a hundred excellently chosen illustrations are included, though the reproduction of them is not always as clear as it might have been. The first part of D. P. Kirby's book on Anglo-Saxon England[2] gives a chronological description of the political and religious history of the period, clear and balanced, but not particularly exciting. The second part, on government and society, literature and the arts, agriculture and commerce, is a good deal more interesting, and most readers will find something new in it. A wide variety of sources throws into relief both the practical reality of daily living at that time, and the influence of geography on the

social and political history, while a number of well-reproduced illustrations adds to the value of the book. H. M. Porter[3] gives a detailed account of what is known of the Saxon conquest of Somerset and Devon. The beginning of it is to be ascribed to Centwine, and its completion to Ine. The conquest of Cornwall took much longer, and there were native kings there until the beginning of the tenth century. But in both cases it seems likely that the occupation was as much a matter of gradual infiltration as of military conquest. Eleanor Duckett[4] provides a scholarly account of the political and cultural history of Europe in the tenth century which places Anglo-Saxon England in wider European context. The book contains much information on the literary, religious, architectural, and artistic survivals from the period but the author who has a wide knowledge of both primary and secondary sources, wears her learning lightly, and has succeeded in writing a particularly interesting book. C. Albertson's Anglo-Saxon heroes are the early saints.[5] He gives translations of the

[3] *The Saxon Conquest of Somerset and Devon*, by H. M. Porter. Bath: James Brodie. pp. 87. 15s.

[4] *Death and Life in the Tenth Century*, by Eleanor Duckett. Michigan U.P. pp. x+359. $8.75.

[5] *Anglo-Saxon Saints and Heroes*, by C. Albertson. Fordham U.P. pp. xv+347. $7.50.

[1] *A Social History of England from 55 B.C. to A.D. 1215*, by R. Arnold. Longmans. pp. xvi+423. 63s.

[2] *The Making of Early England*, by D. P. Kirby. Batsford. pp. 320. 45s.

Latin lives of six of them—Cuthbert, Wilfred, Guthlac, Ceolfrith, Willibald, and Boniface, along with Bede's *Lives of the Abbots*—to each of which is prefixed a brief introduction. The translations are good, and the notes give valuable information on the background, whether religious, social, or political, as also on the various literary influences. A general introduction connects the Anglo-Saxon heroic age with other similar periods, and shows the various influences, whether from Rome, the Germanic heroic age, the Celts, or even Byzantium, which helped to shape its special characteristics. More particularly, it makes clear the reason for the heroic cast of much of the Anglo-Saxon religious literature: the young nobles brought with them to the cloister the ideals of their secular life, and they transferred these to their religious life. An important and scholarly, if sometimes rather provocative, collection of essays on various aspects of Anglo-Saxon England comes from E. John.[6] The articles range from wide surveys of general topics, such as the reality behind the title of *bretwealda*, the problem of folkland, or the structure of Anglo-Saxon society, to detailed studies of various textual problems. In addition to the usual sources, the author makes good use of linguistic evidence and of Old English literature. Altogether the book adds much to our knowledge of Anglo-Saxon society, placing it in a European rather than a merely insular setting. L. Whitbread, 'After Bede: The Influence and Dissemination of his Doomsday Verses' (*Archiv*), describes the different versions of the Latin poem, gives the locations of surviving manuscripts, and lists the possible borrowings. In 'Wulfstan *Cantor* and Anglo-Saxon

Law',[7] Dorothy Whitelock comments on two passages in the Latin verse life of St. Swithun by Wulfstan. The first throws additional light on the Laws of Edgar, providing evidence of a lost edict, whilst the second gives information on the preliminaries to trial by combat.

W. G. Hoskins[8] gives excellent advice for the amateur archaeologist, showing what clues should be looked for on the ground, and where these can be followed up by the use of documents ranging from Anglo-Saxon charters to estate maps. Anglo-Saxon subjects are often used as illustrations of method, though the book is of course much wider in intention and fact that this, and there is also a useful chapter on place-names and topography. Vera I. Evison, in 'The Dover Ring-Sword and Other Sword-Rings and Beads' (*Archaeologia*), lists the known examples of sword-beads from England, and the ring-swords from Western Europe. It appears that the custom of wearing a large bead on the sword, brought to England by the Franks, must have been in fashion as early as the fifth century, and that the sword-ring was also introduced by the same people at about the same time. Janet M. Bately adds a discussion of the runes on the Gilton pommel, and concludes that no satisfactory interpretation of them has yet been suggested. 'Swords and Runes in South-East England' (*The Antiquaries Journal*) by Sonia C. Hawkes and R. I. Page deals with a hitherto unrecognized runic inscription on a sixth-century pommel from Sarre, and reconsiders those on the pommel from Gilton and the scabbard from Chessell

[6] *Orbis Britanniae*, by Eric John. Leicester U.P. pp. xii+303. 42*s*.

[7] In *Nordica et Anglica. Studies in Honor of Stefán Einarsson*, ed. A. H. Orrick. The Hague: Mouton. pp. 196. 50 Guilders. Henceforward abbreviated as *Nordica*.

[8] *Fieldwork in Local History*, by W. G. Hoskins. Faber. pp. 192. 25*s*.

Down. It then discusses the theory that the knowledge of runes did not arrive in this country until the advent of Christianity, long after the invasion period, but a survey of early runic inscriptions provides neither archaeological nor runological evidence for such a theory. In 'Six Old English Runic Inscriptions Reconsidered' (*Nordica*) K. Schneider offers interpretations of the inscriptions on the *scanmodu* coin, the Chessell Down scabbard mount, the Gilton pommel, the Derbyshire bone-plate, the Coquet Island ring, and the Æðered ring. They are taken to be of a magic or magico-religious nature, and assigned to various dates ranging from *c*. 500 to the first half of the eighth century. R. E. Kaske claims that the inscriptions on 'The Silver Spoons of Sutton Hoo' (*S*) are the work of different engravers, and that the SAULOS of the second is merely a bad attempt to copy from memory the PAULOS on the first. O. K. Werckmeister,[9] from a comparison of two early eighth-century miniatures in the *Echternach Gospels* with two in the *Book of Kells* from the end of the same century, all by Northumbrian artists, attempts to demonstrate a connexion between the illuminations and the spiritual climate of the time. He concludes that the illuminations similarly show the change from the preponderantly ascetic attitude of the time of Cassian to the mainly contemplative one of the time of Cassiodorus. Whether or not the author makes out his case, he has some interesting suggestions, illustrated by good plates, on the illuminations and on the spiritual ideals of the time.

J. D. A. Ogilvy[10] has considerably expanded his valuable but long out of print *Books Known to Anglo-Latin Writers*. An interestingly written account of what is known of the Anglo-Saxon libraries is followed by a list of disasters to English libraries up to about 1300. The following catalogue of books is arranged alphabetically by authors, or by titles for anonymous works; bibles or parts of bibles are reasonably enough excluded, as also works by native authors, since in both cases they were certainly known in this country. On the other hand, anonymous works of possible English origin, those of probable or certain Irish origin, and those by Boniface and Alcuin are rightly included. Every kind of evidence is used: borrowing by writers who remained in this country, provenance of manuscripts, the presence of English glosses, the use of the insular script, etc. Often enough the evidence is not conclusive, but the author has preferred to err on the side of comprehensiveness. The result is a long and detailed list of works probably or certainly known to English writers of the period which will be of immense value to all concerned with any aspect of Anglo-Saxon life or thought. No doubt it may be possible in the future to make additions to the various lists, but these are likely to be comparatively unimportant.

Hitherto *Sweet's Anglo-Saxon Reader* contained a remarkably good selection of texts, but the notes were scanty, and the glossary not easy to use. Consequently Dorothy Whitelock, the latest editor,[11] has made few changes in the texts, and these few

---

[9] *Irisch-northumbrische Buchmalerei des 8Jahrhunderts und monastische Spiritualität*, by Otto-Karl Werckmeister. Berlin: de Gruyter. pp. xii+186. 48 plates. DM 48.

[10] *Books Known to the English, 597–1066*, by J. D. A. Ogilvy. Mediaeval Academy of America. pp. xx+300. $7.50.

[11] *Sweet's Anglo-Saxon Reader in Prose and Verse*, revised by Dorothy Whitelock. O.U.P. xiii+404. 25s.

are a decided improvement. The last extract from Boethius is replaced by one of Alfred's original additions; a different Ælfric homily provides an example of his exegetical style; a more interesting charter and a more certainly authentic writ replace former examples; while the non-West Saxon texts include a further specimen of early Kentish and a new passage from the *Lindisfarne Gospels*. In addition, the *Dream of the Rood* is now complete, the whole of the annal for 755 is given, and a slightly different selection from the *Laws of Ine*. The introductions to the various passages have been greatly expanded, bibliographical references brought up to date, and the textual notes are far fuller than in the earlier editions. In the glossary the words are now given in the forms in which they appear in the texts, along with any necessary cross-references. The net result of Professor Whitelock's skilful revision is that while the good points of the original edition are retained, its drawbacks for the student have now been eliminated.

C. L. Wrenn's *A Study of Old English Literature*[12] passes quickly over the non-literary remains, but deals in detail with the rest, and especially with the poetry. It is not easy to find something new to say about the latter, but the author manages it, so much so that more of his illuminating remarks on the literary qualities would have been welcome. He seems rather out of sympathy with the prose, and perhaps there is more to be said for it than he allows. But on the whole it is the introductory chapters which will be found the most interesting and original. There is a good account of Anglo-Saxon culture, and a suggestive chapter on the continuity of English

[12] *A Study of Old English Literature*, by C. L. Wrenn. Harrap. pp. xi+283. 42s.

poetry; the Germanic heroic tradition is well described, and a section on form and style, dealing mainly with the poetry, gives a good description of metrical and stylistic characteristics. Throughout, the author is concerned to demonstrate the connexions of Old English literature with later developments, and to show how different aspects of Anglo-Saxon studies can be used to throw light on each other. The result is a useful, and more than that an interesting, book on the subject. J. J. Campbell, 'Knowledge of Rhetorical Figures in Anglo-Saxon England' (*JEGP*), argues that even the early poetry was influenced by Latin rhetoric, with which any educated Old English poet would have come into contact. Evidence is produced to show that the teaching of Latin in England was more widespread than is usually assumed, and Jackson describes the kind of teaching, especially in grammar, that would have been normal. The interest of the English in Latin poetry between the eighth and the eleventh centuries is demonstrated, and three manuscripts of Leofric of Exeter give examples of the kind of glossed text in which the commentator was at pains to explain technical matters about poetry. Consequently, the very manuscripts in which the Anglo-Saxons read their Latin poetry would help to carry further the reader's instruction in figurative techniques. In 'The Canons of Old English Criticism' (*ELH*) S. B. Greenfield urges greater attention to the contribution made by grammatical elements to literary structure and texture, especially in poetry. Two current trends in the criticism of Old English poetry discourage this: the methods of both the allegorical and the oral-formulaic schools. The latter inevitably concentrates on the grammatical patterns that a poem has in common with other poems, and so decides that Old English poetry is not to be evaluated by ordinary critical standards. The validity of this approach is examined, and it is decided that in fact the recognition of the formulaic or traditional nature of Old English poetry enlarges the scope and promotes the art of the critic. Greenfield then analyses two passages from *Beowulf* to show that a close analysis of verbal and grammatical patterns is not incompatible with the nature of Old English poetry. In dealing with it there is no need to reject the ordinary canons of literary judgement, nor need we evolve new critical methods, apart from those applicable to all English poetry. Elsewhere, in 'Grammar and Meaning in Poetry' (*PMLA*), the same author, by an examination of various passages from Old English poetry, illustrates the ways in which grammatical analysis can illuminate poetic meaning and effect in the realm of syntactic ambiguity. He gives a further example of this in 'Grendel's Approach to Heorot: Syntax and Poetry'[13] where, by a detailed analysis of lines 702b–736a, he shows how the poet's manipulation of diction and syntax achieves subtle effects in bringing Grendel, Beowulf, and the warriors from a polarity of position, action, and attitude, to confrontation. In 'Old English Formulas and Systems' (*ES*), D. K. Fry attempts a re-definition of the formula, though without any great success. J. B. Bessinger, Jr., 'The Sutton Hoo Harp Replica and Old English Musical Verse' (*Nordica*), describes the reconstructed harp, and comments on its probable use in the recitation of poetry, while J. Nist, 'Metrical Uses of the Harp in *Beowulf*' (*Old English Poetry*, see

footnote 13), argues that it was used more particularly to strengthen weak measures, and to heighten the emotional tone by means of heavily emphasizing the syncopation.

E. T. Donaldson, in his prose translation of *Beowulf*,[14] attempts with some success to reproduce as far as possible the word order, speech rhythm, and imagery of the poem. By these means it is possible to preserve the most striking characteristics of the original, its remarkable richness of rhetorical elaboration alternating with, and often combined with, the barest simplicity of statement. The introduction places the poem in its social setting and discusses some problems of translation. Constance B. Hieatt[15] is content to render it into clear straightforward prose, and she includes also *Brunanburh*, *Maldon*, *The Wanderer*, *Deor*, *Judith*, *The Dream of the Rood*, and *The Seafarer*. The last of these is given in the very free version by Ezra Pound, so that the reader can compare the advantages of verse and prose in the translation of Old English poetry. An introduction gives a general account of the characteristics of Old English verse, with special reference to *Beowulf*, and of the society which produced it. Also to be noticed is an interesting and suggestive essay 'On Translating Beowulf' (*Old English Poetry*), by B. Raffel.

J. C. Pope's edition of *Cædmon's Hymn*, *Brunanburh*, *Maldon*, *The Dream of the Rood*, *The Wanderer*, *The Seafarer*, and *Deor*[16] normalizes the language, but gives the manuscript

[13] In *Old English Poetry*, ed. R. P. Creed. Brown U.P. pp. xii+332. $10.

[14] *Beowulf*, by E. T. Donaldson. Longmans. pp. xv+58. 7s. 6d.
[15] *Beowulf and Other Old English Poems*, by Constance B. Hieatt. New York: Odyssey Press. pp. vii+119. $1.25.
[16] *Seven Old English Poems*, by J. C. Pope. New York: Bobbs-Merrill. pp. xii+213. $3.25.

readings in the footnotes. The commentary includes a general introduction to each poem, with useful textual notes, while a detailed account of Old English versification and a comprehensive glossary are also provided. J. B. Bessinger's revision of Magoun's edition of *Beowulf* and *Judith*[17] includes also the *Fight at Finnesburg* and lines 35–49 of *Widsith*. No textual apparatus or notes are given, but misprints in the earlier edition have been corrected, and some inconsistencies removed in the normalization of the texts to early West Saxon.

Jane A. Leake[18] brings together evidence to suggest that the Geats of *Beowulf* have nothing to do with the obscure Gautar of southern Sweden or with the Jutes, but are to be identified with the Getae, a tribe of ancient Thrace. Medieval writers, dependent on classical and patristic sources, amplified references to a mysterious northern people whom they placed somewhere in Scandinavia and associated with the Goths, the last having themselves been confused with the Getae and with the biblical Gog-Magog. The linguistic evidence for the identification of Geats and Gautar is hardly as conclusive as it is sometimes thought to be, and there is little real support for such an identification. Inevitably the author's arguments vary a good deal in strength, and there are awkward gaps in her evidence, though perhaps no more than in the traditional theory. At the least, even if Geats and Gautar were identical, it seems possible that their appearance in *Beowulf* owes as much to the influence of the literary Getae as to memories of the Scandinavian tribe. R. E. Kaske, 'The *Eotenas* in *Beowulf*' (*Old English Poetry*), argues that the word in its various cases is always to be rendered 'giants', and that throughout the Finn episode the term is to be taken as a hostile epithet for the Frisians.

An examination of the 'Structure and Thematic Development in *Beowulf*' (*Proceedings of the Royal Irish Academy*) leads E. Carrigan to divide the different sections into ten groups which are then analysed in some detail. He concludes that their symmetrical grouping is so closely related to the thematic progression of the poem that it can hardly be due to coincidence; the fights themselves are described in groups of five sections, and in addition the first and the last of the fights have each a companion group of five sections. But whilst *Beowulf* is a unity, with a due subordination of parts to the whole, the poem can never be reduced to an explicit moral idea without doing violence to its very meaning. Literary analysis has too often substituted for the poem's design a pattern of ideas abstracted from it, and so avoided the central task of seeing how the poet shaped his traditional themes into a unique work of art. A. Bonjour's 'Jottings on *Beowulf* and the Aesthetic Approach' (*Old English Poetry*) is a reply to Magoun's theory that the poem is made up of two independent poems by different authors, joined together by a third. In the same volume L. D. Benson's 'The Pagan Coloring of *Beowulf*' examines the distinctively pagan element in the poem, and points out that, at the time of its probable composition, the dominant attitude of Christian Anglo-Saxons towards the Germanic pagans was one of interest, sympathy, and occasionally even admiration. This was the period during which the English church was engaged in an

---

[17] *Beowulf and Judith*, ed. F. P. Magoun, revised by J. B. Bessinger, Jr. Harvard U.P. pp. viii+107.

[18] *The Geats of Beowulf*, by Jane A. Leake. Wisconsin U.P. pp. xi+212.

intense activity on the continent, sending missionaries to the Frisians, Danes, Old Saxons, and tribes of central Germany. A knowledge of pagan customs could have come to the author from the continent, and by means of it he was able to provide local colour. He could also capitalize on the general interest in pagandom that the missions had aroused, and by providing vivid accounts of rites, such as cremation, of which his audience had only heard, he would engage their attention for his more important purposes. C. Moorman emphasizes 'The Essential Paganism of *Beowulf*' (*MLQ*). Although tinged with Christianity, it differs from the thoroughly Christian poems of the period in subject, narrative line, and tone. Its major theme of man's determined but futile struggle against a malevolent environment, its reflexion of a code of loyalty to lord and kin, its glorification of prowess and courage, suggest that the nominally Christian author was imbued rather with mythological pessimism than with Christian hope. N. D. Isaacs examines 'The Convention of Personification in *Beowulf*' (*Old English Poetry*), and claims that the figures fall into two major divisions: personifications and inversions of personification. Examples are given of both types, and he then treats more particularly the personification of armour and weapons and, in rather less detail, that of the beasts of battle, other animals, ships, etc. P. B. Taylor deals with 'Themes of Death in *Beowulf*' (*Old English Poetry*) under various headings: the discovery of death, the fatal venture, the sorrowful journey, and the song of death. It would appear that the repetition of certain formulas and formulaic systems to compose themes contributes to the poem's effectiveness in that the repetition immediately establishes a parallelism of ideas and an identification of one element of the text with another. In addition, the theme carries to a particular context the sense of previous contexts in which it has appeared, and acts as a unifying principle. L. Whitbread, '*Beowulf* and Archaeology. Two Footnotes' (*NM*), suggests that Grendel's pouch made of dragon skins is a reflexion of the author's obvious interest in the dragon lore of funeral mounds, while the fact that only ten days were taken to erect Beowulf's barrow would indicate that it refers to a sepulchral chamber of wood set up over funeral remains. A careful examination of 'Post-Consonantal l m n r and Metrical Practice in *Beowulf*' (*Nordica*) leads W. P. Lehmann to the conclusion that after light syllables, when from Primitive Germanic /l m n r/, they are not required as distinct syllables for the metre. But after a light syllable in Primitive Germanic, when they are preceded by a vowel, they may be metrically necessary, while after heavy syllables the consonants were always syllabic. R. Willard and Elinor D. Clemons examine 'Bliss's Light Verses in the *Beowulf*' (*JEGP*), and argue that Bliss was so concerned with word stress that he sometimes overlooked such things as phrasal or clausal stress, or varying linguistic patterns. Consequently many of the so-called 'light verses' can be regarded as having the regular two lifts.

Notes on the text of *Beowulf* include J. L. Baird on 'The Uses of Ignorance: "Beowulf" 435, 2330' (*NQ*). In both passages the author uses his hero's ignorance of something as a means of characterization. Beowulf, by rejecting the use of weapons against Grendel, shows his courage, since no one then knows of Grendel's invulnerability. In the second case he shows his humility by taking upon himself a feud whose true cause he learned later. J. R. Byers, Jr., 'A Possible Emendation of *Beowulf* 461b' (*PQ*), reads *wine-gara* for *gara*, and translates 'then the people of the friendly spears were not able to keep him for fear of revenge', and Jane Crawford takes '"Scirwered": "Beowulf" 496a' (*NQ*) as a single word 'adorned with radiance', describing the ale cup being carried in by a servant. In 'Hrothgar's Tears' (*MP*) T. L. Wright claims that the insertion of *nō* in line 1875 suggests an inconsequence in the portrayal of Hrothgar, and that *ā* or *eft* would be more convincing, since Hrothgar's tears would then express recognition, not regret. J. Norton, 'Tolkien, Beowulf, and the Poet: A Problem in Point of View' (*ES*), criticizes Tolkien's evaluation of Beowulf's speech to his retainers, while the first of M. Rissanen's 'Two Notes on Old English Poetic Texts' (*NM*) argues for the translation 'one (song of lament) after another' for the *an æfter anum* of *Beowulf* 2461, and in the second that *til anum*, Ruthwell Cross III 3, has the meaning 'together, in the same place'. From T. Westphalen comes a very detailed discussion of a particularly difficult passage in *Beowulf*.[19] The introductory chapter deals generally with *Beowulf* textual criticism, with the manuscript, and with the particular problems posed by f. 201 on which the passage occurs. The theory that the lines had been freshened up by earlier editors is considered, and the respective editions of Thorpe (1830) and Sievers (1930) are compared. After this, each half-line is taken in turn and exhaustively commented on, with a final summary of the conclusions and an edition of the lines in question. Chapter 3 deals

with the probable Geatish woman, her identity, the connexion of the episode with the Germanic dirge, and the significance of the episode within the poem as a whole. Comprehensive bibliographies are given, while a separate supplement contains tables summarizing the different emendations that have been suggested at different times, and the various translations. T. F. Mustanoja also deals with 'The Unnamed Woman's Song of Mourning over Beowulf and the Tradition of Ritual Lamentation' (*NM*), especially with the suggested reading *Geatisc meowle* 3150. He then examines the whole passage in the light of the development of the custom of lamentation for the dead. There is no evidence to identify the woman with any specific person; the author is merely describing the solemn rites observed at the funeral of a great Germanic hero, part of these consisting of a lament sung by a woman. Whether she was a relative or a professional mourner is irrelevant; it is simply an essential traditional feature of such a funeral ceremony, and so had to be included in the description. The only remaining work on the heroic poetry is K. Malone's 'The Franks Casket and the Date of *Widsith*' (*Nordica*), in which he considers the theory that the composition of the poem is to be dated between 930 and 940. The Franks Casket is taken to be the work of a heathen Englishman living in sixth-century Gaul, and its mixture of biblical and classical material would indicate that an English poet of the same date might well have composed a poem listing not only Germanic tribes but also biblical peoples.

E. B. Irving, Jr., 'Image and Meaning in the Elegies' (*Old English Poetry*), examines some recurrent images, more particularly that of a

---

[19] *Beowulf 3150–55. Textkritik und Editionsgeschichte*, by T. Westphalen. München: Fink. pp. xi+382.

ruin, those clustering round the theme of exile, and those concerned with physical suffering and danger. It is hoped that the investigation may throw light on the kind of meaning generated by a particular combination of commonplaces in a given poem. 'A Theme in *The Wanderer*' (*MÆ*) by R. Fowler is concerned with whether there is in the poem some unifying device which establishes the mutual relevance and coherence of the separate ideas in it. It would seem that the explicit theme is not merely the mutability of all things on earth, but transcends this to state the permanence of what is spiritual. Moreover, various double function references within the text allow the poem to be read in two ways; as a straightforward Christian poem arguing that the world is transient and heaven permanent, and as a lament on mutability as it affects the nobles and retainers of heroic society. B. Mitchell, 'An Old English Syntactical Reverie: "The Wanderer", Lines 22 and 34–36' (*NM*), disallows Leslie's appeal to lines 34–36 as supporting evidence for the emendation of *mine* to *minne* in line 22 since this implies greater knowledge than we possess of Old English syntax and semantics. In '"The Seafarer" 109–115a' (*ES*) N. D. Isaacs suggests that all previous commentators have here misread the antecedents of *he*, *hine*, and *his*. *He* refers to the enemy, *hine* and *his* to the Christian. The point is that the Christian man must maintain his Christian charity not only towards his friends but even towards his enemies who wish to burn his devoted lord on the funeral pyre, and that consequently religious faith must be stronger than any *comitatus* relationship. Here, too, may be mentioned Cecily Clark's 'Byrhtnoth and Roland: A Contrast' (*N*). As against some recent articles, she suggests the *Chanson de Roland* as the best parallel with, and contrast to, *Maldon*. Compared with Roland, Byrhtnoth is not depicted as a champion of Christianity, still less as a martyr for it. The poet could not deny his hero's Christianity, nor presumably did he wish to do so, but the slightness and vagueness of his references compel us to conclude that he was playing it down in order to depict Germanic heroism with more purity. The poem is essentially a glorification of the military ideals of the *comitatus*, and to call it the celebration of a Christian martyrdom is quite unjustifiable.

On the Christian poetry, A. G. Brodeur, in 'A Study of Diction and Style in Three Anglo-Saxon Narrative Poems' (*Nordica*), claims that the author of the *Andreas* was an excellent poet, with a real flair for vivid, forceful, and sometimes beautiful phrase and image. The author of *Judith* has an astonishingly individual style, with a gift for evoking images and scenes, while the *Exodus* is unique in the quality of the poet's powerful imagination as revealed in its striking figures and its forceful and loaded verbs. All three poems, though containing many traditional formulas, are highly individual in style, and each affords clear evidence of its author's gift for original expression and imagery—evidence which challenges the theory that the language of Old English narrative poetry is overwhelmingly formulaic. B. Mitchell points out that '"Swa" in Cædmon's "Hymn" Line 3' (*NQ*) may be either an anticipatory adverb 'so, thus, in this way', or causal 'because, inasmuch as'. A. Mirsky, 'On the Sources of the Anglo-Saxon *Genesis* and *Exodus*' (*ES*), provides examples, of varying value, to indicate that the authors have made use of the *Talmud*, the *Midrashim*, and ancient Hebrew liturgical poems, though whether directly from Hebrew, or from some written or oral translation, is impossible to decide. R. P. Creed's 'The Art of the Singer: Three Old English Tellings of the Offering of Isaac' (*Old English Poetry*) compares the versions in *Genesis* and *Exodus*, and claims that the former poem is properly completed by this passage. An appendix gives the last 91 lines of *Genesis*, marked for performance to the harp, and with an indication of possible formulas in the author's repertory. F. C. Robinson, 'The OE *Genesis*, 11. 1136–1137' (*Archiv*), brings forward evidence from Middle English poems to show that the lines in question could have the meaning 'since Adam left Paradise'. In 'The Self-Deception of Temptation: Boethian Psychology in *Genesis B*' (*Old English Poetry*) A. Renoir finds in the poem an awareness of the Boethian ideas that evil is its own punishment, so that it thus becomes an effective object lesson on the tragedy of self-deception. J. F. Vickrey proposes 'An Emendation to L[æ]*nes* in *Genesis B* line 258' (*Archiv*), and suggests a similar change at *Beowulf* 1809. 'The Unity of Old English *Daniel*' (*RES*) by R. T. Farrell deals with the question of whether the Songs of Azarias and of the Three Children are to be regarded as interpolations. The usual form of the Easter Vigil or Holy Saturday services would include a reading of Daniel 3, and the two songs would appear in this. Consequently, modern critics have little right to object to the inclusion of what was so important in the liturgy, and equally so in a poem related to this liturgy, on the grounds that such a lyric passage offends our taste.

On the later Christian poetry, L. H. Leiter, '*The Dream of the Rood*: Patterns of Transformation' (*Old English Poetry*), sees the poem as consisting of three identical dramas: the defeat and paradoxical victory of Christ; the cutting down and raising up of the Cross; and the sleep and awakening of the sinful Dreamer. He then deals in detail with the vocabulary of warfare, claiming that the dramatic battle metaphors become symbolic means of redemption. R. D. Stevick examines 'The Meter of *The Dream of the Rood*' (*NM*) with special reference to the expanded lines, while D. P. Farina relates the phrase '"Wædum geweorðod" in "The Dream of the Rood"' (*NQ*) to the medieval custom of re-enacting on Good Friday evenings the lowering of Christ's body from the Cross. The body was wiped with a folded sheet, stained red in places to simulate blood stains. Later, the unfolded sheet was spread upon the cross, and this is what the poet claims to have seen in his dream—a gold-studded cross covered with a cloth. G. C. Britton argues that the difficulties which have arisen about '"Bealuwara Weorc" in the "Dream of the Rood"' (*NM*) are due to the attempt to connect the phrase syntactically with *sarra sorga*. It should rather be regarded as in apposition to *ic*, and translated, 'that I, the work of devils, have suffered grievous sorrows'. J. E. Cross, 'The Conception of the Old English *Phoenix*' (*Old English Poetry*), shows that the Old English poem is an effective medieval homily on the Phoenix, in which the *De ave Phoenice* of Lactantius has been adapted, and ideas from patristic exegesis and polemic, as well as the *Physiologus* literature, have been elaborated to provide distinguishable tropological, anagogical, and typological explanations. D. K. Fry, 'The Heroine on the Beach in *Judith*' (*NM*), discusses briefly the concept of theme in Old English poetry, analysing a number of examples of the theme of the Hero on the Beach as a preliminary to studying its incorporation in *Judith* 186b–204a.

A. Hacikyan[20] deals briefly with riddle literature in general, concludes that the Old English examples are to be attributed to multiple authorship, and that many of them come from the eighth century, the remainder from the ninth or tenth. The literary and social backgrounds are described, and then come twenty-six pages of tables analysing the uses of the definite and demonstrative articles in the *Riddles*, and listing the various suggested solutions. A twenty-two-page bibliography contains a number of items only minimally concerned with the subject. Little new emerges, and although some of the statistics may prove useful, it is difficult to see what the reader is expected to do with them. G. K. Anderson's 'Aldhelm and the *Leiden Riddle*' (*Old English Poetry*) has some general remarks on the two Old English versions of Aldhelm's *De Lorica*, and on Schlutter's re-rendering into Latin of the *Leiden Riddle*. Margaret E. Goldsmith, 'Corroding Treasure: A Note on the Old English "Rhyming Poem" Lines 45–50' (*NQ*), takes *brondhord* as meaning 'burning malice', whilst *efenpynde* should be considered as a participial adjective describing *modes gecynde* and translated 'equally tormenting (to mind and body)'. Of two articles on the minor verse by L. Whitbread, the first, 'Notes on Two Minor Old English Poems' (*ELN*), questions the necessity of emendations by Dobbie and Ure to *The Lord's Prayer II* and *The Gloria I*, while the second provides a number of 'Text-Notes on the

Old English Poem *Judgment Day II*' (*ES*).

The only work on the *Old English Chronicle* is an article by R. Derolez in which he describes 'An Epitome of the *Anglo-Saxon Chronicle* in Lambert of Saint-Omer's *Liber Floridus*' (*ES*). Janet M. Bately examines 'The Relationship between the MSS. of the Old English Orosius' (*ES*), and concludes that Lauderdale and Cotton are derived from the same parent by way of a hypothetical manuscript, the latter being also the ancestor of the French poem by Calendre. In 'Two New Sources for Blickling Homilies' (*NQ*) R. MacG. Dawson shows that part of VIII and IX are from Caesarius of Arles and Adamnan's *De Locis Sanctis* respectively.

J. C. Pope's edition of Ælfric[21] is the first of two volumes which are to contain twenty-one previously unedited homilies and some shorter pieces. The manuscripts of Ælfric's works are described in detail, and tables show the distribution of the texts in them. The evidence of authorship is considered, and then comes a particularly interesting section on Ælfric's rhythmical prose. Other subjects treated include an investigation of the canon, the date and range of the texts here edited, and an examination of their sources. A brief discussion of the language is followed by an account of the glosses in the manuscripts, and more particularly of the so-called 'tremulous' Worcester hand. In the present volume are editions of twelve homilies, each preceded by an introduction, and accompanied by valuable textual notes. The homilies are printed in metrical lines and provided with a full apparatus. This is a particularly

---

[20] *A Linguistic and Literary Analysis of Old English Riddles*, by A. Hacikyan. Montreal: Casalini. pp. viii+94. 1966. $5.50.

[21] *Homilies of Ælfric. A Supplementary Collection. Vol. I*, ed. J. C. Pope. E.E.T.S. No. 259. O.U.P. pp. xvii+491. 84s.

important edition which, when complete, will increase considerably our knowledge, not only of Ælfric and his writings, but of many other aspects of Old English. M. Grünberg presents a useful edition of the so-called *West Saxon Gospels*[22] from C.U.L. Ii. 2. 11, with variants from other manuscripts. These are described in the introduction, and then comes the edition in which a Latin text accompanies the St. Matthew. A detailed commentary on the first gospel deals with the language, the method and style of the translation, and the vocabulary. A tentative diagram illustrates the relationship of the manuscripts, and it would appear that the St. Matthew, at any rate, is based on an early gloss which, if not entirely Anglian, was of

Anglian colouring. The first complete version was probably a product of the Alfredian literary movement, it was often copied, and at least three more or less independent revisions were made in the course of time. Certainly it is clear that the translation can have had no connexion with Ælfric. A. S. C. Ross makes a detailed analysis of Aldred's forms of '"This" in the *Lindisfarne Gospels* and the *Durham Ritual*' (*NQ*), since these often differ from those in standard Old English.

M. Murphy shows that Abraham Wheloc's Edition of 'Bede's History in Old English' (*SN*) was published primarily to provide arguments against Catholicism, and in his notes Wheloc tried to demonstrate that Anglo-Saxon Christianity was closer to the Anglicanism of his day than it was to Catholicism. In addition, note should also be made of the list by F. C. Robinson of 'Old English Research in Progress: 1966-7' (*NM*).

[22] *The West Saxon Gospels: A Study of the Gospel of St. Matthew with the Text of the Four Gospels*, by M. Grünberg. Amsterdam: Scheltema & Holkema. pp. 414. 30 Florins.

IV

Middle English: excluding Chaucer

G. C. BRITTON

First mention must go this year to K. Varty's fascinating and lavishly-illustrated book on Reynard the fox in medieval English art.[1] It is not only informative, but a joy to read and look at. He traces briefly Reynard's literary career from the twelfth-century Latin *Ysengrimus* by the Fleming Nivard, who used material from earlier Greek and Latin stories, and the French poem of Pierre de St. Cloud, to the fifteenth century. In visual art the fox appears in manuscript illustration, in glass, or carved in wood or stone. He is shown hunted, with his prey thrown over his back; taking refuge in a tree; carrying off Chanteclere, pursued by a farmer's wife and men, and losing him; in episodes from the beast fables; as a false priest or friar, often preaching to birds; representing the cunning of the Devil; in association with the ape; as a physician; as a minstrel, and in various other ways. In the series of illustrations on the Bestiary fox are juxtaposed some stills from a modern scientific film showing the fox feigning dead in order to attract and seize the crow. The text relates these vigorous and often delightful examples of Reynard iconography to extant literary texts: Latin, French, Italian, Flemish, German, English. The English literary records are unaccountably

scanty, in view of the large number of visual representations, of which Mr. Varty is convinced he has not collected by any means all. One very early appearance of the hunted fox can be added to the list, that in *The Owl and the Nightingale*, as can the fourteenth-century *Gawain* episode. Middle English also, of course, had a version of *The Bestiary*. Also copiously illustrated is *The Flowering of the Middle Ages*.[2] No pains have been spared to make this compendium as entertaining, informative, and authoritative as possible. Although it is not directly to do with literature, students will find it a stimulating and serious survey of the cultural background to their study.

The second edition, with factual and bibliographical supplement, of 'The Middle Ages' volume of Baugh's *History*[3] is much to be welcomed, especially in its paperback form. R. W. Ackerman gives a selective survey of work on 'Middle English Literature to 1400' (cf. *YW* xlvii. 96), which should be useful both as a guide to the beginner and a reminder to

---

[1] *Reynard the Fox. A Study of the Fox in Medieval English Art*, by K. Varty. Leicester U.P. pp. 169. Plates: 1 colour, 169 monochrome. 105s.

[2] *The Flowering of the Middle Ages*, ed. Joan Evans, with chapters by T. S. R. Boase, C. Brooke, J. Harvey, C. Hohler, R. Hunt, D. King, A. Martindale and G. Zarnecki. Thames & Hudson (1966). pp. 360. 631 illustrations (192 in colour). £8 8s.

[3] *A Literary History of England*, ed. A. C. Baugh. 2nd ed. Vol. 1, *The Middle Ages*, by K. Malone and A. C. Baugh. Routledge. pp. x+312+(30)+xv. Paperback. 18s.

the more advanced student.[4] The first volume of a new edition of Wells's *Manual* appears.[5] The present writer regrets that he has not yet seen a copy, but it has been praised, on the whole, by reviewers. Sixteenth-century material, where appropriate, is included, and there are many corrections and revisions.

The posthumous collection of essays by C. S. Lewis[6] unfortunately escaped mention in *YW* xlvii. The two lectures 'Imagination and thought in the Middle Ages' 'amount almost to a précis of *The Discarded Image*', but were specially prepared for an audience of scientists. In 'The genesis of a medieval book', Lewis examines the process, 'wholly foreign to modern literature, but normal in the literature of the Middle Ages', by which Laȝamon's *Brut* and *Sawles Warde* came into being. The work of Geoffrey, 'an author of mediocre talent and no taste', is reworked with care and vigour by Wace. In his turn, and with the aid of Welsh and English traditions, Laȝamon expanded on Wace—though we do not know exactly what was in the redaction of Wace he used. The identification of the work and personality of a single author is therefore impossible, and in this the *Brut* is typical of most medieval literature. Partially Old English in metre, it is almost wholly so in style and temper, though British in its conscious sympathies. Not that

Arthur could or can be linked with race. Though heavier and more plangent than Wace, more barbaric and less civilized, the *Brut* is also more sensitive and less callous. In dramatic intensity, in its use of vigorous, even passionate, similes, and in its expansion in human terms of the Arthurian sections, it is superior. *Sawles Warde* is based on an unexpected allegorical treatment, possibly by Hugo of St. Victor, of a New Testament passage. The additions are not original, but the imaginative and dramatic treatment is. Criticism of medieval literature must be of the book, not the author. Neither in the *Brut* nor in *Sawles Warde* have we either originality or fidelity in their modern senses. Authorship is truly 'shared'; as the *Brut* is a modification of Wace, so itself it is modified by Wace. The process is typical. The ingredients of a medieval story exist in so far as they contribute to the total work: otherwise they become merely the abstract products of analysis. In 'De Audiendis Poetis', Lewis urges the necessity of historical knowledge and of imaginative and emotional adjustments in order to respond fully, as a lover of literature, not a historian, to a medieval poem. A purely 'modern' response (of whatever period) will bring its own rewards, but 'newer and fresher enjoyments' will come from a journey beyond it. Best is, as far as possible, to combine the two. He rejects both the theological approach (e.g. that *Piers* is a great sermon, and therefore a great poem), and the anthropological approach. Whatever truth lies in the identification of the remote mythical origin of certain literary themes or items, it adds nothing to, it may even detract from, the poem's impact upon us (on the other hand, the poem may illuminate the myth). But Mr. Speirs's

[4] *The Medieval Literature of Western Europe. A Review of Research, Mainly 1930–1960.* General ed. J. H. Fisher. New York U.P. and Univ. London Press, for M.L.A. (1966). pp. xvi+432. $6.50.

[5] *A Manual of the Writings in Middle English 1050–1500*, ed. J. B. Severs. Archon Books, the Shoestring Press, for Conn. Acad. Arts and Science. New Haven. Fascicule 1, 'Romances'. pp. 338. $10.50.

[6] *Studies in Medieval and Renaissance Literature*, by C. S. Lewis, collected by W. Hooper. Cambridge U.P. (1966). pp. xii+196. 30s. $5.95.

E

warning against taking the 'ferlies' of medieval romance as 'sports of fancy' must be regarded. We have recently developed inhibitions against taking them seriously, against feeling their sense of mystery, and these must be broken down. If this can be done by an apparently rational appeal, then there is value in that. But the literary effect must not be mistaken for something other than it is.

In 'Anglicanism and anthropology' (*Southern Folklore Quarterly*), F. L. Utley gives credit to C. S. Lewis and J. Speirs as two of a vanguard which showed that medieval literature is of interest to other than linguists. But 'Speirs is a very doubtful anthropologist', and the year spirit is an imaginative figment which he 'seizes upon as the straw to build a house to keep out the big bad wolf of prosaic anthropology and philological sobriety'. Though Lewis's attack on Speirs was forceful and pointed, he lacked discrimination in linking him with Loomis, to whom the Grail Quest had great spiritual significances, especially for those of the Christian faith. We must not reduce medieval literature to 'one-sided modern moralities'; it has a grasp of the wholeness of life. In 'Middle English misunderstood' (*Ang*), R. H. Robbins attacks some of what he thinks of as the irrationalities and unjustified assumptions of Speirs's criticism of medieval poetry. Speirs disparages, while depending on, the work of some earlier scholars, and ignores others. He rejects the study of the language, and at the same time talks as if it had a life of its own distinct from its users and makers. 'By stressing anthropology and certain technical aspects of writing, [pure literary criticism] urges readers to ignore what literature says. It avoids the areas of thought and people—it does not have to pass judgement except on fertility myths

and metrical rhythms. The critic so minded, interested only in "the unique value of this poem as a poem", can then, under the mask of critical impartiality, introduce his personal predilections.'

T. Silverstein calls for moderation in the allegorical approach in 'Allegory and Literary Form' (*PMLA*). Modern allegorists often confuse allegory with Lewis's symbolism. An author's *interpretatio* will make the allegorical nature of a work certain, but in such cases the *littera* is often merely a base for the discourse, which dictates the form. But analogies between works are often misleading. Many allegorical works are based on the *littera* of a journey. It does not follow that all literary journeys are to be interpreted allegorically. Is there evidence that Gawain's journey is allegorical? To interpret it so may, and does, lead to neglect of literal excellencies, turning a profound *littera* into an allegorical commonplace. P. Beichner asks, in 'The Allegorical Interpretation of Medieval Literature' (*PMLA*), how far the allegorical method should be applied to writings not primarily allegories. Morals or allegorical interpretations could be and often were applied to tales not originally bearing them. It does not follow that the *moralitas* was recognized at their every occurrence: in fact, it was probably not. On the other hand, animals, biblical or historical characters, proper names, etc., were often endowed by custom with symbolic meanings which were not easily shed. We must use our judgement as to when those meanings are to be recognized.

W. O. Evans (*MS*) shows with wide reference that '"Cortaysye" in Middle English' refers rather to virtue, often specifically Christian, than to courtly love, unless the context explicitly requires the latter.

Kindness, consideration for others, peaceableness, hospitality, truthfulness, dutifulness, help to define its conscious area, but it may simply be formalized into 'the right thing to do' in certain circumstances. Its conventional significance is most common in the sphere of chivalry (although some writers see conventional patterns of behaviour as part of a universal order). It does not, in fact, occur very frequently in courtly-love contexts, though one of its most interesting appearances is in *Sir Gawain*, which tells us most about it in the temptation scenes. God is, of course, 'courteous'—even when exacting punishment, for courtesy involves proper action. But His sacrifice shows that 'measure' is not an element in courtesy where charity is in question. *Cortaysye* is, finally, the divine spark which enables men to act in love towards each other and towards God, and to live a good life. It cannot include anything sinful: thus the *cortaysye* of Bercilak's lady is an aberration from Gawain's true *cortaysye*.

S. Wenzel (*MS*) considers the occurrence together of 'The three enemies of man', the world, the flesh and the devil. The origin of the topos is uncertain, though the triad may be found in St. Augustine's Sermon 158. But it does not appear often before the year 1000, and may have become better known by its appearance in the formula of renunciation used by the Benedictines. Its great importance, however, was due to St. Bernard and Hugh of St. Victor. Later the three enemies are connected with the temptations of Christ and of Adam, and with the seven cardinal sins. Their appearance in literature often involves a battle image, as in the *Château d'Amour*. Langland incorporates them twice into larger images (B VIII, B XVI), but it is the

drama which realizes their literary potentialities, as in the *Castle of Perseverance* and the moralities. Nevertheless, their function in literature never becomes very important. They offer no possibility of profound psychological insight, and remain something of a formula. Prof. Wenzel extends his 1966 treatment of *acedia* (*YW* xlvii. 73–4).[7] The medieval idea of sloth finds its origin in the 'psychic exhaustion and listlessness' experienced by the Egyptian desert fathers in the fourth century. The identification of *acedia* with the noon-day demon lasted to the end of the Middle Ages. The introduction of *acedia* to the West was basically the work of Cassian, and it was thought of at first as a peculiarly monastic vice, to be dealt with by bodily work and spiritual fortitude. Its dual nature, therefore, was recognized from the first. *Acedia* as such finds no place in the Gregorian list of vices, but *tristitia*, with which it has much in common, does. It is the twelfth century that gives the fusion a logical and psychological basis. Like other vices, it results from the failure to accept good and reject evil appetites. A shrinking from the necessary labour to attain spiritual good will lead to sloth and despair. It is an aversion to Divine Good itself, and is opposite to joy in God. Only the assent of reason to it makes it mortal. As the origin of other vices, it is also capital. Possible physiological origins, the lack of ability rather than will, are recognized. Bodily laziness, however, is merely a symptom. Although it would be wrong to see a simple progress from a spiritual to a fleshly meaning, there are writers who emphasize one aspect rather than another, and the physical aspect is

[7] *The Sin of Sloth:* Acedia *in Medieval Thought and Literature*, by S. Wenzel. North Carolina U.P. pp. xii+269. $7.50

often stressed in the preacher's 'character' or picture of the slothful man. Gower uses the allegorical figure in the *Mirour de l'Ome*, but he also uses other standard devices, such as *exempla* or animal symbols. He also balances the spiritual and worldly faults that result from the vice. The ways in which Sloth attacks man are portrayed dramatically in such works as Deguileville's *Pélérinage*. There is no intensive literary and personal exploration of *acedia*, however, though it is often mentioned and used. Dante puts its victims on the fourth terrace of purgatory where are those who loved great good with little intensity (*lento amore*). Its purgation is by means of eager action, moved from the will within. A disease of the will must be cured by the will. Dante incorporates the concept into poetical, political and personal patterns. Langland's treatment is much less coherent. He is not intellectual master of the concept, and feels it. No major structural principle is given by the seven sins: they are not stations on the pilgrim's way. Thus the allegories which contain Sloth are linked only by 'the poet's putative dream experience'. Langland's characterization of Sloth is close to the popular image: 'sloth means negligence both in man's relationship with God, and in his dealings with his fellow man and society'. The concept is that of the penitentials. In *Passus* XX he is the offspring of Life and Fortune, a unique genealogy, and married to Wanhope. Failure to make restitution can lead to wanhope, though Robert the robber triumphs over this despair by his faith in Christ. In the moralities the sins become dramatis personae. Sloth is opposed in *The Castle of Perseverance* by *Besynesse*; he drains the moat of the water of grace. *Mankind's* temptation follows the popular idea of the psychology of the

vice, though it is not mentioned. Sloth is here part of man's inner disposition, not an allegorical figure. Enough has been said to show the importance of Prof. Wenzel's subject, and the careful, learned, and illuminated path he shows through its mazes.

Leeds Studies in English makes a welcome return with a New Series. M. F. Wakelin contributes a description, more complete than that in Wells or Horstmann, of the manuscripts of John Mirk's *Festial*, including a map of provisional locations supplied by Prof. Angus McIntosh. As one would expect, most are from the North Midlands. In 'Rhetoric and Style: a bibliographical guide', R. C. Alston and J. L. Rosier include a most useful section on 'The medieval tradition'. J. J. Murphy writes on 'The literary implications of instruction in the verbal arts in 14th-century England', the verbal arts including 'any . . . discipline that could teach a person how to read or speak'. He rejects Manly's view (*Chaucer and the Rhetoricians*, London, 1926) of the major role of Geoffrey of Vinsauf. The *ars grammatica*, especially as taught in Donatus, dominated the trivium; it is in the third section of the *Ars Maior* that a fourteenth-century English writer would become acquainted with figures and tropes. The popular *Graecismus* of Evrard of Bethune also has appropriate sections. Exactly what poets were read in schools is still to be determined, but the pupils produced exercises in both verse and prose. The school background of our fourteenth-century writers needs closer and more careful examination.

K. Humphries describes the 'Distribution of books in the English West Midlands in the later Middle Ages' (*Libri*), i.e. *c.* 1000–*c.* 1400, using the evidence of manuscripts, *ex libris* inscriptions, press marks, catalogues and wills (neither very important for the W. Mids.), and later lists. The earlier books consist of the Bible and commentaries, some works by the Fathers, and (at Worcester) much Old English material. Florence and Bede, of course, appear. Classical texts are few, but Priscian is found. A change comes in the thirteenth century with the growth of the universities and professional book production, the spread of Aristotelian learning and the growth of the mendicant orders. Books become more difficult to place. To the old nucleus are added such books as Peter Lombard's *Sentences*, the *Historia Scholastica* and other aids to preaching and Bible study, works on logic, civil and canon law, and medicine. In thirteenth-century Worcester interest in Old English continues. There is little classical study until the fourteenth century, when literary interest, though small, increases. Apart from Worcester, the peak of monastic influence seems to have been reached in the twelfth century.

K. Sajavaara discusses 'The relationship of the Vernon and Simeon manuscripts' (*NM*), concluding that the two were produced in the same scriptorium, though whether S depends on V, or both on a common original, cannot be decided. Perhaps S depends partly on V, and partly on V's exemplar, which in its turn has a common parent with B.M. Add. MS. 37787. This, Vernon, and Simeon are from North Worcestershire, probably from the Cistercian Bordesley Abbey.

Bennett and Smithers's new anthology, *Early Middle English Verse and Prose*[8] is the Clarendon Press's long-awaited companion to Sisam's *Fourteenth Century Verse and Prose*. Unlike other M.E. readers in common use today, this new one reproduces works wherever possible in full (e.g. the whole of *The Fox and the Wolf*, *Dame Sirith*, *The Life of Saint Kenelm*, *The Land of Cokaygne*, *Sawles Warde*), and otherwise in generous selections (e.g. ten pages allotted to *The Peterborough Chronicle*, twenty-one to *Ancrene Wisse*), chosen with care and discrimination. The introduction consists of forty pages on the language (containing fresh and stimulating thinking), but sadly only nine devoted to the literary background. Each text has its own brief introduction, and there are 165 pages of commentary, linguistic, interpretative, and textual, including select bibliographies for each text. In the first edition (the second will be discussed in vol. XLIX), misprints are unfortunately common, and not all are trivial. Professor Davis's glossary is first-rate and happily free of misprints.

A. W. Baldwin's 'Henry II and *The Owl and the Nightingale*' (*JEGP*), rejecting other theories as ignoring the facts and the 'historical milieu', puts forward her own: that the poem is a satiric commentary on the Henry-Becket controversy, the nightingale representing the king and the owl the archbishop. 'This peace' refers to the peace between the church and state post-1174 (the poem being written in 1174–5), the king's soul being in need of mercy for his part in the saint's martyrdom. The Owl-Thomas is a Christ-figure, but the Nightingale-Henry fails to see this. The king (Henry) punishes the knight (Thomas) excessively for quartering the Nightingale who led his bride (the Church) astray. Nicholas is a false judge who loved Nightingales (the king), and his request for several

---

[8] *Early Middle English Verse and Prose*, ed. J. A. W. Bennett and G. V. Smithers. With a glossary by N. Davis. Oxford. Clarendon Press (1966). pp. lviii + 620. 42*s*.

livings 'flaunted [*sic*] the law'. In the passage on marriage the Owl 'supported the roving wife against the roving husband'. G. B. Kinneavy ('Fortune, Providence and the Owl', *SP*) finds the owl rash, illogical, hypocritical, and proud to the point of blasphemy in her defensive speech on her powers of prognostication. He compares her views on Fortune and Providence with those of Boethius, who 'is quite clear regarding the proper view for the Christian to assume'. The owl cannot be considered the logical victor: the truth lies between her and the nightingale. In the most illuminating of the year's articles on the poem, M. Angela Carson draws attention to 'Rhetorical structure in *The Owl and the Nightingale*' (*S*). The poem's purpose is to make a plea for preferment for Nicholas, and it is thus an example of deliberative argument aimed at moving the reader to action. In addition, Nicholas is praised directly in epideictic passages, and indirectly at the forensic level by indicating his qualities of character and judgement. Nicholas's worth is the birds' sole area of agreement. The poet reveals a knowledge of English legal procedure and of contemporary issues, and adorns it by fable and maxim.

K. Sajavaara summarizes fact and conjecture about Grosseteste, and pleads for more study of one so important to the understanding of the later Middle Ages.[9] The basic theme of his *Château d'Amour*, dated here after, rather than before, 1230, is the securing of souls redeemed by Christ: a consuming interest in Grosseteste's work. The allegories (as we now realize is often so in medieval

poems) are not consistently carried through, and are dropped when they interfere with the historical narrative. As compared with his sources in Bernard and *Rex et Famulus*, Grosseteste feudalizes and legalizes the allegory of the Four Daughters of God by introducing the theory (then fast falling out of favour) of 'the Devil's rights'; this enables him to develop also the 'King and Thrall' theme as allegory. A third allegory of the Virgin as 'Château d'Amour' is enriched and also brought up to date. As well as closely-translated extracts in *Cursor Mundi*, four full or partial ME. versions are known: *Castel of Love*, best represented by the Vernon MS., a close rendering, S.W. Mids. of *c.* 1300; *Myrour of Lewed Men*, a free rendering, by a monk of Sawley, W. Riding, of the second half of the fourteenth century; *King and Four Daughters*, very close, Nth. or N.E. Mids., of the first half of the fifteenth century; *Four Daughters*, much altered, using sources other than *Château*, Nth. or N.E. Mids., of the second half of the fourteenth century. Typical translation procedures are examined, and *Castle* is found to be more connected and consistent, often more poetic and varied in imagery, than *Château*. The four versions are printed with emended forms and syntactical and lexical variants at the foot. Explanatory and textual notes and a Glossary of 'words not immediately intelligible' conclude a painstaking and most useful volume. Sajavaara (*NM*) also brings additional evidence for 'The use of Robert Grosseteste's *Château d'Amour* as a source of the *Cursor Mundi*', i.e. in lines 701–10, 16949–17100, 18661–18750, increasing from 748 to 1000 the number of *Cursor Mundi* lines recognized as derived from the *Château*. The translation is mostly close. An examination of all texts

[9] *The Middle English Translations of Robert Grosseteste's 'Château d'Amour'*, ed. K. Sajavaara. Mémoires de la Société Néophilologique de Helsinki, 32. pp. 434. $7.00.

of the translated passages will probably necessitate a revision of Hupe's stemmata. R. C. Dales discusses (*MS*) 'Rober Grosseteste's views on astrology'. He seems to have accepted some of its doctrines in youth, even writing before 1209 a work on forecasting the weather by its help. In *De Luce* he is still concerned, if not with astrology, with astral influence on worldly affairs. As his interest in mathematics grew, however, his belief in the tenets of the astrologers decreased, until *c.* 1235 in the *Hexaemeron* he rejects them completely—while, however, still maintaining that observation of the heavens helps in forecasting the weather. Even if astrology had some basis, contemporary observations are not precise enough to be reliable; but, in fact, it denies God's omnipotence, man's free will and man's dignity as God's image. Though he concedes that the stars may influence the body, his final condemnation of astrology is absolute.

E. Salter concludes (*MP*) her article on 'The alliterative revival' (*YW* xlvii, 76). Though alliterative verse may be provincial in dialect, it was not so in outlook. It gives 'contemporary relevance and splendour to an old metre', and seems to be the product of a cultural milieu rich and sophisticated, though regionally based; such a culture as must have existed in Gaunt's castles of the Midlands and the North. To assume that it was not known and appreciated in London is to ignore the constant comings and goings of aristocratic and learned classes. D. V. Harrington points out the rich visual details of some of the 'Personifications in *Death and Life*' (*NM*), and the significant development of the two main figures in the course of the poem which gives emotional force to Christ's victory. Life is revealed as not merely life on earth, but everlasting life: in this second character she conquers Death. In general, however, the poet makes no attempt to turn his abstractions into characters. This helps him to subordinate minor elements in the poem, and to achieve a tight and economical structure.

In 'The *Gawain*-Poet: A General Appreciation of Four Poems' (*EC*) D. S. Brewer shows that in each of the poems the tension arises between self-regard, which leads to self-destruction, and that positive virtue of control which results in an affirmation of the ultimate reality of life. Relationships between persons are actually conditioned *within* the individual; the 'courteous' action, in which Christian virtue is the controlling force, releases an outpouring of good to others. The poet's love of life is shown in his zestful descriptions, his eager interest in technical detail, his love of splendour. His humour is ironic, but never satirical; he so loves virtue that his 'evil' characters (e.g. Bertilak) are ultimately unconvincing as such; his 'most characteristic attitude . . . is *praise*'.

The second edition of Tolkien and Gordon's *Sir Gawain*[10] is to be welcomed. Norman Davis's revision has been thorough, though the lines of the original book have been preserved. The introduction has been largely rewritten, and the notes and appendixes also to a considerable extent. The text has been carefully revised: it incorporates some ten readings from Gollancz and others; a fresh collation with the manuscript has produced three new, and plainly superior, readings; and over twenty new emendations (besides significant alterations to the punctuation) are

[10] *Sir Gawain and the Green Knight*, ed. J. R. R. Tolkien and E. V. Gordon. 2nd ed., rev. N. Davis. Oxford: Clarendon Press. pp. xxvii+232. 35*s*

introduced, more than half of which have not been suggested before. The beginner's difficulties are slightly eased by printing 3 as *z* when that letter is intended. The whole has been entirely reset in a new and larger format.

M. Borroff offers a translation of *Sir Gawain*[11] which is both accurate and sensitive. Of course, all is not perfect. For instance, one does not expect the bob to carry much meaning, as it has to do at 2206–7: 'or else I am much / misled' (685–6 is much more in the style: 'When goodly Sir Gawain was gone from the court / that day'). The eternal shock of 150 *And oueral enker grene* (which gains by the emptiness of 149) is dissipated by 'For man and gear and all / Were green as green could be'. Newcomers to *Gawain*, and old hands too, will find the translation and the short introduction stimulating. There is a useful appendix on metrical form.

C. Moorman makes a study of the literary figure of the knight in the work of some major writers.[12] The concept of chivalry confronted the knight with a code of contradictory ethics, and the best writers were aware of this. The modern concept of that chivalric code which still influences our actions is often given a shock by the fact of how the knights actually behaved. What was first a necessary professional military caste developed into an uncontrollable gangster class, later still mellowed by the ideals of Christian knight and courtly lover. The latter conflicted not only with

the former, but also with the knight's ancient duty to his lord, whose lady he was now supposed to court. But he must now become skilled in courtly arts, fit for hall as well as field, for bower—and for literature. The suitor-knight becomes a questing knight, a type virtually originated and most gloriously described by Chrétien: the heroic honour of *Roland* and the chivalry of *Yvain* belong to different worlds. Whereas the epic hero is urged on by destiny, the romance hero has no historic role to play out. But the journey of the knight-errant is a metaphor of transition from youthful ignorance and innocence to self-knowledge, maturity and personal redemption. Its mythic character may be entirely subconscious in the Middle Ages. The basic conflict of love and honour is exploited almost at the end of the romance tradition in *Troilus*, in which 'courtly love disintegrates before the realities of everyday life and passion', and *Sir Gawain*, in which we see 'the effects of courtly love upon society'. Gawain's quest is spiritual rather than physical. At the end he knows himself and the nature of chivalry. The chivalry of Arthur and his court is tested against the chivalry of the Green Knight and his, to the advantage of the latter, for Arthur is unfit for the test, and Gawain's success is partial. Morgan's test, although it does not destroy Guinevere, warns the court of the dangers of wantonness and unfaithfulness. This the initiated Gawain sees: the court does not. But they are faults which are to bring about the end of Arthur's court. 'The poem is semi-allegorical in method.' Mr. Moorman has chapters on Chaucer's 'Philosophical Knight', Malory's 'Tragic Knight', Spenser's 'Allegorical Knight', and 'The Last Knights'. But after the fifteenth century the concern for the ethical dilemmas of

[11] *Sir Gawain and the Green Knight. A New Verse Translation*, by Marie Borroff. New York: W. W. Norton. pp. xvi+62. (Pub. in England 1968 by Longmans, Green & Co. Paperback. 9*s*. 6*d*.).

[12] *A Knyght There Was. The Evolution of the Knight in Literature*, by C. Moorman. Kentucky U.P. pp. x+170. $6.00.

knighthood is no longer central. The heroic myth was revitalized in the knightly quest. When that quest had lost its factual referent it had outlived its relevance and become mere archaism.

G. M. Shedd, in 'Knight in Tarnished Armour' (*MLR*), considers *Sir Gawain* to contain a criticism of the chivalric code. Gawain succeeds in terms of the code at the first test; in the seduction scenes the same virtues of courage, honour, loyalty, and courtesy (not chastity) are being tested. He succumbs to fear and fails to keep his troth with Bertilak, but at first does not recognize this failure. Only at the green chapel does he realize that our true opponent is no monster, but the man within, that following the code cannot lead to human perfection. Bertilak's forgiveness of his human failure merely aggravates his feeling; his fellow courtiers, lacking his experience, fail to understand it. A. S. Champion (*MLQ*) thinks that *Gawain* reflects 'the great religious question of the fourteenth century—whether salvation is achieved by divine grace or human merit'. Since the Green Knight nicks him, his attempt to save himself by accepting the girdle has clearly failed [*sic*]. The signs of his shame are an acknowledgement that he depends on outside help for his safety. The court gladly acknowledges this truth by adopting the green sash. The poet's other works, especially *Pearl*, expound the same view. J. M. Shuttleworth ('On *Gawain's* hagiology', *Discourse*) asserts that it is a 'consciously Christian poem': its mythic element has been exaggerated. Each of the four invocations of saints in the poem is appropriate to the context; e.g. the gatekeeper swears by St. Peter. The audience would have grasped this at once. R. Lass writes on '"Man's

Heaven": the Symbolism of Gawain's Shield' (*MS*, 1966). The pentangle is both *five*, i.e. the number of natural man, and *one*, which indicates (a) imperfect self-sufficiency, and (b) the possibility of transcending the physical and imperfect. The pentads (640 ff.) are threefold: physical, religious, courtly; woven together they make a perfect Christian knight. Five also represents quintessence, or 'mannys heuen', which transcends the four parts of which he is composed. Gawain seeks the perfection 'quae unit nos Deo', attainable only by approximating to Christ, the most perfect of men. That is why the Virgin's picture is also on the shield, for she is the one flesh through which perfection was attained. The concrete fact balances the abstract emblem. G. B. Pace ('Physiognomy and *Sir Gawain*', *ELN*; cf. *YW* xlvi. 71–2) suggests that Morgan le Fay's *blake broȝes* (961) show her to be in her character as 'seductive *amie*', thus foreshadowing the final resolution, and making her and Bertilak's lady 'opposite side of the same coin'. All readers of *Sir Gawain* (and some other poems) will be profitably entertained by M. Thiébaux's article on 'The medieval chase' (*S*). E. C. Johnston (*Language Quarterly*) discusses 'The signification of the Pronoun of Address in *Sir Gawain and the Green Knight*'. 'You' is plural and polite, 'thou' singular and familiar. The Green Knight shows arrogance by using 'thou' to Arthur and Gawain. Gawain consistently addresses the lady as 'you', but her practice varies, and probably significantly. On the whole, however, the rule is not strictly observed, except by the perfectly polite Gawain. P. Haworth suggests (*NQ*) that '*Warthe* in *Sir Gawain*' 715–16 is probably a variant of *wath* (ON *vaðð*) 'ford'.

In her book on *The Pearl*,[13] Miss Kean tries to 'show how an English poet of the late fourteenth century, writing on a devotional theme, set about his work . . . to indicate the kind of material he had to work on, and to show how he organized his poem'. She explores the connotations and depths of groups of associative images in order to establish the theme of the poem: 'the meaning of mortality, its place in the divine scheme and the moral problems it sets the individual'. Through associative images, the symbolic significance of various items is extended beyond the obvious. The poet is as fascinated by complexity of imagery as by complexity of form. For instance, in the proem all the images are meaningfully interlinked in the theme of mortality and regeneration. To isolate a brief example, the cycle of plant growth and decay is seen by Tertullian and St. Bernard as a symbol of physical resurrection and immortality; the poet exploits this. The Dreamer hopes that the plant-life growing from the grave will not decay. He has still not seen that only through this very cycle of decay and regeneration may true immortality be attained. The question of whether the poem is elegiac or allegorical does not arise; the proem establishes that it is about the death of a loved person which has caused irrational grief. The Dreamer's instruction continues via 'The Dream' to 'The Revelation'; he is led to a vision of the New Jerusalem. When he returns to the garden, he has acknowledged at last what he refused to acknowledge at first: truth, and the voice of reason. By means of the personal experience (feigned or real) of the mourner we are brought to the final Christian

affirmation. Whether or not we follow Miss Kean happily into every corner of her exploration, we must feel the conviction which, as a whole, this book holds. In an important and closely-argued article, which cannot be summarized, M-S. Røstvig argues for 'Numerical composition in *Pearl*' (*ES*): 'the technique of casting one's writing in a form conditioned by numbers selected with a view to their symbolic aptness'. Particularly to be noted is the circularity implied by the total (101) of stanzas: the completion of one cycle (100) and the beginning of the next; the lack of *concatenatio* between XII and XIII, symbolizing the movement from this life to the next, between which there is no bridge; the extra stanza of XV, which, since it describes the perfection of the Lamb of God, needs 6, 'the first number of perfection'. 'The second part (i.e. XIII–XX) effects a conscious lifting of the symbolism to a higher, anagogical level.' A. Giudi finds 'Il meglio di *Pearl*' for the modern reader in the first, descriptive, section (*Annali Istituto Orientale di Napoli, Sezione Germanica* IX, 1966). The didactic section is less poetically interesting. This first section has qualities reminiscent of Dante, whom the poet could have read. He is not convinced that *Pearl* and *Sir Gawain* are by the same poet, though they have in common a preciosity of description; however, *Pearl*, by the symbolic use of description, transforms reality in a way that *Sir Gawain* does not attempt. It is this which repays the effort to overcome linguistic difficulties and the modern dislike of the poet's mannerist style. E. Vasta suggests (*JEGP*) that *fede* (*Pearl* 29) is to be translated 'fed', i.e. the narrator expresses the wish that flowers *may* not feed on the lost Pearl. He wishes, against universal law, his Pearl's corruption to be

[13] *The Pearl. An Interpretation*, by P. M. Kean. London: Routledge. New York: Barnes & Noble. pp. x+246. 40s.

suspended; he has not yet become reconciled with reason, with his loss, and with himself. N. Davis (*RES*) adds further instances to his note on *Pearl* 1208 (*YW* xlvii. 79), but quotes two usages, one literary, one archiepiscopal, in which 'God's blessing and mine' is used other than by parent to child. Sister M. V. Hillmann's edition and translation of *The Pearl* was first published in 1961, but escaped notice in *YW*. It is now deservedly reissued[14] with a short introduction and up-dated bibliography. Sister Mary Vincent's interpretation still has value, though perhaps few accept that the pearl is literally a jewel. Mr. Vasta's introduction outlines some of what has been said about the poem since. The text is carefully edited, the translation, though influenced, as is natural, by the interpretation, runs well and is stimulating. Stimulating also, and informative, are the notes. This reissue will be welcomed by those who, although not ignorant of Middle English, quail before the difficulties of *Pearl*. *Pearl* scholars will find that they often return to it.

E. M. Kelly (*ELN*) draws 'Parallels between the Middle English *Patience* and *Hymnus Ieiunantium* of Prudentius'—an analogue hitherto overlooked. Correspondences in detail make it likely, as it was possible, that the *Gawain*-poet knew the *Hymnus*. O. G. Hill revives the theory (Emerson, *PMLA* 10, H. Bateson) which regards the pseudo-Tertullian 'Late Latin *De Jona* as a source for *Patience*', (specifically, lines 61–304). He thinks Liljegren (*Englische Studien* 48) wrong in supposing that *De Jona* does not mention lightning

or the smell in the whale's belly, and that *Patience* has nothing to correspond to the meeting of waves and clouds. Other parallels are more forceful than Liljegren admits.

V. F. Petronella (*JEGP*) considers 'Style as a vehicle for meaning' in *St. Erkenwald*, showing how the manipulation of conjunction and verb in the prologue emphasizes the transformation of St. Paul's from a heathen to a Christian temple, foreshadowing the poem's theme of 'the transformation of a starving pagan soul to a nourished pagan soul'. Thought-links are made through alliterative links; climax is emphasized by the 'two-lined "stanza"' 167–8. The movement of the judge's soul from dark to light is anticipated by the saint's actions in London, and at the end there is the transformation of grief to joy. Other unifying features of the poem are: the use of words denoting 'work'; the use of the word 'name' (all are relatively universalized figures except the named Erkenwald; it is the name of Christ which enables the judge to be re-identified as a saved soul); the use of descriptions which appeal to the ear; and the use of paradox.

In 'Piers Plowman and *The Simonie*' (*Archiv*, 1966) E. Salter suggests that Langland's debt to earlier and contemporary alliterative poetry may have been greater than we have suspected. In particular, *The Simonie* from the Auchinleck MS., though only partly alliterative, reminds one verbally and in its metrical and syntactical structures of *Piers*. It introduces abstract concepts into a realistic setting; its concept 'Truth' could have given an idea for development to Langland; and its closing picture of Pride riding through the land could be a rough sketch for Passus XX. The inclusion of *The Simonie* in Auchinleck shows the acceptability of such complaint and satire poems

---

[14] *The Pearl. Mediaeval Text with a Literal Translation*, by Sister M. V. Hillman. Intro. and add. Bibl. by E. Vasta. Notre Dame U.P. pp. xxiv+175. Paperback. $1.95. 15s. 6d.

to fourteenth-century audiences. R. St.-Jacques (*Révue de l'Université d'Ottawa*) examines the links between 'Langland's Christ-Knight and the Liturgy'. Some liturgical sources have already been recognized (*Isaiah* 63, 1–7; *Pangue Lingua*; *Victimae Paschali*; *Fulgens praeclara*), but in service books, commentaries on the liturgy, and liturgical sermons there are others. Christ is seen as equipped with weapons (sometimes the cross is one); the crown of thorns is a helmet; He spoils His defeated enemy; the Mass is figuratively seen as a battle. Such are the sources of passages in XVI, XVIII, XIX. XVIII 22–5 reminds us that liturgical vestments were symbolically equated with the incarnation and armour, and XVIII 10–16 that liturgical processions were given a military meaning, and also symbolized the Incarnation and the Passion. This use of the liturgy shows that *Piers* was intended for a wide audience. Langland drew on emotional associations common to all. A. V. C. Schmidt, in 'A Note on the *A* Text of "Piers Plowman"', Passus X 91–4' (*NQ*), suggests that it refers to *Romans* 14, 23 (*goddis worde*) and its commentary (*holi writ*) by Richard of St. Victor, in which it is said that to act against conscience (here = 'faith') is mortal sin. This view, and Langland's exact words, appear in a manuscript of the thirteenth-century *Summa de Vitiis* of Jean de la Rochelle. P. L. Heyworth (*MÆ*) considers the Wycliffite *Rejoinder* to *Friar Daw's Reply* to Jack Upland (Bodl. MS. Digby 41) to be a holograph, with original interpolations by another hand. The fact that one passage (Wright 95. 2 ff.) in *Rejoinder* and the interpolation at that point seem to echo *Piers Plowman* X 249 ff. may indicate the wide currency, and, in some cases, detailed knowledge, of *Piers* in the fifteenth century.

R. W. V. Elliott discusses 'The topography of *Wynnere and Wastoure*' (*ES*), whose dramatic qualities have been noticed, and which includes allegorical figures appropriate to the morality play. The description of the setting implies a grassy plain surrounded by an artificial earthwork, i.e. a circular theatre such as was used for the *Castle of Perseverance*. It is relevant that Chaucer calls Theseus's circular lists a 'theatre'.

D. Mehl[15] tries to drive through the field of romance criticism some paths which do not turn back upon themselves. What are romances like? The French romance helps little; French classic forms gave example and stimulus, but the English romance had a different public, less formally courtly. In fact, courtly elements tend to take on a fairy-tale quality. It is literary, though perhaps showing oral influence, and not confined to professional recitation. The diversity of the romances makes definition difficult, and contemporary applications of the term hardly help. Often they simply imply 'dass der Begriff *romance* stets mit einem bestimmter Helden in Beziehung gebracht wurde'. They are closely associated with Saints' lives; while the romances have an implicit moral and didactic purpose (which often alone gives coherence and meaningfulness to the plot), the legends, under their influence, become less devotional and more moral, and so the distinction is further blurred (perhaps there were minstrel versions of romances in less pious strain?). Nor is it always easy to divide romance from chronicle.

[15] *Die mittelenglischen Romanzen des 13 and 14. Jahrhunderts*, by D. Mehl. *Anglistische Forschungen* Heft 93. Heidelberg: Carl Winter. pp. 229. (A 'revised and expanded English version' has now (1969; for 1968) appeared, *viz. The Middle English Romances of the Thirteenth and Fourteenth Centuries*. Routledge. pp. x + 300. £2 10*s*.)

In both cases the emphasis on incident and plot may help to distinguish the romance, and its episodic structure and oral devices of backward and forward reference to further define it. Problems of classification are equally difficult. Classifications so far suggested are unsatisfactory or insufficiently evidenced. Mehl suggests an interim division on grounds of length, each type having its special characteristics. The shorter (500–1200 lines; 'besonders typisch für die englische Form der romantischem Verzahlung') were probably to be read at a sitting, sometimes with intervals. They are condensed versions of novels, or they deal with a single episode at length in epic manner. Their subjects are the life of a hero, an episode showing a hero's superiority, or the story of a family, lovers, or a group of friends. Some are concerned with heroes so virtuous as to be almost saintly, or with innocent women triumphing in adversity. Often God intervenes with a miracle. Although emphasis is usually on the plot, these latter are homiletic in nature. Less common are the longer romances, mostly northern in origin, often dealing with heroic deeds from the English past as models to the present. This group contains some of the most effective of the M.E. romances, notably *Sir Gawain*. The last group of 'Versromanze', such as *Beues*, range from five to twelve thousand lines. They are often compilations, the time-scale is long, and though they may deal essentially with one hero, there is little attention to unity. Agglomeration of episodes rather than epic pace accounts for their length. They are highly literary. It is clear that Professor Mehl's book will be essential reading for anyone wishing to understand the Middle English romances.

A. C. Baugh re-examines our thought on 'The Middle English romance. Some questions of creation, presentation and preservation' (*S*). Almost all are for an audience; it does not follow, in spite of popular style, references to minstrels, or commonplace formulas, that they are composed by minstrels, though some may have been. In fact, they were usually composed in writing, though for oral delivery (the primary method of secular publication) by minstrels at feasts, or for entertainment in hall, parlour or alehouse—perhaps even out of doors. Unprofessional readings amongst friends are also portrayed. The romances were felt to offer entertainment which provided pleasure with profit. They were certainly sung by professionals, probably recited also, and certainly sometimes from a written text. There seem to have been rests and intermissions—which affects discussion of romance structure. Variations in cognate texts are due not merely to scribal errors, which can usually be recognized, but also to imperfect memorization by minstrels whose concern for exact verbal faithfulness was small. The extracts from various romances in A. C. Gibbs's collection[16] are 'not an anthology, but extended quotation illustrating an argument about the nature of romance'. They are 'examples of (romances) at their moment of truth'. In accordance with the policy of the series, 'unnecessary encumbrances such as obsolete letters and manuscript errors' are eliminated. The introduction includes remarks on romance in general and on each of the poems from which extracts are taken. Variations from the manuscript are noted beneath the text, and difficulties in the text itself are

[16] *Middle English Romances*, ed. A. C. Gibbs. *York Medieval Texts.* London: Arnold. Evanston (Ill.): Northwestern U.P. (1966). pp. 180. Paperback, 12*s*. 6*d*.

dealt with in footnotes. There is a select Bibliography and a Glossary. H. Schelp's book on the romances[17] arrived too late for proper consideration in the present volume, and will be dealt with in Vol. xlix. It includes chapters on *Havelok*, *Sir Ysumbras*, *Robert of Sicily*, *Sir Gowther*, *Sir Cleges*, *Emare*, *Florence of Rome* 'and other romances of virtuous women', *Guy of Warwick*, romances of Alexander, Arthur, Troy and Thebes.

J. Finlayson (*S*) rejects the dating 1365 for *Morte Arthure*. The fashions portrayed are of too uncertain date to support it. The poet may have been influenced by the events of the Hundred Years War, but probably by way of the later chroniclers, who romanticized them. Particularly interesting is the Chandos Herald's *Life of the Black Prince*, *c*. 1385, for it offers some hitherto unremarked parallels. There is nothing to prevent us dating the poem (as did Brock) to the last quarter of the fourteenth century, or even later. W. J. R. Brown shows (*MÆ*) that any future discussion of the relationship between the '*Chevalere Assigne* and the *Naissance du Chevalier au Cygne*' must take into account the long redaction of the *Béatrix* version of the *Naissance*. Though the *Chevalere* is clearly based on a *Béatrix* version, none of the surviving redactions is its immediate source. M. Mills (*MÆ*) points out the inconsistency between Havelok's account of Grim at 1417–26 and Grim's rough treatment of him earlier in the poem. He brings evidence from Hartmann's *Gregorius* and Wirnt's *Wigalois* of the character-type of the 'brutal fisherman' and his wife. The main traits seem

[17] *Exemplarische Romanzen im Mittelenglischen*, by H. Schelp. *Palaestra* Bd. 246. Vandenhoeck & Ruprecht. pp. 263. DM 38.00.

to be: he wishes to become rich, is willing to connive at the hero's death, is anxious to get about his own business, treats the hero roughly, strips him, changes heart after the hero's noble nature is revealed by sign or talisman. Although no single version shows all these, *Havelok* comes nearest; its major variation is that Grim is also the type of hired assassin who jibs at carrying out the job. Even in the French versions, Grim is the friend of pirates, who murder Havelok's mother, though Grim saves the boy. The 'brutal fisherman' theme has introduced inconsistency, but also excitement, to *Havelok*. R. W. Hanning shows the structural use of the tale's elements to be more skilful in *Havelok* than in its analogues (*SP*). The three common elements of romantic plot (the hero's progress from loss to recovery; his growth to maturity; his love relationship with a similarly-deprived partner) are marked by the careful disposition of feasts (for without food a man may not grow), feats of strength (the last having a social as well as a personal significance), and recognitions of the king-mark (each case coming at a crucial point and relieving suspense). Havelok's low point is the offering of *manred* to Godard, his rising point Ubbe's offering of *manred* to him. Other themes are the crucial role of Goldboru's love and the contrast of the 'social' and 'personal' power of kingship. J. C. Hirsh writes on 'Pride as Theme in *Sir Launfal*' (*NQ*). Marie's theme in *Lanval* is 'the reciprocating power of love and devotion'. In *Landevale* the hero repents his extravagance, but the same impetuosity leads him to betray the fairy who rescued him from its consequences. The emphasis is on repentance and the grace of forgiveness. In Chestre's *Sir Launfal*, the theme has changed again to one of 'noble pride'. Fairy intervention is here the reward for endurance, and the end shows Launfal's victory over forces that would attack his honour. K. R. Gros Louis sees 'The Significance of Sir Orfeo's Self-exile' (*RES*) to lie in his acceptance of Heurodis's death, his humility, and the strength of his sacrifice for true love. He makes no search, as do other Orpheus-figures, for his wife; she is restored to him as an act of grace in recognition of his sacrifice, and for this he is properly grateful. His experience leads him to a juster appraisal of his kingly power. Quantitatively it has proved ineffective: the thousand knights could not prevent the abduction. Its quality is shown by the faithful steward. D. A. Wright contributes 'A note on *in ich ways*' in *Sir Orfeo* Auch. 119–20 (*NQ*). She rejects Sisam's emendation to *palys/wȳs*, and quotes parallels from *Brut* 18702 and elsewhere to show that *in ich ways* is a blend of the adverbial genitive (continued from OE.) and a prepositional phrase. E. C. York comments on '*Sir Tristrem* 2225–33' (*Ex*) in light of legal procedure: *men seyd* means 'people said' (i.e. not the formal accusation); the bishop acted as intermediary, ameliorating somewhat the harshness of the preliminary decision as to trial by ordeal by attributing it to the queen herself (*sche thougt*).

D. Schueler contends that the advanced 'Age of the lover in Gower's *Confessio Amantis*' (*MÆ*) is explicit and implicit from the beginning of the poem. Thus his wretchedness, his desire to escape from his love, his lack of heroism, and the jealous impulse towards backbiting are not the casual results of Gower's changing attitude towards courtly love, but an adaptation of the code to the age of the lover. But the shock of self-realization is reserved to the end.

A. Renoir begins the reassessment of Lydgate which he thinks the poet deserves,[18] working mainly with the *Troy Book*, the *Fall of Princes* and the *Siege of Thebes*. He finds neither a master nor a bore, but 'a competent craftsman who occasionally rises to a high level of poetic felicity'. His popularity in his own day was great, and persisted into the early seventeenth century. In the eighteenth he was praised for his versification, but Percy began, and Ritson continued, those accusations of prolixity and dullness that have stuck to him since, though 'he has been more often abused than read'. Had the subject matter and style appealed, no doubt Percy and Ritson would have wanted more, not less, and both these appealed to his earlier readers. In such an enormous output dull passages are bound to occur, but he can express human suffering with persuasive sympathy, and, as Gray said, 'raise the more tender emotions of the mind'. He is a competent courtly-love poet, he can portray physical action, and suit imagery to context. Perhaps simply the fact that he was not Chaucer disappointed his later critics. He always acknowledged Chaucer as his master, but his debt is greatest in his early works. Though much in him was medieval, it is rather as a transitional than as a medieval poet that we must judge him. Chaucer knew the names of many of the classical gods, but he took them in less than earnest. Lydgate's understanding of the classics may have been no greater than that of his predecessors, but he had a serious respect for them: 'in the *Siege of Thebes* . . . he methodically

[18] *The Poetry of John Lydgate*, by A. Renoir. Cambridge (Mass.): Harvard U.P. London: Routledge. pp. x+172. 30s.

modified his original in favour of classical antiquity'. He also introduced a nationalistic feeling absent from his French original. Though he expressed the old monastic and courtly attitudes towards women, he also saw them not as members of a category, but as human beings entitled to be respected and judged as individuals. Towards the end of his life he became concerned with the nature of kingship and the concept of the ideal prince. These are the subjects that ensured his popularity in the Renaissance. In style, it was his diction rather than his medieval rhetoric that appealed. The Renaissance also understood better than we that Lydgate had to include in his text what would now be Introduction, Notes and Appendices. What seems mere prolixity now may have been sheer necessity then. Omitted from *YW* xlvii was J. Norton-Smith's selection of Lydgate's poems.[19] The problem of selecting from so large a corpus has been faced by choosing eight shorter poems, *The Temple of Glas* complete, and three samples from longer works. Lydgate's interests and style are well represented. There is a short but good introduction, a select bibliography, excellent notes, a glossary, and a concise appendix on the poet's aureate diction. M. Schlauch draws attention to the 'Stylistic attributes of John Lydgate's prose' (*Jakobson Essays*)[20] in *The Serpent of Division*, which mixes translation and original passages. His characteristic small effects are: the use, more extensively than in his original, of doublets and verbal repetition, both common late medieval devices; the use of grammatically parallel phrases; minor inversions, often throwing emphasis on the adverb (seemingly an idiosyncrasy). The use of alliteration and *cursus*-forms is not striking. In larger elements he shows loose structure and longwindedness, though not all his examples of *amplificatio* are mere padding. More work on such prose texts is needed before statements can safely be made about fifteenth-century prose style. In 'Some Readers of John Trevisa' (*NQ*) R. A. Dwyer suggests that Chaucer's and Lydgate's use of *pillars* (rather than *boundes*) for the Pillars of Hercules shows them to have read Trevisa's passage in *Polychronicon* where the same usage is found. Lydgate also mistakes (as does Trevisa) *Cacus* for *cattus* (*Troy Book* I, 591). In '*The Assembly of Gods* and Christine de Pisan' (*ELN*), C. F. Bühler assigns the poem (once attributed to Lydgate) to the third quarter of the fifteenth century, for the poet's source for the goddess *Othea* (304) must have been Christine's *Épître d'Othéa*. There are other significant parallels.

E. M. Thornley compares 'The Middle English penitential lyric and Hoccleve's autobiographical poetry' (*NM*), specifically, *La Male Regle*, in which he exploits and parodies what must have been the widely-recognized conventions of the 'homiletic' (as opposed to the 'prayer') type of lyric: the first-person opening; the address to the Deity; the equation of youth with sin, and age with repentance; the metaphor of the sinner as God's knight; the exemplification of some or all of the cardinal sins; the intention of amendment, making of satisfaction (his poverty), and plea for absolution (i.e. relief of his poverty). The effectiveness of the parody shows the genre of penitential lyric to have had a recognized literary status. J. Mitchell contends that 'The

---

[19] *John Lydgate. Poems*, ed. J. Norton-Smith. Clarendon Medieval and Tudor Series. Clarendon Press (1966). pp. xvi+202. 32*s*. 6*d*.

[20] See chap. II, footnote 1.

autobiographical element in Hoccleve' (*MLQ*) cannot always be put down, as it can so often in the works of contemporaries and predecessors, to pure convention. He reveals a human if unflattering portrait of an individual.

One purpose J. R. Simon has in editing *The Kingis Quair*[21] is to make available to French students a poem from a neglected period of our literature; the purpose is sufficient in itself, but he does more. His text is closer to the manuscript than either Skeat's or Mackenzie's. For instance, he refrains from Skeat's practice of mending the metre by adding, or marking, final -*e*. (He agrees, however, with Skeat over the interpretation of 'tall *s*'). He sticks more rigidly than they to the manuscript orthography, though, in spite of his words on p. 251, one doubts the value of distinguishing supposed *y* (as in *yat* 3.2, etc., Skeat *that*) from þ (e.g. 55.5 *þat*). Necessary emendation is made (e.g. the transposition of lines 185.4 and 5), but conjectural emendation shunned, e.g. manuscript *In lufe and cunnyng ar to full pleasaunce* 185.6 (Skeat emended to *cummyn*, followed by Mackenzie). Unfortunately, M. Simon's notes are as brief as his predecessors'; there is no discussion, and the translation speaks for itself: 'En amour, sont venus à plein contentement'. In 47.5 even the translation shirks the problem. In spite of occasional (and minor) uncertainties which could only be resolved by reference to the manuscript, the text gives every sign of being a reliable transcription, and the interesting punctuation of scribe 1 is better represented than elsewhere. A most valuable introduction deals with the manuscript,

the present state of *Kingis Quair* studies, and extensively with graphematics, morphology, syntax, style, and versification. Both the graphematics and the syntax sections break new ground. On the evidence of the morphology, M. Simon would contend that the text, however mixed, comes from a Scottish pen. There is a critical study of the poem's narrative, descriptive, lyric and didactic aspects. It would be presumptuous to attempt to assess the Modern French translation; its existence means that the glossary need not be full, and consequently cannot be used as an *index verborum*. The edition contributes to our knowledge and understanding of a major text of Scottish literature.

Sister Mary Jeremy suggests (*ELN*) that '*Mon*' in "Foweles in the frith"', line 3, is not a verb ('must'), but a noun ('man') in apposition to *I*, making a contrast with the birds and the fishes. D. Luisi (*Ex*) sees 'Foweles in the frith' as contrasting the natural order in lines 1 and 2 with the excess of the poet's sorrow, which is contrary to that order. A. G. Rigg corrects *M.E.D.* on 'The letter "C" and the date of Easter' (*ELN*), pointing out that C signifies 7 March, and that the instructions in the poem for finding the date of Easter (Robbins, *Secular Lyrics*, p. 63) work on this basis. He examines significant variants in the various manuscripts of the poem, showing how some make nonsense of the calculation. F. Riddy shows 'The provenance of *Quia amore langueo*' (*RES*) to be North Midlands, thus rejecting Brown's contention that the version of Douce 322 'fairly represents its original form'. As B.M. Add. MS. 37409, the nearest in dialect to the original, is corrupt, it should be supplemented by Douce and corrected by the other manuscripts. R. H.

---

[21] *Le Livre du Roi (The Kingis Quair), attribué à Jacques 1er* ed. J. R. Simon. *Bibliothèque de Philogie Germanique* XXI. Paris; Aubier Montaigne. pp. 359. 2 plates.

Bowers prints, with notes, 'A Middle English poem on the nine virtues' (*Southern Folklore Quarterly*) (*Index* 212) from C.U.L. MS. Dd. 1.1. in which Christ appears as a moral teacher. The original seven virtues (either the Ciceronian quartet plus the Pauline trio, or the Seven Gifts of the Holy Ghost) did not stand neatly opposed to the cardinal sins, and could be augmented and varied, as in this poem. The poet dislikes bodily penance, but shows a puritan strain. He has a concern for lay souls which sets him apart from the worldliness of many fifteenth-century didactic writers. The poem reflects the taste of the English for mnemonic didactic verse. Bowers also prints, with short introduction and notes, some 'Middle English verses on the founding of the Carthusian order' (*S*) from B.M. Add. MS. 37049 (*Index* 435). V. J. Scattergood prints with notes 'An unpublished Middle English poem' (*Archiv*, 1966) a 70-line description of Rome (not in *Index*) recorded with a version of *The Stations of Rome* on the back of Bicester Priory Bursar's Accounts Roll in the Public Records Office. N.E. Mids. in origin, it is in a fifteenth-century hand, and shows some corruption and scribal changes. It may have been used as a guide for pilgrims. D. Gray quotes (*NQ*) 'A Middle English verse at Warkworth' (near Banbury), apparently a line from *Index* 1703. R. E. Nichols offers in modernized spelling the sections on 'Procreation, pregnancy and parturition' from the Middle English translation of *Sidrak and Bokkus* in B.M. MS. Lansdowne 793 (*Medical History*). Perhaps one of the most interesting points for readers of romance is the author's contention (I. 53) that only a woman who is 'hot of kind' and 'great liking hath to man' is likely to bear more than one child (or two? It is not clear) at a birth.

A. Zettersten draws attention to 'The Middle English lyrics in the Wellcome Library' (*NM*), including two medical poems of the Loscombe MS., which W. Heuser (*Die Kildare-Gedichte*) thought to be lost, and a poem on three of the nine worthies, here printed (*Index Supp.* 1322.5). A. G. Rigg prints with translation and explanatory notes a Latin poem 'The Stories of the Cities' (*Ang*) from the fifteenth-century Trinity Coll. Camb. MS. 0.9.38, previously printed with errors in Wright and Halliwell's *Reliquiae Antiquae* II, 178. It dates from before 1401, and characterizes seven English cities. He prints also '"Jam nunc in proximo": a Latin mortality poem' (*MÆ*) which, in one of its three manuscripts (Trin. Coll. MS., above), is followed by a short macaronic stanza. R. R. Raymo prints (*ELN*) *Quod the Devill to the Frier*, a fragment of anti-mendicant satire from C.U.L. MS. Ff vi 31.

RenD (formerly *Research Opportunities in Renaissance Drama*) now includes a section on 'Medieval Drama'. Besides a list of 'Current Projects' and an article on Digby MS. 133 (which falls outside the chronological scope of this chapter), we find S. J. Kahrl on 'Medieval drama in Louth' and A. C. Gay on 'The "Stage" and the staging of the N-town plays'. Kahrl suggests we should pay more attention to the religious guilds as bodies responsible for the production of medieval cycle drama, as was the case at Lincoln. Since they were religious fraternities, their record and account books largely disappeared in Tudor times, unlike those of the craft guilds. But some have survived, and it is clear that at Louth the well-endowed religious guilds had a major part in cycle production in the early sixteenth century. Evidence from elsewhere supports the suggestion that the Lincoln pattern of a religious guild dominant in the production over the craft guilds may be common in the county. Gray contends that Southern's definition of 'place' is appropriate to the N-town plays, that 'the whole cycle bears evidence of "place-and-scaffold" staging', and that the word 'stage' here refers only to 'scaffold'. P. S. Macaulay (*Studia Germanica Gandensia*, 1966) discusses 'The play of the Harrowing of Hell as a climax in the English mystery cycles'. The Harrowing is basic to the concept of redemption. By attempting Christ's death, the Devil, who did not clearly recognize His divine nature, overreached himself and lost his power over the souls of men. Christ's sacrifice is shown to redeem the good who lived before as well as after it: 'the fusion of all human Time is represented by the Harrowing'. The theological importance is obvious. The cycle playwrights seized on its dramatic potential also. Sister M. P. Forrest considers 'The role of the expositor Contemplacio in the St. Anne's Day plays of the Hegge Cycle' (*MS*, 1966), the only major character of his kind in the medieval mysteries. He binds the sequence into one structurally independent play, and 'speaks with the authority of an accepted preacher' (one is reminded of the quasi-Augustinian voice in *Sermo contra Judaeos*). His name reveals him as an allegorical figure of devout meditation, and so interpreter of scriptural story and exhorter to good action. In his prayers (sometimes of great lyric force), expositions, and blessings, he resembles the priest; like the voice of the Church, his is the voice of mankind, and he intercedes for all. R. Weimann (*SJW*) discusses 'Realismus und Simultankonvention im Misteriendrama', with special reference to the Towneley Shepherds'

Plays, finding there a unity of realistic, liturgical, religious and conventional elements from both church and mimic drama. He draws attention to the way in which realistic transference is made from the 'epic' monologues addressed to the audience to dramatic dialogue, thus making dramatically more believable 'die simultane Konvention' of the mystery plays. Mak himself may be a mimic throwback, but his episode is concerned with themes central to the play: the shepherds' wretchedness, and domestic discord. Much of the comic-realistic element has sources in folk-lore or contemporary life. No conflict is recognized between dramatic illusion and conventional speeches; mythical past and real present, Palestine and Yorkshire, exist simultaneously. Artistic unity lies in the inner relationship of the parts. Anachronism is itself the means by which the biblical reveals the contemporary story. As the lyric fervour of the Bethlehem scene shows, the poet is fundamentally Christian. Nevertheless he is concerned rather with realism than myth. The balance between ritual and mimesis has changed. The Christian message is confronted with contemporary actuality. M. J. Young (*Speech Monographs*) examines the evidence regarding 'The York pageant-wagon', and concludes that the action of a specific play normally focused on a single wagon (though possibly two were on rare occasions used). Occasionally actors used the street also. The wagons were of one storey, 10–12 feet above the floor, and probably 10 × 20 feet in area. The devices and ornamentation were neither primitive nor crude. Articles by K. M. Cameron and S. J. Kahrl on 'Staging the N-town Cycle' (*TN*), by C. Davidson on 'The Unity of the Wakefield *Mactacio Abel*' (*T*), and by E. B. Canteloupe and R Griffith on 'The Gifts of the

Shepherds in the Wakefield *Secunda Pastorum*: an Iconographical Interpretation' (*MS*, 1966) are dealt with in chapter VI.

E. J. Dobson, in 'The date and composition of *Ancrene Wisse*' (*PBA*, 1966), detects signs that attention is being paid in the work to the Lateran Council rulings of 1215, and suggests a date of 1215–22, though the only safe *terminus ante quem* is provided by the Corpus MS., i.e. 1230. Nero is probably closest to the original, which underwent three kinds of changes: deliberate changes not by the author; scribal changes; changes by redactor(s). These last are probably made by the original author for the original (but enlarged) community. The exceptional textual purity of Corpus suggests it may be a copy of the author's autograph. Of the two revisers of Cleopatra, B was also probably the author himself. Thus the original (1215–22) was corrected and revised (as shown in Cleopatra), and culminated in the revised Corpus version (of which Corpus MS. is a fair copy) from 1228–30.

Professor Hodgson[22] draws attention away from the self-seeking clerics of *Piers Plowman* and the *Canterbury Tales* to the 'spirit of unworldly devotion' as shown in Rolle, the author of the *Cloud of Unknowing*, and Hilton. The heirs of a stable doctrine and a tradition of vernacular religious prose, they tried to map the way to a direct experience of God. Dominant in all is God's love, mightier than reason. Rolle's work is directly personal, and his message is one of assurance. Although his mystical experiences were probably less profound than he thought, his influence, in religion and as a prose-writer, was great. The author of the

Cloud was a sterner personality rigorously following the negative way of contemplation. Only when contact with the world of reason and the senses is severed can contact with God, by His grace, be made; the seeker must enter the cloud of unknowing. Though profundities have to be expressed, the expression is simple, direct, and untechnical; nevertheless, the author's teaching is for the few chosen by grace. Hilton is a gentler teacher with a wider appeal, concerned with the growth of spiritual man from the fallen into the highest state. His imagery is abundant and integral to his thought. Through self-knowledge, rejection of sin, and persistence in the path to regeneration, the soul's reconciliation with God is to be sought. Love and knowledge are the reward. Prof. Hodgson gives clear guidance in a difficult field. J. E. Milosh makes an attempt to analyse Hilton's teaching and set it in its background for the specialist and the general reader. He examines especially the technical terminology Hilton used, and compares it with that of his contemporaries.[23]

Dr. Aarts puts forth a useful edition of the Westminster School Lib. MS. 3 of the Pater Noster treatise (once thought to be by Richard Rolle), followed by variants from five other manuscripts.[24] There is an extensive introduction dealing with the manuscripts, the language (the provenance and date of the original are tentatively suggested as S. E. Mids. before 1408), the literary background and quality, and the place of the Pater Noster in Middle

---

[22] *Three 14th-century English Mystics,* by P. Hodgson. Writers and Their Work: No. 196. Longmans, Green & Co. pp. 47. 3*s*. 6*d*.

[23] *The Scale of Perfection and the English Mystical Tradition,* by J. E. Milosh. Wisconsin U.P. (1966). pp. viii+216. $6.50. 49*s*.

[24] *þe Pater Noster of Richard Ermyte. A Late Middle English Exposition of the Lord's Prayer,* by F. G. A. M. Aarts. The Hague: Nijhoff. pp. cxiv+174. One plate. Guilders 30.60.

English literature. Completing the volume are notes and glossary, an appendix showing in parallel columns, and in fuller form than in the 'Variants', a short passage as it appears in the various manuscripts, a bibliography and indexes.

Professor Kuriyagawa revises and enlarges his 1958 edition (*YW* xxxix. 78) of Hilton's *Chapters on Perfection*,[25] printing 'one of the oldest and best' manuscripts, Bibl. Nat. MS. anglais 41, with significant variants from the eight other medieval manuscripts at its foot. He proposes a tentative stemma, and describes the language of his selected text in terms of the standard grammars. Though some of the statements about phonology are assumptions undemonstrable from this text, the ultimate placing in the E. Mids. is reasonable. There are some explanatory and textual notes and a selective glossary.

G. Leff's 'John Wyclif: the path to dissent' (*PBA*, 1966) describes clearly the process by which Wyclif became 'the greatest heresiarch of the later Middle Ages'. His real break with the past was not in his reverence for the Bible, but in his rejection of the Church as the arbiter of truth. T. Dyson in 'Wyclif Reviewed' (*Church Quarterly Review*) poses the question 'A prophet or a great man?', and tries to give a balanced answer. At last we have a reliable general edition of Mandeville.[26] The text is based on MS. Cotton Titus C XVI, supplemented from two manuscripts of the Defective Version. Some obsolete letter-forms are modernized, and scribal errors and omissions are corrected. Rejected manuscript readings are placed below the text. There are two commentaries, textual and general, a selective gloss, and a short introduction.

Numerous prints and manuscripts attest the popularity of Thomas (or Robert) Wimbledon's sermon delivered at Paul's Cross in 1388(?). Miss Knight[27] seeks to establish the text on the basis of the English manuscripts, of which MS. C.C.C.C. 357, having 'the fewest number of individual variants' is 'closest to the reconstructed common original'. She thus prints an emended C, with rejected readings and important variants at its foot. 'In most cases the majority reading determines a questionable word', a method which turns out to be as good as any in this particular text. Once, at least, the principle of *difficilior lectio* is applied, if somewhat mechanically: C's minority *lowere* (equated with *louerd*!) *of comunytes* is preferred to *leders*, *lorde* or *reuler*. Huntingdon's *lawere* ('law-giver'?) *or ruler* may give the clue, though *O.E.D.* first quotes this meaning from More. C's dialect is looked at, mostly in the light of Mackenzie. The section contains such remarks as 'OE *æ* of both origins is shortened to both ä and *ĕ*'; '*world* and *worchyng* are characteristic of West Midlands'. Some of the etymologies in the gloss are astonishing, e.g *fayrhed* < OE *fæger* + *hēafod*. The sermon is examined in the light of medieval principles of sermon construction, and there is an inconclusive section on Wimbledon's reading. The notes identify some of his references and quotations. N. H. Owen also publishes the same text with

[25] *Walter Hilton's Eight Chapters on Perfection*, ed. F. Kuriyagawa. Studies in the Humanities and Social Relations 9. Tokyo: Keio Institute of Cultural and Linguistic Studies. pp. lii+58. 8 plates.

[26] *Mandeville's Travels*, ed. M. C. Seymour. Oxford; Clarendon Press. pp. xxi+303. 55s.

[27] *Wimbledon's Sermon Redde Rationem Villicationis Tue: A Middle English Sermon of the Fourteenth Century*, ed. Ione K. Knight. Duquesne Studies, Philological Series 9. Duquesne U.P. pp. viii+147. $7.95. (For Sundén's 1925 edition, see *YW* vi. 102).

editorial emendations and footnotes (MS, 1966). The structure of the sermon and the manuscript are briefly described. J. V. Fleming prints 'A Middle English treatise on the nature of man' (*NQ*) from MS. Garret 143, Firestone Lib., Princeton U. (not in Wells).

V

Middle English: Chaucer

JOYCE BAZIRE and DAVID MILLS

1. GENERAL

The first supplement to D. D. Griffith's *Bibliography of Chaucer, 1908–53* (*YW* xxxvi. 76), compiled by William R. Crawford,[1] is prefaced by a useful introduction on 'New Directions in Chaucer Criticism', a survey of the productions of the ten years covered by the book. It is obviously possible for Crawford, in such a brief space, to discuss only a few of the many works. Robertson and Huppé are dealt with fairly briefly, and more significant to the author are the works of Muscatine, Payne, and Talbot Donaldson, and those expressing views on the *persona* of the *Tales* and *Troilus*. The Bibliography itself follows almost the same pattern as Griffith's, to which page references are supplied, though in the case of 'Chaucer the Pilgrim' a new section is indicated. Some of the changes in the list of Abbreviations would seem to reflect new journals covering this field.

A companion volume to the Cambridge editions of selected tales, *Chaucer's World*,[2] by Maurice Hussey, provides an excellent background for the *Canterbury Tales*. Its 125 illustrations are drawn from a variety of sources—manuscripts such as the Ellesmere, with its miniatures of the pilgrims, or the Duc de Berri's Book

of Hours; features of church architecture, such as misericords, bosses, grotesques, and stained glass; aerial photographs to show old features of the countryside now obscured at ground level; buildings such as the Merchant Venturers' Guildhall, York; paintings, such as those of Brueghel. The accompanying text 'explains the significance of the pictures in relation to Chaucer's writing and his times, drawing the reader's attention to details which the untutored eye might miss'. The greater part is concerned with the individual pilgrims, and their particular backgrounds. Under 'The Militant Church', for instance, are collected comments on the Parson, the parish church, church imagery (wall-paintings, stained glass); and here are found illustrations of the Seven Deadly Sins, which of course appear in the *Parson's Tale*. The rest of the book is devoted to background material, such as maps and the pilgrims' route, or a description of medieval Canterbury and the cathedral there.

In *Chaucer and the Liturgy*[3] Beverly Boyd examines Chaucer's references to the liturgy under the headings 'Ecclesiastical Calendar', 'References to Saints', 'The Liturgy of the Sacraments', and 'The Canonical Hours'; an opening chapter defines terms and justifies the choice of the Use of

---

[1] *Bibliography of Chaucer, 1954–63*, compiled by William R. Crawford. Washington U.P. pp. xlix + 144. 37s. 6d.

[2] *Chaucer's World*, by Maurice Hussey. C.U.P. pp. 172. 35s; paperback 15s.

[3] *Chaucer and the Liturgy*, by Beverly Boyd. Philadelphia: Dorrance & Co. pp. vii + 88. 12 plates. $4.

Sarum as basis for the study. A number of interesting incidental points emerge—for example, that *Troilus* I, 169–72 may show the use of a dominical letter or that the Prioress's *service dyvyne* expressly relates to the canonical hours and is a link with her tale and its prologue. More generally, Miss Boyd stresses Chaucer's secular, but not disrespectful, use of the liturgy.

After briefly considering the evolution of the dream-vision form and medieval dream-interpretation, Constance B. Hieatt[4] examines the attitudes mainly of Chaucer, but also of his contemporaries, to dreams. She goes on to note the compatibility of modern psychological approaches to dreams and the medieval attitudes, and then proceeds to examine a number of dream-poems. In a comparison of *Pearl* and the *Book of the Duchess*, she notes the blending, fusion and double-meaning in *Pearl*, and the parallelism, fusion, and inversion in the *Book of the Duchess*, and suggests that their purposes are different and that their real affinity is as dream-literature. In a brief examination of Chaucer's further experiments, she refers to the humorous use of the device in the *Hous of Fame*, the combination of psychological and humorous functions in the *Parlement of Foules*, and the playful effect in the Prologue to the *Legend of Good Women*. Subsequent chapters examine *Piers Plowman*, *Winner and Waster* and the *Parlement of the Thre Ages*, and the final chapter examines the compatibility of dream-vision and allegorical method and notes new extensions of the form in the fifteenth century.

R. M. Jordan's *Chaucer and the Shape of Creation: the Aesthetic Possibilities of Inorganic Structure*[5] attempts 'to define the essential features of Chaucerian narrative and to provide an aesthetic rationale which is more relevant to the Chaucerian facts than are the principles of narrative art which have generally prevailed in criticism since Henry James'. Chapters I–III trace the development of the medieval ideas of 'inorganic structure' from the Platonic tradition of aesthetics, especially in the *Timaeus*, and compare the emphasis on structure and iconography in the Gothic cathedral. The concept of inorganic structure is then applied to *Troilus* in an important essay emphasizing the structural function of the narrator, who divides the story into sections by his interventions, relates it to the central theme of the nature of love, and emphasizes the finite nature of the fiction; finally, Troilus is set within a divine framework and the reader's attention 'moves past the narrator to the poetic and moral sensibility behind that role, a sensibility now embodied in the poem and even named'. The rest of the book concentrates on the *Tales*. Jordan sees the idea of accommodation, rather than of journey-order or of dramatic effect, as the key to Chaucer's technique and stresses the role of the narrator and the frequent inconsistencies in presentation. These views are then developed in individual studies. The *Merchant's Tale* is analysed as a series of interacting rhetorical sections with 'reality' finally intruding upon 'fiction'. A stimulating study of the *Knight's Tale* emphasizes the formality both

[4] *The Realism of Dream Visions: The Poetic Exploitation of the Dream-Experience in Chaucer and His Contemporaries*, by Constance B. Hieatt. The Hague and Paris: Mouton & Co. pp. 117. 14 Guilders.

[5] *Chaucer and the Shape of Creation: the Aesthetic Possibilities of Inorganic Structure*, by R. M. Jordan. Harvard U.P. pp. xviii + 257. 66s. 6d. and $6.95.

of Theseus's world and of the tale's rhetorical structure. In the first part a narrative balance focuses upon Palamon and Arcite in turn but proceeds from, and returns to, the figure of Theseus; the second part is a rhetorical structure, especially in the temple-descriptions where structural balance is more important than narrative development or semantic significance. The narrator intrudes, especially in the funeral-account which stresses structure at the expense of fictional illusion. A detailed analysis of the final scene illustrates the structural complexity of the *Miller's Tale*, while the discussion of the *Clerk's Tale* develops the idea that 'the tale rests upon two contradictory sets of assumptions, realistic *and* symbolic'. The *Wife of Bath's Prologue* does not present a character but three distinct aspects of antifeminism — concupiscence, sovereignty and feminine wiliness. The *Parson's Tale* is important for what it is—a penitential framework comprehending all forms of human conduct, just as the *General Prologue* comprehends all human society; both share the same structural principle, but the *Parson's Tale* finally points the true way, to a reality of revealed truth.

M. W. Grose has provided in *Chaucer*[6] an introductory volume to a study of the poet. The first chapters are concerned with background material under such headings as 'Social Life', 'Science'; and in three later ones there is commentary on Chaucer's works. As the author acknowledges, ideas have been 'plundered' from many sources, and a book very useful within its set limits has been produced.

'What Arnold suspected when he

charged Chaucer with lack of high seriousness was that life seemed to Chaucer more often than not a series of different games, none of them ultimately real or serious.' R. A. Lanham ('Game, Play, and High Seriousness in Chaucer's Poetry' [*ES*]) suggests that game-aspects are useful for the study of love, rhetoric, and war in Chaucer's poetry. The journey in the *Tales* is a pilgrimage but also a game; Lanham looks particularly at the *Knight's Tale* where the two games of love and war illuminate each other's follies, and at the Wife of Bath who enjoys the game of sex, but still more the game of rhetoric; he considers briefly the tales of the Miller, Man of Law, and Clerk. *Troilus* has love, rhetoric, and war, but war is unchallenged and there are two primary games, 'the aristocratic game of conflict' and 'the bourgeois one of pleasure'; 'the tragedy of the poem . . . is fundamentally a social rather than an individual one'.

C. A. Owen ('The Problem of Free Will in Chaucer's Narratives' [*PQ*]) sees a correlation between the interaction of destiny and free will in the universe and of form and character in a poem. He traces Chaucer's development from the mechanical universe of *The Complaint of Mars* and the emerging pattern of destiny in the *Knight's Tale*, which thwarts freewill, to *Troilus*. In that poem the outcome is known from the start, but not to the characters, while the formal symmetry of the work, suggestive of inevitable growth and decay, is offset by the emphasis upon the thoughts, speeches, and individuality of the characters who bear responsibility for their choices. These are actual events told by an observing narrator who finally exhorts the reader to Christian faith. In the *Tales*, where Owen notes the role of

---

[6] *Literature in Perspective: Chaucer*, by M. W. Grose. Evans Brothers. pp. 160. 8*s*. 6*d*.

the Host, the main formal pattern is the interaction of the characters and the tales and there is no predetermined formal pattern or stress on destiny.

G. W. Dunleavy ('The Wound and the Comforter: the Consolations of Geoffrey Chaucer' [*PLL*]) argues that Boethian philosophy may have helped Chaucer to serve uncongenial masters. He notes the influence of Boethian philosophy in some of the *Tales* and in *Truth*, and particularly emphasizes the presentation in Chaucer's works of the poet as physician or comforter to invisible wounds.

After discussing briefly the main features of Statius's *Thebaid*, Paul M. Clogan notes how Chaucer's use of its classical and mythological materials up to and including the *Hous of Fame* changes in *Troilus*, where they are used to develop tone and atmosphere, and in the *Knight's Tale*, where there is a transformation into a courtly romance style; he uses the influence of Statius as an argument for Manly's dating of the *Complaint of Mars* in 1385 against French's in 1376 ('Chaucer's Use of the "Thebaid"' [*EM*]). Clogan has also contributed a preliminary list of 131 glossed manuscripts of Statius's *Thebaid* in 'Medieval Glossed Manuscripts of the *Thebaid*' (*Manuscripta*).

Phaeton Press have reprinted Hubertis M. Cummings's *The Indebtedness of Chaucer's Works to the Italian Works of Boccaccio (a Review and Summary)*,[7] first published in 1916. It presents in detail the evidence for the influence of the *Filostrato* and *Teseide* on Chaucer's work, considering at the same time the changes made by Chaucer. Influence from

other Boccaccian works is discussed and disclaimed. There is a chapter on the problem of 'Lollius' who is identified with Boccaccio.

Other reprinted works received include Sister M. Madeleva's *A Lost Language and Other Essays on Chaucer*,[8] discussed in *YW* xxxii. 59, and a photographic reprint of Claes Schaar's *The Golden Mirror*.[9] Schaar's work, discussed in *YW* xxxvi. 77–8, is reissued now with an index. Nevill Coghill's *The Poet Chaucer*[10] in the main contains little substantial alteration or additional material, apart from a section on the Physician and Manciple.

H. M. Smyser ('Chaucer's Use of *Gin* and *Do*' [*S*]) argues that *gin* is used for metre and rhyme, not for any intensive descriptive function, and that *do* is mainly causative in Chaucer. Gero Bauer ('Historisches Präsens und Vergegenwärtigung des epischen Geschehens: Ein erzähltechnischer Kunstgriff Chaucers' [*Ang*]) argues against the older idea of a historical present and distinguishes between non-functional occurrences of this present form and examples in which it serves a stylistic function, which he discusses.

Merle Fifield ('Chaucer the Theater-goer' [*PLL*]) briefly notes Chaucer's acquaintance with scaffold-stage, arena-stage, and court-revel, and examines the revel in the tales of the Franklin, Merchant, and Squire.

[7] *The Indebtedness of Chaucer's Works to the Italian Works of Boccaccio (a Review and Summary)*, by Hubertis M. Cummings. New York: Phaeton Press. pp. vii+202. $7.50. (A reprint of the same book was made by Haskell House in 1965).

[8] *A Lost Language and Other Essays on Chaucer*, by Sister M. Madeleva. Russell & Russell. pp. 147. $7.50.

[9] *The Golden Mirror: Studies in Chaucer's Descriptive Technique and its Literary Background*, by Claes Schaar. Skrifter Utgivna av Kungl. Humanistika Vetenskapssamfundet i Lund LIV. pp. viii+557+XIV. Sw. Cr. 70; cloth 80.

[10] *The Poet Chaucer*, by Nevill Coghill. (Opus 23 Oxford Paperbacks University Series). 2nd edition. O.U.P. pp. xi+145. 7s. 6d.

In an article dealing with Hoccleve ('The Autobiographical Element in Hoccleve' [*MLQ*]) Jerome Mitchell refers to the narrator in Chaucer's dream-poems, and more specifically to the realistic and humorous autobiographical passages in the *Hous of Fame* which may have provided a hint for Hoccleve's technique.

Rossell Hope Robbins has found a Chaucer allusion in a poem in MS. Douce 290 which he prints in 'A Late-Sixteenth-Century Chaucer Allusion (Douce MS. 290), (*Chau R*).

2. CANTERBURY TALES

Paul G. Ruggiers's *The Art of the Canterbury Tales*,[11] noticed in *YW* xlvi. 89–90, now appears as a paperback.

Richard L. Hoffman sets out in *Ovid and the Canterbury Tales*[12] to establish his claim that 'Chaucer seems to have fancied himself an English Ovid'. He directs his attention to the *Canterbury Tales* since the general assumption has been that Ovid's influence was not especially pronounced in that work, as it had been in earlier works. Not only has Hoffman considered what may be termed direct influence, but also the interpretation placed on Ovid in the late Middle Ages, which may supply some indication of Chaucer's purpose in using a particular allusion. Not all material was taken direct from Ovid, but came to Chaucer through an intermediate source, such as *Le Roman de la Rose*; consequently its use there is of more significance than its use in Ovid. Ovid's contribution 'to certain medieval literary traditions and iconological conventions' has

also been studied. At the outset Hoffman suggests that the structure of the *Canterbury Tales*, tales within a framework, may owe a debt to Ovid, and cites several possible analogues which among them show certain resemblances, e.g. the purpose in telling the tales, the idea of a reward at the conclusion. More important still is his expounding of the idea that love is the theme of all the tales, though two different kinds of love are involved, celestial and terrestrial. Just as Augustine speaks of *caritas* and *cupiditas*, so Ovid describes the two aspects of Venus, though *cupiditas* has a wider connotation than terrestrial love. In the remainder of the book, devoted to the *Prologue* and individual tales, Hoffman examines the two authors critically, for example pointing out occasionally that a claim made for Ovidian influence by an earlier scholar cannot be maintained, or explaining how an apparent confusion in Chaucer may have arisen, such as his use of *Calistopee* instead of *Callisto*. Altogether this is a useful contribution to Chaucer studies.

Two articles discuss the order of the *Tales*. In 'The Case Against the "Bradshaw Shift"; or, the Mystery of the Manuscript in the Trunk' (*PLL*), John Gardner supports the order in the Ellesmere Manuscript, maintaining that Chaucer modified his plan as the work progressed, and giving a hypothetical account of how the sequence from Fragment II to Fragment VII may have evolved. He suggests that Fragment VII derives its consistence from its theme, 'the significance of wealth and position in the world, ultimately a debate on Fortune', and argues that 'every one of the tales in Fragments II–V comments directly on the interrelated ideas of *constancy* and *patience*' and that they have their starting point

---

[11] *The Art of the Canterbury Tales*, by Paul G. Ruggiers. Wisconsin U.P. pp. xviii+265. $2.95. 22s. 6d.
[12] *Ovid and the Canterbury Tales*, by Richard L. Hoffman. 1966. Pennsylvania U.P. and O.U.P. pp. xii+217. $6.

in the *Man of Law's Tale*. Finally he sees Fragment VI as beginning an account of renunciation of which Fragment VII and the later Fragments are a part, and concludes by offering an overall summary of the thematic structure of the Ellesmere sequence. Lee S. Cox in 'A Question of Order in *The Canterbury Tales*' (*Chau R*) suggests that the interrupter in the Man of Law's endlink was intended to be the Wife of Bath; firstly, the *S* reference often used to support ascription to the Shipman was scribal, a result of the scribe's receiving his manuscript in batches and misunderstanding Chaucer's intention, and secondly, although the original Wife's tale would be an appropriate antithesis to the Man of Law's approach, 'the second is far more precise in parallel and rebuttal to the tale about Constance'.

Muriel Kolinsky ('Pronouns of Address and the Status of Pilgrims in the *Canterbury Tales*' [*PLL*]) correlates the use of 'ye' and 'thou' with the order of portraits in the *Prologue*; the basis is speeches to and from the Host and the results are presented in two tables.

Rossell Hope Robbins in 'A New Chaucer Analogue: the Legend of of Ugolino' (*Trivium*) prints a text of the legend in a late fifteenth-century form which incorporates lines from Chaucer. Robbins examines the quotations from the *Monk's Tale* and overtones from the tales of the Man of Law and Clerk, noting especially the expansion of Chaucer's version by 'non-structural embellishment'.

The theme of the Marriage Group is seen by D. S. Silvia ('Geoffrey Chaucer on the Subject of Men, Women, Marriage, and *Gentilesse*' [*RLV*]) as *gentilesse*. The *Tale of Melibee* and the *Franklin's Tale* present the same kind of marriage, manifesting the God-given quality of *gentilesse*, while other stories in the group treat the theme of sovereignty as objections to this thesis. The stories are further linked by a number of recurring motifs—nature and sovereignty, man's sinful condition and the need for good advice.

Alan T. Gaylord examines Fragment VII, which he regards as remarkably complete, in '*Sentence and Solaas* in Fragment VII of the *Canterbury Tales*: Harry Bailey as Horseback Editor' (*PMLA*). Harry shows a concern for the principles of arrangement of tales and Gaylord considers the meanings of *sentence* and *solaas*, which Harry mentions, in the tales in general and in Fragment VII in particular, where the two types are kept separate. It is this Fragment that makes 'the best of two worlds of "sentence" and "solaas"'.

In 'An Old French Analogue to General Prologue 1–18' (*PQ*), John A. Rea points out the verbal similarities between the *General Prologue* 1–18 and Adenet le Roi's *Berte aus Grans Pies* 1–11; the latter passage is associated with spring and pilgrimage, existed in an English fourteenth-century manuscript, and Chaucer knew the author's *Cleomadés*.

Although the concept of teaching and being taught may have been suggested to Chaucer by the work of Jean de Meun or John of Salisbury, both of whom are indebted to Chalcidius's translation of Plato's *Timaeus* (in which Plato's meaning has been broadened), Chauncey Wood argues in 'Chaucer's Clerk and Chalcidius' (*ELN*) that the debt to Jean de Meun is greater.

Kathleen L. Scott in 'Sow-and-Bagpipe Imagery in the Miller's Portrait' (*RES*) explores the possible connotations of such imagery.

'Two Notes on Chaucer's Arcite' (*ELN*) by Richard L. Hoffman concern a parallel with the story of

Joshua in Arcite's return to Thebes and his disguise, and a connexion with Samson and his death in Arcite's mention of his own uncut hair. In his discussion of 'The Topic of the *Knight's Tale*' (*Chau R*) W. F. Bolton suggests that nothing overt in the tale (e.g. the code of courtly love) represents the topic, and he then explores the several possibilities. His conclusion is that 'it is a series of questions, requests, demands, inquiries, for only a few of which explicit answers are provided'. D. V. Harrington's 'Rhetoric and Meaning in Chaucer's *Knight's Tale*' (*PLL*) attempts to demonstrate that the tale is organized as a *demande d'amour* by analysing its rhetoric to show how distracting details are excluded from the problem by a use of rhetorical devices. Anna Hargest-Gorzelak makes 'A Brief Comparison of the *Knight's Tale* and *Sir Gawain and the Green Knight*' (*Roczniki Humanistyczne*) in which she indicates that in the case of Chaucer's work form dominates the author, whereas the *Gawain*-poet dominates 'a highly organized form'. Under the heading, 'The Philosophical Knight *The Canterbury Tales*' Charles Moorman has incorporated in *A Knyght there was*[13] an article noticed in *YW* xlvi. 91.

John B. Friedman's article, 'A Reading of Chaucer's *Reeve's Tale*' (*Chau R*) concentrates on the animal comparisons (thirteen in number), the use of some of which can make the tale a story of vices humbled by each other. The handling of the horse-episode at the beginning suggests that such an interpretation was intended, one concerned with the ungoverned passions of man, particularly the sins of pride, wrath, and lust. The meaning and use of the term 'quiting' in the *Tales* is examined

first by Sheila Delany in 'Clerks and Quiting in the *Reeve's Tale*' (*MS*), and then the social status of clerks in medieval times. She then turns to the Reeve's clerks and the effectiveness of their appearance as heroes because of their ambivalent social position. The reading, *complyn* (A 4171), of some manuscripts, as against *coupling*, is defended by Robert M. Correale in 'Chaucer's Parody of Compline in the *Reeve's Tale*' (*Chau R*), where he shows what further ironic depth could be added to the interpretation if this were accepted as the correct reading. In 'The Reeve's Polemic' (*Wascana Review*) R. W. Harvey contrasts the *Reeve's Tale* with that of the Miller, 'in its own way so complete and satisfying', which delights the pilgrims. The Reeve's, however, is twisted and polemical, directed against the Miller, but does not achieve its object. While 'the Miller is creative through a healthy, however low, spirit of love', the Reeve's impulse is to destroy.

R. E. Lewis ('Glosses to the *Man of Law's Tale* from Pope Innocent III's *De Miseria Humane Conditionis*' [*SP*]) concludes, after examining the relationship of Innocent's original, the gloss, and Chaucer's paraphrase in the tale, that the glosses were written either by Chaucer himself or under his supervision. Alfred David argues in 'The Man of Law vs. Chaucer: A Case in Poetics' (*PMLA*) that in the Man of Law's doubts concerning his ability to tell a 'thrifty' story may be reflected Chaucer's own uncertainty about his work, which contained tales of differing types, and also his reply to criticism. The tales are, however, fittingly brought to a close by the *Parson's Tale*. In a lengthy article Chauncey Wood discusses 'Chaucer's Man of Law as Interpreter' (*Traditio*), since that pilgrim frequently com-

---

[13] *A Knyght there was*, by Charles Moorman. Kentucky U.P. pp. viii+170 $6.

ments on his tale, reacting much more emotionally than his heroine to the trials she undergoes, and, by his misinterpretation, making his tale a satire on himself. Whereas Custance can pray for strength to overcome trial, the Man of Law expects deliverance from the trial, being unaware of any necessity for it. Wood discusses passages from Innocent's *De Miseria* and Bernard Silvestris, and also the astrological imagery used at the time of Custance's departure from Rome, where the Man of Law misinterprets or misuses his material. Wood argues that Chaucer, in making changes in the tale from the source, did so with the teller in mind, and both emphasized the story's moral further and also charged the narrative with suspense. He maintains as well that the Man of Law has attempted to turn the story of Custance into a simple love-story.

D. S. Silvia argues in 'The Wife of Bath's Marital State' (*NQ*) that the usual assumption that Jankyn is dead is incorrect. Instead he thinks that once Alice has overmastered Jankyn, her love for him fades and that she is keeping her eyes open at the time of the pilgrimage for someone to replace him when he dies. However, as A. V. C. Schmidt points out (under the same heading, later in *NQ*), Silvia has not taken into account the Wife's tale, which suggests that she came to enjoy true happiness with her fifth husband, and so it was only after his death that she started the search for a sixth. Norman N. Holland approaches the tale from the psycho-analytical point of view in 'Meaning as Transformation: The Wife of Bath's Tale' (*CE*) and explores the different meanings of the tale. Its three phases are concerned with *maistrie*, and Holland sums it up thus: It 'starts with phallic aggres-

sive sexuality, regresses to a more primitive relation between taboo mother and passive son and finally progresses to genital mutuality'.

In 'The Summoner's Prologue: An Iconographic Adjustment' (*Chau R*), John V. Fleming traces the iconographic filiation of the Summoner's anecdote concerning the friars who were gathered under the devil's tail, and establishes that the story had strong mendicant overtones and was peculiarly related to the lay fraternities. And this anecdote in the Summoner's Prologue leads the way to the subject of the tale. Roy J. Pearcy examines in 'Chaucer's "An Impossibile" ("Summoner's Tale" III, 2231)' (*NQ*) the background of the problem posed by Thomas, and suggests that all fits the pattern of the *impossibile*, and two apparent difficulties support, rather than refute, such a reading. Albert E. Hartung defends the interpretation of *hostes* (*CT* III [D] 1755) and *swan* (*CT* III [D] 1930) with their customary meanings in 'Two Notes on the Summoner's Tale: Hosts and Swans' (*ELN*).

In 'How Old is Chaucer's Clerk?' (*TSE*) Huling E. Ussery argues against the commonest view that he was a young scholar. He considers those to whom the epithet *clerk* might be applied, evidence of the Clerk's professional attainments, his fictive connexion with Petrarch, abilities, rank among the pilgrims, alongside what is known of English logicians and clerkly ideals in the fourteenth century.

Malcolm Pittock argues in 'The Merchant's Tale' (*EC*) that here is exemplified tension between tale and teller, and that, although the moral values are obscured to a certain extent, they are not completely so. He shows how January is guilty of mortal lechery, despite his own confusion about this, and likewise

May and Damian, though their sin is the result of natural not drug-induced desire. Furthermore, the episode of Pluto and Proserpina serves to lessen the condemnation. But although the tale seems to be concerned with different kinds of lechery, the Merchant, not understanding the true significance, intends it to be interpreted as an illustration of *wyves cursednesse* and, as a result, confuses it. Karl P. Wentersdorf notes 'A Spanish Analogue of the Pear-Tree Episode in the *Merchant's Tale*' (*MP*), probably transferred from Spain during the sixteenth century to Puerto Rico where it was first recorded. The purpose of A. E. Hartung's 'The Non-Comic *Merchant's Tale*, Maximianus, and the Sources' (*MS*) is to discover by examining Chaucer's handling of his sources what light is thrown on his attitude to the tale. He briefly examines other interpretations of the tale, and then studies it in three parts: January's state of mind before he has selected May (here he discusses, instead of the *Miroir de Mariage*, the *Elegiae Maximiani* in respect of old age, especially as it affects sexual potency), the relationship between January and May (referring here to Boccaccio's *Ameto*) and finally the blindness and the pear-tree episode with the Novellino-analogue. Writing on 'Constantinus Africanus and Chaucer's *Merchant's Tale*' (*PQ*), Paul Delany comments on Constantinus's exposition of the physiology of intercourse and of various remedies for impotence, and also on January's attitude to marriage. In 'Another French Source for *The Merchant's Tale*' (*Romance Notes*) Joseph E. Grennen suggests that *Le livre du chevalier de La Tour-Landry* (or some similar work) may supply certain details not found in 'source-passages' in Deschamps. Robert A.

Wichert comments on 'Chaucer's *The Merchant's Tale*, 1662' (*Ex*).

The connexions between 'Chaucer's Squire, the "Roman de la Rose", and the "Romaunt"' (*NQ*) are investigated by John V. Fleming.

'The difficulty of perceiving truth in a world of illusions' is the theme of Russell A. Peck's 'Sovereignty and the Two Worlds of the *Franklin's Tale*' (*Chau R*). He adopts a more cynical attitude than is usual to the tale and its teller, maintaining both that the view of life of Dorigen and Arveragus is perverted and also that the Franklin misunderstands his story. The Franklin (who must not be equated with Chaucer) deceives himself, and here lies the key to the understanding of his tale. Arveragus, concerned greatly with appearances, is significantly different from his counterpart in *Il Filocolo*, and from his perversion of right order in the matter of sovereignty derive the problems of the other characters. Dorigen lives in a world of illusions, though these are eventually shattered. Their marriage has been against the ordering of the Creator, and the magician's illusion only completes the game played by the others. Through the Christian analogues which Peck notes, Chaucer himself is stressing the overriding Providence which maintains order despite men's illusive games. Contrasting with Peck, Harry Berger, Jr., continues his examination of the 'The F-Fragment of the *Canterbury Tales*: Part II' (*Chau R*), being concerned here almost solely with the *Franklin's Tale*. He comments on the Franklin's descriptions of place and behaviour in the light of their relevance to the tale, and then discusses the overall pattern of the work, 'one of withdrawal and return—into and out of a very literary world'. He also comments on the fact that the Franklin's attention appears to shift from his audience to his subject and back again, and on the effect that this has as he becomes involved in it. None the less the Franklin by his comments makes clear his own attitude at various points, for example with reference to the practice of magic, interrupting particularly in the central portion of the tale. Robert B. Burlin in 'The Art of Chaucer's Franklin' (*N*) points out that the underlying theme of the *Franklin's Tale* is not the teller's own vice, but rather his imperfect virtue; both the tone of the tale and the exposition of his limitations are good-humoured and kind. Like some earlier writers he views the Franklin as a practical man of affairs with aristocratic aspirations that he cannot fully understand. His choice of a Breton lay, his use of rhetoric, the portrayal of the main characters, 'elegant but artificial puppets', support this view and also reveal the Franklin's (as opposed to Chaucer's) concept of the ideal marriage. The first problem Chauncey Wood considers in 'Of Time and Tide in the *Franklin's Tale*' (*PQ*, 1966) is whether or not the rocks actually disappeared or only seemed to because of a high tide, and he discusses medieval beliefs concerning tides. Wood suggests that we should question the magic, and then the clerk's claim to *gentilesse*. This is bound up with the Franklin's approach to *gentilesse* and his delight in a tale of far-off days. His tale in many respects can be interpreted as a tale of appearances and reality and reflects the Franklin's own 'disturbed vision' of the world. Thomas J. Hatton cites two passages in Froissart which resemble events in the *Franklin's Tale* and throw light on the evaluation of the sacrifices of the knight, squire, and magician. ('Magic and Honor in *The Franklin's Tale*' [*PLL*].)

In 'Jephthah's Daughter and Chaucer's Virginia' (*Chau R*) Richard L. Hoffman makes several suggestions: that the reference to Jephthah's daughter is inappropriate in the context and therefore confirms the Physician's ignorance of the Bible (mentioned in the *General Prologue*); that Jephthah's rash and foolish vow is paralleled by Dorigen's and may indicate that the *Physician's Tale* should directly follow the Franklin's (as it does in the Ellesmere Manuscript); and that both Jephthah and his daughter may parallel Virginius and Virginia, in that allegorically both pairs suggest Christ and his flesh, with symbolic representations of the Crucifixion in that both daughters are sacrificed. Hoffman's other article, 'Pygmalion in the *Physician's Tale*' (*ANQ*) examines the connexion with the Ovidian version of the story.

Ian Bishop confines his article, 'The Narrative Art of *The Pardoner's Tale*' (*MÆ*), almost wholly to the tale proper. After carefully discussing economy in characterization, description, and narrative, Bishop turns to two other points of interest—'a double perspective and a unifying irony'. In 'Chaucer's Pardoner and the Hare' (*ELN*), Edward C. Schweitzer Jr. comments on the implications of the comparison between the Pardoner and that animal. Nancy H. Owen's argument in 'The Pardoner's Introduction, Prologue and Tale' (*JEGP*) is that the Pardoner's sermon-like Prologue and Tale are enclosed within a fabliau-framework. She examines their development and then explains why she considers the introduction to the tale and the final exchange between the Pardoner and Host to be of fabliau-quality. Robert E. Nichols, Jr., moves away from the usual discussion over 'The Pardoner's Ale and Cake' (*PMLA*), regarding it as an artistic device which helps to integrate the Introduction, Prologue, and Tale; further, it both foreshadows, and is part of, the theme of gluttony in respect of food and drink. Finally it is 'an aspect of a Eucharistic motif' by which the ironic portrait of the Pardoner and his exemplum is reinforced.

A clear connexion between commercial life and sexual activity is shown to exist by Bernard S. Levy in 'The Quaint World of *The Shipman's Tale*' (*SSF*). In their business activities the techniques used by the merchant and monk are parallel and these are finally used by the wife in her dealings with her husband.

In a discussion of the allegorical meaning of the *Tale of Melibee* ('The Allegory of the *Tale of Melibee*' [*Chau R*]), Paul Strohm finds in the idea of charity, which he exemplifies from the Church Fathers, the authority for Prudence's advice to Melibee not to fight the three temptations. He also considers the significance of the name Sophie ('knowledge, wisdom'), which he sees as a precise definition of thematic importance.

An attempt by William C. Strange ('*The Monk's Tale*: a generous view' [*Chau R*]) to justify the *Monk's Tale* sees it as a tension between the Christian view of Fortune as the agent of a just God and Fortuna, the arbitrary goddess. There is, from the worldly monk, a developing unease, seen in the oscillation of the role of Fortune in the stories. The unease is not understood by the Host, though recognized by the Knight, but the Nun's Priest, wittily building on the problem, offers a solution—to eschew worldly pride—and a comic balance to the earlier tragedies. In a short examination of the *Prologue*-portrait of the Monk, the terms of description, and the ideas behind his story

('Chauntecleer and the Monk: Two False Knights' [*PLL*]), T. J. Hatton suggests that Chauntecleer is the mirror of the Monk and points the lesson which he is to learn.

Bernard S. Levy and George R. Adams in 'Chauntecleer's Paradise Lost and Regained' (*MS*) develop the interpretation, already suggested elsewhere, of the *Nun's Priest's Tale* as a comic version of the Fall. In addition to mentioning further points which reinforce this interpretation, they develop the theme of the Crucifixion and Resurrection, so that the tale seems to suggest the possibility for salvation inherent in the Fall. K. Varty's study of artistic representations of the Reynard Legend[14] includes a chapter on The Fox and The Cock which illustrates the currency of stories like the *Nun's Priest's Tale*.

Russell A. Peck ('The Ideas of "Entente" and Translation in Chaucer's *Second Nun's Tale*' [*An M*]) considers writing as a literary answer to idleness, an idea in the *Book of the Duchess*. Starting from a consideration of the meaning of *entente* and *translation* in literature and reality, he analyses the *Second Nun's Tale* and concludes with a discussion of the *Canon's Yeoman's Tale* as its antithesis.

K. Michael Olmert ('*The Canon's Yeoman's Tale;* an interpretation' [*An M*]) examines the tale of the Canon's Yeoman in three ways. Firstly, he relates it to the wide moral context of the pilgrimage and the immediate context of the *Second Nun's Tale*. Secondly, he discusses the impression given by Chaucer in the opening description, the Host, and the Yeoman. Thirdly, he examines in some detail the tale itself, where moral, tropological, and anagogical significances are emphasized.

[14] *Reynard the Fox*, by K. Varty. Leicester U.P. pp. 169. 105s.

The Canon is identified with the devil and the parallel with the priest of the story is drawn. In his study of the same tale ('*The Canon's Yeoman's Prologue and Tale:* An Interpretation' [*PQ*]) John Gardner concentrates on the Canon's Yeoman who, in his opening discussion of pride and his parable relating to the devil, comes to renounce alchemy. The Yeoman's manner is not to speak openly but to hint by metaphor and pun, and this ambiguity of manner is continued in the ambiguous identifications in the tale which are traced in terms of true religion and the false religion of alchemy; the priest of the tale is the equivalent both of the Canon and of the Yeoman. A suggestion that Part II of the *Canon's Yeoman's Tale* may not originate with Chaucer is made by W. B. Folch-Pi in 'Ramón Llull's "Fèlix" and Chaucer's "Canon's Yeoman's Tale"' (*NQ*), and this may account for the fact that Part II has often been said not to fit properly into the tale. Barry Sanders corrects an O.E.D. entry in '"Point": "Canon's Yeoman's Tale" 927' (*NQ*).

R. A. Peck begins with the Parson's Prologue ('Number Symbolism in the Prologue to Chaucer's *Parson's Tale*' [*ES*]) and notes the symbolic force of the calculation of time—to focus the reader on penance and to link the sequence to a religious end—and of the numbers in the Prologue, 11. 1–12.

3. TROILUS AND CRISEYDE

Peter Elbow discusses the speeches at IV. 958–1082 and III. 813–40 in his article, 'Two Boethian Speeches in *Troilus and Criseyde* and Chaucerian Irony',[15] and presents a study of

[15] In *Literary Criticism and Historical Understanding: Selected Papers from the English Institute,* ed. with a foreword by Phillip Damon. Columbia U.P. pp. vii+190. 50s.

Chaucer's irony. In a stimulating analysis he examines the reader's responses to these speeches—his acceptance of their literal truth, his rejection of this truth by an ironical stress on the opposite idea which is made in the poem, and his final acceptance of their truth at a deeper level through the distancing effect of character-contrast and narrative technique.

According to Anthony E. Farnham ('Chaucerian Irony and the Ending of the *Troilus*' [*Chau R*]), Pandarus and Troilus deceive Criseyde, and Criseyde in her turn betrays Troilus. Earthly love is imperfect beside divine love, but it is feigned also as an imitation of divine love and, as at the end of Book III, it is a means whereby man can come to some understanding of perfect love. As such, the conclusion of the poem is 'a consummate example of Chaucerian irony'.

The instability of this world, briefly noted at the start of the poem, is fully recognized at the end. Charles Berryman's 'The Ironic Design of Fortune in *Troilus and Criseyde*' (*Chau R*) briefly reviews the positions of the three leading characters and the narrator, and examines the balance between the heart and truth in Troilus and in Criseyde. 'Chaucer's poem is a celebration of the unstable and attractive world "that passeth soone as flowres faire".'

In 'Myth as Paradigm in *Troilus and Criseyde*' (*PLL*) E. H. Kelly suggests that the association of Deiphebus and Helen in Book II recalls their relationship in the *Odyssey* and points to Criseyde's abandonment of Troilus for Diomede.

John J. McNally in 'Chaucer's Topsy-Turvy Dante' (*Studies in Medieval Culture* [1966]) argues that *Troilus*, which is influenced by Dante both in method and in treatment, explores 'the absurd doctrine of courtly love' by utilizing the religious ideas of the *Commedia* to convey an erotic adventure which presupposes their converse.

Stanley B. Greenfield ('The Role of Calkas in *Troilus and Criseyde*' [*MÆ*]) sees Calkas as an example of 'the contemplation of juxtaposed, not necessarily resolved values' characteristic of the whole poem. He is presented as a man of science whose words heighten the sense of doom, but he is also reduced by the manner of presentation. Like Pandarus, his relative, he is astrologically orientated in his schemes (again suggesting the link of science and absurdity), he is blind and unable to govern his passions, and he is 'thematic and structural counterpoint to the Trojan Prince'; unlike Troilus, he is clearsighted and uses the stars to his own end, but he is blind to the consequences of his deeds, while Troilus finally ascends outside the framework of destiny.

In 'Literature and Sexuality: Book III of Chaucer's *Troilus*' (*The Massachusetts Review*) Donald R. Howard stresses the complexity of Chaucer's account of the first night of love compared with that of Boccaccio. The account incorporates a variety of attitudes to love by the characters, the narrator and contemporary society and religion. The lies and deceits practised in the love-affair and the stable but misplaced trust of Troilus are discussed by W. F. Bolton in the wider context of a false pagan religion and of the story of Troy, itself a series of betrayals ('Treason in *Troilus*' [*Archiv*, 1966]).

Thomas Jay Garbáty lists in 'The *Pamphilus* Tradition in Ruiz and Chaucer' (*PQ*) the parallels between the fourteenth-century Latin dramatic poem *Pamphilus* and Books I–III of *Troilus*, and further notes varia-

tions from the *Pamphilus*-version found in both *Troilus* and *Libro de Buen Amore* of Juan Ruiz which suggests that this latter work may have influenced Chaucer. Neil D. Isaacs discusses the phrase '"On Six and Sevene"' (*Troilus* IV, 622)' (*ANQ*).

4. OTHER WORKS

In 'Chaucer as a Pawn in *The Book of the Duchess*' (*ANQ*) Beryl Rowland suggests that *fers* has a threefold significance, an interesting reference being to the promotion of Chaucer the commoner 'from pawn to *fers*'. In 'The Apotheosis of Blanche in *The Book of the Duchess*' (*JEGP*), James I. Wimsatt provides a useful discussion of the tradition in which Chaucer was working in his description of Blanche, as well as particular commentary on Chaucer's description, and relates this to descriptions of the Virgin, showing what Chaucer has achieved by this means. Ovid's influence on the same poem has long been recognized but in Wimsatt's other article, 'The Sources of Chaucer's "Seys and Alcyone"' (*MÆ*), he argues that, although confined mainly to the Cave of Sleep episode, Statius's influence is considerable. The other two probable sources he discusses are the *Æneid* and *Le Roman de la Rose*, with some mention also of *Ovid moralisé*. Finally he maintains that examination of the use made of sources in the Seys-episode and the rest of the poem suggests that the former was not an early composition later fitted into the *Book of the Duchess*. The connexion between medieval art and poetry is explored by Julia G. Ebel, with particular reference to 'Chaucer's *The Book of the Duchess*' (*CE*). She argues that the poem is organized in three successive planes, each with a main figure analogous to the others, though showing increasing significance. From the realism of the first plane we move through story to the 'focal dream', and the planes are further linked by echoes of each other. Poetic convention too is used in different ways in these planes. Without any 'paraphrasable—or moral—impact' the planes lead to a heightened awareness of the poem's central figure, the Black Knight. In 'Easing of the "Hert" in the *Book of the Duchess*' (*Chau R*), M. Angela Carson, O.S.U., stresses that Chaucer prepares the reader for the 'emotional resonances' of the Knight's account and contrasts this with the lack of preparation in the story of Alcyone. In her second article, 'The Sovereignty of Octovyen in the *Book of the Duchess*' (*An M*), she suggests that Octovyen should be identified primarily with the British king, Octavian, and, through the Welsh Eudav, which translates the name, she would establish a connexion with the Celtic Other World of Annwn; she further suggests that, by a confusion of Augustus and Auguselus, Octavian becomes associated with the hunter Arawn. Various French poems have in the past been cited as sources in part for the *Book of the Duchess*. In 'Le *Bleu Chevalier* de Froissart et le *Livre de la Duchess* de Chaucer' (*Romania*) Normand R. Cartier reconsiders some of these sources, but his main purpose is to show the evidence on which it can be maintained that Froissart's *Bleu Chevalier* provided the central idea of the poem as well as several other innovations.

In 'Science and Poetry in Chaucer's *House of Fame*' (*An M*) Joseph E. Grennen compares the Eagle's attack with the symptoms of apoplexy, a comic potential recognized by Chaucer, and compares the Eagle's lecture with the physical theory of sound, suggesting that there is a strong likelihood that Chaucer was indebted to Burley's *Expositio . . . in libros octo de physico auditu* for the basis, which is worked out falsely in the poem. An examination of the development of the idea of *fantome* and the use of the term in Middle English forms the basis for Sheila Delany's study of the term and concept in the *Hous of Fame* where all the senses of the term are applicable ('"Phantom" and the *House of Fame*' [*Chau R*]). Barry Sanders argues in 'Love's Crack-up: *The House of Fame*' (*PLL*) that thematically love for others is replaced by love for self and that this is reflected in the poem's inner structure and its superstructure of invocations; his article analyses in turn inner structure and superstructure and leads to the conclusion that 'courtly love must be reinstated as a way of getting back to a holier kind of love'. David H. Zucker examines in 'The Detached and Judging Narrator in Chaucer's *House of Fame*' (*Thoth*) the changing role of the poet-dreamer as he passes through a quest for 'love-in-the-world' to a statement of mutability and the recognition that a just quest must fail in an imperfect world; 'the poem's extreme consciousness of its own art is a way of looking at life'. There is a brief comparison with *The Rape of the Lock*. In 'Scholastic Logic in Chaucer's *House of Fame*' (*Chau R*) William S. Wilson suggests that Book III of the *Hous of Fame* 'illustrates the techniques of medieval logic on a medieval dialectician, the goddess of Fame'.

James J. Wilhelm ('The Narrator and His Narrative in Chaucer's *Parlement*' [*Chau R*]) notes the tripartite structure of the *Parlement*, comparing it to the primary time progressions of literature—spiritual, romantic and realistic. A brief comparison with *Pervigilium Veneris* leads to an emphasis on the isolation of the narrator in the *Parlement* and his need for love, a point on which Wilhelm agrees with Donaldson.

In a long article on the *Legend of Good Women* ('Chaucer's Good Woman' [*Chau R*]) Pat T. Overbeck examines the characteristics of Chaucer's ideal Good Woman which provides the thematic unity for the legends; comparisons are drawn with other pictures of the Good Woman and with other Chaucerian heroines and the parodic format and comic intent of the work are discussed.

In the introduction to his parallel-text edition of *The Romaunt of the Rose* and *Le Roman de la Rose*[16] Ronald Sutherland argues that Fragment A goes back to a different group of French manuscripts from fragments B and C and that, while A was the work of a Londoner, perhaps Chaucer, B and C were the work of a northerner, and the resulting poem was put together by a later reviser. The edition gives a postulated manuscript genealogy and a note on editorial practice; the texts are presented in two columns—the 1532 Thynne

text with minor variations and a composite *Roman* text, basically two manuscripts (one for A, the other for B/C). Where necessary, French versions closer to the Middle English poem are printed instead of the 'Base' manuscript. The edition has full textual notes and a Bibliography.

In 'The Date of Chaucer's Final Annuity and of the "Complaint to his Empty Purse"' (*MP*), Sumner Ferris argues that the confirmation of Chaucer's annuity, dated 13 October 1399, was issued only in February 1400 and that the *Complaint* is also of this later date.

In a study of the complaint-genre ('Chaucer's *Complaint*, a Genre Descended from the *Heroides*' [CL]), Nancy Dean looks at the *complainte* in medieval literature, contrasting Ovid's manner seen especially in the *Heroides*. The Black Knight's lament exploits the ideal based on reality, a concept not acceptable to the Dreamer, and develops to the realization of the ideal as reality. The *Complaint of Mars* produces a comic effect in its astrological emphasis but a serious treatment in Mars's complaint which shows the universality of woe in love; the effect is aided by the audience's familiarity with the story.

---

[16] '*The Romaunt of the Rose*' and '*Le Roman de la Rose*': *A Parallel-Text Edition*, by Ronald Sutherland. Basil Blackwell. pp. xxxix + 202. 52*s*. 6*d*.

VI

The Renaissance

B. E. C. DAVIS

The Age of the Renaissance[1] is a miscellany of essays, lavishly produced and illustrated, by a group of scholars, on different facets and aspects of the Renaissance throughout Western Europe from the fourteenth to the close of the sixteenth century. The illustrations, many of which are in colour, are reproduced from contemporary paintings, drawings, and wood cuts, a full-page frontispiece preceding each chapter, and numerous illustrations accompanying the text. In an editorial introduction Denys Hay notes the seeming paradox between achievement in art and culture, on the one hand, and, on the other, political and social unrest, the independent sources and courses of Reformation and Renaissance, the all-pervading influence of Italy, and its relatively retarded impact in England. Three essays deal with the movement in Italy, Nicolai Rubinstein discussing the character and evolution of humanism in Florence, 'cradle of the Renaissance', Cecil Grayson its extension to other Italian towns, and Peter Murray its impact on Italian art from Masaccio to Mannerism. Others cover the new learning and scholarship stemming from Italian humanism (Roberto Weiss); 'Challenges to traditional Christianity' (Delio Cantimori); 'Cultural values in a troubled age', characterizing the Renaissance in France, (I. D. McFarlane); Ren-

aissance and Reformation in Germany (G. R. Potter); 'An Age of Gold' in Spain (A. A. Parker); 'Art and Artists in Northern Europe' (L. D. Ettlinger); and 'A World Elsewhere', discovering new horizons, mental and geographical (John Hale). 'Tradition and Change', the leading motif of Joel Hurstfield's essay on 'English Society under the Tudors', is figured in a frontispiece illustration of Pietro Torrigiani's monument of Henry VII and his Queen at Westminster, erected against an architectural setting of medieval perpendicular. 'Over a large field inspiration came from domestic sources and Italian influence at first was minimal', as may be gathered from records of visiting Italians, and, conversely, from attacks by English writers on Italianization. While Hurstfield somewhat overstresses this 'built-in resistance to alien influences', the strength of native tradition in the blending of old and new cultures is indisputable, and pertinently illustrated in the essentially Christian context of early English humanism, testified in the wording of the foundation deeds of Corpus Christi College, Oxford. From this angle one may concede that the life and work of More showed an unworkable attempt at compromise between Christian ideals and Renaissance politics, but, on this very ground, reject Hurstfield's pronouncement that 'Cheke was as good a Protestant as Thomas More was a Catholic', in the face of the former's

[1] *The Age of the Renaissance*, ed. by Denys Hay. Thames and Hudson. pp. 359 + ill. and maps. £8 8s.

public recantation. Other topics discussed within this essay include the English gentleman, the flowering of language in writings of every sort, including state documents, patronage, Royal Progresses and their significance, the city of London in politics and culture, Puritans, and the emerging of a new society. The illustrations include one of 'the mystery of Longleat', a unique specimen of consistent classicism, half a century earlier than the work of Inigo Jones, details of London from drawings of Antony van der Wyngaerde, and specimens of costumes and fashions from Joris Hofnägel's panorama of English society in Bermondsey (1569). The essays are interrelated at many points of contact and through cross-currents of common interest, the illustrations enhancing the effect of unified motive and continuous argument. Publishers and contributors alike are to be congratulated upon the production of this handsome volume, which should serve as a stimulating companion to Renaissance studies for readers of widely different tastes and interests.

Andrew Martindale's *Man and the Renaissance*,[2] though concerned mainly with Italy, includes a section on art north of the Alps, besides substantial commentary on contacts between art and humanism at different phases of their development. Developing from the prospect of 'International Gothic Art', the common heritage of Italy and the North about 1400, the theme is one of 'change' rather than of 'renaissance'. 'Indeed it is possible that the concept of "Renaissance" is a hindrance to understanding . . . and destroys the idea of continuity in Italian art itself by discounting those elements which

bind the art to its immediate past.' On this premiss, the immediate purpose of Renaissance artists was not at first the archaeological reconstruction of an antique style, and only at a later stage 'scholarship really did join hands with artistic creation, with decisive and far-reaching effects'. With the spread of the Renaissance beyond the Alps, Italian standards and taste became adapted to local needs and idioms, and by 1475 Flemish painting had become a new species of 'international court style', its most impressive extant monument in England being the murals in Eton College chapel, probably by a Flemish artist, here illustrated by a reproduction of one depicting a miracle of the Virgin. Holbein's portrait of Henry VIII (1542), illustrated in a full-page colour reproduction, provides a specimen of the status picture, which 'has much in common with Bronzino's court portraits of the Medici and with the work of court artists, such as Jacob Seisnegger'. At the same time, 'architecture in the late Gothic tradition was at least as inventive and exciting as anything found in Italy, whether its culmination is taken to be the English Perpendicular style or the achievements of the mason in Germany'. It may be questioned whether, to contemporaries, the interior of King's College Chapel in Cambridge would have appeared to be less splendid than that of the Sistine Chapel in Rome. The spread of Italian ideas in England, in Martindale's view, was uneven, spasmodic, unpredictable, and almost always through a foreign intermediary, an impression which he supports by noting that John Shute's *First and Chief Groundes of Architecture* is heavily indebted to Flemish sources. This is a useful book, which fulfils the author's intention in making accessible illustrations, with commentary,

[2] *Man and the Renaissance*, by Andrew Martindale. Landmarks of the World's Arts. Hamlyn. pp. 176. 30s.

of diverse and distinctive forms of Renaissance visual art.

Robert Ergang's *The Renaissance*[3] is presented as 'an interpretive account of the beginnings of our modern civilization', based on the premiss that 'secularization of life, thought, and culture is the essence of the Renaissance'. Surveying, over twenty chapters, politics, scholarship, arts, natural science, and geographical discovery throughout Western Europe from the twelfth to the sixteenth century, he finds, as the basic motive directing thought and outlook throughout this period, a growing spirit of secularism. The rise of the modern secular state, with the decline of the Papacy, as exemplified in the emergence of national sovereignty under the Tudors, is an historical fact. But Ergang's assessment of Renaissance literature and culture overstresses the predominance of secularism, and takes too little account of the medieval heritage. Arbitrary discrimination between old and new forces, religious and secular, gives rise to distortion and oversimplification. The chapter entitled 'The Role of the Medieval Church', labouring the 'strong religious strain' and 'otherworldly attitude' in education and literature, by-passes the great body of medieval secular literature, and the general inadequacy of this part of the book is indicated by the extraordinary statement that early vernacular English literature is 'almost entirely in verse form'. On the other hand, the note of 'secularism' in the Renaissance is persistently overplayed. The account of English literature ignores the distinctive Christian humanism that inspires much outstanding work of this period, including the writings of More, translations of the Bible, politico-religious works

of divines from Cranmer to Hooker, and few readers are likely to accept without qualification the pronouncement that the spirit of Shakespeare's writings is 'thoroughly secular'. Intended as a guide for teachers and students pursuing joint courses on history, literature, and the arts, Ergang's book has the merits and defects of its kind. It supplies information from standard authorities over a wide range of topics, including medieval and Renaissance music, too often neglected in general surveys of this period. The classified bibliography should facilitate fuller and closer study. On the debit side must be set absence of reference to sources, including those of quotations and translations, factual errors (for instance a false etymology to 'mystery'), and descents into naïvety: 'Palgrave, the nineteenth-century English poet'; 'musical instruments were not, of course, invented in the Renaissance period'. The usefulness of the illustrations is seriously impaired through poor reproduction.

M. L. Bush's *Renaissance, Reformation and the Outer World*[4] is an all-round survey of cross-currents in politics, religion, and culture between 1450 and 1660, from the conflict between the expanding Ottoman Empire and Latin Christendom at the close of the Middle Ages to the emerging of new reactionary forces reflected in counter-reformation, natural science, mannerism, and baroque. Specific topics examined include relations between crown, nobility, and commons precipitated in the War of the Roses, the transition from the medieval warrior to the Renaissance gentleman, correlation of classical with Christian scholarship fulfilled in biblical translations, the consolida-

[3] *The Renaissance*, by Robert Ergang. Van Nostrand. pp. x+447. 84s.

[4] *Renaissance, Reformation and the Outer World*, by M. L. Bush. Blandford. pp. 387. 30s. cloth, 15s. paper.

tion of Western empires resulting from geographical discovery, and reaction against humanism in diverse cults of 'oddity'. The text is enlivened and clarified by reproductions of maps and portraits.

Aspects of Medieval and Renaissance Music,[5] a Birthday Offering to Gustave Reese, edited by Jan La Rue, is a rich and varied miscellany of articles, opening with a prefatory note, by Fredrich Blume, on 'The Greater World of Gustave Reese'. Three articles are concerned with music and musicians in England. Denis Stevens, discussing 'Polyphonic Tropers' in England, traces the influence of plainsong upon the trope, defined as 'interpolation into a liturgical text', in form, texture, and performance. Vincent Duckles examines the evolution and distinctive features of 'The English Musical Elegy of the late Renaissance', tracing the tradition of elegy from Horace through Petrarch, and the habit, peculiarly English, of blending literary with musical elements, the purpose of music being 'not to obliterate melancholy, but to render it more exquisite', John Case, in *The Praise of Musicke*, amplifying the view that music has power to intensify feeling. The sense of melancholy is perceptible in part-songs of Tallis and lutenist songbooks, and the characteristic 'funeral-song' of the later Elizabethans and Jacobeans foreshadowed in songs of Richard Farrant, Robert Parsons, and others of their time, who provided laments and deathsongs for the choirboys at Blackfriars during the 1570s. Between the Elizabethan and the Jacobean elegy Duckles finds a contrast typical of the two eras. For the Elizabethan, the

elegy was 'a positive thing, an expression of his insatiable appetite for life, while for the Jacobean mind it led to a resigned and sometimes bitter commentary on the futility of existence'. 'Byrd, Tallis and the Art of Imitation', by Joseph Kerman, illustrates the development of imitation as a convention from Fairfax and the composers of the Eton College Manuscript, who use it only sporadically, through Tallis and Munday, who use it regularly, though freely and flexibly, in large votive anthems, more rigidly in psalms and smaller motets, where imitation bears the weight of structure, and finally, at its extreme, in the 'fearful symmetry' of Robert White. In contrast with Tallis, who is 'sober, assured, deeply individual', Byrd is 'coarse, busy, brash, and rather anonymous in feeling', but Byrd's achievement and artistry in contrapuntal action and harmonic lucidity served as mainspring to the 'great historical fact' of 'the wonderful widening of horizons in British music of the 1570s'. This compilation has much to offer readers on many different aspects of medieval and Renaissance music, including its contacts with literature. Its value as a work of reference would have been greatly enhanced by the inclusion of a general index.

In 'The Allegorical Interpretation of Renaissance Literature' (*PMLA*) Rhodes Dunlap illustrates different uses of allegory as 'a prime element in that free and golden world of the imagination, the proper world of all right poetry which Sidney praises', reflecting a common basic notion of figure in all things, 'a vastly pervasive mode, a notoriously impressive mode' but 'a mode of limited expressiveness', conveyed in language that was seldom clear or precise. A particular application of allegory-cum-analogy widely represented throughout this

[5] *Aspects of Medieval and Renaissance Music.* A Birthday Offering to Gustave Reese, ed. by Jan La Rue. O.U.P. pp. xvii+891. £12 12s.

period is examined by Paul Archambault in 'The Analogy of the "Body" in Renaissance Political Literature' (*Bibliothèque d'Humanisme et Renaissance*), which traces the evolution of this figure from its ancient background and antetypes, including the writings of John of Salisbury, Giraldus Cambrensis, Dante, and Marsilius of Padua, who together 'had made of the organic analogy a weapon for the defence of limited or tempered monarchy and the rights of the community'. Sir John Fortescue, comparing the organization of government with that of physical and terrestrial bodies, finds the tempered 'political' English monarchy, as opposed to absolutism, to conform to nature. Erasmus uses the analogy 'in such a way as to make of the Prince a physician and of the Republic a patient', though he shares the common Renaissance distaste for the perversion of monarchy into tyranny. In Starkey's *Dialogue* the analogy of the body is 'the very skeleton of the treatise', one of the most outspoken of its time, 'clearly intended as an attack upon tyranny and hereditary monarchical succession, and as an apology for the primacy of law and the ideal of mixed government'. The analogy is not merely an instrument of thought, but 'becomes an entire system of expression'. The rest of the article refers to later continental writers of the Renaissance, concluding with a suggestion that an exhaustive study of this analogy in its later manifestations might lead us 'to the threshold of our own age'.

English Society and Government in the Fifteenth Century[6] comprises six essays selected from *History To-Day*

[6] *English Society and Government in the Fifteenth Century*. A Selection of Articles from *History To-Day* with an original introductory essay by C. M. D. Crowder. Oliver & Boyd. pp. 155. 10s. 6d.

by C. M. D. Crowder, who contributes an introduction on 'England at the Close of the Middle Ages'. The subjects treated are 'The Historian and his Archives' (G. Barraclough), 'The Peasants' Revolt of 1381' (W. L. Warren), 'The Council of 1407 and the Problem of Calais' (J. L. Kirby), 'Nibley Green, 1470: the last Private Battle Fought in England' (Jonathan Blow), 'The Character of Richard III' (A. R. Myers), and 'William Caxton: Mercer, Translator, and Master Printer' (Dorothy Margaret Stuart). In the evolution of English society and government during this troubled period Crowder perceives the genesis of British social democracy, 'a measure of economic and social levelling through a more even spread of wealth and prosperity among the merchant class, as represented by Thomas Betson and the Pastons, who profited from economic and political conditions during the Wars of the Roses. The essays on the revolt of 1381 and the private war between the Berkeleys and the Talbots culminating in 1470 give accounts of two widely different class conflicts, both of which stemmed originally from conditions of land tenure during the later Middle Ages. The character of Richard III is assessed as one of complexity in an age of contradictions; the responsibilities and perils of a royal minority aroused in Richard's nature 'elements of fear, ambition, and impulsive ruthlessness, which led him further and further along the path of immediate expediency at the expense of duty and honour', otherwise he might have been remembered as 'an able and energetic administrator, a brave and skilful soldier, a faithful brother and affectionate father, a kind and generous man of culture'. In her account of Caxton and his achievement Miss Stuart notes the significance of courtly patronage extended to his ventures under both Yorkist and Tudor regimes, some of the major difficulties confronting him in an age of disruption, the familiar style of his addresses to his readers, and his 'essential Englishness'.

The King's Great Matter,[7] by G. de C. Parmiter, makes a new contribution to the considerable body of recent work on the squalid background and circumstances of Henry VIII's divorce from Catherine of Aragon, the central theme and lines of argument being indicated in the sub-title, 'A Study of Anglo-Papal Relations 1527–1534'. The author, a barrister-at-law, focuses interest on legal factors of the case together with its political and diplomatic repercussions. Its domestic setting and the individuals involved are referred to, for the most part, only in so far as they may bear upon the 'great matter' under examination. Of this we are given a full account, with details of each stage in the process of the suit: early divided counsel concerning Henry's marriage, proceedings of the decretal commission and the legatine court, endless delay through negotiations of both rival parties with Rome and European powers, consultations with universities, submission of the clergy, and the final breach with Rome with its consequence, the superseding of a universal by a national Church. The record of successive attack and counter-attack at some points makes heavy reading, but the central argument runs clear, and the record, viewed as a whole, is objective and well balanced, the author having taken into account Roman and Spanish documents as well as the more familiar English sources. Though personalities are subordinated to events and intrigues in which they were involved, pertinent references are made to the conduct, thence to the characters, of leading protagonists, more particularly to Catherine, Wolsey, Cromwell, and Cranmer, assessed in the context of particular incidents with which they were concerned. The new documentary evidence assembled in Parmiter's book throws lurid light on the network of intrigue encompassing the Divorce and, in the process, on the ruthlessness and double dealing that characterized contemporary politics and politicians, the decline and fall of Wolsey, the 'villainous scheme' of a mock-trial to which the Queen was subjected, and the aftermath of the 'Great Matter', Henry's reconstitution of the English Church. A brief index of documents is appended, but there is no bibliography. An outstanding example of successful opportunism thriving under four successive Tudor monarchs figures as the subject of Arthur Joseph Slavin's *Politics and Profit. A Study of Sir Ralph Sadler 1507–1547*,[8] which covers a phase in the early career of 'a first-rate man in the second flight of Henrician politics'. In view of the tendency in previous biographies of Sadler to concentrate on his public life under Elizabeth, the present work, centring on his earlier years, aims at throwing light on the conditions which made such a career possible. This 'heir to a fair inheritance' appears successively as 'sorcerer's apprentice', liaison agent between Cromwell and the Crown, 'Cromwell's heir in things political', envoy to the Scots, beneficiary in the Henrician landmarket. His career represents 'a kind of *cursus honorum*' through routine administrative and diplomatic work,

---

[7] *The King's Great Matter. A Study of Anglo-Papal Relations 1527–1534*, by Geoffrey de C. Parmiter. Longmans. pp. xiii + 322. 60s

[8] *Politics and Profit. A Study of Sir Ralph Sadler 1507–1547*, by Arthur Joseph Slavin. C.U.P., 1966. pp. xvi + 238. £2 10s.

in the course of which he held 'dozens of offices, a handful at the highest level'. The biography fulfils its author's intention in telling us 'something useful of the art of patronage, politics, and the pursuit of profit as an end in life'. The portrait it presents is that of a highly successful Tudor politician, consistent with the textbook pattern of political expediency, whose 'virtues were those of moderation in all things, if virtues they were in an age of excess'.

Elizabeth Queen of England,[9] by Neville Williams, Assistant Keeper at the Public Record Office, is presented as 'a new synthesis, a reinterpretation of Elizabeth in the light of recent scholarship and new evidence', no full-scale life of Elizabeth having appeared for a generation, despite the attention that has been paid to Elizabethan statesmen and to the political, social, and economic history of this period. It is intended to be read as 'specifically a life of the Queen, not a chronicle of her times, certainly not a social history of her age'. Preoccupation with the life, character, and personality of the heroine is underlined throughout in chapter titles, for instance, 'God's Creature', 'As Good a Courage as Ever My Father Had', 'La Plus Fine Femme du Monde', 'The Splendiferous Planet', 'The Daughter of Debate', 'The Great Lioness'. Two opening chapters give an account of Elizabeth's life prior to her succession, her changing fortunes in the cold war with her elder sister, education under Cheke and Ascham, flirtatious romps with Thomas Seymour, residence with William Cecil at Hatfield, a youth so chequered with danger and instability that 'for the rest of her life self-preservation became her first

care'. The record of her reign is one of continual crises, domestic and international, making incessant demand upon her resourcefulness in statecraft and political judgement. The 'Anglican settlement', an attempt at compromise between Catholic tradition and Protestant reform, was achieved largely through her success in withstanding the rival pressures of recusants and puritans. The long-term problem of succession was bedevilled by conflicting interests, personal taste against political discretion, with the sinister presence in the background of Mary, Queen of Scots, and her partisans. The struggle with Spain, culminating with the defeat of the Armada, was followed by a golden age of splendour and achievement, but the final phase, for the Queen, was one of disillusion, figured in the defection of Essex, who found, to his amazement, that he could not tame 'the Great Lioness', whose unequalled experience of the arts of government inclined her 'to make decisions more clearly than at any time'. The story of the greatest Tudor monarch necessarily takes into account the role she played in public life, in wielding her realm, and controlling the fortunes of the nation. In descriptions of her bearing and relations with her family, her ministers, and her subjects at different social grades, we catch glimpses of her character, personality, and tastes. A chapter on the royal court, residences, and progresses conveys a vivid picture of Elizabeth in her role of Virgin Queen, the cynosure of chivalric devotion, her love of crowds and pageantry, ceremonial and dress, masques and tilt-yards. The blend of parsimony and extravagance in her attitude is particularly evident in the record of the royal progresses, which served both to gratify the Queen's personal tastes and as a measure of statecraft. This is

[9] *Elizabeth Queen of England*, by Neville Williams. Weidenfeld & Nicolson. pp. xii + 388. 50s.

an important addition to historical studies, scholarly, readable, and worthy of its theme.

Roy Strong's *Holbein and Henry VIII*[10] strikes a new line of approach to the political and religious revolution of the 1530s by demonstrating the force and significance of imperial propaganda in the King's patronage of art, which, like all his policies, was directed primarily to the exaltation and publicizing of the Tudor myth. The author's point of departure is 'that rare piece' (so designated by Evelyn), Hogarth's wall-painting of the apotheosis of the Tudor dynasty in Whitehall Palace, records of which survive in a fragmentary cartoon of part of the original drawing, now in the National Portrait Gallery, and in two seventeenth-century copies on canvas, much condensed, by Remigius van Leemput. 'The figure that dominates the scene, legs astride like some latter-day colossus, is the King. Henry VIII is our touchstone . . . an expression at once of the King's magnificence and of his power. A small army of painters, sculptors, architects, and craftsmen was employed throughout the 1530s to manifest in terms of painting, stone, wood, metal, glass, and fabric the hard facts of a political and religious revolution.' It is against this background that we are advised to reconsider Holbein's work as court artist during his second visit to England, in contrast to that of the first, when he was moving in the tranquil, pious circle of Sir Thomas More. His definitive image of Henry is that of 'Novus Constantinus', who, having overthrown the enemy, ushers in a new age of 'imperial' purity. It is the image presented in different terms by political pamphleteers and reformers, by writers like Rastell, Starkey, and Morison, encouraged by Cromwell to defend the power of the Crown in things ecclesiastical and the triumph of the King over the Pope. It was in this context, we are reminded, that Polydore Vergil's *Anglica Historia*, completed in 1513, was brought up to date in 1533, laying new emphasis on the imperial theme. In Holbein's title-page to the 1536 Bible the King figures as purveyor of the word of God, another Moses and Daniel, the keys of heaven being grasped by all the apostles, not by Peter alone. The illustrations to Cranmer's Catechism, depicting scribes and pharisees dressed as monks, totally anachronistic in 1548, revert to the anti-monastic campaign of the thirties. Surviving portraits of Henry in the double role of *imperator* and chevalier Strong compares with Donatello's St. George and Perugino's St. Michael, which follow a favourite formula for heroic virtue in fifteenth-century Florence, figuring 'knightly triumph against tremendous, often supernatural powers'. By contrast with the Orchard Gallery frescoes, preserved in copies at Hampton Court, emblems of a 'dying medievalism', Holbein's masterpiece at Whitehall stands 'on the cool, classic heights of pure renaissance classicism', within the tradition 'which runs direct from Mantegna, and reaches fruition in Raphael's stanze'. Space allows barely adequate notice of this compact, stimulating study on lines which offer ample scope for further research. The illustrations, essential for the purpose of reference, in quality leave much to be desired.

Concerning the European background and context to Holbein's work in England, readers may refer to John Pope-Hennessy's *The Portrait in the Renaissance*,[11] based on a

---

[10] *Holbein and Henry VIII*, by Roy Strong. The Paul Mellon Foundation for British Art. Routledge & Kegan Paul. pp. 75+pl. 40s.

[11] *The Portrait in the Renaissance*, by John Pope-Hennessy. Phaidon Press. pp. 348. £3 15s.

course of lectures given under the A. W. Mellon foundation. The basic purpose of Renaissance portraiture as contrasted with that of the Middle Ages, in the author's view, was monumental, as appears in the Sistine Chapel frescoes, which depict scenes and characters drawn from contemporary life, and medals and busts imitated from those of antiquity. Humanism is reflected under different aspects, dramatic, figurative, and philosophical, the favourite portrayal of women in profile (deemed most flattering) giving them a character 'almost dematerialized'. The range and lines of investigation are indicated in chapter titles: 'The Cult of Personality', 'The Motions of the Mind', 'The Court Portrait', 'Image and Emblem', 'Donor and Participant'. Of special interest to English readers are references to Erasmus, whose 'abiding interest in his own appearance' and in portraiture generally is indicated in his correspondence with More over the diptych of himself and Aegidius, designed as a gift to More. It was at the instigation of Erasmus, Pope-Hennessy suggests, that Holbein lodged with More during the winter of 1526, Erasmus having already expressed the view, as early as 1519, that it was 'no less a task to portray More than it would be to portray Alexander the Great or Achilles'. A full account is given of the drawing and painting of the More family group, with comments on origins and analogues of these portraits, which convey 'much more than the record of a domestic relationship', confirming Erasmus's comparison of More's household to Plato's Academy and his appraisal of Holbein's painting as an encomium of this aspect of More's life. In the conventional iconography of Holbein's later works as court painter to Henry VIII Pope-Hennessy detects the survival of an earlier English tradition, an image about which there was nothing admirable; 'it was an icon, proud, hieratic, menacing'. Note is taken of the work of early Italian artists in England, particularly of Torrigiani at Westminster, and of Nicholas Hilliard, whose 'captivating intimacy' in his finest portraits reveals unsuspected possibilities in portrait-drawing through a water-soluble medium. This is a fresh and an illuminating study, of wide expanse and excellently produced, with much to offer readers of all tastes interested in Renaissance art.

Peter Le Huray's *Music and the Reformation in England 1549–1660*[12] traces the development of liturgical and devotional music in England during a golden age of musical achievement. The first part is concerned with changes in the function and style of church music resulting from the Reformation, taking into account the introduction of services in the vernacular under Henry VIII and Edward VI, Puritan opposition and economic pressure affecting church music under Elizabeth, the records, character, and significance of music in the Chapel Royal, problems affecting performance, and the development of new techniques. The second part, based largely on exploration of musical sources by the author in collaboration with Ralph Daniel, of Indiana University, consists of a detailed study of extant church music and composers of the Edwardian and early Elizabethan eras, followed by a survey of the vast repertory of services, anthems, and devotional songs composed from 1580 onwards, with special reference to the works of Byrd, Tomkins, Child, and pioneers of *stile nuovo*

[12] *Music and the Reformation in England 1549–1660*, by Peter Le Huray. Herbert Jenkins. pp. viii+454. 63s.

adapted to sacred music. The record is informative and valuable, throwing light both upon intrinsic features of works discussed and on the contribution of music to services of the English Church for a century after the Reformation. Of particular interest for historians of music and literature alike are the chapters on music in 'the order of Common Prayer as it is to be sung in Churches' and on Edwardian and early Elizabethan source-books, in connexion with which considerable attention is given to the gradual transition in liturgy from Latin to the vernacular and from old to new orders of service, with greater attention to music in expressive terms, as intimated in Ascham's comparison of oratory with singing and Archbishop Parker's injunction to those who used his Psalter 'to conjoin a sad tune and song with a sad psalm, and a joyful tune and song with a joyful psalm'. In general, as might be expected, the reformers favoured greater simplicity in music for public worship, Cranmer advocating note-against-note chanting as 'more sober and distinct' than the elaborate style of the older Latin service-books, and the more radical Puritans of the Elizabethan era condemning virtually all church music of the traditional type. 'As an ornament of daily worship, music was a lively issue in the vestiarian controversy, and there were many who looked forward to the eventual abolition of non-congregational music altogether.' The evidence assembled in this book goes to prove that the monumental achievement in church music of the English Renaissance can be credited to the efforts of a few great masters and of many lesser lights, working in the face of strong internal opposition and external economic pressure. In despite of episcopal directives against contrapuntal and harmonized singing by 'singing men and squeaking choristers' of cathedral choirs, the course of English church music, both in quality and popularity, was one of steady advance and triumph against puritan prejudice, so far as to gain the approbation of Hooker as 'a thing which always heretofore the best men and wisest governors of God's people did think they could never commend enough'. Le Huray's study is an important contribution to English musicology, containing much new material, including many musical examples here published for the first time. It contains sixteen half-tone illustrations, a list of sixteenth- and seventeenth-century texts containing devotional music, classified lists of modern editions, and a general bibliography.

A survey of work on bibliographical topics may suitably open with notice of *Fifty Essays in Fifteenth- and Sixteenth-Century Bibliography,*[13] by Victor Scholderer, who 'has always, and most gratefully, walked in the footsteps of Robert Proctor, the greatest modern British incunabulist'. Most of the essays are within the field of German printing and humanism, but reference is made to standard works of scholarship on early printing in England, including E. Gordon Duff's *Printers . . . of Westminster and London from 1476 to 1535* (1906) and the Bibliographical Society's Monograph no. XVIII, a Bibliography of fifteenth-century English books, based on Duff's first-hand collation of books in libraries scattered all over the country. Note is made also of Seymour de Ricci's *Census of Caxtons* (Bibliographical Society Monograph no. XV), W. J. B. Crotch's edition of Caxton's Pro-

[13] *Fifty Essays in Fifteenth and Sixteenth Century Bibliography,* by Victor Scholderer, ed. by Dennis E. Rhodes. Amsterdam: Menno Hertzberger, 1966. pp. 302. £8.

logues and Epilogues (E.E.T.S.) and George P. Winship's *William Caxton and the first English Press*. An essay on 'The Works of Dionysius Cartusianus' discusses correspondence between Theodoricus Loer, 'vicarius' of the Carthusian house in Cologne, and the house of the Order in London at the time of the Dissolution, apprehension of which is reflected both in these letters and in dedications designed to win favour from the King and from Cromwell.

Printing, Selling and Reading: 1450–1550,[14] by Rudolf Hirsch, is offered as 'a survey of problems which followed in the wake of printing', with special reference to social and intellectual developments related to new mass production of books. Topics touched upon include continuity between the craft gild and the printing profession, status and personalities of printer-publishers, economic and legal implications of the new book trade, and selection of texts in different countries to meet national or local taste and demand. A distinctive factor affecting publication and circulation of books in England was the assumption of control by secular authorities and the early suppression of imported Protestant, vernacular works of a controversial nature, most notably Tyndale's New Testament. Discussing the influence of printed literature on literacy in England, Hirsch notes a trend towards a common language, excluding dialectal words and provincial usages. Illustrations include reproductions of an early eulogy of the new invention and of the earliest extant portrait of an author in a printed work. Much of the ground covered has already been treated, from different aspects, by H. J.

Chaytor, A. W. Pollard, and H. S. Bennett, the last of whom is accorded only perfunctory reference, but a considerable body of new material is presented on production costs, business management, type faces, and other kindred topics. The obvious potential value of a study comprising so much in the way of detailed records and statistics is greatly impaired through lack of a bibliography and the provision only of an index of names and selected titles.

Printing and the Mind of Man[15] is defined in its sub-title, 'A Descriptive Catalogue Illustrating the Impact of Printing on the Evolution of Western Civilization during Five Centuries'. The catalogue was provided for the Inland Printing Machinery and Allied Trades Exhibition of 1963, illustrating, for the benefit both of the printing industry and the general public, the internal development and technical progress of printing as a craft, its external development in printing and illustration as applied art, and the impact of printing on the mind of man with consequent effect on his history. It is not offered as a bibliographical reference book, the editors aiming at 'precision without pedantry'. The list of four hundred and sixty-six entries begins with the opening sentences of Gutenberg's Bible, and closes with the 'Lion's Voice' of Winston Churchill addressing the House of Commons on 20 August, 1940. In an Introduction, 'Fiat Lux', Denys Hay dwells on the relations of printing to literacy and education, dealings between publisher-printer and author, and changes

---

[14] *Printing Selling and Reading, 1450–1550*, by Rudolf Hirsch. Wiesbaden: Harrassowitz. pp. viii+165. DM 28.

[15] *Printing and the Mind of Man. The Impact of Printing on five centuries of Western civilization*, ed. by John Carter and Percy H. Muir, with the help of Nicolas Barker, H. A. Feisenberger, Howard Nixon, and S. H. Steinberg. Introduction by Denys Hay. Cassell. pp. 280. £7 7s.

in the status of authorship. The selection of entries from within so vast a field as pertinent to a theme of such range and diversity inevitably reflects the group taste of the compilers, and doubtless every methodical reader will be startled alike by admissions and omissions. Some partiality in favour of English writers is, perhaps, only to be expected, and clearly the relative values of content and style differ widely in different passages selected. The general character of the collection may be gauged from excerpts from works within the scope of this chapter, which include Malory's *Morte Darthur*, *Utopia*, Henry VIII's *Assertio Septem Sacramentarum*, Tyndale's *New Testament*, Lily's *English Grammar*, *The Book of Common Prayer*, the Geneva Bible, Foxe's *Actes and Monuments*, and Ascham's *Schoolmaster*.

Edward Arber's compilation of transcripts from the Stationers' Company Registers contains a large amount of supplementary material, contemporary and authoritative, designed to illumine the text but neither chronologically arranged nor indexed. W. W. Greg's *A Companion to Arber*[16] provides a Calendar to these documents, giving 'a more or less connected survey of matters scattered in no particular order in Arber'. Along with these Greg has included calendar descriptions of other related documents, drawn from the Burghley papers and State Papers Domestic in the Public Record Office, transcribed from photostat copies. His work on Arber formed the basis of lectures given in Oxford and published in 1956 under the title *Some Aspects and Problems of London Publishing be-*

tween 1550 and 1650. One section from the present work, on 'Licensers for the Press to 1640', has already been published by O.U.P. (*YW* xxxvii. 109).

N. F. Blake discusses 'Caxton's copytext of Gower's *Confessio Amantis*' (*Ang*), considering that, though Gower may have been one of Caxton's favourite authors, his handling of *Confessio Amantis* has never been adequately investigated. Rejecting the general acceptance of Macaulay's assumption that Caxton used at least three manuscripts, Blake argues that, as in his editions of Chaucer and Lydgate, he used only one, as might be expected in view of the haste in which, necessarily, he tackled editorial work. Scholars agree that the manuscripts of *Confessio Amantis* may be reduced to three major recensions, one of which, preserved in Magdalen College Oxford MS. 213, Blake accepts as probably the basis of Caxton's text, but in an intermediate form; if Caxton had consulted more than one manuscript, it is likely that his collation would have been more careful.

P. L. Heyworth's 'The Earliest Black-letter Editions of *Jack Upland*' (*HLQ*) views in new perspective a fifteenth-century tract against friars, 'one of the lesser monuments of post-Wyclifian Lollardy', which, unlike most of its kind, was printed during the early sixteenth century, probably about 1536. Two extant copies of the first edition belong, respectively, to the Huntington Library and that of Gonville and Caius College, Cambridge, the composite volume containing the print at Cambridge giving evidence that the printer was James Nicolson, who was active between 1535 and 1538. Why, about 1536, was *Upland* accorded the dignity of print denied to scores of similar pieces, Henry VIII having no love of reform

[16] *A Companion to Arber*. Being a calendar of documents in Edward Arber's *Transcript of the Registers of the Company of Stationers of London, 1554–1640*, ed. by W. W. Greg. Clarendon Press. pp. 451. £5 15s. 6d.

for its own sake? Heyworth finds an explanation in the title-page and the colophon *Cum privilegio Regali*, intimating the royal policy of encouraging propaganda against Rome and the religious orders. '*Upland* owes most of its modest reputation to its early attribution to Chaucer, but its real importance is political rather than literary. . . . It represents the peculiarly Henrician element in the pattern of the English Reformation.' John M. Fletcher draws attention to 'Nicholas Harpsfield's Note of Cranmer's Recantation' (*Transactions of the Cambridge Bibliographical Society*) among jottings in a copy of sermons by Michael of Hungary bearing Harpsfield's signature, preserved in the library of St. John's College, Cambridge. Comparison with the printed version of the recantation, issued early in 1566, shows that Harpsfield's note is predominantly sound, only occasionally changing word-order. Accompanying notes, possibly by Harpsfield, refer to the proceedings against Cranmer and the title and estate of Cardinal Pole, to whom Harpsfield was deeply devoted. Julia G. Ebel's 'A Numerical Survey of Elizabethan Translations' (*Lib*) is designed 'to clarify the setting in which the translations of excellence and repute appeared, and in the light of which their quality is determined'. The list is provisional, and based upon S.T.C. with supplements. The date-limit, 1560–1603, follows in succession from that of H. S. Bennett's *English Books and Readers*.

The recent purchase by Rutgers University Library of an incunabulum has prompted an article, by Anne Slater, 'Dives and Pauper: Orthodoxy and Liberalism'. (*Journal of the Rutgers University Library*), describing the book and discussing its content. The copy is one of de Worde's edition (1496), with a considerable number of printer's errors and plates unevenly inked. A sixteenth-century hand has erased references to Catholic practices and to the Pope, adding scurrilous comments, though without spoiling the sense. A later hand has consistently glossed references to the pastor's obligations towards his flock. Discussing the text, Miss Slater notes that the preface does not, as in other dialogues of the period, anticipate the theme of the main work to follow, but shows the status of the two disputants, each of whom figures as a character in his own right. The dialogue is intended to please as well as to edify, giving glimpses both of the writer's character and of contemporary English life. The author was 'almost certainly a preacher', attaching even more importance to the sermon than to the Mass. He would appear to have been 'both of his times and ahead of them', judging from his debating of such matters as witchcraft, marriage, the position of women, and continuity between Judaic and Christian rites and liturgies. Though not a particularly original thinker, 'he often articulates common sense conclusions, drawn from personal observation'. 'Juliana Berners and *The Boke of St. Albans*' (*RES*), by Rachel Hands, is based on material for an edition. Analysis of the book's content, which comprises four treatises, one in prose on hawks, one in verse on hunting, and two in prose on heraldry, has led Miss Hands to the conclusion 'that the St. Albans compiler had before him three separate and independent treatises, using part of a third to supplement them'. The appearance of the name 'Juliana Berners' at the end of the hunting poem has led to its attribution to someone of this name, often with the hawking treatise as well. Comparison of the several texts, however, suggests that this name belongs rather to the prose treatise, notwithstanding the fact that part of the poem, but only a part, is a dialogue between a 'dame' and a child. It would appear that the compiler based his work on three main texts, a revision of the well known 'Prince Edward's Book', the poem on hunting, and the 'Iulyan Barne' treatise, so identified in the colophon of the Pepys text. A side interest is raised by Malory's note, in his tale of Sir Tristram: 'And therefore the booke of venery, of hawkynge and huntynge is called the booke of sir Trystrams'.

Bulletin de la Faculté des Lettres de Strasbourg contains a review, by G. Lambrechts, of Paul Bacquet's *Un Contemporain d'Elizabeth I: Thomas Sackville* (*YW* xlvii 131, 132), suggesting, on stylistic grounds, a re-arrangement of the respective parts in *Gorboduc* assigned by Bacquet to Norton and Sackville, and the probability that Sackville envisaged modifications of Baldwin's project for *A Mirroure for Magistrates*, on grounds both literary and political. He questions Bacquet's assessment of Sackville as the best poet between Chaucer and Spenser in favour of Wyatt. L. Forster, seeking for information on 'The Translator of *The Theatre for Worldlings*' (*ES*), found one reference to Theodore or Dierick Roest in the contemporary records of the Dutch church in London. On the strength of known personal relations between Richard Mulcaster and Emanuel Van Meleren, a Dutchman, he suggests that the former may have introduced a fellow-countryman of the latter, named Roest, to his pupil, Edmund Spenser, and that the background to the translation is Anglo-Dutch rather than Anglo-French. The evidence for these suggestions, as the author himself admits, is largely speculative.

Sir Thomas Malory. King Arthur and his Knights[17] is a selection, edited by R. T. Davies, of about one sixth of the Winchester MS. text of Malory, including excerpts from the tales of King Arthur, Launcelot and Guenevere, Gareth, Tristram, and the Sankgreall. The text is taken primarily from a microfilm copy of the Winchester MS., the opening and close, missing in the MS., from H. O. Sommer's edition (1889). It is amplified with Caxton's Preface and Epilogue to *Morte Darthur*, a genealogical table, five pages of textual and explanatory notes, and a glossary. An introduction summarizes the content of Malory's work, with brief comments on its background and style, and on what is known of the author. As the selection is clearly intended for the non-specialist, spelling, punctuation, paragraph division, and arrangement of speeches have been modernized. 'What Malory means by order and how it relates to tragedy' is the main concern of Stephen J. Miko's 'Malory and the Chivalric Order' (*MÆ*, 1966). Malory's world, he suggests, is one of appearances, in which shame is essentially a matter of public knowledge, appearance triumphing over reality, even becoming reality. 'Blood as a vital source' is the mainspring of Malory's stories, knights act before they think, with a 'magnificent naïvety' typified in Lancelot; men are known by their deeds, and, apart from the Graal theme, there is little evidence of God's providential presence. The character most nearly conforming with the traditional pattern is probably Gawain, who recognizes in himself the 'tragic flaw', or moral defect. 'What Malory finally creates might be called a tragic emulsion. There is no reso-

[17] *Sir Thomas Malory. King Arthur and his Knights*, a selection from what has been known as *Le Morte Darthur*, made and edited by R. T. Davies. Faber. pp. 271. 30s.

lution, no peripeteia, merely a defeat. Man is defeated, chaos wins.' Argument on these lines is forcefully and well supported, but many readers may feel that it is one-sided, and fails as an overall interpretation of *mores* in *Morte Darthur*.

Charles Moorman's *A Knyght There Was*[18] is designed to trace changing concepts of knighthood and knight errantry in outstanding works of the Middle Ages and the Renaissance 'as a means of coming to grips with the particular themes and patterns of the major writers treated'. Its scope is indicated by the chapter headings: 'The First Knights. *La Chanson de Roland*', 'The Uses of Love. Chrétien's Knights', 'The Stained Knight. *Sir Gawain and the Green Knight*', 'The Philosophical Knight. *The Canterbury Tales*', 'The Tragic Knight. Malory's *Morte Darthur*', 'The Allegorical Knight. *The Faerie Queene*', 'The Last Knights. Shakespeare and after'. Within this context, *Morte Darthur* appears, on the one hand, as a plea to fifteenth-century knights to learn a lesson from the past, on the other as a tragic portrayal of chivalry's failure to attain perfection. Along three main lines of narrative, figuring the knight as soldier, Christian, and lover, Malory pursues a single great theme, 'the rise, flowering, decay, and fall of a well-nigh perfect earthly civilization'. He sees the whole myth of the hero, not just the particular *mores* of the Arthurian court, in tragic terms. 'From Roland to Lancelot we have moved from success to failure, from heroic comedy to tragedy.'

[18] *A Knyght There Was*. The Evolution of the Knight in Literature, by Charles Moorman. Kentucky U.P. pp. viii+170. $6.

[19] *Friendship's Garland. Essays Presented to Mario Praz on his Seventieth Birthday*, ed. by Vittorio Gabrieli with a Bibliography of his Published Writings. Two Vols. Rome, 1966. Edizioni di Storia e Letteratura. Raccolta di Studi e Testi, 106. pp. clvii+304 and 460. L.15,000.

Friendship's Garland,[19] a collection of essays presented to Mario Praz, includes a note by Eugene Vinaver on 'Epic and Tragic Patterns in Malory', reflecting on a radio talk by Praz, with added comments on the modernity and tragic character of Malory's story, demonstrated in Praz's Italian rendering of the Arthur-Bedwere episode.

Harvard U.P. has issued an edition of Caxton's *Aesop*,[20] with notes and glossary by R. T. Lenaghan. In his introduction the editor surveys Caxton's work as 'a historical anthology of the medieval Aesopic fable', based primarily on Steinhowel's collection, but drawing also from other sources, which are classified into seven parts. Examination of Caxton's prose suggests that he made use of a French intermediary, anglicizing many of the original French words, but otherwise seeking to render the fables directly in English. The woodcuts in the present edition are reproduced from a facsimile edition of the German *Esopus* printed at Augsburg in 1477, being far superior to those in Caxton's; but Caxton's frontispiece and four of his illustrations are reproduced in an appendix.

In 'The Mirror of the World and MS. Royal 19 A IX' (*N*), N. F. Blake notes an interesting discrepancy between Caxton's translation and this manuscript, generally accepted as his original. In translating, Caxton omitted the name of the bookseller, Jehan de Bruges, but added 'the month of June' to the year 1464, the year of issue. From this evidence Blake suggests that Caxton may have bought the manuscript from Jehan in June, 1464, and that it remained in his possession until 1481, the date of his translation. If this assumption is

[20] *Caxton's Aesop*, ed. with an Introduction and Notes, by R. T. Lenaghan. Harvard U.P. pp. 264. $7.50.

correct, it provides evidence that Caxton was interested in manuscripts before he turned to translation. In 'Two New Caxton Documents' (*NQ*), Blake reproduces entries in the Journal Books of the Common Council of the City of London, which show how closely Caxton worked with other mercers, how much he benefited from membership of the Mercers' Company, the frequency of his visits between London and the Low Countries, and the wide range of his trading interests, which included pewter as well as cloth and wool. Discussing 'The Source of Caxton's *Paris and Vienne*' (*PQ*), J. Finlayson notes many agreements with a French version in the British Museum, printed by Jacques Moderne in Lyons. He produces evidence suggesting that Moderne's text derives from a source closer to Caxton than the version of a similar romance preserved in Bibliothèque Nationale, accepted as Caxton's original by Leech in his E.E.T.S. edition. Other articles on Caxton by Blake and Dorothy M. Stuart have been noticed above.

Martin Holmes's 'Edward Hall and his "Chronicle"' (*E & S*) gives illustrations of Hall's characteristic flair for eye-witness description of courtly scenes, of pageantry, and of dress associated with jousts, masques, and other ceremonial occasions, of battles, as in that of the hand-to-hand fighting at Flodden, of sporting events, and of comic episodes in the drama of public affairs. The Shakespearian cycle of histories, apart from *King John*, covers the same period as Hall's Chronicle, and Shakespeare follows Hall rather than Holinshed, who himself acknowledges indebtedness to Hall. A leading motive, alike in Hall and in Shakespeare, is the evil wrought by rebellion. 'To Holinshed he could go, and did go, for corroborative evidence, and odd details recorded by other writers, but the first impression of the story must have come unquestionably from the older chronicler.' Hall, not Holinshed, represents the clerical support for the French war under Henry V as an astute manœuvre to distract attention from taxing church property. An objective intimated throughout the Chronicle is the emerging of Henry VIII as 'indubitate flower and very heir' of the two royal houses of Lancaster and York.

The Letter Book of Robert Joseph,[21] the manuscript of which was discovered by Dom Hugh Aveling in the National Library of Wales, has now been published under his editorship, in conjunction with W. A. Pantin, who supplies an introduction, annotations to the text, and three appendixes. The letters, which cover a period of two to three years between Joseph's two sojourns at Oxford, provide a unique autobiographical record of a monk-scholar with affiliations both at Evesham and the University on the eve of the Dissolution, throwing light upon his personality, learning, and tastes, intercourse between monks and scholars, day-to-day affairs in the monastery, and the influence of university studies on monastic life. They are clearly intended not as ephemeral, fugitive notes, but to be collected and preserved in a letter-book, following the precedent of patristic and recent humanistic writers. A devotee of the new learning and its protagonists, notably Erasmus, Joseph frequently extols the benefits of letter-writing, and deplores discouragement of the letter-writing habit by certain abbots. Captivated

[21] *The Letter Book of Robert Joseph, Monk-scholar of Evesham and Gloucester College Oxford, 1530–33*, ed. by Dom Hugh Aveling and W. A. Pantin. Oxford Historical Society. New Series, Vol. XIX. Clarendon Press. pp. lv+300. 42*s*.

by the spell of Oxford, he supplies much needed information on conditions of university life, the placing of students in halls, relations between tutors and pupils, and orders of studies. The personality reflected in his letters, as assessed by the editors, is that of 'a middle-of-the-road man, respectable, studious, kindly, moderately devout . . . a likeable man, who had likeable predilections', in fact not far removed from the ideal parish priest he portrays in one of his letters.

Thomas Paynell's translation of the *De Contemptu Mundi*[22] of Erasmus, published in 1533 by Thomas Berthelet, has been reproduced in facsimile from a copy belonging to Princeton University Library. In an introduction William James Hirten discusses the occasion and background of the original, dated 1488–9 (in particular the identity of 'Jodocus', or 'Joyce', in Paynell's translation), and the preface and twelfth chapter, both of which, in purport, seem inconsistent with the rest of the treatise in stressing the abuses rather than the virtues of the monastic life, and so reflecting Erasmus's changed attitude towards contemporary religious institutions, particularly monasticism. Viewed as a whole, 'though *De Contemptu Mundi* does reveal Erasmus as temperamentally unfitted for the monastic life, it offers nothing to prove that he was incapable of appreciating the ideals of such a life or that he lacked sincerity while writing the first eleven chapters of the treatise'. Paynell's dedicatory address to Mary, Queen Dowager of France, suggests that he was inspired to make the translation by genuine desire to serve the cause of religion and the monastic ideal. His writing is characterized by liberal use of English idiom, skilfully blended with Latinism. Though, in Hirten's view, his ability as a translator is but mediocre, 'it was Paynell's achievement to be one of the few men of learning during the pre-Elizabethan period to make translation the major part of their literary activity'. In a note on 'Antedatings from Nicholas Udall's Translation of Erasmus's *Apophthegmes*' (*NQ*), G. A. Starr lists a hundred and fifty-seven words, apart from 'apophthegmes' itself, antedating entries in *O.E.D.*

Some Forerunners of the Newspaper in England 1476–1622,[23] by M. A. Schaaber, first published in 1929 by the University of Pennsylvania Press, has been reprinted. Proffered as 'rather a first assault, tentative and incomplete than an inclusive or definitive account of the news printed before the evolution of the newspaper in England', it is concerned solely with printed news, circulated during the first two centuries after the invention of printing. Material is classified into official news, represented by state documents, proclamations, and the like; partisan news in the form of religious and political propaganda; news on affairs of state such as trials for treason; exciting, popular news on court scandals, murders, witchcraft, and so forth; 'translated' news of neighbouring states, particularly France and the Netherlands; and news to inform or to instruct. The concluding chapters are concerned with purveyors of news, professional and private, publishers, and the immediate forbears of the newspaper, in particular serials,

[22] '*De Contemptu Mundi*' (*1488?*), by *Desiderius Erasmus*, translated by Thomas Paynell. A Reproduction of the Berthelet Edition of 1533 with an introduction by William James Hirten. Scholars' Facsimiles and Reprints. Gainesville, Florida. pp. xliv + 178. $7.50.

[23] *Some Forerunners of the Newspaper in England 1476–1622*, by M. A. Schaaber. Cass (1966). pp. vii + 368. 65s.

miscellanies, and corantos. Viewed as a whole, the record demonstrates the influence of continental practice on English reporting, the use of the press under the Tudors in the art of governing, circulation of news in verse, particularly in broadside ballads, and the role of printers and publishers, 'the real heroes of this history'. Notwithstanding the large body of work on early news literature published during the last forty years, Schaaber's book retains much of its value as an illustrative background survey. Phoebe Sheavyn's *The Literary Profession in the Elizabethan Age*,[24] first published in 1909, has been reissued in a second edition, revised throughout by J. W. Saunders in conjunction with the author, who has seen the proofs. In the original edition the author defines her work as 'a series of studies upon certain aspects of the whole question of authorship and the conditions amid which it was pursued . . . confined to what may perhaps be styled, for want of a good English word, "belles-lettres"—to the "literature of power", as distinguished from the "literature of knowledge". In the second edition its range has been extended to include playwrights, translators, historians, and authors of controversial works published under courtly patronage. Footnotes have been overhauled and brought up to date with references to standard recent editions and authorities. Original texts of quotations replace the somewhat hybrid versions in the first edition. With these additions and revisions, the book as now presented should fulfil the editor's intention in providing a better tool for scholars while retaining the flavour of the original work, a useful guide within a

field of literary studies still unreasonably neglected.

The content of *Moreana* this year exceeds the average by nearly a half, in consequence of the inclusion of a much enlarged issue as a birthday *festschrift* for Miss Elizabeth Rogers, editor of the *Collected Letters* of More. Appropriately several articles refer to More's letters, recorded details concerning his character and conduct, and other material relating to his biography. R. J. Schoeck surveys features and structure in the letters against the background of rhetorical and epistolary convention, medieval and humanistic, suggesting lines for further research. H. S. Herbruggen argues, from internal and external evidence, that More was the addressee of a letter generally assumed to be addressed to Wolsey. M. P. Sullivan hails the correspondence as 'The Now and Future Goldmine' for biographers and bibliographers. E. E. Reynolds writes on T. E. Bridgett, More's first modern biographer, P. G. Bietenholz on 'A Protestant presentation of More, 1581' by Richard Dinoth in *Adversaria Historica*, and Louis B. Wright gives a note on R. W. Chambers. R. S. Sylvester traces the reflection of 'More's literary personality in his early works'. D. Sargent gives instances of More's 'singularity', and Henri Queffélec offers a discriminating review of Zinnemann's film, 'A Man for All Seasons'. Biographical topics treated include 'Sir Thomas More and the Nun of Kent' (J. D. M. Derrett), 'Sir Thomas More and Doctors' Commons' (Pearl Hogrefe), a letter from More to Cromwell, referring to Anne Boleyn (A. Castelli), and Sir Richard Morison's 'Apology for an Execution' in *Apomaxis Calumniarum* (W. G. Zeeveld). In 'Some Notes on the First Edition of *Utopia*' M. E. Kronenburg records

[24] *The Literary Profession in the Elizabethan Age*, by Phoebe Sheavyn, revised throughout by J. W. Saunders. Manchester U.P. pp. x + 248. 35*s*.

twenty-two surviving copies and their location. R. W. Zandvoort, comparing the English translations of *Utopia* by G. C. Richards and Paul Turner, prefers the latter's as more concise and nearer the style of the original. Henri Brugmans's 'Morus *Utopia* . . . en Verder' and André Merlaud's '*L'Utopie*. Une bouteille à la mer' survey, from different aspects, More's ideal commonwealth against the backgrounds of sixteenth-century politics and modern socialism. Articles by Silvio Zavala and Marcel Bataillon are devoted to the 'Utopian' Vasco de Quiroga. G. Marc'Hadour presents 'a rough anatomy' of extant copies of the 1557 *Workes* folio preliminary to a full collation, Clarence Miller a brief history of the holograph of More's *Expositio Passionis*, and Geraint Gruffyd a Welsh version of a prayer by More, printed in 1587. Paul Sawada lists works by, or on, More in Biblioteka Lenina, Moscow, and, under the title 'The Praise of Realpolitik' answers Hermann Oncken's proposition of a 'revised *Utopia*', superimposing a 'power state' over the 'peace state' of the original, a proposition virtually, though not specifically, answered by Leslie Paul in a note on 'More and Machiavelli'. Topics discussed concerning More's public career and conduct are 'More at Cambrai' (H. Meulon), 'More and the General Council' (Denys Hay), 'More and the Opposition to Henry VIII' (G. R. Elton). Other papers deal with his associations with John Fisher (E. Surtz), Dame Christian Colet (J. B. Trapp), and Linacre (G. Marc' Hadour). Marie-Claire Robineau, O.P., reproduces Richard Hyrde's address to Frances Staverton prefixed to Margaret Roper's translation of Erasmus's *Pater*, together with her own translation into French. Under the title 'Erasmus *Pacificator* and

Girolamo Vida', Mario A. di Cesare reproduces, with comments, two letters addressed to English officials by Hilary Bertulph, previously an assistant to Erasmus, included within a pirated edition of Vida's *Scacchia*.

In 'Sir Thomas More and Lucian. An Interpretation of *Utopia*' (*Archiv*, 1966) T. S. Dorsch draws parallels, in attitude, objective, and technique, between *Utopia* and Lucian's *True History*. More's satire, intended and treated by his contemporaries as a work of entertainment, is characterized, like Lucian's, by fantasy, comedy, and irony, giving the effect of verisimilitude after the manner of a 'pretty Lucianic' dialogue. Utopian attitudes and customs pertaining to religion, warfare, and social organization, treated in reverse as *reductio ad absurdum*, appear fully consistent with More's opinions as expressed in his writings and conduct. Read as mock-serious Lucianic satire, *Utopia* is 'entirely consistent in spirit and method, and it is always possible to see what its author is driving at'. Over More's real intention there must always be wide diversity of opinion, and some may feel him to have been more equivocal than this article would suggest, but the argument is forcefully presented, and much' of it carries conviction. 'Aspects of More's Latin Style in *Utopia*' (*S Ren*), by Edward Surtz, supplements the introduction to the Yale edition through analysing 'the selection and arrangement of words and phrases, which betray the intellectual, emotional, and artistic cast of the author'. The analysis suggests that the style imitates that of the dialogue, the length and character of sentences reflecting the ebb and flow of thought and feeling. More's vocabulary is 'overwhelmingly classical', and his use of rhetorical devices conforms generally with principles enjoined by Erasmus. Ward Allen, in

'Speculations on St. Thomas More's Use of Hesychius' (*PQ*), calls attention to Hythloday's statement that the Utopians 'have no dictionaries except those of Hesychius and Dioscorides', and suggests that More made use of Hesychius in his invention of make-up words, puns, and features savouring of Mithraism and Gnosticism in the pre-Utopian Abraxa. Rainer Pineas discusses 'Thomas More's Controversy with Simon Fish' (*SEL*), publicized in Fish's *A Supplycacioun for Beggars* and More's answer *The Supplicacioun of Soules*. In attacking clergy for allegedly subversive activities, Fish employs 'reportorial technique' similar to that of Skelton and Saint German; More, in replying, uses his opponent's technique together with others, including the appeal to history and the device, popular with contemporary polemicists, of 'remolding the record of past events to suit his needs'. In 'Thomas Murner, Thomas More, and the First Expression of More's Ecclesiology' (*S Ren*) John M. Headley describes Murner's relations with More through their common polemical activities against Luther, particularly through Murner's defence of Henry VIII's *Assertio*, which he translated into German. Their works show similarity in stylistic features and methods of attack, belong to the same intellectual world, and show common understanding of the Catholic Church and its organization.

Jean Servier's *Histoire de l'Utopie*[25] gives a chronological and critical account of successive concepts and portrayals of the ideal state, in particular Plato's Republic, the Jewish vision of a promised land, Augustine's City of God, Utopia and other Renaissance works inspired by scientific and geographical discovery, Faustian, Marxist, and post-Marxist schemes of the nineteenth and twentieth centuries. Covering wide diversity in religion, culture, and outlook, the record shows remarkable consistency in aspiration towards an ideal millennium and in symbols used to express it. As the title indicates, this is an overall historical survey of the Utopian idea, and the representative works discussed are examined extrinsically rather than intrinsically. On *Utopia* it is suggestive in presenting More's fantasy within a threefold context, retrospective, contemporary, and prospective. Marian Frackowiak's *Poglady Economiczne Tomasza More*[26] strikes a new line of approach to More's concepts of society and economy. Living in an age of transition from feudalism towards capitalism, More perceived the ill effects of undue emphasis on the profit motive with the dynamic growth of market economy, unjust distribution of wealth, the rapacity and extravagance of court and magnates, wars waged by the ruling classes entailing ruinous taxation and fines. With clear-sighted vision he realized that the reforms touched upon in Book I of *Utopia* would not, of themselves, remove the source of evils, or prevent them from recurring. Book II sets forth 'his maximum programme of reform', a social and an economic system based on public ownership. But More's economic theory is unscientific through his failure to understand the value of money, which, like Lycurgus, Plato, and many early Christian writers, he denounced on ethical grounds. Regarding money and bullion solely as a source of unhappiness and social

[25] *Histoire de l'Utopie. Idées*, by Jean Servier. Paris: Gallimard. pp. 381. Fr. 4.95.

[26] *Poglady Economiczne Tomasza More*, by Marian Frackowiak. Poznan: Praca Wydana z Zasilku Polskiej Akademii Nauk. pp. 114. zł 24.50

problems, he made the same mistake as the Luddites, blind to the fact that development of a market economy leads to great productivity and provides effective incentives inducing people to increase their skills and to work harder.

The reissue, with translation, of Richard Pace's *De Fructu qui ex Doctrina Percipitur*[27] for the first time since its original publication in 1517 makes accessible a *tour de force* of English humanism memorable both in itself and for the light it throws upon the author and his circle. Pace's satire on 'The Benefits of a Liberal Education', intended, in the first instance, for his pupils at St. Paul's School, amounts to a farrago against pretenders to learning, parading commonplaces of humanistic pedantry in a 'whirlygig of rhetoric', under the guise of surface wisdom. The present editor correlates it with *The Praise of Folly* and *Epistolae Obscurorum Virorum*, though with qualifications. 'The very form of his book, so distressingly incoherent to Erasmus, mirrors perfectly his artful attempts to dodge a decision on the central problem that disturbs him.' It allows him full scope for self-expression and self-advertisement concerning his experiences, environment, and contemporaries. For the modern reader, 'it brings to life the day-to-day affairs of the humanist milieu as do few other literary works of the period. . . . The relevance of his book to the general predicament of the court humanist in the Renaissance cannot be ignored'. The Latin text of this edition is based on the Yale copy of the original, spelling and punctuation being generally retained. In translation, the editor aims first at accuracy, but using modern sentence structure, idiom, and slang where necessary for clarification. The commentary is concerned chiefly with locating and verifying Pace's quotations. 'A medley of humanistic gossip', his book is both instructive and entertaining. Its reappearance should awaken interest in his other writings, hitherto neglected.

Pace's minor works include an English translation of the English sermon against Luther preached at Paul's Cross, on 12 May, 1521, by John Fisher, the subject of a new authoritative study by Edward Surtz.[28] The author's aim is to present this neglected scholar and patron of scholars against the intellectual background of Renaissance and Reformation, 'to ascertain his precise position on such key points as the nature and function of a university, humanism and scholasticism, Greek and Hebrew, corruption and reformation', showing repercussions of these issues in political and religious controversy. Fisher figures successively in the roles of Catholic humanist, ecclesiastical protagonist, and royal antagonist, the first epitomized in the statutes of Christ's and St. John's College, Cambridge, the second in the three *Magdalens* and religious polemic works, the third in action rather than in pamphlet, Fisher's last works, written from prison, being, like More's, non-controversial and devotional. Less accomplished in the three ancient languages than Erasmus and Reuchlin, 'he is their admirer, their helper, their defender, their user', and praised by Erasmus as 'distinguished for virtue as much as for learning,

[27] *De Fructu qui ex Doctrina Percipitur, (The Benefits of a Liberal Education)*, by Richard Pace, ed. and tr. by Frank Manley and Richard S. Sylvester. New York: Ungar. pp. xxvi+190. $8.50.

[28] *The Works and Days of John Fisher. An Introduction to the Position of St. John Fisher (1469–1535), Bishop of Rochester, in the English Renaissance and the Reformation*, by Edward Surtz S. J. Harvard U.P. pp. xvii+572. $15.

qualities in which he has no superior among living men'. His present biographer notes the flexibility of Fisher's literary style, which he adapts to different structural patterns and to different degrees of emotional impact, with general orientation towards the manner of Holy Scripture. His theology tended towards 'the hybrid scholastic humanist type', his methods of argument consistently follow those of the schoolmen. Always the professional theologian, as a preacher he offered 'new bottles for old wine', which established his continental reputation as 'a pre-Tridentine classic'.

The Centaur Press has issued a verbatim reprint of Mombert's edition of Tyndale's *Five Books of Moses*,[29] with a new introduction by F. F. Bruce. Mombert's edition is based partly on the original edition of 1530, and partly on a copy embodying the 1534 text of Genesis and the 1530 texts of the other four books. The text is preceded by extensive prolegomena relating to Tyndale's life and works. Bruce's introduction to the present reprint comprises a brief note on Mombert, followed by a longer account of Tyndale and the printing of his translations, with comments on the woodcut illustrations, and on distinctive features of Tyndale's style both in translation and in 'salty marginalia', which, along with thrusts of anti-papal satire, include straight comments, showing a sound grasp of biblical interpretation. The reappearance of this important edition of an English prose classic, long overdue, should be widely welcomed.

Assessing 'William Tyndale's re-

sponse to the Hebraic Tradition' (*S Ren*), Dahlia M. Karpman analyses his treatment of the first six chapters of Exodus as crucial in the formation of Hebraic theology, finding that his mistakes are such as to make it improbable that the Hebrew Bible was his primary original, and concluding that he consulted it on some points. Allowing that he knew some Hebrew, at least from dictionaries, she notes the stress he lays on the language of the original for the purpose of translation; contrary to the views of some recent authorities, she finds his renderings free from polemical intention. His awareness of Hebrew scholarship is evident from his Prologue to Exodus, which embodies concepts definitely Hebraic and follows the method of the preacher, using texts as prefatory to doctrinal commitment. Miss Karpman concludes that, though not fluent, Tyndale was definitely familiar with Hebrew scholarship, and 'gave to that scholarship a benediction, thus giving it an authority that would increase through the century'. Anthea Hume discusses 'William Roye's *Brefe Dialoge* (1527). An English Version of a Strasburg Catechism' (*Harvard Theological Review*), which she compares with the original, by Wolfgang Capito, published in Strasburg in two versions, German and Latin. Roye makes one bold alteration by reversing the roles of parent and child, making the former 'answerer' and the latter 'questioner'. The tone is markedly more anticlerical than in the original, and additions demonstrate Roye's characteristic mannerisms, addiction to neologizing, Tudor propensity for paired synonyms, and exhibitionism in clustering polysyllabic words. In sum, the tract, a statement of Protestant beliefs in small compass seems 'not inappropriate to the English situation, as seen by

[29] *William Tyndale's Five Books of Moses called The Pentateuch*, ed. by James Isidor Mombert, . . ., ed. with new Introduction by F. F. Bruce. Centaur Press. and S. Illinois U.P. pp. cliv + 635. £6 6s. $22.50.

the first group of English Protestant exiles'. *A History of the Geneva Bible*[30] stems from a chance encounter of the author, Lewis L. Lupton, with a copy in a Chichester bookshop. It gives a summary account of the background, evolution, character, and influence of the Geneva Bible, the communities and rivalries of its compilers, first over matters of doctrine and later over liturgy and ecclesiology, but all within the context of acceptance of the Bible as 'the crucial and integral basis of Christian faith'. Commenting on the excellent craftsmanship of the compilers, Lupton illustrates his text liberally with reproductions of engravings and woodcuts of initial letters. Enthusiasm sometimes betrays him into injudicious generalization ('Calvinism is as modern today as when it was penned'), and the annotations are superficial. Fuller quotation illustrating the language and style of the Bible would have been welcome. Within its limits, as a summary account of an important episode in the course of the English Reformation, the book may serve its purpose.

The Reformation in England to the Accession of Queen Elizabeth[31] is an anthology of contemporary documents, edited by A. G. Dickens and Dorothy Carr, to be followed by a volume covering the Elizabethan settlement and the religious history of Elizabeth's reign. The selection is designed to show the significance both of state intervention and of trends and interests in Tudor society favouring the development of Protestantism in England. The introduction, surveying the background to these documents, takes note of the growth of anticlericalism during the early sixteenth century, the persistence of the Lollard heresy, demand for the education of clergy and laity in the vernacular Scriptures, the spread of reformed dogma and practices, and their adoption by court magnates such as Protector Somerset. The documents, arranged in roughly chronological order, are classified as related to late Lollardy and early Protestantism, the breach with Rome, Dissolution of the monasteries, the Edwardian reforms, and the Marian reaction. They include excerpts from polemical writings of the early reformers, acts, articles, and injunctions under Henry VIII, the Edwardian Acts of Uniformity, and the Marian Injunctions and Acts of Repeal. This is an important contribution to a projected series of studies, which should prove useful for reference in connexion with political, social, and literary history alike.

Pearl Hogrefe's *The Life and Times of Sir Thomas Elyot*[32] is a comprehensive study, demonstrating the part played by Elyot in public affairs, with emphasis on what the author regards as English features in his writings and conduct. The first part gives a record of his ancestry and family background, based partly upon unpublished material, followed by an account of his legal training and education in legislature, politics, and humanism, and his early work as a public servant. The record throws light on matters relating to the Inns of Chancery and the court, the universities, opportunities for study in London, the nature of Elyot's commissions at home and abroad, and conflicting loyalties necessitated through his support of the King. This section

[30] *A History of the Geneva Bible*. Vol. I. *The Quarrel*, by Lewis Lupton. Fauconberg Press. pp. 120. 21*s*.

[31] *The Reformation in England to the Accession of Elizabeth I. Documents of Modern History*, ed. by A. G. Dickens and Dorothy Carr. Arnold. pp. viii+167. 25*s*.

[32] *The Life and Times of Sir Thomas Elyot, Englishman*, by Pearl Hogrefe. Iowa State U.P. pp. xii+410. $6.50.

is followed by detailed examination of each of Elyot's literary works in chronological order, with special consideration of their political and cultural context and relation to Elyot's personal experiences, and of analogues in works by other writers. Dissenting from the view that Elyot changed the first three chapters of *The Governour* in order to please the King and Cromwell, Miss Hogrefe recognizes the impact upon his work of the Tudor concept of government and of bias towards an aristocracy, perhaps 'conditioned somewhat by early contacts with manor life in the West Country'. While drawing on numerous writers to support his arguments, he 'quickly becomes his own man and writes as an Englishman to other Englishmen', with English high seriousness, concepts of law, and tastes in arts and exercises. The record of his dealings with the King and Cromwell in connexion with the royal divorce, particularly his letter to Cromwell concerning his acquaintance with More, leaves his reputation as a political time-server no better than before. 'Elyot was not the man to become a martyr', though, we are reminded, he may have been seeking to bring the King to a sense of his responsibilities in *Of the Knowledge that Maketh a Wise Man*. General assessment of Elyot's personality takes note of his reticence and conservative persistence, his interests in the arts, and, along with a love of friendship, 'a loneliness of spirit'. His literary influence is traced mainly to his contribution towards developing the English vocabulary, particularly in *The Book of the Governour, The Castle of Health*, and the *Dictionary*. As an all-round study of Elyot this book supplements more specialized recent studies, though it suffers from overprotracted paraphrase and commentary. The bibliography, though admittedly selective, should have included entries of first editions of Elyot's works.

Facsimile reproductions of *The Doctrinal of Princes, Pasquil the Playne, The Bankette of Sapience*, and *The Image of Governance*, bound together to form a single volume, entitled *Four Political Treatises*,[33] have appeared in the Scholars' Facsimiles and Reprints series. None of them has been printed since the sixteenth century. The texts are reproduced from the editions prepared by Thomas Berthelet. Introducing them, the editor, Lillian Gottesman, notes their relation to *The Governour*, to which they form a sequel in discussing the utilization of such studies as *The Governour* prescribes for the service of state. By translating an oration of Isocrates as *The Doctrinal of Princes*, 'Elyot could accomplish two purposes, one expressed, and one more subtle', the former to 'assaie' the rendering of a Greek oration in English, the latter to admonish the king on his responsibilities. *Pasquil the Playne* 'is a thinly veiled evaluation of contemporary politics', though elsewhere Elyot denies that the characters in his pasquinade allude to specific persons. *The Bankette of Sapience* and *The Image of Governance*, the one a collection of wise sayings, the other a life of Alexander Severus depicted as an outstanding example of the good governor, reveal Elyot still as counsellor to the King, though indirectly and by inference. 'The expressed purposes or aims of all the writings are very simple', and

[33] *Four Political Treatises. The Doctrinal of Princes (1533), Pasquil the Playne (1533), The Bankette of Sapience (1534). The Image of Governance (1541)*, by Sir Thomas Elyot. Facsimile Reproductions with an Introduction by Lillian Gottesman. Gainesville, Florida: Scholars' Facsimiles and Reprints. pp. xiv+426. $10.

in each case succinctly stated by Elyot himself.

Laurence V. Ryan provides an appropriate sequel to his *Roger Ascham*, published in 1963, in an edition of *The Schoolmaster*,[34] with modernized text and spelling. The text is based on the first edition of 1570, with a few corrections of minor errors from the second of 1571. A few of Ascham's longer periods have been broken up, some of his shorter elliptical sentences have been incorporated with others, and his heavy pointing has been lightened where it would appear quaint in a modern edition. Quotations have been left unaltered, except in cases of obvious misspellings and misplacing of Greek accents. Translations from Greek and Latin have been supplied in the notes where not provided by Ascham himself. Marginal notes have been ignored, except where erroneous attribution calls for comment. A substantial introduction gives an account of Ascham's career and an assessment of *The Schoolmaster* as a contribution to educational literature of the English Renaissance. The modernized spelling and comment should certainly facilitate the reading and study of Ascham's work, though it is doubtful whether the editor has fulfilled his intention of 'not changing too drastically its Elizabethan character'.

English Writers on Education, 1480–1603[35] is the title assigned to a facsimile reproduction of Foster Watson's *Notices of Some Early English Writers on Education*, which appeared in four parts between 1902 and 1906 in the Annual Reports of the U.S. Commission of Education. Watson's title for this compilation is misleading, as he includes many works by foreign writers, though the majority were published in England, and all of them had some impact on the theory or practice of education in England. In substance the compilation consists of an account, not consistently chronological, of works on education published during the Tudor period, assembled and indexed under the names of their authors, with full bibliographical descriptions, summaries of contents, and references to related works. Introducing the work, R. D. Pepper refers to Watson's pioneer studies on the history of education, along with those of A. F. Leach and T. W. Baldwin, noting in particular his work on Vives. Though much of the information in these articles is now out of date, the new edition is fully justified, and should serve its purpose, to quote the editor, in providing 'a handbook of information on the most widely read educational treatises of the sixteenth century'. *A Treatise of Morall Philosophie*,[36] by William Baldwin, was even more of an Elizabethan bestseller than his better known venture, *A Mirrour for Magistrates*, running to twenty-two editions against the *Mirrour*'s fourteen, the successive editions being continually revised. The facsimile under review reproduces the sixth edition, containing a version enlarged by Thomas Palfrey-

[34] *The Schoolmaster (1570)*, by Roger Ascham, ed. by Laurence V. Ryan. Folger Shakespeare Library. Cornell U.P. pp. xlii + 167. $7.50.

[35] *English Writers on Education, 1480–1603, A Source Book*, compiled by Foster Watson. Facsimile Reproduction with an Introduction by Robert D. Pepper. Gainesville, Florida: Scholars' Facsimiles and Reprints. pp. xiii + 153. $8.

[36] *A Treatise of Morall Philosophie Wherein Is Contained the Worthy Sayings of Philosophers, Emperours, Kings and Orators: Their Lives and Answers (1547)*, by William Baldwin enlarged by Thomas Palfreyman. A Facsimile Reproduction of the edition of 1620 with an Introduction by Robert Hood Bowers. Gainesville, Florida: Scholars' Facsimiles and Reprints. pp. xiii + 399. $10.

man. In an introduction, Robert Hood Bowers notes the relation of Baldwin's treatise with other similar collections of ethical commonplaces, culled from Pagan and Christian sources, their continuity with medieval cultural and literary traditions, their educational function 'as one of many short cuts to self-improvement for the rising middle classes . . . whose thirst for culture has always sustained the publishing industry'.

In 'The Assembly of Gods and Christine de Pisan' (ELN) Curt F. Bühler notes that the name 'Othea', for which Triggs, in the E.E.T.S. edition suggested the substitution of 'Athena', appears frequently in Christine de Pisan's Épître d'Othéa, where the goddess bearing this name is described in terms very similar to those in the Assembly. He suggests that the author used Christine's text as a source on the score both of this and other points of similarity, for instance the deities' appearances in the same order and the representation of Atropos as a masculine being. Whether the author used the French original or the English translation by Stephen Scrope is left an open question.

Reviewing 'Some aspects of the early Renaissance in Scotland' (Forum for Modern Language Studies), John MacQueen stresses the contribution of the newly founded Scottish universities to the literary achievement of fifteenth- and sixteenth-century writers, many of whom were probably graduates. The 'regrettable tendency' to speak of 'Scottish Chaucerians' gives a one-sided estimate of their achievement, and our knowledge of other Scots poets is confined to incidental references by Dunbar and Lindsay, and limited extant remains, apart from the Bannatyne MS., an incomplete anthology, the contents of which are difficult to date. Among major contributors to the Renaissance in Scotland and their achievement MacQueen signals out Henryson, his 'aureate' language compounded of medieval and humanistic elements, and the social satire of his Fables, which foreshadows that of More in Utopia; John Major and his friend Gavin Douglas, whose works throw light on the intellectual climate of the age; Hector Boece, first principal of the University of Aberdeen, who 'brought to his post the humanist interests and enthusiasms which he shared with Erasmus', and supplied Shakespeare, through Holinshed, with the plot of Macbeth; and Alexander Scott, one of whose poems may be connected with one of Wyatt's in the Egerton MS. A survey of cultural and educational conditions in Scotland with narrower focus introduces MacQueen's Robert Henryson. A Study of the Major Narrative Poems,[37] where he suggests that Henryson may have studied at a continental university, as his name does not appear in any Scottish university register. Evidence of his poems shows him to have been well acquainted with Chaucer and his school, Scottish alliterative poetry, some French poetry, and works printed by Caxton. The Testament reveals some knowledge of medicine, and the Fables suggest the possibility of legal training. References to papal institutions give evidence of first-hand knowledge, possibly gleaned through study of canon and civil law. An interesting section correlates Henryson's poetic technique with King James's Reulis and Cautelis, particularly in connexion with diction and the grading of style and substance, brief in Orpheus and Eurydice, most complex in The Testament.

[37] Robert Henryson. A Study of the Major Narrative Poems, by John MacQueen. O.U.P pp. 229. 30s.

'Morals' to the *Fables* show borrowings from Boethius and Boccaccio. With good reason MacQueen bases his text on the Bannatyne MS. in preference to the Bassandyne print. *Poems of Robert Henryson*, selected and edited by Charles Elliott (*YW*, xliv. 119), has been reissued in paperback.[38]

'A Further Source for Henryson's "Fabillis" (*NQ*), suggested by I. W. A. Jamieson, is the *Fabulae* of Odo of Cheriton, an English priest writing about 1320 and drawing on *Le Roman de Renart* and other bestiary sources. 'The Fox tryed before the Lyon', in which MacQueen traces a debt to Caxton's *Reynard*, Jamieson compares with Odo's version, which, he considers, is 'quite unlike any other version of the story, except Henryson's, whose major formal characteristic, like Odo's, 'seems to be his constant combining of traditional genres and stories into new wholes'. In 'Henryson and the Thre Prestis of Peblis' (*N*) Donald MacDonald argues for the attribution of this poem to Henryson on textual and other grounds. In the Asloan MS., which contains the first three hundred and fifty-nine lines, Henryson is well represented, and internal evidence convinces the writer that the satire, dating from the 1480s, is directed against James III and his court. The social and political criticism which it embodies resembles that in Henryson's *Fables*, the style, like his, is rapid, easy, economical, dramatic. In support of his argument MacDonald draws from the *Fables* numerous parallels in phrasing and satirical portraiture. Comparing 'Henryson's *Testament of Cresseid* and Heywood's *A Woman Killed with Kindness*'

(*Renaissance Quarterly*), John J. McDermott finds probability that the reading of Henryson's poem effected 'a strong residual aesthetic experience in Heywood's dramatic imagination' through the common motives of a faithless woman killed by remorse at her wronged mate's kindness, and the erection by the injured man to her memory of a marble tombstone engraved with golden letters. Support to his thesis is adduced from the continuing popularity of *The Testament* and a casual reference to Cressida's leprosy in Heywood's *The Iron Age*.

Tom Scott's *Late Medieval Scots Poetry*[39] provides a representative collection from the fifteenth and sixteenth centuries, demonstrating the continuity of medieval traditions, and including, besides the work of 'Scottish Chaucerians', those of their less adventurous successors, Maitland, Scott, Montgomerie, Hume, and Boyd. The historical survey in the Introduction is retrospective rather than prospective, concerned with the medieval heritage and antecedents of these poets rather than their response to the new forces of humanism, and this would account for an over-protracted sketch of traditions in narrative, fable, and the motif of *amour courtois*. More pertinent and useful are comments on the distinctive Scottish notion of the poet as 'makar', or practical artist, and 'seer', or visionary in the recording of facts, represented in Thomas the Rhymer and Barbour, whose *Bruce* could have served as 'a military manual which still had validity as a sheer practical guide to the art of war as late as Flodden'. The Introduction includes brief notes on language and

---

[38] *Poems of Robert Henryson*, selected and ed. with an Introduction, Notes, and Glossary, by Charles Elliot. Clarendon Press. pp. 184. 12s. 6d.

[39] *Late Medieval Scots Poetry. A Selection from the Makars and their Heirs down to 1610*, ed. with an Introduction, Notes and Glossary, by Tom Scott. Heinemann. pp. vii+207. 21s.

metre, and a longer section on political and social conditions in Scotland throughout this period, noting their repercussions on poetry. A glossary is appended, but commentary on individual poems is confined to brief introductory notes on each.

'Dunbar and Villon—A Comparison and a Contrast' (*MLR*), by A. M. Kinghorn, opens with a summary of earlier comparisons of the two poets following J. G. Mackay's study of 1889. Comparing Dunbar's *Lament for the Makars* with Villon's 'Où sont?' ballades, we feel that Dunbar is more 'pastoral', Villon more 'self-detached'. In self-expression Kinghorn finds Dunbar more solitary, Villon citing, by contrast, many names of companions and acquaintances. Dunbar shows a medieval distrust of externals, Villon accepts life as he sees it, since 'unlike Dunbar he is not a self-centred moralist' never hammering home the moral in Dunbar's preaching manner. Dunbar's ribaldry is aimed not at love, which he regarded with reverence, but at its association with marriage; Villon is less fastidious, and his treatment is usually crude. In elegiac poetry Dunbar is more abstract, Villon concrete and personal. *Two Scots Chaucerians*,[40] by H. Harvey Wood (in the 'Writers and Their Work' series), gives summary accounts of Henryson and Dunbar, with critical commentaries and select bibliographies.

The Scottish Text Society edition of *The Shorter Poems of Gavin Douglas*,[41] edited by Priscilla J. Bawcutt, contains *The Palice of Honour, Conscience*, probably by

Douglas, and *King Hart*, traditionally assigned to him, though of doubtful authorship. The London and Edinburgh editions of *The Palice of Honour*, published respectively in 1553 and 1579, are printed in parallel, preceded by the Davidson fragments. *King Hart* is edited from the single manuscript, preserved in the Maitland Folio, belonging to the Pepysian Library at Magdalene College, Cambridge, the edition being in 'critical' rather than 'diplomatic' form. The introduction comments on the date, language, verse, and literary background of each of the three poems, and presents a strong case against Douglas's authorship of *King Hart*. The text is followed by notes, an appendix giving emendations made in the margins of the copy of *The Palice of Honour*, 1579 text, in the National Library of Scotland, a glossary, and an index of names.

Reconsidering the associations of 'Skelton and Sheriff Hutton' (*ELN*), Melvin J. Tucker is led to the conclusion that Skelton's stay at the castle, which forms the setting to *The Garland of Laurel*, took place in the 1490s rather than in 1522–3, as commonly supposed, if we suppose that the poem refers to incidents taking place while the Howards were in residence. The suggested date of composition, if accepted, entails revision of accepted views as to the identification of characters in the poem with members of the Howard family. David V. Harrington discusses difficulties in connexion with 'Manerly Margery' (*Ex*) due to inadequate punctuation and unclear division of voices in the extant music. The real point at issue is the identification of the speaker of the lines in the refrain, which have been assigned alternatively to Margery and to the clerk. With such a division of speakers, set off by contrasting punctuations, the poem may be read

---

[40] *Two Scots Chaucerians. Robert Henryson. William Dunbar*, by H. Harvey Wood. Writers and Their Work: No. 201. Longmans. pp. 48. 3s. 6d.

[41] *The Shorter Poems of Gavin Douglas*, ed. by Priscilla J. Bawcutt. The Scottish Text Society. Blackwood. pp. lxxxvii+298.

I

as 'dialogue between a sophisticated clerk and a servant girl, with two bumpkins . . . silently standing by'. Elaine Spina's 'Skeltonic Meter in *Elynour Rumming*' (*SP*) is an inquiry into the character of Skelton's metre as deducible from his works as a whole, which show a wide degree of variation between two-, three-, and four-stress lines, suggestive of a poet who enjoyed metrical experimentation. 'Although the reader wants some rule, it also appears that the ear is intolerant of total regularity.' In *Elynour Rumming* Miss Spina prefers a two-stress measure throughout, feeling 'that the sound has great wit, speed, and vitality appropriate to the subject'. In this poem two-beat reading may satisfy 'the ear, the mind, and the evidence', conveying the desired effect of wild bacchanalian noise and movement.

A *Tradition of Poetry*,[42] by John Buxton, comprises a series of eight essays on English poets from Wyatt to Lady Winchilsea, designed to show the response of these poets to the social tradition which recognized poetry as an accomplishment suitable for a gentleman, and to the literary tradition which ran in parallel. Wyatt's poetry, notwithstanding its courtly setting, modulates freely into a familiar style, 'somewhat plain', as in his first satire and adaptations of carols and old songs, characterized by racy and colloquial language, deriving from native sources. Though significant to his own century in naturalizing Renaissance courtly fashions in English poetry, he writes most easily in a native lyrical style, and, at his best, 'the two personalities miraculously fuse and combine'. In Surrey 'there is nothing of the native, and therefore medieval, tradition . . . it is all classical grace and

polish'. His translation of Virgil, in Buxton's view, had more effect on his style than his translations from Italian; his own rich resources in vocabulary and syntax were necessary to such translation. 'The reader of Surrey, like the reader of Milton, as of Virgil, is invited to pay attention to the choice and placing of words, is always on duty.' Comparison of the versions of Petrarch by Wyatt and Surrey demonstrates the difference between 'a poet who has understood Petrarch's art, and one who has merely understood the meaning of his words'. Revaluation of Surrey, we are advised, is overdue, in virtue of his achievement as an innovator 'who pointed the way to poets who had greater gifts and more time'. Concerning Gascoigne, the critic's aim is 'to discover again the promise of his poetry, and the cause of its lack of fulfilment, an inquiry which incidentally reveals to us a courtier, soldier, and scholar, who, however feckless and disappointing in each role, at least kept a certain engaging candour, an unwillingness to be deceived, even by himself'. Douglas L. Peterson's *The English Lyric from Wyatt to Donne*,[43] which stems from Yvor Winters's demonstration of the plain and ornate styles of the English Renaissance, traces the confluence of the two styles in Tottel's *Miscellany*, and Elizabethan poetry, early and late. Opening with a summary description of stylistic devices in the medieval lyric, it demonstrates their persistence throughout the sixteenth century, when poetry was still regarded as a stylistic discipline, its ramifications being extended through study of rhetoric. Wyatt, by nature inclined to plain rather than eloquent style,

[42] *A Tradition of Poetry*, by John Buxton. Macmillan. pp. ix+190. 30s.

[43] *The English Lyric from Wyatt to Donne. A History of the Plain and Eloquent Styles*, by Douglas L. Peterson. Princeton U.P. pp. 391. $8.50.

treats Petrarchan conceit as 'something more than a novel invention', using it rather as a means of analysing feeling, and, in the process, of organizing a poem. His translations, 'original in the best sense of the Renaissance doctrine of imitation', introduced to the English lyric a mode of closely-reasoned introspection which anticipates by twenty-five years the technique of later Elizabethans. The irony of Wyatt was sustained and reasserted by Googe, Turberville, Gascoigne, and Ralegh, but the courtly influence is still evident, for instance, in *A Handful of Pleasant Delights*, which, in Peterson's opinion, was published for the benefit of courtiers, and not, as Rollins considered, for the vulgar. In sum, 'the emergence of the plain style as the dominant lyric tradition marks the end of the Court's domination of the lyric'.

English Poetry in the Sixteenth Century,[44] by Maurice Evans, first published in 1955, has been rewritten and is now reissued, retaining only the chapter on historical poetry and occasional excerpts from the others. The two opening chapters, on 'Crosscurrents of the Renaissance', and 'Poetic Theory and Practice' cover familiar ground, the blending of humanism and scholasticism, Pagan and Christian thought, widening of the vernacular and predominance of the London dialect, the impact on criticism of rhetoric and the cult of imitation. The others are devoted to the principal poets from Skelton to Shakespeare and his contemporaries, assessed on traditional and, in places, over-simplified lines. Skelton, 'perhaps the most considerable poet between Chaucer and Shakespeare . . . points both forward and back';

Wyatt 'launched English poetry on a new career in the field of the sonnet'; the Court of Henry VIII 'was not essentially different from that of Eleanor of Aquitaine'. Running judgements of this sort are, unhappily, too numerous. However, for readers not put off by them the book may well have something to offer.

Friendship's Garland[45] includes an essay, 'Una Fonte Petrarchesca de Sir Thomas Wyatt', by Sergio Baldi, comparing Wyatt's 'Though I my self be bridilled of my mynde' with its original in Vellutello's edition of Petrarch (1525). Concurring with Patricia Thomson's view that Wyatt may have availed himself of Vellutello's commentary in the earlier version, from the evidence of comparison of the versions in the Egerton and Devonshire manuscripts, Baldi concludes that Wyatt based the later one directly on the original text of Petrarch. Discussing 'The Texts of Wyatt's Penitential Psalms' (*NQ*) after collating the three manuscript texts with the edition published in 1549–50, Kenneth Muir prints selected variants, which have led him to the conclusion that the majority of the poems in the Egerton MS. were copied by a scribe before Wyatt went to Spain, though not in chronological order; the poems added by Wyatt, he considers, were written after 1537. 'The Mind in the Poem: Wyatt's "They Fle from Me"' (*SEL*), by Donald M. Friedman, reopens discussion on this enigmatic poem, which he reads as an example of one of Wyatt's favourite techniques, 'a dramatization of the mind of an imagined figure . . . attempting to deal with the experience of faithlessness'. He regards the poem as 'the most highly developed and most brilliantly successful of these dramatic "essaies"', analysing diverse

---

[44] *English Poetry in the Sixteenth Century*, by Maurice Evans. Hutchinson. pp. 184. Cloth 30*s*. Paperback 12*s*. 6*d*.

[45] *Friendship's Garland:* v. footnote 19.

moods, as it evolves, with great resourcefulness in metaphor and vocabulary. Winifred Maynard's 'To Smithe of Camden' (*RES*) refers to the inscription at the end of a poem in the Arundel Harington MS. of Tudor poetry generally attributed to Wyatt. Miss Hughey had suggested that this might refer to the tune, and in this article Miss Maynard recounts the gruesome story in Foxe's *Actes and Monuments* of Henry Smith, also of Camden, with the suggestion that this may have formed the theme of a broadside ballad, thence giving occasion for a popular tune. Raymond Southall, regarding 'Wyatt's "Ye Olde Mule"' (*ELN*) as a studied insult, antithetical to the more complimentary and servile poems of courtly love, rates it as one of Wyatt's finest performances, effective enough if read literally, doubly so as the implications of syntax and vocabulary reveal the full measure of the insult and Wyatt's wit.

The Poetry of Walter Haddon,[46] edited by Charles J. Lees, follows the 1567 and 1576 editions, collated with extant manuscript copies. It reintroduces the works of an accomplished Latinist, amplified with full notes on his life and achievement as versatile scholar and educator, public servant, reformer, and poet. His appointment successively to academic posts at the highest level – Master of Trinity Hall, Regius Professor of Law, Public Orator, and Vice-Chancellor at Cambridge, President of Magdalen College, Oxford, a record supported by the internal evidence of his writings and tributes from his contemporaries, justifies the present editor's claim that 'Haddon was one of the most influential educators of his day'. His

[46] *The Poetry of Walter Haddon*, ed. by Charles J. Lees, S.M. The Hague: Mouton. Studies in English Literature Vol. XLVI. pp. 314. $11.75.

poetry provides large-scale evidence of the principle of imitation in practical and creative operation, with free embellishment by means of rhetorical figure and poetic licence. In partial disagreement with Leicester Bradner, Lees notes affinities between Haddon's epistles and those of Horace, though we miss the Horatian urbanity. His conception of war, even allowing for its Christian context, is 'not totally divorced from Virgil's', but in assessing his poems as a whole as specimens of imitation we must take into account his preoccupation with versifying passages from Scripture. 'Haddon mirrors his own day. To read his poetry is to take a trip through the England of his lifetime.' The new edition, well produced and documented, should serve the purpose for which it was intended.

'John Heywood and Sir John Davies: A Change in the Tradition of the Sixteenth-Century Satiric Epigram' (*Satire News Letter*), by Joseph C. Baldwin, draws a contrast between Heywood's *Epigrams* and those of Sir John Davies, the former being in style and tone medieval, the latter imitated from classical analogues. Heywood figures as a jester, indulging the popular English taste for rude and homely humour. His epigrams can be classified as allegorical, proverbial, humorous, and abusive, the first, which include fables, apologues, and parables combining humour with instruction, the second providing a source for similitudes and allegories, the third marked by jocundity and skilful use of narration, the last and largest group attacking the usual butts of medieval flyting. Deriving from medieval fableaux, jest-books, and exempla, their satire is mainly impersonal, giving only occasional glimpses of the contemporary English scene. With Sir John Davies, however, 'the satirical epigram assumes its major character as a medium of social satire, a character which no other literary form can express with such compression, wit, and polish'. 'An Unknown Contemporary Epitaph of Thomas Mason (d. 1559)' (*NQ*), by David H. Thomas, brings to light an epitaph in French, which Thomas translates, of Thomas Mason, son of Sir John Mason, Chancellor of the University of Oxford, whose tomb, in Winchester Cathedral, bears a Latin inscription and who is referred to as recently deceased by Jasper Heywood in his dedication to Sir John Mason of his *Thyestes*. In Lloyd E. Berry's 'Richard Hakluyt and Turberville's Poems on Russia' (*PBSA*) attention is called to Hakluyt's omission, in *Principal Navigations*, from Turberville's poetical account of his voyage to Russia in 1568–9, of his attack on the morals of Russian peasants, an omission parallel with Hakluyt's similar treatment of Giles Fletcher's *Of the Russe Commonwealth*, both prunings doubtless prompted by fear of offending the Muscovites. Roger A. Geimer contributes 'A Note on the Birthdate of Thomas Churchyard' (*NQ*), reckoning the date, from internal and external evidence, as not earlier than 1523. Other information on Churchyard, collected by Merrill H. Goldwyn is embodied in 'Notes on the Biography of Thomas Churchyard' (*RES*, 1966), 'Thomas Churchyard's "Marriages"' (*NQ*), and 'Some Unpublished Manuscripts by Thomas Churchyard' (*SP*).

Ten Miracle Plays,[47] edited by R. G. Thomas, designed primarily for the benefit of younger students, is composed of plays not readily available in anthologies, selected with the object of demonstrating both the wide range and individual excellence of the plays as well as their function in a pageant cycle. Each of the main cycles is represented, and most of the plays are produced in their entirety, with modern punctuation. In his introduction the editor comments on the origins of medieval drama, staging, elements of comedy, and the 'grand design' of man's spiritual history from his Creation to the Day of Judgement. The meaning of the text is clarified by footnotes and a glossary.

Discussing 'The Unity of the Wakefield "Mactacio Abel"' (*T*), Clifford Davidson contends that this play, like the whole Corpus Christi cycle, represents the wholeness of God's plan of salvation, a central motive to which the farcical interlude is merely incidental. Cain is an antitype of the saint, acting as he does because of the Fall, his appearance with the plough figuring God's curse against Adam, and his final despair foreshadowing that of Judas at the sacrifice of Christ, typified in Abel. Eugene B. Cantelupe and Richard Griffith offer an 'Iconographical Interpretation' of 'The Gifts of the Shepherds in the Wakefield *Secunda Pastorum*' (*MS*, 1966), suggesting that the three gifts are unified both in significance and in their relation to the number of the rustics and to their salutations, all participating in the triadic structure signifying the Trinity. The cherry, the bird, and the ball, symbolizing (respectively) resurrection, the winged soul, and sovereignty, and, at the highest level, the Three Persons of the Trinity 'complement each other, characterize the rustic donors, and underscore the moral interest of the play'.

Discussing 'Structure and Tone in the *Second Shepherds' Play*' (*Educational Theatre Journal*), John Gardner argues that production should

---

[47] *Ten Miracle Plays*, ed. by R. G. Thomas. (York Medieval Texts.) Arnold. pp. 166. Cloth 25*s*. Paperback 12*s*. 6*d*.

emphasize the symbolical Christian significance in the play of the number three, figured in the representation of law, charity, and wonder, the three adorations of the Holy Child, and the three symbolical gifts. Mak and Gill serve as foil to the Holy Family, their actions and character epitomizing the worldly fall from order. The coherence of the play, generally regarded as disjointed, is reinforced through tone and symbolic characterization. 'Symbol and Structure in the *Secunda Pastorum*' (*Comparative Drama*), by Lawrence J. Ross, is focused on the liturgical attributes of the play, which, he suggests, give the key to its proper representation, with the secular characters grouped round the icon of the Nativity as chorus, greeting the Child in successive 'Hail!' lyrics, and offering symbolic gifts. Viewed in this light, the preliminary farce becomes an integral part of the play, introducing a figural kind of comic irony. In 'The "Stage" and the Staging of the N-town Plays' (*RORD*) Ann Cooper Gay pursues the findings of Wickham and Southern, applying the latter's definition of 'place' and his theories of 'stages' and stations to the N-town plays, which, she considers, give distinct evidence of place- and scaffold-staging. The difference between these plays and those of other cycles, Chester, for instance, 'lies not so much in its "stage" but in its staging'. Stanley J. Kahrl, in 'Medieval Drama in Louth', *(RORD)*, calls attention to the important part played by religious gilds, as well as craft-gilds, demonstrated by records of payments to these gilds for their services to pageant production, the survival of the 'Boy Bishop' custom till 1524, and other evidence of active participation by specific gilds until 1528. Speculating on the authorship of Louth plays, he suggests that they may have been written by a school-master. Their cessation was probably precipitated through the loss of endowments to religious fraternities. Researches by Kenneth Cameron and Stanley J. Kahrl on 'Staging the N-Town Cycle' (*TN*), based on the evidence of banns, language, prosody, and stage directions, lead to the conclusion that, from this aspect, the Cycle cannot be treated as a unified whole, but represents staging in a state of flux. They suggest that, in its extant form, it is a pastiche of proto-cyclic plays, revisions of these combining processional and 'round' staging (the Marian group), and a still later group (the Passion cycle) revised for central staging. Further topics discussed are the joint interest of civic and religious authorities in plays at Lincoln, the actors taking part, and the possibility of performance at a central station within the Minster Close. The article is to be continued in a later issue.

John Conley suggests that 'The Reference to Judas Maccabeus in *Everyman*' (*NQ*), which is not in the *Elckerlijk*, may allude to Judas in his role as one of the Nine Worthies, and, coming from Strength, is 'obviously ironical'. D. C. Baker and J. L. Murphy write on 'The Late Medieval Plays of MS. Digby 133' (*RORD*), discussing their origins, transmission, text, and mutual relation, preliminary to a projected edition. From water-marks and other evidence they date *Wisdom* 1490–1500, and the other plays ten to twenty years later. It would appear that, at one time, the collection was in the monastery at Bury, possibly a centre of interest in drama during this period. John Hazel Smith, in 'Seneca's Tragedies: A Tentative Checklist of Fifteenth-, Sixteenth-, and Seventeenth-Century Printings' (*RORD*), classifies them under collected and partial editions in Latin, translations, paraphrases, and imitations, with an appendix listing renaissance manuscripts. He notes the diligence and ingenuity of earlier editors in emending corrupt texts and in their commentaries, which, though often merely exegetical, curious, or irrelevant, are sometimes critically significant.

A Satire of the Three Estates[48] has been adapted by Matthew McDiarmid from Robert Kemp's acting text made for the 1948 Edinburgh Festival production. A brief introduction gives an account of the author, the text, and content of the play. The text conveniently is printed on right-hand pages, faced on the left by notes on vocabulary, allusions, and analogues. It follows, in the main, Robert Charteris's 1602 edition, but 'the evident interference of Anglicizing printers' with that edition has persuaded the present editor, in some instances, to adopt some earlier readings. A few of the passages excised by Kemp have been restored, and the actual words of Lindsay retained, though spelling has been brought nearer to that of later and more familiar Scottish poetry. The editor has aimed at presenting Lindsay's masterpiece 'in an acting version that speaks only his language and gives a just idea of his dramatic intention and achievement', a worthy venture which should draw encouragement from the outstanding success of the Edinburgh Festival production. '*Gammer Gurton's Needle*. Comedy not Quite of the Lowest Order?' (*SEL*), by R. W. Ingram, stems from a phrase in a grudging tribute by H. Bradley. Assessing the comedy more highly, Ingram notes the skilful fusion of physical and verbal combat in a tangle of quarrels and misunderstandings, brought to a head when, in detective-story fashion, suspects and accusers face one another, the effective use of noise and movement, neat linguistic turns and word-games. In sum, the author 'found an excellent medium for his talents and left a better thing than he found'. Donald C. Mullin's 'An Observation on the Origin of the Elizabethan Theatre' (*ETJ*) calls attention to the significance of the baiting-ring as a formative influence on the architectural design of the three-tier open Elizabethan theatre. He suggests that adaptation of the 'Roman' arena baiting-ring for theatrical purposes through the introduction of a platform and tiring-house 'is only one more logical step in the direction of the faintly understood form of the Roman theatre'.

---

[48] *A Satire of the Three Estates*, by Sir David Lindsay. A play adapted, with Introduction and Notes by Matthew McDiarmid. Heinemann pp. 171. 21*s*.

VII

Shakespeare

NIGEL ALEXANDER

1. BIBLIOGRAPHIES

There are four major attempts to provide a comprehensive annual bibliography of books and articles on Shakespeare but the volume of published material is so great that all must be consulted, and even then there are likely to be some items which have escaped the vigilance of the compilers. The Modern Language Association is now proposing to collect abstracts of articles published in a large number of journals, and it is to be hoped that some scheme of publishing these will be arranged.

The three major bibliographies for 1967 are Rudolph E. Habenicht's essential 'Shakespeare: An Annotated World Bibliography for 1967' (*Sh Q* 1968) which lists 1168 items including reviews and has a new and welcome section for 'Selected Reprints'. Harrison T. Meserole is responsible for the '1967 MLA International Bibliography' (*PMLA* 1968) while 'Literature of the Renaissance in 1967' (*SP* 1968) appears under the general editorship of Dennis G. Donovan. The *Deutsche Shakespeare-Gesellschaft West Jahrbuch*[1] contains a 'Shakespeare-Bibliographie für 1966 mit Nachträgen aus früheren Jahren' by Wilhelm Kindervater. Selective Bibliographies are published by the major American and British Shakespeare annuals. In *Shakespeare Studies III*,[2] the survey of 'Significant Articles, Monographs and Reviews' by J. Leeds Barroll is now an established and important feature which is both remarkably up-to-date and gives very full abstracts of the chosen articles. In *Shakespeare Survey 20*[3] J. K. Walton, Norman Sanders and Stanley Wells continue 'The Year's Contributions to Shakespearian Study' with a survey of books and articles published in 1965 and 1966.

Other useful bibliographies are 'The Year's Contribution to English Renaissance Textual Study' (*Manuscripta*) by William C. McAvoy, and M. A. Shaaber's 'Recent Studies in Elizabethan and Jacobean Drama' (*SEL*).

Work in progress is reported on by W. R. Elton in *Shakespearean Research Opportunities*[4] and S. Schoenbaum in *Research Opportunities in*

[1] *Deutsche Shakespeare-Gesellschaft West Jahrbuch, 1967*, ed. by Hermann Heuer, with Ernest T. Sehrt and Rudolf Stamm. Heidelberg: Quelle & Meyer. pp. 382.

The compiler of a bibliography is dependent upon the help of editors of journals and their contributors. I am particularly grateful to Harrison T. Meserole and Robert Weimann and to the other editors and authors who sent me copies and offprints.

[2] *Shakespeare Studies III: An Annual Gathering of Research, Criticism and Reviews*, ed. by J. Leeds Barroll. Cincinnati. U.P. pp. 370. $10.00.

[3] *Shakespeare Survey 20: Shakespearian and Other Tragedy*, ed. by Kenneth Muir. C.U.P. pp. x+188. 45s. $8.50.

[4] *Shakespearean Research Opportunities: Report of the Modern Language Association of America Conference*, ed. by W. R. Elton. Riverside: Dept. of English, University of California. pp. 97.

Renaissance Drama.[5] Elton also includes a new and extremely important bibliography entitled 'Shakespeare and Renaissance Intellectual Contexts: a Selective, Annotated List 1966–67', containing articles which might otherwise escape attention.

2. EDITIONS

The Arden Shakespeare continues to make its appearance in paperback and some important editions have been added to the series this year. The two parts of *King Henry IV*[6] edited by A. R. Humphreys are interesting studies in two extremely difficult texts, though it is a little surprising that an editor who acknowledges the Folger Shakespeare Library should have collated his text from the Kökeritz-Prouty facsimile. *King John*[7] edited by E. A. J. Honigmann is a pioneering edition whose account of the relationship between Shakespeare's play and *The Troublesome Raigne* is now accepted by many other editors. J. W. Lever's edition of *Measure for Measure* and G. K. Hunter's of *All's Well That Ends Well* provide most useful commentary and notes upon plays that are coming to be regarded as comic masterpieces rather than 'problem' comedies. *Henry IV Part I*[8] edited by H. M. Richmond is the first of a new series. The text has

been carefully established and the introduction and notes are clearly aimed at an American undergraduate audience. Although not as full as the notes to the Arden editions, they are on occasions more informative and certainly provide a fuller, and therefore more useful, commentary than is available in the other standard paperback editions. It is a pity that this series will not be generally available in Britain.

Under the general editorship of T. J. B. Spencer the Penguin press have at last decided to replace their old and unsatisfactory edition edited by G. B. Harrison. The first six plays[9] published are *Coriolanus, Julius Caesar, Macbeth, The Merchant of Venice, A Midsummer Night's Dream* and *Romeo and Juliet.* In the text of *Romeo and Juliet,* the difficult problems of contamination and the frequent compositorial or authorial duplication have been well handled. It seems a pity that it has not been part of the general editor's policy to treat the original stage directions as part of the text but to allow the directions to depend upon the theatrical imagination of his editors. The commentary in some of these texts is not as informative as it might be. When more of the series have appeared it will be possible to judge whether we have gained or lost by the fact that Penguin's copyright arrangements make this series available in Britain and the admirable Pelican edition under the editorship of Alfred Harbage available only in the United States.

[5] *Research Opportunities in Renaissance Drama: The Report of the Modern Language Association Conference,* ed. by S. Schoenbaum. Evanston: Northwestern University Press. pp. 168.

[6] *King Henry IV Part I,* ed. by A. R. Humphreys (1966) pp. lxxxii+203. *King Henry IV Part II,* ed. by A. R. Humphreys. pp. xcii+242. (The Arden Shakespeare Paperbacks) Methuen. Each vol. 8s. 6d.

[7] *King John,* ed. E. A. J. Honigmann. pp. lxxvi+176. *All's Well That Ends Well,* ed. by G. K. Hunter. pp. lx+152. *Measure for Measure,* ed. by J. W. Lever. pp. xcviii+203. (The Arden Shakespeare Paperbacks) Methuen. 7s. 6d. and 8s. 6d.

[8] *Henry IV Part One,* ed. by H. M. Richmond. Indianapolis. Bobbs-Merrill. pp. xxxii+176. $1.45.

[9] *Coriolanus,* ed. by G. R. Hibbard. pp. 264. *Julius Caesar,* ed. by Norman Sanders. pp. 252. *Macbeth,* ed. by G. K. Hunter. pp. 200. *The Merchant of Venice,* ed. by W. Moelwyn Merchant. pp. 214. *A Midsummer Night's Dream,* ed. by Stanley Wells. pp. 171. *Romeo and Juliet,* ed. by T. J. B. Spencer. pp. 295. (The New Penguin Shakespeare) Penguin Books. 4s. 6d. and 6s.

In comparison with the New Penguin, the pages of the latest volumes of the Signet edition appear cramped and difficult to read. In their editions of *Henry VI, Part One* and *Henry VI, Part Two*[10] the editors, Lawrence V. Ryan and Arthur Freeman, pay little attention to the question of authorship of these plays but concentrate on establishing and explaining the text. It seems a pity that Hereward T. Price's important study of *1 Henry VI* was not included in the critical commentary.

With such excellent texts available in fairly cheap paperback editions the justification for such a series as the University Tutorial Press's South Bank Shakespeare must be that it explains Shakespeare's language more fully for the benefit of schools. In the two current volumes[11] it can hardly be said that this is done in such a fashion that it justifies the extra expense.

3. GENERAL WORKS AND COLLECTIONS OF ESSAYS

A reprint has appeared of the third (1870) edition of E. A. Abbott's *A Shakespearian Grammar*,[12] which is still one of the few studies of its kind available and which remains useful provided that it is treated with care and disagreement.

Elizabethan Poetry[13] ed. by Paul Alpers contains 'Shakespeare's Banquet of Sense' by W. B. C. Watkins; 'Shakespeare's Sonnets' by L. C. Knights; 'An Essay on the Sonnets' by C. L. Barber. This is an extremely valuable collection. Two important papers are included in a collection of essays presented to H. D. F. Kitto, *Classical Drama and Its Influence*.[14] B. L. Joseph writes on '*The Spanish Tragedy* and *Hamlet*: Two Exercises in English Seneca', and in 'Neo-Classical Drama and the Reformation in England' Glynne Wickham provides an interesting and informative short account of the different attitudes to classical drama both in England and on the Continent which influenced the development of the English drama. In 'The Forming of the Early Comedies' (*SRO*) John Arthos emphasizes the importance of music and dancing to the development of the comic drama and suggests that a new approach to Shakespeare's achievement might be made by investigating these matters. Georg Lukács writes on 'Die Szenik bei Shakespeare' in *Homo Homini Homo*.[15] M. C. Bradbrook considers Shakespeare's use of spectacle in 'Shakespeare's Primitive Art'.[16] Arguing that 'As his poetic imagination subdued itself to what it worked in, the visual and scenic basis of his art became absorbed into his poetry' Professor Bradbrook justifies the use of the 'Icon' of spectacle within a poetic

---

[10] *Henry VI, Part One*, ed. by Lawrence V. Ryan. pp. 222. *Henry VI, Part Two*, ed. by Arthur Freeman. pp. 224. (The Signet Classic Shakespeare) New English Library. Each vol. 3s. 6d.

[11] *Henry the Fourth, Part I*, ed. by C. W. R. Moseley and V. E. Neuburg. pp. 228. *Richard II*, ed. by B. W. Derbyshire. pp. 192. (The South Bank Shakespeare) London. University Tutorial Press. Each vol. 7s. 6d.

[12] *A Shakespearian Grammar*, by E. A. Abbott. New York: Dover Publications. London: Constable. pp. xxiv+511. $2.75. 26s. 6d.

[13] *Elizabethan Poetry: Modern Essays in Criticism*, ed. by Paul J. Alpers. O.U.P. pp. 524. 17s. 6d.

[14] *Classical Drama and Its Influence: Essays Presented to H. D. F. Kitto*, ed. by M. J. Anderson. London: Methuen 1965. pp. x+277.

[15] *Homo homini homo: Festschrift für Joseph E. Drexel*, ed. by W. R. Beyer. Munich: Beck. 1966. pp. 329. DM 24.

[16] 'Shakespeare's Primitive Art', by M. C. Bradbrook in *Proceedings of the British Academy*, Vol. LI (1965) O.U.P. 1966. pp. xxii+519.

drama pointing out that 'The compelling power of that part of ourself which we do not desire to meet can return only in such images'. This is an extremely interesting and important lecture. In *A Shakespeare Encyclopaedia*[17] Oscar J. Campbell and Edward G. Quinn offer 'in a single volume all the information available about every feature of Shakespeare's life and works'. This is clearly an impossible task and yet it is an important one to attempt. One can only concur with J. C. Maxwell in his review (*RES* 1968) that, while 'the number of readily corrigible errors is rather higher than it ought to have been', yet 'the student will find more of his questions answered here than in any other single book'. Wolfgang Clemen's 'Past and Future in Shakespeare's Drama'[18] is an important contribution to the understanding of Shakespeare's construction, since it is a study of 'the relationship between past and future' which 'opens up an approach to the time structure in the plays; it is closely connected not only with the art of preparation, of exposition and suspense, but also with the fundamental principles of composition'. With the increased interest in how much the Elizabethan theatre owed to the Greek and Latin classics it is satisfactory to have a paperback edition of Tom F. Driver's *The Sense of History in Greek and Shakespearean Drama*[19] while another welcome reprint is T. F. Thiselton Dyer's *Folk-Lore of Shakespeare*.[20]

In *Shakespeare and Society*[21] Terence Eagleton argues that 'our own experience has now reached a point where I believe we are able to understand Shakespeare in ways not possible before, and where this understanding is simultaneously an insight into our own condition'. His book is an examination of *Troilus and Cressida, Hamlet, Measure for Measure, Coriolanus, Antony and Cleopatra, Macbeth, The Winter's Tale* and *The Tempest,* a selection which is itself an interesting comment on recent critical attitudes to Shakespeare. This examination of 'the tension between spontaneous life and society' contains some important insights, but the general theme is not sufficiently sustained to produce the expected coherent critical argument, and the book as a whole fails in its attempt to 'deepen our own understanding, and to recognize new ways forward'. *Shakespeare's Life and Times*[22] by Roland M. Frye is intended 'to convey as vivid an impression of Shakespeare's life as we can now create on the basis of the available evidence'. The book is lavishly produced and it is a great help to have illustrations which are at least sixteenth- and seventeenth-century. The available evidence, however, should surely have restrained the author from reproducing John C. Adams's model of the Globe stage. Northrop Frye's *Fools of Time: Studies in Shakespearian Tragedy*[23] is an extended examination of the pattern and structure of Shakespearian tragedy which

[17] *A Shakespeare Encyclopaedia*, ed. by Oscar James Campbell and Edward G. Quinn. London: Methuen. 1966. pp. xv + 1014. £5.

[18] 'Past and Future in Shakespeare's Drama', by Wolfgang Clemen in *Proceedings of the British Academy*, Vol. LII. (1966) O.U.P.

[19] *The Sense of History in Greek and Shakespearean Drama*, by Tom F. Driver. New York. Columbia U.P. pp. 231. 16*s*.

[20] *Folk-Lore of Shakespeare*, by T. F. Thiselton Dyer. New York: Dover Publications. pp. x + 526. $2.50. 24*s*.

[21] *Shakespeare and Society*, by Terence Eagleton. London: Chatto & Windus. pp. 208. 25*s*.

[22] *Shakespeare's Life and Times: A Pictorial Record*, by Roland M. Frye. London: Faber & Faber. Princeton U.P. 42*s*.

[23] *Fools of Time: Studies in Shakespearian Tragedy*, by Northrop Frye. Toronto U.P. pp. viii + 121.

argues that this pattern is responsible for the way in which the audience experience the play, and that it is this experience as it is lived through that constitutes the 'meaning' of the play. Under the title of *A Companion to Arber*[24] Cyprian Blagden and I. G. Philip have edited some of the papers collected by Sir Walter Greg for the Lyell lectures in 1954–5. This is a chronological calendar of all the documents contained in Arber together with a summary of their contents and also includes a large number of supplementary documents, not in Arber's transcript, which are set out in full. It is a major work of scholarship which will be of permanent value. In *The Early Shakespeare*[25] A. C. Hamilton examines the three parts of *Henry VI, Titus Andronicus, The Comedy of Errors, The Two Gentlemen of Verona, Love's Labour's Lost, Venus and Adonis, Lucrece, Richard III, Romeo and Juliet,* and *A Midsummer Night's Dream*, arguing that '*Richard III* is not an early attempt to write an English *Macbeth*, nor is *Romeo and Juliet* a youthful *Antony and Cleopatra*. Each of the early plays surprises us by differing from the others, just as the later plays, even those written as a group, do not compete with each other', Hamilton treats the poems as works of art in their own right as well as important evidence for the development of Shakespeare's art. This leads him to pay proper attention to Shakespeare's use of Ovid in both *Titus Andronicus* and *The*

Comedy of Errors. The book ends with a consideration of *Romeo and Juliet*, in which its placing with the early plays 'allows the proper recognition of its own achievement and its appreciation on its own terms, not at the expense of the early plays or in spite of the later plays'. A similar examination of *A Midsummer Night's Dream* demonstrates that 'The play accommodates all responses, from the most imaginative to the most literal. Its relationship to the early plays, particularly to the comedies, may show why and how it satisfies'. This is an important contribution to criticism.

In *Studies in Honor of DeWitt T. Starnes*[26] T. W. Baldwin writes on '*Errors and Marprelate*', Robert L. Montgomery studies 'Shakespeare's Gaudy: The Method of *The Rape of Lucrece*', Leonard F. Dean argues in '*Richard II* to *Henry V*: A Closer View' that 'the attempt to simplify Shakespeare's English history plays into an example of the History Play with a single overriding theme obstructs our appreciation of the actual variety of dramatic mode and structure in the plays, their thematic richness, and the remarkable effects which occur when contrasting modes within a play interact co-operatively. We are "better educated" by Shakespeare, as Northrop Frye puts it, than by his sources'. Fredson Bowers examines 'Death in Victory: Shakespeare's Tragic Reconciliations' in a paper which is largely devoted to *Hamlet* while Hardin Craig in 'Shakespeare and the All-inclusive Law of Nature' fails to define his terms in any very useful fashion but concludes that 'One

---

[24] *A Companion to Arber. Being a Calendar of Documents in Edward Arber's Transcript of the Registers of the Company of Stationers of London, 1554–1640*, edited by W. W. Greg assisted by C. P. Blagden and I. G. Philip. Oxford: Clarendon and O.U.P. pp. 451. £5 15s. 6d.
[25] *The Early Shakespeare*, by A. C. Hamilton. San Marino: The Huntington Library. pp. x+237. $6.50.

[26] *Studies in Honor of DeWitt T. Starnes*, ed. by Thomas P. Harrison, Archibald A. Hill, Ernest C. Mossner and James Sledd. Austin: Texas U.P. pp. 295. $7.50. 71s. 6d. Hereafter referred to as *Starnes Studies*.

at least feels that, if Shakespeare and Ben Jonson were not debating the issue between drama as the product of Nature and drama as the independent invention of man, they ought to have been'.

In *Eos*[27] edited by Arthur T. Hatto, T. J. B. Spencer contributes the article on the dawn parting theme in English poetry and finds that the tradition illuminates both *Romeo and Juliet* and *Troilus and Cressida*.

Rudolf Hirsch's *Printing, Selling and Reading 1450–1550*[28] is not without faults (see the review in *TLS* 21 Sept. 1967), but will be of interest to all students of Shakespeare in that it studies the state of printing in Europe, examining important topics such as the cost of production, the selling of books and national and local characteristics of the book trade.

An important paper by L. C. Knights appears in *The Hidden Harmony: Essays in Honor of Philip Wheelwright*.[29] In considering 'The Thought of Shakespeare' Knights argues that 'Shakespeare's "thought" is not something that can be extracted from the body of his work or discursively paraphrased' because it involves 'the attitudes embodied in the different speakers in their complex relationships, the implicit comment of action on profession, emotional overtones, perhaps things even more elusive'. Professor Knights concludes that 'Perhaps what we have to do is

attempt to re-define "thought"', and this essay is an important first step in a new bearing in Knights's own dramatic criticism.

The Proceedings of the IVth Congress of the International Comparative Literature Association[30] contain a number of papers on Shakespeare. Oswald LeWinter writes on 'Shakespeare on the continent: the cosmopolitan fortunes of nationalism' and argues that 'Shakespeare's *Richard III* has no other protagonist than history, history to which the moral order is completely irrelevant', and then points out that 'The European mind of the eighteenth and nineteenth centuries could not conceive of such a Shakespeare'. This point is illustrated by a comparison with the Richard of Christian Felix Weisse. In 'The sonnet—a cosmopolitan literary form —in the Renaissance' Robert M. Burgess attempts 'to consolidate within a few pages a vast amount of information concerning the origin and spread of the sonnet, as a cosmopolitan literary form, during the period of the Renaissance'. The condensed nature of this information means that it is unlikely that the article will contain information on Shakespeare's sonnets which is new to readers of the *Year's Work*—but it illustrates the European importance of the genre since the sonnet was written from Amsterdam to Yugoslavia. In 'Shakespeare and national traits in Slavic literatures' Constantin Bida considers the difficulties of interpretation which must arise when Shakespeare's works are considered in the context of a completely different literary aesthetic. Such historical considerations account, for example,

[27] *Eos: An Enquiry into the Theme of Lovers' Meetings and Partings at Dawn in Poetry*, ed. by Arthur T. Hatto. The Hague: Mouton. 1965. pp. 854.

[28] *Printing, Selling and Reading 1450–1550*, by Rudolf Hirsch. Wiesbaden: Harrassowitz. pp. viii+165. DM 28.

[29] *The Hidden Harmony: Essays in Honor of Philip Wheelwright*, ed. by Oliver Johnson, David Harrah, Peter Fuss and Theodore Guleserian. New York: Odyssey Press. pp. 195. $6.25.

[30] *Proceedings of the IVth Congress of the International Comparative Literature Association*, ed. by François Jost. The Hague: Mouton. 1966. 2 Vols. pp. xxxii+1459. 250 Guilders.

for Tolstoy's attack on Shakespeare. Marvin Rosenberg touches on Shakespearian tragedy in his interesting 'Tragedy—departures from Aristotelian imitation' while Eric LaGuardia distinguishes between Renaissance and Medieval figural imitation in 'Figural imitation in English renaissance poetry'. Max Bluestone examines the dramatic structure of *Othello* in order to illustrate 'Means of imitation in dramatic adaptation of prose fiction: the example of *Othello*'.

G. W. Keeton's *Shakespeare's Legal and Political Background*[31] is an extremely interesting and important book. The account, however, of the legal terms used in the graveyard scene in *Hamlet* is not as complete as it might be and does not supersede W. L. Rushton's account in *Shakespeare's Legal Maxims*. While the author modestly asserts that 'beyond the legal and political ideas reflected in them he has no wish to express judgement upon the plays themselves' he cannot avoid doing so, and his judgements are often questionable. It is disturbing that a legal mind which has presumably examined the evidence should be able to assert that '*Henry VI* is not a good play, and it is commonly supposed that Shakespeare's share in it was small', while Quiller-Couch's views upon the text and structure of *Measure for Measure* are treated with a respect which they have never deserved. Yet, with these reservations, any student of Shakespeare will find this an indispensable work of reference provided that he consults it for its legal rather than its literary opinions.

G. Wilson Knight has collected a series of his essays on Shakespeare and religion and has published them under the title of *Shakespeare and Religion*.[32] The main interest of this book is in the introduction which is written as a reply to R. M. Frye's critique of 'The School of Knight' in *Shakespeare and Christian Doctrine*. It now appears that 'my collection shows how I have been for forty years labouring to liberate the Ariel powers, the spirit-powers, of Shakespearian drama for our use. There has been need for continual reiteration and continual defence. The liberation of new powers, however salutary those powers, in all ages arouses a bitter opposition; and of that there has been no lack'. These Ariel powers are not identical with orthodox Christianity, since 'In Shakespeare orthodox Christianity may at any moment, if the story allows it, appear with accepted sanction; but though his thought and imagery may tend towards the medieval, in human delineation, plot, action and dramatic conception he is of the Renaissance; and he has much in common with the dramatists of ancient Greece. Like those, he is concerned, as the medieval Church was not, with the Dionysian and erotic energies, with politics and power-quests and dramatic supermen.' One is left with the uneasy impression that Christianity and Shakespeare, as well as Byron and Nietzsche, are being interpreted in a pattern which leads unerringly towards a new prophet and that this prophet bears some resemblance to the author of this book. The book contains the six radio talks given in 1964 which Knight himself calls 'the heart of my life's work on Shakespeare' and, in an appendix, letters published in the *Times Literary Supplement* and reviews published in a variety of journals. As the author himself says at the end of his Introduction, 'There is much left unsettled'.

[31] *Shakespeare's Legal and Political Background*, by George W. Keeton. London: Pitman. pp. viii+417. 63s.

[32] *Shakespeare and Religion: Essays of Forty Years*, by G. Wilson Knight. London: Routledge & Kegan Paul. pp. ix+374. 45s.

Jan Kott's *Shakespeare Our Contemporary*[33] (*YW* xlv 138) now appears in paperback in a second edition which contains new chapters on *Othello* and *As You Like It*. The chapter on *Othello* is important and has already appeared in *Études Anglaises* for 1964. There is a considerable discrepancy between this French translation and the English version on p. 89 where the French appears to give very much better sense. This is a work of criticism which has been violently attacked as unhistorical and as violently defended. It is an interesting addition to the continuing debate about art and nature which Shakespeare himself dramatized from *Love's Labour's Lost* to *The Winter's Tale* and which has no known conclusion.

Another welcome reprint is J. B. Leishman's *Themes and Variations in Shakespeare's Sonnets*[34] which now appears in paperback. The book does not attempt to be either a history of Elizabethan poetry or a 'definitive' study of Shakespeare's sonnets. It does compare certain themes and variations in Shakespeare's sonnets with the work of other poets from the classics to the Elizabethans for the purpose of literary criticism. As the author says 'nowhere else is comparison so possible and so profitable'.

Laurence Lerner's volume on *Shakespeare's Comedies*[35] in the Penguin Shakespeare Library is accurately subtitled *An Anthology of Modern Criticism* since some of the extracts are extremely short. Nine plays are treated, excluding the last plays and the so-called problem comedies—a selection which the editor says reflects merely the wish to have plenty of space and not an elaborate theory of comedy. In an anthology of this kind where 'excellence' is said to be the criterion, everyone will be surprised to find that some critics have been included and others omitted, but the book unquestionably fulfils the editor's purpose in that it will invite, not discourage, further reading.

In *The World and Art of Shakespeare*[36] Adam A. Mendilow and Alice Shalvi have produced a book 'based on teaching Shakespeare at various levels to students in the Department of English at the Hebrew University and we hope that the need to clarify Shakespeare and his world to the foreign student may have resulted in some novel insights'. It has certainly resulted in an admirably clear account of Shakespeare's life and the stage for which he wrote, together with interesting and well balanced chapters on the plays. Shakespeare's England is sufficiently remote from the students at any university for one to wish that this excellent introduction could be published at a price that they might be expected to pay.

The reprints in one volume of A. W. Pollard's *Shakespeare's Fight with the Pirates* and *Shakespeare's Hand in the Play of Sir Thomas More*[37] are of essential works which ought to be on the shelves of every serious student of Shakespeare.

Norman Rabkin's *Shakespeare and*

[33] *Shakespeare Our Contemporary*, by Jan Kott. London: Methuen. pp. xi+308. 35s. 18s. paperback.

[34] *Themes and Variations in Shakespeare's Sonnets*, by J. B. Leishman. London: Hutchinson. pp. 254. 15s.

[35] *Shakespeare's Comedies*, ed. Laurence Lerner. Harmondsworth: Penguin Shakespeare Library. pp. 346. 7s. 6d.

[36] *The World and Art of Shakespeare*, by Adam A. Mendilow and Alice Shalvi. Jerusalem: Israel U.P. New York: D. Davey. pp. viii+285. 42s.

[37] *Shakespeare's Fight with the Pirates* and *Shakespeare's Hand in the Play of Sir Thomas More*, by A. W. Pollard. C.U.P. pp. xxviii+110 and viii+244. 60s.

the *Common Understanding*[38] is one of the most important books on Shakespeare published this year. The title is an indirect acknowledgement of J. Robert Oppenheimer's *Science and the Common Understanding*, and Rabkin is seeking to apply the concept of 'complementarity' to literary criticism. In Rabkin's view this suggests that 'reality when fully understood is more complicated than any simple, logical and coherent reading of it, yet of such a nature that we find ourselves forced constantly to make, and to profit from, simple, logical and coherent readings'. The argument from science to art is still merely an analogy and some may consider it no argument at all. It does, however, confer a great benefit upon the critic because it makes him examine the plays not as the unsubtle statement of some great truth about the world, whether that truth is held to reside in the 'world picture' of Shakespeare's time or in the critic's individual intuition, but as dramatized debates which are concerned with vital human problems which cannot be 'solved' now and for all time but which each individual must somehow answer for himself. The book is mainly concerned with *Hamlet, Troilus and Cressida, Othello, Richard II, Julius Caesar, Coriolanus, Romeo and Juliet, Pericles, Cymbeline, The Winter's Tale* and *The Tempest*. All of these Rabkin treats as 'problem' plays in the same sense that, for him, *Hamlet* is a 'problem' play; 'I am going to argue that what makes it a problem is precisely what makes it Shakespearean. I am going to argue furthermore that the particular nature of the utterly characteristic kind of problem that Shakespeare establishes

in *Hamlet* is responsible for what makes successive generations who agree on little else continue to find him more relevant to their own problems than they do many of their contemporaries.' Rabkin's discussion will illuminate the plays even for those who do not accept his initial scientific analogy.

On Shakespeare's Stage[39] by George F. Reynolds is the text of four lectures given at the Stratford Summer School in 1954. As the editor says, 'the ideas expressed in this book are no longer new', but it is still a good book to turn to for a judicious summing up of the state of knowledge about the Elizabethan theatre— though new views and new discoveries may mean that the views put forward here may have to be modified in the near future.

H. M. Richmond's *Shakespeare's Political Plays*[40] is an interesting discussion of the history plays, *Julius Caesar,* and *Coriolanus.* Mr Richmond's brief half-page account of what he puts forward as the complexities of Shakespeare's personal life may cause the reader to doubt the author's own historical sense. This account in no way supersedes M. M. Reese's *The Cease of Majesty.*

Anne Righter's important *Shakespeare and the Idea of the Play*[41] now makes a welcome appearance in paperback.

In *Shakespeare and English History*[42] William H. Rogers clearly

---

[38] *Shakespeare and the Common Understanding*, by Norman Rabkin. New York: Free Press. London: Collier-Macmillan. pp. x + 267. 25*s*.

[39] *On Shakespeare's Stage*, by George F. Reynolds, ed. by Richard F. Knaub. Boulder: Colorado U.P. pp. 109. $3.95.

[40] *Shakespeare's Political Plays*, by H. M. Richmond. New York: Random House. pp. 241. $1.95.

[41] *Shakespeare and the Idea of the Play*, by Anne Righter. Harmondsworth: Penguin Shakespeare Library. pp. 200. 5*s*.

[42] *Shakespeare and English History*, by William H. Rogers. Totowa: Littlefield, Adams. 1966. pp. vi + 149. $1.75.

intends to provide a volume which may be prescribed on courses on the History plays in North American Universities. It undertakes to provide information at a fairly elementary level which is both necessary and desirable for those who have little or no acquaintance with English history. It is, however, unfortunately true that a book like this is now as necessary for British universities. This one will not quite do – it is too full of expressions like 'the magical touches by which Shakespeare created the imperishable likenesses of his historical characters'—but there is unquestionably a market for books which can provide reliable and basic information.

The Jahrbuch of the Deutsche-Shakespeare Gesellschaft West (footnote 1) is largely devoted to accounts of criticism of stage performances. The papers given at the 1966 meeting of the society in Basel by Claus Bremer, Horst Oppel, Leopold Lindtberg and Ernst Theodor Sehrt are published under the title of 'Podiumsgespräch über Theater und Forschung im Dienste Shakespeares' with a summary of the discussion by Ernst Theodor Sehrt. Karl S. Guthke writing on 'Shakespeare im Urteil der deutschen Theaterkritik des 18. Jahrhunderts', gives an interesting account of German theatrical criticism of performances in the eighteenth century. Robert Hapgood considers Clement Scott's contribution in 'His Heart upon His Sleeve: Clement Scott as a Reviewer of Shakespearian Productions'. William Archer is treated by Hans Schmid in 'Die werktreue Aufführung: Zur Shakespeare-Kritik William Archers', Theodor Fontane as a critic of English performances is discussed by Peter Michelsen in 'Theodor Fontane als Kritiker englisher Shakespeare-Aufführungen' while Fritz Martini examines 'Shake-speare-Aufführungen im Spiegel der Kritik Otto Brahms und Alfred Kerrs'. Peter Loeffler gives an account of 'Bernhard Diebold als Shakespeare-Kritiker'. John Russell Brown looks at 'English Criticism of Shakespeare Performances Today' while Stanley Wells considers 'Shakespeare's Text on the Modern Stage'. Hanns Braun studies 'Ein Shakespeare von innen. Zu Günther Herzfeld-Wüstoffs gesprochen Interpretationen'. In 'Die Funktionen der Gerichtsszene bei Shakespeare und in der Tradition des älteren englischen Dramas' N. Christoph de Nagy examines trial scenes in the classical drama from Aeschylus to Seneca and their use in the Chester and Coventry cycles as well as work such as *The Castle of Perseverance* and *Appius and Virginia* before passing on to an examination of Shakespeare's handling of such scenes. The discussion includes not only such obvious set scenes as those in *Measure for Measure* or *The Merchant of Venice* or *Richard II* but also the effect of justice as administered by Theseus in *A Midsummer Night's Dream* or by the Prince in *Romeo and Juliet*. Rudolph Böhm examines the use of slander scenes in 'Die Verleumdungsszene bei Shakespeare' considering *King Lear II* i 39–87 in detail before surveying the numerous other examples.

In *Shakespeare Jahrbuch*[43] Martin Lehnert writes on 'Shakespeare und Chaucer' and studies the two poets' use of classical poetry, their treatment of characters and ideas, their arts of language, and the varying historical and linguistic conditions of their reputations in the seventeenth century and after. Rolf Rohmer discusses Lessing's contribution to the

---

[43] *Shakespeare Jahrbuch*, ed. by Anselm Schlösser and Armin-Gerd Kuckhoff. Bd. 103. Weimar: Böhlaus. pp. 302.

understanding of Shakespeare in Germany in 'Lessing und Shakespeare', Wolfgang Stellmacher in 'Der junge Herder und Shakespeare' considers Herder's opinion of Shakespeare as 'a poet of history' while in 'Deutsche Klassik und Shakespeare' Wilhelm Girnus argues that Shakespeare has been an overwhelming inspiration for modern German literature: Werther, Götz, Wallenstein, and Faust are unthinkable without a Shakespearian 'Kontaktmetamorphose'. In 'Shakespeare's Sonnets and Pastoral Poetry' Paul A. Bates argues that the sonnets are composed of two plots—the Poet, Fair Youth and Rival Poet in the first 126 sonnets and the Poet, Youth and Dark Lady in the second series. This scheme owes a great deal to the pastoral tradition and to the poetry of Richard Barnfield. Alick West examines 'The Importance of Shakespeare in the Contemporary English Theatre' and appears to find it in the fact that 'We have seen that men have power to end capitalism through socialist revolution'. Robert Weimann studies 'Realismus und Simultankonvention im Misteriendrama, Mimesis, Parodie und Utopie in den Towneley-Hirtenszenen' and describes the interplay of illusion and convention in the drama of the *Prima* and *Secunda Pastorum*. Walther Martin in 'Shakespeare und Cervantes' inquires into their respective attitudes to feudal chivalry and the concept of 'honour', paying special attention to Falstaff and Thersites. *The Two Gentlemen of Verona* is the subject of Anselm Schlösser's paper 'Betrachtungen über *Die beiden Veroneser*' which considers the play in the light of the general theme of love and friendship and the contemporary concept of the gentleman. In 'Über die *Timon*-Bearbeitungen von Dalberg (1789) und Hans Rothe', Dieter Hoffmeier considers two adaptations of the text of *Timon of Athens* while Dieter Görne studies the 1964/5 productions of *The Winter's Tale* and *The Tempest* at the National Theatre in Weimar in 'Bemerkungen zur Konzeption der Aufführungen des *Wintermärchens* und des *Sturms* am Deutschen Nationaltheater Weimar 1964/65'. In an important article 'Notate zu Bertolt Brechts Bearbeitung von Shakespeares *Coriolan*, zur Bühnenfassung und zur Inszenierung des Berliner Ensembles', Dieter Hoffmeier studies the principles of Brecht's adaptation of *Coriolanus* as well as those of the Berliner Ensemble production which is based on it.

Shakespeare Studies III (see footnote 2) contains 'Dr Fludd's Engravings and their Beholders' by Herbert Berry; 'The Language of Paradox in *Romeo and Juliet*' by Joseph S. M. J. Chang; 'A Crux and No Crux in *Hamlet* I iii Safty: Sanctity (21) and Beguide: Beguile (131)' by Thomas Clayton; 'A Re-examination of the "Patient" Pericles' by Thelma N. Greenfield; 'The Two Worlds of Shakespearean Comedy' by Sherman Hawkins; 'A Note on the Aural Errors in the First Quarto of *King Lear*' by Patricia Ingham; 'Bond Slaves and Counterfeits: Shakespeare's *Measure for Measure*' by R. J. Kaufmann; 'The Marriage of True Minds: Truth and Error in Sonnet 116' by Hilton Landry; 'The Masque of Greatness' by Ruth Nevo; 'Prince Hal and Francis: The Imitation of an Action' by J. D. Shuchter; 'The Stage in Robert Fludd's Memory System' by Frances A. Yates; 'Review Article. The New Arden *Henry VI*, Parts I, II, and III' by Robert K. Turner, Jr.; 'Shakespeare's Other Ovid: A Reproduction of Commentary on Metamorphoses I-IV' as well as a number of important reviews.

The articles by Herbert Berry and Frances A. Yates are both concerned with the five engravings of what appear to be stages in Robert Fludd's *Ars Memoriae* (1619) and both refer to I. A. Shapiro's article in *Shakespeare Studies II* (*YW* xlvii. 143–4). Berry believes that at present it is not possible to use Fludd's engravings as evidence for the English stage and suspects that 'they are a mélange which is generally continental'. He argues that 'we should not juggle the details of the engravings to fit other evidence or our own theories' and he believes that 'Miss Yates has played this game so diligently that in her reconstruction almost nothing remains of Fludd's detailed engraving save four doorways, the general shape of the oriel, the battlements and the facing on the walls'. The engravings, then, represent neither the Globe, as Miss Yates has claimed, nor the Blackfriars—as argued by Shapiro. In her own article Miss Yates examines a number of points where Shapiro appears to have misunderstood her original arguments. She then goes on to argue that 'the Jacobean stage belonged into the memory system and was to be used in the mnemonics' and that Robert Fludd argues against the use of imaginary buildings in the art of memory. Miss Yates draws attention to a passage in which 'the reader is here clearly warned that Fludd will use real, and not imaginary, buildings in his art of memory, that cubicles within those buildings will be based on reality, and that five memory places on a cubicle wall will be real places on a real wall'. This can hardly be described as 'juggled' evidence, and it seems possible to argue that we must interpret the engravings in Fludd's book in accordance with the evidence of his text. None of Miss Yates's opponents have so far shown any sign of engaging with these problems.

Sherman Hawkins uses an archetypal approach to Shakespearian comedy and adds to Northrop Frye's classification of the 'green world' comedies what he calls the 'alternate pattern'. 'In the comedies we are now describing, the characters stay put, but they are visited by outsiders, who upset the routine of the community into which they come.' The main examples are *Love's Labour's Lost, Much Ado about Nothing, Twelfth Night* and *The Comedy of Errors*. The purpose of this distinction, we are told, is really directed at the four major tragedies which divide 'with almost embarrassing neatness' into tragedies of the 'closed' or of the 'green' world. Mr Hawkins says that 'the detailed workings of these patterns in the tragedies is matter for a longer study'. On this evidence it is not one that the reader is likely to look forward to with much enthusiasm.

A large part of the volume is given up to the reproduction of George Sandys' commentary on Books I–IV of the Metamorphoses from *Ovid's Metamorphosis. Englished, Mythologiz'd And Represented in Figures* (1630). This is intended 'to continue what will be an annual exploration of such material as may increase our understanding of well-known traditions'. It is certainly important that attention should be drawn to Sandys and his work, but the extracts here published, including the dedication and prefatory poems, are not a text which can be used with any confidence for scholarly purposes, while the interests of the layman might be better served by exposition instead of reproduction. One suspects that this is therefore a large and expensive part of the volume which will never be used. The 'exploration' promised by the editor is very necessary but this apology for scholarly proceeding hardly provides it. Among the excellent reviews contained in this volume special attention ought to be drawn to R. W. Dent's consideration of J. M. Nosworthy's *Shakespeare's Occasional Plays* (*YW* xlvi. 143).

Shakespeare Studies: Volume 5[44] published by the Shakespeare Society of Japan contains 'Time and Truth in *King Lear*' by Soji Iwasaki; '*King Lear* and Its Tragic Pattern' by Toshikazu Oyama; 'The Homiletic Tradition in Shakespeare's Plays' by Peter Milward S. J. and 'The Three Themes in One Harmonious Chord' by Takako Uchiyama. These articles will be discussed under the separate plays.

Shakespeare Survey 20 (see footnote 3) contains 'Shakespeare, Fletcher and Baroque Tragedy' by Marco Mincoff; 'Seneca and the Elizabethans: A Case-study in "Influence"' by G. K. Hunter; 'George Chapman: Tragedy and the Providential View of History' by G. R. Hibbard; 'Critical Disagreement about Oedipus and Hamlet' by Nigel Alexander; 'Shakespeare's Thematic Modes of Speech: *Richard II* to *Henry V*' by Robert Hapgood; 'Anarchy and Order in *Richard III* and *King John*' by Ronald Berman; 'The Staging of Parody and Parallels in *1 Henry IV*' by John Shaw; 'Shakespeare's Unnecessary Characters' by Arthur C. Sprague; 'Walter Whiter's Notes on Shakespeare' by Mary Bell; 'Shakespeare's *Romeo and Juliet*: Its Spanish Source' by Oscar M. Villarejo; 'The Grieves Shakespearian Scene Designs' by Sybil Rosenfeld; 'Shakespeare on the Modern Stage: Past Significance and Present Meaning' by Robert Weimann; 'Shakespeare in Brazil' by Barbara Heliodora C. de M. F. de Almeida; 'Recent Shakespeare Performances in Romania' by Alexandru

Dutu; 'Shakespeare, the Twentieth Century and "Behaviourism"' by Gareth L. Evans, and 'The Year's Contribution to Shakespearian Study' as previously mentioned.

In comparing Shakespearian and other tragedy Marco Mincoff argues that 'what stands out most markedly is the different approach to the presentation of man himself—man seen in the round as an individual, differentiated in his reactions and behaviour, in the aura of imagery that he carries with him, in his very speech rhythms, as with Othello and Iago, and man at most rather superficially differentiated into a few basic types, as a conductor of various currents of emotion, reacting seismographically to every little impulse'. This article presents an interesting view of the relation of the Beaumont and Fletcher plays to Elizabethan tragedy and to the later tragedy whose chief representative in England was Dryden. *The Maid's Tragedy* is particularly well handled.

G. K. Hunter considers that J. W. Cunliffe's 'The Influence of Seneca on Elizabethan Tragedy' (1893) still represents the 'common assumptions' about the influence of Seneca and sets out, first, to dispute the relevance of many of the supposed parallel passages cited by Cunliffe. In *The Spanish Tragedy* and *Titus Andronicus* 'Seneca all but disappears into the engulfing sea of Ovidian and quasi-Ovidian imitation', and the Elizabethan theatre owes more to the Gothic tradition, so that one can see, 'inside a single acting tradition, a gradual but continuous adaptation of the discursive and moralizing drama of the late Middle Ages into the polydimensional story-drama of mature theatre'.

Robert Hapgood's thesis is that 'just as Shakespeare's characters in a given play tend to use the same words and images, they also tend to use the

[44] *Shakespeare Studies: Volume Five* (1966–1967) ed. by Jiro Ozu. Tokyo: The Shakespeare Society of Japan. pp. 156.

same 'modes' of speech. For instance *Hamlet*, one of the few plays in which this characteristic has been noted, is full of questions'. He goes on to examine the 'modes' used in *Richard II, 1 Henry IV, 2 Henry IV* and *Henry V*. The 'mode' of *Richard II* is denunciation and the varying modes of the plays then proceed through 'retrospection', 'true and false report' and 'dispute'. 'What stands out most of all is the sequence of anti-modes which Shakespeare gives Harry Monmouth: in a world of retrospection, his is the voice of the future; in a world of false report, his speech is direct and true; in a world of dispute, his call is to concord. Whatever the prevailing mode, and however advanced the general decay of language, Shakespeare always lets us hear in his voice its heroic opposite.'

Ronald Berman distinguishes *Richard III* and *King John* from the other history plays 'by tough, cynical and realistic wit on the part of those whose business it is to maintain the idealized image of monarchy'. Both plays end 'with a kind of apotheosis in which history is visualized as the servant of law. They have confronted the egocentric, anarchic nature of the individual with the ideals of order. Yet their real issues have been neither the "monstrosity" of Richard nor the ruthlessness of the Bastard, but the rationalism and materialism which are *representative* qualities of humanity'.

Arthur C. Sprague examines the 'easy assurance on the playwright's part that the company for whom he wrote was able to cope with a great many minor roles, as many conceivably as he cared to insert'. The parts of Lovel in *Richard III*, Gloucester in *Henry V*, Cicero, Cinna the Poet and the Second Poet in *Julius Caesar*, the Third Murderer in *Macbeth*, the Archbishop of York in *1 Henry IV*, Barnadine in *Measure for Measure*, Fabian in *Twelfth Night* and Peto in *I Henry IV* are studied—parts which served a variety of purposes, sometimes with purposes 'closely related to the gravest concerns of the play' whose purposes 'are easy to detect', although in some cases 'we can only guess at them—and with no great confidence that we have guessed right'.

Mary Bell studies a collection of notebooks and loose papers of Walter Whiter in the Cambridge University Library which contains 'further comments on textual and interpretative problems in at least twenty-four of Shakespeare's plays, excluding some of the histories and all of the Roman tragedies'. This provides interesting light on the *Specimen of a Commentary on Shakespeare* recently reprinted, and it is arguable that 'Whiter deserves more credit than he is usually allowed for having laid the foundations of many so-called "modern" trends of thought on Shakespeare'.

Sybil Rosenfeld gives an account of the work of the Grieve family up to the death of J. H. Grieve in 1845. There are eight designs only among the more than six hundred designs in the University of London Library which are assigned to Shakespeare in a contemporary hand. These designs are discussed and illustrated.

In an important article Robert Weimann argues that 'Today *any* Shakespeare staging has to come to terms with the tension between Renaissance values and modern evaluations. But this contradiction is not necessarily frustrating, and it may well be said that it constitutes an important element in the resulting production'. This means that the director and the critic must take account of both, since 'the modernized Shakespeare is no more acceptable than the museum version'. The way in which this can be achieved is then illustrated by a discussion of two productions of *Hamlet* in the GDR at the Deutsches Theater, Berlin, and Städtische Theater, Karl-Marx-Stadt.

Barbara de Almeida comments on the 'short and sad story of Shakespeare in Brazil', and Alexandru Dutu discusses recent performances and translations of the plays in Romania. Gareth L. Evans discusses the recent work of the Royal Shakespeare Company at Stratford.

Joseph Satin's account of *Shakespeare and His Sources*[45] will no doubt be widely used by undergraduates who are unable to obtain Geoffrey Bullough's *Narrative and Dramatic Sources of Shakespeare*. This book does not claim to be so comprehensive since it only deals with *Richard III, Richard II, The Merchant of Venice, 1Henry IV, 2Henry IV, Henry V, Julius Caesar, Twelfth Night, Hamlet, Othello, King Lear, Macbeth*, and *Antony and Cleopatra*. It is, however, a little disturbing to find the *True Tragedy of Richard III* given among the 'sources' of *Richard III* when the only argument that can be adduced for this is that 'Another basic source for *Richard III* is *The True Tragedy of Richard III*, an anonymous play first published in 1594 in the wake of the success of *Richard III* but certainly written much earlier, as its dramatic crudeness attests'. Professor Satin's choice is, however, in the main judicious and the book will be a useful one.

S. Schoenbaum has an interesting paper on 'Editing English Dramatic Texts' in *Editing Sixteenth Century Texts*,[46] which is a survey of current practice and problems, including dis-cussion of some of the series of Renaissance texts which are now in progress.

Peter J. Seng's *The Vocal Songs in the Plays of Shakespeare*[47] is a scholarly and important book. It gives the text of all the songs reproduced from the earliest authoritative editions, a general critical commentary arranged according to date, a textual commentary arranged according to date, information about music for the song (although no music is actually printed in this volume), information concerning sources or analogues for the song, and a discussion of the dramatic function of the song in the play. A great deal of information is thus brought together in one volume for convenient reference. There are, of course, a number of omissions. It is surprising, for example, to find in the commentary on *Love's Labour's Lost* v ii 904–921 no reference to J. W. Lever's 'Three Notes on Shakespeare's Plants' (*RES* 1952) with its comment on the colour ascribed to 'lady-smocks', and while it is consistent editorial policy not to include the Witches' songs from *Macbeth* (since no certain text for them exists) it is inconvenient not to have any information about them available in such a volume.

J. L. Styan's *Shakespeare's Stagecraft*[48] is a disappointing book. It is more often Mr Styan's stagecraft that is in question than Shakespeare's, and the book tends to include observations at the level of 'Total theatre implies a total assault upon the spectator's mind and senses. Othello and Iago are black and white to increase our sensitivity to their

[45] *Shakespeare and His Sources*, by Joseph Satin. 1966. Boston: Houghton Mifflin. pp. xii+623.

[46] *Editing Sixteenth Century Texts: Papers Given at the Editorial Conference, University of Toronto 1965*, ed. by R. J. Schoeck, Toronto U.P. 1966. pp. 137. $5.00.

[47] *The Vocal Songs in The Plays of Shakespeare: A Critical History*, by Peter J. Seng. Cambridge: Harvard U.P. pp. xix+314. $8.95.

[48] *Shakespeare's Stagecraft*, by J. L. Styan. Cambridge U.P. pp. viii+244. 45s. $7.95.

qualities of good and evil'. This is a pity, because the basic thesis of the book ('It is Shakespeare's habit to build upon the actor's living contribution to the scene and allow the actor to build upon his own keen suggestions') is important and should certainly govern our approach to the plays.

Claus Uhlig's *Traditionelle Denkformen in Shakespeares tragischer Kunst*[49] is concerned with traditional concepts such as Conscience, the Love–Lust opposition, Time, and Grief, and traces Shakespeare's treatment of them through the poems and many of the plays. Since it is a dissertation, much of the material is extremely condensed, but Dr. Uhlig's reading has been wide and his many references to Renaissance literature are valuable and illuminating.

In *Discussions of Shakespeare's Romantic Comedy*[50] Herbert Weil has collected 'Shakespearean Comedy' by Lord David Cecil; 'General Observations on the Comedies' by Samuel Johnson; 'The Virtues of Malvolio' by Charles Lamb; 'Too Good-Natured for Comedy' by William Hazlitt; 'Romantic Nonsense' by George Bernard Shaw; 'Two Comedies' by Francis Fergusson; '*Much Ado About Nothing*' by A. P. Rossiter; 'The Success of *Much Ado About Nothing*' by Graham Storey; '*As You Like It*' by Helen Gardner; 'The Alliance of Seriousness and Levity in *As You Like It*' by C. L. Barber; 'Rosalind and Touchstone' by Harold C. Goddard; 'Touchstone Defended' by John Palmer; '*Twelfth Night*' by

G. K. Hunter; 'The Design of *Twelfth Night* and Its Sources' by L. G. Salingar; 'The Masks of *Twelfth Night*' by Joseph H. Summers; '*Twelfth Night* and the Morality of Indulgence' by John Hollander; 'Comic Myth in Shakespeare' by Northrop Frye. The editor contributes an introduction which is itself an interesting essay on Shakespearian Comedy.

Shakespeare und die Tradition des Volkstheaters[51] by Robert Weimann is a re-interpretation of Shakespeare and the popular dramatic tradition. It is concerned with the traditional function and structure of word-play, proverb, 'aside', couplet, nonsense, madness, and clowning. It examines figures such as Jack Finney, Garcio, the Vice, and Herod, and structural principles such as that of 'polarity' and the double plot. It takes account of the sociology and dramaturgy of the 'scene individible': the platform stage and the synthesis of realism and convention, illusion and audience awareness. It considers Tarlton, Shakespeare and popular myth; and the popular tradition and contemporary criticism. One can only regret that there will not soon be an English translation available.

Walter Whiter's *A Specimen of a Commentary on Shakespeare*[52] has now been edited by Alan Over and Mary Bell. It offers the text of the 1794 edition as it had been revised by the author, although it was never published in this revised form. The work consists of a first section containing notes on *As You Like It* and a second section which is 'An Attempt to Explain and Illustrate Various

[49] *Traditionelle Denkformen in Shakespeares tragischer Kunst*, by Claus Uhlig. (Britannica et Americana Band 15). Hamburg: Cram, de Gruyter & Co. pp. ix + 206.

[50] *Discussions of Shakespeare's Romantic Comedy* ed. by Herbert Weil, Jr. Boston: D. C. Heath. London: Harrap. pp. xvii + 142. 15s. 6d.

[51] *Shakespeare und die Tradition des Volkstheaters*, by Robert Weimann. Berlin: Henschelverlag. pp. 552.

[52] *A Specimen of a Commentary on Shakespeare* (1794), by Walter Whiter. ed. by Alan Over and Mary Bell. London: Methuen. pp. 304. 65s.

Passages of Shakespeare on a New Principle of Criticism, derived from Mr Locke's Doctrine of the Association of Ideas'. This is an important work, and the editors have done a very valuable service in again presenting it to students of Shakespeare.

Although there are only five references to Shakespeare in the index of Edgar Wind's new edition of *Pagan Mysteries in the Renaissance*[53] it is an essential book for any understanding of the Renaissance and its drama. This impressive and fascinating work of scholarship examines the symbolism of some of the great works of art of Botticelli and Michelangelo and their use of the hermetic symbolism. The full application of these discoveries to English Renaissance drama has still to be made.

4. GENERAL ARTICLES

In 'Why Not Costume Shakespeare According to Shakespeare' (*ETJ*) Lucy Barton argues for the use of the kind of costume clearly indicated by the text of the plays on the ground that this helps the actor; 'Wearing English Renaissance garments with confidence he uses them and is used by them to make visible to the audience the spoken word, that text which is the reason for the presentation of Shakespeare'.

A number of important questions for the editor of any English text are considered by F. W. Bateson in his 'Editorial Commentary' (*EC*). His views provoked a reply from J. C. Maxwell which is printed together with Bateson's reply under the title of 'Textual Criticism and its Problems'. Elinor Bevan studies the Elizabethan and Renaissance attitude to revenge in 'Revenge, Forgiveness and the Gentleman' (*REL*) and makes

the important distinction that 'Passionate revenge, undertaken in passion, should be avoided by an exercise of self-restraint and temperance: the conflict being one between emotion and intellect. But revenge deliberately undertaken for honour's sake cannot be prevented by self-restraint for, theoretically, it contains no element of passion to be controlled'. Ian Donaldson discusses the relation of Shakespeare criticism to stage presentation in 'Shakespeare Observed' (*Oxford Review*), and in an important article 'The Arts of Memory and Poetry' (*ES*) J. A. van Dorsten relates the Renaissance arts of memory, discussed by Frances A. Yates in her book *The Art of Memory* (*YW* xlvii. 1966), to Sir Philip Sidney's *Defence of Poetry* showing that the arguments which Sidney uses show an awareness of the memory arts.

John W. Draper studies 'Shakespeare and the Problem of Evil' (*Philological Papers* 1966) and traces a development up to *Antony and Cleopatra* and *Coriolanus*, where 'at last Shakespeare attributes Evil to causes more universal than mere social non-conformity and more subjective than the astrological science of his day'. Since Mr Draper's footnotes contain thirty-four references to his own writings, no one should be in any doubt about his opinions on these matters.

William Empson, reviewing Maynard Mack's *King Lear in Our Time*, observed that the variant spellings of 'bastard': 'barstard' at *King Lear* I. ii. 10 reflected a general distinction between high-born bastards and low-born barstards. This caused a further comment by J. C. Maxwell and a reply by Empson 'Bastards and Barstards' (*EC*).

Stanley G. Eskin in 'Politics in Shakespeare's Plays' (*Bu R*) argues that 'The political themes in English

---

[53] *Pagan Mysteries in the Renaissance*, by Edgar Wind. Harmondsworth: Penguin Books. pp. xiii+345. 25s.

Renaissance drama range between two poles: one, the representation and glorification of the Renaissance monarchic principle particularized in the House of Tudor; the other, the utterly deteriorated political chaos of Webster, Tourneur, and some of Shakespeare'. From this there follows the distinction that 'The Roman plays, then, are not at all touched by the great Renaissance ideal of a static order. The politics of the Roman plays are a politics of flux with no redemption in sight from the flux'.

G. Blakemore Evans offers 'New Evidence on the Provenance of the Padua Prompt-Books of Shakespeare's *Macbeth, Measure for Measure* and *Winter's Tale*' (*SB*).

In an important note 'Bacon-Shakespeare: The Tobie Matthew Postscript' (*Sh Q*) J. P. Feil dates Matthew's letter to Bacon in April or early May 1619 when Matthew was in Belgium and points out that the postscript contains no reference to Francis Bacon but is concerned with Robert Southwell who was at that time on the continent using the alias Thomas Bacon. Ann D. Ferguson in 'A Brief Comparison of Supernatural Elements in *Richard III* and *Macbeth*' (*Gordon Review* IX 1966) considers that 'Shakespeare's basic grasp of the function of the supernatural in his dramas is essentially the same, whether early or late in his writing'. Fresh evidence about the 'best bed' is produced by Elaine W. Fowler who shows in 'The Earl of Bedford's "Best" Bed' (*Sh Q*) that in his will of September 20th 1585 the Earl left his best bed not to his wife but to 'my Lady of Cumberland, my daughter, wife to the said Earl'.

Arthur Efron and Robert Hapgood engage in a dialogue on 'Shakespeare's Negated Myths?' (*Paunch* 1966) debating Efron's argument that in Shakespeare's plays 'the ritual renewal is never going to happen'. 'Introducing Shakespeare' (*EJ*) by John F. Gleason describes his success in using the sonnets as an introduction to the study of Shakespeare. Richard Harrier adds to C. H. Hobday's study in *Sh Q* XVI (*YW* xlvi. 156) in 'Another Note on "Why the Sweets Melted"' (*Sh Q*) by suggesting that the sweets thrown at pageants may be part of the association between melting sweets and flattery. J. Hardy examines the eighteenth-century concept, derived from the Renaissance, that poetry should instruct as well as delight and finds one of its main effects in the quest for self knowledge, in 'The "Poet of Nature" and Self-Knowledge: One Aspect of Johnson's Moral Reading of Shakespeare' (*UT Q*). In 'The Villain and the Happy End of Shakespeare Comedy' (*RP* 1966) T. Walter Herbert examines the way in which the villain is, in the early comedies, 'convincingly deprived of all his power' until in *Twelfth Night* 'Shakespeare has taken some pains for the first time to incorporate the authentic unchanged enemy of joy into the world that permits a happy ending for young lovers' so that 'Happiness at the end of the later comedies exists in a perilous world. Viola, Mariana, Perdita, and Miranda must sustain their happiness in a world where villains play considerable roles'.

'Shakespeare, Richard Edwards and the Virtues Reconciled' (*JEGP*) by Allan Holaday is concerned with the allegory of the Parliament of Heaven and the expressed conflict between Justice and Mercy in Tudor-Stuart drama. The connexion between this allegory and Richard Edwards's *Damon and Pythias* is discussed; 'it supplies a useful commentary on several cryptic episodes in other works, among them the trial scene in the *Merchant of*

Venice', but this commentary is not elaborated.

It is a little surprising to find *Macbeth* described as a 'tentative venture into the field of witchcraft' by R. Holmes in 'Shakespeare and Witchcraft' (*QR*) but there is a useful table showing the relationship between plays and witchcraft from 1550 to 1650.

'On the Indifferent and One-Way Variants in Shakespeare' (*Lib*) by E. A. J. Honigmann is an article of major importance for all future editors of Renaissance dramatic texts. At the moment 'the fashionable course is to put one's faith in the better text, following it whenever the variants seem to be truly indifferent – on the assumption that in any one text the general mass of indifferent and substantive variants will be corrupt in much the same proportions'. Instead 'an editor ought to study the indifferent variants together with substantive ones as a single group. For the manifest errors in the group may well reveal a predisposition to error in one text, or in one compositor or copyist. At the very worst the incidence of manifest errors will indicate whether or not the generally inferior text (if any) is also inferior in this category'. In fact the editor must go further than this, since the whole question of indifferent variants 'must be pegged down by the fact of the printing house before we can hope to discuss it profitably'. Consequently 'Before editing any single play surviving in two good texts one must check on all its indifferent variants in the other Quartos and the whole Folio and, if necessary, in other books produced by the printers of the two substantive versions. Having isolated post-authorial substitutions one may then turn to the indifferent variants that remain, using, I repeat, much more editorial freedom than was allowed by the better-text theory'. The examples offered amply support and justify these statements and if the editor's labours are made more arduous they may also be made more exact.

Richard Hosley studies 'Elizabethan Theatres and Audiences' (*Research Opportunities in Renaissance Drama*), and reminds us that a survey of the theatres must include the inn yards, the 'academic' theatres, and the Court theatres, as well as the public and private theatres. The size, shape, and capacity of these buildings are considered and a particularly interesting study is made of the way in which the King's Men were probably responsible for the gradual introduction of the customs of the private theatre into the public ones. This paper provides an introduction to the revaluation of our knowledge of the Elizabethan theatres that is now in progress.

Lois Josephs, in 'Shakespeare and a Coleridgean Synthesis: Cleopatra, Leontes and Falstaff' (*Sh Q*), attempts to reconstruct some of the fragments concerning Cleopatra, Leontes and Falstaff which, 'obviously related to his critical method and provocative enough to excite interest, emerge in Coleridge's criticism' into a valid critical interpretation.

In an important article William S. Kable studies 'The Influence of Justification on Spelling in Jaggard's Compositor B'. (*SB*) This study is based upon the comprehensive analysis which Kable has made of the spellings of Jaggard's compositor B in the Pavier Quartos.

David Klein argues that the standard 'two hour traffic' of the Elizabethan stage was in fact much closer to three hours in 'Time Allotted for an Elizabethan Performance' (*Sh Q*) while in 'De longues notes sur de brefs passages shakespeariens' (*Ea*),

G. Lambin is concerned with a number of passages in *All's Well That Ends Well*. The names Charbon and Poysam (I iii 48–60) are explained by a French proverb (although a similar explanation already appears in the New Arden edition) and the retention of Astringer in the stage direction at V i is advocated. The voyage of Pericles is also examined and related to the reasons that caused *Pericles* to be performed before the ambassador of the King of France.

In 'The Dramatists' Independence' (*Research Opportunities in Renaissance Drama*) Clifford Leech is concerned to stress 'the influence of a genre or sub-genre that became established through some major new work – *Tamburlaine* or *Hamlet*, for example—with the corollary that a prime influence on the dramatists came from within their own profession as writers: they were perhaps as much concerned with the idea of a particular kind of play as with providing suitable fare for the Globe or the Red Bull, suitable parts for this or that player'. This is a difficult subject since the evidence on which this kind of influence depends is difficult to assess, but the approach is suggestive and interesting. Richard Levin offers a new view of 'The Unity of Elizabethan Multiple-Plot Drama' (*ELH*) which concentrates upon *As You Like It* and *King Lear*.

'T. S. Eliot and Shakespeare' (*Criticism*) by Phillip Marcus, though more concerned with Eliot than with Shakespeare, is of great interest as a clear, systematic account of Eliot's criticism of Shakespeare which reveals, as the author claims, 'not only a number of highly interesting and idiosyncratic responses to Shakespeare's work, but also a clear and striking evolution of Eliot's views that illuminate at several points his own

changing perspectives as a thinker and writer'.

Louis Marder has a very timely article on 'Problems of Computer Scholarship' (*SNL*) arguing that it is extremely necessary to reach some kind of international agreement on the coding system for Shakespeare's works and that a Computer Conference on Shakespeare ought to be arranged to see if some of the problems of Shakespearian scholarship could not be solved on a co-operative basis. The need for this is emphasized by further articles (in *SNL*) by Marder on 'Shakespeare Concordances: 1787-1967', 'The Spevack Shakespeare Concordance' and by T. H. Howard-Hill, 'Shakespeare: The Clarendon Press Concordance'. To have two new concordances seems an unnecessary duplication of expensive effort, and they will not be compatible since they are keyed to different editions of the works of Shakespeare.

Professor Marder also claims to have discovered a new 'authenticated' copy of the Stratford bust in 'The Stratford Bust—A New Authenticated Copy' (*NQ*)—a unique copy made by Lewis Nochalls Cottingham.

Sister Marian Frances studies the way in which 'Shakespeare uses prayer as insight into character motivation, situation, and as a means of foreshadowing' in 'Prayer as Insight in Shakespeare' (*Gordon Review* IX).

In '"Black Chaos": Shakespeare and Muretus' (*NQ*) J. C. Maxwell comments on the lines 'black chaos comes again' (*Venus and Adonis* 1020) and 'chaos is come again', (*Othello* III iii 93) 'and shows that T. W. Baldwin mistranslates a line from Muretus in his comment on these passages—a mistake perhaps caused by his failure to consult the fullest version of Malone's note on the passage. 'Unavoided' (*NQ*) by the same author questions whether the use of this word in the sense of 'unavoidable' or 'inevitable' can be, as the OED suggests, confined to Shakespeare.

In 'Shakespeare Today: Two Talks for Radio' (*HAB*) G. S. McCaughey suggests that 'certain obvious questions, not so much new as unanswered, have been totally lost sight of'. One must assume that some of these questions re-emerge in this discussion of *Henry V* and the comedies.

In 'John Shakespeare's "Spiritual Testament"' (*Sh Q*) James G. Mc-Manaway discusses the recent discovery of an English printing of the formulary used in the 'Spiritual Testament' of John Shakespeare transcribed and printed by Malone in his 1790 edition of Shakespeare. Printed in 1638, its title is *The Contract and Testament of the Soule* and it indicates that 'the five leaves of the Spiritual Testament sent to Malone must have been genuine, even though the identity of the testator cannot now be established'.

Alexandra Mason discusses the fact that Cuthbert Burbage was fined for not taking up knighthood on the accession of Charles I in 'The Social Status of Theatrical People' (*Sh Q*) and concludes that 'In 1639 a theatre proprietor could be considered eligible for knighthood at least for purposes of taxation'.

In an important article Kenneth Muir examines 'Image and Symbol in Shakespeare's Histories' (*BJRL*) observing that 'the stage imagery (in *Richard III*) throws light on Richard's role and character. His hypocrisy may be regarded as the application of the actor's art to real life'. The conclusion of this study shows that 'there is no iterative imagery in the earliest Histories; that there are traces of it in *Richard III* and a whole complex of patterns of imagery in *Richard II*; that there is iterative imagery in

King John, which, however, throws little light on the theme of the play; that there is no such imagery in *1 Henry IV*; that the sickness imagery of *2 Henry IV* contributes a great deal to its atmosphere; and that the weighing down and shipwreck imagery of *Henry VIII* would seem to indicate that if there were two authors they worked in close harmony'.

Readers of Joan Mulholland's interesting article '"Thou" and "You" in Shakespeare: A Study in the Second Person Pronoun' (*ES*) should not miss the correction on p. 163.

Gerd Müller studies 'Brecht, Shakespeare und das epische Theater' (*Moderna Språk*) and in a brief article gives an account of Brecht's theories of Shakespeare, some reasons for finding them unsatisfactory, and relates them to Gunter Grass's *The Plebeians Rehearse the Revolution.*

Norman Nathan considers that production of the plays is the best way to reveal the craft of the dramatist, in 'Shakespeare: "The Play's the Thing"' (*EJ*).

In 'Shakespeare's Dress in His Portraits' (*Sh Q*) J. L. Nevinson examines the details of dress shown in the Chandos portrait, the wall monument at Stratford and the Droeshout engraving and concludes that 'The suggestion that the costume of the Droeshout engraving is in no way derived from the Stratford monument cannot be accepted'.

In 'Shakespeare at Work in his Theatre' (*ETJ*) B. Iden Payne sets out to ask the question 'whether, in constructing his plays, he held in mind and made use of the facilities of the theatre in which they were performed', but the actual article is more concerned with the application of what the author calls 'modified Elizabethan staging' to *The Merchant of Venice.*

Robert K. Presson discusses 'Two Types of Dreams in the Elizabethan Drama, and their Heritage: *Somnium Animale* and the Prick-of-Conscience' (*SEL*) and examines their place in *Romeo and Juliet, 1 Henry IV, 2 Henry VI*, and *Richard III*. This is a clear, interesting and important article.

In examining Arend van Buchell's copy of De Witt's sketch of the Swan theatre again, D. F. Rowan in 'The "Swan" Revisited' (*Research Opportunities in Renaissance Drama*) gives a historical survey of the difficulties raised by the drawing and the theories which attempt to explain them. As he says, 'the vast bulk of this important work remains to be done'.

John Sibly studies 'The Duty of Revenge in Tudor and Stuart Drama' (*REL*) and argues that 'The Elizabethans and Jacobeans made a clear distinction, taken for granted in most of their plays, between a king who ruled badly, even one whose title was perhaps weak, and a usurper or a regicide; one who had gained the throne by killing the previous occupant.'

In 'Their Exits and Re-entrances' (*Sh Q*) Irwin Smith points out that, in general, 'Shakespeare avoided having a character enter the stage at the beginning of an act or scene after having been on-stage at the end of the preceding act or scene'. A distinction, he says however, must be made between the Globe, where such a re-entrance would involve a character walking back on to the stage immediately he had left it, and the Blackfriars where the act divisions make such a re-entry possible. The re-entrance of Prospero and Ariel in Acts IV and V of *The Tempest* is clearly due to the performance at the Blackfriars. The article considers sixteen possible violations of this apparent law of re-entry. 'Shakespeare's Last Plays: Facts and Problems' (*Shakespearean Research Opportunities*) by Hallett Smith indicates ways in which a useful contribution can still be made to the study of Shakespeare's last plays.

'Hero and Villain in Shakespeare: on Dualism and Tragedy' (*TSL*) by Marvin Spevack is a demonstration that 'tragic drama, although distinctively of western origin and assuredly a life-and-death struggle, is not finally the dualistic conflict we often make it out to be'. It is shown that 'In the ten dramas which are generally recognized as tragedies, for example, Shakespeare's restraint in employing villains is striking, especially when we consider the weight which he and his contemporaries placed on boldly conceived characters, exciting dramatic situations, and vivid, if not melodramatic, theatrical effects'. Spevack concludes that 'the scarcity of fixed oppositions is consistent with an attitude which considers dualism too simple, too insensitive, and perhaps even too inaccurate a representation of and response to tragedy'.

In 'Anthony and John Nash: Shakespeare's Legatees' (*NQ*) Christopher Whitfield investigates two brothers who were left small legacies in Shakespeare's will to buy mourning rings and shows that they were moderately well-off country gentlemen. In the same journal Whitfield also provides information on 'The Stratford Riots of 1619 and Richard Dover of Evesham: Robert Dover and Sir Baptist Hicks'.

'The Cockpit Reconstructed' (*New Theatre Magazine*) is an important article by Glynne Wickham which deduces from F. P. Wilson's transcript of the Office of Works accounts that the Cockpit in Court as remodelled by Inigo Jones for Charles I opened as early as October 1630 and that we are now equipped with a plan and elevation that can be directly compared with the De Witt drawing and the plans for the Hope and Fortune. Shakespeare's company was the first to use the new theatre in 1630.

'Two "Missing" Shakespeare Documents' (*NQ*) by Michael Wilding reports the presence of the wills of Robert Arden and his second wife Agnes Arden, mother of Mary Arden, in the Worcestershire Record Office.

George P. Wilson in 'Shakespeare and Southern Folklore' (*Ga R*) shows that 'a great deal of folklore in the South is also found in Shakespeare'.

5. INDIVIDUAL PLAYS AND POEMS

All's Well That Ends Well

Josephine Waters Bennett examines 'New Techniques of Comedy in *All's Well That Ends Well*' (*ShQ*) and argues that the play shows 'a marked advance in technique' over *Measure for Measure*. That there is a deliberate relationship between the plays is shown by the repetition of the bed-trick but in this case the part of Helena and the author's careful control of the sympathies of the audience make it a better play. In the event 'Shakespeare has carried even further in this play than in *Measure for Measure* his experiments in representing serious and potentially tragic (or at least fatal) situations so controlled by various artifices as to prevent sympathy from destroying comedy'. This article is an important step in the overdue revaluation of this play.

Antony and Cleopatra

'Dramatic Irony in Antony and Cleopatra' (*Sh Q*) by William Blissett, a paper given to the Renaissance Society of America in Cleveland in 1962, cannot be said to increase our understanding of the play. John P. Cutts examines I ii 25 in 'Char-

mian's "Excellent Fortune"' (*ANQ*) and links the scriptural reference which Zielinski saw in this passage to Elizabeth, mother of John the Baptist.

In 'The Masque of Greatness' (*Sh St*) Ruth Nevo observes that 'it is by now a commonplace that popular pageant and court masque—in its heyday in England at the time of Shakespeare's late plays—combined to form the theatrical imagination of the time. Yet, even when one is prepared to find the poet-dramatist and the masque-librettist sharing a world of symbols and images, the resemblance between Cleopatra's dream of Antony and Jonson's *Masque of Hymen* (written for the Twelfth Night of 1605 to celebrate the ill-starred marriage of Essex to the Lady Frances Howard) is startling'. The article argues that it is this 'theatre-metaphor of the masque in the final Act' which determines the relationship of the various elements in the play. H. W. Piper in 'Shakespeare's *Antony and Cleopatra* V ii 279–281' (*Ex*) examines the Christian symbolism of 'robe' and 'crown' and compares St. Mark 14.25 'drink no more of the fruit of the vine'.

As You Like It

'Ducdame' (*Sh Q*) by Richard Knowles is an extremely interesting examination of the possible meanings of Jacques's invocation. The balance of the evidence seems to lie in favour of duc d'âme (s). In '*As You Like It* as the Augustans Liked It' (*ANQ*) LeRoy J. Morrissey discusses Charles Johnson's adaptation of 1723, *Love in a Forest*. It is significant that in cutting away the 'low' characters Johnson also cut away the comedy. II iii 59–60 is the subject of H. J. Oliver's 'An Alleged Variant in *As You Like It*' (*NQ*). Furness records the variant 'neede' for 'meede' in his copy of the

Folio but further examination makes it seem probable that this is due to erasure in that particular copy and that the variant 'neede' does not occur.

The Comedy of Errors

In an important article Louise G. Clubb studies 'Italian Comedy and *The Comedy of Errors*' (*CL*). 'Examining *The Comedy of Errors* against the background of Italian tradition, as Baldwin suggests, reveals that the form is anything but archaistic. The complexity answers the demands of Italian regular comedy in general, and the character of its unity reflects the *commedia grave* in particular.' The article concludes that, while it cannot be proved that Shakespeare knew Italian comedy, the structure of *The Comedy of Errors* is consistent with a close, up-to-date, and accurate knowledge of it. T. W. Baldwin, in '*Errors* and Marprelate' (*Starnes Studies*) points out that there are two jests used in *The Comedy of Errors* which are also found in the Marprelate controversy. 'In *Errors*, Shakespeare presents the first known instance in England of the labelled type, as the mountebank Dr Pinch, an exorcist (religious) mountebank. Lyly's *Pappe*, hardly more than two weeks before November 5, 1589, perpetrates a pun on *finis-funis*—an end by a rope. Shakespeare's *Errors* puns on a "ropes end", whose "end" was to have its "end" applied to a victim's "end" in a flogging. Here are two prominent jests in the Marprelate controversy, in August and October of 1589, which have equally prominent analogues in *Errors*'. On this and other pieces of evidence Baldwin proposes 'toward Christmas 1589' as the date for the play.

Coriolanus

'The End of *Coriolanus*' (*ELH*) is studied by E. A. Colman while Bernhard Kytzler suggests a source for some of the names in 'Classical Names in Shakespeare's *Coriolanus*' (*Archiv*). H. D. F. Kitto devotes a chapter to *Coriolanus* in *Poiesis*.[54] The argument is that 'Shakespeare's "meaning", being typical of his own age, soon became and long remained inaccessible, because unfashionable, with the result that one of his most magnificent plays has often been undervalued; further, that our best means of regaining contact with his remote sixteenth-century mind is, again, to look steadily at his *poiesis*'. Coriolanus, it turns out, like the Ajax of Sophocles, cannot think 'as becomes a mortal man'. Shakespeare's 'mind was on the passions or vices that are contrary to the harmony of Nature and therefore must work mischief: it is only when we see this that everything in the play comes into focus, makes its proper contribution to the whole, and forms a powerful unity'. A contrary opinion is expressed by J. C. F. Littlewood in two articles on '*Coriolanus*' (*Cambridge Quarterly*). 'Critics have surely been misguided in attempting to define what Shakespeare himself does not reveal—the full significance of Coriolanus' life and death.' The play has, in general, been overvalued, he asserts. Michael McCanles's article 'The Dialectic of Transcendence in Shakespeare's *Coriolanus*' (*PMLA*) is complementary to Kenneth Burke's '*Coriolanus*—and the Delights of Faction' (*HR*) (*YW* xlvii. 150) and argues that if we construct 'a scale of values in which praise and power are the controlling values, we will have both the controlling scheme of the action of *Coriolanus* and a good part of its theme as well'. In this play 'what we

[54] *Poiesis*, by H. D. F. Kitto (Sather Classical Lectures: Vol. 36). Berkeley and Los Angeles: California U.P. Cambridge U.P. pp. x+407. 50s.

watch is the inexorable working out of a love perverted into a drive towards power, from which few in the play seem redeemable'.

Cymbeline

'*Cymbeline* and Coterie Dramaturgy' (*ELH*) by Arthur C. Kirsch states that the circumstances of its presentation at the Blackfriars theatre have had a definite effect upon the structure of the play. Barbara A. Mowat laments in '*Cymbeline*: Crude Dramaturgy and Aesthetic Distance' (*Renaissance Papers* 1966) the fact that 'new knowledge of the effects of theatricality on audience engagement and detachment' has so far had very little effect upon criticism of Shakespeare. By a close study of Act I, scene v, she attempts to show that 'Shakespeare uses presentational conventions, deliberately made artificial, in order to provide just that distancing needed for his Romance story'.

Hamlet

Nigel Alexander discusses 'Critical Disagreement about Oedipus and Hamlet' (*Sh S*). In 'Hamlet's Oedipus Complex: A Query' (*SNL*) Dominick I. Bongiorno asks why, if Hamlet is suffering from an Oedipus complex, he shows no hesitation in killing Polonius behind the arras believing him to be the King. In later issues Robert F. Fleissner, Bernard Grebanier, J. C. Maxwell, Harry Slochower and David R. Cheyney all make suggestions while Louis Marder provides a final summing-up attributing Hamlet's action to 'rage and frustration'. Fredson Bowers adds another chapter to his own moralized version of *Hamlet* in 'Death in Victory: Shakespeare's Tragic Reconciliations' (*Starnes Studies*). For this critic Hamlet's 'tragic error is the impulsive killing of Polonius in mistake for the King' and 'this error is

Hamlet's alienation from Heaven by his inability to wait upon a non-criminal revenge that God would have arranged for His minister'. It is concluded that 'The tragic experience of Hamlet, therefore, exhibits error and then reconciliation through a return to God's plan'.

The main question that concerns Carol J. Carlisle in 'Hamlet's "Cruelty" in the Nunnery Scene: The Actors' Views' (*Sh Q*) is 'how can Hamlet's apparent cruelty in the nunnery scene be explained (or explained away)?' The article considers the attitudes of various celebrated actors to this problem. 'A Crux and No Crux in *Hamlet* I. iii: Safty: Sanctity (21) and Beguide: Beguile (131)' (*Sh St*) by Thomas Clayton offers reasons for emending 'the safety/sanctity of the /this whole state' to 'surety' and for reading 'beguile' with the Folio in 'the better to beguide/beguill'. In '*Hamlet*, III ii 146' (*RES*) Jane Crawford suggests that 'munching malice' is the phrase that must lie behind the 'munching *Mallico*' of Q2 or '*Miching Malico*' of F. John W. Draper's *The Hamlet of Shakespeare's Audience*[55] is now reprinted from the original edition of 1939. It claims to set out the Hamlet that Shakespeare wrote, but some doubts may be entertained about a scholarly endeavour which gives as an account of the relationships between the texts—'the first quarto would seem rather clearly to be an early Shakespearean version in somewhat mangled form; and the folio would seem to be a revision of the later quartos. Thus, not only the play as a whole, but specific characters and situations can more or less be traced from Shakespeare's source through one or more revisions at his hands;

[55] *The Hamlet of Shakespeare's Audience*, by John W. Draper. New York: Octagon. London: Frank Cass 1966. pp. x+254. 63s.

and his changes, so far as we can infer them, furnish a useful clue as to his meaning and artistic purpose'. It is not, unfortunately, possible to make any such inference.

The name Corambis in the first Quarto may be derived from '*crambe repetita*: twice cooked cabbage' Doris V. Falk suggests in 'Proverbs and the Polonius Destiny' (*Sh Q*). The type of the advice of the wise father to his son is David's advice to Solomon and the irony of the 'Polonius Destiny' is that all of Polonius's wise saws have a double meaning and he is always unable to take his own good advice. A. L. French argues in clear and convincing fashion in 'Hamlet's Nunnery' (*ES*) that the lines (III i 121–152) do not make any sense unless the nunnery referred to means 'a community or body of nuns'. A distinction must be made, according to M. D. Faber in 'Shakespeare's Ghosts' (*ANQ*), between the Ghost of Act I, which is a 'real' or 'genuine' ghost and the ghost which Hamlet sees in his mother's closet and which is simply the product of his own mind.

The Prayer scene is the subject of William Frossberg's study 'Shakespeare's *Hamlet* III iii 36–72' (*Ex*). It is ironic that 'under the very circumstances most conducive to the relaxation of our judgement of him, Claudius compels our deepest judgement'. 'Slings and Arrows' (*REL*) by Katharine Garvin examines III i 56–60 and compares passages from books IV and V of Caesar's *De Bello Gallico* translated by Arthur Golding in 1565. It is argued that this parallel makes it unlikely that Hamlet is simply referring to suicide. In '*Hamlet* and the Emperor's New Clothes' (*EJ*) Ronald Goba expresses his belief that 'Hamlet, and anything like it, should be taken out of the high school English class'.

A reprint appears of '*The Sources*

of *Hamlet*'[56] by Sir Israel Gollancz, first published in 1926. It contains an essay tracing the story, as well as the relevant sections from Saxo Grammaticus in Latin and English and Belleforest's *Histoires Tragiques* with the translation printed in 1608.

In 'The Ghost of Dr Johnson: L. C. Knights and D. A. Traversi on *Hamlet*' (*EC*) P. R. Grover accuses both critics of indulging in unconscious 'character' criticism. Referring in particular to Knights, Grover complains that 'he believes Hamlet should have behaved differently. The play then becomes a text for the reading of lay sermons, and Hamlet's characteristics are examined to show their weaknesses. For all the qualifications that Hamlet is a character in a play we are being invited to see his conduct as appropriate or inappropriate in life'. It is perhaps difficult to see how any critic can avoid this kind of consideration, but the article certainly exposes some flagrant contradictions in critical method.

E. B. Hungerford examines '*Hamlet*: The Word at the Center' (*TriQuarterly*) and discovers 'a kind of verbal center in the word *act*'. 'Act' or 'action', however, covers a wide area and this article is particularly illuminating both on the 'action' of the duel and the 'buried metaphor' of the 'action' of firing a cannon which Claudius uses to describe it to Laertes. This is an interesting close analysis of some important passages in the play.

'The Concept of the "King's Two Bodies" in *Hamlet*' (*Sh Q*) by Jerah Johnson is an important explanation of IV ii 26, 'The body is with the King, but the King is not with the body', relying on F. W. Maitland's *The King's Two Bodies* and Ernst H.

[56] *The Sources of Hamlet: With an Essay on the Legend*, by Sir Israel Gollancz. London: Frank Cass. pp. x+321. 35s.

Kantorowicz's *The King's Two Bodies, A Study in Mediaeval Political Theology*. A distinction is made between the 'body natural' and the 'body politic' in the person of the King.

In his comparison between '*The Spanish Tragedy* and *Hamlet*: Two Exercises in English Seneca' (see footnote 14) B. L. Joseph argues that the great difference between these plays is not in construction but in conception and that 'What Kyd inherited from Seneca makes a very imperfect play. Shakespeare utilizes his inheritance to create a first-class tragedy'. This is because Kyd accepts in his play that 'Revenge rules the world working deviously through human beings and Fortune', whereas Shakespeare writes as if the world 'is subject to the onslaughts of evil, but is never out of the control of Providence'.

Time and its relation to drama is one of Jan Kott's chief concerns in 'Hamlet and Orestes' (*PMLA*). He points out that 'the situation in tragedy is in the present, but it has behind it a past that defines it, and a future that has been forecast'. It is within this framework that the hero has to make his choice and the article is a comparison of the choices which face Hamlet and Orestes in their task of revenge. The article concludes that the roles of these characters is different since the choice facing Hamlet is that 'he can and must choose between the Hamlet who will kill and the Hamlet who will not. He is in a compulsory situation involving two parts, both imposed from outside. Neither is acceptable to him. Both would alienate him from society, either as a man who has killed or as a son who has not avenged his father'. This is an important article with a clear grasp of vital dramatic principles.

Hamlet is the main example in

Peter Milward's 'The Homiletic Tradition in Shakespeare's Plays with Special Reference to *Hamlet*' (*Shakespeare Studies*, Japan) and he offers 'a random selection which may suggest the remarkable proximity of *Hamlet* to the living homiletic tradition in England'. The close correspondence between Shakespeare's language and the language of the homilies makes these parallels more convincing than many similar suggestions.

Vincent F. Petronella in 'Shakespeare's *Hamlet*' (*Ex*) draws attention to the fact that 'the grouping of the triumphant and the non-triumphant in the affair between the houses of Denmark and Norway creates a chiasmic structure that spans the length of the play'. This note offers additional evidence for taking seriously the character of Fortinbras.

Hamlet and Revenge[57] by Eleanor Prosser is an interesting and important book which seeks to establish that the Elizabethans' and Shakespeare's attitude towards private revenge was quite unequivocal—they condemned it—and that the Ghost has all the marks of a demon from hell. Hamlet himself comes to reject 'his intention of usurping God's function' and 'is now ready to become the willing minister of Heaven. He has put himself at the disposal of God to use as, in His knowledge, He shall see fit'. There are, however, a number of difficulties associated with this approach, and one becomes evident when Hamlet's seventh soliloquy has to be discussed. The difficulty is dismissed; 'The soliloquy clearly neither makes logical nor dramatic sense in Shakespeare's final version of the play'. Fredson Bowers adopts the same position. It is true that it does not quite fit into the morality play of

[57] *Hamlet and Revenge*, by Eleanor Prosser. California: Stanford U.P. London: O.U.P. pp. xiv+287. 45s.

Hamlet favoured by these critics, but not all readers of the play will be convinced that they have here revealed Shakespeare's 'final' intentions. In '*Ecce Signum!* Hamlet's Handsaw Again' (*Renaissance Papers* 1965) Dale B. J. Randall argues that it should be a handsaw that Hamlet knows from a hawk and compares passages from *1 Henry IV* to substantiate the claim that the passage is concerned with a pun on counterfeit friendship. '*Hamlet*, 1703' (*NQ*) by J. G. Saunders points out that 'it is difficult to ascertain whether there were two, three, or more editions dated 1703'. Levin L. Schücking's *The Meaning of Hamlet*[58], translated by Graham Rawson, is reissued. This is an important book for the historian of Shakespearian criticism, but there are other and better works now for the student.

Charles H. Shattuck in 'Edwin Booth's *Hamlet*: A New Promptbook' (*HLB*) announces that 'The Harvard Theatre Collection has acquired Booth's own souvenir promptbook of 1870, the text cut exactly as it was played, the basic stage business professionally recorded, and Charles Witham's watercolours of all ten of the sets'. '*Narcissus* and the Folio text of *Hamlet*' (*NQ*) by G. Sjögren suggests that *Narcissus*, staged at St. John's College, Oxford, on Twelfth Night 1602/3 contains a possible allusion to the fencing match in *Hamlet*. Marvin Spevack in 'Hamlet and Imagery: The Mind's Eye' (*NS* 1966) draws attention to the way in which Hamlet uses the imagery of the visible world in order to illuminate his own inner world of thought. In 'Paperback Editions of *Hamlet*: The Limits of Editorial Eclecticism' (*CE*)

Vern Torczon examines the way in which editors of recent paperback editions have handled Hamlet's speech to Ophelia (III ii 142). He finds their methods inconsistent, but presents no clear editorial policy of his own which might help to resolve such difficulties. Robert Weimann studies the mixture of 'madness' and 'impertinency' in 'Rede-Konventionen des Vice von *Mankind* bis *Hamlet*' (*ZAA*) and traces the origin and development of this tradition in popular morality plays. *Hamlet and the Philosophy of Literary Criticism*[59] by Morris Weitz now makes a welcome appearance in paperback. This important book has not yet had the attention from literary critics that it deserves.

Henry IV

Justice and Law are the concerns of W. H. Auden in 'Le Chien du Prince' (*Preuves*), an essay mainly concerned with Falstaff. Fredson Bowers examines 'Hal and Francis in *King Henry IV*, Part I' (*Ren P* 1965) and offers as the point of the exchange between Hal, Poins, and Francis the view that 'If one seeks for the cause of Hal's impatience, almost his frustration, in this scene, then, it is because the "action" that he knows is ahead is so slow in coming and he must still play his part in the taverns until the time arrives for him to demonstrate how the controlled strength for national good that reason directs is superior to the mindless activity of a Francis-Percy, who has never learned to exercise his godlike reason in speech or in deeds'. 'Shakespeare's Source for *2 Henry IV* II i' (*ANQ*) by L. S. Champion argues that this is a case of direct borrowing from *The Famous Victories*. The

[58] *The Meaning of Hamlet*, by Levin L. Schücking, translated from the German by Graham Rawson. London; Allen & Unwin. pp. x+195. 35*s*.

[59] *Hamlet and the Philosophy of Literary Criticism*, by Morris Weitz. New York: Meridian Books. pp. xvi+335. $2.25.

parallel is not, however, exact enough to make this a certain 'source'.

Alan G. Cross attempts to make the 'I know you all' soliloquy more dramatically acceptable by arguing that it shows evidence of authorial revision in 'The Text of Hal's First Soliloquy' (*EM*). Bridget Gellert provides more convincing evidence in 'The Melancholy of Moor-Ditch: A Gloss of *1 Henry IV* I ii 87–88' (*Sh Q*) where she quotes Robert Anton's *Philosophers Satyrs* (1616) in support of her argument that 'Moorfields, the haunt of beggars and cashiered soldiers, was commonly associated with melancholy. In their exchange of other melancholy associations Hal manages to get in a cruel thrust by suggesting that Falstaff's future will be with the decayed soldiers and poverty-stricken folk who frequent Moorfields'. 'Falstaff on an 18th Century Battlefield' (*TN*) by Christian P. Gruber examines pictorial representations as evidence of actual staging practice. 'The Play-within-a-Play in *1 Henry IV*' (*Sh Q*) by Richard L. McGuire examines Falstaff and Hal playing at King in II iv, and argues that this game is not merely a parody but that the 'play' is one of the ways in which Hal comes to realize his own role.

In an interesting article Charles Mitchell studies 'The Education of the True Prince' (*TSL*). Falstaff is essential to his education since 'with Falstaff's help, Hal discovers both his common weakness as a man and his special strength as a man, which together enable him to be the true prince. The weaknesses which Hal permits himself are associated with Falstaff's physical appetites; the weakness which Hal does not allow himself is associated with Falstaff's comic wit, which is related to Falstaff's flouting of moral consciousness'. Both the Hal-Francis scene and the Hal-Falstaff playing at King are considered by John Shaw in 'The Staging of Parody and Parallels in *1 Henry IV* (*Sh S*). He asks, 'What evidence might there be to suggest that the physical staging of the two scenes, and the acting, emphasized and clarified their relationships?' It is concluded that 'it is not extreme to suggest that careful attention was paid to the blocking, the use of gestures and properties, and the use of voice in putting parallel scenes on the stage'. The Francis scene is also the subject of J. D. Shuchter's 'Prince Hal and Francis: The Imitation of an Action' (*Sh St*). It is here considered not as parallel with the Hotspur scenes but as an interview similar to the one between Hal and Falstaff and Hal and his father: 'it is clear that the dialogue between Hal and Francis *plays* as an interview, and when one has seen it, it is hard not to think back to it when the mock interviews with Falstaff come on'. He concludes, 'For Hal playing is a way of knowing; dramatizing a situation is a way of clarifying the various positions within the conflict or of learning what the conflict really is.' C. G. Thayer in 'Shakespeare's Second Tetralogy: An Underground Report' (*Ohio University Review*) argues that the plays are a careful political scheme opposed to the Tudor doctrine of non-resistance to a monarch and that Bolingbroke should be treated as the centre of *Henry IV*.

Henry V

Harold F. Hutchinson discusses 'Shakespeare and Henry V' (*History Today*).

Henry VI

In '"I Am But Shadow of Myself": Ceremony and Design in *1 Henry VI*' (*MLQ*) Sigurd Burckhardt examines the function of the scene between

Talbot and the Countess of Auvergne at II iii, with respect both to the structure of this play and to its significance in Shakespeare's development as a dramatist. 'Trapping', 'sight' and 'hand-arm' imagery is studied by J. L. Calderwood in 'Shakespeare's Evolving Imagery: 2 Henry VI' (ES).

'Rough Notes on Editions Collated for 1 Henry VI' (Shakespearean Research Opportunities 1966) by G. B. Evans is a check list compiled fifteen years ago in the course of work on the Variorum 1 Henry VI and is offered 'only as a possible stimulus for future work'. Guy Lambrechts intends to demonstrate in 'La Composition de la Première Partie de Henri VI' (Recherches Anglaises et Americaines) that the play cannot have been written solely by Shakespeare. The only grounds offered are the doubtful ones of stylistic detail, but on this basis a thorough disintegration is proposed with each scene set out and ascribed to Nashe or Greene as well as Shakespeare. The thesis is that Nashe and Greene collaborated on the play and that their effort was revised by Shakespeare. It is not possible to demonstrate this thesis on the evidence offered by this article.

In an important review article Robert K. Turner Jr. (Sh St) considers Andrew S. Cairncross's Arden editions of the three Henry VI plays.

Henry VIII

R. Berman in 'King Henry the Eighth: History and Romance' (ES) considers that 'what is essential is that life and the royal line continue, that the play culminates in a last scene which quite transcends the ordinary subject of drama'.

Julius Caesar

'Hero and theme in Julius Caesar' (Rivista di Letterature Moderne e Comparate) by John W. Draper argues that 'The theme of Julius Caesar would seem to be the requirement of a Divine Right monarch for the stability of government that alone could bring peace and prosperity; but none of the persons of the tragedy, either by birth or character, appears as God-Anointed'. Johannes Ebert finds the tragic centre of the play in the way in which the same words, used in different contexts, mean entirely opposed things to many of the characters in the play. These meanings are studied in "Liberty! Freedom!" (Julius Caesar III i): 'Versuch einer schulischen Interpretation' (NS 1966). In 'Hamartia, Brutus, and the failure of Personal Confrontation' (Person) J. L. Halio examines the choices which he considers were open to Brutus and argues that Brutus failed to confront Caesar in the same way that he did confront Cassius with his crimes in the quarrel scene. J. C. Maxwell, 'The Name of Brutus' (NQ), refers to the derivation of the Latin adjective 'brutus' given in Cooper's Thesaurus and suggests that 'it is tempting to see a recollection of this in III ii 106–7'. Michael G. Southwell argues in 'Dawn in Brutus' Orchard' (ELN) that the discussion is 'a simple substitute for a discussion between Brutus and Cassius'.

King John

Ronald Berman's 'Anarchy and Order in Richard III and King John' (Sh S) has already been noted.

King Lear

Commenting on the Centaur image Michael Andrews in 'Lear's Wheel of Fire and Centaur's Daughters' (Renaissance Papers 1965) argues that 'the salient fact to recall is that Centaur-crimes are also notorious for being violations of the sacred ties binding guest and host. We have only to remember the conduct of Goneril and Regan to see that in this as in other respects the Centaur image is conspicuously appropriate'. 'The Influence of Hobbes on Nahum Tate's *King Lear*' (*SEL*) is examined by James Black who points out that Edmund was seen as an example of 'natural' man. However, 'while Tate's treatment of Edmund grows out of a close familiarity with Hobbes's works, the result tends towards a perpetuation of the misconception about the philosopher's ideas'. A speech delivered by Alexander Blok at the Bolshoi theatre in 1920 is translated by Daniel Gerould as 'Shakespeare's *King Lear*: A speech to the Actors' (*ETJ*) while the same number of the journal also contains Jacques Copeau's '*King Lear* at the Théâtre Antoine' translated by B. Dukore and D. Gerould.

The John Coffin Memorial Lecture for 1966 was delivered by Helen Gardner under the title *King Lear*.[60] While regarding the play as the greatest of the tragedies Dame Helen also argues that 'we might see it as a mighty universal comedy on the great subject of all comedy: man's blindness and folly, his childish ignorance of himself. No other tragedy gives us this sense of the world as a great stage of fools. But no tragedy also so turns us upside down and confuses our notions of what is wisdom and what is folly'. There are various responses possible to the play and we may agree with both Bradley, who emphasized the virtues of Lear and Cordelia, and Granville Barker, who felt the play's appalling cruelty because, as Lear asks, '"Is there any cause in nature that makes these hard hearts?"' The question is unanswerable, as are so many of the questions that are asked in this play. There is no

answer either to a question that is not asked: "Is there any cause in nature that makes these gentle Hearts"?' The scene ends with Shakespeare's 'secular Pieta', a sight which offers us no consolation 'for there is none which this world, the world of the play, can offer'. Consolation, however, is discovered in the play by Marilyn Gaull who argues in 'Love and Order in *King Lear*' (*ETJ*) that 'Lear created the condition for rebellion by those whom he was enjoined to control. By extension, through his failure to be ruled by reason, he alienated himself from divine love and forfeited his sovereignty over his own baser passions'. It is Kent, Cordelia and Edgar, the three exiles, maintainers of the 'three basic relationships of an ordered society', who express divine love in the play.

Daniel C. Gerould studies 'Literary Values in Theatrical Performances: *King Lear* on Stage' (*ETJ*) by examining the Moscow State Jewish Theatre Production of February 10th 1935. John Golata compares '*Père Goriot* and *King Lear*' (*EJ*). In 'King Lear and his Comforters' (*EC*) Andor Gomme is commenting on J. D. Rosenberg's article of the same title (*EC* 1966).

The interesting suggestion that the idea behind 'Ripeness is all' may be found in E.K.'s remarks on the emblem to November in *The Shepheardes Calender* is offered among 'Replies' (*NQ*) by W. L. Godshalk. Patricia Ingham in 'A Note on the Aural Errors in the First Quarto of *King Lear*' (*Sh St*) suggests a classification for the various kinds of aural errors contained in the Quarto and argues that 'unmistakably aural errors are fewer than generally supposed, and that whoever was responsible for them used an advanced or vulgar form of speech'. 'Time and Truth in *King Lear*' (*Shakespeare Studies*,

---

[60] *King Lear: The John Coffin Memorial Lecture 1966*, by Helen Gardner. London: Athlone Press. pp. 28. 5s.

Japan) by Soji Iwasaki is an examination of the relevance of the emblem 'Veritas filia temporis' to King Lear and suggests that 'Cordelia is truth, and she is driven away from the world by untruthful speeches mistakenly approved by childish innocence or even ignorance, till at last time comes and brings her back to the world, now as the confirmed truth'.

Paul Jorgensen's *Lear's Self-Discovery*[61] is an interesting and important book. He is concerned, in the first instance, with Elizabethan views of 'self-knowledge' and examines a number of works which, while they are in no way sources, are part of the intellectual context in which King Lear was written. He thus draws attention to the real intellectual questions which are raised in the play, and suggests that they may not have received proper attention because Shakespeare had developed a new and less obvious technique than the soliloquy for presenting them to his audience—the extended meditation. The virtue of the book is that, whatever one may think of the interpretation of events offered, it points to elements which are unquestionably in the play and which any interpretation has to account for.

Waldo F. McNeir analyses 'The Last Lines of *King Lear* V iii 320–327' (*ELN*) and assigns them according to the context of the dramatic moment. 324–5 are given to Albany as showing understanding of Kent's attitude and his refusal to govern, while the last lines remain with Edgar. This division, as is admitted, has no basis in either Q or F. Another textual problem is studied by James G. McManaway in 'A Reading in *King Lear*' (*NQ*), where it is argued that 'body' rather than 'bed' should be the reading at IV ii 28. Supporting evidence is cited

from *The Massacre at Paris* and *Arden of Feversham*. H. A. Mason continues to publish his forthcoming book in instalments in *CQ* and three articles this year are concerned with a revaluation of *King Lear*: 'The Central Stream', 'Manipulating Our Sympathies' and 'Radical Incoherence?'. They are concerned with important problems, and it is a pity that these objections to *King Lear*: are not themselves more coherently expressed. Elizabethan demonology is related to the play by Toshikazu Oyama in '*King Lear* and its Tragic Pattern' (*Shakespeare Studies*, Japan). Lear's vow 'by all the mysteries of Hecate' means 'that Lear has already dedicated his soul to Hecate' and the play is therefore interpreted in these terms.

Russell A. Peck in 'Edgar's Pilgrimage: High Comedy in *King Lear*' (*SEL*) considers that 'Edgar might with profit be viewed as the most important figure in the sub-plot, perhaps even the second most central figure in the play', and that 'An awareness of Edgar's growth to a full character is essential to understanding Lear's growth'. 'And We Were Left Darkling: Notes on *King Lear*' (*A Sch*) by Lawrence Raab makes an illuminating comparison between Lear's scenes of madness on the heath and Hamlet's scene in the graveyard. That 'Bradley's ideas are still highly regarded by the critics of this generation' is the thesis of Jean T. Spikes in 'Bradleyism at Mid-Century: The Death of King Lear' (*So Q*). A fairly pessimistic reading of the play is offered by Betty K. Stuart in 'Truth and Tragedy in *King Lear*' (*Sh Q*). In this play 'Given a life without meaning, let alone happiness, Shakespeare emphasizes the struggle for life and truth. Such a struggle is mad and vain, but the power of the language makes it significant'. In 'The Fool's Prophecy' (*Sh Q*) Sheldon P. Zitner

---

[61] *Lear's Self-Discovery*, by Paul A. Jorgensen. Berkeley: California U.P. pp. vii + 154. $4.50.

argues that the prophecy at III ii 79–95 is genuine.

Love's Labour's Lost

'The Dialogues of Spring and Winter: A Key to the Unity of *Love's Labour's Lost*' (*Sh Q*) by Catherine M. McLay is concerned with the two songs which end the play and which 'hold a key to the interpretation of the central themes'. 'The season of love is at once the season of jealousy and folly, as symbolized by the cuckoo. On the other hand, the season of winter, associated with age and sterility, becomes the season of wisdom as represented by the owl'.

A similar interpretation is offered by Joseph Westlund in 'Fancy and Achievement in *Love's Labour's Lost*' (*Sh Q*). 'Nowhere is the thematic design of the play more evident, or more beautifully worked out, than in the songs with which the comedy ends.' It is this preference for winter, the owl and reason, rather than the world of spring and the cuckoo which explains the plan of the 'academy' in the play.

Lucrece

'Shakespeare's Gaudy: The Method of *The Rape of Lucrece*' by Robert L. Montgomery Jr. (*Starnes Studies*) argues that 'Shakespeare's method approaches the borders of allegory through the occasional enlarging of his characters into figures and through his destruction of the potential verisimilitude of the crucial scenes in the poem, but if the method stops short of allegory, it is due to the variety of tasks Shakespeare seems to be attempting'.

Macbeth

In '"Appal" in *Macbeth* III iv 60' (*ELN*) Dennis Biggins points out that *O.E.D.* gives this passage the sense of 'to cause the heart to sink, etc.'. He argues that it is derived from OF *apallir* 'to make pale', and that the line means that Banquo's ghost would make the devil turn from black to white. Herbert R. Coursen Jr. argues in 'In Deepest Consequence: *Macbeth*' (*Sh Q*) that 'the power beneath the surface, then, is the myth of the fall from a state of grace, whether the fall from the beneficent light of God or the expulsion from paradise on Earth. The myth has three basic manifestations in *Macbeth*: moral decision, feminine persuasion, and cosmic retribution'. 'Kemble's Production of *Macbeth* 1794' (*TN*) is studied by Joseph W. Donohue Jr. 'As We Three Meet Again' (*EJ*) by Marion Gleason points out that in *Macbeth* 'everything is done double and suffered double with astonishing consistency'. Richard Jaarsma in 'The Tragedy of Banquo' (*L&P*) supports Bradley's opinion that in the course of the play Banquo becomes Macbeth's accomplice—even if only through maintaining silence. Shakespeare's possible acquaintance with Dante's *Inferno* is examined by Harry Morris in '*Macbeth*, Dante, and the Greatest Evil' (*TSL*). 'Macbeth on Sleep: "Sore Labour's Bath" and Sidney's *Astrophil and Stella* XXXIX' (*NQ*) by Jean Robertson assembles useful parallels from Sir Thomas Wyatt and others, and argues that if Shakespeare is indebted to Sidney then he must have been content with the reading of the 1591 Q 'The bathing place of wits' which was changed to 'baiting' in 1598. *ETJ* publishes the text of Bernard Shaw's skit on *Macbeth*. Written for Gerald Du Maurier and Lillah McCarthy, it was never produced. Finally, Ulrich Suerbaum examines 'Die dramatischen Funktionen der Lady Macbeth' (*Poetica*).

Measure for Measure

'The Theme of Government in

Measure for Measure' (*Paunch* 1966) by Robert D. Callahan argues that 'At best, I think we have to regard *Measure for Measure* as suggesting, but failing to dramatize, an alternative to imposed "government", Claudio's "sensible warm motion" self-regulated and free'. Ronald Berman studies the play in 'Shakespeare and the Law' (*Sh Q*) and points out that 'whatever "doctrine" there is in the play depends on certain Pauline ethical and psychological formulations. The Letter of Paul to the Romans does not "explain" this complex play, but it does illuminate both the sensuality and the righteousness of the protagonists. *Romans* does not furnish a scheme that simplifies; in fact it points to things unresolvable in the natural condition. In a sense, that is its importance; it furnishes the "problem" of a problem play'. This is an illuminating article. Coleridge's attitude to the play is examined by George L. Geckle in 'Coleridge on *Measure for Measure*' (*Sh Q*)—it failed to give him pleasure because it exasperated his sense of decency and justice. 'Bond Slaves and Counterfeits: Shakespeare's *Measure for Measure*' (*Sh St*) by R. J. Kaufmann puts forward the view that 'the play is literally and in many shadings of figure about bondage, but where bondage is psychic these bonds may not be loosed save by self-understanding. The intransigent Barnadine thus becomes thematically intelligible as an emblematic representation of the pure state of bondage'. '*Measure for Measure*: A Case for the Scottish Solomon' (*MLQ*) by Peter Alexander is a review article which considers D. L. Stevenson's *The Achievement of Measure for Measure*, J. W. Bennett's *Measure for Measure as Royal Entertainment* and William B. Toole's *Shakespeare's Problem Plays*.

The Merchant of Venice

An important period in the theatrical history of the play is studied by William S. E. Coleman in 'Post-Restoration Shylocks Prior to Macklin' (*TS*). He points out that 'From early 1701 to 1741 a truncated and drastically rewritten version of the play, adapted by George Granville and re-titled *The Jew Of Venice*, held the London stage'. A connexion between Antonio and the fortunes of a Genoese, Orazio Pallavicino, is traced by John W. Draper in 'Shakespeare's Antonio and the Queen's Finance' (*N*). A rather different view of the trial scene from G. W. Keeton's in *Shakespeare's Legal and Political Background* is taken by Robert Hapgood in 'Portia and *The Merchant of Venice*: The Gentle Bond' (*MLQ*). He argues that Portia's exceptions are within the spirit of the law. Lawrence W. Hyman comments on Thomas H. Fujimura's 'Mode and Structure in the *Merchant of Venice*' (*PMLA* 1966) in 'Antonio in the *Merchant of Venice*' (*PMLA*). In '*Merchant of Venice* IV i 128' (*NQ*) Paul Merchant defends the reading 'inexecrable' by comparing it with the A-version of Marlowe's *Dr Faustus*.

A Midsummer Night's Dream

'Bottom and Titania' (*Sh Q*) by John A. Allen argues that 'Bottom's presence in *A Midsummer Night's Dream* has the effect of short-circuiting attempts to draw a moral from the play, based upon a supposed possibility of choosing between the reasonable and the fanciful as the basis for conducting human affairs' and concludes that 'if *A Midsummer Night's Dream* has a message, it is as inarticulate as Bottom's—or as eloquent'. This same problem receives attention in David P. Young's interesting study *Something of Great*

Constancy: The Art of A Midsummer Night's Dream.[62] 'Thus it is that the clowns, without retracting an ounce of their clownishness, reveal a complex series of comic association. Their taste brings to mind the worst excesses of Elizabethan verse; their notions of drama, the least successful features of a stagecraft only recently outworn; and their attempts at decorum and rhetorical glamour, the danger of preferring critical theory to practical experience and common sense.' Although this is an interesting study of the play it is questionable if it adds very much to R. W. Dent's analysis in 'Imagination in a *Midsummer Night's Dream*' (*Sh Q* 1964). G. M. Lee in 'Plotinus and Shakespeare' (*NQ*) reports on Tudor Vianu's suggestion in 'Manierism si Asianism' (*Studii Clasice* Bucharest, V, 1963) that Plotinus's conception of 'internal form' (ἔνδον εἶδος) has influenced Shakespeare in this play.

Much Ado About Nothing

In 'The Church Scene in *Much Ado*: The Absence of Antonio' (*NQ*) J. C. Maxwell points out that 'the opening dialogue between Leonato and Antonio in V i cannot plausibly take place between two speakers both of whom know that Hero is alive'. 'Illusion and Metamorphosis in *Much Ado About Nothing*' (*Sh Q*) by Paul and Miriam Mueschke is an extremely interesting article which argues that 'the theme of this comedy is honor, that its spirit is less joyous than reflective, and that courtship, a peripheral concern, is presented as an imminent threat to masculine honor. Once the accent on honor is established, interest in the witty lovers becomes subordinated to interest in the troubled lovers; John, the malevolent match-breaker becomes more than a nominal villain; the main plot focuses less on the birth and growth of love than on the death and rebirth of love'. The play is thus related to some of the central concerns of the histories and tragedies. Denzell S. Smith in 'The Command "Kill Claudio" in *Much Ado About Nothing*' (*ELN*) argues that it marks a development in the characters of Beatrice and Benedick. They are less selfish and more prepared to come to terms with real problems; Beatrice accepts her womanliness and it makes the position of these lovers less cliché-ridden at the same time as involving them in the main plot. The play, according to John Wain in 'The Shakespearean Lie-detector: Thoughts on *Much Ado About Nothing*.' (*CQ*), is a failure—'The typical Shakespearean failure is a play at once lop-sided and brilliant—so brilliant that the lop-sidedness does not keep it from being acted and read'. The problem of Claudio is insoluble and the altar scene is 'a central spot of infection'. It appears that 'Shakespeare has fallen into his old trap of beginning to handle a story without realizing that at bottom it simply does not interest him'.

Othello

Shakespeare's use of Cinthio's novella is considered by Mariella Cavalchini in 'Intorno alle fonti dell' '*Othello* (*Rivista di Letterature Moderne e Comparate*) where she argues that Shakespeare probably read the story in Italian and draws attention to some interesting parallel expressions. 'Othello's Angels: The *Ars Moriendi*' (*ELH*) by Bettie A. Doebler points out that 'the second scene of the last act of *Othello* invokes the *ars moriendi* tradition, a popular tradi-

---

[62] *Something of Great Constancy: The Art of A Midsummer Night's Dream*, by David P. Young. Yale Studies in English. Vol. 164. New Haven: Yale U.P. pp. xii + 190. $5.00. 37s. 6d.

tion of comfort for the dying which stands in ironic contrast to Othello's own violent and despairing death'. Wayne Dodd examines II i 200 in '"But I'll Set Down the Pegs That Make This Music"' (*NM*).

The concept of *infamia* as set out in John Livingstone's *Infamia in the decretists from Rufinus to Johannes Teutonicus* (Ph. D. Wisconsin, 1962) is used by Madeleine Doran in an excellent and important article 'Good Name in *Othello*' (*SEL*) which argues that 'a man's good name is a property he was born with: that it is a commodity that can be lost or taken away; that if so it is replaced by another, infamy, which is just as positive'. Consequently 'it is no wonder, then, that Othello's last speech is an attempt to set the record straight. It is not an excuse, not a plea for anything less than justice; but it is a plea that his name be cleared of false imputation'. In 'The Context of Othello's Tragedy' (*So R*) Michael Echeruo makes an attempt 'to show how Othello's blackness affects the play in material ways. It will be shown that Shakespeare's Othello conforms more or less to the stock Elizabethan notions of the Moor. Finally an attempt will be made to assess the usefulness of recent attempts at a symbolic or Christian reading of the play'. Othello's 'tragic type' is expressed by III iii 90–92 argues Toshikazu Oyama in 'Tragic Fate of Othello's World of Consciousness' (*Ang*). 'The tragic irony is two-fold. First, it is one of the best examples of Othello's characteristic way of thinking, although Othello himself is not aware that this is his tragedy. "Love or perdition" is what he exclaims. He admits no middle ways, as Hamlet does.' Rodney Poisson considers '*Othello* V ii 347: "The Base Indian" Yet Again' (*MLR*), quoting a passage from Thomas Milles's *The Treasurie*

of Auncient and Moderne Times (1613–19) which states that Indians took no account of pearls. Milles also explains how Moors use pearls in their medicines. Poisson also examines II iii 161–163 in '"Which Heaven Has Forbid The Ottomites"' (*Sh Q*) arguing that Othello's words refer to the Turkish military prohibition on duelling.

Pericles

'Shakespeare's Miracle Play' (*Sh Q*) by Howard Felperin argues that 'When an artist believes he has apprehended the unalterable laws that govern the moral and mortal world, he must resort to the dark conceit of allegory, which is alone capable of presenting things as they are, given the belief that things are a certain way'. Neither these laws nor the dark conceit are much illuminated by this article. Thelma N. Greenfield conducts 'a Re-Examination of the "Patient" Pericles' (*Sh St*) and observes 'I feel that certain weaknesses appear in the arguments which support Pericles (however virtuous he is) as an extraordinary example of patience, for too often the play emphasizes his avoidance of and retreat from misfortunes rather than his patient endurance of them'. In 'The Imagery of *Pericles* and what it tells us' (*Ball State University Forum*) Gerald J. Schiffhorst disagrees with Spurgeon's analysis and argues that 'the number, types and efficacy of the images and clusters in the first two as well as the last three acts point to work that seems indisputably Shakespearean'. James O. Wood has a series of notes in 'Notes on *Pericles* Act I and II' and '*Pericles* I ii' (*NQ*).

Richard II

John R. Elliott Jr. takes issue with E.M.W. Tillyard's view of the play as

'Shakespeare's Picture of the Middle Ages' in 'Richard II and the Medieval' (*Renaissance Papers* 1965) and points out that 'as a result of his conception of kingship, Richard's attitude towards his land and his subjects is one that completely defies the traditional view of the relationship between monarch and people'. He then argues that Shakespeare 'gives a much more traditional answer to the problem of the nature and extent of royal authority. Where Tudor theorists saw order in the state as fundamentally a matter of obedience, Shakespeare saw it as a matter of responsibility and of keeping a due balance between the sources of political power'. In 'Who Deposed Richard the Second?' (*EC*) A. L. French argues that the King is himself responsible—'at no one's prompting but his own, he has deposed himself'; and that this has an important effect upon the play—'the trouble with *Richard II* is that it suffers from what we might call double vision, giving us one truth in one place and another in another, with apparently equal weight and conviction'.

A masterly introduction to the play and its problems is provided by A. R. Humphreys in No. 31 of the *Studies in English Literature* series. *Shakespeare: Richard II*[63] offers information on the English history play and the sources as well as an intelligent commentary on the action itself. This is an important reading of the play. G. Lambrechts, in 'Sur deux prétendues sources de *Richard II*' (*Ea*), argues that the evidence for calling *Woodstock* and Daniel's *Civil Wars* 'sources' for *Richard II* is totally inadequate. Richard's responsibility for Gloucester's murder is discussed by J. C. Maxwell in '*Richard II* IV i

[63] *Shakespeare: Richard II*, by A. R. Humphreys. *(Studies in English Literature 31)*, London: Arnold. pp. 64. 8s. 6d.

11–12' (*NQ*). 'That it is proverbially *kings*' arms that are long makes this a covert resumption of the notion, already important in I i, that the real responsibility is the king's, and that Mowbray was merely his agent.' The play's themes are studied by Takako Uchiyama in 'The Three Themes in One Harmonious Chord' (*Shakespeare Studies*, Japan). 'These three main themes: 1) the fall of England, 2) the political doctrine of the Tudors, 3) the tragedy of the person of Richard II, may serve as keys to unlock the treasure hidden in the play.' 'The unique experience is, therefore, the result of the poetic harmony that Shakespeare has produced uniting the three main themes into one harmonious chord.' 'Charles Kean's Production of *Richard II*' (*ETJ*) by M. Glen Wilson reconstructs the production of 1857 and discusses Kean's work at the Princess Theatre from 1850 to 1859.

Richard III

A new magazine published by Monash University contains '"Determined to Prove a Villain"': Character, Action and Irony in *Richard III*' (*Komos*) by Jennifer Strauss. An interesting defence of his own position on the text of *Richard III* is provided by J. K. Walton in the course of a review of Fredson Bowers's *Bibliography and Textual Criticism* (*NQ*).

Romeo and Juliet

Standish Henning studies 'The Printer of *Romeo and Juliet* Q1' (*PBSA* 1966). In 'How Many Children Had Lady Capulet' (*Sh Q*) Richard Hosley emends I iii 71–73 from 'your mother' to 'a mother' on the grounds that all the evidence of the play is that Lady Capulet is old or middle-aged except these lines— which make her twenty-eight. 'The emendation requires the assumption that Capulet and his wife, beginning some time after her marriage to him at the age of about fourteen, have had several children, only one of whom (Juliet) has survived. (Juliet, of course, would be one of the last, if not the last, of these.) The assumption accords with Capulet's line, "Earth hath swallowed all my hopes but she" (I ii 14). The purpose of Joseph S. M. J. Chang's 'The Language of Paradox in *Romeo and Juliet*' (*Sh St*) is to 'demonstrate that the play is controlled by the Petrarchan contrarieties, which are realized both rhetorically and by the action', and that 'the play exploits a love-centered situation to explore problems of larger import, the abiding concerns of time, death and immortal aspiration'. The article concludes that 'as in the sonnets, love is used as a vehicle for representing, simultaneously, man's subjection to time and decay and man's ability to transcend the limits prescribed by his mortal nature'.

Dreams, in *Romeo and Juliet*, come true and Warren D. Smith in 'Romeo's Final Dream' (*MLR*) argues that Romeo's dream also represents the symbolic 'truth' of the play. This is an interesting examination of the wedding bed/grave and love and death theme through the imagery of womb/tomb and the herb rosemary. The golden statues at the end of the play are an indication that the families can never understand a love that extinguishes even the sun. 'Shakespeare's *Romeo and Juliet*: Its Spanish Source' (*Sh S*) by Oscar M. Villarejo attempts to show that Lope de Vega's *Castelvines y Monteses* 'must be linked to Shakespeare's play'. The evidence, as is usual in such cases, consists of verbal similarities and parallel scenes, but these hardly warrant the elaborate weight of inference and conclusion that he rests upon them.

Sonnets

In 'Shakespeare's Sonnets in a New Light' (*SN*) Lorentz Eckhoff argues that the unity of the sonnets depends upon the friend and the lady being creations of the poet's own imagination devised to express the theme of 'perfect love'. Jean Fuzier provides a detailed examination of Sonnet I in 'Poesie et Perplexité: Réflexions sur un Sonnet de Shakespeare' (*LLM*). Samuel Hux examines 'Shakespeare's Sonnet CXXXVIII' (*Ex*) and compares its use of double meanings and its attitude to love to the 'foolish' love of *Antony and Cleopatra*. 'The Marriage of True Minds: Truth and Error in Sonnet 116' (*Sh St*) by Hilton Landry argues that 'the natural context of 116 is a fairly large group of poems beginning with Sonnet 109' and proposes a radical reinterpretation of the sonnet. 'The poet is the remover in question, the one who has changed his allegiance in the recent past, and the one in whom alteration is to be found. It is his friend's love for him which must not alter in the face of alteration or be inclined to seek a new object.' C.-P. Laurent in 'Les Sonnets de Shakespeare: Étude d'une Désillusion' (*LLM*) argues that the struggle between the friend and the lady represents a failure by Shakespeare to achieve a balance between good and evil in his soul. 'A Seventeenth-Century Manuscript of Shakespeare's *Sonnet 128*' (*NQ*) is discussed by R. H. Robbins who points out that 'though this MS has no discernible bearing on the authorship or authenticity of the *Sonnets* it has some incidental value as an illustration of what poets of the day constantly feared: that unless they speedily issued authoritative editions they would become known to the world only in diluted and garbled form'. The influence of Shakespeare on Keats is studied by J.-C. Sallé in

'Shakespeare's Sonnet 27 and Keats's *Bright Star*' (*NQ*). This sonnet is heavily marked in the copy of the poems which belonged to Keats. 'Shakespeare's "Well": A Note on Sonnet 73' (*SNL*) by Kenneth Seib suggests that 'well' in line 14 could be a noun as well as an adverb and thus could bring into the poem imagery suggestive of 'life-spring' and 'the reviving waters of life, the source of man's eternal salvation'. J. C. Maxwell in '"Rebel Powers": Shakespeare and Daniel' (*NQ*) suggests that Sonnet 146 may contain an echo of Daniel's *Cleopatra*.

The Tempest

Wolfgang Baumgart examines 'Prospero'[64] and compares and contrasts the character of that magician with Marlowe's Faustus. John W. Draper suggests in 'Monsieur Caliban' (*RLC* 1966) that Shakespeare may have obtained some of the details of his remarkable extensive description of Caliban's physical appearance from Jean de Léry's *Histoire d'un Voyage en la Terre du Brazil* (?1578).

The Dream of Prospero[65] by D. G. James sees *The Tempest* as a logical development from *Hamlet* and *King Lear*, and this book is itself, therefore, a logical extension of the author's previous *The Dream of Learning*. He discusses how Shakespeare's mind worked on the tradition of magic and demonology and on the reports which were coming in from the New World. Caliban is the child of a witch and the devil but he also owes a great deal to descriptions of the North American Indian. Perhaps the most remarkable feature of the book is the

identification of Francis Bacon as the author of the reports on Virginia which usually go under the titles of *A True and Sincere Declaration* (1609) and *A True Declaration* (1610). The end of the play may represent 'the mind of Europe saying farewell to magic as a part of its imagination of the world' but the farewell to magic suggests that 'we are still left with a mystery'.

In dealing with magic James has been indebted to the work of Dr. Frances Yates, and A. D. Nuttall has also made use of her work in his recent book *Two Concepts of Allegory*.[66] This is 'an inquiry into certain conceptual questions missed, in the first place, by the allegoristic critics of *The Tempest*, and, in the second place, by allegorical and quasi-allegorical poetry in general. My argument has the further consequence of suggesting that allegory and metaphysics are in practice more closely allied than is commonly supposed'. This, therefore, is a book which uses *The Tempest* as the major example in a larger inquiry—but it is an important inquiry which, if Mr. Nuttall is correct, will have far-reaching consequences for literary criticism. The chapter on 'The Use of the Imagination in the Sixteenth and Seventeenth Centuries' alone would have established this as a major work of criticism.

Jacob Korg studies 'The Rage of Caliban' (*UTQ*) while in '*The Tempest* and *The Wasteland*' (*AL*) Ronald Tamplin argues that the play is a major source for Eliot's poem.

Timon of Athens

'*Timon of Athens* and Morality Drama' (*CLA*) by David M. Bergeron studies the relationship between the

[64] *Festschrift für Richard Alewyn*, ed. by Herbert Singer and Benno von Wiese. Cologne: Böhlau. pp. xiv+423. DM 58.
[65] *The Dream of Prospero*, D. G. James. O.U.P. pp. viii+174. 32s. 6d.

[66] *Two Concepts of Allegory*, by A. D. Nuttall. New York: Barnes & Noble. London: Routledge. pp. xii+175. 35s.

form of Shakespeare's play and *Everyman*. Leonard Goldstein considers that the handling of 'Alcibiades' Revolt in *Timon of Athens*' (*ZAA*) 'indicates a growing interest and sympathy for the people as an active political force', and the aim is to 'evaluate this change in attitude which has two aspects: an interest in the strong man as benevolent ruler, and an apparent growing interest in the common people'. 'Desperate Debts' (*NQ*) by J. C. Maxwell cites another occurrence of the term used at *Timon* III iv 103 in Thomas Middleton's *Michaelmas Term*. In '*Timon of Athens* and the Growth of Discrimination' (*MLR*) R. Swigg sees the play as a process 'of the degradation of feeling, of its manipulated regulation by grosser values'. The pervading imagery of quantity and counting, even in references to love and honour, indicates that 'a commercial view of life' dominates a more idealistic one. Timon's crisis arises from this confusion of values, and the second half of the play shows a movement towards discrimination and the growth of moral responsibility.

Troilus and Cressida

'Affirmation in *Troilus and Cressida*' (*Discourse*) by William B. Bache offers the final answer of charity to the problems of man's inhumanity to man represented in the action. Nevill Coghill's letter on '*Troilus and Cressida*' (*TLS* 19 Jan.) questioning the veracity of Bonian and Walley and explaining the reasons that lay, in his opinion, behind the Prologue started an acrimonious correspondence which appeared in the issues of 16th February, 2 March, 9 March, 30 March, 6 April, 20 April and 4 May. Arlin J. Hikin argues in 'Texture in *Troilus and Cressida*' (*ETJ*) that 'its characters are sometimes absurd and sometimes noble; and in these very

paradoxes lies a rich texture of repeated patterns that is the play's strength'. 'Cressida, Achilles and the Finite Deed' (*Ea*) by Charles Lyons examines the way in which all 'energy' in the play, whether sexual energy or the desire for fame, is consumed in the actual act and that consequently there can never be any sense of triumph in the world of *Troilus and Cressida*. In 'Essence and Existence in Shakespeare's *Troilus and Cressida*' (*PQ*) J. Oates Smith argues that 'what is withheld—and deliberately withheld—is "poetic justice"' so that 'like Gulliver's Travels, it works towards establishing all mankind as its satiric object'.

Twelfth Night

The way in which language is used is the chief concern of Terence Eagleton in 'Language and Reality in *Twelfth Night*' (*CQ*). 'Reason—reality—can be expressed only in language and yet is falsified by language; without language there can be no reason, yet with language there can be none either—to speak or keep silent is equally illusory' and consequently 'the Clown's sanity—his reality—springs from the fact that he fulfils a settled role consistently, and it is the lack of such consistency in the play as a whole which suggests that illusion and insanity are general conditions'. 'Art and Nature in *Twelfth Night*' (*CQ*) by D. J. Palmer develops the thesis that 'in *Twelfth Night* the conception of metamorphosis informs Shakespeare's use of disguise, and its function as a particular kind of change in a world subject to changefulness is similar in spirit to that of Ovid's stories', and this is used to produce 'a play in which nature and art are constantly changing places'. The play's dramatic irony is examined by Elias Schwartz in '*Twelfth Night* and the Meaning of Shakespearean Comedy'

(*CE*), who points out that 'it presents a vision not of types which depart from some social code or rationalized moral system, but of the ultimate absurdity of human life. It sees human beings, even at their best, as limited mortal creatures, and rather than lamenting this truth, celebrates it, rejoices in it'. In 'Maluolio's a Peg-a-Ramsie' (*ELN*) James O. Wood argues that this phrase, as used in ballads, means 'a watchful hovering woman'.

The Two Noble Kinsmen

'Shakespeare's Song and Masque Hand in *The Two Noble Kinsmen*' (*EM*) by John P. Cutts argues the case for Shakespearian authorship from internal evidence.

The Winter's Tale

Kate Hotine argues in 'Shakespeare's *Winter's Tale*' (*Contemporary Review*) that the play is an allegory of the Gunpowder Plot.

VIII

Later Elizabethan and Early Stuart Drama

BERNARD HARRIS

EDITIONS

This year's Malone Society publication (which is by the Society's chronology their issue for 1965) is Munday's *The Death of Robert Earl of Huntingdon*.[1] J. C. Meagher, an experienced traveller in these parts, admits that he has been unsuccessful in his attempts 'to divide the authorship of the two Huntingdon plays by tests of prosody, rhyme, ending-types, punctuation, spelling, interjections, stage-directions, dramaturgical techniques, and other phenomena'. He is able to offer, however, two hypotheses: 'A. The extant text of *The Death* is all by Munday, and the work for which Chettle was paid was either added at a later stage of composition or devoted to the representation of King Richard's funeral, which was originally intended to form part of this play (see *Downfall* 2826–9) but subsequently became a separate play with Chettle as part-author (Henslowe's Diary, fols. 46–46v). B. The extant text is primarily the work of Munday, and Chettle's contribution was either very small or reworked by Munday.'

Seven texts have appeared in the Regents Renaissance Drama

series.[2] All are welcome, none more so than J. D. Jump's edition of both parts of Marlowe's *Tamburlaine*. The introduction contains the interesting remark that 'Part I could have been successfully performed on a simple platform stage, but the full resources of a well-equipped London theater would have been needed for Part II'. Jump acknowledges that we may 'have our doubts about the ethics of the play in which Marlowe's Tamburlaine is held up for our almost unbounded admiration; but we can have no doubts about our immediate, spontaneous sympathy with the eager aspiration that was so important a part of what Marlowe was trying to express through him'. Beaurline's introduction to *Epicoene* contains many comments valuable for the understanding of the conditions of the drama in this period. Of Jonson's

[1] *The Death of Robert Earl of Huntingdon*, by Anthony Munday, ed. by John C. Meagher. The Malone Society Reprints, 1965 (1967). O.U.P. for Members of the Society. pp. xvi+95.

[2] Regents Renaissance Drama Series. General editor, Cyrus Hoy; advisory editor, G. E. Bentley. *Tamburlaine the Great*, Parts I and II, by Christopher Marlowe, ed. by John D. Jump. pp. xxvi+205. *Epicoene, or The Silent Woman*, by Ben Jonson, ed. by L. A. Beaurline, pp. xxiii+159. *The Revenger's Tragedy*, by Cyril Tourneur, ed. by Lawrence J. Ross. pp. xxxii+130. *The Widow's Tears*, by George Chapman, ed. by Ethel M. Smeak. pp. xxvi+119. *Michaelmas Term*, by Thomas Middleton, ed. by Richard Levin. pp. xxv+139. *The Changeling*, by Thomas Middleton, ed. by George W. Williams. pp. xxiv+112. *The Antipodes*, by Richard Brome, ed. by Ann Haaker. pp. xxi+138. Nebraska U.P. 1966: Edward Arnold 1967. Paperback. Each 10s. 6d.

specific aims he finds that the plan 'of the whole play is a tissue of afflictions visited upon hermaphroditical monsters, an elaborate game of vexation copiously filled with variety'. And he concludes that 'Some deep cynicism, some reserve of self-mockery, of loathing and contempt, seems to lurk beneath the dazzling artifice' of *Epicoene*. 'The central theme' of *The Revenger's Tragedy*, argues L. J. Ross, 'realized through its pattern of ironic reversals, and everywhere evident in the turns and exchanges of its metaphoric language, is transformation'. This concept is examined in terms of the play's structure, action and imagery. The introduction dwells, very properly, on the strengths of the play, exemplified in the famous passage at III. v. 71–81, of which the editor notes that its 'awesome concentration of almost palpable meaning would seem inevitably to have come from profoundly and immediately jarred, if richly traditional, simplicities of vision'. Ethel M. Smeak observes that 'In some ways, *The Widow's Tears* seems to be one more of Chapman's experiments in the dramatic form—his attempt to give a valid portrayal of a Machiavellian character and a true interpretation of Machiavelli's philosophy as it can, and must be, applied to everyday life'. It is good to have a work of such interest available again, and a similar welcome is offered to Middleton's *Michaelmas Term*. In his appraisal of this piece Richard Levin notes that 'The setting of *Michaelmas Term* is the actual life of Jacobean London, vividly rendered by an accomplished satirist with a keen eye for the kind of detail that embodies and exemplifies his social milieu'. But he also recognizes that Middleton's portrait 'goes beyond the visible surfaces of London in Term-time to record the more basic "reality" underlying them—the economic revolution that was gradually transforming a feudal society into a capitalistic one through the transfer of wealth and power from the landed gentry to the rising urban middle class'. Levin's account is not confined, however, to the social realism conveyed in this comedy, but is instructive about the technical construction and the relationship of the plots. George Walton Williams sees *The Changeling* as a 'singularly successful' collaborative effort, and argues that 'The association of the comic plot with the tragic plot may be ascribed without question to the collaborating authors, who have related the two widely disparate plots structurally, tonally, thematically, and metaphorically with a subtlety and effectiveness that lets them speak as one on the unifying concept of transformation, or the condition of being a changeling'. His discussion of the play is perceptive, particularly about the inter-relationship of imagery and action, though Tomlinson's study might have been mentioned. Ann Haaker well presents Brome as a dramatist, in her edition of *The Antipodes*, dealing with his relationship with his predecessor and with his public, and the nature of his comedy. She finds that 'With skill and ingenuity, Brome applies Jonson's precepts to prove his own comic muse a gentle surgeon who finds the cause of the pain, heals the wound, and preserves the man'. Instead of escape 'Brome admonishes recognition of follies and truths in everyday life in the true comic spirit, which is to say, void of passion. Only then can wit, love, mirth, and health bring harmony and enjoyment to life'.

The year's New Mermaids are concerned with Greene, Marlowe, Marston and Tourneur.[3] Again one must welcome the presence of a less familiar text in this popular series and it is good to have *James the Fourth* available. J. A. Lavin's introduction is a very useful discussion both of the tradition of the theatre which Greene worked in, and to which he contributed this example of 'homiletic comedy', and of the historical criticism which the play has received. The play is certainly worth recalling as a demonstration of the dramatic handling of the framework tale and the taste of the audience for the popular theatre. W. M. Merchant's introduction to his text of *Edward II* stresses its unity of themes and treatment. Beginning from the title-pages of the 1594 and 1598 editions, with their triple citations of the tragic motivations of Edward, Mortimer and Gaveston, he notes that 'All three involve the tragic fall of men in high estate but all three are different in their implication both in individual moral responsibility and in the assumption of a moral universe (or its absence)'. Merchant makes valuable comparative use of Drayton's poem in determining the nature of the play's themes, challenges much received opinion with the declaration that 'the dramatic verse of *Edward II* has a range of effects unattempted in the other plays', and offers brief but helpful comment on the play's tone and structure. As editor of *The Malcontent* the present writer may perhaps be permitted to confess that on p. xii he has given the date of Marston's father-in-law's will as the date of death, and that, through further compression, his blanket acknowledgement to Davenport's *The Poems of John Marston* as biographical authority has stifled proper recognition of the researches of J–M Axelrad on this and other particulars. Brian Gibbons suggests that we may see the form of *The Revenger's Tragedy* most clearly 'by relating it to three kinds of drama then popular: Senecan revenge tragedy, "Comicall Satyre" in the style of Marston and intrigue comedy in the style of Middleton'. His account of the play's action, however, is notable for its attention to specific qualities rather than general categories. Noting the play's 'alternation between energetic, high-spirited action and brooding, slow-paced scenes of meditation on death, revenge and evil', he sees this 'disturbing duality' as deriving from medieval traditions of meditation and classical and literary traditions of satire: the duality is carried within Vindice's personality, that 'witty deviser of schemes' and an 'anguished and melancholy mourner'. Gibbons's analysis of Tourneur's 'deliberately stylized and mannered technique' is accompanied by emblematic representations of some of the major themes of this dramatized Dance of Death.

Another edition of *Edward II* has been provided by Roma Gill.[4] Her introduction is a brief but thorough discussion of familiar problems broached by this work, in which she argues that 'Irony and deflation are the characteristic modes of this play', that 'Frustration and weakness are Marlowe's themes in *Edward II*', but contends against the declared disappointment of critics that 'In their disappointment they minimize the importance of suffering, suffering no

[3] The New Mermaids. General editors Philip Brockbank and Brian Morris. *James the Fourth*, by Robert Greene, ed. by J. A. Lavin. pp. xxv+102. *Edward II*, by Christopher Marlowe, ed. by W. M. Merchant. pp. xxx +108. *The Malcontent*, by John Marston, ed. by Bernard Harris. pp. xxxvii+105. *The Revenger's Tragedy*, by Cyril Tourneur, ed. by Brian Gibbons. pp. xxxv+108. Benn. Paperback. Each 9s. 6d.

[4] *Edward II*, by Christoper Marlowe, ed. by Roma Gill. pp. 195. O.U.P. 10s. 6d.

longer an intoxicant (as it was in *Tamburlaine*) but the object of terror and pity'.

Mouton continue their Studies in English Literature series with J. H. Dorenkamp's edition of *Beggars Bush*.[5] Dorenkamp makes use of a manuscript version in his scholarly-prepared old-spelling text of an unfamiliar play, and gives a scrupulous account of its printing problems. The critical commentary might well have been longer in view of the relationships suggested for some of the play's allusions. Editor and publishers are to be congratulated, however, on making available a work which, under several guises, was known on the stage into the nineteenth century. This is a highly selective series and inclusion within it of dramatic texts deserves full encouragement.

There are four Jonson offerings. Maurice Hussey's old-spelling text of *The Divell is an Asse* is doubly welcome, as placing this work within the range of students and doing justice to a play long neglected on the stage.[6] It is to be hoped that Hussey's brief introduction will revive interest in Jonson's later plays. Hussey is especially adept in providing points of comparison, unbelaboured, between Jonson's society and our own, so that the play's topical concerns become matters for further rumination. David Cook's edition of *Volpone*, a cogently conceived and presented modern text, has been reissued in paperback.[7] J. B. Steane has

provided a student-orientated edition of *The Alchemist*, with commendable vivacity in its introduction and discriminating attention to the necessary commentary.[8] F. H. Mares has contributed a full-scale modern edition of *The Alchemist* to the Revels series.[9] He places the work economically on 'the rising graph of Jonson's geniality', and makes an extremely clear analysis of the play's construction, attentive both to its theatricality and its morality. To illustrate this double and reciprocal critical skill one may quote the following passage: 'The laboratory—though it is never seen, or need not be —is the symbol at the centre of the play. It is the dream factory, the most potent instrument of delusion, and its presence and location are firmly established early in the play. This one fixed point in space obliged Jonson to have others: the two doors, right and left, one to the outside world, one to the "back way". (One to the forum, one to the country, in Roman comedy.) Jonson the scholar was no doubt pleased to construct a play that fitted so neatly the neo-classical prescriptions for unity of time, place, and action; Jonson the man of the theatre turned these strict limitations to brilliant account in contriving comic stage-business—comings and goings, quick changes, unexpected entries, double takes and so on. But scholar and theatre craftsman are both subservient to the imaginative artist, who saw the apparatus for making gold— the get-rich-quick machine—as the central symbol of a play about human greed and credulity, and their inevitable consequence in disappointment and loss.' The edition is furnished

---

[5] *Beggars Bush*, by John Fletcher and Philip Massinger, ed. by John H. Dorenkamp. The Hague: Mouton. pp. 202. 25 Guilders.

[6] *The Divell is an Asse*, by Ben Jonson, ed. by Maurice Hussey. University Tutorial Press. pp. xxxi+159. 8*s*. 6*d*.

[7] *Volpone*, by Ben Jonson, ed. by David Cook. Methuen: University Paperbacks. pp. 256. 9*s*. 6*d*.

[8] *The Alchemist*, by Ben Jonson, ed. by J. B. Steane. C.U.P. pp. 153. 10*s*. 6*d*.

[9] *The Alchemist*, by Ben Jonson, ed. by F. H. Mares. Methuen. pp. lxxix+208. 30*s*.

with an appropriately detailed stage-history, and a precisely full discussion of the textual problems raised by modernization.

STUDIES OF THE MASQUE

Interest in the masque has been a feature of this year's work, and it seems convenient to group together here a volume containing essays and editions, a study of Jonson's masques, and several related articles. Colleagues and pupils of Allardyce Nicoll have produced in his honour a book designed to have a more practical focus and function than is sometimes to be met with in the category of such offerings; the result is *A Book of Masques*.[10] This contains a General Introduction to the masque by G. E. Bentley, a concluding essay on 'These Pretty Devices' (a study of masques in plays) by Inga-Stina Ewbank, forty-nine pages of illustrations chosen by Sybil Rosenfeld, and the modernized texts of fourteen masques. As a contributor to this volume the present writer can only hope that its range and interest may be sufficiently conveyed by listing the contents of the volume. These are: Samuel Daniel's *The Vision of the Twelve Goddesses*, edited by Joan Rees; Jonson's *Oberon, the Fairy Prince*, edited by Richard Hosley; Jonson's *Love Freed from Ignorance and Folly*, edited by Norman Sanders; Thomas Campion's *The Lords' Masque*, edited by I. A. Shapiro; Francis Beaumont's *The Masque of the Inner Temple and Gray's Inn*, edited by Philip Edwards; *The Masque of Flowers*, edited by E. A. J. Honigmann; William Browne's *The Masque of the Inner Temple (Ulysses and Circe)*, edited by R. F. Hill; Jonson's *Lovers Made Men*, edited by

Stanley Wells; Jonson's *Pleasure Reconciled to Virtue*, edited by R. A. Foakes; Thomas Middleton's *The Inner Temple Masque, or Masque of Heroes*, edited by the late R. C. Bald; James Shirley's *The Triumph of Peace*, edited by Clifford Leech; Thomas Nabbes's *The Spring's Glory*, edited by John Russell Brown; Inigo Jones's and William Davenant's *Salmacida Spolia*, edited by T. J. B. Spencer; James Shirley's *Cupid and Death*, edited by B. A. Harris.

John C. Meagher has written an introductory study of Jonson's masques.[11] His title-page and chapter-headings are suitably adorned by sketches of masque figures found in the material of Inigo Jones, for the special emphasis of this work is on the practical achievement of Jonson. There is some neglect of earlier historians of the masque, and some surprising omissions among modern commentators, notably Edgar Wind. Presumably, although noted, Stephen Orgel's study appeared too late for assimilation. Nevertheless, this is a useful criticism of Jonson's masques, especially valuable for its chapters on 'Music', 'Dance', and 'Light'; for though the documentation under all these aspects could be extended, there is sound reason for attempting this kind of succinct judgement. Meagher's Preface utters a warning, which his book heeds, and which needs to be kept in mind by writers on this most difficult dramatic form, namely, that if Jonson's masques are 'as it has generally been conceded, the finest flower of the (pre-Miltonic, if you will) English masque tradition, their proper understanding must begin in discovering from what roots and in what air they grew'. Within the limits defined in the preface this book makes

[10] *A Book of Masques*. General editor, T. J. B. Spencer, with the assistance of S. W. Wells. C.U.P. pp. xv+448. 70s.

[11] *Method and Meaning in Jonson's Masques*, by John C. Meagher. University of Notre Dame Press. pp. ix+214. $6.50.

a valuable contribution to a study currently active and much in need of its proper scholarship.

Harriett Hawkins, in 'Jonson's use of traditional dream theory in *The Vision of Delight*' (*MP*), makes justified employment of Macrobius's classification of dreams into five major types, arguing that 'Throughout the masque, the analogous relationships Jonson establishes between audience and dreamers, maskers and dream figures, allow him to organize scenes according to specific types of dreams and to effect an ending in which his artistic world of poetry and dreams merges with the world of duty and action, in which the ideal merges with the factual'.

In her brief 'Note sur la legende de Sabrina dans le *Comus* de Milton' (*Ea*), M. T. Jones-Davies usefully reviews Milton's available knowledge of English literary sources in Lodge and *Locrine*. Meagher's trepidation—that our understanding of the masque may be seduced by Milton before it has hope of approaching Jonson—may be overcome if we come to Milton's work with the respect for its power of enchantment induced by Richard Neuse's discussion of 'Metamorphosis and Symbolic Action in *Comus*' (*ELH*). This article contests Enid Welsford's dictum that 'difference in structure corresponds to a difference in spirit between *Comus* and the Court Masque; the masque is a dramatized dance, Comus is a dramatized debate'. Neuse comments: 'This idea of the poem's structure seems to me, if not incorrect, at least drastically incomplete.' For it ignores the sequel, wherein 'the symbolic and ritual scenes of the Lady's paralysis and liberation by Sabrina present a genuine complication and resolution initiated by the original clash between the Lady and Comus'. Acknowledging Orgel's view that *Comus* 'fulfils per-

fectly the demands of the Jonsonian masque form', Neuse brings fresh scholarship and criticism to bear in his own account. B. Rajan's '*Comus*: The Inglorious Likeness' (*UTQ*) is a closely argued, and sometimes opaquely written, defence of the serious doctrine of the masque and Milton's dramatic achievement of 'doctrinal and imaginative balance'.

BOOKS AND ARTICLES

A. H. Sackton's study of Jonson's rhetorical language has been reprinted.[12] Although not put to much use by Jonson's recent editors, the book has some merit, particularly the two central chapters on 'Jargon'. B. N. De Luna's book on *Catiline* is a very detailed account of the historical context of that play in terms of Gunpowder Plot, the characters of the conspirators and the issues of state.[13] Indeed the book goes well beyond the relationship of the play and its times, to matters of Jonson's personal standing with his fellows, the vast range of literary allusiveness found in much literature rarely searched so thoroughly, and also takes us into the complex literature of conspiratorial allusion in the later part of the seventeenth century. The results of patient and wide-ranging research into this complex period is a book of value both for incidental discoveries and for its general thesis of the interpretation to be put upon unexpected, or unsuspected, congruencies of fact, fiction, documentation, and suggestion. The large number of references made to *Catiline* during the seventeenth century certainly

[12] *Rhetoric as a Dramatic Language in Ben Jonson*, by Alexander H. Sackton. Cass. pp. viii+182. 75*s*.
[13] *Jonson's Romish Plot: a study of 'Catiline' and its Historical Context*, by B. N. De Luna. Oxford: Clarendon Press. pp. ix+415. 65*s*.

indicate the contemporary evaluation, and may explain subsequent neglect, of this play.

Ian Fletcher has written on Beaumont and Fletcher.[14] His range is well judged, the bibliography useful and critical comment particularly rewarding on *The Faithful Shepherdess, The Maid's Tragedy* and *Valentinian*. The author concludes with an interesting opinion about reasons for earlier failure to appreciate the work of these collaborators, and their stage neglect, seeing their most important achievement in 'exploiting the paradoxes of drama and life' in a manner which Pirandello found 'absorbing'. Beaumont and Fletcher 'are keenly interested in a topic which fascinates the modern world, that is the problem of identity and the playing out of roles, or, to put it another way, the refusal of the average human being to live as an individual when faced with painful challenges'. Marco Mincoff has a valuable study of 'Shakespeare, Fletcher and Baroque Tragedy' (*Sh S*), with some especially close insights into Fletcher's conduct of scene and sense of structure.

Two short monographs must be mentioned. Bertil Johansson has written on law and lawyers particularly as represented in the plays of Jonson and Middleton, helpfully bringing together statements by writers on law, evidence of legal practice and the representation of these matters in plays.[15] Donald S. Lawless has studied Massinger's biography, and scrupulously assessed what is known, the possible and probable associates, and the nature of the evidence upon which we may construct Massinger's biographical relationships.[16]

Jacques Ramel amplifies knowledge of Thomas Hughes, John Lancaster, Master Penruddock, Francis Flower and Nicholas Trotte, in 'Biographical Notices on the authors of "The Misfortunes of Arthur" (1588)' (*NQ*): and R. E. Brettle surveys evidence for satirical occasional poems in 'John Marston and the Duke of Buckingham, 1627–1628' (*NQ*).

Two textual and bibliographical studies are of major importance for their respective works; they are George R. Price's 'The Early Editions of *A trick to catch the old one*' (*Lib*), and Robert K. Turner's 'The Text of Heywood's *The fair maid of the West*' (*Lib*).

Two essays of general importance for literary themes in the drama of this period have come from G. K. Hunter, in 'Seneca and the Elizabethans: A Case-study in "Influence"' (*Sh S*), and John Sibly in 'The Duty of Revenge in Tudor and Stuart Drama' (*REL*).

Among articles on the early drama Richard Hosley has contributed an excellent demonstration of method in his inquiry into 'The Authorship of *Fedele and Fortunio*' (*HLQ*); he supports the theory of Munday's authorship with a list of 'at least eight circumstances' which seem confirmatory. David M. Bevington makes an interesting case for interpreting indirect address in 'John Lyly and Queen Elizabeth: Royal Flattery in *Campaspe* and *Saphao and Phao*' (*Renaissance Papers*). One may here

[14] *Beaumont and Fletcher,* by Ian Fletcher. Writers and their Work: No. 199. Longmans. Paperback. pp. 60. 3*s.* 6*d.*

[15] *Law and Lawyers in Elizabethan England, as evidenced in the plays of Ben Jonson and Thomas Middleton,* by Bertil Johansson. Stockholm Studies in English XVIII. Stockholm: Almqvist and Wiksell. pp. 65. Sw. Kr. 15.

[16] *Philip Massinger and his Associates,* by Donald S. Lawless. Ball State Monograph Number 10. Indiana: Ball State University. pp. ix+67.

perhaps mention that Lyly's works are available again in reprint.[17]

In 'Shakespeare, Richards, and the Virtues Reconciled' (*JEGP*), Allan Holaday argues for 'conscious allusion' to the Parliament in Heaven in several episodes in Tudor-Stuart drama, instancing 'the dumb show before Act III of Lyly's *Endimion*, the trial scene in *Swetnam the Woman-Hater*, and perhaps that in Peele's *The Arraignment of Paris*', but basing his main argument on the evidence provided in Richard Edwards's *Damon and Pithias*. Hans Walter Gabler has brought together some patterns of verbal and character relationship between Greene and Marlowe, though not them alone, in 'Imitation und Parodie in Greenes *Orlando Furioso*' (*Ang*). Siegfried Wyler makes suggestive use of some aspects of modern linguistic inquiry in 'Marlowe's Technique of Communication with his Audience, as seen in his *Tamburlaine Part I*' (*ES*); the conclusion summarizes the author's concern with a 'system of word signals, the semantic field of "power", and the carefully handled interplay of its constituents'. J. C. Maxwell has done his duty in keeping lines of communication clear by listing errors, failures in modernization and possible emendations in the World's Classics edition of Robert Davenport's *King John and Matilda*, in *Elizabethan History Plays*, in 'Notes on Davenport's "King John and Matilda"' (*NQ*).

John J. McDermott argues that Henryson's *Testament* may have 'importantly shaped Heywood's conception of the death of Anne Frankford', and provided the final plot detail of the tombstone 'erected to the memory of the faithless woman by her injured mate', in 'Henryson's *Testament of Cresseid* and Heywood's *A Woman Killed with Kindness*' (*Renaissance Quarterly*).

R. G. Howarth links evidence for a new death date for John Webster in 1638 with further considerations leading him to reject any claim for Heywood to have a share in 'Webster's *Appius and Virginia*' (*PQ*), which he finds 'Webster's most satisfactory work of dramatic art'.

Among Jonson studies Arthur Freeman points out that the reference to 'The Fox' in Parrot's *The Mous-Trap* of 1606 is apparently 'The earliest allusion to "Volpone"' (*NQ*), and adds other theatrical references from this literature. Lloyd L. Mills delineates the dramatic and symbolic context in his 'Clarification of Broker's use of "A perfect sanguine" in "The Staple of News"' (*NQ*). In 'Jonson's "Knaue of Clubs" and "The Play of the Cards"' (*MLR*), Alan C. Dessen draws convincing evidence from references to old and new ways of representing the Vices in *The Staple of News* to support the claim that 'the existence of *dramatis personae* derived from the deck of cards'.

Two substantial articles have appeared on one of Jonson's major plays. I. Donaldson, in '"A Martyrs Resolution": Jonson's *Epicoene*' (*RES*), persuades us that 'As in Jonson's court masques, and also perhaps in some of his other stage plays, the decorum of the play seems to be governed by the nature of a festive occasion which the play depicts; an occasion which gives certain "laws" and "licence"—to use terms of which Jonson was fond—both to methods of the dramatist writing the play and to the action of characters within it.' Donaldson observes that 'Unlike *Volpone* or *The Alchemist*, *Epicoene* does not seem to

---

[17] *The Complete Works of John Lyly*, ed. by R. Warwick Bond. 3 Vols. Oxford: Clarendon Press. £12 12s.

be a play about the acquisition of money. It seems more accurate to see it as a play about the persecution of a misanthrope'. The 'leading action' is concerned with the breaking down of Morose's isolation and the punishment of his misanthropy by means of 'a viciously high-spirited festive ceremony'. Donaldson not only studies the contexts which traditions of contemporary festive customs provide for the play, but brings *Epicoene* into thematic relationship with other of Jonson's plays, and most interestingly with the masque. L. G. Salingar, in 'Farce and Fashion in "The Silent Woman"' (*E&S*), approaches the work from considerations of classical comedy, definitions of farce and comedy, Dryden's criticism, and comparative use of the scheme of Aretino's *Marescalco*. Placing Morose as 'a petty tyrant', Salingar notes that 'if Morose deserves some of his neighbours, they also deserve him'. The essay is valuable for its discussion of the topic of 'sociability' in the conditions of London life, and argues that 'among the many Jacobean comedies touching on the subject, only *The Silent Woman* breaks through generalities to a sharp, animated farcical portrayal of the discomforts and vexations of metropolitan life'.

Philip J. Finkelpearl makes telling points, both of detail and proper generalization, about another aspect of ceremonious foolery in his arguments for 'The use of the Middle Temple's Christmas Revels in Marston's *The Fawne*' (*SP*), and Harry Keyishian makes many useful comparative notes on 'Dekker's *Whore* and Marston's *Courtesan*' (*ELN*).

In a general review of 'George Chapman: tragedy and the providential view of history' (*Sh S*), G. R. Hibbard locates the 'peculiar interest' of this dramatist in two things: 'first, all his tragedies are historical, in the

sense that they are set in a definite time—four out of the five in very recent time—and deal mainly with characters and situations that had actually existed, and about which a good deal was known; and, secondly, the experience they embody and explore seems to me to spring in no small measure from the tension that is created in them by conflicting attitudes to historical material and to history itself'. Raymond B. Waddington, in 'Prometheus and Hercules: the dialectic of *Bussy D'Ambois*' (*ELH*), shows the importance of the Prometheus analogy for understanding the character of Bussy. The article is notable for its range of detailed reference, from the work of Chapman and his contemporaries, from ancient and modern commentators; but though the result is often compressed writing, the analysis of the intricate imagery and the use of myth in this play contributes fresh critical perception and historical understanding. P. Bement, in 'The Imagery of Darkness and of Light in Chapman's *Bussy D'Ambois*' (*SP*), distinguishes between the senses in which day and night are referred to in the first act of the play, and the 'false night' of man's 'moral confusion and his blindness to truth' in the later four acts of the play.

Dorothy M. Farr, in a lucidly argued piece on 'The Changeling' (*MLR*), sees Middleton, with Rowley, engaged in 'an unusual experiment', that of 'transmuting' the mediocrity of 'the experience of a group of ordinary people whose fate is the natural consequence of their obtuseness and simplicity' into poetry 'which could form the material of a tragic drama, and in using the methods and attitudes of comedy to produce the effects of tragedy'. This essay is persuasive about the characters, the psychology of Middleton's presentation, and the distinctions made between Webster's art and Middleton's. Dorothea Kehler has an interesting discussion of the significance and use of 'Rings and Jewels in *The Changeling*' (*ELN*). David George's investigation of 'The problem of Middleton's "The Witch" and its sources' (*NQ*) enables him to argue for a date nearer to 1614 for its composition.

Roma Gill, in 'Collaboration and Revision in Massinger's *A Very Woman*' (*RES*), redirects inquiry from what she believes was a false clue to source hunters planted over a century ago by Rapp in Tübingen, and re-locates the basic plot of *A Very Woman* in 'Book VIII of *The Mirror of Knighthood* (Part III, Book iii of the original), attributed to M. Martinez and translated into English by one L.A. in 1599'. Ranging more widely Alan G. Gross has examined some categories of 'Social Change and Philip Massinger' (*SEL*).

Klaus Peter Steiger, in '"May a Man be Caught with Faces?"'. The Convention of "Heart" and "Face" in Fletcher and Rowley's *The Maid in the Mill*' (*E&S*), ranges direct analysis alongside use of *Much Ado* and Fletcher's employment of Lope de Vega to accumulate 'sufficient evidence for the assumption that Fletcher intentionally insinuated his main theme, the symbolism of eye and face, into the subplot and the play within the play'.

Two articles worth consulting for Webster criticism are James P. Driscoll's examination of the theme of 'Integrity of Life in *The Duchess of Malfi*' (*Dram S*), and Frank B. Fieler's consideration of 'The Eight Madmen in *The Duchess of Malfi*' (*SEL*).

In notes of possible Ford source material N. W. Bawcutt offers Nero's defence of his decision to marry

Poppaea, in *Octavia*, as a model for a line in Giovanni's counter argument to the Friar, in 'Seneca and Ford's "'Tis Pity She's A Whore"' (*NQ*); and F. M. Burelbach, Jr., in '"The Truth" in John Ford's "The Broken Heart" Revisited' (*NQ*), finds most of the elements of the relationship between Orgilus-Penthea-Bassanes in an example cited by Lord Cesar Gonzago in Book III of Hoby's translation of Castiglione's *Courtier*.

David M. Bergeron's 'Anthony Munday: Pageant Poet to the City of London' (*HLQ*), examines Munday's important contribution to Jacobean civic pageantry, providing comment about the circumstances of actual pageants, analysing their emblematic, antiquarian, historical and dramatic intentions. The discussions of *The Triumphes of Re-United Britania, Chruso-thriambos* and *Chrysanaleia* are full and usefully illustrative of the fact that Munday brought to his pageant-making an 'historical sense of continuity'.

K. R. Richards has written a sensitively phrased comparison of 'Joseph Rutter's *The Shepherd's Holiday* and the *Silvanire* of Jean de Mairet' (*Ang*). Rutter's work is more than placed in the sequence of d'Urfe, Mairet and analogues; it is studied for itself in a way that it deserves as 'one of the very few English pastorals accorded not only a court production, but a professional performance on the London public stage'.

Richard Levin has contributed a useful survey of critical arguments about 'The Unity of Elizabethan Multiple-Plot Drama' (*ELH*), and made what, in that survey, he calls an isolated demonstration of a specific example, in 'The Triple Plot of *Hyde Park*' (*MLR*). The skilful working out of the modes of plotting in Shirley's play justifies Levin's interest in theory, and his summary of the purpose of the three plots is admirable: 'It appears, then, that this triple-plot structure has been designed to encompass three traditional species of comedy. The main plot is a sophisticated or "high" comedy of clever intrigue, appealing primarily to the intellect; the second is a sentimental comedy that is directed to our ethical sensibilities; and the third a simple comedy of situation that depends mainly, like most other plots of this type, upon coincidence, disguise, and sheer spectacle.'

This last quality is seen by Albert Wertheim, in 'The Presentation of James Shirley's "St. Patrick for Ireland" at the first Irish Playhouse' (*NQ*), as the true link between the three plots of that remarkable work, of miracle-worker, evil magician, and two pairs of lovers. Wertheim is surprised at Shirley's decision to let St. Patrick perform, '*on stage*, his famous deed of driving the serpents from Ireland', and thinks that 'presentation of the serpents on stage would have been no mean feat for Caroline stagecraft even in England, and Shirley was clearly aware that these serpents plus the sudden sinking of the magician would provide a breath-taking finale for the Dublin theatre-goers'. But surely the English theatre that could stage the marvels of Faustus, and the magic of fairies, could already manage serpents.

IX

The Later Tudor Period, Excluding Drama

PATRICIA THOMSON

GENERAL

Phoebe Sheavyn's *The Literary Profession in the Elizabethan Age* (1909) was a pioneer study. Her findings and material, though modified and amplified by her successors during a period of over fifty years, are still of interest, so that this year's second edition[1] has been a worth-while enterprise, and all the more so because the text has been revised throughout by J. W. Saunders, himself an authority on the subject (*YW* xlv 207). The book retains its original form. It was not designed as a complete survey, but as a series of essays on aspects of the literary profession: private patronage, official censorship, dealings with publishers, work for the public theatres, other means of livelihood, relations amongst authors, and their rapport with the reading public. Dr. Sheavyn deliberately restricted herself to belles-lettres, which has had its disadvantages for the reviser. It is more fully realized now than in 1909 that certain other branches of literature offered more opportunities to the professional author: religious polemic and translation, for example, were in demand from government, patron, or publisher, and were, in fact, quite often commissioned. Saunders has corrected the emphasis here, as far as was possible within the limits of Dr. Sheavyn's plan. He has also added to her comments on the drama, for he sees this as the most fertile ground in the Elizabethan and early Stuart period for the growth of a literary profession. It ensured a rather less niggardly remuneration than other literary genres, as well as independence of private patronage. By contrast the court, with its gentlemanly amateurishness and tendency to eschew print, was inimical to professionalism. Saunders has also brought the literary (but not the historical) references up to date, using the best modern editions. But 'this remains', he insists, 'Dr. Sheavyn's book'.

One of the most popular of handbooks of rhetoric, to judge by its constant reprinting between 1586 and 1626, was Angel Day's *The English Secretary*,[2] which has been republished in facsimile from his 'fresh renouation', set out 'in far more orderly manner', of 1599. It is easy to see why it was popular. In addition to the fact, brought out by R. O. Evans in his short introduction, that it is simpler than Sherry's or Peacham's work, it is obviously useful. It instructs the learner efficiently in proper letter-writing. After an introduction with tips on style, how to address a bishop etc., Day gives specimen letters of various kinds, descriptive, laudatory, vituperative,

---

[1] *The Literary Profession in the Elizabethan Age*, by Phoebe Sheavyn. 2nd ed., revised by J. W. Saunders. Manchester U.P. Barnes and Noble. pp. x+248. 35*s*. $6.50.

[2] *The English Secretary*, by Angel Day. Introd. by Robert O. Evans. Scholars' Facsimiles and Reprints. Gainesville, Florida. pp. xiii+8+148+133+5. $8.

consolatory, persuasive, dissuasive, conciliatory, monitory etc. At the end he adds a *Declaration*, a list of the schemes, figures, and tropes used, with definitions. In view of the current interest in Elizabethan rhetoric and the impact of its study on works of literature, Day's book, hitherto rare, is welcome.

Robert Ralstone Cawley's 'Studies in the Influence of the Voyagers on Elizabethan Literature', first published in 1940 (*YW* xxi 147–8), reappears this year.[3] He considers, first, the ancient and medieval heritage, continuing with an attempt to estimate how the material provided by the voyagers was used by Greene, Dekker, Beaumont and Fletcher, Shakespeare, Bacon, and Davenant. There is also a chapter on maps, and another on 'The Spirit of the Voyagers', which communicates, through quotation from a variety of poets, prose-writers, and dramatists, the great enthusiasm even of the armchair travellers.

That the interest of emblem books, and, more important, the prevalence of the emblematic way of thinking are now so generally recognized by students of Elizabethan literature is thanks largely to Rosemary Freeman's authoritative book, originally published in 1948 (*YW* xxix 182). A second impression[4] makes a welcome appearance this year. The book spans the period from 1586, when the first emblem book, a translation, appeared, to the end of the seventeenth century, when emblem books ceased to be popular, at least with adults, and when, simultaneously, the mode of

allegory lost its strength. Miss Freeman marks out two phases in the earlier history of the emblem books in England, the first inaugurated by Whitney in 1586, the second, with its more inward stress and more literary character, by Quarles in 1635. She also connects both with English allegory and lyric. The pages on Spenser and Herbert, particularly, yield an insight into an age for which poetry was 'a speaking picture', and in which the emblematic, allegorical, or symbolic significance of things described in words had priority, while the claims of descriptive verisimilitude of the modern kind were felt with much less force.

The last of three papers on allegory, all printed in *PMLA*, is Rhodes Dunlap's on 'The Allegorical Interpretation of Renaissance Literature' (referring to Shakespeare, Spenser, Tasso, Jonson and others).

Rudolf Gottfried's 'Autobiography and Art: An Elizabethan Borderland'[5] starts with the first known autobiography proper in English, Thomas Whythorne's (1576), in which what would appear to be stereotyped poems are included in the context of his life, a technique similar to Gascoigne's in *The Adventures of Master F. J.* (1573). He proceeds to the sonnet sequence and pastoral. *Astrophel and Stella* and Spenser's shorter poems provide good examples of poetry rich in allusions to their authors' lives, and in which actuality and circumstance are wedded to a literary tradition.

Douglas L. Peterson analyses *The English Lyric from Wyatt to Donne*[6]

---

[3] *Unpathed Waters. Studies in the Influence of the Voyagers on Elizabethan Literature*, by Robert Ralstone Cawley. Octagon Books. Frank Cass & Co. Ltd. pp. viii+285. $7.50.

[4] *English Emblem Books*, by Rosemary Freeman. Chatto and Windus. pp. xiv+256. 63*s*.

[5] In *Literary Criticism and Historical Understanding: Selected Papers from the English Institute*, ed. by Phillip Damon. Columbia U.P. pp. vii+190. $5.50.

[6] *The English Lyric from Wyatt to Donne. A History of the Plain and Eloquent Styles*, by Douglas L. Peterson. Princeton U.P. 68*s*.

in terms of the plain and eloquent traditions inherited from the middle ages, categories which he prefers to C. S. Lewis's 'drab' and 'golden'. In the sixteenth century the plain style was still considered adequate to the expression of ideas, and is often used with effect, as by Raleigh in 'The Lie'. The eloquent style, meanwhile, continues up to 1580 to be dominated by ornamental rhetoric, and Peterson finds evidence that the handbooks of rhetoric were used not only by the 'Tottel' poets but by Shakespeare in his sonnets. After discussing Tottel's 'Miscellany' and Wyatt, he proceeds to illustrate his thesis in the work of the three chief early Elizabethan lyrists, Googe, Gascoigne, and Turberville, in whose work he discovers an 'experimentation with structure' which makes them more than mere imitators of 'Tottel': Gascoigne's 'The Constancie of a Lover' marks an advance in 'control of style', while his 'Wodmanship' and 'Memories 3' are selected for special praise as the first successful long lyrics of the century. This chapter also comments on the lyrical miscellanies of the 1560s and 1570s. With the next chapter, on Sidney's *Astrophel and Stella* and Spenser's *Amoretti*, a break marked by new refinements in language and technique is noticed. Peterson comments on the current dissatisfaction with love poetry as either vacuous or licentious, and its consequences for poetry. Sidney makes love poetry itself more serious in content, distinguishing, for example, the operation of reason and will in the lover's psychology. Spenser brings into at least some of his sonnets his own distinctive synthesis of Platonic and Christian ideas. Later chapters are on Shakespeare's Sonnets, Fulke Greville's *Caelica* and John Donne. Greville, standing about midway between Sidney and Donne, provides

an interesting case: beginning his sequence as a courtly lover, he soon displays his dissatisfaction with 'courtly' attitudes, eventually rejecting his mistresses for God, and even in the early sonnets he adopts the plain instead of the eloquent style more usually adopted by sixteenth-century love-poets in the Petrarchan tradition. Peterson has done well to emphasize the continuance of the plain lyric manner in this period, and is perhaps correct in his insistence that the eloquent Petrarchan manner has received an undue share of attention.

Eric La Guardia in 'Figural Imitation in English Renaissance Poetry'[7] explains that the mimetic poet participates in two worlds, Sidney's golden and brazen worlds, or the ideal and the mundane. He illustrates the point from the treatment of nature, love, and art in various poems, such as Greville's *Mustapha*, Spenser's *Faerie Queene*, and the lyrics of Herbert and Marvell.

In Paul J. Alpers's edition[8] of 'Modern Essays in Criticism' of Elizabethan poetry, the items have been chosen for an interest 'primarily critical'. It is divided into three sections: Poetics, 'Individual Poets and Modes', and *The Faerie Queene*. All except two (those on Spenser by Roger Sale and Martha Craig) have been published before. Those of general interest are to be noted here, those on individual poets, or works, in the appropriate places below. Rosemond Tuve's '"Imitation" and Images' comes from her important book, *Elizabethan and Metaphysical*

[7] In *Actes du IV Congrès de l'Association Internationale de Littérature Comparée*, ed. by François Jost. Mouton & Co. 1966. pp. xxxii+1459.   250 Guilders.

[8] *Elizabethan Poetry. Modern Essays in Criticism*, ed. by Paul J. Alpers. O.U.P. pp. 524. $2.50 (paperback).

Imagery (*YW* xxviii 162–4). I. A. Richards's 'The Places and Figures' is reprinted from *Speculative Instruments*.[9] Yvor Winters's 'The Sixteenth-Century Lyric in England: A Critical and Historical Reinterpretation' combines two essays published in *Poetry* (1939). Howard Baker's 'The Formation of the Heroic Medium' is from his *Induction to Tragedy* (1939). William Empson's 'Donne and the Rhetorical Tradition', (from *KR*, 1939), L. C. Knights's 'Shakespeare's Sonnets' (from *Explorations*, reviewed in *YW* xxvii 119, 132), and C. L. Barber's 'An Essay on the Sonnets' (from *The Laurel Shakespeare: The Sonnets*, reviewed in *YW* xlii 103), are also, for the sake of completeness, mentioned here, though their subjects belong to other chapters.

Lu Emily Pearson's *Elizabethan Love Conventions*[10] of 1933 (*YW* xiv 221–2), republished this year, surveys first the sources in Provence, Italy, and medieval England, then the Petrarchan and anti-Petrarchan 'currents' in Elizabethan love poetry. Major sonneteers from Sidney to Shakespeare, and a good many minor ones, are studied in some detail, the weight being thrown usually on their contribution to the 'philosophy of love'. This is a balanced and clear study of its subject, but, inevitably, in view of the amount of work produced by scholars during the last three decades, it appears old-fashioned: 'Leave me ô Love', for example, is taken as a fitting conclusion to *Astrophel and Stella*, though the author does, of course, realize that it was not originally published as part of Sidney's sequence.

Maren-Sofie Røstvig in a letter to the editor of *SEL* destroys certain prevalent misconceptions about Renaissance numerology, such as that it 'must needs be occult'. This is followed by a brief, civil protest, by Douglas Bush, against Røstvig's numerological reading of certain poems and his method.

E. H. Fellowes's edition of English madrigal verse and lute songs has been extensively revised and enlarged by Frederick W. Sternfeld and David Greer.[11] It now contains the texts of most madrigal collections and song books published between 1588 (when Byrd's first set virtually brought the English madrigal into being) and 1632. It is divided into two parts: madrigals, including some part-songs which are not strictly Italianate madrigals; and airs or solo songs with lute accompaniment. Ten new collections are added to Fellowes's editions of 1920 and 1929, and his texts have been rechecked with the original copies. As before, the texts are modernized. The notes now combine Fellowes's information with facts discovered since 1929.

Elizabethan Lyrical Poets,[12] edited by Patricia Thomson, is an anthology designed for sixth-formers and undergraduates, with texts in modernized spelling, introduction, and explanatory notes. The emphasis falls on eight major lyrists, Spenser, Sidney, Raleigh, Daniel, Drayton, Shakespeare, Donne, and Campion.

Julia G. Ebel (*Lib*) has attempted a

[9] *Speculative Instruments*, by I. A. Richards. Chicago U.P. Routledge & Kegan Paul. 1955. pp. 216. $4.50. 21*s*.

[10] *Elizabethan Love Conventions*, by Lu Emily Pearson. Barnes & Noble. Allen & Unwin. pp. xi+365. $7.50. 52*s*. 6*d*.

[11] *English Madrigal Verse 1588–1632*, ed. by E. H. Fellowes. Revised and enlarged by Frederick W. Sternfeld and David Greer. 3rd edition. O.U.P. pp. xxx+798. £4 10*s*.

[12] *Elizabethan Lyrical Poets*, ed. by Patricia Thomson. Routledge & Kegan Paul. pp. xv+219. 18*s*; limp, 11*s*. 6*d*.

numerical survey, with charts, of translations done between 1560 and 1603. This inevitably draws attention to the setting in which the famous translations (North's, Florio's etc.) appeared.

Robert D. Pepper (*Lib*) attempts an interpretation of the hitherto un-noticed and rather obscure sentence of instruction to Thomas Vautrol-lier's publisher in the two surviving copies of Francis Clement's *The Petie Schole* (1587).

Robert Illing (*NQ*) indicates dis-crepancies between the original text of Est's Psalter (1592) and the edition published in 1844 by the Musical Antiquarian Society.

M. C. Smith (*Bibliothèque d'Hum-anisme et Renaissance*) aims to show how Ronsard came to write *Elegies*, dedicated to Queen Elizabeth, Robert Dudley, and William Cecil, and how he changed his text as political cir-cumstances changed.

James VI's youthful treatise, *Reulis*, is related by Ronald D. S. Jack (*English*) to other examples of Renais-sance critical theory (by Trissino, Vida, Du Bellay, Puttenham, Gas-coigne etc.) and shown to be at once an attempt to bring Scottish poetry into the European mainstream and a nationalistic plea for 'a Scottish poetic and linguistic autonomy'. It is, of course, relatively limited in scope in that, like Gascoigne, James con-centrates largely on rhetoric and technique.

Arthur F. Kinney (*SEL*), aware that Gosson's *Schoole of Abuse* prompted the first important Eng-lish criticism, asks what in it so stimulated and concerned his con-temporaries. Re-examining the text he shows that Gosson 'introduces a new complex of issues in his attack, touching upon social, economic, and legal concerns as well as ethical con-cerns', and that 'in style . . . there

appears a consistent rhetorical struc-ture in the ordering of ideas'.

SIDNEY

Franco Marenco (*Filologia e Let-teratura*) considers the current revival of interest in Sidney, covering books published in 1965-6.

J. A. van Dorsten (*ES*) starts with strong and just appreciation of Fran-ces Yates's recent work on the art of memory (*YW* xlvii 171), before going on to a search for '"speaking pic-tures" that resemble mnemonic *imag-ines*' in the work of Sidney.

Mary R. Mahl (*TLS*, 21 Dec) reports on the Norwich Sidney MS. (as a newly discovered MS. of Sid-ney's *Apology* is to be called). It is a substantive text, unrelated to the Penshurst MS. or to the editions of 1595 by Olney and by Ponsonby. A facsimile edition will appear in due course.

Russell A. Fraser (*SAQ*), who sees devotion to the uses of life as the essence of humanism, defines Sidney as the humanist *par excellence*: in theory in the *Apology*, and in practice in *Arcadia*, art is of value because it is exemplary.

Franco Marenco (*EM* 1966) inter-prets *Arcadia* as an allegory of human life inspired by Calvinistic thought: the Arcadian setting, both attractive and repulsive as it is, the world, in which the two princes live as the soul lives prisoner of the senses.

Nancy R. Lindheim (*SP*) takes the opportunity afforded by the hundred pages of retrospective narrative in Book II of the revised *Arcadia* 'to examine Sidney's complex sense of structure': the elements of moral choice, conflict, the emergence and exercise of virtue, all important themes of his, help to explain the complexity.

In his book on *Sidney's Poetic*

Development,[13] Neil L. Rudenstine illustrates an unbroken continuity from the *Arcadia* poems and the contemporaneous *Certain Sonnets* to *Astrophel and Stella*. A point well made is that these works have concerns in common with each other and also with those of Sidney's own early years as known to us through his correspondence with Hubert Languet. For example, the conflicting claims of retirement and the active life, of duty and desire, or reason and passion, forge important links. Another of Rudenstine's theses is that the ornate rhetoric of some of the *Arcadia* poems is not a sign of immature experimentation, or mere delight in 'decoration', but that it is, in its context, intentional, purposeful, and 'functional'. At this stage Sidney is, in any case, by no means incapable of the plain, colloquial, and dramatic manner, in which rhetorical figures are reduced to a minimum: not only the rustic songs, but also those of Philisides (Sidney's fictional self and the forerunner of Astrophel) demonstrate this. It is good to have a chapter on *Certain Sonnets*, which has attracted little critical attention, and the arrangement of which, in accordance with form and theme, has hitherto passed unnoticed. Rudenstine is also right to give attention to Sidney's critical theories in connexion with his poetic practice, and particularly to his 'anti-Ciceronian' emphasis on the pre-eminence of subject matter, and to his important comment on *Energia* in the *Apology*. The quality of *Energia*, that which in poetry is 'tuned to the highest key of passion' (Sidney's own words), is most clearly manifest in *Astrophel and Stella*. The last six chapters are given to various aspects of, or groups of poems in, this work. Analyses of stress and rhyme

patterns and other stylistic details from Sidney's poems, though they do not always sustain interest, provide factual backing for Rudenstine's main points. His is a comprehensive study, omitting (except for an appendix on dating) only the translation of the Psalms. An essay on 'Sidney and Energia' from this book is in Alpers's collection (see note 8), in which is David Kalstone's 'Sir Philip Sidney: The Petrarchan Vision', reprinted from his book on *Sidney's Poetry* (*YW* xlvi 180–1).

A short note on the mysterious *Arcadia* listed by Ramage, supposedly of 1599, in fact a copy of the 1613 *Arcadia*, and once the property of Pope, is provided by Bent Juel-Jensen (*BC*). He also describes in *Lib* an unrecorded issue of *Arcadia* in 1638, 'a reprint of the 1633 edition printed for Simon Waterson and Robert Young, and probably by Young'.

Short analyses of the sonnets 'And have I heard her say?' and 'Leave me, ô Love, which reachest but to dust', both from Sidney's *Certain Sonnets*, are by Paul K. Dempsey and Leland Ryken respectively, and appear in *Ex*.

Elizabeth Dipple's essay on Sidney's eclogues, in *Literary Monographs*,[14] has not been available for review.

William A. Ringler assumed that Sidney would have disapproved of Edward IV, and that therefore his sonnet on his character and career (*Astrophel and Stella*, no. 75) is not to be taken at its face value—an assumption questioned by T. G. A. Nelson (*AUMLA*), who points out that the king's public image in the sixteenth century was not bad, and sometimes positively good.

---

[13] *Sidney's Poetic Development*, by Neil L. Rudenstine. Harvard U.P. pp. x+313. $6.95.

[14] *Literary Monographs I*, ed. by Eric Rothstein and Thomas K. Dunseath. Wisconsin U.P.

Jean Robertson (*NQ*) goes into the possibility of Shakespeare's debt in *Macbeth* (II ii 37–40) to Sidney's sonnet on sleep (*Astrophel and Stella*, no. 39).

Franco Marenco, in two articles in *Filologia e Letteratura*, gives an appreciation of Sidney's achievement in *Astrophel and Stella* (which he compares to that of Caravaggio's painting 'Amore vittorioso'), stressing his use of commonplaces, conventional arguments and conceits, and, at the same time, his originality, especially in directing his interest not only to love but to morals and to life as a whole.

Astrophil and Stella,[15] edited by Max Putzel, has not been available for review.

SPENSER

Harold Fromm (*EM*, 1966) makes a spirited attack, intended to provoke the powers-that-be, on the 'unfounded notion of Spenser as a great poet', which, he thinks, is merely a truism inherited from the past. He places Spenser in the category of dull and talented, and not in that of the 'powerful and original' Shakespeare, Milton, and Wordsworth.

E. Paul Alworth's essay on 'Spenser's Concept of Nature' appears in *His Firm Estate*,[16] a collection which has not been available for review. Hallett Smith's '*The Shepheardes Calender* and Pastoral Poetry', from his book *Elizabethan Poetry* (*YW* xxxiii 149) is reprinted in Alpers's collection of essays (see note 8).

G. Wilson Knight's essay on Spenser, published in 1939, reappears

this year in his *Poets of Action*.[17] There can be no doubt that the author of *The Shepheardes Calender* (already full of his typical profusion and 'upgushing of poetic life') and of the *Hymnes* and *The Faerie Queene* is one such. In the *Hymnes*, imagery of light, fire, scintillation, and sun accompanies the synthesis, characteristic of Renaissance poetry, of Christian and erotic feeling. In *The Faerie Queene* the erotic impulse is yet more dynamic, accompanying the Spenserian concern with the whole problem of action. Knight writes appreciatively of these aspects of Spenser's work, at the same time advancing strong criticisms of the lack of design, structure, and direction in *The Faerie Queene*.

Spenser's *Fowre Hymnes* and *Epithalamion* come together in an edition[18] by Enid Welsford whose aim in making this unusual combination is to expound Spenser's doctrine of love in several of its contrasting forms. The exposition is given chiefly in an introduction of ninety-one pages, though there are also explanatory notes, as well as two appendixes (on the text and on Hieatt's numerological reading of *Epithalamion*). The *Fowre Hymnes* are related to a complex of traditions, the Platonic, the medieval romantic, the Renaissance Neoplatonic, the Christian, and the Protestant Christian. Each of the four represents a different aspect of the love theme, but together they form, Miss Welsford believes, a unified whole, a 'dramatic poem', in which two ideas of love, the love for a woman and the love for God, are both shown to be good and

[15] *Astrophil and Stella*, by Sir Philip Sidney. Ed. by Max Putzel. Doubleday. Anchor Books. pp. xxxii+208. $1.25.

[16] *His Firm Estate*, ed. by Donald E. Hayden. Univ. of Tulsa, Oklahoma.

[17] *Poets of Action*, by G. Wilson Knight. Barnes & Noble. Methuen. pp. xvi+302. $8.50*s*.

[18] *Fowre Hymnes; Epithalamion: A Study of Spenser's Doctrine of Love*, by Edmund Spenser. Ed. and introduced by Enid Welsford. Blackwell. pp. ix+215. 45*s*.

true. *Epithalamion* is related to a more narrowly literary tradition, that of the nuptial hymn through the ages; and here Spenser presents yet another aspect of the love theme, seeing himself and his bride, as he does in the Easter Day sonnet in *Amoretti*, 'as part of a larger whole which includes both earth and heaven'.

Charles Bowie Millican's study[19] 'in the contemporaneous background for Spenser's use of the Arthurian legend', originally published in 1932, has been reprinted this year with a few revisions and the addition of references to Ralph Knevett, who attempted a continuation of *The Faerie Queene*. The book surveys the cult of Arthur from the accession of Henry VII, supposedly his descendant, to the death of Charles I. There was prolonged controversy amongst historians over the historicity of Arthur, as well as of Brutus and the whole 'British' legend, and it was naturally to the advantage of the Tudor monarchs, and even of the Stuarts, to foster belief in all this. The Arthurian motif appears in various patriotic shows, as, for example, in the one given before Elizabeth in 1575 at Kenilworth, and the one celebrating the creation of Henry as Prince of Wales in 1610. There seems also to have been, in Spenser's day, a 'Round Table' of Archers in London, while at Cambridge, where he was a student, the belief that Arthur founded the university was current. There was much, therefore, to foster interest in the Arthurian legend, and to make it inevitable that it should embody, for him as for others, the spirited patriotism characteristic of his age.

Spenser's Images of Life[20] is not the important book on C. S. Lewis's favourite author which he could and would have written. It is an interesting, short book on *The Faerie Queene* built up by Alastair Fowler, with great labour and discretion, from Lewis's lecture notes. The view that 'the poem is . . . very often to be regarded as a verbalization of Pageant' is likely to be acceptable at a time when the relevance of iconography to Renaissance literary studies is increasingly recognized. Amongst the images or icons Lewis analyses are the False Cupid (III xi 48), who, being armed, contrasts with those images in which Cupid has laid aside his weapons. He presents an image of cruel, evil love, that of 'polite adultery', from Ovid on. His other anti-types are Venus as hermaphrodite (IV x 41), Scudamour and Amoret in embrace in the cancelled stanzas of Book III, and Nature in the Mutability cantos, all representing *natura unialis*. Lewis makes a particularly valuable discrimination between the features characteristic of his images of good and evil in general. The former are often of veiled and mysterious character, unveiled in solitary places (Belphoebe), or at moments of achievement (Una at the end of Book I). They are often gay, spontaneous, and fertile, always connected with order, sometimes naïve. Above all, in contrast to the images of evil, they are energetic. Unlike Shakespeare and Milton, Spenser does not characterize evil by energy. It is represented as relaxation or the death-wish (Despair), defect (Abessa) or disease (Malbecco), frenzy (Pyrochles), vacancy (the empty rooms in the House of Busirane), and as a disgusting thing (Error). Mutability is

[19] *Spenser and the Table Round*, by Charles Bowie Millican. Frank Cass & Co. Ltd. pp. x+237. 75s.

[20] *Spenser's Images of Life*, by C. S. Lewis. Ed. by Alastair Fowler. C.U.P. pp. ix+144. 21s. $3.95.

the exception that proves the rule. Lewis also considers the story of *The Faerie Queene*, referring especially to Florimell's and Arthur's stories; and he analyses Britomart's dream at Isis Church.

Elizabeth A. F. Watson's *Spenser*[21] belongs to a series, 'Literature in Perspective', which aims at giving straightforward, lucid accounts, avoiding critical jargon, of various writers. Her short, informative book has succeeded admirably in these respects. The first three chapters remove certain difficulties in the path of the newcomer to Spenser. They provide relevant 'background' material. Spenser's ambition to write a national epic, aspects of his life (such as his education and his life in Ireland) bearing on his work, the function of his allegory, his literary models, his use of classical philosophy and his own conception of the world, are the main subjects covered. The fourth chapter proceeds to a running commentary on each of the books of *The Faerie Queene*, while the fifth covers all the other poems. There is no fault to find in this unpretentious book, except that the Bibliography and Index are rather sketchy, and the contents of the former occasionally odd.

Paul J. Alpers's bulky book[22] on the poetry of *The Faerie Queene* is not, as we might expect, primarily concerned with evaluation of poetic passages; rather, simply, to refocus attention on the poetry, instead of, for example, on the narrative. He refuses to judge it as narrative poetry in any case, preferring the 'rhetorical mode' in which each stanza is taken

as an address to the reader, eliciting a response from him, modifying or complicating his feelings and attitudes. Spenser's is, he believes, not even pictorial poetry in the sense that it renders real visual experience: Spenser's 'speaking pictures' create a psychological experience in the reader. This is an interesting thesis, though sometimes Alpers's reader may hope to get away from its limitations, and, after all, have it both ways. In the Phedon episode in Book II 'the climax of the episode is not an action at all, but a rhetorical scheme, a formal arrangement of words—precisely a stanza of poetry and nothing else'. The emphasis on the stanza, on the rhetoric, and the words is welcome, but are we forbidden any interest in the connexions of stanza and stanza, in the unwinding of the stories? Why that 'nothing else'? From the third chapter, headed 'Spenser's Poetic Language', onwards, the reader feels more secure. Here there is useful comparison between *The Faerie Queene* and both Marlowe's *Hero and Leander* and Drayton's *The Barons Warres*, and comment on structural and grammatical ambiguity as 'a genuine poetic resource for Spenser'. Alpers goes on to consider the 'organization' (what most scholars call the 'structure') of the poem. There are thought-provoking chapters on 'the Sixteenth-Century Reader', and on Spenser's use of Ariosto. Alpers believes that various responses, other than the narrow moralistic one illustrated in Golding's comments on Ovid, were found in Spenser's period. Spenser himself was not limited to the platitudinous allegorizing way of reading *Orlando Furioso* (for example, Toscanella's). A valuable detailed examination of his rehandling of Ariosto's material shows that though he took suggestions from the allegorists, his reading

[21] *Spenser*, by Elizabeth A. F. Watson. Literature in Perspective. Evans Bros. Ltd. pp. 176. 16s. 8s. 6d. (paperback).

[22] *The Poetry of 'The Faerie Queene'*, by Paul J. Alpers. Princeton U.P. pp. ix+415. $12.50. £5 19s.

was more fully responsive and intelligent: he transmutes his original as Jonson transmuted Horace. The iconography of *The Faerie Queene* receives due attention, Alpers showing that Spenser does not simply treat conventional symbols as an 'established code'. Parts of the poem also get detailed consideration: the Cave of Mammon in Book II, the theme of heroism in Book I, and the 'Heroic and Pastoral' in Book III.

The Faerie Queene naturally figures prominently in Charles Moorman's account[23] of 'the evolution of the knight in literature'. Though he takes Hawes's Graunde Amoure as the link between Chaucer's knight and Spenser's knights, he is struck more by the distinctiveness and uniqueness of the morally conceived and allegorical heroes of *The Faerie Queene*. A contrast with Ariosto bears this out: 'Bradamante is chaste, but Britomart is chastity'. Within the English tradition a similar contrast between Malory's and Spenser's knights is to be observed.

Veselin Kostić in an article of one hundred pages in *EM* (1966) discusses Spenser's use of Ariosto, with reference to the development of critical ideas (imitation, theory of epic, function of poetry etc.) between *Orlando Furioso* and *The Faerie Queene*. Finally he asks the question whether Ariosto really was a suitable model for Spenser, and answers it in the negative. In the sixteenth century *Orlando Furioso* was the only modern epic considered worthy of imitation. But Spenser has no true affinity with its author.

Roger Sale in his essay on 'Spenser's Undramatic Poetry' in Alpers's collection (see note 8) starts with a reminder that the term 'dramatic' is not, of necessity, more approbative

[23] *A Knyght There Was*, by Charles Moorman. Kentucky U.P. pp. viii+170. $6.

than 'undramatic'. He then gives a description of Spenser's poetry, based upon 'a sense of the kind of undramatic verse it is'. He first explains that 'The author of an undramatic work is certain and does not need his story to discover a sense of life he already commands'. Spenser has this kind of 'certainty' in abundance. 'We read on and on in *The Faerie Queene* not to find out what happens to a particular character but to follow Spenser's sequence, the evenness and unhurriedness of which is the mark of his assurance that he knows what life is like.' Sale also gives interesting examples, particularly of Spenser's repetitions of adjectives.

Martha Craig's essay (based on her unpublished doctoral dissertation: Yale University, June, 1959) on 'The Secret Wit of Spenser's Language' also appears in Alpers's collection (see note 8). She encounters the difficulty that 'for many readers the language of *The Faerie Queene* is at best merely curious or quaint, at worst hollow and contorted'. She successfully applies the ideas about language set forth in Plato's *Cratylus*: 'Plato's etymologizing expedient explains the sort of archaizing Spenser does in *The Faerie Queene*.' She is especially good on names. For example, 'Orgoglio is not from heaven and earth' (as it is according to the mythographers) 'but merely from earth and air'. He is born of *Gea* (earth), but his sire is *aella* (stormy wind), or alternatively *aiolos* (shifting, changeable). Most of Dr. Craig's illustrations are from Book I, but there are also some others from other parts of *The Faerie Queene*.

W. B. C. Watkins's 'Shakespeare's Banquet of Sense' from his *Shakespeare and Spenser* (*YW* xxxi 109–110) is yet another essay in Alpers's collection (see note 8): it contains, of course, only a few pages on *The Faerie Queene*.

D. Douglas Waters (*Renaissance Quarterly*), studying the relations of Duessa with the Red Cross Knight (in *The Faerie Queene* Book I) at the fountain, and also Orgoglio in his castle, makes the point that the physical is a symbol of the spiritual fornication. Duessa also fits in with Spenser's theological allegory: she is, he believes, influenced by the tradition of the mass personified as a whore.

Harry Rusche (*SEL*) thinks that Despair (in Book I) has received undue emphasis as allegedly the Red Cross Knight's chief adversary, and so takes up Pauline Parker's point that Pride has this role. Despair, error, hypocrisy, falsehood and faithlessness are subordinate to it. Pride maintains its traditional primacy.

Spenser's emblem of Gluttony (*The Faerie Queene*, I iv 21) includes the feature of the long neck, which has been traced back to Aristotle's account of the glutton Philoxenus, who wished for a throat as long as a crane's in order to enjoy his food the more. Malcolm H. South (*MLR*) uses Sir Thomas Browne's comment on Philoxenus to illuminate Spenser's conceit.

J. C. Maxwell (*NQ*) identifies the Virgilian echo (*Aeneid*, VI 127) in *The Faerie Queene*, II iii 41 8–9.

R. M. Cummings (*JWCI*) and Jerry Leath Mills (*NQ*) both tackle Spenser's arithmological stanza (*The Faerie Queene*, II ix 22). Cummings suggests that it is 'an exercise not in plane but in solid geometry'. He adduces a hitherto unnoticed parallel from Francesco Colonna's *Hyperotomachia Poliphili* (1499), from which he supplies the relevant illustration of a structure partly resembling the House of Alma. There are also similarities in the allegorical comment.

Mills suggests that the description of the House of Alma is assigned to the twenty-second stanza of this book and canto because twenty-two is associated with moderation or temperance by Isidore and his successors. Alastair Fowler's opinion, in his extensive study of the numerology of *The Faerie Queene* (*YW* xlv 211–212) was that twenty-two symbolized the soul.

Jack B. Oruch (*SP*), writing on that neglected sub-genre, the river marriage, offers comment on Spenser's 'Epithalamion Thamesis' (never published and perhaps never written), the Thames-Medway marriage pageant in *The Faerie Queene* (IV xi 11–53) and the river marriage myths in *Colin Clouts Come Home Againe* and the Mutability cantos, as well as on the fragments of the anonymous 'De Connubio Tamae et Isis', printed in the early editions of Camden's *Britannia*.

Arnold Williams's *Flower on a Lowly Stalk*,[24] a study of *The Faerie Queene* Book VI, the book of 'courtesy', has not been available for review.

Spenser's treatment of the Garden of Adonis and the trial of Mutability is covered in about five pages in Frank Kermode's far-ranging account[25] of 'ends' and 'apocalypses' in fiction: the first, he shows, deals 'with the sempiternity of earthly forms, and the second with the dilation of being in these forms under the shadow of a final end'.

OTHER POETS

The minor epic or epyllion (as it is now often called) has received, in

[24] *Flower on a Lowly Stalk: the Sixth Book of 'The Faerie Queene'*, by Arnold Williams. Michigan State U.P. pp. 144. $5.75.
[25] *The Sense of an Ending. Studies in the Theory of Fiction*, by Frank Kermode. Bryn Mawr College. O.U.P. pp. x+187. $5.75 (Canada $6.35).

recent years, increasing recognition as a distinct Elizabethan literary genre. Elizabeth Story Donno's collection, published in 1963 (*YW* xliv 186) is now supplemented by Paul W. Miller's *Seven Minor Epics of the English Renaissance*.[26] The short narrative poems by Dunstan Gale, Richard Lynche, William Barksted, Samuel Page, and two anonymous poets, together spanning the years from 1596 to 1624, are reproduced in facsimile. Though, traditionally, Ovid is the storehouse for the Elizabethan epyllion, only three of the stories in this collection derive from the *Metamorphoses*. Perhaps that well was running dry by the end of the sixteenth century. At any rate, Lynche seems to have derived the material for *Dom Diego and Mirrha* from Bandello, via Painter, while the anonymous *Philos and Licia* and Page's *Amos and Laura*, though both indebted to *Hero and Leander*, seem to be original stories. The influence of Marlowe, Shakespeare, and, in Lynche's case, of Lodge, is apparent in metre, style, and tone. These 'Ovidian' stories are generally simple in outline, though richly ornamented, and expressive of extremes of romantic passion.

A similar, but fortunately in content different, volume is Nigel Alexander's edition of *Elizbethan Narrative Verse*,[27] covering the period 1560–1610. Except for Marlowe's *Hero and Leander*, this contains poems not readily available in print: the anonymous *Fable of Ovid treting of Narcissus*, Lodge's *Scillaes Metamorphosis*, Chapman's and Henry Petowe's continuations of *Hero and Leander*, Chapman's *Ovids Banquet of Sence*, Francis Beaumont's *Salmacis and Hermaphroditus*, Henry Willoby's *Willobie his Avisa*, Daniel's *Complaint of Rosamund*, two of Drayton's *Heroicall Epistles*, and Giles Fletcher's *Christs Victorie and Triumph*. A good deal of the emphasis again falls on the Ovidian element in narrative poetry. English Ovidian poetry has, Alexander believes, 'dramatic range and possibilities' of a kind not recognized by Carew in the well-known attack on Elizabethan mythological poetry in his elegy on Donne. For one thing there was more than one way of interpreting, and hence of imitating, Ovid.

I meane to shewe, accordying to my wytte

That Ovyd by this tale no follye mente,

says Golding, following in the tradition of *Ovide moralisé*. Lodge and Marlowe delight in the world of mythology, but the latter does not stop at delight, and presents, with typical ambiguity, various different attitudes to the story of Hero and Leander. Willoby uses the Ovidian framework to throw into relief a Christian heroine whose virtue withstands pressure from suitors of all kinds and nations: she is unlike Marlowe's Hero, Shakespeare's Venus, and most Ovidian heroines in this respect. Alexander does not, in any case, limit himself to the Ovidian. Daniel's *Complaint of Rosamund* and Fletcher's *Christs Victorie* are narrative poems of a different order and source, the first derived from English, the second from biblical history. The texts, in old spelling, are accompanied by an introduction and notes, alike useful.

John Buxton's book[28] of elegant

[26] *Seven Minor Epics of the English Renaissance* (1596–1624), introduced by Paul W. Miller. Scholars' Facsimiles & Reprints. pp. xxvii+272. $8.

[27] *Elizabethan Narrative Verse*, ed. by Nigel Alexander. Edward Arnold. pp. ix+ 338. 42*s*.

[28] *A Tradition of Poetry*, by John Buxton. London: Macmillan; New York: St. Martin's Press. pp. ix+189. 30*s*. $6.95.

essays on gentlemen-poets (plus one lady) includes a newly minted one on Gascoigne and a revision of the one on Drayton originally published as the introduction to his poems (1953). Gascoigne deserves all the attention he has received here, for, though he can hardly be thought of as an undiscovered genius, he is surely the most interesting of writers of the period between the deaths of Wyatt and Surrey and the emergence of Sidney and Spenser, and this because he is varied, lively, and original. He translated Ariosto and Dolce, wrote sonnets in the Surrey form, and a variety of other lyrics, a satire, *The Steele Glas* (in blank verse), a vivid journalistic account (in prose) of the siege of Antwerp, and the thoughtful, practical, *Certayne Notes of Instruction concerning the making of verse or ryme in English*, 'the first piece of critical writing by an English poet'. Buxton's essay on Drayton gives a well-balanced survey of the different genres to which this thoroughgoing professional applied himself, the pastoral, the sonnet, the historical poem, the topographical. He stresses Drayton's responsiveness to his age, as well as his individual qualities, the Englishness of his pastorals, the skill in describing narrative action etc.

Jörg Schönert's article (*Ang*) on the revisions made by Drayton to his sonnet sequence, *Idea*, in successive editions from 1594 to 1619, illustrates various changes in form and style, and the variety of influences and tendencies ('Elizabethan', 'metaphysical', etc.) in his work.

Cecil Seronsy's biographical and critical study *Samuel Daniel*[29] has been anticipated not only by his own articles, which are incorporated in it, but by Joan Rees's book, published

after its completion but well before its publication (*YW* xlv 218). It provides, nevertheless, a useful, short, comprehensive account of Daniel's poems, plays, masques, literary criticism, and his prose history of England, all set neatly within the framework of his life in noble homes, at court, or in retirement. Seronsy stresses Daniel's innovativeness, so that he appears more original, more of the *avant garde*, than in previous studies: if not absolutely the first, he was at least amongst the first to attempt the sonnet sequence, verse epistle, historical poem, Senecan closet drama, pastoral drama, and masque in England. Seronsy also gives him praise where praise is due. His claim that *Cleopatra* is the best of the plays of its type is, though doubtless correct, not fully substantiated by comparison with its rivals, and his appraisal of *Civil Wars* is rather cursory. But he certainly carries conviction in his study of *Musophilus* and the six verse epistles of 1603, Daniel's 'crowning achievements', in the appraisal of *Ulysses and the Siren*, and, most of all, in the excellent analysis of the funeral poem on the death of Daniel's patron, the Earl of Devonshire, a poem combining elegiac and epic modes with features of the seventeenth-century 'character'. There is also a judicious summing-up in the last chapter covering diction, rhetoric, versification, metaphor, and aspects of Daniel's 'thought' with special reference to his unique sense of history.

Since the complete poems of Robert Southwell were last edited in 1872, when A. B. Grosart's edition appeared, the work[30] originally undertaken by James H. McDonald and then extensively revised and completed by Nancy Pollard Brown is of

---

[29] *Samuel Daniel*, by Cecil Seronsy. Twayne Publishers, Inc. pp. 198. $3.95.

[30] *The Poems of Robert Southwell, S. J.*, ed. by James H. McDonald and Nancy Pollard Brown. O.U.P. pp. cvi+180. 55s. $8.80.

obvious value. Southwell, even when given the O.U.P.'s handsomest V.I.P. treatment, retains the unmistakable marks of the good but minor poet. His output was small, his effects rarely sustained, and even his longest and most ambitious poem, *Saint Peter's Complaint* (792 lines), contains many monotonous passages, besides being, as a whole, shapeless. He is still, in fact, chiefly to be remembered for the anthology piece, 'The burning Babe', and some other lyrics, such as 'A vale of teares', which deserve to be equally well known. Miss Brown presents a selective text based on the early printed collections, and, for the poems not included in them, on MS. copies, the most important of which is the Stonyhurst MS. She provides a full collation, and a commentary combining textual and explanatory notes. The latter are generally useful, though one must question the suggestion that the 'Anna' mentioned in one version of 'Decease release' could be Anne of Denmark. Miss Brown reorders the lyrics in accordance with the MS. tradition (which, in this respect, she prefers to that of the printed editions). She also raises certain new doubts about the Southwell canon. The first editor of the lyrics is, she believes, reliable, and accordingly suspicion is cast on the poems he did not print, the three in *Mæoniæ*.

With this standard edition of Southwell's poems, it is convenient to have a paperback reprint of the standard biography of the poet by Christopher Devlin.[31] The story of his education abroad, his return to England as a Jesuit priest, his mission, capture, trial, and martyrdom is of interest on many levels, moving in itself, and historically illuminating. In the years before Hooker made the Anglican *via media* a rallying point, there were many good reasons for deviation to Puritan separatism or Catholic recusancy, and Southwell's own reckoning was that about a third of the nation clung to the 'old religion', for whose sake, however, only a few were willing to risk disembowelling. Devlin brings out well the Catholic missionaries' endeavour to exercise religious, without political, influence, though their plea that they were not traitors to the Queen often fell on deaf ears. He also deals clearly with the doctrine of equivocation which has given Southwell, its exponent, a certain notoriety. Southwell's character and civilized ways emerge freshly from these pages in spite of the difficulty presented by a person whose piety was not relieved by any marked quirks. His poetry is not dealt with in detail, though there is a discussion of his possible influence on Shakespeare and other contemporaries.

F. M. McKay (*NQ*) offers a brief note on Peter Mowle, the compiler of Oscott College MS. E. 3. 11 (containing poetry by the two recusant poets, Southwell and Alabaster).

C. S. Lewis's 'Hero and Leander', on the poem by Marlowe and Chapman, originally published in *PBA* (1952) is reprinted in Alpers's collection of essays (see note 8).

Joseph C. Baldwin has written on 'John Heywood and Sir John Davies: a change in the Tradition of the sixteenth-century Satiric Epigram' (*Satire Newsletter*).

Wesley Trimpi (*JEGP*) examines 'all the available conditions' favouring the particular reading of Nashe's line 'Brightnesse falls from the ayre' that he thinks 'emerge as the most probable', *i.e.* he rejects, as far as he can, the arguments of those who support 'hayre' for 'ayre'.

Cesare G. Cecioni (*Rivista di*

---

[31] *The Life of Robert Southwell*, by Christopher Devlin. Watergate Edition. Sidgwick and Jackson. pp. x+367. 17s. 6d.

letterature moderne e comparate) elaborates the argument, originally put forward in the introduction to his edition of Thomas Watson's *Hekatompathia* (Catania 1964), that Frances Walsingham was the poet's inspiration. He adduces particularly the MS. variant 'Franc' (for *Dame*) in the line 'All this deere *Dame* befals me for thy sake'.

Roger A. Geimer (*NQ*) works out the birth date, 1523, of Thomas Churchyard, and Merrill H. Goldwyn (*NQ*) extracts from *A Pitefull Complaint* (1579) an autobiographical account of his marriage. To *SP* Goldwyn contributes quotations from, and descriptions, of four unpublished MSS. of Churchyard, one letter and one poem in his own hand, two items in those of copyists.

Thomas George (*NQ*) exposes Samuel Rowland's plagiaristic habits in a detailed comparison between his *The Betraying of Christ* (1598) and the translation (1595 and 1597) of Guevara's *The Mount of Caluarie*.

David W. Lindsay (*SSL*) provides a short textual note, covering stanza division, punctuation, and two questionable readings in the Scottish Text Society edition by Alexander Lawson (1902), on Alexander Hume's *Of the Day Estivall*, one of the best of Scottish sixteenth-century poems.

OTHER PROSE WRITERS

Facsimiles of the B.M.'s copies of two prose works[32] by Raleigh, the very short *Last Fight of the Reuenge* (1591) and the much longer *Discouerie of Guiana* (1596), are printed together and published by the new Scolar Press. Both are stirring, topical works. The first, starting with an attack on the Spaniards and their 'vaine glorious vaunts' proceeds to a vigorous defence of Sir Richard Grenville who died as a result of his vain endeavour to preserve his ship *The Revenge*: 'he hath ended his life honourable in respect of the reputation wonne to his nation and country'. The second, a description of Raleigh's exploration of Guiana, is an eloquent plea to England to annexe it as a colony, and an attempt to sell its advantages by all means, fact and rhetoric, in his power. The chief is, of course, the dazzling promise of gold, which always fixated Raleigh's mind, and which, in one passage, he rates as a *desideratum* higher than bread. But, besides, he urges the value of the other trading commodities in Guiana, its fertility, food supplies, sport, healthy climate, the facts that it is only six weeks' journey from England, that an expedition can be manned by younger brothers, and will not cost much. Raleigh, not now enjoying the 'more happy times' of earlier years, is obviously committed heart and soul to the project. Guiana is 'a Country that hath yet her Maydenhead . . . I neuer saw a more beawtifull countrey'.

Dekker's prose pamphlets would probably never have been written had not the plague driven him out of the theatre and had he not been chronically short of that commodity, money, that Raleigh valued so highly. Yet they were certainly worth writing and no less certainly worth reprinting in a modern edition. E. D. Pendry's selection[33] includes in full *The Wonderful Year*, *The Gull's Horn-Book*, *Penny-Wise, Pound-Foolish*, and *Lantern and Candlelight*, his text of the

---

[32] *A Report of the Truth of the Fight about the Iles of the Açores (The Last Fight of the Reuenge); The Discouerie of the Large, Rich, and Bewtiful Empyre of Guiana*, by Sir Walter Raleigh. Scolar Press. pp. 28+16+111. 29*s*.

[33] '*The Wonderful Year*', '*The Gull's Horn-Book*', '*Penny-Wise, Pound-Foolish*', '*Villainies Discovered by Lantern and Candlelight*', *and Selected Writings*, by Thomas Dekker. Ed. by E. D. Pendry. Arnold. pp. ix+374. 50*s*.

last named being particularly useful in that this is the first reprint of the complete work. In his short introduction he makes the point that Dekker is 'essentially a writer of artifice'. Graphic as his descriptions are, with their air of first-hand recording and their circumstantial detail, he is obviously also the skilled contriver of literary effects. *The Wonderful Year*, proceeding from the death of Elizabeth in March 1603 to the accession of James, and thence to the plague which soon after devastated London, is full of contrast illustrating 'the short-lived felicity of man'. Dekker thinks in dramatic and moral terms; the sketch of the bride who sickens on her wedding day illustrates both. He is also more frequently critical and bitter than used to be supposed, as his comments on London's plague-time doctors show. In addition to the four pamphlets given in full, Pendry includes tales extracted from *The Raven's Almanac* and *A Knight's Conjuring*, in which Dekker's narrative art is displayed to advantage. The volume concludes with notes on sources and text, and a glossary.

The seven anti-episcopal pamphlets by 'Martin Marprelate gentleman' are conveniently brought together, in facsimile, in one volume.[34] First come the two, published in 1588, attacking Dr. John Bridges, his 'most senceles book', listing *Certaine Minerall and Metaphysical Schoolpoints* that ought to be defended by the established church. *Hay any worke for Cooper, Theses Martinianae, The iust censure and reproofe of Martin Iunior*, and *The Protestatyon of Martin Marprelat*, all of 1589, follow. Martin is much more interesting as a prose

writer than as a theologian, as a satirist than as a critic. Who, not already of his party, will be won over by his shot at 'the Canterburie Caiphas, with the rest of his Antichristian beasts'? Yet his lively, cheeky, and personal abuse is still readable in the same way as Nashe's is.

G. K. Hunter's 'Humanism and Courtship', from his book *John Lyly* (*YW* xliii 160–1) is reprinted in Alpers's collection of essays (see note 8).

There are two items on Nashe's *Unfortunate Traveller* to report. N. W. Bawcutt (*NQ*) draws attention to an anecdote in Jean Bodin's *The Republic* as a possible source (one of several) of the revenge story told in Cutwolfe's confession. Richard A. Lanham (*SSF*) considers 'Jack Wilton's personality as the central form' of Nashe's novel. This hero is, of course, the author's fictional spokesman. Lanham discerns a 'consistent pattern of anti-social violence' which, he thinks, may 'have come from the unique expressive demands that Nashe's personality and social situation made on his personality'.

In his *Groatsworth of Wit* Greene urges three men to change their way of life, though without naming them. Two are generally agreed to be Marlowe and Peele, but the 'Young Juvenal' has not been successfully identified. Philip Drew (*SEL*) argues thoroughly, but inconclusively, the claims of Nashe and Lodge.

Norman Sanders (*NQ*) takes up H. C. Hart's hint that Robert Greene's pamphlet *Farewell to Follie* (1591) relies on Pierre de la Primaudaye's *The French Academie* (translated, 1586): he shows that more than seventy sections are borrowed from this source.

Leonard Forster (*ES*) writes on the prose section in *The Theatre for*

---

[34] *The Martin Marprelate Tracts (1588–1589)*, by Martin Marprelate (pseudonym), Scolar Press. pp. ii+54+46+2+53+31+32+3. 48s.

Worldlings (1568), or rather, of its translator Theodore Roest, a friend of Spenser's schoolmaster Richard Mulcaster.

Maria G. Bellorini (*Aevum*) has written a short article, in Italian, on the evidence of Italian culture in Sir Thomas North's background; for example, his brother Roger knew the language well, and Thomas himself may have had contacts with Castelvetro.

X

The Earlier Stuart and the Commonwealth Period, Excluding Drama

AGNES M. C. LATHAM

Of the *Seven Minor Epics of the English Renaissance*,[1] reprinted at Gainesville, only one was published before 1607, so they fall within the seventeenth century, though they stem from *Hero and Leander* and *Venus and Adonis*, and are in the Ovidian tradition. An introduction by Paul W. Miller discusses authorship, sources, formal characteristics and literary value. The writer notes how freely the poets invent and embroider, yet always within a classical framework, using frequent mythological allusions to naturalize their stories in the Ovidian world. He does not always sufficiently recognize the tendency of the genre towards the *faux naïve* and the Elizabethan delight in the tragicomical. Dunstan Gale's *Pyramus and Thisbe* is surely not unintentionally bathetic. *Poets of the Early Seventeenth Century*[2] edited by Bernard and Elizabeth Davis, dispenses with Donne, who is reserved for another volume. The procession of poets follows very coherently from Jonson and William Browne through Herrick to Marvell, with the religious poets making a distinctive but not an alien contribution. English poetry, it appears, might not have been very different had Donne never written. The editors, however, pay due attention to the metaphysical strain. Their introduction and biographical notes are terse, graceful and admirably informative.

In the second edition of *The Metaphysical Poets*,[3] Helen Gardner has taken occasion to substitute the text of her recent volume of Donne's *Elegies and Songs and Sonnets*. There is not much change otherwise. She is still under fire for her handling of Donne. In 'Donne in the New Edition' (*Crit Q*), William Empson makes clear his disagreement with some of her emendations, with her new dating, and with her views on the relationship of manuscripts. He considers that the Donne he admires, the daring exploiter of the idea of plural worlds in space, has been unwarrantably bowdlerized. In 'Dr Gardner's Dating of the *Songs and Sonets*' (*EIC*), A. L. French, after examining the evidence adduced by Dame Helen, decides that her dating is wholly speculative and insufficient. Alan MacColl (*EIC*) defends the text, in 'Critical Forum', against the criticisms of Mark Roberts and is answered at some length by an unrepentant Roberts.

[1] *Seven Minor Epics of the English Renaissance (1596–1624)*. Facsimile Reproductions with an Introduction by Paul W. Miller. Gainesville. Florida. Scholars' Facsimiles and Reprints. pp. xxvii +272. $8.00.

[2] *Poets of the Early Seventeenth Century*, ed. by Bernard and Elizabeth Davis. Routledge English Texts. pp. x+246. 18s.

[3] *The Metaphysical Poets*. Selected and ed. by Helen Gardner. O.U.P. pp. xxxvi+309. 27s. 6d.

A leading article in *TLS*, 6 April, 'Ill Donne: Well Donne. Scholarship and Para-Scholarship', commends Dame Helen's work, though with some strictures. Her dating in particular is declared unacceptable, but she is praised for offering solid scholarship, rather than the shows of erudition and flights of fancy said to disfigure some recent work on Donne. On 24 Aug. Dame Helen made a good-humoured reply, commenting with feeling on the difficulty of her task—Donne has been 'explicated' more often than he has been edited or annotated—and going on to expand points of disagreement between herself, the anonymous *TLS* reviewer, and Mark Roberts. On 7 Sept. there is a brief reply by Roberts.

It is unlikely that W. Milgate, who has completed an edition of Donne's satires, epigrams and verse letters for the Clarendon Press,[4] will encounter a comparable critical barrage. The poems with which he is concerned are less familiar and less fiercely cherished than the lyrics. He will not, however, have them dismissed as by-products or aberrations. In the satires Donne has produced a sustained imitation of a classical genre, naturalizing it in the crowded, busy, corrupt world of Jacobean London. There is plenty of sheer fun alongside a genuine moral and religious gravity. Promise of the lyrical Donne is seen in the skilful portrayal of changing moods and in the critical, often ironic, awareness that can accompany an intense absorption in a dramatically imagined experience. The *Progress of the Soul* is 'a kind of anti-epic, with incidental, but continual, satiric comment'. In it can be seen a power of natural description such as Donne is often declared to lack. It is mock-heroic, and should not be read as an expression of portentous gloom and real despair. Two ideas were saved to serve on future occasions. The satire on dangerous innovators appears in *Ignatius his Conclave* and the spiritual journey in *The Second Anniversary*. The verse epistles are equally a new kind in English. Donne writes seriously to his men friends, with a deep concern for a quality he calls integrity. For women he has a strain of inventive hyperbole which witnesses both to his affection and their understanding. There is no falseness or obsequiousness. 'It would be strange if a poet who so persuasively and shrewdly wrote of the need for, or existence of, integrity in others should have abjectly surrendered his own.' In addition to the critical introduction there is an extensive textual introduction and commentary.

I. A. Shapiro's 'Donne in 1605–06' (*TLS* 26 Jan.) offers a tentative account of a journey abroad which Donne made with Sir Walter Chute. At the same time his wife left Pyrford, where she had been living with her cousin, Sir Francis Wolley, and stayed for some time at Peckham, the home of her married sister. Wolley, who was an extremely wealthy man, bequeathed nothing to Donne though he knew he was in sore straits. This and the move from Pyrford contradict Walton's account of Wolley's 'love and bounty' to Donne and suggest an estrangement.

In *John Donne. Conservative Revolutionary*,[5] N. J. C. Andreasen argues that Donne's habit of looking at both sides of a question must have enabled him in the end to present a synthesis. She distinguishes three traditions in his work. They are the cynical

---

[4] *John Donne. The Satires, Epigrams and Verse Letters*, ed. with introduction and commentary by W. Milgate. Clarendon Press. pp. lxxvii+296. 63s.

[5] *John Donne. Conservative Revolutionary*, by N. J. C. Andreasen. Princeton U.P. pp. ix+249. $6.95.

Ovidian, the masochistic Petrarchan, and the Christian Platonist, which corrects the two extremes. Donne's greatness as a poet lies in his power to 'capture these varieties of emotional experience from the inside'. This does not mean that he approves of them. The poems that glory in lust and those that are sated and disillusioned by it are equally condemnations, and so are the Petrarchan poems that project so magnificently the blasphemous conviction that love is all. The poems of 'good love' are curious in that they are the most technically advanced and at the same time the most traditional in the vision they express. Donne had probably always cherished this vision but had kept it hidden behind a mask of irony until he was so polished a poet that he need not fear the charge of banality.

Susumu Nomachi, in 'John Donne: Struggle behind the Mask of Sarcasm. Endless Pursuit of Sin and Death' (*Critical Studies*, Gakushin University, Tokyo) finds Donne in his early days trying to assert the claims of the particular against the general, and opposing a life of pleasure to the threat of death. Later he came to identify the self-assertion of the particular with sin, and death no longer appeared terrible. The particular is imperfect until it is united with the general, which alone can impart immortality.

P. G. Stanwood reports to *TLS*, 19 Oct., 'A Donne Discovery'. It is a Latin epigram in a manuscript in Durham Cathedral Library, which satirizes the canonization of St. Ignatius Loyola in 1622, and is attributed to 'Dr Dun. Deane of Paules'. Another manuscript discovery, reported by A. M. Gibbs in 'A Davenant Imitation of Donne?' (*RES*), relates to a poem modelled on 'Go and catch a falling star' and

assigned in Ashmole's hand to Davenant.

In 'Donne's "Peece of Chronicle"' (*RES*), William H. Matchett suggests that 'peece' may reflect the meaning of 'a fortified place', which would contrast effectively with the 'pretty rooms' the lovers build in sonnets. It also glances at the meanings of 'masterpiece' and 'fragment'. In 'Donne's "To his Mistress going to bed", 45' (*Ex*), Harold Love shows that the mention of a white linen sheet leads naturally to the idea of penance. Elias Schwartz, considering 'Donne's "Holy Sonnets", XIV' (*Ex*), denies that this sonnet is constructed upon the doctrine of the Trinity and argues for the three functional images of the tinker, the besieged town, and the rape. Richard E. Hughes is interested in 'The Woman in Donne's *Anniversaries*' (*ELH*). He thinks there is an important association with St. Lucy, with her martyrdom on the shortest day, and with the symbol of light. Elizabeth Drury died on St. Lucy's day but the poems are not about her. She received the tribute of a commonplace funeral elegy. The poems are meditative and intensely private, and Donne came to regret that they were ever published. They are about his own rebirth. Alexander Sackton supports the view that Donne thought of poetry as very private. 'Donne and the Privacy of Verse' (*SEL*), is based mainly upon evidence in the verse epistles.

John Donne. Selected Prose[6] is an anthology begun by Evelyn Simpson and completed by Helen Gardner and Timothy Healy. It consists of selections from the whole range of Donne's prose works including his letters. Two sermons are printed

---

[6] *John Donne: Selected Prose*. Chosen by Evelyn Simpson. Ed. by Helen Gardner and Timothy Healy. Clarendon Press. pp. xvi + 397. 55s.

entire, 'Death's Duell' and the Lent Sermon of February 12, 1630. Special attention has been paid to passages which will illustrate Donne's style and thought, and to those which notably parallel his verse.

In 'Time and Place in Donne's Sermons' (*PMLA*), William Gifford examines two sermons to show how topical Donne could be, and with what art he suited his discourse to his congregation. He spoke against ambition and covetousness at Court soon after parliament had debated the abuse of patents and Bacon had been charged with taking bribes. To an audience of the governors and children of Christ's Hospital he spoke of non-payment of tithes and told his mixed audience of aldermen and charity children that they each had their part in God's eternal plan. In '"Decency" and "Zeal" in Sermons of John Donne' (*TSLL*), Madelon E. Heatherington notes how frequently Donne urges an appropriate blending of moderation and zeal. Each needs the other. His approbation of a rightly applied zeal places him 'slightly left of the conservative Anglican *via media*'. In 'Donne's Debt to the Great Tradition: Old and New in his Treatment of Death' (*Ang*), Bettie Anne Doebler examines in particular Donne's sermon on the death of King James, showing how much he owed to tradition and how much was personal. Janel M. Mueller's 'A Borrowing of Donne's Christmas Sermon of 1621' (*HLQ*) shows by close comparison that John Cosin was borrowing heavily from Donne when he preached before the exiled English court at Paris in 1651.

R. S. Thomas supplies a frankly devotional preface to sixty-nine poems by Herbert.[7] He values the poet for what he has to say and that is how Herbert, at any rate, would wish it. He finds in his work 'the simplicity and gravity of great poetry' and 'a proof of the eternal beauty of holiness'. Joseph H. Summers has set out the whole of Herbert's English poetry in a scholarly booklet.[8] The introduction shows him confident of Herbert's appeal even to the uninstructed reader. He concentrates on an interpretation of 'The Church Porch', which seems to him the hardest of Herbert's poems for the present day.

In 'A Note on Herbert's "The Collar"' (*NQ*), Wolfgang Weiss suggests that when Herbert used the image of a 'rope of sands' he had in mind the supposed derivation of 'religion' from 'ligare'. Both rope and collar are images of thraldom, which the last lines of the poem dispel. In 'Herbert's "The Collar" and Shakespeare's *1 Henry IV*' (*ANQ*), William J. Brown notes a correspondence between Herbert's double meanings and Shakespeare's. Collar can refer to religious restraint and to choler, meaning either anger or melancholy. Roberts W. French, in 'Herbert's *Vertue*' (*Ex*), suggests that 'coal' means glowing coal and not ashes. Only in this sense can it be an image of a soul that 'lives'.

E. L. Marilla makes some observations on 'The Mysticism of Henry Vaughan' (*RES*). He rejects R. A. Durr's contention that Vaughan turned to religious poetry after experiencing a sudden conversion. Vaughan was throughout his life inclined to piety, particularly so in 1655, when he wrote the introduction to *Silex Scintillans*. His conversion was a gradual turning from a world in which there was nothing left for him

---

[7] *A Choice of George Herbert's Verse*, ed. with an introduction by R. S. Thomas. Faber. pp. 95. Paperback 6s. 6d. Cloth 21s.

[8] *The Selected Poetry of George Herbert*, ed. by J. H. Summers. Signet Classics. pp. xxxviii+288. 10s.

and his kind. Günther Wiese finds 'A New Source for Henry Vaughan's "Man in Darkness"' (*NQ*). He refers it to a Latin poem which appeared in 1632 in Robert Bolton's *The Four Last Things*. In 'Henry Vaughan's Apology for Darkness' (*SEL*), S. Sandbank investigates Vaughan's use of images of darkness as complementary to light. It reflects many antitheses—of night and day, affliction and blessing, sin and forgiveness, flint and fire, life and death, as well as the more conventional good and evil. The final stress is always on the light and the glory. Anthony Low suggests that in 'Vaughan's *The Morning Watch*' (*Ex*) the image of the lamp, which is the divine spark in the soul, should be interpreted with the help of the poem called *The Lampe*. Here the watch faithfully kept by the Wise Virgins is what preserves the spark. Ted-Larry Pebworth solves 'The Problem of *Restagnates* in Henry Vaughan's "The Water-fall"' (*PLL*) by rejecting the meaning cited in the *OED*, 'to become stagnant again', in favour of the Latin sense of 'overflow'. The water is purified in falling as man is in dying.

Robert Harrison considers 'Erotic Imagery in Crashaw's "Musick's Duell"' (*SCN*). He complains that Crashaw is too often regarded simply as a religious poet, and that critics who declare his poetry free of sexual passion are overlooking 'Musick's Duell'. Though it originated in a Jesuit textbook, Crashaw contrives to add strong sexual suggestions, which counterpoint the musical terminology. Leland Chambers, 'In Defense of "The Weeper"' (*PLL*), points to the reciprocal metaphor on which the poem is based, the weeping eyes of the Magdalen and the bleeding wound in the Sacred Heart. Contrary to Convention, the Magdalen symbolizes God's love for man,

and much that seems like excess in the poem is acceptable once its true subject is revealed.

H. Neville Davies, in 'Quarles's Hybrid Strain' (*ELN*), offers a musicianly interpretation of Quarles's "Invocation" (*First Book of Emblemes*, 1635). Quarles proposed to tune his theorbo 'four notes higher' and join the seraphim in 'high-bred'—by which he also meant 'hybrid'—strains, uniting heaven and earth.

In 'Plagiarism by Thomas Jordan' (*NQ*), Patricia A. Pinsent shows Jordan, a known plagiary, reissuing as his own, under the title *Divine Raptures* (1646), a work by an obscure poet, James Day, which had been published in 1637 as *A New Spring of Divine Poetrie*. Since the verse is mediocre and Jordan names no dedicatee, it is hard to see what he gained.

Robert D. Richardson, Jr., praises 'The Puritan Poetry of Anne Bradstreet' (*TSLL*), and will not have her viewed simply as a phenomenon. She wrote true poetry, the product of her Puritan sensibility. Her doubts and struggles are not evidence that she rebelled against the Puritan way of life. The problem of how to live in the world while not being of it propounds itself inevitably to one of her faith. In her best poetry, notably in 'Contemplations', she achieved the difficult balance. Her poems have been edited by Jeannine Hensley from the Boston edition of 1678 and from manuscript sources.[9] The poems were first published in London in 1650 as *The Tenth Muse, Lately Sprung Up In America*. A foreword by Adrienne Rich notes that there was much amateur versifying in New England. Anne, who reared eight

[9] *The Works of Anne Bradstreet*, ed. by Jeannine Hensley. Foreword by Adrienne Rich. O.U.P. and Harvard U.P. pp. xxxvii + 320. 48s.

children and kept house 'at edge of wilderness', used poetry at first to protect herself from her raw, new experiences. As she gained confidence her poems began to reflect the simple events of a woman's life and the landscape of America. They are 'genuine, delicate minor poems', essentially Puritan and feminine.

Earl Miner discusses 'The Death of Innocence in Marvell's *Nymph Complaining for the Death of Her Faun*' (*MP*). He sees the fawn as 'an analogue for the damaged innocence of the Nymph'. A likely source is the shooting of Silvia's pet stag by Ascanius in *Aeneid* VII, which finally starts the war of Latins and Trojans. The story may have had a similar political significance for Marvell, a small personal tragedy which is part of an infinitely greater and more important action. Much of the innocence and charm of the old world must inevitably be sacrificed in founding a new. The poem, like others written at this time, is 'enigmatic', since the feelings it shows are not wholly favourable to those in power.

In 'Andrew Marvell: The Poem as Green World' (*Forum*), Harry Berger, Jr., interprets three poems of pastoral withdrawal. The nymph lamenting her fawn escapes into the safe world of art. Like Pygmalion in reverse she turns herself to stone. In the dewdrop we see two different kinds of withdrawal. The dewdrop feels insecure on earth, the soul is disdainfully superior. When Marvell changes his analogy from dew to manna, nature and spirit cease to be hostile. Finally, in the Horatian Ode, Marvell simultaneously justifies the politician's engagement in the world and the poet's desire to withdraw. The politician is humanized by being given something of the poet. In 'Marvell's "Garden": Still Another Interpretation' (*MLQ*), Berger hopes to show

'that Marvell's vaunted wit has an entirely different character and purpose when viewed as a form of phenomenological *action* than it does when viewed as a form of "metaphysical" statement'. What Marvell is really withdrawing into is his poem. He only imagines himself in the sensual nirvana of a garden. While he is doing this—which is how 'meanwhile' must be interpreted—his mind is indulging itself in its own kind of pleasure. It masters the world by ensuring that it is self-created. When in the last stanza he returns to an actual garden, it is a return from 'manic languor' to a real world.

Daniel Stempel offers a rather different interpretation. In 'The Garden: Marvell's Cartesian Ecstasy' (*JHI*), he suggests that Marvell was playing with the ideas of Descartes. He must have heard them discussed on his travels abroad and perhaps also by his Cambridge contemporary, Henry More, or his mathematical friend, Dr. Pell. 'This sharp separation of soul from body in order to define the nature and function of cognition is not Platonic—it is Cartesian.' Anybody might have described the fertile external world as 'a green Shade'. Only a Cartesian could reduce it to 'a green Thought'. The poem is not, of course, a serious statement of philosophical belief.

In 'The Actor and the Man of Action: Marvell's Horatian Ode' (*CS*), C. K. Stead sees unconscious tensions in the poem, which account for its deep appeal and for differing critical interpretations. When Marvell finally resolved his inward conflicts and abandoned his poetical royalism, he abandoned poetry. Indeed, the duality disappears before the Ode itself is ended, and lines which might at first sight suggest sarcasm, such as the praise for Cromwell's dealings with the Irish, must be taken quite literally. Readers rightly feel this part of the poem to be inferior. The heroic mode pales after the tragic. George de F. Lord is similarly interested in the problems which beset Marvell. In 'From Contemplation to Action: Marvell's Poetical Career' (*PQ*), he finds Marvell learning that a man must be ready to leave the garden and enter public affairs in order to defend the values that the garden represents, and that only a man who knows these values is fit for public service.

The debt of later poets to Marvell is noted by E. E. Duncan-Jones, in 'Smart and Marvell' (*NQ*) and by P. J. C. Field, in 'Marvell and "The Rape of the Lock"' (ibid.). There are allusions to Marvell and to Hull in Smart's *Jubilate Agno* and parallels between *The Rape of the Lock* and Marvell's *Third Advice to a Painter* and *A Poem on the Death of O.C.*

A poet deeply stirred by the defeat of the royalist cause was John Cleveland. His poems have been edited by Brian Morris and Eleanor Withington.[10] He does not seem to have consented to publication, and the first thing his editors have had to do is to establish the canon, and to assign many poems which have passed as his to other authors. A slender collection remains, to which they append a commentary. The introduction considers Cleveland's rather curious reputation, which veered from high praise of his 'strong lines' to Dryden's attack on him for giving 'common thoughts in abstruse words'. Except as a satirist he was never a serious poet. He was 'a fantastic yet elegant eccentric', and his chief characteristic is his fecundity of invention.

[10] *The Poems of John Cleveland*, ed. by Brian Morris and Eleanor Withington. Clarendon Press. pp. lxxvii + 175. 60s.

In 'Art and Nature: Herrick and History' (*EIC*), William Leigh Godshalk contests Richard Ross's account (*EIC*, 1965) of Herrick's attitude to art and nature, in which nature is 'raw external reality', whereas in the earlier renaissance it had been a norm of which art is a corruption. In 'Robert Herrick's Classical Ceremony' (*ELH*), Robert H. Deming argues that Herrick's classicism is not so much a pagan hedonism as a natural feeling for ceremony, which he satisfies from both pagan and Christian sources, achieving a humanistic fusion. He does not use ceremony as a scholar but as a poet, and he is always aware of historical distance. He could see both Roman and Christian sacrifices as, on a simple level, akin. A. A. Cowan supplies 'A Note on "The Hock-Cart" by Robert Herrick' (*SCN*) in which he discusses the last five lines. He points out puns on *feed* and *fee* = 'a tribute to a feudal superior', and on *pain* and *bread*, occurring in a statement of an idealized relationship between cattle, labourers, Lord Mildmay and the Lord of Heaven. The whole poem is mock-serious and solidly Christian. Roger B. Rollins has detected 'A Thief in Herrick's "Hesperides"' (*NQ*). He finds Chamberlain apparently plagiarizing Herrick in his 'Praise of a Country Life'. Though a lesser poet, Chamberlain was in many ways temperamentally close to Herrick.

'The Lyric as Song: Lovelace's "Orpheus to Beasts"' (*CS* 1966) is an analysis by Katherine Duncan-Jones of what at first seems a slight piece, to show how 'the true sense of each line emerges only after the next is completed, as in music where the rationale of an individual phrase is made evident only by its neighbour'. Pauline Palmer has listed a number of parallel passages in which Lovelace has borrowed from Carew and weakened the force of his borrowings. This appears as 'Lovelace: Some Unnoticed Allusions to Carew' (*NQ*).

The musicians who set seventeenth-century songs are discussed by experts, in *Words to Music*,[11] two papers read at a Clark Library Seminar. In 'English Song and the Challenge of Italian Monody', Vincent Duckles declares that 'obscure as they are, the English composers of the mid-seventeenth century were among the most literate musicians who ever lived'. It is doubtful whether this was altogether good for their music, but it is worth looking at their songs in their own right, and not just as steps on the road to opera. Duckles transcribes Lanier's setting of some verses on Hero and Leander (c. 1628–1630) and shows how the music is so closely wedded to the text that it would be meaningless in any other context. He compares it with Lawes's *Theseus and Ariadne* and an Italian *Complaint of Dido*. Distraught heroines on lone sea-shores proved irresistible to composers of the period. Later in the century, Purcell, refusing to be hampered by the words of songs, showed very great skill in altering and adapting them to musical requirements. This subject is expanded in Franklin B. Zimmerman's contribution, 'Sound and Sense in Purcell's "Single Songs"'. Both writers deal admirably with material not too familiar to the literary critic.

Two articles on the philosophy of music appear in *JWCI*. In 'The Musical Theory and Philosophy of Robert Fludd', Peter J. Ammann discusses, with many illustrative plates, the important part which music played in Fludd's thinking. In 'Kepler's Celestial Music', D. P. Walker considers some of the peculiarities of Kepler's *musica mundana*. Kepler was the first to give music a meaning and a value, apart from any words that might be set to it. It is Man's imitation in little of the harmony to which God has tuned his whole creation.

Books and articles dealing with prose writers are so various this year that it seems better to deal with them in categories rather than in approximately chronological order. The philosophers will come first, then the stylists great and small, and finally some miscellaneous historical material. The prose of Milton and Donne is dealt with immediately after their poetry.

J. A. Mazzeo's *Renaissance and Revolution*[12] presents a rich, various and stimulating panorama of renaissance culture. He devotes individual chapters to Machiavelli, Castiglione, Bacon and Hobbes. He accepts that Bacon's greatness lay in ideology, not in method, and shows how his sweeping vision, at times so penetrating and at others so blind, was further complicated by the misinterpretations and selectiveness of his followers. The emergent Puritan middle classes found it reassuring to be able to pursue science without its affecting revelation, and they were delighted to exchange the old aristocratic and contemplative learning for something that seemed to them eminently practical, utilitarian and democratic. Beside Bacon's dry light Hobbes appears impassioned. It is true that he applied the methods and postulates of natural science to man and society, which seems a cool pro-

[11] *Words to Music.* Papers on English Seventeenth-Century Song Read at a Clark Library Seminar, 11 December 1965, by Vincent Duckles and Franklin B. Zimmerman. With an Introduction by Walter H. Rubsamen. California U.P. for the William Andrews Clark Memorial Library. pp. 93.

[12] *Renaissance and Revolution. The Remaking of European Thought*, by Joseph Anthony Mazzeo. Secker. pp. xi+349. 45*s*.

cedure, but he was motivated by his terrifying vision of anarchy as the alternative to stable government and of the basic nature of man. 'Hobbes was a great psychologist, whose knowledge is in the service of unmasking mankind, a master diagnostician of the various forms of the pathology of conscience.' His assertions of religious orthodoxy were probably simply an instance of a man taking his own medicine. He had seen so much sectarian strife that he advocated, and himself practised, outward submission to the religion of the state. What he had not seen was modern absolutism. He assumed that the supreme authority would be rational and would be exercised with as little interference in private life as possible. Vast areas, to Hobbes, were private. The last chapter in Mazzeo's book is devoted to one of the most powerful of the new currents of thought which entered the world in the seventeenth century, the idea of progress, of a melioration which was not cyclical or other-worldly, but was measurable, demonstrable, and, in the opinion of some optimists, inevitable.

Judah Birman claims, in 'The *New Atlantis*, Bacon's Utopia of Science' (*PLL*), that the two allegories, of the founding of Bensalem and of its Christianization, are important to the understanding of Bacon's thought. Science, in the person of the Father, recognizes revelation, and God recognizes science when he sends it.

Bernard Gert, in 'Hobbes's Psychological Egoism' (*JHI*), denies that Hobbes's political theory is dependent on egoistic psychology. Hobbes chose to begin at the lowest point and face the worst. He could do this calmly because there is also a better. Men do have good impulses and will listen, in sufficient numbers, to an appeal to honour contracts and obli-

gations. On this Hobbes builds his state. He believed human nature was malleable, and only his pessimism and his tautological egoism (i.e. what I do is always what I want to do, because in fact I do it) have concealed this. John M. Steadman has a note on '*Leviathan* and Renaissance Etymology' (*JHI*) to show that Hobbes's use of the term was unconventional but not unprecedented.

G. M. Story has selected, from the earliest printed editions, twelve sermons of Lancelot Andrewes.[13] Andrewes, he says, rose through scholarship as much as through pulpit eloquence. He was deeply learned in languages, an inspired teacher, but too moderate and unworldly for ecclesiastical politics and not at all happy when called upon to engage in Anglican apologetics. He was no leader and he had no enemies, for everyone acknowledged his spiritual purity and intensity. In his sermons he developed a powerful and laconic prose, which is more admired than read today. It is not easy to present it in excerpts, and it is highly impersonal, with little appeal to the unbeliever. Andrewes expounds Christian doctrine. His tone is joyful, his scholarship deep and his emphasis central. Many of the attacks on his style are really directed against his church and cannot be rated as literary criticism. As prose, his sermons are superb, showing 'such compressed fullness that it may be doubted whether English letters can provide a parallel'.

In 'Master Holdsworth and "A Knowledge Very Useful and Necessary"' (*QJS*), Eugene E. White examines Holdsworth's 'Directions for Studies in the Universitie', with

---

[13] *Lancelot Andrewes. Sermons.* Selected and ed. with an Introduction by G. M. Story. Oxford: Clarendon Press. pp. lii+295. 52s. 6d.

special reference to the place allotted to oral and written communication. Holdsworth recommends that every afternoon should be devoted to oratory, since it is of predominant importance in study and life. Laura Crowell, in 'Three *Plain* Speakers in Stuart England' (*QJS*), looks at John Pym, John Preston and Stephen Marshall as characteristic of the forceful plain speaking of the Puritan party. Raymond P. Stearns, in 'Hugh Peter was a Wit' (*PAAS*), gives an account of Peter's jesting manner in sermons, which his enemies used against him when they published *The Tales and Jests of Mr. Hugh Peters* and *Hugh Peters Figaries* in 1660. His wit had a moral purpose, appealed to his illiterate audiences, and was generally harmless, though it outraged many of his co-religionists and put a weapon in the hands of his political antagonists. He had doubtless learned the decorum of wit at school.

In 'Robert Burton, Anglican Minister' (*RP*), Dennis G. Donovan claims that 'it is the sincere expression of a sensitive, competent minister which informs the true spirit of *The Anatomy of Melancholy*'. Burton recommended a middle way, stressing mercy and submission. He thought 'thundering Ministers' did much harm. Religion should console. He deplored the temporal power of the Pope and the superstition of Jews and Mahometans, but attacked only faults of excess. In 'Some Additional Corrections of Shilleto's Edition of Burton's "The Anatomy of Melancholy"' (*NQ*) Donovan submits a list of errors not previously noted, occurring in the last section of the work.

Leonard Nathanson writes finely on Sir Thomas Browne,[14] clarifying

[14] *The Strategy of Truth. A Study of Sir Thomas Browne*, by Leonard Nathanson. Chicago U.P. pp. ix+241. $5.95.

what readers have long been confusedly aware of, notably 'that style is an effect and not the cause of excellence'. He finds Browne's habitual ways of thinking both interesting and definable. The most important thing to know about him is that he was a Christian Platonist, alert to new currents of thought but adjusting them always to a Platonist epistemology, an ascending scale through custom and nature to Idea. 'His outlook is conditioned by the assumption of the relatedness and superiority of revelation to reason. This means more than belief in the adequacy of Scripture as an explanation of the world. It means that the truths Scripture propounds to faith are ultimately rational and that the workings of nature, analysable by reason, can be traced up to the divine.' Such a belief imparts to *Vulgar Errors* its characteristically old-fashioned flavour. *Religio Medici* is fascinating because its innumerable oppositions display a pattern or 'action', not of choices but of 'interdependent necessities'. We see the reconciliation of apparently incompatible religious and intellectual postures by a highly personal application of the traditional Christian and Platonic valuation of their relative levels of truth, presented 'in the form of a mimetic essay'. *Urn Burial*, Browne's other surpassing work, is not unrelated to *The Garden of Cyrus*, but modern criticism has been too hasty in declaring one incomplete without the other. *The Garden of Cyrus* is a graceful Platonic exercise, wanting in depth. *Urn Burial* is a work of Browne's highest and most calculated art. The prefatory dedication makes clear that it is not to be an archaeological pamphlet which takes wings at the end. The problem of values is intrinsic and 'the actual process for discovering how the futility of human effort can be transcended operates as an action within the work and is experienced as such by the reader'.

In 'A Note on Spenser and Sir Thomas Browne' (*NQ*), Malcolm H. South finds Spenser representing Gluttony with the neck of a crane, a conceit derived ultimately from the glutton Philoxenus in the *Nicomachean Ethics*. Browne, in *Vulgar Errors*, looks at the matter more scientifically and points out that taste is situated in the tongue not the neck. Spenser none the less effectively expresses the dehumanizing nature of gluttony.

P. H. Hardacre's '17th-century materials in the Public Record Office, acquired by gift, deposit or purchase' (*SCN*), summarizes the principal seventeenth-century items from the list recently published by the List and Index Society. The title of Julia G. Ebel's 'The Family of Love: Sources of Its History in England' (*HLQ*) is self-explanatory.

David B. Quinn edits George Percy's *Observations on Virginia*.[15] Purchas, who first printed them, seems to have used selections from Percy's journal, begun in 1606, which describes the first Jamestown settlement. Quinn supposes that the earlier part, a connected and optimistic narrative, was sent home with Newport in June 1607. After that the account degenerates into tragic and disconnected jottings, as one after another the settlers died of fever and famine. F. E. Halliday's *A Cornish Chronicle*[16] is based on two newly

discovered manuscripts of Richard Carew the younger, not to be confused with his father, who wrote the *Survey of Cornwall*. Richard is chiefly concerned to pass on to his family his experience of God's providence and the methods whereby he preserved his health, a subject in which he was obsessively interested.

In 'A Seventeenth-Century Controversy: Extremism vs. Moderation' (*TSLL*), Rudolf Kirk shows Bishop Hall, before he was attacked by Milton and the Smectymnuans, engaged in a similar contest with a violent Puritan called Henry Burton. Hall, who was valiantly defending the *via media*, was constantly accused of Roman sympathies. In 'The Impeachment of Roger Maynwaring' (*HLQ*), Harry F. Snapp claims that the proceedings against Maynwaring in 1628, and all that followed, are a valuable demonstration of the positions of Parliament and Crown. Maynwaring, chaplain to King Charles, preached an extreme doctrine of divine right, which ensured him every favour under the king, whereas under Parliament he was reduced to beggary. His sermons were ordered to be burnt even though they had been published at the king's special desire. In 'Clement Walker and the History of Independency. Some notes on the use of pamphlets in historical propaganda' (*NQ*), R. E. Maddison examines Walker's *History of Independency* which, in the guise of a history, was an attack on the Independents. Walker quoted extensively from printed pamphlets, broadsides and government publications of earlier years, thus convicting his opponents out of their own mouths of having betrayed their party. The stir caused by his book shows how effective was his simple procedure. Paul J. Pinckney, in 'Bradshaw and

---

[15] *Observations Gathered out of 'A Discourse of the Plantation of the Southern Colony in Virginia by the English, 1606'. Written by that honorable gentleman, Master George Percy.* Ed. by David B. Quinn. Virginia U.P. for The Association for the Preservation of Virginia Antiquities. pp. xv+27. $1.

[16] *A Cornish Chronicle*, by F. E. Halliday. Newton Abbot: David and Charles. pp. 171. 30s.

Cromwell in 1656' (*HLQ*), quotes in full a manuscript from Lord Braye's collection, in which Bradshaw gives an account of his meeting with Cromwell and the council of state in August 1656.

Philip A. Knachel has edited *Eikon Basilike*,[17] a book which by the Restoration had gone through thirty-nine English editions besides Continental editions and translations. *Eikonoklastes*, in contrast, appeared twice only, with a French translation commissioned and paid for by Parliament. In 1690 came the evidence of the Anglesey Memorandum, establishing Bishop Gauden as the author. Knachel accepts Madan's argument that the book was a remodelling of an original work by the king, to which there is the testimony of many eye-witnesses who saw him engaged on it.

MILTON

The bulk of Milton studies is now considerable. The year 1967, marking the tercentenary of the publication of *Paradise Lost*, has evoked numerous tributes, notably *Th'Upright Heart and Pure*, edited by Amadeus P. Fiore,[18] *Le Paradis Perdu*,[19] edited by Jacques Blondel, and special issues of some periodicals (e.g. *HLQ*, *Ea*). The articles in these collections are separately noticed in the appropriate places.

[17] *Eikon Basilike. The Portraiture of His Sacred Majesty in His Solitudes and Sufferings*, ed. by Philip A. Knachel. Cornell U.P. for the Folger Shakespeare Library. Folger Documents of Tudor and Stuart Civilization. pp. xxxii+201. [1966].

[18] *Th'Upright Heart and Pure. Essays on John Milton Commemorating the Tercentenary of the Publication of Paradise Lost*. Ed. by Amadeus P. Fiore, O.F.M. Duquesne Studies. Philological Series 10. Duquesne U.P. pp. 149. $5.95.

[19] *Le Paradisé Perdu, 1667–1967*. Etudes réunies et presentées par Jacques Blondel. Paris: Minard. pp. 276. Fr. 28.

(*a*) *General*

In a study of twentieth-century criticism,[20] Patrick Murray finds that the attack upon the poet of *Paradise Lost* has done his reputation in the end nothing but good. The seeds of hostility were already present in the nineteenth century. Now the objections to the Grand Style, to Milton's theology, to his personality, and to his narrative techniques have been openly stated, and countered with something other than platitudes. Murray claims that the most important positive contribution of our time is towards the rehabilitation of Milton's thought. It is hard to believe that he was for long considered to show no intellectual power. It is even more surprising to learn that for over twenty-five years T. S. Eliot's theory of 'a dissociation of sensibility' was never publicly queried by any responsible critic but appeared to be universally accepted as a proven historical fact. Thanks to Murray we now know who said precisely when and where. What was thought is another matter.

Robert West, in 'Milton as Philosophical Poet' (*Th'Upright Heart*), examines what right Milton had to teach and what lesson he felt competent to give. It was not the world view emerging from the new science and its philosophers (though it appears from later notices in the section that he had some affinities there). Armed with the Bible, much reading and a powerful and disciplined mind, Milton was confident of the judgements he made. They were concerned with central issues and he had subjected them to prolonged criticism. What philosopher could do more?

Edward Le Comte, in 'Milton as Satirist and Wit' (*Th'Upright Heart*), looks at an aspect of Milton little

[20] *Milton: The Modern Phase. A Study of Twentieth-Century Criticism*, by Patrick Murray. Longmans. pp. 163. 30s.

studied and often deplored, his gift for wit and satire. He claims for him a humour more hilarious than bitter.

In 'Theoretics or Polemics? Milton Criticism and the "Dramatic Axiom"' (*PMLA*), Roger B. Wilkenfeld investigates the common charge that Milton's poems are 'not dramatic' which is too often made without pausing for a definition and always in a pejorative sense. Since there is no adjective from narrative (n), it is not easy to marshal a defence. In 'Aspects de l'Imagination de Milton' (*Ea*), Jean-Jacques Mayoux contends that Milton writes the dialogue of Adam and Eve, parting and meeting again, like a great comic dramatist, humanizing it to a point which agrees ill with the disaster it represents. He notes many contradictions in Milton's imagery, particularly his imagery of Nature, who appears sometimes guilty, sometimes sympathetic to good, and apparently Satanic when most bountiful. Milton's feelings lead him to sympathize with the sin of Satan and Eve, but he sees that it *is* sin, and he must therefore stress the sinfulness. His genius for poetry and caricature is due to the devil within, and he makes the Fall a dark comedy.

John M. Major, in 'Milton's View of Rhetoric' (*SP*), traces a growing hostility in Milton's attitude, despite his early training and his admiration for an eloquent style. Showy rhetoric belongs to the tempters and a plain style to the truth-tellers. Plato, Augustine, Bacon and Jonson joined with Milton's Puritan outlook to direct him towards plain speaking. Russell Fraser, 'On Milton's Poetry' (*YR*), is interested in Milton as 'the poet of esthetic scientism', who tried to refashion language 'to convey the truth with absolute totality and precision'. In contradiction of the rationality he sought, his rejection of

particulars, which are the mind's proper nutriment, betrayed him to a private vision and to something like 'blood prescience'.

John Holloway, in '*Paradise Lost* and the Quest for Reality' (*FMLS*), sees a clear link between Milton and Bacon. Milton was strongly intellectual, optimistic, a hater of quibbles and useless speculation. He was a master of the plain style, that necessary part of epic copiousness and variety, and he can surpass Shakespeare in economy. Where Shakespear is concrete and imaginative, Milton is factual and precise, with 'a curious kind of curt delicacy'. In his treatment of his subject he is constantly asking questions to which he supplies exact answers. For him, Genesis is a book to learn from rather than to teach from. He is unlike Bacon in that he does not divert his quest for insight from the mysteries of religion but presses on into them as far as he can go. Truth is to be adventured for. This, Holloway would have us agree, is a modern mind.

In 'John Milton, Poète vivant?' (*Ea*), Henri Fluchère argues once more the charges brought by Eliot and Leavis against Milton's diction, which he thinks have not yet been adequately met. B. A. Wright's 'A Note on Milton's Diction' (*Th'Upright Heart*) supplies a sample list of words which Milton uses in senses not recognized or poorly glossed by editors. His diction was not flat, generalized and artificial, and was more like Shakespeare's than is generally believed. Thomas Wheeler, in 'Milton's Blank Verse Couplets' (*JEGP*), notes that Milton avoids balance and antithesis in couplets which actually rhyme, but uses them freely in what are, in effect, blank verse couplets. These tend to be disdainful in tone and are often in the mouths of 'enemies', their epigrammatic neatness implying falsehood. An example is 'The mind is its own place' (*Paradise Lost* I, 254–5).

In 'Milton and Thomas Ellwood' (*Milton Newsletter*), Elizabeth T. McLaughlin gives an account of Milton's friend which is much to his credit. She prints his ninety-three-line epitaph on Milton as an early critical evaluation of the poet. It is not possible to praise Ellwood's verses, but he was an intelligent reader, and his failure to find in *Paradise Lost* much about Paradise regained was not so stupid as it is often made out to be. Presumably Milton acknowledged some similarity of views when he bequeathed to Ellwood his valuable manuscript collection of letters addressed to Cromwell. Ellwood, by this time deeply immersed in the affairs of the Quaker community, and engaged upon editing the journals of George Fox and others, never found time to publish them.

(b) Minor Poems

In 'Poesie Italiane di Milton' (*Studi Secenteschi* 1966), Sergio Baldi prints a text of the Italian sonnets with parallel passages from Italian poets. Linguistically, there is a striking debt to Tasso. Baldi declares Milton's Italian to be almost faultless. It is specifically literary, a language of the poets. Such a mastery could not have been achieved at second hand, with the Geneva-born Diodati as teacher. Baldi leans therefore to the theory that though the juvenile sentiments of the sonnets suggest an early date, they must have been given final form after Milton had visited Italy. John T. Shawcross, in 'Milton's Italian Sonnets: An Interpretation' (*UWR*), notes the Christian imagery of the sonnets and suggests that Aemilia was not a real person but personifies the inspiration which can raise a man to emulate heavenly beauty and love.

In 'Milton's Sonnet XIX Reconsidered' (*TSLL*), Joseph Pequigney suggests a dramatic rather than a closely autobiographical reading. It is a despondent poem which reaches no simple conclusion. The nature of the useless talent is never specified.

In 'The Metaphysical Milton (1625–1631)' (*TSLL*), William J. Roscelli seeks for evidence of metaphysical conceits, i.e. such as make an ingenious comparison between dissimilar things, and finds them in some early poems. John T. Shawcross, in 'A Note on Milton's Hobson Poems' (*RES*), gives an account of the printed and manuscript texts of the two Hobson poems and of a third which may possibly be Milton's too.

Richard Neuse considers 'Metamorphosis and Symbolic Action in *Comus*' (*ELH*). He thinks Milton is not showing man's lower and higher natures in conflict, but harmoniously responsive, as in the image of the Tree of Life (*Paradise Lost* V, 479–87). Sabrina, representing the unconscious life of nature, is able to release the Lady from the paralysing limitations of pure spirit. In 'Note sur la Légende de Sabrina dans le *Comus* de Milton' (*Ea*), M. T. Jones-Davies suggests that Milton's Sabrina may have been influenced by Lodge and by the anonymous *Locrine*. In 'Comus and Bryce Blair's *Vision of Theodorus Verax*' (*Milton Newsletter*), Charles C. Mish describes a hitherto unnoticed translation of Erycius Puteanus's *Comus*. It is the sole recorded work of Bryce Blair, who published it in 1671, without acknowledging its source and without, apparently, knowing Milton's masque.

B. Rajan, in 'Lycidas: The Shattering of the Leaves' (*SP*), considers *Lycidas* an extremely complicated and artificial poem, whose technical accomplishment is wholly at the service of its inner meaning. A menacing violence, glimpsed first in the rude shattering of the leaves, is forced to yield to order. The turning point comes with the angel of the guarded mount, and the end displays a compassion unique in Milton. In 'Milton's *Lycidas*, 192' (*Ex*), Joseph Anthony Wittreich, Jr., considers the verb in 'twich't his Mantle blue', and the possible senses of pulling a cloak tight or plucking a stringed instrument, or, when it is read intransitively, of a convulsive movement and a swift departure. These senses echo phrases used earlier in the poem, as the rhyme words appear to echo rhymes with which the poem opens. In 'A Background in Folklore for the "Blind Mouths" Passage in *Lycidas* (ll. 113–31)' (*Milton Newsletter*), Frank L. Huntley, noting some folk-motifs that underlie the poem, suggests that the linking of false prelates with wolves may be associated with the stories of Ysemgrim, the wolf, whose characteristics are his stupidity and greed.

(c) Paradise Lost

An important book by Dennis H. Burden, *The Logical Epic*,[21] pays tribute to Milton's intellectual qualities, in particular his determination to present a logical and coherent argument in *Paradise Lost*. He wanted to show a Christian world, ordered by God's providence. Chance, fate and fortune belong to the random world of paganism, which is the devil's kingdom. Nothing in *Paradise Lost* must happen by pure chance. Hence, for instance, Eve's encounter with the serpent is the consequence of her own determination to work alone. Many literary kinds have presented the world of chance and

offered a wrong view of events. Milton plays off the opposing viewpoints one against the other. The Satanic version of the story often appears beautiful and seductive, but the logic of the poem shows that it must be rejected. It is because the last two books demonstrate providence in world history, without this double vision, that readers complain of flatness. Far from being unaware of the paradoxes inherent in his story, Milton calls special attention to them, to a hell of fire which gives no light, the sanctuary-lamps for a God who can see without them, and above all to the great paradox of free-will and predestination. His constant recourse to the gifts and limitations of the angels is to show that man also has gifts and limitations. Angels feel hungry, like Eve, crave love, like Adam. Human beings are not put into the world with insuperable handicaps.

Stanley E. Fish, in *Surprised by Sin*,[22] goes over some very similar ground, making rather more open war on those who, though they read the poem sensitively and attentively, do not go all the way with Milton. His concern is to show how Milton entangles his reader so that he is constantly himself making the moral choices the poem propounds and having to admit that he has chosen, or is sorely tempted to choose, badly. This discomfited reader does everything he can to resist heavenly disposition. John Peter has said of Adam's transgression that 'only by inverting our own natures and values can we even begin to reproach him'; but this, Fish contends, is exactly what Milton is asking us to do. He agrees with Burden that the tension alters in the

[21] *The Logical Epic. A Study of the Argument of 'Paradise Lost'*, by Dennis H. Burden. pp. ix+206. Routledge. 32s.

[22] *Surprised by Sin. The Reader in 'Paradise Lost'*, by Stanley E. Fish. London: Macmillan. New York: St. Martin's Press. pp. 344. 50s.

last books, which relate providential history in a more traditional and didactic manner.

In *Milton and the Renaissance Hero*,[23] John M. Steadman explores the critique of conventional epic patterns which he sees to be inherent in Milton's three major poems. Milton carries further the kind of criticism which is present in the *Aeneid*, where Turnus is modelled upon Achilles in order to show the superiority of Aeneas. Steadman shows Milton reinterpreting the great epic virtues. True fortitude is not brute force but dependence on God, and strength can be displayed in weakness. Wisdom may mean obeying a revelation not always understood. A leader must learn to be a servant. Love, so important in renaissance epic, is central to the action of Milton's poem, but romantic submission to woman is completely discredited by becoming the main motive of the Fall. Satan may appear magnanimous but he fails in the first test of magnanimity. He does not know himself. The heroic role of Messiah gradually becomes clear. That Adam fails is the measure of Milton's epic heresy. He radically altered the heroic poem when he based it on 'the cornerstone of Protestant ethics, the "vanity of human motives"'.

Gunnar Qvarnström's *The Enchanted Palace*[24] is an application of numerology to *Paradise Lost*. Milton's admiration for Pythagoras, his skill in music, his use in the text of numbers which invite symbolic interpretation, and his devotion to Augustine, all support the probability that the sym-metry observable in the structure of the poem was consciously determined. The most striking instance of this is the discovery that Christ's enthronement in the Chariot of Paternal Deity occurs exactly midway. Just before this Christ has a speech of 23 lines on justice, and another just after, of the same length and tenor. His first speech in the poem is of 23 lines on mercy and so is his last. The figure 23, according to Pietro Bongo's *Numerorum Mysteria*, signifies the joint operation of justice and mercy. A poet who can thus adjust his work to numerological significances must be 'capable of shaping his subject-matter with great formal precision, yet without loss of poetic intensity'. Milton was such a poet. In correspondence in *SEL*, Maren-Sofie Røstvig defends the application of numerology to literature against Douglas Bush and Ernest Sirluck. She argues that numerological interpretations are valid when the contents of a poem invite or support them. The judge of this, Bush retorts, must be 'the committed numerologist'.

Comments on the theology of *Paradise Lost* may well begin with '*Paradise Lost*: "Arian Document" or Christian Poem?' (*Ea*), in which James H. Sims argues in detail, against Kelley, that Milton was not a dogmatist first and a poet second. In '*Paradise Lost*': *a deliberate epic*,[25] Ernest Sirluck claims that Milton meant what he said when he declared he would justify the works of God to man, and that this was not another way of saying that he would assert eternal Providence. He accepted the risks inherent in asking tremendous questions. Our sympathy with Satan focuses our discontent in the face of

[23] *Milton and the Renaissance Hero*, by John M. Steadman. Clarendon Press. pp. xx+209. 30s.

[24] *The Enchanted Palace. Some Structural Aspects of Paradise Lost*, by Gunnar Qvarnström. Stockholm: Almqvist and Wiksell. pp. 189. Sw. Kr. 29.

[25] *Paradise Lost: a deliberate epic*, by Ernest Sirluck. Heffer. Churchill College Overseas Fellowship Lecture. Number One. pp. 30. 6s.

Milton's justification. Man, Milton tells us, damns himself. Adam sinned with his eyes wide open. Thereafter God has renewed man's free will and promised increasing assistance to all who turn to him. 'It is not Adam's choice but his own that determines each man's eternal portion.'

Pierre Legouis, in 'Dryden, plus miltonien que Milton?' (*Ea*), finds one place in *The State of Innocence* where Dryden has equalled if not excelled Milton. When Adam talks with Raphael and Gabriel about predestination and free will, Gabriel exclaims 'And who but man should judge of man's free state?'. Harry Neumann makes an interesting comparison in 'Milton's Adam and Dostoyevsky's Grand Inquisitor on the Problem of Freedom before God' (*Personalist*). Unlike the rationalists, Adam knows his free will is not his own creation. He owes this best part of himself to God and the consequent sense of inadequacy makes him crave society. Hence he clings to Eve and falls with her. 'The tragic combination of humble piety and human need are the ingredients of Adam's dilemma.' Dostoevsky's Inquisitor is also aware of this human longing for society and the horror of making an independent decision. He thinks man will never learn, whereas Milton hopes he may. Both are agreed that it depends on man himself, for God will never force him to be free.

In 'Milton and Prevenient Grace' (*SEL*), Jackson C. Boswell, quoting *De Doctrina Christiana*, argues that Milton believed in prevenient grace as well as in predestination. God cannot save man from making a wrong decision, but he can and does, by the inward workings of grace, incline him towards a right one. Nor does grace come after the recipient has shown himself worthy. It is what

enables him to be so. 'The Beginning of Adam's Repentance' (*PQ*), by George M. Muldrow, stresses the importance of Adam's restoration to grace, which makes him fully the hero and gives effective embodiment to the love and mercy that are often thought of as lacking in the poem or merely expository. He examines in detail X, 720–844 and Satan's soliloquy on Mount Niphates, alongside *Christian Doctrine*. Satan talks about repentance, Adam experiences it. In 'The Salvation of Satan' (*JHI*), C. A. Patrides traces the long history of a belief, first advanced by Clement of Alexandria, that Satan may yet find grace. Since God's love must necessarily be limitless, Satan's deserts should not be in question. Origen argued that all God's creation must ultimately come to good, but neither Milton nor Donne could envisage Satan forgiven.

William B. Hunter, Jr., in 'The Heresies of Satan' (*Th'Upright Heart*), shows that Satan, unlike Marlowe's Mephistophilis, who must first acknowledge a strictly orthodox God before he can deny him, is an archheretic. Instances are his refusal to believe God is omnipotent, and his tendency to ignore the very existence of the Son, in the manner of the monarchian heretics.

M. Y. Hughes, in 'Merit in *Paradise Lost*' (*HLQ*), considers the nature of the Son's transcendence, which Satan and modern critics challenge and which is so important in *Paradise Lost*. He wonders whether there had not perhaps been conflicts in heaven before, just as there had certainly been thoughts less than angelic in the minds of Satan and Mammon. Paul Rozenberg's 'Don, Amour et Sujétion' (*Le Paradis Perdu*) examines the difficult problems involved in the 'debt immense of endless gratitude' owed by all Creation to the

Creator. In 'The Dramatic Function of the Son in *Paradise Lost*: A Commentary on Milton's "Trinitarianism"' (*JEGP*), Stella P. Revard finds that 'The foundation of Milton's Trinity is not identity of origin, but unanimity of Heart—the bond of love'. The Son is a created being and mutable. We watch him ascending 'from good to better', as Satan descends. Adam, Eve, and Satan will not sacrifice self. The Son's proffered sacrifice for man is genuine. Without the omniscience of the Father he cannot know what will happen when he takes on himself man's penalty. But he does know God's nature.

In 'Free Love and Free will in *Paradise Lost*' (*SEL*), Barry E. Gross investigates the relations of Adam and Eve, unable to be happy because they are lost in self-love. In 'Something More About the Erotic Motive in *Paradise Lost*' (*TSE*), Purvis E. Boyette distinguishes erotic love in man from 'passion' or 'lust'. If the pair love as they should, Eve can help Adam to realize himself and so to love God. In 'Sexual Metaphor in Milton's Cosmogony, Physics and Ontology' (*RP*), Boyette shows Milton humanizing the universe and spiritualizing the facts of life. There is a higher value than human love, but it is an extension of what we know through human love. John T. Shawcross, in 'The Metaphor of Inspiration in *Paradise Lost*' (*Th'Upright Heart*), examines Milton's use of the common metaphor of the union of God and Man in terms of sexual intercourse. Nathaniel H. Henry, in 'The Mystery of Milton's Muse' (*RP*), objects to too limited an interpretation of the Muse which Milton invoked. In so far as the concept is theological at all and not purely literary, it 'reflects the light of all

parts of a complicated and interrelated Trinity'.

Mother Mary Christopher Pecheux, in 'The Second Adam and the Church in *Paradise Lost*' (*ELH*), shows Milton paralleling Eve with the Church, while Sin, the second member of the infernal Trinity, becomes its antitype.

K. W. Grandsen, in '*Paradise Lost* and the Aeneid' (*EIC*), makes a detailed comparison of the way Virgil adapts Homer's epic to the purposes of a doctrinal and historical poem and Milton in his turn adapts Virgil. He is particularly interested in the complex time-schemes of the poems. Manocher Aryanpur, in '*Paradise Lost* and *The Odyssey*' (*TSLL*), traces affinities between the two poems consequent upon a similarity in the stories they relate.

Sister Mary Irma Corcoran could charge critics before 1945 with treating Milton's work as more humanist than religious. That the case is altered is in part due to her informative treatise, *Milton's Paradise with Reference to the Hexameral Background*, now in print again.[26] She indicates what was available to Milton in the work of the Fathers and exegetes, and comments on what he accepted, which was much, and some points on which he differed. For instance, he derived Eve's soul as well as her body from Adam, in whose image and glory he says she was made. His insistence on the innocence of sexual pleasure in Paradise is not linked with procreation, and his angels do not embrace in order to multiply, as Gregory of Nyssa would have it, but simply to express love. Most post-Reformation exegetes placed the consummation of the first marriage after the Fall,

[26] *Milton's Paradise with Reference to the Hexameral Background*, by Sister Mary Irma Corcoran. Catholic U. of America Press. Second edition. pp. x+139.

to avoid the embarrassment of a child conceived in Paradise and free of sin, the physical perfection of the parents implying that conception would take place. This is a problem that Milton ignores.

A facsimile of Giovannino Francesco Loredano's *Life of Adam*[27] has been issued as an interesting analogue of *Paradise Lost*, 'more typical of the tradition of literature on Genesis' and 'probably the most comprehensive fictional treatment of the Fall before Milton'.

Irene Samuel, in *Dante and Milton*,[28] compares the poets in a wider context than is provided by mere verbal parallels. 'If Milton was impressed by Dante's treatment of a given matter,' she declares, 'the whole treatment left its traces on his whole treatment of like matter.' Milton knew Dante well, an unusual thing in seventeenth-century England. It is obvious—though critics have not always found it so—that poems different in nature will show differences in treatment. If Milton has no Beatrice, Dante has no Eve. Dante's poem looks back on a world with a history. Milton looks forward to a history about to begin. Dante is more concerned with heaven and Milton with earth. Even the 'Paradise within' is something that man can hope to enjoy here and now, whereas Dante's Paradise is out of this world. Hence the Purgatorio is in many respects the most influential book for Milton. Here he found congenial views on love, free will, and politics. Dante lays most stress on habit and Milton

on conscious choice. They diverge because they are individuals, though they are treating much common material and fetching it frequently from common sources. A comparison can assist in defining their individuality and leaves one contemplating two different kinds of good, not a better and a worse. Raymond Tschumi, in 'De Dante à Milton' (*Le Paradis Perdu*), makes his own comparison of the way the two poets treat parallel subjects. In a wider discussion he shows Milton internalizing his fable and revealing 'things invisible', often things contradictory, to a point beyond which no epic could thereafter afford to go. He finished the epic as a viable kind, but left literature a new world to move in.

Wayne Shumaker's '*Paradise Lost* and the Italian Epic Tradition' (*Le Paradis Perdu*) is concerned with 'certain epic precedents that Milton chose not to follow'. When he abandoned the romantic Italian epic, he abandoned intricacy of plot, multiplicity of persons, great length, magic and hermetic science, honour and romantic love as motives, and rhymed stanzas as verse form. In 'Milton and Fairfax's Tasso' (*RLC* 1966), A. Bartlett Giamatti points out that Milton was not only influenced in general by Tasso, but in particular by Fairfax's translation, and gives instances. Edward Weismiller, in 'Materials Dark and Crude: A Partial Genealogy for Milton's Satan' (*HLQ*) notes further parallels, which confirm Milton's attachment to Tasso despite his dismissal of war as a heroic argument. Tasso's pagan heroes, Argantes and Soliman, are akin to Satan in that the virtues they display are of an essentially military kind, such as can reside equally in the evil and the good.

John D. Demaray, in 'The Thrones of Satan and God: Backgrounds to

---

[27] *The Life of Adam (1640)*, by Giovannino Francesco Loredano. A facsimile reproduction of the English translation of 1659 with an introduction by Roy C. Flannagan with John Arthos. Gainesville, Florida. Scholars' Facsimiles and Reprints. pp. xxi+86. $6.

[28] *Dante and Milton. The 'Commedia' and 'Paradise Lost'*, by Irene Samuel. O.U.P. and Cornell U.P. pp. x+297. 60s.

Divine Opposition in *Paradise Lost*' (*HLQ*), traces a strong masque-influence. Pandemonium rises like an exhalation, God enthroned in light is a noble spectator, the angels dance and feast, and the descendants of Cain (Book IX) present an anti-masque. Stella Revard, in 'Milton's Eve and the Evah of Sir William Alexander's *Doomes-day*' (*PLL*), suggests that in Alexander's epic, published in London in 1637, Milton could have found a picture of Eve which emphasizes her physical beauty and wholesomeness, much as he does himself.

Roger Lejosne, in 'Satan Républicain' (*Le Paradis Perdu*), finds Milton permitting sound republican arguments even from the devil. Were God a human tyrant, some of them would put Milton's own political position fairly enough. Lejosne does not suggest that Milton was ignorant of this. In 'Point of View in *Paradise Lost*: Books I–IV' (*RP*), William A. McQueen notes how the poem, beginning in hell, promises conflict because we see Omnipotence with Satan's eyes. The narrator's comments suggest that there may be another viewpoint, and in Book III we have the God's eye view. After this we slowly readjust our attitude to Satan, as his actions betray the falseness of his first appearance.

John W. Crawford, in 'Another Biblical Allusion in *Paradise Lost*' (*SCN*), gives reasons why Moloch (II, 65–70) can speak of 'Tartarean Sulphur' and 'strange fire'. In Leviticus 10: 1, 2, the favoured sons of Aaron 'offered strange fire before the Lord', a presumption for which they were punished when divine fire destroyed them. In 'Homeric Parody at the Gates of Milton's Hell' (*MLR*), John E. Seaman sees Satan's encounter with Death as a fine parody of Iliad VI, 119–236. Diomedes hesitates

to encounter Glaukos for fear that he may be fighting a God. Glaukos reassures him, they find they are old friends, and there is no battle.

Merritt Y. Hughes, in 'Milton's Limbo of Vanity' (*Th'Upright Heart*), considers probable sources, particularly Plato's vision of Er and Dante's wind-blown souls of the uncommitted. Irene Samuel also treats the parallel with Dante at some length.[28] J. E. Parish, in 'Milton and the Rape of Proserpina' (*ES*), traces several allusions to Ovid's story. In Book IX, for instance, Eve mourns that she must leave her flowers when she leaves Paradise. Parish shows how Milton required Eve to be Ceres as well as Proserpina, and how skilfully he shifted the emphasis in his imagery to this end. In 'Le Merveilleux dans le Paradis miltonien Chant IV.' (*Ea*), Jacques Blondel examines the way in which Milton used Christian marvels seriously, so that 'l'Eden ne sera pas un jardin fantastique mais un continuel enchantement'. In 'Milton et l'Eden' (*Le Paradis Perdu*), Blondel is similarly concerned to put Eden outside the realm of mere dreaming. Its enormous bliss evokes a sense of loss deeper than nostalgic fantasy, and at the same time holds the promise of renewal, of the interior Paradise. In 'Three Notes on Eve's Dream in *Paradise Lost*' (*PQ*), A. B. Chambers discusses the decorum of Satan's toad-disguise, his appearance to Eve as an angel, and his tempting her through her ear. Manfred Weidhorn, in 'The Anxiety Dream in Literature from Homer to Milton' (*SP*), examines Eve's dream. Although supposedly induced by Satan, perhaps to preserve the prelapsarian innocence of the dreamer, it is very natural, and may be interpreted as a wish-fulfilment. It intensifies the reality of Eve's free will. Warned by it of her evil potential, she can take full responsibility for her waking acts.

Stella Revard, in 'Milton's Critique of Heroic Warfare in *Paradise Lost* V and VI' (*SEL*), analyses Milton's purposes in describing a battle which at first appears ordered and heroic, but soon disintegrates into disorder, pain and fear. After Satan has parodied God the Creator by inventing gunpowder, the war becomes cosmic and completely destructive. Good and evil have clashed for the first time in the poem. Adam and Eve have seen the consequences of disobedience, and Satan's disingenuous account of the struggle has been replaced by something more factual. In 'Christian Heroism in *Paradise Lost*' (*CQ*), Stanley Fish says that by the time we come to the War in Heaven we should no longer entertain expectations based on 'assumptions about the importance and effectiveness of physical action'. The angels may seem to be fighting pointlessly since God can dispense with their service, but they do not fail to give it. Their will is free and it is bent to serve. The perpetual limitation of the sphere in which they act illustrates the fact that true heroism requires no large battlefield. It is non-spatial. For Adam and Eve it is confined to not eating the apple, for Milton to accepting the limitations of his own lot.

In 'Satan "Now Dragon Grown" (*Paradise Lost*, X, 529)' (*Ea*), M. Y. Hughes considers the way Milton prepares for Satan's sudden transformation and the propriety of this scene in which deceit has been deceived. In '*Paradise Lost*: The Hill of History' (*HLQ*), Balachandra Rajan undertakes a defence of Books XI and XII. One can fairly ask, he thinks, that they should be joyful, and within the strict logic of the poem their message is reassuring, certainly not humbling or intimidating, since Adam and Eve are already humbled. As evil strengthens in history, so does good. The Incarnation is God's grand alliance with man for the defeat of evil. Law is superseded by 'an inner righteousness, which issues in order instead of reluctantly yielding to it'. The Paradise Within is the opposite of Satan's perverted 'Myself am Hell'. But good does not triumph easily and 'there are times the tone approaches weariness'.

Jean Gillett, in 'Remarques sur un Concours entre Traducteurs de Milton, sous l'Empire' (*Le Paradis Perdu*), describes some not very successful attempts to put Milton into neo-classical French verse. For the eighteenth century, Milton propounded no problems beyond the technical and aesthetic, which leaves him hardly recognizable to the modern reader. In 'A Note on Two Translations of *Paradise Lost*' (*RLC*), Edward Ifkovic compares the Spanish translation of Juan de Escoiquiz, in 1812, with the French-English version which Delille published in 1805, and finds the Spaniard apt to translate Delille's French in preference to Milton's English.

Articles by Max Milner, 'Le Satan de Milton et l'Epopée Romantique Française', Jacques Seebacher, 'Comment peut-on être Milton?', and Robert Couffignat, '*Le Paradis Perdu* de Victor Hugo à Pierre-Jean Jouve', are concerned with the influence of Milton on French poets (*Le Paradis Perdu*).

(d) Samson Agonistes and Paradise Regained

In 'The Tragic Glass: Milton, Minturno and the *Condition Humaine*', (*Th'Upright Heart*), John M. Steadman relates the apparent pessimism of Milton's last poems to his choice of literary form and content rather than to his personal disappointments. They are tragic because they are tragedies. There is suffering because heroes must suffer in order to display heroism. They stress the paradoxes of man's condition and the consolations of religion because of their theological subject and intent. Like Minturno, Milton saw tragedy as a mirror of man's estate and a way of teaching patience in adversity. Man's original dignity and present misery are sharply contrasted in order to proceed logically to the Christian remedy.

In 'Bruising the Serpent: Milton as a Tragic Poet' (*Centennial Review*), R. J. Kaufmann agrees with Johnson that *Samson Agonistes* is structurally unsatisfying. Coherent it may be, but 'human choices are so completely absorbed in divine ones that the catastrophe is the play'. Moreover Samson's regeneration is final. He is exempt from new error. This is too diagrammatic, too facile for tragedy. Samson is a cult-hero, who gets his reward.

In 'Sea, Snake, Flower, and Flame in *Samson Agonistes*' (*MLR*), John Carey claims that the imagery contradicts the play's apparent values in a way which shows Milton, at a deep level, critical of his hero. In 'On the Pronunciation of Names in *Samson Agonistes*' (HLQ), James Thorpe argues that the three names, Dalila, Manoah and Harapha are to be stressed on the first syllable.

George M. Muldrow, in 'An Irony in *Paradise Regained*' (*PLL*), distinguishes two kinds of knowing, 'savoir' and 'connaître'. Satan, who suspects Christ's identity, puts it to the test of experience with ironic effect, for it was in this way that he taught Adam and Eve to 'know' evil. Thomas Langford, in 'The Temptations in *Paradise Regained*' (*TSLL*), contends that, far from being in doubt, Satan is aware and deeply fearful of Christ's identity. Fear

governs all his manœuvres. In 'Jerusalem and Athens: The Temptation of Learning in *Paradise Regained*' (*Th' Upright Heart*), B. Rajan shows the place of this unbiblical temptation in the poem's logic. Satan, who has failed with the kingdoms of the world, moves into Christ's own territory with the offer of a kingdom not of this world. He has, however, no wisdom which is not worldly. Christ is to bring a new light into the world and he cannot surrender his power 'to the very substance which it is supposed to transform'.

(e) Prose Works

In 'Time, Place, Persons: The Background for Milton's *Of Reformation*' (*SEL*), Robert F. Duvall investigates Milton's quarrel with the bishops and sees his tract as 'inspired by a desire for reform which will free a particular poet in a particular time and place to sing the lasting strains of God's judgments in England'. Leo Miller, in 'Milton's *Reason of Church Government*, Book I, Chapter 5' (*Ex*), notes how Milton, alluding to the parable of the tares, uses the name of a weed with which he was more familiar when he speaks of the 'glorious poppy . . . insulting over the good corne'. Kester Svendsen, in 'Milton and the Hundred Articles against Alexander More', (*Th' Upright Heart*), discusses and reproduces, from documents at Geneva, some of the charges against More which formed the basis of Milton's attack in *Pro Se Defensio*, that 'awesome document in the rhetoric of character assassination'.

Emile Saillens, in 'Coup d'œil sur les débuts de Milton en France' (*Ea*), says that Milton was first known as a political pamphleteer. The Latin defences were admired, but *Eikonoklastes* showed up badly beside *Eikon*

Basilike, and Milton's abuse of his countrymen gave no good impression of the revolution. Milton did, however, influence an abortive revolt in Bordeaux, led by an English republican colonel. Seignobos has said of the Bordeaux Constitution: 'C'est la plus ancienne déclaration des droits de l'homme écrite en français et elle est l'oeuvre d'un Anglais.'

'The Composition of Milton's *De Doctrina Christiana*—the First Stage' (*Th'Upright Heart*), by Maurice Kelley, traces the work back to the 'perfect System of Divinity', collected from Amesius and Wollebius, which Edward Phillips says Milton used to dictate to his pupils on Sundays. The lost 'Index Theologicus', referred to in the surviving Commonplace Book, presumably contained notes on secular reading and was concerned with temporal aspects of the Church. Kelley's account of 'The Recovery, Printing, and Reception of Milton's *Christian Doctrine*' (*HLQ*) tells us that the work was translated, edited, printed, and very widely reviewed within two years of its being discovered. It was something of a shock and a disappointment, but it did not reduce the popularity of *Paradise Lost*. It was not used at all seriously in the interpretation of Milton's poem until about 1920, though the first reviewers had seen its relevance.

XI

The Restoration Period

P. MALEKIN

1. GENERAL

(a) *Drama*

Restoration tragedies have not worn well. Insight into why, together with a defence of the modest merits of these plays, is provided by Eric Rothstein's *Restoration Tragedy: Form and the Process of Change*.[1] The heroic play was outdone by the sentimental in emotional appeal and in splendour of spectacle by opera. It was displaced by a more natural and domestic type of tragedy, better able to arouse the concernment of the audience that contemporary aesthetic theory was beginning to require. Here love and honour cease to be the prerogative of hero and heroine and the language begins to express the subjective perceptions of the characters. While the main action narrows in scope, the range of characters increases and comic incident is introduced and integrated. The plots still tend to be arbitrary, but in the best plays of the kind, such as *Venice Preserv'd, Don Sebastian*, and to some extent *The Mourning Bride*, the imagery or the themes embodied in the incidents set the key-note for the ending. A strain of pastoral idealism partially compensates for the heroes' lack of self-sufficiency, but the concentration of the language on what the characters feel, at the expense of what is objectively true, leads to a general lack of moral force. Rothstein relates his general contentions to specific instances and bases his argument on detailed analysis; his book is a solid piece of scholarship and is both concise and comprehensive.

In 'Libertin und Heroischer Held' (*Anglia*) Ulrich Broich stresses the necessity of relating Restoration comedy meaningfully to its contemporary, the heroic play. He sees the two as actuality and ideal, the former parodying and complementing the latter; in both genres, however, despite the contrast in setting and action, the hero and heroine, mutually in love, are surrounded by a network of other love relationships, and the hero struggles for a throne or fortune as well as possession of the heroine. Moreover the solipsistic codes of honour and of sexual conquest both demand of the heroes an unusual control and self-mastery. The Spanish sources, real and imaginary, of thirty-one Restoration plays are usefully noted by Floriana T. Hogan in *RECTR*. Cecil V. Deane's study of the rhymed heroic play and its relationship to French and English critical theory is a recognized classic in its field and has now been reprinted.[2]

The rhetorical patterns in Restoration prologues and epilogues are

---

[1] *Restoration Tragedy: Form and the Process of Change*, by Eric Rothstein. Madison, Milwaukee, and London: Wisconsin U.P. pp. xii+194. 62*s*. $6.50.

[2] *Dramatic Theory and the Rhymed Heroic Play*, by Cecil V. Deane. Frank Cass and Barnes & Noble. pp. vi+235. 45*s*. $7.50.

analysed in a paper by Emmett L. Avery.[3] He describes the way in which Restoration dramatists picture themselves as pilots, captains and merchant adventurers, as soldiers to be tested in battle, as subjects suing to their kings, as prisoners before their judges, as lovers, as sinners seeking forgiveness. The audience at whom this extraordinary ingenuity of address was directed is discussed by Harold Love in 'The Myth of the Restoration Audience' (*Komos*). Following up Avery's earlier attack on the notion of a frivolous, limited, and dissolute Restoration theatre audience (*YW* xlvii. 210), he points out that prologues and epilogues haranguing the beastliness of the audience imply an audience not altogether beastly, for it is the sympathy of the audience which is being sought. He supports Avery's evidence from Pepys with citations of Hooke's diary and Marvell's satires, and he posits an audience wider and more sensible than the colourful clique described by Beljame and subsequently accepted as historical fact.

Three articles have a bearing on the design of stages in use during the Restoration. Glynne Wickham's 'The Cockpit Reconstructed' (*New Theatre Magazine*) establishes that the stage of Inigo Jones's Cockpit Theatre had a railed apron and was backed by a two-storied façade with five doors below, the middle one being considerably larger than the others, and a single central window above. Donald C. Mullin in 'The Theatre Royal, Bridges Street: A Conjectural Restoration' (*ETJ*) argues that the first Theatre Royal was probably built by Webb to a Serlian-type plan with a wide

proscenium backed by wings in grooves; the Wren sketch 81 at All Souls is probably for alterations and enlargements to this stage in 1665–6. Mullin and Bruce Koenig also argue in 'Christopher Wren's Theatre Royal' (*TN*) that the frontispiece to *Ariane*, showing a stage with an apron about four feet deep, gives a reasonably accurate impression of the stage of the Theatre Royal when Wren rebuilt it after the fire of 1672. Eleanore Boswell's *The Restoration Court Stage*, which originally appeared in 1932 (*YW* xiii. 222–4) and remains a major piece of scholarship in its field, has received a timely reprint.[4]

What Davenant and Betterton did to *Macbeth* is recorded and disliked by Dennis Bartholomeusz in 'The Davenant-Betterton *Macbeth*' (*Komos*). Odell's judgements were a little kinder. 'These extra bits in the play really detract terribly from its nobility; they are extremely theatrical and very badly written. They no doubt acted well, and consequently were retained for many years.' Odell's *Shakespeare from Betterton to Irving* (*YW* ii. 66–7) of course covers far more than Restoration stage practice; although corrected in details since its first appearance, it remains an invaluable compendium of good-humoured erudition, and its publication as a paperback is to be welcomed.[5] Another of the older standard works on Restoration and eighteenth-century stage practice, Noyes's *Ben Jonson and the English*

---

[3] 'Rhetorical Patterns in Restoration Prologues and Epilogues', by Emmett L. Avery in *Essays in American and English Literature Presented to Bruce Robert McElderry, Jr.*, ed. by Max Schultz *et al.* Ohio U.P.

[4] *The Restoration Court Stage 1660–1702: With a Particular Account of the Production of 'Calisto'*, by Eleanore Boswell. Allen & Unwin and Barnes & Noble, 1966. pp. xviii + 370. 70s. $12.50.

[5] *Shakespeare from Betterton to Irving*, by George C. D. Odell. Constable and Dover Publications, 1966. Vol. I, pp. xx + 456. Vol. II, pp. viii + 498. Paperback 24s. each. $4.75 each.

Stage (*YW* xvi. 209–10), forms part of the valuable series of reprinted works on the Restoration published by Benjamin Blom.[6]

A brief survey of 'Restoration Theatre Scholarship 1960–66' is contributed to *RECTR* by Edward A. Langhans, who expresses pious hopes for the finding of new manuscript material, and P. F. Vernon contributes to the same periodical a list of London theses and dissertations on the theatre of the Restoration and eighteenth century as an addendum to the list of Carl J. Stratman (*RECTR* 1963).

(b) *Poetry*

In *The Honest Muse* Rachel Trickett focuses on the increasing importance of truth to fact and of honesty, in the sense of integrity, both as a subject of praise and as an assumed virtue of the poet in the tradition of Augustan verse.[7] In panegyric Dryden continues the older celebration of public figures as symbols of honour and nobility but begins to attune this to personal fact, while in satire he combines the declamation of Juvenal with the easy intimacy and assumed sincerity of the dramatic prologues and epilogues. In elegies such as 'To the Memory of Mr. Oldham' direct truthfulness is given dignity and force by an epic awareness of the inevitability of death. In their satires, satirical epistles, and town eclogues, Oldham and Rochester developed the free stance of assumed impartiality, handed on later to Pope, and the vivid use of contemporary instances which Pope was to find so useful. Although Miss Trickett is at her best on Johnson and the last phase of Augustan verse, her survey of Restoration poetry is impressive in its sense of historical development; she is not, however, entirely in sympathy with the period, and some of her passing judgements, especially those on Restoration comedy, are less than just.

Ronald Paulson's *The Fictions of Satire* has an even wider historical sweep, from primitive ritual to the sophisticated satires of Swift.[8] Paulson notes the way in which Oldham turns to advantage the natural suspicion of a satirist's motives by making the railing villain of the first and third of the *Satyrs upon the Jesuits* condemn himself through his attacks on Protestantism, while the poet is merely a detached narrator. Travesty is used in Butler's *Hudibras*, Cotton's *Scarronides*, and the court satires of Rochester to express and expose illusory moral assumptions. The pro-court satire of *Absalom and Achitophel* defends the ideals of the court party while attacking human inadequacies, and its mock-heroic world is orderly, as opposed to the fundamentally absurd world of *Mac Flecknoe*. General historical theses lurk rather than lodge in Paulson's book and its virtue lies not in the comprehensiveness of its survey but in the flashes of insight which fitfully illumine particular works and particular historical connexions.

Ralph Cohen in considering 'The Augustan Mode in English Poetry' (*Eighteenth Century Studies*) emphasizes Dryden's use of spatial process as a means of linking present and past. Peter Thorpe attacks 'Some Fallacies in the Study of Augustan

---

[6] *Ben Jonson on the English Stage 1660–1776*, by Robert Gale Noyes. Benjamin Blom. pp. viii+351. 90s. $12.50.

[7] *The Honest Muse: A Study in Augustan Verse*, by Rachel Trickett. Oxford: Clarendon Press. pp. 309. 50s. $8.80.

[8] *The Fictions of Satire*, by Ronald Paulson. The Johns Hopkins Press. O.U.P. pp. ix+228. 66s. 6d. $7.

Poetry' (*Criticism*): the 'organic fallacy', a tendency to interpret poems such as Dryden's 'To my Honour'd Friend Dr. Charleton' as organic wholes, whereas they are really discursive poems which create the impression of unity by leaving the main point to the end; the 'ambivalence fallacy' which turns dialectic into ambiguity, whereas the Augustans' achievement was clarity and the praise of the golden mean between paradoxical extremes; and the 'Metaphysical fallacy' which stresses ambivalence, irony, and paradox, and tends to see the Augustans as descendants of the Metaphysicals whom they in fact rejected. Somewhat generally argued, Thorpe's position is nevertheless sensible, which cannot be said of some of the extremes he is attacking. The main points relevant to the Restoration in Ian Watt's three broadcast talks on the Augustans, published in the *Listener*, concern the differing applications of the Augustan political analogy, according to whether Augustus is regarded as peace-bringer and patron of the arts, or tyrant and destroyer of liberty, and the practical use of irony in enabling a writer to address both men of sense and the mob in one set of words with two distinct meanings. Patronage and the various interpretations of the political analogy are also discussed by Howard Erskine-Hill in considerable detail (*RMS*). He points to Waller's praise of Cromwell and Dryden's of Charles II as peace-makers, and to the association, from *Astraea Redux* onwards, of the Augustan with the Golden Age. The seventeenth- and eighteenth-century critics themselves, whether they located their Augustan ages in the reigns of Charles, William and Mary, or Anne, all valued common language, common experience, regularity, polish, and per-

manence in poetry. The Augustan analogy sprang naturally from shared aspirations, but the light it cast could expose poetic and political virtues or vices according to the eye that perceived them.

(c) *Prose and Bibliography*

The collection of lectures and papers by R. S. Crane contains a number of sections bearing on the Restoration.[9] His chapters on 'The Rivalry of Letters and Natural Philosophy in the Seventeenth Century' and 'The Quarrel of the Ancients and Moderns and Its Consequences' sketch the widening of the subject-matter of the humanities to include modern literatures and sciences, the development of an historical approach to art, and the growth in the Restoration and eighteenth centuries of the idea of progress and of a philosophy of history. The well-known 'Suggestions towards the Genealogy of the "Man of Feeling"' reprinted from *ELH*, discusses the influence exerted by the Latitudinarian divines of the Restoration, who emphasized natural benevolence and a community of essential belief, in reaction to the Stoics' praise of unmoved charity, Hobbes's conception of a natural state of war, and the insistence of the Puritans on reprobation and on justification by faith alone. A note on Locke's *Essay* challenges the notion that Locke regarded the human mind as a merely passive recipient of ideas and sense impressions, while 'On Writing the History of Criticism in England, 1650–1800' uses a discussion of the work of Saintsbury and Atkins to recommend an analysis of the pairs of critical opposites current in that

[9] *The Idea of the Humanities, and Other Essays Critical and Historical*, by Ronald S. Crane. Chicago U.P. Vol. I, pp. xxii+311. Vol. II, pp. viii+332. £5 5s. $15.

period, and an attempt to see what questions the critics sought to answer when they applied these to particular works. All these papers must be seen in the context of Crane's somewhat strenuous methodology, whereby he sees the aesthetic and educational theories of the past and of our own period as related in a historical continuum; it has the advantage of preventing our own assumptions from being inflated into absolutes, of preventing indeed the kind of naïvely facile, moral and aesthetic judgement that has too often been made on the Restoration.

The literary history of the Restoration and eighteenth century by George Sherburn and Donald F. Bond remains the most informative and comprehensive of the modern histories; it is now usefully reprinted as a paperback.[10] It is natural that some of the judgements and assumptions of fact in Francis Gallaway's study of English classicism should no longer be acceptable today, but it too remains a valuable attempt to interrelate literature, philosophy, science and the classical heritage, and it is gratifying to record its appearance as a paperback.[11]

In 'Augustinianism and Empiricism' (*Eighteenth Century Studies*), Donald Greene suggests that 'neoclassicism' and 'the age of reason, should be abandoned as historical terms, and believes that more useful points of reference for understanding the period can be found in an Augustinian sense of man's moral weakness, with the resulting need for constant self-examination, and the empirical distrust of human reason exhibited in the experimental philosophy, Bacon, Locke, Cowley's ode 'To the Royal Society', Dryden's poem to Charleton, and many later works. As a corrective this view is valuable, but in opposing to the Augustinian-empiricist attitude a minority 'Stoic-rationalism' and linking with this Adam Smith, Mandeville, Shaftesbury and Rousseau, Greene surely runs the risk of establishing a terminology as distorting as the one he is attempting to oust. William H. Halewood, in '"The Reach of Art" in Augustan Poetic Theory'[12] holds that poets from Dryden onwards may have owed their idea of genius contravening the rules in part to similar conceptions in Renaissance treatises of painting, and that they may also have been influenced by the Platonic concept of the painter as inspired by divine grace and of painting as approaching the perfection of divine ideas. The idea of the sister arts may have been encouraged by the desire of poets to profit from the prestige of Renaissance painting, the only branch of modern art generally acknowledged to have rivalled the achievement of the ancients. A 'Restoration and 18th Century Theatre Research Bibliography for 1966', indexed and briefly but helpfully annotated, has been prepared by Edmund A. Napieralski (*RECTR*).

2. DRYDEN
(a) *General*

In papers read to a Clark Library Seminar Charles E. Ward discusses the challenges to Dryden's biographer, the difficulty of establishing

---

[10] *A Literary History of England,* ed. by Albert C. Baugh. Vol. III, *The Restoration and the Eighteenth Century*, by George Sherburn and Donald F. Bond. Routledge. pp. x+699–1108+[41]+xxi. 25s.

[11] *Reason, Rule, and Revolt in English Classicism*, by Francis Gallaway. Kentucky U.P. 1966. (Kentucky Paperback 105) pp. xii+371. $2.75.

[12] In *Studies in Criticism and Aesthetics, 1660–1800. Essays in Honor of Samuel Holt Monk*, ed. by Howard Anderson and John S. Shea. Minnesota U.P. Hereafter referred to as *Monk Studies*.

facts and degrees of probability, the perplexities arising from doubtful references to Dryden, and the task of evaluating references, particularly hostile ones, as well as problems of general interpretation, selection and comparative emphasis. H. T. Swedenberg discusses the similar problems facing an editor, and illustrates the consequent frustrations by recounting his attempts to discover from works of history whether the description of Shaftesbury's virtues as a judge in *Absalom and Achitophel* should be taken literally or ironically; the historical accounts turned out to be based on a literal reading of Dryden.[13] Bruce King, in 'Dryden's Ark: The Influence of Filmer' (*SEL*), contends that Filmer's theory of divinely instituted patriarchal monarchies descending from Adam to Noah's sons after the flood did in fact have an important influence on Dryden. He traces it particularly in *Absalom and Achitophel* and *The Spanish Friar*, as well as in many other poems, plays, and prose writings; the cumulative force of his evidence is convincing, however dubious some isolated details may be. Gian Carlo Roscioni, in 'Sir Robert Howard's "Skeptical Curiosity"' (*MP*), points to Howard's religious scepticism and his advocacy of rational progress, as an underestimated influence on Dryden, and George Falle, in 'Sir Walter Scott as Editor of Dryden and Swift' (*UTQ*), pays a genial tribute to the critical insight and extensive historical annotation in Scott's edition of Dryden.

(b) *Poetry*

Earl Miner has produced a major study of Dryden's poetry, which he sees as centring on the relationship between mortal man, immortal fame or achievement, and, beyond both, eternity.[14] Dryden's poetry is therefore primarily public poetry. The historical panegyrics on Cromwell and Charles lead up to the expression of a providential and royalist view of history in *Annus Mirabilis*, at whose climax Charles's prayer is answered by the new order arising from the purifying fire. In *All for Love* the public and private worlds are reconciled in death as the Romans adopt the virtues of personal friendship and Antony and Cleopatra die in the Roman fashion, but for love. Controlling metaphors are traced in *Mac Flecknoe, Absalom and Achitophel* and *The Hind and the Panther*; in the latter poem a certain absurdity is intentional and there are witty shifts from tenor to vehicle. Before Dryden's conversion to Roman Catholicism his historical metaphors are usually based on analogies with other periods of history; after it a more baroque fable and myth predominate. The late *Fables* are bound together by the themes of love and arms. Miner's book supplies the need for a comprehensive study of Dryden utilizing the increased scholarly and critical grasp of Dryden's poetic techniques that has developed of recent years, and it replaces Mark Van Doren's dated study; it does not, however, have the civilized grace and thoroughly integrated organization of its predecessor.

H. T. Swedenberg charts 'Dryden's Obsessive Concern with the Heroic' and its panegyrical, historical, and satirical sub-variants.[15] R. G. Peter-

---

[13] *John Dryden. Papers Read at a Clark Library Seminar, February 25, 1967*, by Charles E. Ward and H. T. Swedenberg. Los Angeles: Clark Memorial Library, University of California. pp. vii+44. Paperback.

[14] *Dryden's Poetry*, by Earl Miner. Bloomington: Indiana U.P. pp. xx+354. 95*s.* $10.

[15] In *Essays in English Literature of the Classical Period Presented to Dougald MacMillan*, ed. by Daniel W. Patterson and Albrecht B. Strauss. (*SP* Extra Series No. 4) Chapel Hill: North Carolina U.P. Hereafter referred to as *MacMillan Essays*.

son's 'Larger Manners and Events: Sallust and Virgil in *Absalom and Achitophel*' (*PMLA*) is a pleasing and exhaustive study of the use of references to classical literature in the poem, and shows in particular that, 'The moral history of Sallustian monograph fused with the mythic and panegyrical history of Virgilian epic and pastoral' to raise the characters to the heroic stature and significance of Roman figures; this is a welcome restatement of the Roman side of the poem, which has been rather under-emphasized recently. Shadwell attacked Dryden's heroic characters and witty comedies, advocating instead characterization based on humours; Michael W. Alssid, in 'Shadwell's *Mac Flecknoe*' (*SEL*), illuminates the ingenious way in which Dryden uses this against him by turning Shadwell himself into a humour. He also detects in line 205 a reference to Shadwell's *Psyche*, dedicated to Monmouth and possibly intended to support the latter's political ambitions. In giving this work by implication a diabolical origin, *Mac Flecknoe* looks forward to developments in *Absalom and Achitophel* and *The Medall*. Stanley Archer comments on lines 47–48 of the poem (*Ex*). In 'Dryden's "Enchanted Isle" and Shadwell's "Dominion"' (*MacMillan* Essays), Aline Mackenzie Taylor moots the idea that the identification in *Mac Flecknoe* of the area of Shadwell's dominion as the open seas between Ireland and Barbados may be directed at Shadwell's successful adaptation of the Dryden-Davenant *Tempest*, published without Shadwell's name, but with Dryden's preface and prologue, in 1674; the success of this opera may have soured Dryden into leaving the stage.

Current attention to the structural principles of Dryden's poetry is shown in many articles. A. E. Wallace Maurer (*PLL* 1966) considers *Astraea Redux* to be planned as a classical oration to a grand assembly of the English, the Continental powers, and Charles II. S. A. Golden in 'Dryden's Praise of Dr. Charleton' (*Hermathena* CIII. 1966) challenges Wasserman's political interpretation, believing rather that the poem does precisely what its full title claims, and tracing the simplicity of the style, the political references, and the list of British scientists back to Charleton's beliefs, scientific work, personal friendships, and royalist convictions, and to the actual details of *Chorea gigantum* to which the poem was prefixed. This interpretation accounts for the details of the poem and has the added virtue of simplicity. By detailed comparison with the actual medal commemorating Shaftesbury's acquittal, Maurer (*PLL* 1966) elucidates Dryden's *The Medall*, where the obverse portrait of Shaftesbury is 'corrected' by depicting Shaftesbury as governed by an ever-changing seditious will, and the reverse picture of London rejoicing is replaced by scenes and an inscription showing London and the whole of England on the verge of a disaster. An important discussion of the numerological and musical structure of the 'Song for St. Cecilia's Day, 1687' is undertaken by Alastair Fowler and Douglas Brooks in *EIC*. The eight stanzas represent an octave of which the eighth (eight being associated with eternity and regeneration) ushers in eternity and is distinguished from the preceding as an italicized grand chorus. Stanza seven with seven lines and stanza two with nine correspond in their references to Orpheus and Jubal, seven carrying the numerological significance of body, nine of spirit. The cyclic structure of the whole, from creation to dissolution in an octave, is echoed in the division of the first stanza into two sections of ten and five lines (the numerical relationship of a note to its octave), and the 'Diapason closing full in man' leads on to the central stanzas where the effects of music on the four temperaments, the choleric, melancholic, phlegmatic, and sanguine are described in stanzas three to six. The analysis is extremely detailed, and some of the detail is more ingenious than convincing, but on the whole Fowler and Brooks illuminate the poem brilliantly, their numerology strengthening and supporting the natural structure of the poem and appropriately enriching its meaning. Earl Miner argues in *HLQ* that 'Dryden's ode on Mrs. Anastasia Stafford' was written about December 1687, notes the Biblical parallels linked with Anastasia and her bridegroom by Dryden, and believes that the poem, which moves from past to present tense, probably had an ending on analogy with the Killigrew ode, a prophecy possibly concerning the bride and children. In 'Rhetoric and Meaning in *Religio Laici*' (*PMLA*), J. W. Corder analyses the poem as judicial oratory, the section *confirmatio-confutatio* answering the Deists, the traditionalists, and the zealots, while the final *peroratio*, advocating a golden mean, emphasizes the need to accept the good to be found in the Deist and traditionalist positions.

The alterations to 'Chaucer in Dryden's *Fables*' (*Monk Studies*) are examined by Earl Miner and explained in terms of *fabula, argumentum*, and *historia*, the rhetorical subdivisions of *narratio*. In *TSLL* Percy G. Adams considers Dryden's alliteration, consonance, and assonance, and their relationship to the music and meaning of the verse. Pierre Legouis, in 'Dryden plus

Miltonien que Milton' (*Ea*), explores the possible meanings of the line, 'And who but man should judge of man's free state?', and the editors of *NQ* provide information about a possible echo of Dryden by Pope. In *Dryden e Teocrito*[16] Silvano Gerevini compares Dryden's translations of Theocritus with the originals and with the translations of Creech. He stresses the struggle between classical measure and baroque exuberance in the translations of Dryden, and studies Dryden's amplifications in some detail, with resulting insight into Dryden not only as a translator, but also as a poet. Creech's personal relations with Dryden are treated briefly in the introduction, and his versions are conveniently reprinted in an appendix.

(c) Drama

An attractive, two-volume selection of four of Dryden's comedies and four of his tragedies has been edited by L. A. Beaurline and Fredson Bowers for the Curtain Playwrights series,[17] and it makes an interesting contrast to the California Dryden. The general introductions to the two volumes sketch rather boldly the place filled by Dryden's dramas in literary history. There is also a separate introduction to each play, that to *The Indian Emperour* drawing

[16] *Dryden e Teocrito: Barocco e Neoclassicismo nella Restaurazione Inglese*, by Silvano Gerevini. Milan: U. Mursia. pp. 157. Lire 2,200.
[17] *Four Comedies* and *Four Tragedies*, by John Dryden, ed. by L. A. Beaurline and Fredson Bowers. Chicago and London: University of Chicago Press. (Curtain Playwrights.) pp. ix+367. 90s. $10. pp. ix+412. 99s. $10.95. The comedies are: *Secret Love, Sir Martin Mar-All, An Evening's Love, Marriage a-la-Mode*. The tragedies are: *The Indian Emperour, Aureng-Zebe, All for Love, Don Sebastian*.

heavily on the California Dryden, while the preface to *All for Love* provides a stimulating and sound discussion of the relationship of Dryden's play to Shakespeare's; on the whole the separate introductions are independent, and if not startlingly new, very much to the point and soundly reasoned. Unlike the California Dryden this edition uses the Trinity College manuscript as copytext for *The Indian Emperour*. The elaborate commentary and detailed textual notes of the monumental California edition are of course absent, but the annotations at the bottom of the page cover a great many basic points which are taken for granted and ignored in the fuller scholarly edition. The selection is well printed, easily legible, and easily handled; it can in short be heartily recommended as a sound edition suitable for all but the most exhaustive scholarly study.

In 'Alexas in *All for Love*: His Genealogy and Function' (*SP*) Howard D. Weinbrot traces his descent from the eunuch Photinus who intrigues to murder Pompey in many of the Roman histories and earlier dramatic versions of the life of Cleopatra. In Dryden's *All for Love*, however, Alexas is contrasted with Ventidius, Dryden's own creation; the one is associated with polish, cowardice, and the unnatural fertility of Cleopatra and Egypt, while the other links with rugged, martial manhood, with Octavia, her children, and Rome. After the arrival of Octavia the counterturn comes when Ventidius tries to use Egyptian guile; Alexas continues true to his character in trying to save himself, and when the others are dead goes to grace Caesar's triumph. He serves dramatically to bring out the nobility of the protagonists in a contest of good and evil. In discussing 'Dryden's *All for*

Love and Sedley's *Antony and Cleopatra*' (*NQ*), Neville Davies also notes Alexas's relationship to Sedley's Photinus, but holds that Ventidius is based on Sedley's characters, Canidius and Lucilius. The good faith of Cleopatra and the love of the messenger for her, together with his later confession of his own guilt and Cleopatra's innocence, are among the important parallels, although the borrowings are integrated in a tighter structure by Dryden. The contention of the California Dryden that the Duke of Newcastle was part author is supported by F. H. Moore in his study of 'The Composition of *Sir Martin Mar-all* (*MacMillan Essays*). He points to the clashing time schemes of the main plot and subplots, the evidence of the cancelled scene between Moody and Swallow at the end of the first act, and the difference in characterization and standard of language between Acts I to III and Acts IV and V. He believes that Dryden and Newcastle agreed on the outline of the play, Newcastle wrote the first three acts, Dryden the last two, and that Dryden then worked over the whole again.

(d) *Prose*

A well-chosen selection of Dryden's prose criticism, especially his criticism on drama has been edited in a sound modernized text by Arthur C. Kirsch.[18] Latin quotations are translated, brief but adequate notes are provided, and a short bibliography is included. A very sensible introduction summarizes the state of knowledge concerning Dryden's critical genesis and places him firmly and

[18] *Literary Criticism of John Dryden*, ed. by Arthur C. Kirsch. Lincoln: Nebraska U. P. 1966. (Regents Critics Series.) pp. xvii + 174. Cloth $4.95. Paperback $1.95.

fairly in his historical context. This is an extremely useful one-volume edition.

Karl J. Höltgen[19] traces Dryden's nimble spaniel of poetic fancy back to Huartes's refined or elevated imagination like a spaniel (misconstrued by the English translations as 'Swift imagination') and beyond this to the *imaginatio* of classical psychology, combined with the *inventio* of Quintilian and Cicero, which sought out the *loci* where arguments were hidden. In 'Dryden's Critical Vocabulary: The Imitation of Nature' (*PLL*, 1966), Mary Thale classifies the various meanings of Dryden's phrase and shows how he exploits its ambiguities in *An Essay of Dramatic Poesy* to harmonize the conflicting claims of ancients and moderns, French and English, classical principles and English practice; in *A Parallel of Poetry and Painting* it is similarly used to reconcile the sister arts. Stanley Archer, also in *PLL* (1966), vindicates Malone's identifications of 'The Persons in *An Essay of Dramatic Poesy*', while granting that the representation of living persons is subordinated to the function of the characters as mouthpieces for 'preconceived and reasonably coherent critical positions. In *NQ* Wallace Maurer retracts an earlier statement that Dryden, in his 'Defence of the Paper Written by the Duchess of York', had misremembered a passage from Lord Herbert of Cherbury.

3. OTHER AUTHORS

(a) *Poets*

The *Gyldenstolpe Manuscript Mis-*cellany,[20] containing poems by Rochester and others, has been published in a careful facsimile, introduced and annotated by Bror Danielsson and David M. Vieth. Vieth contributes an interesting account of the nature of such miscellanies and the public for which they were designed. In keeping with the importance he attaches to manuscript versions of Restoration poems, he attributes a high degree of accuracy to the facsimile's texts of many of the major poems of Rochester and his annotations contain numerous cross-references to his own *Attribution in Restoration Poetry*. Many of the poems appear in sequences of statement and reply by various hands. Altogether this is a handsomely produced volume which helps to convey something of the ambience which shaped much Restoration poetry. An older book with a strong bearing on Rochester is Wilson's *Court Wits of the Restoration* (*YW* xxix. 198–9), which did much to clear the wits of legendary scandal, and which has now been reprinted, together with many other important works of Restoration scholarship, by Frank Cass.[21]

Another Restoration facsimile is that of the 1686 volume of poems by Mrs. Anne Killigrew,[22] with a helpful and unpretentious introduction by Richard Morton. Killigrew is certainly a minor poetess, but she does

[19] 'John Drydens "Nimble Spaniel": Zur Schnelligkeit der *Inventio* und *Imaginatio*' in *Lebende Antike: Symposion für Rudolf Sühnel*, ed. by Horst Meller and Hans-Joachim Zimmermann. Berlin: Schmidt.

[20] *The Gyldenstolpe Manuscript Miscellany of Poems by John Wilmot, Earl of Rochester, and other Restoration Authors*, ed. by Bror Danielsson and David M. Vieth. Stockholm: Almqvist & Wiksell. Stockholm Studies in English XVII. pp. xxvii+385. Sw. Kr. 70.

[21] *The Court Wits of the Restoration: An Introduction*, by John Harold Wilson. Frank Cass. pp. vi+264. 84s.

[22] *Poems (1686)*, by Mrs. Anne Killigrew. A facsimile reproduction with an introduction by Richard Morton. Scholars' Facsimiles and Reprints. Gainesville: Florida. pp. xii+ [20]+100. $6.

have a distinctive quality; she has lucidity and occasional strength, often together with a certain awkwardness, and she is a trifle Denhamesque, without having the consummate skill in versification of Denham at his best. Though minor, this is a useful addition to reprints from the period.

John Buxton's *A Tradition of Poetry*[23] is concerned with those writers, from Wyatt to Winchelsea, who wrote poetry not as professionals, but because the composition of verses was a natural part of civilized living. Among them Waller and Cotton are considered. Buxton sympathizes with the outlook of these authors, and the strength of his book is its sense of their poetry as part of the daily life of men. His account, however, needs complementing by more technical, if less civilized, studies, and it would have been improved if his denigratory remarks on the modern world, however true, had been omitted in favour of a policy of allowing facts to speak for themselves.

In Alvin I. Dust's 'Charles Cotton's comments on John Collop's Poetry' (*NQ*), one of Cotton's minor poems, 'To Cupid', is demonstrated to be an attack on Collop's 'The Vanity of Courtship'. In *RES* Allan Pritchard prints for the first time 'Six Letters by Cowley', full of charm, learning, and tender raillery, and promises an edition of a newly discovered manuscript of *The Civill Warre*. J. C. Calderhead (*NQ*) traces some lines of stanza X of Cowley's 'The Garden' to Palladius's 'De Ceraso' of the fourth century, and not to Marvell as had previously been suggested. Marvell himself is the subject of comment in 'From Contemplation to Action: Marvell's Poetical Career' (*PQ*) by

George de F. Lord, who holds that even in his earlier poems Marvell had considered the only sufficient reason for leaving retirement to be service of the universal good, embodied politically in a mixed constitution which preserves the rights and liberties of the subject. This constitutional ideal was not fulfilled by the Protectorate or the Restoration, and in consequence, 'The painter poems are didactic injunctions to corrective action which nevertheless embody, though intermittently and sometimes crudely, the lyric, elegiac, and heroic themes of the earlier poems'. When it finally became clear that Charles's aims were not Marvell's, the poet bade farewell to literature in his doggerel lampoons on the king and turned to political action. George Guffey in 'Thomas Traherne on Original Sin' (*NQ*) takes issue with K. W. Salter's interpretation of Traherne's theological position and quotes passages from the *Christian Ethicks* and *Meditations and Devotions upon the Life of Christ* demonstrating Traherne's acceptance of original sin, the necessity of grace and the efficacy of Christ's passion. A previously unpublished poem by Davenant in imitation of Donne is printed by A. M. Gibbs in 'A Davenant Imitation of Donne?' (*RES*), together with a number of notes on the printed and manuscript locations of various Davenant poems.

Boileau's influence on the literature of the Restoration and eighteenth century is great and acknowledged. The 'translation' of the first four cantos of *Le Lutrin*, published in 1682 by N.O. and now reprinted,[24] effectively naturalizes the original; it con-

[23] *A Tradition of Poetry*, by John Buxton. Macmillan and St. Martin's Press. pp. ix + 190. 30*s*. $6.95.

[24] *Le Lutrin: An Heroick Poem Written Originally in French by Monsieur Boileau. Made English by N.O. (1682)*, introduced by Richard Morton. (*ARS*, No. 126.) Los Angeles: Clark Memorial Library, University of California. pp. viii + 41.

tains many comic echoes of earlier English poetry and substitutes for the high propriety of style of the original a rougher expansive exuberance. The version was certainly worth reprinting and Richard Morton provides it with a fitting and just introduction of commendable brevity. Boileau is a key figure in European literary developments of the late seventeenth century and in his study of the contest between Boileau and Charles Perrault Hans Kortum brings out some of the wider implications of the quarrel between the ancients and the moderns.[25] He sees the dispute between the two men not merely as a conflict of ideas, but as a personal conflict related to their social backgrounds, and their economic, political, and social relationships with the centralized power of the French court. Some of the book's assumptions about the forces governing history are extremely questionable, but it makes a most impressive attempt to tackle a literary, cultural, and social event in its full complexity. An equally exacting study of the English ramifications of the quarrel would be enlightening.

(b) Dramatists

Light is shed on the extraordinary relationship between Sir George Etherege and his secretary at Ratisbon in two articles by Frederick Bracher in HLB. He demonstrates that the Harvard letterbooks in the hand of Hugo Hughes, the secretary, are the official ones, while the British Museum manuscript is a further transcript kept by Hughes for his own purposes and including additional damaging material, some of it demonstrably false, concerning Etherege. He makes out a plausible case for believing that this was intended for the Dutch Resident at Ratisbon, and that gentle George's secretary was a spy for the supporters of William of Orange.

Wycherley has been extensively edited of late. Weales's editing of the early quartos in the Complete Plays and Loftis's edition of The Country Wife have now been followed by Leo Hughes's edition of The Plain Dealer.[26] Hughes presents a sound, modernized text, and the annotation is brief but adequate. The introduction comments on the sources, and is enthusiastic about the dramatic virtues of various characters and incidents, but it neither makes the play out to be an integrated whole, nor explains adequately why it is not. This problem is attacked by Ian Donaldson in '"Tables Turned": The Plain Dealer' (EIC). He points to shortcomings in Zimbardo's and Holland's interpretations, analyses the paradoxical plot developments, in which appearances and facts constantly belie one another, and the contradictions in Manly's character, and he sees the various worlds of the play, particularly those of Freeman and Manly, as counterbalancing and judging each other. The final situation, despite some discomfiture of Manly, rewards his wild justice, and he is on the whole sympathetically presented; however, the ending, after so many paradoxical changes of fortune, lacks finality, and Manly is not made sufficiently aware of the dubious morality of his earlier tactics. A. M. Friedson, in 'Wycherley and

[25] Charles Perrault und Nicolas Boileau. Der Antike-Streit im Zeitalter der Klassichen Französischen Literatur, by Hans Kortum. (Neue Beiträge zur Literaturwissenschaft, Band 22.) Berlin, German Democratic Republic: Rütten & Loening, 1966. pp. 211. MDN. 18.

[26] The Plain Dealer, by William Wycherley. ed. by Leo Hughes. Nebraska U.P. and Arnold. (RRestDS.) pp. xxii+183. Cloth 21s, $4.75. Paperback 10s. 6d. $2.66.

Molière: Satirical Point of View in *The Plain Dealer*' (*MP*), points out the important differences between the play and its source, Molière's *Le Misanthrope*, starting with the opening of the French play, a long critique of Alceste, as opposed to the opening contrast between Manly and the despicable Plausible, and ending with Alceste's withdrawal and defeat, as opposed to Manly's triumphant reconciliation with the world; Manly, in part a humour of the blunt sea captain, is comic but not ridiculous, and the satirical target throughout is the corrupt society of the time. This interpretation has the virtue of accounting for all the facts of the play, which the multiple satire theories do not. In 'Wycherley's *The Country Wife*: An Anatomy of Masculinity' (*PLL*, 1966), David M. Vieth provides a clever but unconvincing interpretation of that play, considering Harcourt and Alithea the norms between Margery (nature) and Horner (artifice), Harcourt also standing as the norm of masculinity between the undercommitted Dorilant and the overcommitted Horner; during the analysis Pinchwife is provided with a case history as an insecure male forced by paranoiac fears into the arms of whores. R. Berman in 'The Ethic of *The Country Wife*' (*TSLL*) pleads for greater attention to what is said and thought in the play, and less to what happens, and believes that Horner's response is at least justified logically, as ideals like honour, reputation, friendship, and freedom, 'are remorselessly presented as having no bearing on the conduct of those who invoke them—and, more important, as being really removed from their understanding'. Horner is in some sense analogous to the satirist himself. Joyce Miller (*Scripta Hierosolymitana*) distinguishes between Congreve, who uses

metaphor to establish a climate of values, and Etherege and Wycherley whose true wits are distinguished from their false wits by a capacity to assemble and reassemble significant verbal data at high speed. The opening epigram of *The Country Wife* excludes the supernatural and propounds the hypothesis of a human, biological, sexual urge which only the unhealthy or unnatural refuse to exercise; this hypothesis is then tested in the rest of the play. As such epigrams contain no moral suppositions of which the speaker is unaware, they and the comedy based on them can be accepted or rejected according to the moral predisposition of the audience.

The *Complete Plays* of Congreve have been edited by the late Herbert Davis,[27] whose death was such a loss to Restoration and eighteenth-century scholarship. His text is based on the first quartos, and the simplified textual apparatus records substantive variants and emendations. The annotations are admirably clear and succinct, and have a weight of erudition behind them. There are informative introductions to the separate plays and a general introduction, the main virtues of which are a vivid sense of period and an acute awareness of the perfection of Congreve's language. A. Norman Jeffares has introduced and annotated Bateson's text of *Love for Love*.[28] An analysis of *The Way of the World* is undertaken by Alexandre Maurocordato;[29] he

[27] *The Complete Plays of William Congreve*, ed. by Herbert Davis. Chicago U.P. (Curtain Playwrights.) pp. vii + 503. 112s. 6d. $12.50.

[28] *Love for Love*, by William Congreve, ed. by A. Norman Jeffares. Macmillan and St. Martin's Press. pp. xxi + 144. 8s. 6d.

[29] *Congreve: Ainsi Va le Monde. Étude sur la Structure d'une 'Comedy of Manners'*, by Alexandre Maurocordato. Archives des Lettres Modernes, No. 76. pp. 54. F 6.

finds the action complicated and the characters lacking in development, but considers the play as a whole a brilliant reflection of a society where morality has given way to style and good taste. Gerald Weales in 'The Shadow on Congreve's Surface' (*ETJ*) throws out the suggestion that Vainlove may not be a mere humour but instead a lightly sketched picture of a pervert suffering from impotence or narcissism. The study of Congreve's circle by Kathleen M. Lynch (*YW* xxxii. 196–7) has been reprinted;[30] not all of it, of course, is very relevant to Congreve, but the sections that are remain a testimony to the playwright's consideration and good sense.

The Man of Mode, The Country Wife, and Love for Love are the plays edited for the Penguin volume of *Three Restoration Comedies*, by Gāmini Salgādo.[31] His introduction, based, with acknowledgement, on Holland, contains some misleading generalizations. Holland's work itself (*YW* xl. 180), despite its somewhat *a priori* approach, remains the most distinguished modern study of Restoration comedy and has done immense service to study of the drama of the period; its publication as a paperback is very welcome.[32]

Three less accessible Restoration dramas have now been added to the titles appearing in the Regents Restoration Drama Series. Frederick M. Link has produced a sound edition of Aphra Behn's *The Rover*,[33] with an incisive introduction examining Behn's debt to and improvements on Killigrew. Behn's fondness for witty lovers here finds expression in the Rover and Hellena, whose attitudes are contrasted with the sentimental affection of Belvile and Florinda, and the conventional attitude of Blunt, Pedro, and Antonio to forced and financial matches. The Tory *City Politiques* by John Crowne is edited by John H. Wilson,[34] who is inclined to opt for composite portraits rather than individual identifications for the characters. Lee's *Lucius Junius Brutus*, a Whig play, is edited by John Loftis;[35] his annotations are amusingly coy on occasion, but his introduction is admirably full, with a detailed account of the Roman historical parallels to the Restoration position, and a just appraisal of the play.

Howard S. Collins's *The Comedy of Sir William Davenant*[36] contains a great deal of information on the sources, certain and dubious, of Davenant's work, and a good many generalizations on comedy. The upshot seems to be a claim that Davenant started burlesque and partially anticipated the comedy of manners, and that his comedy is fuller in range than that of Congreve and Etherege. Collins sometimes misuses English, and the book is marred by

[30] *A Congreve Gallery*, by Kathleen M. Lynch. Frank Cass and Octgaon. pp. xiv + 196. 75s. $7.

[31] *Three Restoration Comedies*, ed. by Gāmini Salgādo. (Penguin English Library 27.) Penguin Books. pp. 365. 6s.

[32] *The First Modern Comedies: The Significance of Etherege, Wycherley and Congreve*, by Norman N. Holland. Bloomington: Indiana U.P. (Midland Book 100.) pp. 274. Paperback 25s.

[33] *The Rover*, by Aphra Behn, ed. by Frederick M. Link. (*RRestDS.*) Nebraska U.P. and Arnold. pp. xvi + 144. Cloth 21s. $4.75. Paperback 10s. 6d. $2.66.

[34] *City Politiques*, by John Crowne, ed. by John H. Wilson. (*RRestDS.*) Nebraska U.P. and Arnold. pp. xix + 159. Cloth 21s. $4.75. Paperback 10s. 6d. $2.66.

[35] *Lucius Junius Brutus*, by Nathaniel Lee, ed. by John Loftis. (*RRestDS.*) Nebraska U.P. and Arnold. pp. xxiv + 107. Cloth 21s. $4.75. Paperback 10s. 6d. $2.66.

[36] *The Comedy of Sir William Davenant*, by Howard S. Collins. (Studies in English Literature, vol. XXIV.) The Hague: Mouton. pp. 179. Guilders 22.

numerous misprints. The masque *Salmacida Spolia* by Inigo Jones and Davenant is reprinted by T. J. B. Spencer in *A Book of Masques*,[37] together with the stage plan, scenic sketches and brilliant costume designs. Arthur H. Nethercot's lively account of Davenant's life and theatrical activity (*YW* xx. 104–5)[38] has been reissued with additional notes taking account of recent Davenant research.

Bernard Harris's account of Sir John Vanbrugh is brief but competent.[39] He sees Vanbrugh's plays as essentially comedies of unregenerate human nature, and regretfully concludes that, as opposed to Farquhar's advocacy of divorce, Vanbrugh tends to advocate 'Personal freedom beyond the law'. The short account of the architecture is good. The reprinted Cibber bibliography by L. R. N. Ashley in *RECTR* lists Cibber's works and a selection of the articles and books on him; some of the annotations are so elementary that it is difficult to see precisely for what public it is designed. Cibber's best play, *The Careless Husband*, is edited by William W. Appleton.[40] It contains several notable roles, including Lord Foppington, the descendant of Cibber's own Sir Novelty Fashion, raised to the peerage by Vanbrugh. In its concentration on postmarital problems and the softened tone of its

comedy it is adapted to the emotional climate of the early eighteenth century.

In 'Shadwell and the Anonymous *Timon*' (*NQ*) John Edmunds argues that Shadwell's *Timon* is an adaptation of the old play of that name, and not based only on Shakespeare as has been generally supposed. James Black finds much evidence for 'The Influence of Hobbes on Nahum Tate's *King Lear*' (*SEL*), especially in the characterization of Edmund who is a 'natural' man, typifying Hobbes's conception of the state of war, and set in opposition to the character of Albany. The circumstances of the opening production of the play, and its subsequent stage history during the eighteenth century and later, are explored by Black in *RECTR*. *A Fond Husband* is the subject of 'A D'Urfey Play Dated' *(MP)* by Jack A. Vaughn, who also contributes a survey, not very well written, of D'Urfey's output to *QJS*.

Otway's influence on Hofmannsthal's *Das Gerettete Venedig* is examined by H. R. Klieneberger in *MLR*, while Roger Bauer's '"A Souldier of Fortune": "Als Soldat und Brav"'[41] discusses Goethe's debt to *The Orphan* in the Valentin scene of *Faust*, and the significance of the changes he makes in borrowing from Otway. Thomas B. Stroup traces 'Otway's Bitter Pessimism' (*MacMillan Essays*), holding that, '[It] is basic to the cynicism of his comedy, and in its larger expression gives to all his plays their quality of frustration and futility'. The relationship in *Venice Preserv'd* between the sado-masochism of Antonio and Aquilina, the sexual motives of Pierre and Jaffeir, and references to the Venetian state as a political whore, are examined by

[37] *A Book of Masques: In Honour of Allardyce Nicoll.* See chap. VIII, footnote 10.
[38] *Sir William D'avenant: Poet Laureate and Playwright-Manager*, by Arthur H. Nethercot. New York: Russell & Russell. pp. vii+[7]+488. $12.50.
[39] *Sir John Vanbrugh*, by Bernard Harris. Longmans, for the British Council and the National Book League. (Writers and their Work, No. 197.) pp. 43. 3s. 6d.
[40] *The Careless Husband*, by Colley Cibber, ed. by William W. Appleton. (*RRestDS*.) Nebraska U.P. and Arnold. pp. xvi+135. Cloth 21s. $4.75. Paperback 10s. 6d. $2.66.

[41] In *Festschrift für Richard Alewyn*, ed. by Herbert Singer and Benno von Weise. Cologne: Böhlau.

Gordon Williams in 'The Sex-Death Motive in Otway's *Venice Preserv'd*' (*Trivium*). Frank J. Kearful's 'The Nature of Tragedy in Rowe's *The Fair Penitent*' (*PLL* 1966) sees Rowe as inheriting his use of the pathetic from Otway, Banks, and Southerne, and considers that *Jane Shore* and *The Fair Penitent*, 'are the first attempts to fuse the naturalism of domestic tragedy and the patheticism of "sentimental" tragedy with a new didacticism which is part of the Augustan temper'.

Many older editions of the works of minor Restoration dramatists are being currently reissued by Benjamin Blom. This year's reprints include a copy of the 1664 edition of *Comedies, and Tragedies* by Thomas Killigrew,[42] a reissue of Harbage's book on Killigrew (*YW* xi. 243–4),[43] and a reprint of the nineteenth-century edition of *The Dramatic Works of John Crowne* by Maidment and Logan.[44] Many of the titles in Blom's catalogue are otherwise virtually unobtainable today.

(c) *Prose Authors*

The monumental edition of Elias Ashmole's papers edited by C. H. Josten[45] provides a vivid picture of a fascinating and influential personality and also sheds light on a neglected aspect of Restoration culture. Ashmole was a member of the Royal Society who learnt the Paracelsian art of making sigils or talismans, which he used frequently as cures for various diseases, and he was consulted by many, from King Charles II downwards, when astrological forecasts were required concerning political developments. His scholarship was immense, his curiosity unbounded, and his practical business sense shrewd in the extreme. These various aspects of his activity seem necessarily to conflict from the twentieth-century point of view; from the Restoration point of view they did not.

Irène Simon introduces and edits a selection of the sermons of Barrow,[46] with South and Tillotson to follow. Her introduction is exhaustive and scholarly; she traces the plain style of the post-Restoration Anglicans to the belief that reason, arguing from 'The common notions written by God in the hearts of all men' will produce assent to the essential tenets of Christianity, reason being a certain and public, not a fallible and private, faculty. The plain style aims at ease of communication concerning the essential truths and is a reaction to the Senecan style of Andrewes and his tendency to crumble a text into small pieces, and also to the Biblical imagery and emotionalism of Puritan preaching. The individual characteristics of Barrow, South, and Tillotson are further analysed and a sympathetic account is given of the diffi-

[42] *Comedies and Tragedies (1664)*, by Thomas Killigrew. Benjamin Blom. pp. 576+80. £14 14s. $27.50.

[43] *Thomas Killigrew: Cavalier Dramatist, 1612–83*, by Alfred Harbage. Benjamin Blom. pp. viii+247. 90s. $12.50.

[44] *The Dramatic Works of John Crowne*, ed. by James Maidment and W. H. Logan. Benjamin Blom. Vol. I, pp. xviii+342. Vol. II, pp. 396. Vol. III, pp. 457. Vol. IV, pp. 426. £17 10s. $47.50.

[45] *Elias Ashmole (1617–1692): His Autobiographical and Historical Notes, his Correspondence, and Other Contemporary Sources Relating to his Life and Work*, ed. with a biographical introduction, by C. H. Josten. Oxford: Clarendon Press, 1966. Vol. I, *Biographical Introduction*, pp. xx+306. Vol. II, *Texts 1617–1660*, pp. 309–808. Vol. III, *Texts 1661–1672*, pp. 809–1289. Vol. IV, *Texts 1673–1701*, pp. 1291–1898. Vol. V, *Index*, pp. 1899–2065. £18 18s. $50.60.

[46] *Three Restoration Divines: Barrow, South, Tillotson. Selected Sermons*, ed. by Irène Simon. Paris: Société d'Edition 'Les Belles Lettres'. (Bibliothèque la de Faculté de Philosophie et Lettres de l'Université de Liège, Fascicule CLXXXI.) Vol. I, *Introduction+Barrow: Selected Sermons*, pp. vi+510+20. F 40.

cult decisions they were faced with concerning the relationship between Church and state. Brief biographies of the three are included. The selected sermons are printed in full.

John Bunyan's relationship to covenant thought in the seventeenth century is discussed by Richard L. Greaves in *Church History*. Bunyan, he concludes, held that admission to the covenant of grace came from election by God and not action by man, that the elect could not fall from grace, and that their fulfilment of the moral law was the natural result of their election; he differed from the strict Calvinists primarily in his rejection of a baptismal covenant.

Montague Summers's edition of *Oroonoko and Other Prose Narratives* by Aphra Behn is now reprinted.[47]

4. HISTORY, SCIENCE, ARCHITECTURE

A readable, lively, and informative account of shipping, dockyards, naval administration, the river trades, and a good many Restoration maritime buildings is given by L. A. Wilcox's *Mr. Pepys's Navy*, which also provides numerous illustrations covering a great range of ships and much else.[48] Wilcox places a just emphasis on Pepys's administrative virtues and professional thoroughness, and his book is unusual and unusually pleasurable. Vivid contemporary accounts and illustrations of the kind of fighting for which the great ships of the time were designed are provided in *The Second Dutch War*, together with an historical commentary on the course of the struggle, in which

Sedley, Rochester and other courtiers, took part.[49]

In the *Bulletin of the History of Medicine* C. Webster describes the role played by the College of Physicians in seventeenth-century scientific investigation. The College eventually declined in importance because of the competition of the Royal Society, the loss of its library and museum in the Fire, and its loss of prestige through the Plague. Boyle's work as a physician, an amateur who open-mindedly pursued truth and believed in the predominance of facts over theory, but was not always reliable in his judgement of what was fact, is recounted by Lester S. King.[50]

The fourth volume of *The Correspondence of Isaac Newton*[51] covers the years 1694–1709 and includes a great many letters to Flamsteed, including the notorious outburst of 6 January 1698–9. Newton's greatness as a scientist and difficulty as a man are both brought out in the course of the volume, which gives a vivid sense of the wide range of his interests and of his practical concerns. The editing and production of the book are of the highest standard.

Two papers read to a Clark Library Seminar deal with seventeenth- and eighteenth-century attempts to ex-

---

[47] *Oroonoko & Other Prose Narratives*, by Aphra Behn, ed. by Montague Summers. Benjamin Blom. pp. 524. £3 12s. $8.50.

[48] *Mr. Pepys's Navy*, by L. A. Wilcox, illustrated by the author. Bell, 1966. pp. ix+189. 45s.

[49] *The Second Dutch War: Described in Pictures & Manuscripts of the Time*. Her Majesty's Stationery Office. pp. 43. 6s. 6d.

[50] 'Robert Boyle as an Amateur Physician' in *Medical Investigation in Seventeenth Century England. Papers Read at a Clark Library Seminar, October 14, 1967*, by Charles W. Bodemer and Lester S. King. Los Angeles: Clark Memorial Library, University of California. pp. 55. Paperback.

[51] *The Correspondence of Isaac Newton*, ed. by J. F. Scott. C.U.P. for the Royal Society. Vol. IV, *1694–1709*, pp. xxxii+578. £11 11s. $38.50.

plain the texture of matter.[52] John G. Burke deals with attempts to explain the crystalline shape of snowflakes, and Cyril Stanley Smith describes the speculations about the geometrical shapes which should be attributed to metal atoms in order to explain the granular structure and practical properties of metals. As Smith points out, the seventeenth century was the last period to permit scientific speculations which could neither be reduced to mathematical form nor be verified by experiment; hence part of the fascination of the period, and part of the explanation of its modes of thought.

The second revised edition of Locke's *Two Treatises of Government* edited by Peter Laslett has now appeared.[53] Laslett's brilliant linking of the treatises with Locke's activities as Shaftesbury's secretary, adviser, and friend, brings out the continuity between the reigns of Charles and Anne; the admittedly great differences which also exist between the two reigns were in part caused by Locke himself. That the treatises should be written as replies to Filmer, the main support of Tory thinking, is an indication of their close relationship with the literary and intellectual stream of the times. Locke's conception of the state of nature, in which the executive power of the law of nature rests solely in the hands of the individual, may hardly be establishable as objective truth, but it provided a powerful counter-myth to the theorists of absolute rule, and its stress on the consent

of the governed did much to temper English political life. Wilbur Samuel Howell (*QJS*) shows how Locke affected eighteenth-century views of rhetoric, his criticism of arguments drawn from the traditional topics causing increased attention to specific and logical arguments, and his emphasis on perspicacity, ease, and speed of communication aiding the establishment of the plain style.

M. M. Goldsmith in his perceptive study, *Hobbes's Science of Politics,* elucidates Hobbes's belief that a science of natural bodies, a science of man, and a science of political bodies could all be elaborated systematically on the assumptions and methods of Galilean science.[54] The result was subject to the weakness of Galilean science, the absence of criteria for falsifying the theory by an empirical test. John M. Steadman in '*Leviathan* and Renaissance Etymology' (*JHI*) shows that Hobbes in applying leviathan to the state and its head was following a minor but well-established tradition in mid-seventeenth-century Biblical exegesis.

J. H. Plumb's *The Growth of Political Stability in England 1675–1725* describes the development of the oligarchical political establishment of the period.[55] Geoffrey Holmes and W. A. Speck have gathered an interesting selection of documents which give some idea of the ways in which politics permeated social life at the end of the seventeenth century.[56]

[52] *Atoms, Blacksmiths, and Crystals: Practical and Theoretical Views of the Structure of Matter in the Seventeenth and Eighteenth Centuries. Papers Read at a Clark Library Seminar, November 26, 1966,* by Cyril S. Smith and John G. Burke. Los Angeles: Clark Memorial Library, University of California. pp. 61. Paperback.

[53] *Two Treatises of Government,* by John Locke, ed. by Peter Laslett. Second edition. C.U.P. pp. xvii+525. 70s. $13.50.

[54] *Hobbes's Science of Politics,* by M. M. Goldsmith. New York and London: Columbia U.P. 1966. pp. xv+274. 67s. 6d. $7.50.

[55] *The Growth of Political Stability in England: 1675–1725,* by J. H. Plumb. Macmillan and Houghton Mifflin. pp. xviii+206. 30s.

[56] *The Divided Society: Parties and Politics in England, 1694–1716,* ed. by G. S. Holmes and W. A. Speck. Edward Arnold. (Documents of Modern History.) pp. xii+179. Cloth 25s. Paperback 12s. 6d.

Two papers by Vincent Duckles and Franklin B. Zimmerman deal with the relationship of music to poetry in seventeenth-century song.[57] Duckles notes the great respect paid to the words by Lanier and Lawes in the earlier part of the century. Zimmerman traces Purcell's development from songs where the music is bound by the verse form to the ornamental, melismatic, structures of his last years, where the sense of the words is expressed in purely musical ways and the metrical form no longer dominates. Zimmerman's book on Purcell is a biographical account centring firmly on his musical activity and giving a useful summary of his career.[58]

[57] *Words to Music: Papers on English Seventeenth-Century Song Read at a Clark Library Seminar, December 11, 1965*, by Vincent Duckles and Franklin B. Zimmerman, with an introduction by Walter H. Rubsamen. Los Angeles: Clark Memorial Library, University of California. pp. vi + 93. Paperback.

[58] *Henry Purcell, 1659–1695: His Life and Times*, by Franklin B. Zimmerman. Macmillan and St. Martin's Press. pp. xvii + 429. 70s. $15.

XII

The Eighteenth Century

KEITH WALKER and JOHN CHALKER

THE chapter is arranged as follows:
1. General; 2. Poetry; 3. Prose; 4.
Drama; 5. The Novel. The first four
sections are by Keith Walker: the
last is by John Chalker.

1. GENERAL

Studies in Criticism and Aesthetics,[1]
a Festschrift for Samuel Holt Monk
to mark the thirtieth anniversary of
The Sublime contains essays on Neoclassicism, theories of poetry and
language; Dryden, Shaftesbury,
Addison, Pope, Gray, Thomson,
Johnson and Sterne; and Giovanni
Francesco Barbieri, Reynolds, and
Gainsborough. The book concludes
with a bibliography of Samuel Holt
Monk. In the opening essay B. H.
Bronson asks 'When was Neoclassicism?'. All classical movements are
'*neo*-classical' movements, and the
essence of classicism is the imitation
of Nature, a concept of great flexibility in the eighteenth century which
Bronson follows through poetry,
music, landscape gardening, painting
and sculpture. His idea of 'flexibility'
is taken up by William H. Halewood,
who argues in '"The Reach of Art"
in Augustan Poetic Theory' that
although poets often felt their art to
be representational like painting, the
analogy could work in other ways:
it 'had a clandestine usefulness to

poetry in resisting its danger from a
too narrowly understood mimetic
purpose, in revising its conception of
its nature and function, and incidentally in raising its self-esteem'. 'Philosophical Language and the Theory of
Beauty in the Eighteenth Century' by
Walter J. Hipple pleads for the possibility of aesthetics, and for the continued relevance of eighteenth-century
aesthetics to the debate about the
nature of the beautiful.

'The Naked Science of Language,
1747–1786' by Scott Elledge notes the
counterpoint of ideas of a lexico-
grapher as objective recorder of the
language, and of legislator and guardian of the language, in Johnson's
Plan for an English Dictionary (1747).
Johnson's Dictionary both recorded
the language and had an effect on
how it was used: it is wrong to think
of him as mainly a legislator, or as
legislating in vain. Elledge then turns
to other eighteenth-century writers
on language—James Harris, Joseph
Priestly, Adam Smith, Lord Mon-
boddo, George Campbell, and Hugh
Blair—and shows how their works
contributed to the development of
attitudes and concepts necessary to
the scientific study of language which
began with Sir William Jones's lecture *On the Hindus* (1786).

The essays in *Studies in Criticism
and Aesthetics* on Addison, Pope,
Thomson, Hume, Warburton, Johnson, and Sterne will be noted in the
appropriate place below.

R. S. Crane's collected papers *The*

---

[1] *Studies in Criticism and Aesthetics, 1660–
1800: Essays in Honor of Samuel Holt Monk*,
ed. by Howard Anderson and John S. Shea.
Minnesota U.P. pp. viii+419. $10. Here-
after referred to as *Monk Studies*.

Idea of the Humanities[2] contain such important essays for the study of the eighteenth century as 'Suggestions towards a Genealogy of the "Man of Feeling"', 'Anglican Apologetics and the Idea of Progress 1690–1745', 'Montesquieu and British Thought: Gibbon, Adam Smith, Burke', 'On writing the History of Criticism in England, 1650–1800', and 'The Houyhnhnms, the Yahoos, and the History of Ideas'. All these have been previously published. A new and significant addition in these volumes is a series of ten lectures on 'Shifting Definitions and Evaluations of the Humanities from the Renaissance to the Present' of which two are devoted to the eighteenth century.

George Sherburn's *The Restoration and Eighteenth Century*[3] which used to form a part of A. C. Baugh's *Literary History of England* (1948) has now been re-issued separately, with a bibliographical supplement by D. F. Bond, whose name inexplicably appears on the title page as joint author.

Eighteenth-Century Studies (*ECS*), a new periodical from the University of California at Davis, is concerned with the literature and the arts of the Restoration and eighteenth century. The focus is to be on English and American culture, but it will not neglect the literature of the continent. The first issue contains articles on 'The Augustan Mode in English Poetry', eighteenth-century intellectual history, Hogarth and historical painting, music, and criticism of *Moll*

Flanders: it is to be hoped that this generous variety of subjects will be maintained. The editors allow their contributors such ample elbow-room as positively to provoke longwindedness, but otherwise this is a promising journal.

Essays in English Literature of the Classical Period[4] contains essays on Swift, Pope, and Johnson noted below. In addition there are essays on Otway, on Gentleman Smith (an actor protégé of Garrick's), and on *The Dial*, together with three essays on Dryden's plays.

Another collection of essays, the Proceedings of the David Nichol Smith Seminar at Canberra in 1966, has not been available for inspection.[5]

Peter Gay's huge, erudite, and discursive essay in cultural history, *The Enlightenment . . . The Rise of Modern Paganism,*[6] is concerned with the genealogy of the ideas of the 'philosophies' (Gay deals mainly with the French, but includes all the European thinkers of the Enlightenment) who found in the inspiration of the ancients (notably Lucretius and Cicero) a new world view which was humane, sceptical, and 'pagan'. This sprightly and partial introduction to eighteenth-century thought is illuminating on some English writers, notably Gibbon and Hume, and the polemical 'Bibliographical Essay' is diligent and helpful.

J. W. Johnson's *The Formation of*

[2] *'The Idea of the Humanities' and Other Essays Critical and Historical*, by R. S. Crane. Chicago U.P. 2 vols,: pp. xxii+311; viii+332. $15; £6 15s.

[3] *The Restoration and Eighteenth Century (1660–1798)*, by George Sherburn and Donald F. Bond. (*A Literary History of England*, ed. by Albert C. Baugh, second edition, vol. III.) Appleton-Century-Crofts and Routledge. pp. xii+474. Paperback £1 5s.

[4] *Essays in English Literature of the Classical Period Presented to Dougald MacMillan*, ed. by Daniel W. Patterson and Albrecht B. Strauss. (*Studies in Philology*, extra series no. 4.) North Carolina U.P. pp. 185. Cloth $5. Hereafter referred to as *MacMillan Essays*.

[5] *Studies in the Eighteenth Century*, ed. by R. F. Brissenden. Australian National U.P.

[6] *The Enlightenment: An Interpretation: The Rise of Modern Paganism*, by Peter Gay. Knopf (1966) and Weidenfeld & Nicolson (1967). pp. xviii+572. $8.75. 63s.

English Neo-Classical Thought[7] attempts to 'define' the thought-and-literature of the eighteenth century by examining and redefining its sources and influences. In various chapters Johnson points up very well the pervasive influence of classical and Renaissance ideas of historiography, and shows that Greek, patristic, Byzantine, and Dutch, as well as Latin, influences played their part in forming the eighteenth-century mind. Johnson certainly adds to our notions of the complexities of the age—for instance he shows how ambivalent the word 'Augustan' could be—but his book is unsatisfactory in one important respect. He expends so much time and evidence in establishing the existence of a neglected 'influence' that he has no room left to show how that influence worked in shaping or modifying the imaginative concerns of the neo-classical writer, except in the case of Gibbon, the subject of his last chapter. For Johnson, Gibbon is the 'archetypal Neo-Classicist' and he writes interestingly about the genesis and achievement of *The Decline and Fall*. *The Formation of English Neo-Classical Thought* will remain a useful work which combats received simplifications and opens up neglected possibilities of study.

In 'Augustans on Augustanism: England, 1655–1759' (*RMS*) Howard Erskine-Hill examines (as J. W. Johnson had done) the term 'Augustan', adds important examples of its use to Johnson's list, and shows that Johnson gets details wrong. The word did have a derogatory sense (the Tories attacked George II by stressing the bad side of Octavius) but this was not the main implication of the word.

Susie I. Tucker's study in eighteenth-century vocabulary and usage *Protean Shape*[8] falls into two parts: (a) an examination of comments on and discussions of usage drawn from the periodicals of the time, and (b) a survey of terms and usages from a modern standpoint. (The two parts are not as distinct as this would suggest, because Miss Tucker's 'modern' awareness continually informs her first section.) 'The eighteenth century is a period so near to us,' she writes, 'that we can read its writings without the apparatus needed for even the seventeenth, and yet it is far enough away to make us perpetually on the alert lest we fall into a sudden or routine pitfall. It is therefore an ideal training ground for observant students.' Comment on the language in the eighteenth century was often surprisingly enlightened. The *Monthly Register* criticized Richard Wynne for saying that an active verb 'governs the accusative case' on the grounds that 'nouns in English having no accusative termination, the verb cannot be said to govern that case'. The language examined in *Protean Shape* is not confined to, or even mainly, literary language, but this interesting and brightly written book will increase the reader's sensitivity to the literature of the period.

Colin Clair has edited a very useful volume of selections (the extracts are in alphabetical order of subject) from the chaotic nine-volume *Literary Anecdotes of the Eighteenth Century* by John Nichols.[9]

---

[7] *The Formation of English Neo-Classical Thought*, by James William Johnson. Princeton U.P. and O.U.P. pp. xxiv+359. $9. 83s.

[8] *Protean Shape: A Study in Eighteenth-Century Vocabulary and Usage*, by Susie I. Tucker. U. of London: Athlone Press. pp. xiv+322. 55s.

[9] *Literary Anecdotes of the Eighteenth Century*, by John Nichols. Ed. by Colin Clair. Centaur Press and Southern Illinois U.P. pp. 525. £5 5s.

Ralph Allen made a fortune out of his improvements to the postal service, was a friend of Fielding, Pope and Pitt, and became a type of the Benevolent Man in his lifetime (he even managed to put up with the awful Warburton). He had a 'simple and unspoiled respect for books and authors', but his life touched on many other aspects of the age, and these Benjamin Boyce illuminates in his fascinating and scholarly biography.[10] It is discussed (along with books on Fielding) in Martin C. Battestin's 'Fielding and Ralph Allen: Benevolism and its limits as an eighteenth-century ideal' (*MLQ*).

M. Dorothy George's survey of Georgian caricature *Hogarth to Cruikshank*[11] is a masterly treatment, lavishly illustrated. Her subject is not mainly literary of course, but we see Pope here caricatured by Hogarth in *The Man of Taste* (1731) whitewashing Burlington, and as a triple-crowned monkey with an ape in the anonymous *His Holiness and his Prime Minister*. Johnson appears along with Boswell, Goldsmith, and Mrs. Thrale in a supper-box at Vauxhall in Rowlandson's famous print (wonderfully reproduced in colour), as an owl with ass's ears looking at a bust of Milton and Pope in Gillray's *Old Wisdom Blinking at the Stars* (this was 1782, just after the *Lives of the Poets*) and again in Rowlandson's *Apollo and the Muses, Inflicting Penance on Dr. Pomposo, round Parnassus*. Johnson, pot-bellied, and stripped to the waist, is being chastized. He wears a dunce's cap

bearing the names of the poets in the *Lives*, and is saying 'I acknowledge my transgressions and my sins are before me.' Two winged books are entitled *An Essay on Envy* and *An Essay on the Milk of Human Kindness*. This monstrous and cruel libel tells us a lot about the eighteenth century.

Paolo Rolli came to England in 1715 and later became a secretary of the Royal Academy of Music. He was a librettist for Handel, and a poet; he translated *Paradise Lost* into Italian and got a mention in *The Dunciad*. George E. Dorris gives a very full survey of his activities in *Paolo Rolli and the Italian Circle in London 1715–1744*.[12] He also writes about the Italian opera in England, and recounts the visits here of Antonio Conti, Scipione Maffei, and Antonio Cocchi. There is a checklist of operas produced in London from 1705 to 1744.

2. POETRY

(a) *General*

Rachel Trickett's *The Honest Muse*[13] tries 'to consider some of the attitudes and assumptions underlying the poetry of Dryden, Pope and Johnson, and to see them in relation to the political and intellectual circumstances in which they worked'. The 'attitudes' that Miss Trickett examines are questions of stance, tone, and ethical ideas: the complicated cluster of associations of the concept of honesty, which in Pope 'points to a new idea of worth and virtue' different from 'the older vein of panegyric'. Despite Miss Trickett's firm disclaimer, her book at times

---

[10] *The Benevolent Man: A Life of Ralph Allen of Bath*, by Benjamin Boyce. Harvard U.P. pp. xiv+304+15 pp. of illustrations. $7.95.

[11] *Hogarth to Cruikshank: Social Change in Graphic Satire*, by M. Dorothy George. Allen Lane: Penguin. pp. 224+16 colour plates+201 black and white illustrations. £5 5s.

[12] *Paolo Rolli and the Italian Circle in London 1715–1744*, by George E. Dorris. The Hague: Mouton. pp. 310. 32 Guilders.

[13] *The Honest Muse: A Study in Augustan Verse*, by Rachel Trickett. Oxford: Clarendon Press. pp. x+309. £2 10s. $8.80.

aspires to a history of Augustan poetry (although they are not connected to her theme the points she makes about the connexions of Pope with the poetry of the Restoration are very acute, as is her critique of Johnson's minor poetry). This is an important book in many ways, and it would be wrong to allow the leisurely limpidity of the style to blind us to the significance of her theme or to her sensitivity in dealing with it.

'The Augustan Mode in English Poetry' (*ECS*) by Ralph Cohen is no less than an attempt to define 'the common features of the poetry written from 1660–1750' in order to provide 'a basis for reliable generalizations of poetic habits of thought and expression' in that poetry. Not surprisingly, Cohen's 'definition' is not simple: it runs to ten items tabulated at the end of his essay.

The Poetry of Vision by Patricia Meyer Spacks[14] examines some of the poetry of five eighteenth - century poets of sensibility—Thomson, Collins, Gray, Smart, and Cowper—in order 'to suggest some of the values this poetry holds for the twentieth-century reader by investigating the function in it of visual imagery of various kinds'. It is not obvious that these two aims are the same, and Mrs. Spacks does not always reconcile them satisfactorily, but perhaps she was wise to limit the front of her defence since a general defence often leads to special pleading. (She is very cool about admitting specific objections to the poets she deals with.) The value of the book lies mainly in its individual close readings which are sometimes over-ingenious but can (as in the case of Smart) be very good.

Charles Peake's anthology *Poetry of the Landscape and the Night*[15] tries, in its own way, to do what Mrs. Spacks hoped to do in *The Poetry of Vision*: to concentrate on a theme which would provoke the interest of comparison and to make this non-Augustan poetry accessible to modern readers. Peake selects from all of Mrs. Spacks's poets except Smart, and gives a very just selection of other poems on his themes from Denham to Wordsworth. It is good to have *Cooper's Hill* and *Windsor-Forest* easily accessible between the same covers.

As P. W. K. Stone notes, the history of poetic theory in the late eighteenth century has been thoroughly investigated with the exception of the interesting topic of the theory of poetic composition and style, and in *The Art of Poetry 1750–1820*[16] he attempts to make good this deficiency. He shows how the 'art of poetry' in the eighteenth century is derived from rhetoric, and how its presuppositions were taken over from rhetorical theory. A larger aim of his book is to argue that the Romantics did in fact (despite the trend of recent studies) produce a radically new set of ideas about how poetry should be written: 'the theory we call "Romantic" made its first appearance in Wordsworth's Preface of 1800, and . . . by 1820 it had been elaborated into a fairly complete and consistent body of ideas which stands in sharp contrast to the critical thought of the preceding age'.

Peter Thorpe, in 'Some Fallacies in the Study of Augustan Poetry'

---

[14] *The Poetry of Vision: Five Eighteenth-Century Poets*, by Patricia Meyer Spacks. Harvard U.P. pp. x+237. $6.50. 52s.

[15] *Poetry of the Landscape and the Night: Two Eighteenth-Century Traditions*, ed. by Charles Peake. Arnold (Arnold's English Texts). pp. 191. Cloth 15s.; paper 7s. 6d.

[16] *The Art of Poetry 1750–1820: Theories of poetic composition and style in the late Neo-Classic and early Roman periods*, by P. W. K. Stone. Routledge. pp. vi+202. 40s.

(*Criticism*), suggests that we may be misreading eighteenth-century poetry because of the confusions in our own critical positions. Thorpe's main attack is on the 'Organic Fallacy' (believing that Augustan poetry is like Romantic poetry), the 'Ambivalence Fallacy' (finding fruitful ambiguities) and the 'Metaphysical Fallacy' (praising Augustan poetry for qualities it shares with the seventeenth century). Thorpe scores heavily against Wasserman's reading of Dryden, makes a few points against Mack on Pope, and misunderstands Leavis on Pope.

(b) *Individual poets*

First place on Pope must go to the superb edition of Pope's Homer[17] which completes the Twickenham edition (the volumes are dedicated, appropriately, to the memory of John Butt). Maynard Mack presents the two translations 'in their full historical dress, using as copy-text the text of the original subscriber's quartos'. Pope's original (and important) notes and his index have been retained. Understandably, the editorial apparatus has been confined to textual notes and brief verifications inserted into Pope's notes. A full commentary would have made the work impossibly expensive, but Mack and his contributors give fairly full 'samplings' of such matters as 'deviations from and parallels to the original Greek, comparisons of published texts with the British Museum manu-

script versions, etc.' in the 250-page introduction. This introduction is in six parts: 'A brief account of Pope's Homer' by the general editor, 'Pope's Homer and the Greek learning of his time' by Normal Callan, 'Pope and his English predecessors' by William Frost, general assessments of Pope's achievement in the *Iliad* and *Odyssey* by Douglas Knight and Robert Fagles respectively, and finally a probing essay, again by the general editor, on the relations of Pope's Homer to his life and work. There are no less than nine appendixes. Most deal with the MSS., but there is a vast listing of verbal parallels between Pope and (a) earlier English translators, and (b) earlier English poetry in general, together with a selection of passages from earlier translations, contributed by William Frost. On points of detail, the review by H.-J. Zimmermann (perhaps the only man competent to review these volumes) in *PQ* (1968) should be looked up. Zimmermann contributes 'Alexander Pope und die homerischen Fliegen: Ein Beitrag zur philologischen Entomologie' to *Lebende Antike*[18] which has not been available for inspection.

The first volume of Joseph Warton's essay on Pope makes the absurd charge that Pope was not a true poet because his work cannot endure transposition of the order of the words and still be recognized as poetry. Johnson ignored this charge. Possibly he thought it beneath contempt, but possibly he remembered the refutation of Warton in Percival Stockdale's defence of Pope in his *Inquiry into the Nature and Genuine Laws of Poetry* (1778), an unduly neglected work discussed by John Hardy in a note in *RES*. In 'Joseph

---

[17] *The Iliad of Homer*, by Alexander Pope. Vol. I: Books I-IX; Vol. II: Books X-XXIV. *The Odyssey of Homer*, by Alexander Pope. Vol. I: Books I-XII; Vol. II: Books XIII-XXIV. (*The Twickenham Edition of the Works of Alexander Pope*, Vols. VII-X.) Ed. by Maynard Mack, with Norman Callan, Robert Fagles, William Frost, and Douglas M. Knight. Methuen and Yale U.P. pp. cclii+477+13 plates; xiv+621+9 plates; xviii+460+11 plates; xiv+637+11 plates. £12 12s. each set.

[18] *Lebende Antike: Symposium für Rudolf Sühnel*, ed. by Horst Meller and Hans-Joachim Zimmermann. Berlin: Erich Schmidt. pp. 568.

Warton and his second volume of the *Essay on Pope*' (also in *RES*) Joan Pittock goes into the reasons for the twenty-six-year gap between the two volumes.

James E. Wellington has a careful discussion of 'Pope and Charity' in *PQ*, setting Pope's theories in rough historical perspective and tracing his ideas of charity and the right attitude to the poor. Pope may seem complacent at times, but he comes out far better than others of his time. Wellington makes the point, already noticed by Reuben Brower, that Pope's concern with charity, so intense in the 1730s, is prefigured in parts of the Homer translations.

In an interesting essay 'The Cistern and the Fountain: Art and Reality in Pope and Gray' (*Monk Studies*: see note 1) Irwin Ehrenpreis questions the notion that satire should be general, that the truth or falsity of a doctrine in poetry is irrelevant, and that art is concerned with impersonal internal patterns remote from 'life'. He looks at two works which, although 'self contained' depend 'for their cogency upon allusions to reality': Pope's *Epistle to a Lady* and Gray's *The Bard*.

Horace was Pope's model in his attitude to satire and like Horace Pope evolved a defence of satire. This defence owes much to Horace's, but also extends it. In 'Sermo or Satire: Pope's Definition of His Art' (*Monk Studies*) Lillian Feder thinks that Pope is un-Horatian 'in his determination to withhold nothing, in his pride in his independence, in his forebodings of future spiritual and intellectual darkness, and in his tragic assumption that satire is a "monument" to testify to his prophetic powers'.

In 'The Watch of Judgment: Relativism and *An Essay in Criticism*' (*Monk Studies*) Paul Ramsay offers a pointed commentary, and concludes that relativism 'doesn't really exist' in the poem. 'At its best it is better than a system: brilliant, profound and delightfully tuned. At its worst it is trivial, frivolous, timidly dull, and disorderly.'

Addison C. Bross looks at 'Alexander Pope's Revisions of John Donne's *Satyres*' in *XUS* (1966). He finds that 'many of Pope's changes effect an intensification of bitterness in Donne's *Satyres* and that this heightened bitterness derives in large part from the calm care with which Pope notes the just mathematical precision of injustice'. In 'That Impudent Satire: Pope's Sober Advice' (*MacMillan Essays*: see note 4) John M. Aden argues for a revaluation of the poem as 'a serio-comic poem, relevant to both the moral and satirical vision of its creator, and no mean specimen of his genius'.

Rebecca Price Parkin lists and discusses 'Alexander Pope's Use of Biblical and Ecclesiastical Allusions' in *Studies on Voltaire and the Eighteenth Century*. Kathleen Mahaffey's 'Timon's Villa: Walpole's Houghton' (*TSLL*) presents a detailed and convincing argument for the identification: it was Walpole's supporters who spread it about that Pope had Cannons in mind, the 'soft Dean' is Walpole's friend Henry Bland, Dean of Durham, etc. A. J. Sambrook has a note on 'Pope's Neighbours: An Early Landscape Garden at Richmond' which describes the garden of Petersham Lodge, home of Henry Hyde, Earl of Rochester (*JWCI*).

Other Pope items consist of two on points of scholarship, and seven on points of annotation. 'Alexander Pope's and Sir William Trumbull's Translations of Boethius' by Brian S. Donaghey (*Leeds Studies in English*) reproduces manuscripts from the Brotherton Library. Robert M. Ryley in *PQ* defends the authenticity of the sixteen lines said to have been suppressed at the end of Pope's 'Epistle to Miss Blount, on her leaving the Town, after the Coronation' against the Twickenham editors and Ralph M. Maud in *RES* 1958.

Annotations: 'Pope's "Magus" in Fielding's *Veroniad*: The satire of Walpole' (*PQ*), by Martin C. Battestin, notes that James Sutherland's conjecture that 'Magus' in *Dunciad* IV. 516 may refer to Walpole is confirmed by Fielding's *Veroniad* (1741) which provides an additional source for the figure in Pope. In 'Three Notes on Pope' (*NQ*) James A. Means suggests an echo of Waller in *The Dunciad*, of Denham in *Spring*, and of Dryden in *An Essay on Criticism*. 'Marvell and "The Rape of the Lock"' (*NQ*), by P. J. C. Field, is concerned with parallels between *A Poem on the Death of O. C.* 281–6 and *Rape* III 161–70. 'Pope's *Rape of the Lock*' (*ANQ*), by M. R. Schonhorn, glosses III 21–2. Schonhorn's 'Pope's "Epistle to Augustus" and Ambrose Philips' (*NQ*) glosses line 417. In 'The Lucky Hit in Commerce and Creation: Attenbury and Pope's Sir Balaam' (*NQ*) Howard Erskine-Hill shows that the term 'lucky hit' is not only businessman's language but conveys wider theological significances. Lastly, A. J. Sambrook notes 'A Possible Source for "Master of the Sev'nfold face" in "The Dunciad (B)"' (*NQ*): in *The Scribleriad*.

The Augustan Reprint Society have already reprinted three of the anonymous Grub Street attacks on Pope in 1742: *Sawney and Colley* and *Blast upon Blast* (1960), and *The Blatant Beast* (1965). Now they reprint a Grub Street *defence* (it attacks Cibber, Hervey's ally): the anonymous *Scribleriad*, together with an attack from the court, Lord Hervey's inept verses *The Difference between Verbal and*

Practical Virtue, both first published in 1742.[19]

Samuel Boyse wrote six volumes of verse, and knew Dr. Johnson before he died and sank into a richly deserved oblivion. In 'Portrait of a Grub: Samuel Boyse' (*SEL*) Edward Hart dredges up an account of his life from Shiels, Boswell, and Nichols, without explaining why he thinks the enterprise of any value.

Two items on Thomson can be briefly noted. In a long review article 'The Seasons of Discrimination' (*MP*) Robert Marsh discusses some of the problems raised by Ralph Cohen's *The Art of Discrimination: Thomson's 'The Seasons' and the Language of Criticism*, and Cohen himself has a difficult essay on 'Thomson's Poetry of Space and Time' (*Monk Studies*).

P. L. Carver's biographical articles in *NQ* (1939) have put all students of Collins in his debt. His new book adds to these from wills and other legal documents, but even so his life of Collins[20] is of a modest size. However it recounts all the known facts about Collins, corrects many earlier errors of emphasis, suggests some interesting speculations, and offers some comment on the poems. There is undoubtedly more to be said about Collins, as Earl R. Wasserman demonstrates by bringing the Bible, Renaissance Biblical commentaries, Neoplatonism, and Milton to bear on a reading of 'Collins' "Ode on the Poetical Character"' (*ELH*). Mary Margaret Steward makes an undoubted contribution to scholarship

---

[19] *The Scribleriad (Anonymous) (1742); The Difference Between Verbal and Practical Virtue (1742)*, by Lord Hervey. Introduced by A. J. Sambrook. William Andrews Clark Memorial Library (*A.R.S.* No. 125). pp. xiv+44.

[20] *The Life of a Poet: A Biographical Sketch of William Collins*, by P. L. Carver. With a Foreword by Edmund Blunden. Sidgwick & Jackson. pp. xiv+210. 30*s*.

by showing that Collins's sole surviving letter in MS. should be dated 17 Nov. and not 10 Nov. (*NQ*).

Arthur Johnston's anthology of *Selected Poems of Thomas Gray and William Collins*[21] gives Gray almost complete and everything of substance in Collins except the early *Persian Eclogues*. The annotation is very full: 'that on Collins', James Sutherland writes in his Preface, 'may be said to be more extensive than any hitherto available'. Clearly, Professor Sutherland had forgotten about Professor Wasserman.

There are signs of renewed interest in Smart. Arthur Sherbo's biography[22] gives the fullest and most accurate life of Smart we have yet had. Sherbo's indefatigable industry has turned up a great number of new facts (especially about the details of Smart's confinement) but unfortunately the accumulation of facts— in themselves illuminating—has tended to obscure the course of Sherbo's narrative since Sherbo's gifts of organization and expression do not equal his ability as a researcher. So Father Devlin's inaccurate but deeply intuitive study still remains the best guide to Smart's character. Sherbo's book gives a great deal of comment and annotation to Smart's poetry, but offers little insight into its nature.

In 'Two Pieces Newly Ascribed to Christopher Smart' (*MLR*) Sherbo reprints from *The Christian's Magazine* (1762) a letter possibly from a clergyman to Smart, and from the *Literary Magazine* (1758) a new Smart poem 'To Miss Harriot's

Squirrel', and in *JEGP* Sherbo compares 'Christopher Smart's Three Translations of Horace': two in prose and one in verse. The revisions show Smart was hardworking, and the prose translations illuminate the verse. The dual purpose of all Smart's verse was to confess God's presence and report his praise. In '*Jubilate Agno* and the "Theme of Gratitude"' (*PLL*) Francis D. Adams argues that the antiphonal structure of the poem enacts Smart's stated purpose. John Block Friedman writes of 'The Cosmology of Praise: Smart's *Jubilate Agno*' in *PMLA*, and E. E. Duncan-Jones's 'Smart and Marvell' (*NQ*) notes an allusion in *Jubilate Agno*.

Morris Golden's 'Sterility and Eminence in the Poetry of Charles Churchill' (*JEGP*) asks why Churchill is 'so distinctly a minor poet'. Yvor Winters's fine essay on 'The Poetry of Charles Churchill', first published in *Poetry* 1961 (see *YW* xlii 217) is reprinted in his last book, *Forms of Discovery*.[23]

H. K. Gregory's 'Cowper's Love of Subhuman Nature: A Psychoanalytic Approach' (*PQ*) shows that Cowper cared for animals and plants because he could love them uncomplicated by and play God to them.

One item this year bears on Macpherson: Henry Okun contributes an illustrated study of 'Ossian in Painting' (in Britain; Denmark and Germany; and France, Italy and Russia) to *JWCI*.

In 'Chatterton: The Problem of Rowley Chronology and Its Implications' (*PQ*) Donald S. Taylor postulates that the Rowleyan writings were composed 'between the summer of 1768 and the late spring of 1769', sets out 'a rhythmic sequence of five

[21] *Selected Poems of Thomas Gray and William Collins*, ed. by Arthur Johnston. Arnold (Arnold's English Texts). pp. 222. Cloth 15s. Paperback 7s. 6d.

[22] *Christopher Smart: Scholar of the University*, by Arthur Sherbo. Michigan State U.P. pp. viii + 303. $8.50.

[23] *Forms of Discovery: Critical & Historical Essays on the Forms of the Short Poem in English*, by Yvor Winters. Alan Swallow. pp. xxii + 377. 83s. 6d.

phases' that seem to emerge, and considers the implications of this chronology.

A large new selection from Crabbe's poetry is very welcome. *Tales, 1812, and other Selected Poems*[24] contains *The Village*, parts 1 and 3 of *The Parish Register*, nine letters from *The Borough*, the *Tales* of 1812 complete, *Infancy—A Fragment*, *The World of Dreams*, four of the *Tales of the Hall*, and *In a Neat Cottage*, 'in all, a good third of Crabbe's prolific work' aimed at showing the full range of his powers. Howard Mills prefaces the volume with a fighting introduction which uncovers the complexity of Crabbe's character and pleads for a greater sensitivity in reading his work. In 'Crabbe's Borough: The Process of Montage' (*UTQ*) W. K. Thomas annotates references to bells, effigies, and inns.

Ian C. Walker writes about the 'Scottish Verse in *The Weekly Magazine*' (1768–84) in *SSL*.

G. E. Bentley's superb edition of *Tiriel*[25] brings the text and Blake's designs together for the first time (the manuscript was separated from the drawings early in the nineteenth century) and provides a full and illuminating commentary.

The new Cornell concordance to Blake[26] includes poetry and prose, and is based on the Keynes Nonesuch edition (1957; reprinted by O.U.P.

in 1966, see *YW* xlvii 232). A few words, duly listed, are omitted from the concordance, otherwise everything of Blake is here. Most important, the grammatical context of the listed words is given. Apparently it is difficult to persuade a computer to do this. What computers cannot do is to distinguish between homonyms, and here the editors have not helped it much.

'Pictorial and Poetic Design in Two Songs by Blake' by Thomas E. Connolly and George R. Levine (*PMLA*) examines 'Little Boy Lost' and 'Little Boy Found' together with their engravings. In 'Blake's "Tyger": The Nature of the Beast' (*PQ*) Rodney M. Baine suggests that the tyger symbolizes 'the creation of brutal cruelty in nature and in man'. Also in *PQ* Francis Doherty produces an early foreshadowing of Blake's questioning in 'Tyger' in a poem by Henry Needler, while 'Blake's "Tyger" and Vaughan's "Cock-Crowing"' (*NQ*) by William Harrold investigates another early parallel for Blake's poem. Frederick W. Hilles prints 'A "New" Blake Letter' (*YR*): 16 July 1804 to William Hayley.

3. PROSE

(a) *Swift*

The products of the Swift tercentenary are noted in the following order: biography; editions; volumes of essays devoted to Swift; other books; and articles.

The first volume of Irvin Ehrenpreis's major life of Swift appeared in 1962 (*YW* xliii. 201). The second volume *Dr. Swift*[27] covers the years 1699–1714 'the most interesting chap-

[24] *Tales, 1812, and other Selected Poems*, by George Crabbe. Ed. with an introduction by Howard Mills. C.U.P. pp. xxxviii+446. Cloth 50s. $9.50. Paperback 16s. $2.75.

[25] *William Blake: Tiriel: Facsimile and Transcript of the manuscript, reproduction of the drawings, and a commentary on the poem*, by G. E. Bentley. Oxford: Clarendon Press. pp. xii+94. £3.

[26] *A Concordance to the Writings of William Blake*, ed. by David V. Erdman, with the assistance of John E. Thiesmeyer and Richard J. Wolfe. Cornell U.P. 2 vols: pp. xxxviii+1146; x+1171. £11 17s. 6d.

[27] *Swift: The Man, His Works, and the Age*. Vol 2: *Dr. Swift*, by Irvin Ehrenpreis. Methuen and Harvard U.P. pp. xviii+781. £5 5s.

ters of his life' and the most fully documented. This volume is to be the largest of Ehrenpreis's projected three. The matter here is largely political, expounded in very great detail. Ehrenpreis gives some disturbing evidence of Swift's timeserving, analyses very well his deception by Harley and St. John, and writes sensibly on his political tracts. Indeed the writing throughout this second volume is better than it was in the first, but Ehrenpreis is still plagued by the urge to offer psychological insights which are unconvincing.

The Clarendon Press continue their fully-annotated series of Swift's works with an elaborate edition of his first published book *A Discourse of the Contests and Dissentions Between the Nobles and the Commons in Athens and Rome*[28] by Frank Ellis which sets the pamphlet firmly in its topical historical setting. Ellis chooses as his copy-text the first edition (1701) whereas Herbert Davis chose the 1735 Faulkner text for his edition in the *Prose Writings*. Ellis's edition is reviewed in great detail in *MP* (1968) by Edward Rosenheim.

The final offering of Herbert Davis in the service of Swift for whom he laboured so long is a handsome volume of the poetry in the Oxford Standard Authors series.[29] The text is usually that of the latest authoritative edition (Harold Williams had preferred early printings in his edition) and the poems are arranged in

rough chronological order. A small selection of Swift's poems has been edited by James Reeves.[30]

Penguin Books offer a handy and cheap little edition of *Gulliver's Travels*[31] with a careful modernized text by Peter Dixon, notes by John Chalker, and an introduction by Michael Foot.

Six collections of essays are noticed here. A seventh, Brian Vickers's interesting *The World of Jonathan Swift* was not published until 1968 and will be reviewed next year. A. Norman Jeffares's collection *Fair Liberty was all his Cry*[32] contains fifteen previously published essays (by David Nichol Smith, T. G. Wilson on medical aspects of Swift, Herbert Davis, A. L. Rowse, Virginia Woolf, F. R. Leavis, Kathleen Williams on imagery, J. C. Beckett on Swift and the church, George Orwell, Yeats, Irvin Ehrenpreis, Marjorie Nicolson and Nora M. Mohler, Vivian Mercier, George P. Mayhew, and Mackie L Jarrell), an appraisal of recent Swift scholarship by Ricardo Quintana, a checklist of recent writings on Swift by Claire Lamont, and two new essays. The first of these is a graceful but slight piece by Bonamy Dobrée questioning the image of 'the gloomy dean', and the second a 'Key to the language of the Houyhnhnms in *Gulliver's Travels*' by Marjorie W. Buckley, which seems to this reviewer quite fanciful. By this key we can elucidate the Houyhnhnm word

[30] *Selected Poems of Jonathan Swift*, ed. with an Introduction and commentary by James Reeves. Heinemann (The Poetry Bookshelf). pp. vi+146. 15s.

[31] *Gulliver's Travels*, by Jonathan Swift. Ed. by Peter Dixon and John Chalker with an Introduction by Michael Foot. Penguin Books (The Penguin English Library). pp. 360. 5s.

[32] *Fair Liberty Was All His Cry: A Tercentenary Tribute to Jonathan Swift 1667–1745*, ed. by A. Norman Jeffares. Macmillan. xxii+410. £3 3s.

[28] *A Discourse of the Contests and Dissentions Between the Nobles and the Commons in Athens and Rome With the Consequences They Had upon Both Those States*, by Jonathan Swift. Ed. with an Introduction and Notes Textual, Critical, and Historical by Frank H. Ellis. Oxford: Clarendon Press. pp. xiv+270. 50s. $8.

[29] *Poetical Works*, by Jonathan Swift. Ed. by Herbert Davis. O.U.P. pp. xxx+682. 35s.

R

'Ynlhmnawihlma' ('a continuance of foul or unseasonable weather') as 'You-know-well-home-in-a-while-may'. This volume is welcome for bringing between one cover half a dozen important essays. Few of the essays are, like A. L. Rowse's 'Swift as Poet', totally useless. It is noticeable that here (as elsewhere) scholarly activity is far more lively and more in evidence than a sense of critical engagement with Swift.

Jonathan Swift 1667–1967[33] records the Swift Tercentenary Symposium held in Dublin in April 1967. The essays here are sometimes graceful, sometimes learned, but resolutely minor. The distinguished contributors have probably said all they have to say about Swift elsewhere. Herbert Davis on Swift's character, Irvin Ehrenpreis on Swift and Ireland, Louis A. Landa on Swift as a churchman, James Sutherland on satire in the 'Character of Wharton', and the 'Bickerstaff Papers', Ricardo Quintana on satire in *Gulliver's Travels*, Austin Clark on the poems, Vivian Mercier on Swift's humour, J. N. P. Moore on Swift's philanthropy, J. G. Simms on Ireland in the age of Swift, R. B. McDowell on Swift as a political thinker, and George P. Mayhew on recent Swift scholarship.

Another set of *Tercentenary Essays* comes from the University of Tulsa.[34] David P. French identifies 'C.M.P.G.N.S.T.N.S.' who wrote on Swift in *Gentleman's Magazine* (1757) as the Reverend John Geree, Philip Mahone Griffith writes on 'Dr. Johnson's "Diction of Common Life" and Swift's *Directions to Servants*' (an appendix lists all the entries in the *Dictionary* from *Directions*), Paul J. Ketrick discusses Swift's mental state, Thomas F. Staley writes on Joyce's debt to Swift, Winston Weathers on irony in *A Tale of a Tub*, and Lester F. Zimmerman on Gulliver.

The Spring issue of *Hermathena: A Dublin University Review* is a special Swift number. In a long essay J. K. Walton finds 'The Unity of the *Travels*' in a balance of contrast, shifting perspective, and reversal, as well as in the theme of abuse of power. Christopher Thacker has a piece on Swift's influence on Voltaire and on the personal links between the two writers, and L. H. C. Thomas writes on 'Swift in German Literature' dealing mainly with Herder, Goethe, and Heine. J. V. Luce adds 'A Note on the Composition of Swift's Epitaph'. A special number of the *University Review* (Dublin) devoted to Swift has not been available. The November issue of *Europe* contains fourteen essays on Swift in French.

Louis Tonko Milic's book on *The Style of Jonathan Swift*[35] begins with an angry backward glance at earlier critics of style in general and Swift's in particular who have not agreed with Milic's conception of what style is. Then he examines lists, connecting words, and the balance of the various parts of speech in Swift, and argues, on the basis of his findings (which are drawn up in numerical lists, and pretty, but to this reviewer, incomprehensible, graphs) that *A Letter to a Young Poet* is an authentic work

[33] *Jonathan Swift 1667–1967: A Dublin Tercentenary Tribute*, ed. by Roger McHugh and Philip Edwards. Dublin: Dolmen Press and O.U.P. pp. xx+231+8 pp. of plates. 63s.

[34] *Jonathan Swift: Tercentenary Essays*, by David P. French, Philip Mahone Griffith, Paul J. Ketrick, Thomas F. Staley, Winston Weathers, Lester F. Zimmerman. U. of Tulsa (U. of Tulsa Department of English: Monograph Series no. 3.) pp. vi+73. $2.25.

[35] *A Quantitative Approach to the Style of Jonathan Swift*, by Louis Tonko Milic. The Hague: Mouton (Studies in English Literature XXIII). pp. 317.

of Swift's. Milic's samples are taken from all of Swift's works except the *Proposal* (1712), the *History*, the *Journal to Stella*, the letters and the dialogues in *Polite Conversation*. Milic covers a good deal of ground on the question of assessing style in general and this makes for a certain diffuseness in the early part of his book.

Swift's Tory journalism forms more than a quarter of his work in prose. In *Jonathan Swift as a Tory Pamphleteer*[36] Richard I. Cook studies the polemical tracts (1710–14) that Swift wrote for the Tory campaign leading to the Peace of Utrecht 'for their intrinsic merit as examples of persuasive discourse, for the light they shed on Swift's use of rhetorical techniques during an important period of his development, and for the significant relationships they have with his more famous works.

The third section of Ronald Paulson's *The Fictions of Satire*[37] (a companion volume to his *Satire and the Novel in Eighteenth-Century England*, noticed below in section 5) is devoted to Swift. The whole book is an attempt to isolate some common patterns and figures of satire. Paulson begins with Horace, Juvenal, Lucian, Petronius, Rabelais, and Cervantes, and when he gets to Swift his concern is rather to fit him into his constructions than to say anything very new.

The collection of Swift MSS. (one of the largest in the world) at the Huntington Library contains *inter alia* notes for part of the *History of the Four Last Years*, a fair copy of Swift's *Letter to a young lady on her marriage* (the young lady is Deborah Rochford), transcriptions of *An Epistle to a Lady* and *On Poetry: A Rapsody*, Swift's manuscript version of '*On his own Deafness*', and a fragment of *Polite Conversation*. In *Rage or Raillery*[38] George P. Mayhew gives a full description and discussion of these and other MSS., and a 'Brief Description' of the complete collection.

A comprehensive annotated bibliography of Swift studies published between 1945 and 1965 has been compiled by James J. Stathis.[39] It covers Bibliography, Canon and Edition, Biography, General Criticism, Poetry, Prose, and *Gulliver's Travels*. Unpublished theses are also included, but Stathis does not claim completeness here. A list of 45 additional items is given in Peter J. Schakel's review in *PQ* (1968).

A brilliant article by Robert Martin Adams throws the question of the authorship of *A Tale of a Tub* wide open. In 'Jonathan Swift, Thomas Swift, and the Authorship of *A Tale of a Tub*' (*MP*) he shows conclusively that rejections by earlier editors of Thomas Swift's claim to authorship have been made far too easily, and that Jonathan Swift's claim in the 1710 'Postscript' is not as conclusive as has been thought. Adams draws on annotated copies of the first and third edition (at Cornell and Columbia)—the first in Thomas Swift's hand—which provided the material for Curll's *Key* (1710), and argues that they make a very good case for the assumption that Thomas Swift was the author of the entire narrative allegory—i.e. most of Section II and all of Sections IV, VI and XI of the

---

[36] *Jonathan Swift as a Tory Pamphleteer*, by Richard I. Cook. Washington U.P. pp. xxxiv+157. $6.95.

[37] *The Fictions of Satire*, by Ronald Paulson. The Johns Hopkins Press. pp. x+228. $7. 56s.

[38] *Rage or Raillery: The Swift Manuscripts at the Huntington Library,* by George P. Mayhew, with a foreword by Herbert Davis. Huntington Library. pp. xviii+190. $6.50.

[39] *A Bibliography of Swift Studies 1945–1965*, by James J. Stathis. Vanderbilt U.P. pp. xii+100. $5.

Tale, as well as 'The Mechanical Operation of the Spirit'. This assumption is enforced by consideration of internal evidence in these sections. All future work on *A Tale of a Tub* will have to take this argument into account. In 'Source for *A Tale of a Tub*' (*ANQ*) Karl S. Nagel suggests 'Three men in a tub/The butcher, the baker, the candlestick maker': respectively, Jack, Martin, and Peter.

William Frost's 'The Irony of Swift and Gibbon: A Reply to F. R. Leavis' (*EC*) attempts to show that Leavis's treatment of Swift is 'demonstrably wrong, wrong on its own premises'. Frost agrees that it is the function of Gibbon's irony 'to habituate and reassure', of Swift's 'to defeat habit, to intimidate and demoralize', and asks which represents the greater achievement. 'Swift's Use of Literalization as a Rhetorical Device' (*PMLA*) by Maurice J. Quinlan is concerned with Swift's distinctive combination of pun and metaphor, as 'I could name a Country, which would be glad to eat up our whole Nation' in *A Modest Proposal*.

'On Swift's "Scatological" Poems' by Donald Greene (*Sew*) takes issue with Norman Brown's celebrated chapter in *Life against Death* (1959). Greene reads 'Cassinus and Peter' as 'a devastating satirical *attack* on those who . . . place a high estimation on . . . "the anal function"', and suggests that throughout these poems Swift is mocking 'the excremental vision'.

John B. Shipley shows that 'The Whale', a doubtful poem of Swift's, may be (following Hervey's attribution) by Lord Chesterfield, in 'A Note on the Authorship of *The Whale*' (*RES*). In 'Swift's *Project*: A Religious and Political Satire' (*PMLA*) Leland D. Peterson sets out 'the hitherto unsuspected complexities and ironies, not to mention

comedy' which the *Project for the Advancement of Religion* yields when we inquire into the issues that gave it birth. In 'Jonathan Swift's "Preferments of Ireland" 1713–1714' (*HLQ*) George P. Mayhew reproduces and discusses a new manuscript recently acquired by the Huntington Library, a list of preferments and promotions in the Church of Ireland that Swift had submitted to Harley and the Archbishop of Armagh.

David Hamilton's essay 'Swift, Wagstaff, and the composition of *Polite Conversation*' (*HLQ*) investigates the 'largely ignored' subject of the irony of the Introduction to *Polite Conversation*. 'Jonathan Swift's Proposal Concerning the English Language: A Reconsideration' by Henry W. Sams (*Macmillan Essays*) concerns the political background of Swift's tract.

Two Swift items come in *Lib*: Margaret Weedon records variants from 'An Uncancelled Copy of the First Collected Edition of Swift's Poems', and Paul V. Thompson prints 'An Unpublished Letter from Swift' (to Dr. Delany, 11 July 1726) from a transcript by John Forster. Finally, Richard H. Passon writes about 'Legal Satire in *Gulliver* from *John Bull*' (*ANQ*); Swift's IV v echoes Arbuthnot's *The History of John Bull* chapter VI, and Maurice J. Quinlan has a note on the significances of the names of 'Lemuel Gulliver's Ships' (*PQ*).

(b) *Other prose writers*

Peter Gay's article on Addison 'The Spectator as Actor: Addison in Perspective' (*Encounter*) concedes the justice of the reproachful label 'Victorian', but suggests that there is more to Addison than cosy Sir Roger: his forward looking literary criticism for instance. Above all, his writings had a serious moral purpose and a decisive effect on manners in the larger sense. In an early paper Addison thought that poetry required ornament, but later he came round to the view that simplicity was a characteristic of the sublime, and still later he thought simplicity the mark of excellence in poetry. David A. Hanson's long essay 'Addison on Ornament and Poetic Style' (*Monk Studies*) traces these changes in Addison's thought through his comments on the *Georgics*, Ovid's *Metamorphoses*, and his *Spectator* papers on true wit and on 'Chevy Chase'.

'Addison's "Cartesian" Passage and Nicolas Malebranche' (*PQ*) by Hilbert H. Campbell is about the possible influence of *De la recherche de la vérité* on *Spectator* 417. Addison's books were sold in 1799 and some scholars have doubted the value of the sale catalogue. In *ELN* Hilbert H. Campbell gives reasons for thinking that the library remained relatively intact after Addison's death, and that therefore the catalogue is a reliable index to the range of his books.

'Meaning and Format: Mr. Spectator and his Folio Half-Sheets' (*ELH*) by William Kinsley is an investigation of 'the nature of [*The Spectator's*] medium, the printed folio half-sheet, and the character of Mr. Spectator, especially as it is influenced by that medium'. The single sheet on which the essay was printed is associated with the intimate newsletter or even the private letter, and this perhaps made possible the extraordinarily close relationship between *The Spectator* and its readers.

Rae Blanchard's edition of *Tracts and Pamphlets* by Richard Steele, first published in 1944, has been reprinted.[40]

[40] *Tracts and Pamphlets by Richard Steele*, ed. with notes and commentary by Rae Blanchard. Frank Cass. pp. xviii+664. £8 8s.

The publication of a reprint of the Bohn edition of *The Works of Lord Bolingbroke* occasioned a full-page article in *TLS* entitled 'Not Everyone Loved this Lord', concerned more with Bolingbroke's reputation than his writings.

David Hume promised to write a book on criticism if his *Treatise on Human Nature* was a success. The *Treatise* 'fell *dead-born from the press*', and the book on criticism was never written. Ernest Campbell Mossner's essay 'Hume "Of Criticism"' (*Monk Studies*) attempts to reconstruct what Hume's book would have been like. Since Hume assumed that philosophy and criticism were inseparable, and philosophy could not be learned *a priori* but from experience the book would have provided a purely empirical method of critical judgement based on repeated observations. Drawing carefully on all Hume's extant critical work Mossner is able to show the general outlines of the book Hume never wrote. There is no reason to think that Hume was a distinguished practical critic ('but he is certainly not so poor a critic as has often been alleged') but his book would have developed and synthesized the pregnant hints and fruitful ideas on aesthetics scattered throughout his published works.

An interesting essay on 'The Curiosity of William Oldys: An Approach to the Development of English Literary History' (*PQ*) by Lawrence Lipkin investigated three problems: why we note the fact that Oldys did *not* write the first history of English literature, what he thought literary history should be, and how far Warton and Johnson diverged from Oldys's ideal. Oldys was well qualified to execute the factual and scholarly side of a literary history, and his minute and varied researches leave an intriguing trail through the humane scholarship of the eighteenth century. But Warton was partially to achieve, thanks to the antiquarian researches of Oldys and others, what Oldys himself could not do, for he lacked the gift of organization and shaping of Warton or (still more) Johnson. The virtues of his most distinguished work, the life of Raleigh, 'are apparent most of all in its footnotes'.

It is good to welcome a reprint of G. B. Hill's *Johnsonian Miscellanies*,[41] first published in 1897, both because they provide glimpses of Johnson more true perhaps than Boswell's (we do not feel that Johnson is being manipulated into quotable situations here) and because they report some of Johnson's valuable comments on literature not easily available elsewhere. In a letter to *TLS* J. D. Fleeman commented on the review of these volumes, arguing that Hill's textual editing was deficient, and giving a list of work (some unpublished) done on Johnson biography. (This letter started a controversy which almost immediately drifted away from Johnson and Hill to a consideration of the ethics of the flourishing reprint business.)

J. D. Fleeman's industry continues to put Johnson scholars in his debt. His *Preliminary Handlist of Documents & Manuscripts of Samuel Johnson*[42] is an attempt to list everything in Johnson's handwriting except letters, inscriptions, and marginalia in printed books There are 265 items, and a full index. The author hopes that publication of this handlist will encourage readers to make corrections whenever possible.

Passionate Intelligence: Imagination and Reason in the Work of Samuel Johnson[43] by Arieh Sachs pushes the 'polarity' implied in the title very hard. Sachs presents a heavily medievalized Johnson, the writer of the 'deeply Christian' book *Rasselas*. 'None of his work can be understood apart from his faith.' This thesis leads him into forced readings: 'Rasselas, secretly dreaming of his perfected commonwealth, epitomizes human pride ...' We may agree with Sachs in rejecting the idea that Johnson can be adequately seen as representative of the English 'Common Sense School' without going quite to the opposite extreme. Still Sachs says some interesting things by the way, calling attention to tensions, contradictions, and doubts rather in the tradition of Walter Jackson Bate and W. B. C. Watkins. His themes are 'The Vacuity of Life', 'Cosmic Hierarchy', 'The Art of Forgetfulness', 'Idle Solitude and Diabolical Imagination', 'The General and Particular', 'The Folly of Utopia', and 'The Rationality of Faith'.

Johnson's moral thought is more dutifully examined in Paul Kent Alkon's *Samuel Johnson and Moral Discipline*,[44] a painstaking exposition of the moral ideas of *Rasselas*, the sermons, and the periodical essays, under the headings 'Appetites and Passions', 'Higher Faculties', 'Locke and Johnson', 'Freedom and Voluntary Delusion', 'Moral Discipline', and 'Pulpit, Press, and the Advancement of Learning'.

[41] *Johnsonian Miscellanies*, arranged and edited by George Birkbeck Hill. [With a Foreword by Walter Jackson Bate.] New York: Barnes & Noble, 1966; Constable, [1967]. pp. xx+488; viii+517. £7 7 .

[42] *A Preliminary Handlist of Documents & Manuscripts of Samuel Johnson*, by J. D. Fleeman. Oxford Bibliographical Society: Occasional Publications. no. 2. pp. iv+51. 15s.

[43] *Passionate Intelligence: Imagination and Reason in the Work of Samuel Johnson*, by Arieh Sachs. Johns Hopkins Press and O.U.P. pp. xvi+124. $4.95. 40s.

[44] *Samuel Johnson and Moral Discipline*, by Paul Kent Alkon. Northwestern U.P. pp. xii+219. $6.95.

'Why is Dr. Johnson a great moralist? Where does his strength as a moralist come from?' John Wiltshire asks in his essay 'Dr. Johnson's Seriousness' (*Critical Review*, Melbourne). Wiltshire rejects the standard answer that Johnson is a great Augustan and that his strength lies in 'his authoritative restatement of those truths which men more often need to be reminded of than informed'—this answer covers only a part of Johnson's work. But for Wiltshire *Rasselas* is not 'assured', and its concern is to ponder 'doubts and questions'. This was Johnson's centre, to feel problems intensely and to ask fundamental questions.

Robert Voitle has a very just essay on Johnson and stoicism in *MacMillan Essays* (see note 4) in which he cautions us not to forget that Johnson was both a Christian *and* a Classical humanist. When we do, 'Johnson the neo-Calvinist, or even Johnson the mystic will be lurking right round the corner'.

Despite the high claims for Shakespeare in his *Preface*, Johnson complained that Shakespeare 'seems to write without any moral purpose'. In 'The "Poet of Nature" and Self-Knowledge: One Aspect of Johnson's Moral Reading of Shakespeare' (*UTQ*) John Hardy explores the 'deeper, though less obvious, sense in which Johnson considered Shakespeare a morally instructive poet' adducing Johnson's comments on 'the motives of action' of Shakespeare's characters. Wolfgang Bernard Fleischmann writes briefly about 'Shakespeare, Johnson, and the Dramatic "Unities of Time and Place"' (*MacMillan Essays*).

In 'Johnson as Satirist: A New Look at *The Vanity of Human Wishes*' (*ELH*) Patrick O'Flaherty pothers a great deal over recent criticism of Johnson's poem, defines satire in an absurdly narrow way (which would exclude most of Pope's work from the genre) and decides that satire 'was not Johnson's *natural* mode of expression' and that since Johnson adopts 'the pose of a cynical, bitter satirist' the poem 'must be judged finally a failure'. Howard D. Weinbrot has a note on 'Dr. Johnson's Poems: A New Version of "Medea", lines 193–203, and a New Translation of the Epitaph on Goldsmith' in *NQ*.

Emrys Jones thinks we undervalue *Rasselas* if we find it merely gloomy or neglect its artistry. 'The parts merge together, they work accumulatively, to form a whole larger and more interesting than the parts themselves.' 'The Artistic Form of *Rasselas*' (*RES*) argues that both Johnson's and Sterne's novels 'testify to a similar impatience with closed systems, whether in philosophy or literature', and both 'question the validity of the concept of form in terms of beginning, middle, and end'. Jones sees three 'movements' of sixteen chapters each, with the outer movements in opposition to each other. The final chapter is a witty 'trailing coda': the system is both closed and open; 'the demands of literary form and the demands to life are both met'.

Geoffrey Tillotson has an essay on 'Imlac and the Business of a Poet' (*Monk Studies*), and James B. Misenheimer sets out 'Dr. Johnson's Concept of Literary Fiction' in *MLR*.

Charles Peake's selection from Johnson[45] includes *Rasselas*, four *Rambler*, three *Adventurer*, and five *Idler* essays, and selections from *Review of a Free Inquiry*. There is a long introduction, helpful notes, and

---

[45] '*Rasselas' and Essays*, by Samuel Johnson. Ed. by Charles Peake. Routledge (Routledge's English Texts). pp. xlii+212. Cloth 18s. Paperback 11s. 6d.

a list of familiar words which often cause students difficulty.

'Johnson's *Journey to the Western Islands of Scotland*: A Reconsideration' (*Studies on Voltaire and the Eighteenth Century*) by Clarence Tracy proposes that the *Journey* was original 'because it is a clear-sighted, unsentimental, and first-hand report on . . . a primitive society, devoted to telling the truth, and free from any obsession with myth-making' and 'because it showed the upsetting of his conviction that human experience is everywhere the same and that one's surroundings have no effect on one's personality'. In '"Savage Virtues and Barbarous Grandeur": Johnson and Martin in the Highlands' (*Cornell Library Journal* 1966) Thomas J. Jemielity speculates on the influence on Johnson's *Journey* of Martin Martin's *Description of the Western Isles of Scotland* (1703), a 'curious yet tedious' book, which Johnson had read as a boy. It first incited his desire to go to the Highlands, accompanied him on his travels, and suggested certain topics of inquiry to him. Richard J. Dircks writes on 'Johnson's Knowledge of Ireland' in *NQ*.

Like Keats, Johnson believed that 'English should be kept up' and he also thought that translations from French were great corruptors of the language. In 'No "Dialect of France": Samuel Johnson's Translations from the French' (*UTQ*) John Lawrence Abbott shows that Johnson's translations from French can claim to be independent works in his own language. Abbott looks at the translations of Le Grand's 'Sarpi', Crousaz's 'Commentary' on Pope, 'A Dissertation on the Amozons', 'Dr. Morin', and some medical biographies written for Robert James's *Medicinal Dictionary*, and concludes that they are 'not so much French works rendered into English by Johnson but Johnsonian compositions which happen to derive from French works'.

F. V. Bernard investigates the attribution of various Parliamentary Debates in the *Gentleman's Magazine* between 1738 and 1744 and concludes that Johnson's contributions are confined to 1741–44 ('Johnson and the Authorship of Four Debates', *PMLA*). In 'Common and Superior Sense: A New Attribution to Johnson' (*NQ*) F. V. Bernard finds 'some highly interesting marks of Johnson's hand' in a paper signed 'S.U.' published in *Gentleman's Magazine* (December 1738) entitled 'Observations on the Foregoing'. In the same issue of *NQ* Donald J. Greene reminds us of some forgotten 'Johnsonian Attributions by Alexander Chalmers'.

'The Making of Johnson's *Life of Savage*, 1744' (*Lib*) by J. D. Fleeman is a bibliographical study. Finally, there is 'The "A" Papers in the *Adventurer*: Bonnell Thornton, not Dr. Bathurst, Their Author' (*SP*) by Victor J. Lams. Mahmoud Manzalaoui prints various versions of 'Soame Jenyns' "Epitaph on Dr. Samuel Johnson"' in *NQ*. Mary Margaret Steward examines in some detail Boswell's relationship with the kirk in 'James Boswell and the National Church of Scotland' (*HLQ*), and Eileen C. Davies reprints 'An Epigram on Boswell' from *Jackson's Oxford Journal* 1787 in *NQ*.

John Kerslake's *Mr. Boswell*[46] is the catalogue of the Boswell exhibition at the National Portrait Gallery which the present writer described (anonymously) in *TLS* ('Mr. Boswell Comes to Town').

Mrs. Piozzi's *Observations and*

[46] *Mr. Boswell*, by John Kerslake. The National Portrait Gallery: H.M.S.O. 7s. 6d.

Reflections (1789) is an interesting late example of the genre of eighteenth-century records of the Grand Tour, giving an account of her short journey through France in 1784 and Germany in 1786, and her longer stay in Italy between these two journeys. Herbert Barrows's new edition[47] is a reprint of the first edition. He has also used the corrections and marginal notes of Mrs. Piozzi's own copy. The introduction sets the work in the tradition of traveller's accounts, and there are explanatory notes.

Background of Romanticism: English Philosophical Prose of the Eighteenth Century[48] is an anthology of extracts from hard-to-find works (mainly philosophical) which helped 'shape the thinking of the English Romantics'. It contains selections from William Law, Berkeley, David Hartley, Adam Smith, William Duff, Abraham Tucker, Jacob Bryant, and Godwin. Leonard M. Trawick contributes a short introduction, a helpful reading list, and notes on each writer included.

Adam Ferguson was a Scotch *philosophe*, professor of Philosophy at Edinburgh, and a pioneer of social and political theory. Duncan Forbes's new edition of his *Essay on the History of Civil Society* (1767)[49] reprints the first edition, collated with the seventh (1814). The introduction discusses the ideas of the *Essay* and

its influence on later thinkers. There is a marvellously full index.

Two essays on Warburton can be briefly noted: 'William Warburton as "New Critic"' by Robert M. Ryley in *Studies in Criticism and Aesthetics* (see note 1), and 'The Literary Criticism of William Warburton' by Stephen J. Curry in *ES*.

'Diagonal Handwriting: An Allusion to Swift by Lord Chesterfield' (*NQ*) by C. J. Rawson connects a passage in Chesterfield's letters with *Gulliver's Travels*.

Robert Halsband has published the third and final volume of his great edition of *The Complete Letters of Lady Mary Wortley Montagu*[50] (see also *YW* xlvi: 239 and *YW* xlvii: 237). These letters cover the last eleven years of her life spent mainly in or near Venice until her return to London six months before her death.

Although Gibbon in a famous passage in his *Memoirs* dramatically represents the 'moment of inspiration' of his history, his thoughts had long been tending towards his subject, which indeed was 'the fulfilment of the historical ambitions and questions of a whole generation' as H. R. Trevor-Roper argues in 'The Idea of the Decline and Fall of the Roman Empire', an essay in the Besterman Festschrift.[51] Trevor-Roper discusses the three influences crucial for Gibbon's choice: his discovery of the philosophy of the enlightenment in Lausanne, his reading of Montesquieu, and the general preoccupation of his age with the Middle Ages.

Gerald W. Chapman's *Edmund*

---

[47] *Observations and Reflections Made in the Course of a Journey Through France, Italy, and Germany*, by Hester Lynch Piozzi. Ed. by Herbert Barrows. Michigan U.P. and Cresset Press. pp. xxx+457. $12.50. 90s.

[48] *Background of Romanticism: English Philosophical Prose of the Eighteenth Century*, ed. by Leonard M. Trawick. Indiana U.P. pp. xxviii+221. Boards 64s. Paperback (A 'Midland Book') $2.65. 22s. 6d.

[49] *An Essay on the History of Civil Society 1767*, by Adam Ferguson. Ed. with an Introduction by Duncan Forbes. Edinburgh U.P. 1966. pp. xliv+330.

[50] *The Complete Letters of Lady Mary Wortley Montagu*, ed. by Robert Halsband. Vol. III: *1752–1762*. Oxford: Clarendon Press. pp. xx+408. £4 4s. $13.45.

[51] *The Age of the Enlightenment: Studies presented to Theodore Besterman*, ed. by W. H. Barber, J. H. Brumfitt, R. A. Leigh, R. Shackleton, and S. S. B. Taylor. Oliver & Boyd. pp. xii+468.

Burke: The Practical Imagination[52] approaches its subject in the search of 'sense' rather than 'system'. 'The unity of Burke's thinking is to be sought in its latent character or spirit, in what I have called "practical imagination"—his power to experience the life of a thing in its "organic" complexity, to discriminate its relations, and to act upon (or reverence) its latent good'. Chapman's excellent book is not confined to 'Burke the writer'—a stress that must distort Burke's thought—but is what he calls an 'ideo-biography' which focuses on the five great issues or crises of Burke's career—America, Ireland, Constitutional Reform, France, and India—striving to catch Burke's thought as it was forming and re-forming in its historical context.

Another volume of *The Correspondence of Edmund Burke*[53] must be recorded. It prints 164 letters of Burke's of which 79 were previously unpublished. Letters to Burke are quoted or summarized in the notes.

The handsome volume from Yale which commemorates Horace Walpole's two-hundred-and-fiftieth anniversary[54] contains six essays on 'Walpole as Politician and Political Commentator', seven essays on 'Walpole as Connoisseur and Antiquarian', and six on 'Walpole as a Literary Figure'. These last six are: 'Walpole *versus* Lady Mary' by

Robert Halsband, 'The "Theatre of Geo. 3"' by Charles Beecher Hogan, 'Two Unpublished Fairy Tales by Horace Walpole' by A. Dayle Wallace, 'The Part Played by Horace Walpole and James Boswell in the Quarrel Between Rousseau and Hume: A Reconsideration' by Frederick A. Pottle, 'Walpole and Pearch' by Herbert W. Liebert, and 'Horace Walpole and Edmond Malone' by James M. Osborn.

A third series of the letters of Walpole to Sir Horace Mann has been published, covering the years 1768–79, in the Yale edition of Walpole's letters.[55]

A 'Synoptic Bibliography' of Godwin criticism[56] has been edited by Burton R. Pollin with the aid of an IBM 360/30 computer, useful (among other reasons) because it seems to be able to produce innumerable indexes without either error or omission (there are eleven here). The bibliography consists of 4,314 annotated entries and covers periodicals and books from 1783 to 1966.

Whereas Warton's approach to literary history is antiquarian, Robert Alves's *Sketches of a History of Literature*[57] first published posthumously in Edinburgh in 1794 and destined immediately to be forgotten, is a guide for those wishing instruc-

---

[52] *Edmund Burke: The Practical Imagination*, by Gerald W. Chapman. Harvard U.P. pp. xiv+350. $5.95. 55s. 6d.

[53] *The Correspondence of Edmund Burke*: Vol. VI: *July 1789–December 1791*, ed. by Alfred Cobban and Robert A. Smith. C.U.P. and Chicago U.P. pp. xxvi+495. £6. $13.15.

[54] *Horace Walpole, Writer, Politician, and Connoisseur: Essays on the 250th Anniversary of Walpole's Birth*, ed. by Warren Hunting Smith. Yale U.P. pp. xiv+358+6 illustrations. 135s.

[55] *Horace Walpole's Correspondence with Sir Horace Mann*, Vols. VII-VIII, ed. by W. S. Lewis, Warren Hunting Smith, and George L. Lam, with the assistance of Edwine M. Martz. (*The Yale Edition of Horace Walpole's Correspondence*, ed. W. S. Lewis, Vols. 23-24.) Yale U.P. and O.U.P. pp. viii+517; viii+545, $17.50 each volume.

[56] *Godwin Criticism: A Synoptic Bibliography*, by Burton R. Pollin. Toronto U.P. pp. xlvi+659. $18.50. £8 16s.

[57] *Sketches of a History of Literature* (1794), by Robert Alves. A Facsimile Reproduction with an Introduction by Patrick O'Flaherty. Gainesville, Florida: Scholars' Facsimiles & Reprints. pp. x+310. $8.

tion in forming judgement and taste in reading. Alves trots nimbly through Oriental, Grecian, Roman, Italian, Portuguese, Spanish, French, and German literature in 110 pages before getting down to English and Scotch literature (a further 70 pages). Nineteen short 'literary essays' ('Milton, Shakespeare, Homer, and Virgil compared' etc.) fill up his book, which is now reprinted in an edition by Patrick O'Flaherty.

Walter Whiter, antiquarian and philologist, published his *Specimen of a Commentary on Shakespeare* in 1794. It consisted of notes to *As You Like It* and 'an attempt to explain and illustrate various passages on a new principle of criticism derived from Mr. Locke's doctrine of the association of ideas'. This attempt was neither understood nor welcomed when Whiter issued his book, but recently he has been recognized as a critic who anticipated the serious study of Shakespeare's imagery done in this century, notably by W. A. Armstrong and Wolfgang Clemen. (It is a great loss to Shakespearean criticism that Coleridge gave Whiter's work no more than cursory attention.) Whiter revised his *Specimen* extensively for a second edition which was never published, but his revised text and a mass of MS. material on Shakespeare are now incorporated into a new edition by the late Alan Over and Mary Bell.[58] The extensive introduction considers Whiter and his background, contemporary criticisms of his work, and the relation of the *Specimen* to later criticism. The whole work is an important addition to our knowledge of Shakespeare in the eighteenth century.

[58] *A Specimen of a Commentary on Shakespeare: Being the text of the first (1794) edition revised by the author and never previously published*, by Walter Whiter. Ed. by Alan Over, completed by Mary Bell. Methuen. pp. lxxxii+233. 70s.

4. DRAMA

Despite the popularity of *The Beggar's Opera*, critics have not looked very closely at Gay's other dramatic works, and so *The Beggar's Opera* is seen as an isolated phenomenon, whereas it should be thought of, as Peter Elvet Lewis points out, as 'the culmination of Gay's experiments in dramatic burlesque'. Lewis examines Gay's wide-ranging satire of Restoration and Augustan tragedy in an interesting essay in *DUJ*, 'Gay's Burlesque Method in *The What D'ye Call It*'.

Six new plays are published in the excellent Regents Restoration Drama Series: Cibber's *The Careless Husband* (1705), Steele's *The Tender Husband* (1705), and *The Conscious Lovers* (1723), Fielding's *Historical Register* and *Eurydice Hissed* (1737), and Lillo's *Fatal Curiosity* (1737).[59] ('Further Notes for a Biography of George Lillo' are supplied by C. F. Burgess in *PQ*.)

The Female Wits; or, The Triumvirate of Poets at Rehearsal (1704), an anonymous satire in the manner of Buckingham's *Rehearsal* on women playwrights, is reprinted by *A.R.S.* with an introduction by Lucyle

[59] *The Careless Husband*, by Colley Cibber. Ed. by William W. Appleton. Nebraska U.P. (1966) and Arnold (1967). pp. xvi+135. Boards 21s. Paperback 10s. 6d.
The Tender Husband, by Richard Steele. Ed. by Calhoun Winton. Nebraska U.P. and Arnold. pp. xxii+90. Boards 15s. Paperback 7s. 6d.
The Conscious Lovers, by Richard Steele. Ed. by Shirley Strum Kenny. Nebraska U.P. (1967) and Arnold (1968). pp. xxvi+111. Boards 21s. Paperback 10s. 6d.
The Historical Register for the Year 1736 and *Eurydice Hissed*, by Henry Fielding. Ed. by William W. Appleton. Nebraska U.P. (1967) and Arnold (1968). pp. xviii+83. Boards 21s. Paperback 10s. 6d.
Fatal Curiosity, by George Lillo. Ed. by William H. McBurney. Nebraska U.P. and Arnold. pp. xxvi+69. Boards 21s. Paperback 10s. 6d.

Hook.[60] Also in *A.R.S.* Jean B. Kern transcribes two of Charles Macklin's plays from manuscript copies in the Huntington Library: the popular two-act farce *A Will and No Will*, and *The New Play Criticiz'd*,[61] a 'farcical afterpiece' to Benjamin Hardy's *The Suspicious Husband* (1747).

Edward A. Langhans transcribes 'Three Early Eighteenth-Century Manuscript Promptbooks' (*MP*) from the Bodleian which give some useful information about staging practices in the 1710s and 1720s.

In *RECTR*, Samuel N. Bogorad discusses 'Samuel Foote: The Prospects for a' Life and Works' listing library holdings of material, L. R. N. Ashley gives a bibliography of Colley Cibber, James Black traces the stage history of Tate's *Lear*, Lillian Gottesman writes on 'Garrick's *Institution of the Garter*' and Paul Vernon adds a few theses on Restoration and eighteenth-century theatre from London University to the list given by Carl J. Stratman in *RECTR* in 1963.

Esther K. Sheldon's book on Thomas Sheridan is not a full-length biography since she did not want to duplicate the work done in Wallace A. Bacon's *Elocutionary Career of Thomas Sheridan*. The focus in *Thomas Sheridan of Smock-Alley*[62] is

on Sheridan as a man of the theatre. The book gives a great deal of information on the theatre in Ireland and shows how it influenced the London theatres. There is a list of all plays performed at the Smock-Alley Theatre from 1745 to 1758.

Finally in this section two pieces on Thomas Sheridan's more famous son. In 'The Completion of the School for Scandal' (*TLS*) C. J. L. Price gives clues which point to the possibility that Sheridan was meditating his play as early as 1773. We have definite evidence that he was working on the play in 1777. Other evidence suggests 'that the play was completed rapidly, that some of the characters were based on people that [Sheridan] knew, and that he threw in some important topical references'. Susie I. Tucker gives 'Notes on Sheridan's Vocabulary' in *NQ*.

5. THE NOVEL

In this section the major study of the year is Ronald Paulson's *Satire and the Novel in Eighteenth-Century England*.[63] Paulson sees the history of narrative in the period as a conflict between the conservative values of the satirist, who assumes that man can be judged objectively and that he bears complete responsibility for his actions, and the emerging values of the novelist, who is concerned with the individual responses of a character's consciousness, and who is unwilling to sit in judgement on particular actions. The relationship between satire and the novel is seen in a general way as 'analogous to the relationship between satire and the drama in the early seventeenth century': the novelist uses satiric conventions when he wishes 'to expose reality beneath appearances or

[60] *The Female Wits (Anonymous) (1704)*, Introduced by Lucyle Hook. The William Andrews Clark Memorial Library (*A.R.S.* no. 124). pp. xx+78.

[61] *A Will and No Will, or A Bone for the Lawyers (1746)* and *The New Play Criticiz'd, or The Plague of Envy (1747)*, by Charles Macklin. Introduced by Jean B. Kern. The William Andrews Clark Memorial Library (*A.R.S.* nos 127–8). pp. viii+78.

[62] *Thomas Sheridan of Smock-Alley, Recording His Life as Actor and Theatre Manager in Both Dublin and London; and Including a Smock-Alley Calendar for the Years of His Management*, by Esther K. Sheldon. Princeton U.P. pp. xii+530.

[63] *Satire and the Novel in Eighteenth-Century England*, by Ronald Paulson. Yale U.P. pp. v+318. $8.50. 76s.

motives behind actions', and consequently novels are often generically mixed. In a densely-packed discussion Paulson anlyses the function of satiric conventions in the novel, suggesting finally that 'the most tangible result of the satiric tradition in the eighteenth century . . . was the novel of manners of Jane Austen. Our exploration has followed a series of distinctive types of novel as they grew out of the contact with satiric forms, conventions and impulses; these in turn have been regarded as a kind of evolutionary process culminating in *Pride and Prejudice*'. Many readers will be doubtful about this evolutionary concept (and Paulson himself goes on to express reservations), but this does not invalidate the perceptiveness with which he discusses particular works, and there can be no doubt that this is a major contribution, especially to the study of Fielding and Smollett.

Those interested in the interaction between moral discourse and fiction in Defoe will find *Conjugal Lewdness; or, Matrimonial Whoredom*[64] an interesting volume. Published in 1727 (although begun much earlier), this treatise is the most complete exposition of Defoe's ideas on sex and marriage: it deals directly with many problems that are familiar from *Moll Flanders* or *Roxana*, and often illustrates them through dialogue and the development of dramatic episodes which show great sensitivity to the position of women in society, and a very humane understanding of the marriage relationship. In an introduction Maximilian E. Novak comments both on the place of the book in rela-

tion to contemporary thinking, and also on its 'complete mastery of all the techniques of prose'.

Many of the dramatic episodes in *Conjugal Lewdness* show an interest in subtle and complex moral problems which bears out G. A. Starr's thesis in his valuable and stimulating article, 'From Casuistry to Fiction: The Importance of the *Athenian Mercury*' (*JHI*). Starr analyses several of the ethical problems that Dunton dealt with in his question-and-answer journal, relates them to the tradition of seventeenth-century casuistry, and demonstrates the extent to which they not only anticipate the preoccupations of Defoe's protagonists, but even account for the form of his works. 'Owing to the assumption that life is composed of a series of cases of conscience, each of which must be decided on its own merits, the casuistical method tends to dissolve narrative into a sequence of discrete episodes. It may give each episode internal consistency and considerable vitality, but these very strengths can jeopardize any larger pattern or design the book may have.' An addition to the by now impressive body of criticism which stresses the importance of reading Defoe's fiction within the context of the Puritan tradition is provided by R. W. Ayers's '*Robinson Crusoe*: "Allusive Allegorick History"' (*PMLA*), a study of some of the basic images and symbols of the novel and their relationship to 'traditional Bible exegesis particularly as it was expressed in the pietistic literature of the Puritans in the late 17th and early 18th centuries'. Ayers shows, for example, that Crusoe and his father may be seen as analogues of the son and the father in the parable of the Prodigal Son, or as emblems of Adam and God in a parable of the Fall. Disobedience of the father is the original sin that

[64] *Conjugal Lewdness; or, Matrimonial Whoredom. A Treatise concerning the Use and and Abuse of the Marriage Bed.* (1727), by Daniel Defoe. A Facsimile Reproduction with an Introduction by Maximilian E. Novak. (Scholars Facsimiles and Reprints.) Gainesville, Florida. pp. xiv+406. $10.

causes Crusoe's depravity and leads to his incessant wandering over the face of the earth. Rodney M. Baine's 'Defoe and the Angels' (*TSLL*) follows a similar general tendency to Starr and Ayers in a study of Defoe's angelology which is based mainly on 'A Vision of the Angelick World' (appended to *Serious Reflections . . .* in 1720) and the *Essay on the History and Reality of Apparitions* (1727). These works reveal Defoe as 'a sincere Puritan trying . . . to retain and strengthen all meaningful and credible evidence of Providence, of an invisible world of spirits, and of a communion with God'. M. A. Goldberg, on the other hand, in '*Moll Flanders*: Christian Allegory in a Hobbesian Mode' (*UR*), traces a relationship between Moll's religion and the materialism of Hobbes, and suggests that 'Moll's narrative is not a confessional of her own sins: it is, rather, a confession of the world's sins, from which man may redeem himself—if there is money enough and time'.

John B. Shipley's 'Daniel Defoe and Henry Baker: Some of their Correspondence Again and its Provenance' (*Bodleian Library Record*) comments on new material which provides a more accurate version of Defoe's 'last and most poignant letter'—that of 12 August 1730 to his son-in-law, Henry Baker.

Michael J. C. Echeruo writes on '*Robinson Crusoe, Purchas His Pilgrimes* and the "Novel"' (*ESA*), Pierre Nordon on '*Robinson Crusoe*: unité et contradictions' (*Archives des lettres modernes*), and Konrad Pilgrim 'Zu Defoes Welverständnis im 3. Teil von *Robinson Crusoe*' (*Archiv*). Also to be listed are Minoru Oda's 'Allegory and History: A Study of Daniel Defoe's *Roxana*' (*Memoirs of Osaka Gakugei University*—1966), James E. Rocks's 'Camus Reads Defoe: *A Journal of the Plague Year* as a Source for *The Plague*' (*TSE*), and Ian Watt's 'The Recent Critical Fortunes of *Moll Flanders*' (*ECS*).

T. C. Duncan Eaves and Ben D. Kimpel contribute important information on 'Richardson's Revisions of *Pamela*' (*SB*). They have discovered that Richardson's last and most elaborate revision of the novel, long believed to have been lost, was actually published in 1801 and reprinted in 1810. In this article they present both the evidence for this conclusion and the findings from a collation of this and earlier texts. The revisions are generally towards a greater gentility and accuracy, in which the raciness of Richardson's original conception of Pamela is often toned down. The authors suggest that the first edition is the one that should be reprinted—'it is closer to the Pamela whom Richardson actually imagined, whereas all succeeding texts try to approach the Pamela he thought he should have imagined'. Neither of the currently available texts has any authority. In 'Beauty and Mr. B' (*SEL*), D. C. Muecke suggests that Richardson might have taken the name Colbrand from *Guy of Warwick*, and discusses various similarities between *Pamela* and the story of Beauty and the Beast and other fairy tales. Richardson naturally drew upon 'the stock figures and situations of the kinds of fiction' he was most familiar with.

John A. Dussinger's 'Richardson's "Christian Vocation"' (*PLL*) examines Richardson's religious attitudes which are seen to be opposed to the deist heresy that natural religion alone is sufficient for man's salvation. At the same time he was suspicious of Methodist enthusiasm, and insistent upon the importance of 'Christ's atonement as the model of moral perfection to be imitated by man in as high a degree as is humanly possible'. All three of Richardson's novels, it is argued, 'convey this thesis of the perfectionist hero as the mirror of Christ's vicarious sacrifice'. In 'Richardson's Tragic Muse' (*PQ*), the same author contributes usefully to our understanding of the dramatic background of Richardson's novels. He suggests that Richardson was directly influenced by Rapin's affective theory of tragedy, and analyses numerous examples of the 'distressed-heroine' stereotype to show how common the theme of rape and suicide was. Both the theory and practice of late seventeenth-century drama appear to 'have influenced significantly Richardson's conception of *Clarissa* as a tragedy, particularly his characterization of the pathetic heroine'.

Morris Golden's 'Richardson's Repetitions' (*PMLA*) discusses Richardson's use of recurrent plot devices, situations and character types. In 'Richardson's Helper in Creating the Character of Elias Brand' (*NQ*), T. C. Duncan Eaves and Ben D. Kimpel propose that one R. Smith gave the novelist help with Latin quotations.

The most durable contribution to Fielding scholarship during the year is likely to be the edition of *Joseph Andrews* prepared by Martin C. Battestin for the Wesleyan Edition of the *Works*.[65] The volume, which is produced with great elegance by the Oxford University Press, is 'designed to furnish scholars and other readers both with a reliable text and with all other materials relevant to the history and essential meaning of the text'. The Textual Introduction by Fredson Bowers sets forth the rigorous editorial principles that have been followed, and Battestin's own general

Introduction, which is deliberately designed to be 'historical rather than critical' puts its emphasis on the 'making of the novel—the circumstances of its genesis and composition and the facts of its printing and publication—rather than on its larger meanings'. The fully informative yet compact notes are printed at the foot of each page. This is a volume which sets a new standard for the editing of eighteenth-century fiction.

Although Michael Irwin's *Henry Fielding: the Tentative Realist*[66] is sometimes irritating in its underlying assumptions, it has the merit of raising important critical questions. Irwin's thesis is that 'many of Fielding's chosen narrative techniques were incompatible'—in particular that his occasional attempts at representing life realistically conflict with the kind of distancing that is achieved through the use, for didactic purposes, of mock-heroic, parody, irony and the stylizations appropriate to burlesque and caricature. Irwin opens with chapters on 'Fielding's Moral Position', on didacticism in the plays, and on the influences (dramatic and epic among others) on the novels, and he assembles some useful information economically. He then analyses each of the novels in order to demonstrate the incongruities that occur as Fielding shifts from one order of verisimilitude to another, and he has little difficulty in adducing examples. The problem here, as he recognizes, is to interpret the evidence, and to account for the fact that the novels appear to be much more unified than the critical account would suggest. Irwin rejects the explanation that unity depends upon 'Fielding's careful adjustment of manner and matter', on what will seem to many readers the specious grounds that 'this argument is to

[65] *Joseph Andrews*, ed. by Martin C. Battestin. (The Wesleyan Edition of the Works of Henry Fielding.) O.U.P. pp. xlvii+389. 63s. $10.

[66] *Henry Fielding; the Tentative Realist*, by Michael Irwin. O.U.P. pp. vii+147. 25s.

assume a control of narrative effects unlikely in an author experimenting in a brand-new form and preoccupied with the problem of projecting certain didactic views'. The effect of the novels is less complex, he argues, than many modern critics assume, and the impression of unity springs less from authorial control than from the reader's willingness to engage in an 'automatic sorting process' as he reads, to place each episode in terms of an emerging pattern, and to suppress from his memory those elements which are discordant.

Henry Fielding and the Dry Mock,[67] by George R. Levine, is a study of Fielding's ironical techniques in his work up to and including *Joseph Andrews*. The preliminary analysis of irony in the eighteenth century owes an acknowledged debt to Norman Knox's *The Word Irony and Its Context* (see *YW* xlii. 193), the inevitable starting point for an inquiry of this kind. There is a good section on Fielding's use of the personal technique in his journalism, and this is found to show a high level of technical sophistication, although it has to be admitted that Fielding's use of the device cannot be compared with Swift's in brilliance. A chapter on the techniques of verbal irony applies the methods used by Eleanor Hutchens in her analysis of *Tom Jones* (see *YW* xlvi 248) to the earlier writings, and there is a section on Fielding's use of dramatic irony. The conclusion is that 'it was not until *Joseph Andrews* that Fielding became fully aware of the comic, satiric, and structural potential of irony as a literary device', but that in *Joseph Andrews* 'irony came to be more than a comic, satiric, or structural device, but a mode

integral to the very style of the novel'.

Hamilton Macallister's *Fielding*[68] in the 'Literature in Perspective' series is addressed to the general reader and is intended to give a straightforward account of its subject, avoiding 'critical jargon' and offering enough information to bring the reader 'up to date on critical estimates'. In the commendable search for lucidity the critical method tends to become oversimplified—each novel, for example, is discussed first in terms of structure and then from the point of view of characters and themes, but little attempt is made to deal with style or with the complexities of Fielding's irony perhaps because the technicalities that this would involve might prove daunting. But the book makes sensible use of work by Battestin and Ehrenpreis, and should prove a helpful introduction for A level students and others. There are illustrations by Cruickshank, Hogarth and Rowlandson.

David L. Evans's 'The Theme of Liberty in *Jonathan Wild*' (*PLL*) suggests that, while the ironic inversion of the terms 'goodness' and 'greatness' is certainly essential to Fielding's novel, the antithesis of moral anarchy and moral order is equally important. Wild, 'the man who refuses the law, restraint, conventions, is unwittingly a slave', and Heartfree, 'who accepts the law and allows himself to be confined turns out to enjoy true freedom'. In 'Puffs and Pollitricks: *Jonathan Wild* and the Political Corruption of Language' (*PQ*), Glen W. Hatfield, after discussing some examples of satire directed at the language of politicians in *Joseph Andrews*, *Tom Jones*, and *Amelia*, shows how Fielding re-

---

[67] *Henry Fielding and the Dry Mock: A Study of the Techniques of Irony in His Early Works*, by George R. Levine. The Hague: Mouton. pp. 160. 20 Guilders.

[68] *Fielding*, by Hamilton Macallister. (Literature in Perspective Series.) Evans Bros. pp. 140. 8s. 6d.

sponded, in the person of Gustavus Puffendorf in *The Champion*, to Walpole's manipulations of hack pamphleteers and journalists, and how this led to the attack on political 'greatness' in *Jonathan Wild*. The same author's 'Quacks, Pettyfoggers, and Parsons: Fielding's Case Against the Learned Professions' (*TSLL*) draws on the novels, plays and essays, in order to show Fielding's attitude to the obfuscations of language brought about by the professional jargon of lawyers, doctors and clergymen. He suggests parallels between Fielding's attitude and Locke's.

'Richardson's *Pamela* and Fielding's *Joseph Andrews*' (*EC*) by Douglas Brooks, attempts to show through a detailed study of parallel passages that the relationship between the books is much closer than has generally been supposed. 'Fielding was, in fact, rewriting *Pamela* in his own mode. In its structural symmetry, its comic approach to the psychological, its themes ... Fielding's novel stands as a symbol of Augustanism, opposed to *Pamela*, the real voice of the future.' B. L. Reid's 'Utmost Merriment, Strictest Decency: *Joseph Andrews*' (*Sew*) interprets the novel in terms of two predominant metaphors, the 'horizontal metaphor' of the journey, 'a comic Pilgrim's Progress', and the 'vertical metaphor' of the social scale, which becomes an emblem of the vanity and affectation of the world.

Martin C. Battestin's 'Tom Jones and "His *Egyptian* Majesty": Fielding's Parable of Government' (*PMLA*) is a detailed and informative essay on the gipsy episode in *Tom Jones*. It shows that Fielding's account of the government and system of justice among the gipsies is taken from contemporary accounts of ancient Egyptian society, and that in the novel this society is made to

function with a Swiftian ambiguity. 'On the one hand, it is used satirically to expose by contrast the immorality of English society and the inefficiency of constitutional government; on the other hand the alternative political system the gipsies represent (the Jacobite dream of absolutism) is at once untenable and absurd. Finally, Fielding's rejection of the Tory dream is shown to echo one of the best known apologies for the Hanoverian settlement, Bishop Hoadly's *The Happiness of the Present Establishment, and the Unhappiness of Absolute Monarchy*. 'Bampfylde-Moore Carew and Fielding's King of the Gipsies' (*NQ*) by Tuvia Bloch, makes the point, also established by Battestin, that Bampfylde-Moore Carew's autobiography, regarded by Cross and Dudden as a source for the gipsy episode, in fact itself uses material from *Tom Jones*. In a subsequent letter Angus M. Fraser suggests that the dialect that Fielding gives to his gipsies has some traces of authenticity. 'The Serpent and the Dove: Fielding's Irony and the Prudence Theme of *Tom Jones*' (*MP*), by Glen W. Hatfield, argues that Sophia is to be regarded as the model of 'true prudence'. Daniel J. Schneider writes on 'Sources of Comic Pleasure in *Tom Jones*' (*Connecticut Review*) and Sheridan Baker on 'Bridget Allworthy: the Creative Pressures of Fielding's Plot' (*PMASAL*).

'The Prison and the Dark Beauty of *Amelia*' (*Criticism*), by Peter V. Lepage, discusses images of confinement in *Amelia*, and suggests that 'as a symbol . . . the prison and its analogues connote the tyranny of the social will and the injustice of that will', and also the enshackling power of sexual desire. Fielding uses this symbolism consciously in the central structure of the work: 'the forces whose conflict provides the drama in the novel are imprisonment through falsity and consequent separation of the Booths, in opposition to freedom through charity and faith, and consequent union of the hero and heroine'.

William J. Farrell's 'Fielding's Familiar Style' (*ELH*) argues that, although Fielding's style does have a distancing function, it also, especially in comparison with earlier fiction, has the effect of 'underlining his most important artistic end—fidelity to life itself'. In 'Fielding and the Uses of Style' (*Novel*), Robert Alter gives a detailed analysis of Fielding's consistency in manipulating style in a meaningful way.

Malvin R. Zirker, Jr.'s 'Fielding and Reform in the 1750's' (*SEL*) argues that, although Fielding's position as one of the founders of the British police system is secure, his influence on the Government reforms of the 1750s has been generally exaggerated since the publication of Cross's biography. Fielding's *Enquiry* and, later his *Proposal*, were doubtless written with knowledge of the Government's interests and intentions, but once his 'opinion had been asked and given, the Government may well have concluded its business with him'.

Hugh Amory's 'Henry Fielding's *Epistles to Walpole*: A Re-examination' (*PQ*) discusses the date and significance of the two *Epistles* which appeared for the first time in the *Miscellanies*. 'Two Lost Fielding Manuscripts' (*NQ*), by the same author, refers to a letter and a bond, neither of any intrinsic importance. C. J. Rawson writes on 'Gentlemen and Dancing Masters: Thoughts on Fielding, Chesterfield and the Genteel' (*ECS*), and adduces a possible echo of Fielding by Wordsworth in '*Tom Jones* and *Michael*: A Parallel' (*NQ*). Finally, Philip K. Jason gives

an account, based on a manuscript find in the British Museum, of a play derived from incidents in the first and fourth books of *Joseph Andrews*, which was presented as an afterpiece at Drury Lane in 1778: 'Samuel Jackson Pratt's Unpublished Comedy of *Joseph Andrews*' (*NQ*).

Robert Giddings's *The Tradition of Smollett*[69] is 'an attempt to place Smollett in the context of his tradition, the picaresque tradition, and to provide some appropriate standards by which to evaluate his achievement'. This is a large programme which is only fitfully carried out: to try, as Giddings does, to sum up 'The Picaresque Tradition' in a chapter of twenty pages shows extraordinary boldness in a book supposedly academic. Inevitably, he has to rely on large and disputable generalizations which it would take a great deal of patient argument to substantiate, but which the reader is expected to take on trust. The book suffers also from a certain stridency of tone which invites dissent. This said, however, it should be added that Giddings's enthusiasm for Smollett is well-communicated, and that his analysis, especially in the chapter on 'Structure and Moral Intention' is often helpful. If the book had had a rather more modest aim, it might have been more warmly received.

In 'Stylistic Energy in the Early Smollett' (*SP*), Philip Stevick analyses examples of hyperbole to show how Smollett, one of the least philosophical of novelists, produces 'the altogether convincing appearance of a view of life in a style which can be as hyperbolic as it is only because it expresses values which are deeply felt'.

Two articles discuss Smollett's last novel. David L. Evans's '*Humphry*

[69] *The Tradition of Smollett*, by Robert Giddings. Methuen. pp. 215. 42*s*. $5.50.

Clinker: Smollett's Tempered Augustanism' (*Criticism*) shows how the morose rejection of the world which Bramble displays at the beginning of the novel is modified by his discovery of the necessity of an active, unconcealed engagement in life. Evans traces the influence of Tabitha, Humphry and Charles Dennison in bringing this change about. Dennison, in particular, provides a living example of the successful fusion of Augustan order and business-like industry. 'Looking for Dustwich' (*TSLL*), by Leon V. Driskell, considers the implications of the pair of letters from Jonathan Dustwich and Henry Davis printed at the beginning of *Humphry Clinker*, and suggests that they provide important clues for the interpretation of the novel.

In 'Smollett's Quest for Form' (*MP*), Tuvia Bloch suggests that Smollett, recognizing that *Roderick Random* lacked structural unity, was influenced by *Tom Jones* in his attempts to give a more careful structure to *Peregrine Pickle*, *Fathom* and *Sir Lancelot Greaves*. *Humphry Clinker* represents a successful emancipation from the influence of Fielding. 'Smollett's Microcosms: A Satiric Device in the Novel' (*Satire Newsletter*), by Grant T. Webster, concerns the frequent digressions in Smollett's novels where he creates 'a little world . . . in which a number of humour characters are presented and exposed as frauds'.

There are three articles on matters to do with text and attribution. Damian J. Grant's 'Unpublished Additions to Smollett's *Travels*' (*NQ*) is an account of manuscript additions that Smollett had inserted in his own copy of the first edition. 'Smollett's Translation of *Gil Blas*: A Question of Text' (*ELN*), by John P. Kent, shows that Smollett worked from the first edition of Le Sage's work; and 'New Smollett Attributions in the *Critical Review*' (*NQ*), by Philip J. Klukoff, adduces evidence which suggests that in 1759 Smollett wrote reviews of *Rasselas*, Adam Smith's *Theory of Moral Sentiments*, and Gerard's *Essay on Taste*.

Klukoff also writes on 'Smollett and the *Critical Review*: Criticism of the Novel, 1756–1763' (*SSL*). He argues that Smollett's influence on the criticism of the novel might have been to establish a context within which the novel could be discussed as a serious aesthetic genre. Following the theories of such critics as Adam Smith and Gerard there is, in the *Critical Review*, an emphasis on sympathy as 'a foundation for a theory of morals and a source of judgement', and a concern for 'an organic fusion of form and ethic whereby the moral assertion of the novel is effectively directed by a structural intensity governed by the action of the hero'.

'Tobias Smollett's *Advice* and *Reproof* with Introduction and Notes' (*Thoth*), by Donald M. Korte, reprints the poems from Henley's edition of Smollett's *Works*, and notes parallels with Pope's satires. Two items concern Smollett and medicine. G. S. Rousseau discusses 'Matt Bramble and the Sulphur Controversy in the XVIIIth Century' (*JHI*), and Daniel M. Musher writes on 'The Medical Views of Dr. Tobias Smollett' (*Bulletin of the History of Medicine*).

Paul-Gabriel Boucé contributes three articles: 'Smollett Criticism, 1770–1924: Corrections and Additions' (*NQ*); 'The "Chinese Pilot" and "Sa-rouf" in Smollett's *Atom*' (*ELN*); and 'Smollett and the Expedition Against Rochefort (1757)' (*MP*). Also to be noted is the appearance of *Humphry Clinker* in the 'Penguin

English Library', edited by Angus Ross.[70]

Starting from the proposition that *Tristram Shandy* is both profoundly original and extremely derivative, J. M. Stedmond's *The Comic Art of Laurence Sterne*[71] is a general study of the 'many literary contexts' of the novel. Stedmond discusses the relationship between Sterne and such predecessors as Rabelais and Burton, but also looks forward to make useful comparisons with Joyce, Pound and Proust. In a chapter on 'The Question of Style' he stresses the importance of seventeenth-century baroque prose in providing the well-established conventions which Sterne used in subjecting his artistic medium, language, to a critical scrutiny which attempted 'to keep himself and his reader aware of the compromises necessary in all forms of verbal art'. The chapter on 'Tristram as Satirist' draws comparisons from Swift and Pope. A long section on 'Tristram as Clown' concludes that the 'message' of the book is that of the 'Erasmian clown': 'man can experience the delights of the human state only by subjecting himself to its limitations. If he rebels disproportionately, he may well lapse into frustrated melancholy; if he submits too readily, he may lose himself in tawdry trivialities. But if he can retain his sense of humour and his urge to make the best possible use of his admittedly limited powers, then he can attain a measure of human happiness'. Finally, Stedmond writes on the various functions of Yorick in Sterne's work.

Ian Watt's 'The Comic Syntax of *Tristram Shandy*'[72] is an analysis which stresses the predominance of rhetorical over narrative structures in the book. The ordering principle of the novel is essentially a complex but consistent mode of comic speech which unites all its parts and attitudes, loosely no doubt, but with perfect appropriateness. In 'A Version of Pastoral: Class and Society in *Tristram Shandy*' (*SEL*), Howard Anderson discusses the idyllic quality of the social relationships depicted in *Tristram Shandy*, compared particularly with Defoe and Richardson, and suggests that Sterne uses the pastoral vision to provide an implicit criticism of the ridiculousness and cruelty of narrow class interests and military extravagance, while at the same time exploiting fully the comic aspects of his characters. Ronald Hafter's 'Garrick and *Tristram Shandy*' (*SEL*) traces the relationship between Sterne and Garrick, and finds similarities between Garrick's manner of acting ('charged with feeling, supple, capable of representing fleeting sensations') and the stylistic innovations that mark *Tristram Shandy*. He then shows that the practice of both men was influenced by a concept of the imagination as an emphatic faculty. B. L. Reid writes on 'Sterne and the Absurd Homunculus' (*VQR*). 'In the general histrionic enterprise the master puppeteer Sterne manipulates his puppet-puppeteer Tristram, who manipulates a little troupe of puppet originals who mimic the absurdity of the race in its standard forms.' George Goodwin writes on 'The Comic as a Critique of Reason: *Tristram Shandy*' (*CE*).

In 'The Journey and the Picture: the Art of Sterne and Hogarth'

---

[70] *The Expedition of Humphrey Clinker*, by Tobias Smollett, ed. by Angus Ross. Penguin pp. 414. 6s.

[71] *The Comic Art of Laurence Sterne: Convention and Innovation in Tristram Shandy and A Sentimental Journey*, by John M. Stedmond. Toronto U.P. pp. 178. $5.50.

[72] See *Studies in Criticism and Aesthetics*, note 1.

(*BNYPL*), William Holtz studies the work of the two men to show that 'just as Hogarth, aware of limits imposed by the spatial and static nature of his medium, sought to achieve narrative effects, so Sterne, sensitive to the deficiencies of narrative, attempted to render effects that may well be called spatial and static'. 'Sterne and Hogarth's Analysis of Beauty' (*NQ*), by Marjorie Ryan, discusses the description of Trim reading the sermon, and Hogarth's illustration of it. George P. Landow writes on '*Tristram Shandy* and the Comedy of Context' (*Brigham Young University Studies*), and Graham Petrie supplies a 'Note on the Novel and the Film: Flashbacks in *Tristram Shandy* and *The Pawnbroker*' (*WHR*). Also to be noted are J. E. P. Thomson's 'The Morality of Sterne's Yorick' (*AUMLA*), and William Holtz's 'Pictures for Parson Yorick: Laurence Sterne's London Visit of 1760' (*ECS*).

In a review of the evidence relating to the vexed question of 'William Combe and the *Original Letters of the Late Rev. Mr. Laurence Sterne* (1788)' (*PMLA*), Harlan W. Hamilton concludes that 'the letters as we have them, whether authentic, imitative or mixed, set forth facts about Sterne and Combe which biographers must treat with cautious respect. Much of the writing is imitative overlay, but the occasional particularization and sometimes the style itself must convey tantalizing suggestions of Laurence Sterne's presence just beneath the surface'. Arthur H. Cash's 'Who Was Sterne's Mother?' (*NQ*) gives the results of an elaborate inquiry which tends to support Sterne's statement that his mother was 'the Daughter of no Other than a poor Suttler who followed the Camp in Flanders'.

Both *Tristram Shandy*[73] and *A Sentimental Journey*[74] have appeared during the year in the Penguin English Library. Also to be noted, although it has not been available for review, is a major edition of *A Sentimental Journey*, by Gardner D. Stout, Jr.[75]

Henry Mackenzie's *The Man of Feeling* has been added to the 'Oxford English Novels' series, edited with an Introduction by Brian Vickers.[76] David G. Spencer's 'Henry Mackenzie: a Practical Sentimentalist' (*PLL*) suggests that Mackenzie was a more sensible moralist than he is generally supposed to be. 'His philosophy is simply that to adjust to the world one needs . . . a sympathetic heart, but one needs also a large measure of common sense.' The first novel, *The Man of Feeling*, shows the probable fate in the world of an ideally sympathetic heart, while the second, *The Man of the World*, takes account of the compromises necessary to existence in this world.

Elizabeth Rowe's *Friendship in Death*, a collection of moral short stories, was popular in the eighteenth century, and in 'Mrs. Elizabeth Rowe: the Novel as Polemic' (*PMLA*) John J. Richetti tries to discover why. He concludes that the reason lies in Mrs. Rowe's assertion that 'death, the great problem which rationalism and infidelity cannot solve, is defeated by true and pure love, the great

[73] *The Life and Opinions of Tristram Shandy, Gentleman*, by Laurence Sterne, ed. by Christopher Ricks. Penguin. pp. 659. 7s. 6d.

[74] *A Sentimental Journey through France and Italy*, by Laurence Sterne, ed. by Graham Petrie with an Introduction by A. Alvarez. Penguin. pp. 154. 3s. 6d.

[75] *A Sentimental Journey through France and Italy by Mr. Yorick*, ed. by Gardner D. Stout, Jr. California U.P. pp. xvii+377. $10.

[76] *The Man of Feeling*, by Henry Mackenzie, ed. with an Introduction by Brian Vickers. O.U.P. pp. xxx+137. 21s. $5.

human necessity, which reason cannot explain or eliminate'.

William Park's 'Change in the Criticism of the Novel after 1760' (*PQ*) shows how critical norms changed to accommodate the new kinds of sentimental and romantic fiction that were being produced in the later part of the century.

Finally, it is pleasant to report that Elizabeth Inchbald's *A Simple Story* has been published in the 'Oxford English Novels' series with a sympathetic Introduction by J. M. S. Tompkins.[77]

[77] *A Simple Story*, by Elizabeth Inchbald, ed. with an Introduction by J. M. S. Tompkins. O.U.P. pp. xxx+345. 30*s*. $7.

XIII

The Nineteenth Century

P. M. YARKER and BRIAN LEE

This chapter comprises the following sections: (1) Social and Intellectual Background; (2) Poetry and Drama; (3) Novels and Novelists; (4) Selected Prose Writers. Of these the first two are by P. M. Yarker, and the last two by Brian Lee.

1. SOCIAL AND INTELLECTUAL BACKGROUND

The name of Croker will always sound a harsh note in literary history, and whatever the truth of its effect on Keats himself, few can read the notorious review of *Endymion* without regretting its tone of facile sarcasm, unaccompanied as it was by a critical comment of much worth. Croker, indeed, was not a critic of very great distinction; his talents were of a different sort. *The Croker Papers*, first published in 1884 have been re-edited, with an Introduction, by Bernard Pool,[1] and this selection from his letters, journals, notes of conversations, and speeches in the House, is chiefly interesting for the light thrown on personalities and events at the time when Croker, as First Secretary to the Admiralty, was at the centre of affairs. In particular, his close association with the Duke of Wellington during the Peninsular campaign and afterwards produced some of the Duke's most revealing comments on his life, his armies, and his generalship. Croker was active in

both literature and politics until his death in 1857, and his Papers are a source of information concerning both spheres in the first half of the century. Other sources are the *Creevey Papers* and the *Greville Memoirs*, and a short introduction to these two has been contributed by Joanna Richardson to the 'Writers and their Work' series.[2] Even more important to literary studies is *The Diary of Henry Crabb Robinson*, of which Derek Hudson has made a new abridgement (O.U.P.).

Under the title *The Progress of a Ploughboy* Cobbett's autobiography, edited from his writings by William Reitzel, was published in 1933, and has now been reissued.[3] Cobbett never fulfilled his intention of writing the story of his life, from crow-starver to Member for Oldham, but there is sufficient autobiography in his other work to form a complete account. In the present volume the sources are given in an appendix, and there are very full notes.

'His name is Davy . . . the young chemist, the young everything, the man least ostentatious of first talent that I have ever known.' Southey's characteristic enthusiasm was fully justified, for Davy who might, had he received an appropriate education, 'have advanced chemistry by at least

[1] *The Croker Papers*, ed. by Bernard Pool. Batsford. pp. vii+277. 50s.

[2] *Creevey and Greville*, by Joanna Richardson. Longmans Green. pp. 36. 3s. 6d.

[3] *The Autobiography of William Cobbett*, edited by William Reitzel. Faber & Faber. pp. 272. 9s. 6d.

a hundred years', was considered seriously as a poet by Coleridge and had a marked effect on Wordsworth. A short life, by Sir Harold Hartley, F.R.S.,[4] is of interest not only for the light it throws on his relations with the poets, but also for its account of the state of knowledge of the natural sciences at that time, and the nature and extent of Davy's discoveries.

Richard Henry Horne (he adopted the more legendary 'Hengist' as his middle name quite late in life) is remembered as having snowballed Keats at Dr. Clarke's school, and for some essays, verse drama, and *Orion* his epic poem (1843), which he sold at a farthing a copy to 'mark the contempt into which epic poetry had fallen'. His career was varied, and included service in the Mexican navy during the War of Independence, and activities in the goldfields of Ballarat. A less spectacular aspect is reflected in *Memoirs of a London Doll*, a delightful children's book now reprinted with an Introduction by Margery Fisher,[5] which contains varied scenes of family life and a notable account of the Lord Mayor's Show.

'Principles and Perspective in Jeffrey's Criticism' is the title of an article by P. F. Morgan (*SSL*). John Stuart Mill's literary criticism has attracted far less attention than his other writing, although it is not without importance. In a well-informed study F. P. Sharpless[6] shows, by an examination of Mill's essays in *The Westminster Review* and elsewhere, how his critical

theories related to his thought in general. Bentham's equation of poetry with push-pin was a bad starting point, and Mill never wholly abandoned the Utilitarian approach, nor remitted his hostility to Coleridge. But although his attempt to establish a system of aesthetics on purely empirical lines did not get far, when he turned from poetry to the poet and his audience he had more to offer. Sharpless shows that he had some affinity with Ruskin's ideas in Volume II of *Modern Painters* concerning the nature of beauty, but he was unable to accept Ruskin's ideal basis for it. Instead he returned to standards of utility, and, in his Inaugural Address at St. Andrews in 1867, he related beauty to morality and order. E. S. Dallas, who had certain points in common with Mill, is another neglected critic. In 'What Happened to E. S. Dallas?' (*REL*) Derek Hudson gives a short biographical account, and comments on his idea of criticism as 'the science of pleasure'. E. W. Hirshberg writes on 'G. H. Lewes and A. W. Schlegel: An Important Critical Relationship' (*Language Quarterly*).

Two books deal with universities in the nineteenth century. The diaries of Joseph Romilly, edited by J. P. T. Bury,[7] cover the years 1831 to 1842 at Cambridge. Romilly was Registrary of the University from the first of these dates until 1862, during which period he was closely concerned with affairs, and played a prominent part in the chief University ceremonies, many of which he describes. His regular entries present an alarming picture of University life. Reform was in the air, however, although the present volume ends before the appointment of the Royal

---

[4] *Humphry Davy*, by Sir Harold Hartley, F. R. S. Nelson (1966). pp. 160. 55s.

[5] *Memoirs of a London Doll*, by Richard Henry Horne, with an Introduction and Notes by Margery Fisher. Deutsch. pp. xxx + 143. 21s.

[6] *The Literary Criticism of John Stuart Mill*, by F. P. Sharpless. The Hague: Mouton. pp. 246. 28 Guilders.

[7] *Romilly's Cambridge Diary 1832–42*, ed. by J. P. T. Bury. C.U.P. pp. xv +260. 63s. $12.50.

Commission. John Sparrow's Clark Lectures on Mark Pattison[8] deal closely with Pattison's efforts to guide the reforms at Oxford along what seemed to him the true path, and his bitter disappointment at the way things eventually went. There is an interesting chapter on Pattison and the novelists, dealing with his (putative) portrait as Casaubon in *Middlemarch*, and his more certain identification with Forth in Rhoda Broughton's *Belinda* and Squire Wendover in *Robert Ellesmere* by Mrs. Ward. Sparrow cannot doubt that Casaubon was, in part at least, based on Mark Pattison; but he wonders how George Eliot 'can have failed to know how deep a wound she would inflict'.

Brian M. Murray contributes 'The Authorship of some Unidentified or Disputed Articles in *Blackwoods Magazine*' (*SSL*).

'All these documents reveal the *human* side of life' says E. Royston Pike of his two compilations[9]/[10] of extracts from nineteenth-century Government Reports and other sources. They are, he says 'the raw material of history', and this is true. Nevertheless it is questionable how useful such collections are today. Although many of the extracts are from sufficiently recondite sources, there is a depressing sameness about them all that makes their proliferation pointless. Social history has moved on, and these grim and endlessly repeated details are surely as familiar now as they ever need be. In

'The Radical Ideology of the "New Woman"' (*So R*) Lloyd Fernando discusses the background to the feminist movement in the latter part of the century, and how it was treated by certain novelists.

Marion Miliband's volume of extracts from *The Observer*[11] from 1791 to 1901 is, as Asa Briggs says in his short Introduction, merely 'one person's choice of extracts which catch the eye in the middle of the twentieth century'. A similar, though more restricted, anthology has been compiled by Leonard de Vries from the files of the *Illustrated London News*,[12] which, as Arthur Bryant points out in his Foreword, 'constitute what is probably the most important single pictorial source for the social history of any age or country'.

To commemorate the retirement of G. Kitson Clark, Robert Robson has edited a *Festschrift* of eleven essays on social history.[13] Some are general and others have a particular reference. Among the general essays G. F. A. Best writes on 'Popular Protestantism', commenting on 'the extraordinary wildness and nastiness into which even its more educated adherents ran'. Another Victorian attitude to religion is illustrated in 'The Atheistic Mission, 1840–1900', in which F. B. Smith outlines the Apostolic zeal of such men as Charles Southwell, Holyoake and Bradlaugh. In 'The Uses of Philology' J. W. Burrow relates the growth of philological scholarship to develop-

[8] *Mark Pattison and the Idea of a University*, by John Sparrow. C.U.P. pp. x+149. 30s. $5.50.

[9] *Human Documents of the Industrial Revolution*, ed. by E. Royston Pike. Allen and Unwin. pp. 368. 48s.

[10] *Human Documents of the Victorian Golden Age*, ed. by E. Royston Pike. Allen and Unwin. pp. 378. 48s.

[11] *The Observer of the Nineteenth Century 1791–1901: A Selection*, ed. by Marion Miliband. Longmans. pp. xii+296. 36s.

[12] *Panorama 1842–1865: The world of the early Victorians as seen through the eyes of the Illustrated London News*, ed. by L. de Vries. Murray. pp. 159. 45s.

[13] *Ideas and Institutions of Victorian Britain. Essays in Honour of George Kitson Clark*, ed. by Robert Robson. Bell. pp. viii+343. 63s.

ments in the anthropological and theological fields. The work of F. W. Farrar (later Dean), J. W. Donaldson, Baron Bunsen, and Max Müller is considered in these connexions in some detail. In direct contrast to Best's essay, a lecture by F. R. Selter on *Dissenters and Public Affairs in Mid-Victorian England* outlines the notable impact made by Nonconformists after some forty were elected to Parliament in 1852.[14]

The centenary of the Second Reform Bill brought two very different studies. Far less attention has been paid to the Second than to the First Reform Act, and literary students know it best, perhaps, as associated with the writing of *Culture and Anarchy* through the Hyde Park riots that preceded it. Arnold, says F. B. Smith in one of the books noticed here,[15] thus gave the riots a 'fortuitous notoriety', for they were not an important factor. Smith's book is a straightforward investigation of the defeat of Gladstone's similar proposals in 1866, and the reasons for Disraeli's success the following year. He sees the Act as part of an inevitable process by which institutions were adjusted to meet the emergence of a powerful working class. It was as part of this process, and not as the active pursuit of democracy, that the Conservatives espoused the cause of reform. Yet 'Disraeli, too, had his principles', and it was to defend his belief that the landed gentry 'underpinned British liberty' that he accepted the amendment that 'quadrupled the Ministry's intended enfranchisement', and so shot Niagara. In complete contrast, the other

book, by Maurice Cowling,[16] is a searching and specialized study. Cowling is less concerned with the reform movement generally, but concentrates on the manœuvring of the Parties, and of individuals within the Parties, between October 1865 and August 1867. For, he says, 'in the period under discussion new social forces did not make their impact directly'. Power lay with the political Parties, and the Reform Act was the result of their search for advantage.

Light is thrown on British diplomacy and colonialism from an unusual angle in *Send a Gunboat*, a history of the exploits of these ubiquitous vessels by Antony Poston and John Major.[17] Its main interest in the present chapter is the account given of the Jamaica Rebellion in 1865, and the subsequent controversy about Governor Eyre, notable for the acerbity it produced between Carlyle and Mill. Mill, Darwin, and Huxley favoured the 'Jamaica Committee', campaigning for Eyre's indictment. Carlyle, Ruskin, Tennyson, Dickens, and Kingsley were champions of the 'Eyre Defence Fund'. However, this was merely one of many episodes in which gunboats were embroiled, and which, whatever is thought of the policy they represented, produced much high adventure. Such adventures were the standby of the writers of boys' books, and R. M. Ballantyne, one of the most famous of these, is the subject of a biography by Eric Quayle[18] that has interest beyond his immediate concern. Ballantyne's father was a member of the printing family ruined

---

[14] *Dissenters and Public Affairs in Mid-Victorian England*, by F. R. Selter. Dr. Williams's Trust. pp. 24. 5s.

[15] *The Making of the Second Reform Bill*, by F. B. Smith. C.U.P. pp. 297. 55s. $10.50.

[16] *1867. Disraeli, Gladstone, and Revolution*, by Maurice Cowling. C.U.P. pp. x+451. 70s. $13.50.

[17] *Send a Gunboat*, by Antony Poston and John Major. Longmans. pp. xi+266. 50s.

[18] *Ballantyne the Brave. A Victorian Writer and his Family*, by Eric Quayle. Hart-Davis. pp. 316. 50s.

by Scott's insolvency in 1826. 'Christopher North' was a close friend, and the book has something to say about literary Edinburgh, as well as comment on the background to the stories themselves.

Since its publication in 1907 *William Allingham's Diary* has been a principal source of information and anecdote concerning the great men of the latter part of the century, and especially of Tennyson and Carlyle. It has now been republished with an Introduction by Geoffrey Grigson[19] in which he outlines Allingham's career and discusses his personality and qualities. Allingham was in some ways well-placed for his self-imposed task of recording conversations and noting the peculiarities of prominent men. His reputation as a minor poet, struggling in his post as a junior Customs official, secured him the introductions he sought, and thereafter his persistence and tenacity enabled him to consolidate his gains. Grigson comments rather wryly on his imperviousness to snubs, but we may be thankful for his determination, for to him we owe some of the most familiar impressions and revealing utterances of Tennyson, and, above all, of Carlyle, whom he propitiated with brose, and whose Boswell he aspired to be. In 1873 Allingham succeeded Froude on *Fraser's Magazine* and the scope of his observations widened to include politicians and such men of the moment as Huxley and Tyndall. Recording his own opinions as well as those of others, Allingham shows himself inclined, perhaps, to a rather partisan point of view; '*The Ring and the Book*— What a thing it is!' he exclaims. But his championship of Tennyson, his

hero, was equally uncompromising. The *Diary* has long been out of print, and the new edition is therefore opportune and welcome, the more so as it keeps the pagination of 1907, thus facilitating reference.

John Addington Symonds was a prolific letter-writer, and although many have vanished some two thousand of his letters are known to survive. The task of editing them has been undertaken by H. M. Schueller and R. L. Peters, who have produced the first, covering the years 1844–68[20], of three projected volumes. As they point out, the letters provide 'at once a portrait of an age and a richly detailed account of a Victorian writer's mind and career', although the present volume deals only with his time at Harrow and Balliol, and as a fellow of Magdalen. They have aimed at inclusiveness, and many of the items are mere notes. Others, particularly the weekly letter to his sister, are full and lively accounts of life in Oxford and elsewhere, with much comment on events and personalities. Many, such as those to Mrs. Clough, have an extrinsic interest and historical value, as do Symonds's narratives of certain special occasions, such as the long account of 'An Evening at Woolner's', with Tennyson, Gladstone, and Holman Hunt. The editing is impeccable, and exhaustive notes supplement the text. A recent biography (*YW* xlv. 295) emphasized Symonds's psychological distress; these early letters, however, present a very different figure.

In one of several books on William Morris, Paul Thompson[21] emphasizes the many-sided nature of his genius,

[19] *William Allingham's Diary*, ed. by H. A. Allingham and D. Radford, with an Introduction by Geoffrey Grigson. Centaur P. pp. xii+404. 105*s*.

[20] *The Letters of John Addington Symonds*. Vol. I. 1844–1868, ed. by Herbert M. Schueller and R. L. Peters. Wayne State U.P. pp. 867. $17.50.

[21] *The Work of William Morris*, by Paul Thompson. Heinemann. pp. xvi+300. 63*s*.

discussing each of his main activities in a separate chapter—architecture, furniture, wallpaper and tiles, textiles, stained glass, book-design, poetry, politics—the list seems endless, and in each department Morris's effort was prodigious, though his success and impact varied. His poetry has never received wholehearted acclaim; Thompson praises the 'new verse form, like stammering direct speech', but points out that Morris was quite insensitive to his own art, and owes most of his effects to accident. 'The dramatic opening of *Guinevere* was pure luck, due to a mistake by a printer who started with the second page of the manuscript.' Morris's designs present a different problem. In his study of *William Morris as Designer*[22] Ray Watkinson claims that, through his influence on Van de Velde, Gropius, and the *Bauhaus*, Morris had a direct influence on modern design. 'However much style may have changed, the thread runs unbroken from Morris to our own time', he says. Thompson does not entirely agree. Recent research, he says, has shown that 'Morris was closer to the best designers of his own period and less important in the evolution of the modern movement than had previously been thought.' But, whatever view is taken, books on Morris have an unfailing interest, especially when, like Watkinson's, they are superbly produced and lavishly illustrated. A third book on Morris, by Philip Henderson[23] has not been available for review. In *Country Life* E. Pemming-Rowsell writes on 'Kelmscott Manor Restored', and Andrew Von Hendy has a note on 'Histories and Flowers:

The Organic Unity of William Morris's Late Art' (*VN*).

In his lectures on *Victorian Artists*[24] Quentin Bell points out that the firm of Morris, Marshall, and Faulkner had 'a very decided influence on the art of painting, for it produced that reunion of the arts, that nineteenth-century style which we call . . . *Art Nouveau*'. Bell does not intend the book as an apology for Victorian painting, and among the works he discusses are, he says, some 'detestable paintings', which, nevertheless, have historical value. The main part of the book concerns, of course, the Pre-Raphaelites, beginning with the 'Teutonic influence' of the Nazarenes that inspired the Brotherhood, the techniques they evolved, the importance of Ruskin, and the movement 'from Rossetti to *Art Nouveau*'. The French affinities of the New English Art Club reversed the trend. There is a chapter on 'low art', and the book has a word on many painters now almost forgotten; for, says the author, 'the first duty of the historian is to exhibit the evidence'. One painter not quite forgotten is Luke Fildes, the illustrator of the later Dickens. His handling of *genre* and narrative painting gained him a reputation for social realism in his lifetime which persists to some extent to the present. His biography by his son L. V. Fildes,[25] not only gives a full account of the painting of his most famous canvases, but has much to tell about artistic circles in the latter part of the century.

2. POETRY AND DRAMA

There is no collected edition of Crabbe's poems in print, and a new

[22] *William Morris as Designer*, by Ray Watkinson. Studio Vista. pp. 84+89 plates. 70*s*.

[23] *William Morris: His Life, Work, and Friends*, by Philip Henderson. Thames & Hudson. pp. 388. 63*s*.

[24] *Victorian Artists*, by Quentin Bell. Routledge. pp. xiv+111+123 plates. 50*s*.

[25] *Luke Fildes, R. A. A Victorian Painter*, by L.V. Fildes. Michael Joseph. pp.xiv+241.42*s*.

volume, edited by Howard Mills[26] is therefore welcome. It comprises the *Tales* of 1812, two-thirds of *The Parish Register*, and nearly half of *The Borough*, which, with a few later poems including selections from *Tales of the Hall*, covers most of what he wrote after 1800. In a short Introduction Mills emphasizes the difference between the mode of *The Village* and that of the *Tales*. The earlier work belonged to the age of Johnson and Goldsmith, and Crabbe seemed to Campbell one of the 'giants before the flood'. But, with increasing misfortunes and difficulties, Crabbe's vision became more inward. *The Borough* is a transitional work, 'starting with general social surveys and ending with studies of individuals that lead us directly into the *Tales*'. Of these last, 'Peter Grimes' is the most original, and its originality 'does not lie in a new subject (sadism, nightmare, madness) but a new treatment', by which the objective narrative 'enforces' the inner tragedy. Crabbe was not a 'Romantic' poet; but he did learn from Wordsworth, and such poems as *Infancy* or *Silford Hall* are about the growth of a poet's mind. Nevertheless, Crabbe understood that he must 'find his own language', and avoid direct imitation.

The first volume of a chronology of Wordsworth's life and works has been compiled by Mark L. Reed.[27] It covers the years 1770–79, and two more volumes are in preparation. As Reed points out, the problem in preparing such a work is two-fold: that posed by the dearth of primary facts about certain periods, and that resulting from the wealth of general comment and speculation. Where the

latter kind of evidence is taken judgement in selection of material must be careful. Reed bases his decisions on the degree and quality of documentation available, rather than on the attractiveness of the theory proposed. He carefully weighs the evidence, or criticizes the conjecture, in either footnotes or Appendix, and one can have nothing but praise for the way in which the formidable task has been undertaken. The value of the work, which thus provides a readily accessible compendium of fact and theory about Wordsworth's life, will be sufficiently obvious. Two notable works on Wordsworth have been re-issued in new editions. They are: *The Letters of William and Dorothy Wordsworth: The Early Years 1797–1805*, edited by E. De Selincourt (1955), and now revised by Chester L. Shaver (O.U.P.), and *Wordsworth and Annette Vallon*, by Emile Legouis (1922), now revised by the author after forty-five years (Hamden, Conn., Archon Books). Mary Moorman writes on 'The True Portraiture of William Wordsworth' (*Cornell Library Journal*). In *NQ* C. L. Shaver prints *Three Unpublished Wordsworth Letters*, and D. B. Owen makes an 'Identification of an Allusion in a Wordsworth Letter'. David Bonnell Green prints 'A New Letter to John Taylor: Wordsworth and the Westmoreland Election of 1818' (*MLR*). In 'Stranger in a Strange Land' (*MQ*), M. Montgomery discusses 'Wordsworth in England, 1802'.

In *JEGP* J. A. Finch writes on '*The Ruined Cottage* Restored: Three Stages of Composition, 1795–1798'. C. J. Rawson finds a parallel between '*Tom Jones* and *Michael*' (*NQ*). Barbara Garlitz writes on 'The *Immortality Ode*: Its Cultural Progeny' (*SEL*). In 'The Hewing of *Peter Bell*' (*SEL*) J. E. Jordan studies Wordsworth's revisions in the manuscripts.

---

[26] *Tales, 1812, and Other Selected Poems,* by George Crabbe, ed. by Howard Mills. C.U.P. pp. xxxviii+445. 50s. $9.50.

[27] *Wordsworth: The Chronology of the Early Years,* by Mark L. Reed. Harvard U.P. pp. xi+369. $9.

James A. Jefferson relates passages of *The Prelude* to Burke's categories in 'Wordsworth and the Sublime: The Quest for Interfusion' (*SEL*). D. Ross comments on '*The Prelude* VIII' in *ANQ*. In 'Arcadia Re-Settled: Pastoral Poetry and Romantic Theory' (*SEL*) J. Stevenson shows that to Wordsworth and the Romantics the Golden Age was in the future. Alan Grob writes on 'Wordsworth and Godwin: a Reassessment' (*SIR*).

Making a study of *Wordsworth's Style* Roger Murray[28] examines some poems in the second edition of *Lyrical Ballads* in order to 'demonstrate to some degree how delicately Wordsworth's language responds at the level of grammar and diction to the pulse of feeling'. More than this, he shows how Wordsworth's use of language reflects his insight into 'the life of things'. For example, something of what Wordsworth meant by this expression is revealed by his use of the intransitive verb. The application of this construction to inanimate objects faintly suggests personification, but at the same time it emphasizes the particularity, the 'otherness' of the object. Wordsworth thus avoided the too facile anthropomorphism of much eighteenth-century personification, while yet preserving a vitalist conception. Applied to people, the intransitive use of the verb has something of the opposite effect, for, as in the case of the Leechgatherer for example, it suggests their kinship with 'enduring objects'. Change to the transitive use immediately reverses the effect. 'The only truly abstract thing in Wordsworth is that speechless, imageless moment of pure feeling that . . . occupies the pauses of the poem, its silences', says Murray, and this is the theme of

'Statement by Omission: The Case of *The Prelude*' (*EC*), in which K. Rayan argues that Wordsworth describes the circumstances of an experience and draws conclusions from it, but is silent about the nature of the experience itself. James A. Heffernan writes in *PMLA* on 'Wordsworth and Dennis: The Discrimination of Feelings'. Also in *PMLA* Robert Langbaum discusses 'The Evolution of Soul in Wordsworth's Poetry' in terms of Locke and Hartley. S. C. Gill examines 'Wordsworth's "Never Failing Principle of Joy"' (*ELH*). There is an essay on 'The Preface to *Lyrical Ballads*: A Revolution in Dispute' by J. Scroggins in *Studies in Criticism and Aesthetics: 1660–1800*, edited by A. Howard and J. S. Shea (Minneapolis U.P.). *Wordsworth: A Philosophical Approach*, by Melvin Rader (O.U.P.) has not been available.

The publication of Coleridge's *Notebooks* has brought new evidence of the state of his mind in the decade 1795 to 1804, and this is used by Geoffrey Yarlott in his interpretation of the poetry.[29] 'It is relevant,' he argues, 'to a full understanding of *The Ancient Mariner* that the *life-as-a-voyage* image at its centre has stood as a personal symbol for Coleridge since childhood.' Sometimes Yarlott appears to use the poem to reveal the man, instead of vice versa ('Because the mariner's imagined feelings lay so close to the subliminal sources of the poet's own imagination he was able to express them with startling vivacity'). However, the analysis of the poems is very thorough, and by tracing parallel images from poem to poem he is able to support suggestions of the value certain expressions had for Coleridge. Thus, 'pleasure'

---

[28] *Wordsworth's Style. Figures and Themes in the Lyrical Ballads of 1800*, by R. N. Murray. Nebraska U.P. pp. ix+166. $4.75.

[29] *Coleridge and the Abyssinian Maid*, by Geoffrey Yarlott. London: Methuen. N.Y.: Barnes & Noble. pp. xvi+333. 53s.

evidently bore overtones of moral stricture, and 'stately' or 'bright' suggested artificiality. Kubla's Pleasure-Dome was thus something garish and dead, and not a symbol of creative art, which is represented by the 'shadow-dome', the 'miracle of rare device' mentioned fleetingly in contrast to Kubla's own. Two aspects of Coleridge's character are developed in the book; his need for 'sheet-anchor' friendship, and his uncertain attitude towards women. The chapters concerned with *Dejection* and Sara Hutchinson are particularly interesting. The book ends with a consideration of Coleridge's attitude to the doctrine of 'the whole man'.

William Walsh's study of the poet[30] proceeds on the different lines of an inquiry into the relationship of his various activities. 'Coleridge was a critic with a poet inside him and a philosopher on his back,' says Walsh, and he reviews this composite figure in the three main sections of the book. In the first he is concerned with the 'genuine criticism' as distinct from the 'applied metaphysics', and he examines a number of passages to emphasize the distinction. The essential problem in criticism, says Walsh, 'is that of moving from the particular response to the relevant judgement and back again'. To Coleridge this problem was unusually acute because of his tendency to 'topple into the disaster of abstraction'. Nevertheless, his responses and judgements were usually sound and penetrating. Turning to 'Coleridge and poetry', Walsh sees Coleridge's 'conversational' poems as 'a truly original and independent achievement'. The 'poems of magic', on the other hand, appear to him as examples of 'a traditional

habit'. On Coleridge's abstruser musings Walsh sees his originality in his realization that a new direction must be taken. He was an 'a-political innocent'; yet his political notions were, in his lifetime, an influence in both Europe and America. Walsh ends with a discussion of Coleridge's theory of education, and this aspect is also examined by N. Sinclair in 'Coleridge and Education' (*QQ*). M. J. Kelly writes on 'Coleridge and Dream Phenomenology' (*Massachusetts Studies in English*). Two essays on Coleridge's metaphysics appear in *Friendship's Garland: Essays Presented to Mario Praz,* edited by Vittorio Gabrielli. They are 'Coleridge on Reason and Understanding', by E. Chinol, and 'Coleridge, Fichte, and "Original Apperception"', by G. G. Orsini. D. Keppel-Jones writes on 'Coleridge's Scheme of Reason' in *Literary Monographs,* edited by Eric Rothstein and T. K. Dunseath (Wisconsin U.P.). D. Stempel discusses 'Coleridge and Organic Form: The English Tradition' (*SIR*).

C. G. Martin gives 'A Corrected Text and a Final Version of Coleridge's *Lines to Thelwell*' (*SB*), and in *NQ* he publishes 'An Unpublished Coleridge Letter' and 'Sara Coleridge: An Unpublished Letter'. P. M. Zall examines 'Coleridge's Unpublished Revision of *Osorio*' and discusses 'Sam Spitfire; or Coleridge in *The Satirist*' (both *BNYPL*). In *Cornell Library Journal* Zall writes on 'Coleridge and *Sonnets from Various Authors*'. In 'Coleridge and William Crowe's *Lewesdon Hill*' (*MLR*) C. G. Martin suggests that the poem, referred to in *Biographia Literaria,* influenced *Reflections on having Left a Place of Retirement.* E. San Juan sees 'Coleridge's *The Eolian Harp* as Lyric Paradigm' (*Person*). Maren-Sofie Røstvig writes on '*The Rime of*

---

[30] *Coleridge: The Work and the Relevance,* by William Walsh. Chatto & Windus. pp. 217. 30s.

the *Ancient Mariner* and the Cosmic System of Robert Fludd' (*TSL*), and J. A. Stuart sees 'The Augustinian "Cause of Action" in Coleridge's *Rime of the Ancient Mariner*' (*HTR*). H. H. Meier writes on 'Xanaduvian Residues' (*ES*), and J. Ower discovers 'Another Analogue in Coleridge's *Kubla Khan*' (*NQ*). D. M. Hassler writes on 'Coleridge, Darwin, and the Dome' (*Serif*). In *UR* J. S. Simmons sees Coleridge's *Dejection: An Ode* as 'A Poet's Regeneration'.

E. Sewell has an essay on 'Coleridge: The Method and the Poetry' in *The Poet as Critic*, edited by F. P. W. McDowell (Northwestern U.P.) *Coleridge: A Collection of Critical Essays*, edited by Kathleen Coburn (Prentice-Hall) has not been available for comment.

Kenneth Curry's edition of Southey's letters (*YW* xlvi. 263) is supplemented by 'The Published Letters of Robert Southey: A Checklist' (*BNYPL*). In *NQ* C. G. Martin prints 'Robert Southey: Two Unpublished Letters'.

A brief survey of the life and work of Thomas Moore by Miriam Allen deFord mentions most of his activities and makes short but pertinent comment on his works.[31]

Byron studies were confined to *Childe Harold* and *Don Juan*. K. A. Bruffee writes on 'The Synthetic Hero and the Narrative Structure of *Childe Harold* III' (*SEL*), and J. J. McGann examines 'The Composition, Revision, and Meaning of *Childe Harold's Pilgrimage* III' (*BNYPL*). To 'Routledge English Texts', a series designed for the close study of selected works, the general editor, T. S. Dorsch, has added an edition of the first four Cantos of *Don Juan*, with Notes and an Introduction giving historical and biographical information and a brief

critical comment.[32] C. W. Hagelman, W. Charles, and R. J. Barnes have edited *A Concordance to Byron's Don Juan* (Cornell U.P.). In *NQ* J. D. Jump traces 'Literary Echoes in Byron's *Don Juan*', and H. T. Keenan finds 'Another *Hudibras* allusion in Byron's *Don Juan*', H. C. Maxwell has a note on '*Academician*' referring to *Don Juan* IX 17, and also notes 'More Literary Echoes in *Don Juan*'. R. M. Brownstein writes on 'Byron's *Don Juan*, some Reasons for the Rhymes' (*MLQ*), and in 'Irony Anew, with Occasional Reference to Byron and Browning' (*SEL*) C. Kemper comments on *Don Juan* and *Fifine at the Fair*. T. G. Steffan prints 'Some 1813 Byron Letters' in *KSJ*, and 'Another Doubtful Byron Letter' in *NQ*. T. W. Lombardi prints 'Hogg to Byron to Davenport: An Unpublished Byron Letter' (*BNYPL*). E. L. Brooks contributes 'Two Notes on Byron' (*NQ*).

Although Seymour Reiter includes biography in his study of Shelley[33] only because 'it is necessary to do so to clear the way to Shelley's poetry', this aspect of his book is of more interest than what he calls 'the critical issue'. For he follows Shelley's productive years both chronologically and circumstantially, and relates each poem to its background in a scholarly fashion, bringing together a great deal of information from various sources, and assessing the conjectures of earlier biographers with a judicious eye. The criticism is less interesting. Much space is given to mere summary and in glossing words; references are vague and there are no notes.

The 'reply' in 'Coleridge and

---

[31] *Thomas More*, by Miriam Allen deFord. N.Y.: Twayne. pp. 128.

[32] *Don Juan, Cantos I-IV*, by Lord Byron. Ed. by T. S. Dorsch. Routledge, pp. xxxvi + 169. 18s.

[33] *A Study of Shelley's Poetry*, by Seymour Reiter. New Mexico U.P. pp. xii + 335. $8.85.

Shelley's *Alastor*: A Reply', by T. Webb (*RES*), is to an article by Joseph Raben (*YW* xlvii. 263) emphasizing the influence of *Kubla Khan* on *Alastor*. B. R. Pollin writes on '*Ozymandias* and the Dormouse' (*DR*). In 'Roman Scenes in *Prometheus Unbound* III iv' (*PQ*) D. H. Reiman discusses the origins of some symbolic features in the scene. Eben Bass discusses 'The Fourth Element in *Ode to the West Wind*' (*PLL*). In 'Shelley on Wordsworth: Two Unpublished Stanzas of *Peter Bell the Third*' (*EC*) F. W. Bateson finds support for his well-known theory about Wordsworth and Dorothy. J. D. Margolis finds an echo of *King Lear* in 'Shakespeare and Shelley's Sonnet *England in 1819*' (*ELN*). In 'Shelley's *The Boat on the Serchio*: The Evidence of the Manuscript' (*PQ*) J. Raben suggests that fragments associated with *Rosalind and Helen* were incorporated when Mary Shelley edited the poem. S. R. Swaminathan has a note on 'Shelley's *Triumph of Life*' (*NQ*). In *KSJ* Irving Massey discusses 'The First Edition of Shelley's *Poetical Works* (1839). Some Manuscript Sources', and D. G. Halliburton writes on 'Shelley's "Gothic" Novels'.

Two volumes of Shelley's prose reflect interest in his critical and intellectual opinions. The first is a reissue of David Lee Clark's edition of all Shelley's surviving prose, which first appeared in 1954.[34] Clark's aim was to dispose of two misconceptions: that Shelley was an ineffectual angel, and that he was a radical atheist. His intention was to illustrate the growth of Shelley's mind, and he outlines the stages of this growth in his Introduction. There are copious notes to the text, and each excerpt is introduced by a short Preface. The second book, edited by Bruce R. McElderry,[35] is restricted to Shelley's criticism, and has an Introduction expounding his ideas and commenting on them.

Margaret Crompton's study of *Shelley's Dream Women*[36] covers a great deal of his biography. Only the poetry is omitted—although casual mention is made from time to time of what he was writing. Nevertheless the book is absorbing in its detail, and in the skill with which the evidence is marshalled. Nothing new is added, but the author's assessment of the many theories and opinions that have been voiced about what is mysterious in Shelley's life—about Harriet's fate, for example—adopts, one feels, the reasonable as well as the charitable view. The final part deals with events after Shelley's death until that of Mary in 1851. Also concerned with this period is B. R. Pollin who, in '*Mary Shelley as The Parvenue*' (*REL*) relates her tale 'The Parvenue' in *The Keepsake* (1837) to the circumstances of her life after Shelley's death.

The second (revised) edition of *Shelley at Work* by Neville Rogers has been published by O.U.P. *The Mutiny Within: The Heresies of Percy Bysshe Shelley*, by J. Rieger, is published by Geo. Braziller (N.Y.).

The text of *Shelley, or the Idealist: A Tragi-Comedy* by Ann Jellicoe[37] has been published. This three-act biography is about 'the nature of goodness'.

Keats's biography has for the moment reached saturation point. In

---

[34] *Shelley's Prose: or The Trumpet of a Prophecy*, ed. by David Lee Clark. New Mexico U.P. pp. 385. $3.

[35] *Shelley's Critical Prose*, edited by Bruce R. McElderry. Nebraska U.P. pp. xxiii+183. $5.95 ($2.25 Paperback).

[36] *Shelley's Dream Women*, by Margaret Crompton. Cassell. pp. 301. 42s.

[37] *Shelley, or The Idealist: A Tragi-Comedy*, by Ann Jellicoe. Faber. pp. 111. 16s.

a short but illuminating study of the poet Douglas Bush[38] acknowledges that he does little more than provide a gloss to the work of others, notably that of W. J. Bate (*YW* xliv. 274): but the effect of his scholarly judgement is to bring the story into focus with the poems. Examining these, Bush is most revealing in his outline of the development of Keats's art, and the works that appear to have influenced him at different stages, with 'probable, or possible, literary echoes', and the implications to be drawn from them. In criticism Bush is no less penetrating, though sometimes a little difficult to go along with. It seems inconceivable, for example, that Keats intended to say 'Cool Pastoral', and that 'Cold' was a Freudian slip. The book ends with a summary of the growth of Keats's reputation. A different though similarly brief study by Robin Mayhead[39] carefully avoids the biographical approach, and deals with the poems and letters 'as literary works which are interesting and worthy of detailed scrutiny in themselves'. The treatment of the letters thus, in a separate section, emphasizes their own quality, and yet it does not (nor could it) isolate them from Keats's life and poetry. Starting with Keats's 'sustained interest in all forms of art as subject matter for his poems', Mario D'Avanzo has produced a study of *Keats's Metaphors for the Poetic Imagination*[40] pointing out that 'when read with a full understanding of Keats's metaphors, the poetry reveals depths of meaning hitherto unexplored'. But although a large number of Keats's metaphors are

traced from poem to poem, it cannot be said that the book reaches any such depths. However, D'Avanzo offers interesting interpretations of certain poems, notably *La Belle Dame* and *Ode to Psyche*.

In 'Classicism in Keats's Chapman Sonnet' (*EC*) Garry Wills argues that the 'stilted' classicism of the octave is an apt foil for the 'romantic' sweep of the sestet. In *Literary Monographs* Stuart M. Sperry makes a study of 'Richard Woodhouse's Interleaved and Annotated Copy of Keats's *Poems* (*1817*)'. On *Endymion*, M. D'Avanzo writes on 'Keats's and Virgil's Underworld: Source and Meaning in Book II of *Endymion*' (*KSJ*); B. Chatterjee finds 'Echoes of Cary's Dante in *Endymion*' (*NQ*), and A. Lombardo writes on '*Endymion* e l'esperienza poetica' in *Studi e ricerche di letteratura inglese* (Milan). In 'Keats and Baldwin's *Pantheon*' (*MLR*) Alan Osler points out that 'Baldwin' was William Godwin, and suggests that the book was used in *Endymion* and *Hyperion*. Giving an account of the Pindaric tradition in England, I. A. Gordon, in 'Keats and the English Pindaric' (*REL*), argues that this, rather than the sonnet, was the origin of Keats's ode form. Three articles make studies of the *Ode on Melancholy*: R. Rogers contributes 'Keats's "Strenuous Tongue"': A Study of *Ode on Melancholy*' (*L & P*), B. H. Smith writes on '"Sorrow's Mysteries"': Keat's *Ode on Melancholy*' (*SEL*), and G. L. Little comments on 'Keats's *Ode on Melancholy*' (*Ex*). In *NQ* J. C. Maxwell has notes on 'Porphyro as "Famished Pilgrim"', and '*Hyperion* and *Rejected Addresses*'. H. D. Purcell suggests 'The Probable Origin of a Line in Keats's *Ode to a Nightingale*', J.-C. Sallé compares 'Shakespeare's *Sonnet 27* and Keats's *Bright Star*', and S. R. Swaminathan

[38] *John Keats*, by Douglas Bush. Weidenfeld and Nicolson. pp. 224. 21*s*.
[39] *John Keats*, by Robin Mayhead. C.U.P. pp. 127. 17*s*. 6*d*.
[40] *Keats's Metaphors for the Poetic Imagination*, by Mario L. D'Avanzo. Duke U.P. pp. xii +232. $7.50.

has a note on 'Keats's *Epistle to John Hamilton Reynolds*, Line 14'. In *KSJ* C. Olney writes on 'Keats as John Foster's "Man of Decision"', D. Ormerod discusses '"Nature's Eremite": Keats and the Liturgy of Passion', and D. E. Robinson considers 'A Question of the Imprint of Wedgwood in the Longer Poems of Keats'. In 'Dreamer, Poet, and Poem in *The Fall of Hyperion*' (*PQ*) I. H. Chayes examines the poem in some detail.

A collection of *Critics on Keats*, by Judith O'Neill,[41] begins with short extracts from three 'historical' essays—Lockhart's 'The Cockney School of Poetry', Croker's review of *Endymion*, and Matthew Arnold's essay of 1880. The remaining fourteen extracts suggest the trend of criticism of Keats during the past twenty years, and include passages from Middleton Murry, Lionel Trilling, F. R. Leavis, and Cleanth Brooks.

Several general works on the Romantic poets and Romanticism may be mentioned here. *Backgrounds of Romanticism*, a collection by Leonard Trawick[42] of eight excerpts from eighteenth-century critical and epistemological treatises must find a place not only because these works, or most of them, were read by the poets, but also because the origins of Romanticism in the strong undercurrents of the Enlightenment cannot be too often illustrated. The excerpts include passages from William Law, Berkeley, and Hartley, as well as from William Duff, Abraham Tucker, and Jacob Bryant, whose *Analysis of Antient Mythology* may have influenced Coleridge. Each extract has a brief comment by the compiler, and there is a useful annotated bibliography.

A. K. Thorlby has contributed a volume on *The Romantic Movement*[43] to a series designed to 'study problems in preference to periods' in history. Compiled from the writings of well-known critics, the main section of the book is in three parts: 'The Nominalistic Confusion', with extracts from A. O. Lovejoy, René Wellek, and others; 'The Attempt to Evaluate: Sickness or Health', illustrated from Nietzsche, Croce, Irving Babbitt, F. L. Lucas, and others; and 'The Romantic Period Outside Literature'. There are a number of 'Select Documents'—short excerpts from appropriate sources. In his Introduction Thorlby sees the weakness of Romanticism in its 'seeking the true self by relation not to society but to nature'. In *Eros and the Romantics*[44] Gerald Enscoe sees the whole thing in sexual terms, and interprets it on what are now conventional lines. *Kubla Khan* 'recognizes in almost Freudian terms' the tumult produced by repressed eroticism; Geraldine performed a notable service to Christabel, who 'must be corrupted in order to exist in a corrupt world'. And so on.

Graham Hough's *The Romantic Poets*, first published in 1953, has been reissued in paper covers.[45] A good deal has been done in this field in the last fifteen years, but Hough has contented himself with making some additions to the book lists at the end. The book remains what it always was, a useful general introduction to the criticism and poetry

[41] *Critics on Keats*, ed. by Judith O'Neill. Allen & Unwin. pp. 115. 10*s*. 6*d*.

[42] *Backgrounds of Romanticism*, ed. by Leonard M. Trawick. Indiana U.P. pp. xxvii+221. 51*s*.

[43] *The Romantic Movement*, ed. by A. K. Thorlby. Longmans (1966). pp. 176. 12*s*. 6*d*.

[44] *Eros and the Romantics*, by Gerald Enscoe. The Hague: Mouton. pp. 178. 20 Guilders.

[45] *The Romantic Poets*, by Graham Hough. Hutchinson. pp. 200. 10*s*. 6*d*.

of the period. E. Bernhadt Kabisch makes a survey of 'The Epitaph and the Romantic Poets' (*HLQ*).

Eric Robinson and Geoffrey Summerfield continue their work on Clare (*YW* xlv. 303–4) with a selection from his poetry and prose.[46] In their Introduction they question why Clare, 'a great poet', still lacks the recognition long accorded to others no more worthy. Clare was accused (by Middleton Murry) of wanting 'the principle of inward growth which gives to Wordsworth's most careless work a place within the unity of a great scheme'. But 'recognition of Clare's efforts to comprehend his experience in a scheme of imagery' would have come more readily had not critics been preoccupied with his rusticity. Nevertheless, it is Clare's 'awareness of his own landscape, the directness with which he always sees places of his childhood' that makes the most immediate appeal in these pieces, and his awareness of change gives them poignancy. Here, as the editors point out, the poems are unique, for 'his is almost the only voice that can still be heard from the otherwise silent peasantry of the enclosure years'. Ian Jack has an essay on 'The Poetry of Clare's Sanity' in *Patterns of Love and Courtesy: Essays in Memory of C. S. Lewis*, edited by John Lawlor (Arnold, 1966). David Bonnell Green prints some 'New Letters of John Clare to Taylor and Hussey' (*SP*)

In 'The Three Modes in Tennyson's Prosody' (*PMLA*) A. Ostriker says that 'from 1830 to 1842 Tennyson was composing in three distinct modes'. These were the 'irregular, or ode', the 'stanzaic', and 'sustained' verse. Clarice Short argues in 'Tenny-

son and The Lover's Tale' (*PMLA*) that Boccaccio provided 'but a shadow to the substance of young Alfred Tennyson's personal experience' when the poem was written in 1833. A. P. Antippas refers to Hallam's sonnet *Long hast thou wandered on the happy mountain* in 'Tennyson, Hallam, and *The Palace of Art*' (*VP*). Also in *VP* Alice Chandler writes of autobiographical elements in Lady Clara in 'Cousin Clara Vere de Vere'. In 'The Transcendentalist Problem in Tennyson's Poetry of Debate' (*PQ*) W. D. Shaw discusses *The Two Voices, In Memoriam*, and *The Ancient Sage*, emphasizing that 'one of Tennyson's abiding concerns is how the idealist can act on the basis of *a priori* categories which are merely subjective'. W. Schmiefsky, writing on '*In Memoriam*: Its Seasonal Imagery Reconsidered' (*SEL*), discusses the 'two linked archetypal metaphors, the Heaven-and-Hell type, and the Rebirth type' in the poem. J. Sendry discusses '*In Memoriam* and *Lycidas*' (*PMLA*), arguing that Tennyson followed Milton to a greater, rather than to a less, extent. In *L & P* S. R. Weiner writes on 'The Chord of Self: Tennyson's *Maud*'. *Idylls of the King* attract much attention. W. D. Shaw, in another metaphysical inquiry, 'The Idealist's Dilemma in Tennyson's *Idylls of the King*' (*VP*) discusses the function of Arthur in resolving the problem 'how to have "power on this dead world" without compromising his ideals'. R. Adicks writes on the colour symbolism in 'The Lily Maid and the Scarlet Sleeve' (*UR*). Lawrence Poston considers 'The Two Provinces of Tennyson's *Idylls*' (*Criticism*); H. H. Wilson writes on 'Tennyson: Unscholarly Arthurian' (*VN*); and Clyde de L. Ryals discusses '*Idylls of the King*: Tennyson's New Realism' (*VN*). His volume of

---

[46] *Selected Poetry and Prose of John Clare*, ed. by Eric Robinson and Geoffrey Summerfield. O.U.P. pp. xxxviii+214. 35s.

essays on *Idylls of the King*[47] has not been available for comment. There are notes on 'Tennyson and Hegel on War' by R. W. Noland (*VN*), and 'Tennyson and Geoffrey of Monmouth' by J. M. Gray (*NQ*). J. Solimine writes on 'The Burkean Idea of the State in Tennyson's Poetry: The Vision in Crisis' (*HLQ*). J. H. Buckley writes on 'Tennyson's Irony' (*VN*).

The volume on Tennyson is probably one of the most pertinent in the 'Critical Heritage' series of collected reviews of nineteenth-century authors. Not only did everyone write about Tennyson, but he himself was greatly influenced by their opinions of his poems. This selection, compiled by J. D. Jump,[48] comprises thirty-five complete essays or articles, and includes those of Hallam, 'Christopher North', Croker, Mill, Kingsley, Brimley, Gladstone, Arnold, Hopkins, Swinburne, and many others. Though often severe in their censure of Tennyson, their effect on one reading them today is, curiously, to increase his stature; for it is clear that his contemporaries often failed to approach him. 'Perhaps,' says Jump, 'we can learn something from commentators whose assumptions are very different from our own.' A good many of the essays were contributions to the debates that flourished in Victorian monthlies, and we thus have the benefit of several views on a single question, and a cumulative commentary. The best example of this is in Taine's essay (No. 21) and Swinburne's reply (No. 29), with R. H. Hutton's very thoughtful reply to him (No. 31). Apart from its great value to Tennyson studies, the volume

is a compendium of Victorian critical attitudes. A note on Tennyson's own attitude to criticism of his verse is given by H. P. Sucksmith in 'Tennyson on the Nature of his Own Poetic Genius' (*RMS*), in which he examines some marginalia by Tennyson on an article by J. Churton Collins. E. E. Smith continues the account of the poet's reception in 'Tennyson Criticism, 1923–1966' (*VN*). An extremely useful adjunct to this aspect of Tennyson studies is an Annotated Bibliography prepared by Sir Charles Tennyson and Christine Falls.[49] Their aim has been to assist research, and therefore introductory works have not been included. Tennyson's own publications, other than editions containing useful editorial matter or fragments and poems not included in the collected editions, have also been omitted as have many of the contemporary reviews. However, influential items in this latter category, especially those relating to the dramas, have been included, and very wide coverage is given to subsequent works. The list is divided into useful sections to facilitate reference, and the annotations are both interesting and helpful. This little book will be an invaluable aid to researchers and others interested in the poet.

In his study of Browning's 'Moral-Aesthetic Theory'[50] T. J. Collins is not very much concerned with the theory itself, which he quaintly expresses in current jargon as 'a conscious belief in the man-God synthesis of Christ', but his examination of the early poems is of some interest. These poems also occupy an unduly large part of the volume on Browning contributed by Ioan M.

---

[47] *From the Great Deep: Essays on Idylls of the King*, by Clyde de L. Ryals. Ohio U.P. pp. xii+204.

[48] *Tennyson. The Critical Heritage*, ed. by J. D. Jump. London: Routledge. N.Y.: Barnes & Noble. pp. x+464. 50s.

[49] *Alfred Tennyson: An Annotated Bibliography*, by Sir Charles Tennyson and Christine Falls. Georgia U.P. pp. viii+126. $6.

[50] *Robert Browning's Moral-Aesthetic Theory 1833–1855*, by Thomas J. Collins. Nebraska U.P. pp. x+164. $5.50.

Williams to the 'Literature in Perspecive' series,[51] which apart from this imbalance, is a workmanlike survey. Less acceptable is a patronizing book by Thomas Blackburn,[52] who is prepared to tolerate only a very few of the poems. He gives no cogent reason for his discrimination, but believes that the fact that he exercises it has 'some special relevance' to the present time, implying that the chosen poems are more 'modern' than the rest. Browning's modernity is also the theme of Edward Lucie-Smith's much more thoughtful Introduction to his selection of Browning's poetry.[53] But whereas Blackburn regards modernity as a virtue in itself Lucie-Smith convincingly argues that there has been a serious decline in certain directions since Browning's time. It is interesting to note that his *Choice* includes poems that Blackburn expressly rejects.

In 'Browning's Last Lost Duchess: A Purview' (*VP*) R. F. Fleissner makes a plea for the Duke. J. Solimine comments on 'Browning's *My Last Duchess*' in *Ex*. Christopher Ricks finds 'An Echo of Tennyson in Browning' (*NQ*), an echo of *The Princess* in *Childe Roland*. R. E. Sullivan sees parallels between 'Browning's *Childe Roland* and Dante's *Inferno*' (*VP*). In *PLL* L. M. Thompson discusses 'Biblical Influence in *Childe Roland to the Dark Tower Came*', and R. D. Altick writes on 'Lovers' Finiteness: Browning's *Two in Campagna*' in the same journal. J. McNally contributes a note on 'Suiting Sight and Sound to Sense in *Meeting at Night* and *Parting*

at Morning' (*VP*), and in 'Blue Spurt of a Lighted Match' (*QR*) W. M. Parker discusses the kind of match Browning referred to in this line from *Meeting at Night*. There are two articles on *A Grammarian's Funeral* in *VP*. In 'Dactyls and Curlews: Satire in *A Grammarian's Funeral*' R. L. Kelly argues that the students, not the Grammarian, are the objects of the poem's satire, for they 'are absurdly unaware that the very rhythm of their speech discloses their aesthetic mediocrity'. M. J. Svaglic, on the other hand, argues that the poem should be read with straightforward reference to 'its Platonic dialectic' in 'Browning's Grammarian: Apparent Failure or Real?'. Also in *VP* R. L. Slakey points out, in 'A Note on Browning's *Rabbi Ben Ezra*' that the poem is part of a sermon. J. L. Winter comments on 'Browning's Piper' in *NQ*. In *UTQ* J. Grube writes on 'Browning's *The King*', and R. Gridley discusses 'Browning's Two Guidos'. In 'Another View of *Fifine at the Fair*' (*EC*) Philip Drew comments on Barbara Melchiori's article (*YW* xlvii. 266). In 'Robert Browning's Courtship and the Meditation of Monsieur Leonce Miranda' (*VP*) Barbara Melchiori adds a short note on *Red Cotton Nightcap Country*. R. R. Columbus and C. Kemper discuss 'Browning's Fuddling Apollo, or The Perils of Parleying' (*TSL*), referring to *Apollo and the Fates* and *Fust and His Friends*. In *Cithara* Boyd Litzinger writes on 'Browning's Measure of Man'. It is regretted that the first volume of Maisie Ward's biography of Browning, *Robert Browning and His World: The Private Face. 1812–1861* has not been available for comment.

A descriptive list of the collection of manuscripts and printed books relating to Browning in Texas has

[51] *Robert Browning*, by Ioan M. Williams. Evans. pp. 160. 7s. 6d.

[52] *Robert Browning. A Study of his Poetry*, by Thomas Blackburn. Eyre & Spottiswoode. pp. 210. 35s.

[53] *A Choice of Browning's Verse*, selected by Edward Lucie-Smith. Faber & Faber. pp. 166. 9s. 6d.

been compiled by Warner Barnes,[54] who complains that this collection, the largest in the United States, has been neglected by scholars. If this is so it is a pity, for the evidence exists there to correct certain misconceptions which have persisted since they were started by T. J. Wise. Two hundred and twenty-two unpublished letters are listed here with numerous manuscripts of both Robert and Elizabeth. As Barnes says, 'all Browning's letters, published and unpublished, should be assembled and furnished with a full critical apparatus . . . a variorum study should be made of Elizabeth's poems, reporting all the textual variants and cancelled lines found in these manuscripts'. Park Honan gives the whereabouts of 'The Texts of Fifteen Fugitives by Robert Browning' (*VP*). R. W. Gladish writes on 'Mrs. Browning's Contributions to the New York *Independent*' (*BNYPL*), and F. C. Thomson prints 'Elizabeth Barrett Browning on Spiritualism: A New Letter' (*VN*).

The 'Variorum and Definitive Edition' of *The Poetical and Prose Writings of Edward Fitzgerald*, with an Introduction by Edmund Gosse, originally published in seven volumes in 1902–3, has been reprinted by the Phaeton Press (N.Y.). F. R. Bagley writes on 'Omar Khayyam and Fitzgerald' (*DUJ*).

Romantic Mythologies, a collection of eight essays on nineteenth-century topics, compiled by Ian Fletcher,[55] includes R. A. Forsyth's interesting discussion of Barnes's *Views of Labour and Gold* (*YW* xliv. 276), 'The Conserving Myth of William Barnes'.

A descriptive catalogue of works by and about Clough has been compiled by R. M. Gollin, Walter E. Houghton, and Michael Timko.[56] It is in three parts; the first, by Gollin, deals with Clough's poetry, and lists thirty-seven unpublished items, as well as published poems and collections. Part two, by Houghton, deals with the prose, including unpublished work, and part three, by Timko, is on biography and criticism. Frederick Bowers writes on 'Arthur Hugh Clough: The Modern Mind' (*SEL*). In *NQ* W. V. Harris refers to 'The Curious Provenance of Clough's *Longest Day*', P. G. Scott writes on 'The Text and Structure of Clough's *The Latest Decalogue*', and J. K. Stubbs prints 'An Unpublished Letter of A. H. Clough'.

In his study of Arnold's poetry and prose William A. Madden[57] says 'For all his Hebraism, Arnold was a Romantic in the historical sense of that term, in the direct line of the tradition which holds the creative, unifying power of art above other forms of consciousness'. Later perspectives, he says, have tended to represent Arnold's poetry as more 'moralistic' than in fact it is. 'Arnold's morality needs to be interpreted within the context both of his mid-Victorian environment and of his aesthetic temperament and training.' In other words, Matthew's belief that poetry should be a *magister vitae* was strongly at variance with Dr Arnold's ethical teaching, and so a source of tension. Madden classifies the poems as 'poems of nostalgia', 'dialogue poems', and 'meta-poems', or those

---

[54] *Catalogue of the Browning Collection. The University of Texas*, ed. by Warner Barnes. Texas U.P. (1966). pp. 120. $7.50.

[55] *Romantic Mythologies*, ed. by Ian Fletcher. Routledge. pp. xiii+297. 50s.

[56] *Arthur Hugh Clough. A Descriptive Catalogue: Poetry, Prose, Biography, Criticism*, ed. by R. M. Gollin, Walter E. Houghton, and Michael Timko. New York Public Library. pp. 117. $8.

[57] *Matthew Arnold: A Study of the Aesthetic Temperament in Victorian England*, by William A. Madden. Indiana U.P. pp. xiv+242. 57s. $6.

in which 'a note of hope, a sense of recovery, struggles for expression'. These are closest to his prose writings; but although, when he turned to criticism, Arnold sought to come to terms with his age, 'his rapprochement was only partial'. Two articles link Arnold with his contemporaries. Edward Alexander writes on 'Roles of the Victorian Critic: Matthew Arnold and John Ruskin' in *Selected Papers of the English Institute*, edited by D. Phillip (Columbia U.P.), and W. D. Anderson discusses 'Types of the Classical in Arnold, Tennyson, and Browning' in *Victorian Essays*, edited by W. D. Anderson and T. D. Clareson (Kent State U.P.). This publication also contains an essay by D. A. Culler on 'Arnold on Etna'. In 'Apollo and Arnold's *Empedocles on Etna*' (*REL*) B. Raymond approaches the poem by way of Callicles's lyrics. J. W. Frierson discusses the Shakespeare sonnet in 'The Strayed Reveller of Fox How' (*VP*). R. L. Brooks notes 'An Oriental Detail' in *Sohrab and Rustum* (*ELN*). That 'happiness cannot be achieved if it is pursued directly' is the theme of *The Scholar Gipsy* and *Thyrsis* is the argument of 'Arnold's Passive Questers' (*VP*) by D. L. Eggenschwiler. M. W. Schneider writes on 'The Source of Matthew Arnold's *Balder Dead*', and R. H. Super has a note on 'The Dating of *Dover Beach*' (both *NQ*). R. M. Gollin considers the contemporary meaning of the 'battle by night' and 'sea of Faith' images in '*Dover Beach*: The Back of its Imagery' (*ES*). M. G. Sundell finds a close parallel between '*Tintern Abbey* and *Resignation*' (*VP*), although Arnold's poem is more complex than Wordsworth's. Sundell also writes on 'Arnold's Dramatic Meditations' in *VN*. Flavia M. Alaya makes one of several pleas for a reassessment of Arnold's poems in '"Two Worlds" Revisited: Arnold, Renan, the Mon-

astic Life, and the "Stanzas from the Grande Chartreuse"' (*VP*). She relates the *Stanzas* to Renan's essay on Thomas à Kempis. In *JHI* she discusses 'Arnold and Renan on the Popular Uses of History'. R. Bachem writes on 'Arnold's and Renan's Views on Perfection' (*RLC*). W. S. Johnson considers '*Rugby Chapel*: Arnold as a Filial Poet' (*UR*).

'When one considers the level of argument upon which he conducted his polemics, it seems remote from any concern with accuracy or fairmindedness' says G. Watson in 'Arnold and the Victorian Mind' (*REL*), a plea for a reappraisal of Arnold's criticism of society. R. L. Brooks writes on 'Matthew Arnold "Joseph de Maistre on Russia"' (*HLQ*). In 'How Matthew Arnold Altered "Goethe on Poetry"' (*VP*) C. D. Wright observes an amended passage in Arnold's Notebooks. On Arnold's letters, J. B. Gordon contributes 'Matthew Arnold and the Elcho Family: A Record of a Correspondence' (*NQ*), E. Williamson writes on 'Matthew Arnold's Letters to George Stacey Gibson' (*VN*), and R. L. Brooks has compiled 'Letters of Matthew Arnold: A Supplementary Checklist' (*SP*). '*Bitter Knowledge*' and '*Unconquerable Hope*': *A Thematic Study of Attitudes Towards Life in Matthew Arnold's Poetry 1849–53*, by Erik Frykman (Stockholm, Almqvist and Wiksell, 1966) and *Matthew Arnold: The Poet as Humanist*, by G. R. Stange (Princeton U.P.), have not been available for comment.

Two contrasting views of James Thomson (B.V.) are presented by Charles Vachot and W. D. Schaefer.[58][59] Vachot divides his exhaustive

[58] *James Thomson (1834–1882)*, by Charles Vachot. Paris: Didier (1964). pp. 508. 45 Fr.

[59] *James Thomson (B.V.): Beyond 'The City'*, by W. D. Schaefer. California U.P. and C.U.P. (1965). pp. xvii+208. $4.95.

treatise on the poet into three parts: the man, the poet, and the prose writer, with a section on his personality and opinions. He follows H. S. Salt and other biographers of Thomson in tracing the poet's melancholy and drunkenness to the death of Matilda Willer, the thirteen-year-old girl he knew in Ireland. Schaefer, in his systematic study of Thomson's intellectual development, spares a section of his much more concentrated work to a refutation of this legend. To Vachot, *The City of Dreadful Night* 'est une des rare oeuvres modernes qui soient du même rang que les grands poèmes bibliques', as universal as the Book of Job. Schaefer inclines to the more moderate opinion that critics have usually expressed of the poem, and sees it, in fact, as an obstacle to the recognition of Thomson's true stature. This, he suggests, is more accurately to be measured by his prose work, and he has been assiduous in identifying numerous essays hitherto unnoticed in *Cope's Tobacco Plant* and other journals for which Thomson wrote. Thomson's intellectual progress is followed along three separate but related lines: from orthodoxy to militant atheism; from belief in perfectibility to despair of the human race; and, in criticism, from a romantic outlook to one of bitter pessimism. In 1867 he began to read Leopardi, but, says Schaefer, 'Leopardi did little more than confirm a latent pessimism which was present even during Thomson's most joyous declarations.' Vachot agrees with this, arguing that Leopardi helped him 'à développer, à manifester plus nettement . . . ce que déjà il portait en lui'. Both volumes have extensive bibliographies; Schaefer, in particular, lists some two hundred essays and reviews, many hitherto unrecognized.

The last two volumes of Rossetti's correspondence, edited by Oswald Doughty and J. R. Wahl, making four in all, have been published by O.U.P. Vol. III covers from 1871 to '76, and Vol. IV from 1877 to '82. Harrison Eldredge refers to Sonnet xxxiv of *The House of Life* in 'On an Error in a Sonnet of Rossetti's, (*VP*), and in 'Rossetti's *A Last Confession*' (also *VP*), R. R. Howard claims that, as a dramatic monologue, the poem deserves the 'painstaking attention paid to (and required by) a Browning monologue'. F. N. Lees discusses *The Hill Summit* in 'The Keys are at the Palace: A Note on Criticism and Biography' (*English Institute Essays*). G. Omans throws 'Some Biographical Light on Rossetti's Translation of Villon' (*VN*), and Edward Lucie Smith has an article on 'Dante Gabriel Rossetti' (*Listener*). Rossetti's picture *The Sphinx* is discussed by C. A. Peterson in *Apollo*. *Rosetti and the Pre-Raphaelite Brotherhood*, by G. H. Fleming (Hart-Davis) has not been available for review.

In a long essay on '*The Woods of Westermain*' (*VP*) P. Grunden says that much of the difficulty and density of Meredith's poem 'derives from its habit of self-reference and its creation of a new set of meanings for crucial words'.

R. D. McGhee discusses '*Thalassius*: Swinburne's Poetic Myth' (*VP*), maintaining that 'the myth in *Thalassius* is an attempt to integrate the experiences described in *Poems and Ballads* into a broader vision of life. Also in *VP* G. B. Kinneavy discusses 'Character and Action in Swinburne's *Chastelard*'. Curtis Dahl writes on 'The Composition of Swinburne's Trilogy on Mary Queen of Scots' (*TSL*).

The Windhover attracts the usual attention. In 'The Growth of *The Windhover*' (*PMLA*) E. R. August makes a study of the manuscripts. R. Bates in 'Downdolphinry' (*UTQ*) and R. Fraser in 'The Windhover Again' (Downside Review) discuss the poem. In 'Once More The Windhover' (VP) Boyd Litzinger rejects the view that the falcon is an image of Christ. M. Payne writes on 'Syntactical Analysis and The Windhover' (Ren). 'Hopkins's God's Grandeur 3–4' is discussed by M. Taylor (Ex). P. C. Doherty, in 'Hopkins's Spring and Fall: To a Young Child' (VP), points out the poem is a dramatic monologue, and, as the title suggests, is concerned not only with the Fall of man, but also with his Redemption. G. Müller-Schwefe writes on 'Gerard Manley Hopkins: Spelt from Sybil's Leaves' in Die moderne englische Lyrik, edited by H. Oppel (Berlin, E. Schmidt). P. L. Mariani writes on 'Hopkins's Felix Randall as a Sacramental Vision' (Ren). In 'Hopkins's Dark Sonnets: Another New Expression' (VP) L. Rader analyses the versification to show that the poems indicate not a falling-off but a new development in Hopkins's poetic powers and enthusiasm. Also in VP S. A. Hallgarth traces the 'four chronological groups into which the poems fall' to illustrate Hopkins's 'changing religious attitude', in 'A Study of Hopkins's Use of Nature'. D. Sonstroem writes on 'Making Earnest of Game: G. M. Hopkins and Nonsense Poetry' (MLQ). F. Gibbon discusses 'The Influence of Welsh Prosody on the Poetry of Hopkins' (XUS). Gerard Manley Hopkins: The Classical Background and Critical Reception of his Work, by T. K. Bender (Johns Hopkins U.P.), and Gerard Manley Hopkins by F. N. Lees (Columbia U.P.), both 1966, have not been available for comment. In the fourth edition of Hopkins's Poems[60] W. H. Gardner

and N. H. Mackenzie publish 'all the known poems and fragments', and make a thorough revision of the text. Graham Storey has edited a volume of Selections from poems.[61]

In 'Henley and The Hound of Heaven' (VP) W. D. Schaefer argues that London Voluntaries, particularly the first section, 'Piccadilly', was influenced by Thompson's poem.

Desmond Flower's edition of The Poetical Works of Ernest Dowson, first published in 1934, has been reissued in preparation for an edition of Dowson's letters shortly to appear.[62] J. J. Duffy writes on 'Ernest Dowson and the Failure of Decadence' (UR), and J. B. Gordon discusses the 'Poetic Pilgrimage of Ernest Dowson' (Ren).

In 'Beeny Cliff and Under the Waterfall: An Approach to Hardy's Love Poetry' (VP) A. W. Friedman compares the two poems. Also in VP P. Zietlow comments on the 'variety in Hardy's attitudes' in 'The Tentative Mode of Hardy's Poems'. Irving Howe discusses 'The Short Poems of Thomas Hardy' (So R). A. W. Pitts comments on 'Hardy's Channel Firing' (Ex).

W. H. Auden's anthology of Nineteenth-Century Minor Poets[63] is of interest in several ways. The poems themselves have a remarkable variety; but there is also the question of the category of 'minor poets' in which their authors thus find themselves. Some clearly merit no other title; but others, Clough, for example, or Elizabeth Barrett, or William Morris, though certainly not major poets, seem to require something other than the alternative. Some third category

[60] Poems of Gerard Manley Hopkins, ed. by W. H. Gardner and N. H. Mackenzie. O.U.P. pp. 362. 30s.

[61] Hopkins: Selections, chosen and ed. by Graham Storey. O.U.P. pp. 206. 10s. 6d.

[62] The Poetical Works of Ernest Dowson, ed. by Desmond Flower. Cassell. pp. 295. 30s.

[63] Nineteenth-Century Minor Poets, chosen by W. H. Auden. Faber & Faber. (1966). pp. 408. 50s.

seems required. In his Introduction Auden does not consider this point, although he acknowledges that there are borderline cases. Meredith is one of these. Kipling is excluded as a major poet. An amusing collection of favourite recitations, from Scott to G. R. Sims, has been compiled with an Introduction and commentary by Michael Turner.[64]

The title of Erika Meier's book, *The Function of the Stage Direction in the New Drama from Robertson to Shaw*,[65] is sufficient to explain her purpose. All the dramatists of the later nineteenth century drew to a greater or less extent on the melodramatic conventions of the earlier theatre. By examining the works of Robertson, Pinero, Henry Arthur Jones, Gilbert, Wilde, and Shaw, Meier shows how a complex relationship developed between the dialogue and the stage directions, which were the dramatists means of conveying his realistic intentions. In Robertson there is a notable discrepancy between these two features, and this continues in Pinero and Jones. With Gilbert, however, 'the actual shape of the play-in-performance as conveyed by the stage directions stands in complete contrast with the dialogue' and 'the dialectical relationship between the two is the essence of the play's meaning'. This technique is continued by Wilde in *The Importance of Being Ernest*, where the conventions of melodrama are exploited for ironic purposes. Shaw's elaborate and copious directions have suggested that he 'let the novel encroach on the drama', but Meier argues that on the contrary, 'in his plays stage

directions and dialogue form a perfectly balanced whole'. The book is of interest not only for its thesis but also for the large number of plays discussed.

J. B. Jones writes on 'Gilbert and Sullivan's Serious Satire: More Fact than Fancy' (*WHR*). Jones also discusses 'The Printing of *The Grand Duke*: Notes towards a Gilbert Bibliography' (*PBSA*). Six of Gilbert's plays have been edited by J. W. Stedman.[66]

Interest in Wilde's biography has inevitably spread to those of his parents, and it is only partly fortuitous that they should be the subject of two very different books in one year.[67/68] They were remarkable enough in their own right. Of Dr, later Sir William, Wilde, one of the present authors, Terence White, says 'it fell to his lot . . . to double the roles of the weird sisters and Macbeth'. His notorious private life led to an action for libel by Mary Travers, a discarded mistress, the hearing of which curiously anticipated the trials of his son. As to Lady Wilde, 'Speranza', with her 'gigantism' and posturing, and mismanagement of her children, it seems inevitable that disaster should flow from her ministrations. The present writers both avoid speculation about the effects of purely maternal influence, however, and emphasize the general effects of heredity. White suggests that Oscar inherited a debilitating sentimentality from his father, and in the other book Eric Lambert points out that 'the fatal flaw of the Wildes was moral

[64] *Parlour Poetry*, ed. by Michael R. Turner. Michael Joseph. pp. 264. 30s.

[65] *Realism and Reality. The Function of the Stage Direction in the New Drama from Thomas William Robertson to George Bernard Shaw*, by Erika Meier. Berne: Francke. pp. 334. S.Fr. 38.

[66] *Gilbert Before Sullivan: Six Comic Plays*, ed. by J. W. Stedman. Chicago U.P. pp. 284.

[67] *Mad With Much Heart. A Life of Sir William and Lady Wilde*, by Eric Lambert. Muller. pp. ix + 165. 30s.

[68] *The Parents of Oscar Wilde*, by Terence de Vere White. Hodder & Stoughton. pp. 303. 45s.

cowardice'. Few will dissent from White's assertion that Wilde was 'foredoomed by his parentage'; but if he was indebted to them for his misfortune, or his folly, he also owed them his genius, for they were remarkable people in their own absurd fashion. These books are a contrast in method. Lambert, a novelist, emphasizes the dramatic aspect, with scant attention to minutiae. White, a lawyer, and literary editor of *The Irish Times*, is much more meticulous. His book is full of detail, sometimes irrelevant, and presents a highly interesting acount of Dublin society at the time. Philippe Jullian also discusses 'Les parents d'Oscar Wilde' (*Révue des deux mondes*), which is the first chapter of his book on Wilde.[69]

The *Bibliography of Oscar Wilde* by 'Stuart Mason' (Christopher Millard), first published in 1914, has been reissued, with a new Introduction by T. d'Arch Smith.[70] E. San Juan has published *The Art of Oscar Wilde*.[71] Germaine Beaumont writes on 'Oscar Wilde, comedien et martyr' (*Nouvelles Littératures*), and Ghislain de Diesbach has an article on 'Oscar Wilde entraîné vers la catastrophe' in *Révue de Paris*. Jacob Korg discusses Wilde in 'The Rage of Caliban' (*UTQ*). N. W. Alfred writes on 'Oscar Wilde in Texas' (*TQ*), and P. Jullian has another article on 'Oscar Wilde en Amérique' (*Révue de Paris*). R. Ellmann discusses 'The Critic as Artist in Oscar Wilde' (*Encounter*) and S. Migdal writes on 'The Poseur and the Critic in Some Essays of Oscar Wilde' (*DR*). J. B. Gordon

considers 'Parody as Initiation: the Sad Education of Dorian Gray' (*Criticism*).

John M. East's biography of his grandfather and great uncle, John and Charles East,[72] is full of information about the minor theatres and the tradition of melodrama and pantomime in the last part of the century. These two were well-known as actors and producers in the smaller theatres of London and the provinces, and were especially associated with the Lyric, Hammersmith.

The bibliographies of studies in Victorian literature published each June in *VS* are among the most exhaustive and informative of their kind, particularly in the field of the historical and social background. Originally appearing in *MP*, they were transferred to their present location when *VS* was founded ten years ago. A volume comprising the bibliographies that appeared from 1955 to 1964, edited by R. C. Slack,[73] is therefore greatly to be welcomed, especially as an Index referring to both subjects and contributors has been added, together with an Introduction in which the trend of criticism of Victorian literature during the period is discussed.

3. NOVELS AND NOVELISTS

Two books which formulate general propositions about nineteenth-century fiction and announce a polemical intent in the course of setting out those propositions deserve comparison, even though the material chosen for exemplification in each book is quite different. In the first[74]

---

[69] *Oscar Wilde*, by Philippe Jullian. Paris: Perrin.

[70] *Bibliography of Oscar Wilde*, by Stuart Mason. New edition with an Introduction by Timothy d'Arch Smith. Bertram Rota. pp. vi+xxxix+605. 8 guineas.

[71] *The Art of Oscar Wilde*, by E. San Juan. Princeton U.P. pp. ix+238. 52s.

[72] *Neath the Mask: The Story of the East Family*, by John M. East. Allen & Unwin. pp. 356. 55s.

[73] *Bibliographies of Studies in Victorian Literature for the Ten Years 1955–1964*, ed. R. C. Slack. Illinois U.P. pp. xvi+461. 94s.

[74] *The Truthtellers: Jane Austen, George Eliot, D. H. Lawrence*, by Lawrence Lerner. Chatto & Windus. pp. 291. 35s.

Lawrence Lerner examines in some detail behaviouristic and positivistic views of man and relates them to what he thinks is the novelist's central belief: 'that what we are is how we behave'. The strength of the three novelists Lerner writes about—Jane Austen, George Eliot and D. H. Lawrence—comes out in the way they set about proving this belief in their fiction, for example by probing metaphysical concepts in search of their psychological content. It is this search for 'the common trudge of truth' that emerges as a general defining characteristic: 'To see religious experience as a human phenomenon, to use religion as a metaphor for conduct, can only be truthtelling to the irreligious: or to those whose religion has rejected a transcendent for an imminent God. Since this is the way George Eliot sees religious experience, and since she weakens her grip as a novelist when she ceases to see it this way; since the same is true of Jane Austen and of Lawrence; and since I believe the same is true of all the great "religious" novelists—Dostoyevsky, Bernanos, Mauriac, Greene—it would seem that the novel, on my view, is a kind of confirmation of agnosticism.' In the second half of his book Lerner examines in more detail the three novelists' attitudes to moral experience: Jane Austen's pre-Romantic admiration for the ability to resist impulse: D. H. Lawrence's subversive Romanticism which leads him to surrender to it; and George Eliot's positive Romanticism which sees no clear opposition between impulse and reason.

The novelists whose work is the subject of the second book,[75] Fenimore Cooper, Hawthorne, Dickens, Mrs. Gaskell and Gissing, are also truthtellers, though of a different kind. The authors believe they are alike in the way they directly confront their experience of social change and attempt but fail to assimilate the old to the new in a fictional inclusiveness of vision. Dickens's failure in *Dombey and Son*, it is argued, is a failure of nerve. Seeing so clearly what the consequences of industrialism might be, he recoiled in horror from it and took refuge in the "mysterious simplicities" of family life. Mrs. Gaskell in *North and South* and *Mary Barton* also fails in the last analysis, but again the failure is related to an intensity of imaginative honesty which is ultimately sacrificed to stock political attitudes. Gissing's *The Nether World* was written out of his disillusion with positivism and his acute perception of the eternal nature of social warfare. Moreover, the Victorian standards of personal conduct which could sustain earlier novelists in the face of industrial society, had by this time become irrelevant and the hopelessness of *The Nether World* reflects the only possible honest presentation of the themes he chose. The last essay in the book discusses the debate about fiction between Henry James and Walter Besant and argues that in the eighteen-eighties a middle-class novelist, if he wished to avoid the evasive philanthropism satirized by Gissing, had to become an alienated one.

Two books deal in different ways with the minor fiction of the nineteenth century. In Robert A. Colby's study,[76] a representative selection of great novels including *Waverley, Mansfield Park, Oliver Twist, Pendennis, Villette, The Mill on the Floss*, and *Middlemarch*, is studied in the

---

[75] *Tradition and Tolerance in Nineteenth-Century Fiction*, ed. by David Howard, John Lucas & John Goode. Routledge. pp. 281. 42s.

[76] *Fiction With a Purpose: Major & Minor Nineteenth-Century Novels*, by Robert A. Colby. Indiana U.P. pp. viii+376. 71s.

context of the surrounding minor fiction. In this way Colby purports to reveal important affinities, which are just as important as the divergences, between the greater and lesser writers. He also attempts to trace two con-comitant developments that helped to enhance the prestige of the novel: its growth as an instrument of learn-ing, and the gradual extension of the role of the author. The other book[77] brings together nine essays mainly on Romantic and Victorian novelists including Disraeli, Mrs. Gaskell, Surtees, Peacock, Maria Edgeworth, and Fanny Burney. Its editor is care-ful in his introduction to discriminate between artists of the second rank and those who are second rate, and he goes on to define minor fiction as that in which the world is seen only in terms of the novelist's preoccupa-tions, in contrast to major fiction where the novelist's preoccupations are conceived in terms of the whole world. Most of the contributors to the volume though, do not interest themselves in such general proposi-tions and are content to write essays surveying the careers of their chosen subjects. Charles Shapiro is an excep-tion, and he contrasts *Mary Barton* with *Cranford*, concluding, after a very brief analysis of the former, that its failure lies in its inability to trans-cend its preoccupation with the "condition of England" problem in the way *Cranford* does.

A collection of materials[78] taken from letters, notebooks, reviews, and other sources is intended as supple-mentary reading in the study of the history of the eighteenth and nine-teenth-century novel. The nineteenth-

century novels chosen are: *Emma, The Heart of Midlothian, Wuthering Heights, Vanity Fair, Bleak House, Middlemarch,* and *Jude the Obscure.* Some indication of the range of material presented can be given by citing the readings chosen in respect of one novel. The section on *Bleak House* comprises: an editorial from *The Times* of 1851 on the subject of Chancery reform; an extract from 'On Duty with Inspector Field' published in *Household Words;* Dickens's 'Memoranda and Number Plans for *Bleak House';* H. F. Chorley's review of the novel in *The Athenaeum;* and an extract from a more general essay in *Blackwood's.* As well as isolating some useful fictional source material and helping to relate particular novels to their context, this collection also fulfils its editors' expectations in dramatizing the interaction between private artis-tic purpose and public expectation.

The dogma referred to in the title of Mark D. Hawthorne's new study of Maria Edgeworth[79] is her father's, concerning his theories of eduction; the doubt is her own. Hawthorne's thesis is that Maria Edgeworth's fic-tion constitutes a long attempt to bring together the two in a way that would satisfy both a representative late eighteenth-century rationalist and early nineteenth-century romantic. The result, he claims, is a form of fiction in which meaning is created in the tension between didactic surface and symbolic structure, and one which, in its reconciliation of passion and reason, prefigures the mid-Vic-torian compromise between the two. In pursuing this theme, Hawthorne does not spend any time on Maria Edgeworth's best known novels,

[77] *Minor British Novelists*, ed. by Charles Alva Hoyt. Southern Illinois U.P. pp. xiv + 148. $4.95.

[78] *The English Novel: Background Read-ings*, ed. by Lynn C. Bartlett and William R. Sherwood. New York: Lippincott. pp. xiv + 322.

[79] *Doubt and Dogma in Maria Edgeworth*, by Mark D. Hawthorne. University of Florida Monographs–Humanities. No. 25. University of Florida P. pp. 93.

Castle Rackrent and *The Absentee*, nor on her last work, *Helen*, which recapitulates the position reached years before in *Ormond*, but restricts himself to an analysis of those novels and tales in which the dialectic is developed.

J. F. G. Gornall's two-part essay on 'Marriage, Property and Romance in Jane Austen's Novels' (*HJ*), examines her treatment of selected aspects of a social order based on about twenty-five thousand land-owning families, living on rents and perpetuating themselves through entail and marriage settlements. 'Jane Austen and the Seven Deadly Sins' (*QR*) is the title of a short article by Marion Lochhead which also purports to deal with Jane Austen and moral virtues. Having begun with Pride, however, the author has to squeeze Lechery and Gluttony into a couple of sentences, and has hardly any space left to delineate virtue. Kenneth L. Moler deals with a similar subject in 'The Bennet Girls and Adam Smith on Vanity and Pride' (*PQ*), in which he demonstrates that the scene in Volume I, Chapter V in which various members of the Bennet and Lucas families discuss Mr. Darcy's pride, echoes several passages on pride and vanity that occur in Adam Smith's *Theory of Moral Sentiments*. The same writer has another article on '*Pride and Prejudice*: Jane Austen's "Patrician Hero"' (*SEL*); and a third by Ralph Nash examines 'The Time Scheme for *Pride and Prejudice*' (*ELN*) and concludes that both Chapman and MacKinnon have come too hastily to believe that the novel follows the calendar of 1811–12, and that the available evidence supports equally well, and probably better, a hypothesis of composition and revision by the calendars of 1799 and 1802.

'Of how many subjects of literary study can it be observed that where once articles were to be written, today only books will do.' The author of those words has added one more subject to the list, *Mansfield Park*.[80] The subtitle of his book is 'An Essay in Critical Synthesis' and his aim is to apply to the novel what he calls a 'multi-perspectival' criticism, consisting of sociological, psychological and mythical interpretations. By so doing he believes it possible to avoid the trap of both the Historicist and the anti-Historicist fallacies and to synthesize his readings into an interpretation commensurate with 'the manifold reality of a great novel'. What happens in fact is that the novel proves resistant to the diverse criticisms which cancel each other out rather than coalesce in any synthesis. Fleishman, going against his own critical theory, has also published one of the chapters of his book as an article called '*Mansfield Park in its Time*' (*NCF*).

Janet Burroway, in an essay on 'The Irony of the Insufferable Prig' (*CQ*), argues that critics are wrong either to deny the presence of essential irony in *Mansfield Park* or to dissociate it from the heroine. The irony is simple, and it is in the character of the heroine and her moral situation: Fanny, who is committed to preserving the repose, stability and order of Mansfield Park, has to do so in an active, independent, and self-assertive manner; she is the only character who attaches importance to Sir Thomas Bertram's dominion, and is also the only one who explicitly rejects it. P. R. Lynch also contributes a note about Fanny's qualities of independence and determination, as

[80] *A Reading of Mansfield Park*, by Avrom Fleishman. Vol. 2. Minnesota Monographs in the Humanities. Minnesota U.P. pp. x + 109. $4.

this is manifested in the game of 'Speculation at Mansfield Parsonage' (*NQ*). In 'The Plot of *Emma*' (*EIC*), W. J. Harvey writes about Jane Austen's deliberate delay in revealing the truth about the Frank Churchill-Jane Fairfax relationship, arguing that her choice of strategy was not only a necessary one, but that her technique of mystification also contributes an unusual depth and solidity to the novel and gives it an openness and resonance within the precise limits of its form. W. R. Martin examines 'The Subject of Jane Austen's *Sanditon*' (*ESA*), which he discovers is the contrast between old England—seclusion, repose, stability and health, and the new commercial society—restless, rootless, and self-conscious.

Most of the interest in the *Reports of the Jane Austen Society*[81] centres upon biographical and architectural details connected with the purchase and maintenance of Chawton Cottage, though the annual addresses given by such scholars and writers as Lord David Cecil, L. P. Hartley, and Harold Nicolson range over much wider topics.

James Anderson publishes the third part of his long essay on 'Sir Walter Scott as Historical Novelist' (*SSL*), in which he examines in some detail the historical features of *Old Mortality*, *Rob Roy*, and *The Heart of Midlothian*.

W. M. Parker traces the links between 'Scott and Russian Literature' (*QR*), and discusses in particular the influence of *A Legend of Montrose* upon Zagoskin's *Iuri Miloslavsky*, and the way in which Pushkin makes use of characteristic details from Scott's novels. 'Scott's *Chronicles of the Canongate*' are the subject of an

essay by J. T. Christie in *E & S* in which 'The Surgeon's Daughter' and 'The Highland Widow' are quickly passed over in order to allow the author space to discuss 'The Two Drovers' which he believes to be 'among the best dozen English short stories of the century', and *The Fair Maid of Perth* which 'deserves far more credit than it has been given'. In '*The Bride of Lammermoor*: A Re-examination' (*NCF*), Andrew D. Hook argues that the novel's peculiar interest lies in the clarity with which Scott brings together here the historical and romantic elements, and he goes on to demonstrate a variety of devices which are used to neutralize the more luridly romantic elements of his tale. Other items of interest on Scott include: O. D. Macrae-Gibson's 'Walter Scott, the Auchinleck MS., and MS. Douce 124' (*N*, 1966); and Clell T. Peterson's 'The Writing of Waverley' (*ABC*).

Lionel Madden contributes a study of Peacock to the series *Literature in Perspective*[82] and whilst he is restricted by the scheme governing the form and size of these works, he does make some attempt to reassess him, refuting both the view that sees Peacock's philosophy as incoherent and inconsistent, and also that which portrays him as a simple reactionary. Madden traces the chronological development, through the novels, of Peacock's Epicureanism and Utilitarianism to their culmination in the achieved tranquillity of *Gryll Grange*. The kind of remark Madden is reacting against is exemplified in the introduction to a new edition of *Nightmare Abbey*,[83] where A. R. Tomkins lends his approval to the estimate of

---

[81] *Collected Reports of the Jane Austen Society*, with an Introduction by Elizabeth Jenkins. Wm. Dawson. pp. x+317.

[82] *Thomas Love Peacock*, by Lionel Madden. Evans Bros. pp. 160. 8*s. 6d.*

[83] Peacock's *Nightmare Abbey*, with Introduction and Notes by A. R. Tomkins. Blackie, 1966. pp. viii+97. 5*s. 6d.*

Peacock as 'a wit and stylist of considerable, though sometimes superficial, good sense, with no strong views on anything except the desirability of food, wine, laughter and sunshine'. Other notes and essays of critical, biographical, and bibliographical interest concerning Peacock include: '*The Bee* (1790–1794): A Tour of Crotchet Castle' (*SAB*), by Charles F. Mullett; 'Gladstone's Reading of Thomas Love Peacock' (*NQ*), by U. L. Madden; and 'Contemporary Reviews of Thomas Love Peacock: A Supplementary List for the Years 1805–1820' (*BB*), by William S. Ward.

Winifred Gérin adds a substantial biography[84] to the two she has already published on Branwell and Anne Brontë respectively. This time her subject is Charlotte, upon whose life the standard work is Mrs. Gaskell's. A great deal of Brontë scholarship has been undertaken since 1857, though much of this research has been published in fragmentary articles treating particular biographical and critical aspects. This new biography incorporates in a general study the results of Fannie Ratchford's work on the juvenilia, C. W. Hatfield's editions of the poems, the Wise and Symington edition of the letters, and perhaps most importantly, the Brontë-Heger Letters. Examples of the use made of this twentieth-century scholarship can be found in her chapter 'The Web of Sunny Air', and perhaps more interestingly in the chapter on the narratives of Charlotte's early twenties, 'Zamorna Against all Comers' in which the themes of the great novels, and in particular that of the master-pupil relationship, and characters such as Caroline Vernon and

Mina Laury are analysed. Charlotte Brontë's life has often tempted biographers to write fiction, just as the novels have led critics into the realm of pseudo-biography. This well-documented biography ought to make such excursions more difficult in the future.

Thomas Langford examines 'The Three Pictures in *Jane Eyre*' (*VN*), and suggests that in their scope they portray the three major sections of Jane's life and help to focus the attention of the reader on the three most crucial situations of the novel. Donald H. Ericksen also discusses the way in which 'Imagery as Structure in *Jane Eyre*' (*VN* 1966), helps to give unity to the novel.

As well as a new compilation of critical essays on *Wuthering Heights* edited by Alastair Everitt, which is not available for comment, there are also two new essays on the novel by Irving H. Buchen. In *NCF* he writes about 'Emily Brontë and the Metaphysics of Childhood and Love', discovering in the novel's preoccupation with childhood as the basic stage at which pre-natal immortality dies, certain affinities with the themes of her poetry; and in *VN* about 'Metaphysical and Social Evolution in *Wuthering Heights*', this time examining disparities between the poetry and the fiction that cannot be explained by the generalized nature of poetry and the particularity of the novel, but which can be bridged by Emily Brontë's treatment of evolution in terms that adjust the religious and social as well as the romantic and Victorian aspects of her work. James W. Branch has a note 'Concerning the Last of the Brontës' (*BA*), on Patrick; and Winifred Gérin publishes an interesting essay tracing 'Byron's Influence on the Brontës' (*KSMB*).

Dudley Flamm's annotated biblio-

---

[84] *Charlotte Brontë: The Evolution of Genius,* by Winifred Gérin. Oxford: Clarendon P. pp. xvi+617. 63s. $12.50.

graphy[85] of Thackeray criticism covers the period 1836 to 1901. He discovered some 1,500 items but omitted 800 of these on the grounds that they were reprints, dramatizations and summaries of the novels, books and articles concerning bibliographical problems, accounts in literary histories which do not devote a separate chapter to Thackeray, brief material from publishers' lists, encyclopedia accounts, and newspaper articles. This still leaves over 700 items, a sizeable bibliography of nineteenth-century criticism which, claims its compiler in his long introductory essay 'provides the means by which we can examine the thinking of an era in terms of its social and ethical tenets, as well as in regard to its theories of literature'.

Most of Thackeray's modern critics concentrate their attention on *Vanity Fair*, the exception being Jean Sudrann who writes a general essay on '"The Philosopher's Property": Thackeray and the Use of Time' (*VS*), in which she surveys in some detail his manipulation of the concept of time, finding there 'an importance that springs from his realization, not his denial, of the Victorian social dilemma'. Edgar F. Harden examines 'The Discipline and Significance of Form in *Vanity Fair*' (*PMLA*), and concludes that the novel was constructed by specifically pairing and grouping successive instalments, linking one serial part to another with rhythmic connections. Berhard J. Paris also treats the form of the novel in 'The Psychic Structure of *Vanity Fair*' (*VS*), but the focus of his essay is limited to a psychological analysis of the implied author of the novel, discovering there

an inconsistency in his interpretation of the experience he dramatizes. In '*Vanity Fair* and the London Skyline' (*AUMLA*), Joan Stevens discusses the detail of the cover design of the first number of the monthly-part novel, a wood-cut which has seldom been reproduced in subsequent editions and which provides clues, not only to the setting and central event of the novel, but to its narrative tone and its relevance to English society at the time. Finally, Leslie M. Thompson has an essay on 'Becky Sharp and the Virtues of Sin' (*VN*), in which he argues that Thackeray uses Becky to satirize the narrow, Victorian concept of virtue by revealing to his contemporaries the inadequacy of current notions of chastity.

As the Dickens centenary approaches publishers and scholars alike begin to work up their onslaught upon the reading public. This year sees the publication of six new monographs, a compilation of critical essays, and the reissue of André Maurois's 1934 biography.[86] Maurois was led to publish his lectures on Dickens by a belief that recent critics had unjustly depicted him in an unpleasing light, and that this view deserved to be corrected by the Frenchman's 'straightforward impressions'. The impressions he refers to are those gained by reading the novels, in which he discovers 'proof of a sensitiveness so acute that it is impossible for us reasonably to accept an accusation of cruel or dishonest character'. By the side of Maurois's book, modern studies appear much more sophisticated and specialized, and none more so than Stanley Gerson's,[87] which properly

---

[85] *Thackeray's Critics: An Annotated Bibliography of British and American Criticism 1836–1901*, by Dudley Flamm. N. Carolina U.P. pp. 184. 46s.

[86] *Dickens*, by André Maurois. New York: Ungar. pp. 183. $1.45.

[87] *Sound and Symbol in the Dialogue of the Works of Charles Dickens*, by Stanley Gerson. Stockholm: Almqvist and Wiksell (Stockholm Studies in English XIX). pp.xxxii + 382. Kr. 40.

speaking, is so tangentially relevant to Dickens that it ought to be noticed in a different section of this volume altogether. The subtitle of his study is: A survey of the divergencies from normally received spellings in the dialogue of Dickens's works, together with an investigation into Dickens's methods of conveying an impression of divergent sounds of speech. It is unlikely that any reader of Dickens will want to work his way through this massive, painstaking analysis in order to reassure himself about Dickens's mastery of language or his knowledge of the various types of spoken English that could be heard in his lifetime. The urge towards classification and categorization is not confined to students of language, however. In a new critical study of Dickens,[88] Archibald Coolidge claims that the details of his work are based upon the collection of 25,000 'facts', some of which he prints in his appendix on stock characters and incidents and motifs. At the end of his extensive lists of 'People driven by fear', 'People whose pride is softened', 'Letters telling all' and so on, he admits that his method is not very trustworthy, being at once too subjective and yet too cut and dried. But he believes that from his investigation emerge several patterns which illuminate the way in which Dickens habitually controlled his sprawling and confusing materials. These devices are often the product of the pressures of serial publication and a good deal of Coolidge's work is complementary to that of Tillotson and Butt in *Dickens at Work*. More dubious is his claim to have been the first to discover or to demonstrate that Dickens used impressionism, or that he developed in certain ways as

a symbolist. Nor is he correct in his claim to be the first to describe the instalment patterns of Dickens's novels.

The first volume in the Clarendon Dickens[89] besides being a superb edition and setting what one hopes is not an impossibly high standard for the series, is also a landmark in Dickens scholarship; the culmination of twenty years' work begun by Kathleen Tillotson and the late John Butt. As well as providing all existing documentation relating to the composition of *Oliver Twist*, the editor includes a full bibliography and appendixes dealing with the illustrations, the prefaces, the descriptive headlines, and the novel's reception. There is no attempt made to include explanatory notes or any critical appraisal, but surely the editor is right to hope 'that such appraisal will in future be the more firmly based as a result of our labours'.

Ross Dabney's excellent study of a central theme in Dickens's fiction[90] concentrates mainly upon the last great novels; novels in which Dickens's determination to make a moral analysis of society made him unwilling any longer 'to settle for villains, no matter how vital and fascinating, who are essentially small fish, ugly eccentrics doomed in the nature of things to failure, concomitants of an essentially satisfied view'. Such characters are pushed to the periphery of the action of the later books by larger, more mixed villains, and by institutions which are part of the very fabric of society. Similarly, while Dickens was always fascinated by the theme of mercenary marriage, it was not until mid-way

[88] *Charles Dickens as Serial Novelist*, by Archibald C. Coolidge Jr. Iowa State U.P. pp. xiv+256. $6.

[89] *Oliver Twist*, ed. by Kathleen Tillotson. Oxford: Clarendon Press. 1966. pp. lxv+403. 75s. $12.

[90] *Love and Property in the Novels of Dickens*, by Ross H. Dabney. Chatto & Windus. pp. 176. 21s.

through his career that he became able to place this subject effectively within a general context. In his analysis of *Bleak House, Little Dorrit, Great Expectations,* and *Our Mutual Friend,* Dabney illuminates both Dickens's comprehensive social analysis and the development of his ability to organize his plots.

Christopher Hibbert's biography[91] as its title implies is essentially concerned with Dickens's childhood and the early years of his success; his life and career after 1845 occupying a fairly brief epilogue. In his preface Hibbert disclaims any pretensions to being a Dickens scholar, but this book makes very clear that his knowledge of the novels is profound. This together with his skilful use of letters and documents ensures the complete success of his aim to 'show how he interpreted his youthful experiences both to his readers and to himself'. Humphrey wrote that 'There is no need to emphasize any more, that Dickens used the years of his youth with a persistence and confident exactness'. While critics continue to assert the relation between life and art, one is grateful to Hibbert for so well illustrating it.

In accord with modern critical emphasis, the essays in Martin Price's compilation[92] dealing with individual novels, are for the most part about the later ones: W. J. Harvey on *Bleak House;* Lionel Trilling on *Little Dorrit;* Paul Pickrel on *Great Expectations;* J. Hillis Miller on *Our Mutual Friend;* and Kathleen Tillotson on *Dombey and Son.* There are, however, pieces on *The Pickwick Papers, Oliver Twist,*

and *Martin Chuzzlewit,* by W. H. Auden, John Bayley, and Steven Marcus, as well as more general essays by Angus Wilson, Dorothy Van Ghent, Barbara Hardy, and George H. Ford. This is a good representative, collection of modern Dickens criticism.

J. C. Reid's essay is published as a separate volume in the 'Studies in English Literature' series.[93] His account of the novel is in line with modern orthodoxy which sees *Little Dorrit* as being only incidentally concerned with bureaucratic inefficiency and the Victorian financial structure. Its main motifs, Reid maintains are: 'the corrupting effects of social attitudes, based upon snobbery, privilege and class-divisions, the constraints on the human will imposed by a society so organized, the indifference to human misery bred by class-divisions and the pursuit of money, the illusions with which men bolster up their own egos and hide their true nature from themselves and the supreme positive value of self-abnegating love'.

A large number of articles of general interest on Dickens includes two by Harry Stone: in 'Dickens and the Idea of a Periodical: A History of the Triumphant Will' (*WHR*), he traces and discusses Dickens's experiences and the development of his ideas as an editor of *Bentley's Miscellany, Master Humphrey's Clock,* and *Household Words;* and in 'Dickens and Composite Writing' (*DS*), he prints a further extract from the introduction to his forthcoming edition of Dickens's uncollected writings, the argument of which is that a study of these jointly authored pieces gives a unique opportunity for contrasting Dickens's vision with the "ordinary" vision of his co-authors.

[91] *The Making of Charles Dickens,* by Christopher Hibbert. Longmans. pp. xiv + 321. 45s.

[92] *Dickens: A Collection of Critical Essays,* ed. by Martin Price. Englewood Cliffs, N.J.: Prentice Hall (Twentieth Century Views.) pp. 184. Cloth 46s. 6d. Paperback 18s. 6d.

[93] *Dickens,* by J. C. Reid. Arnold (Studies in English Literature 29). pp. 61. 8s. 6d.

Jerome Thale, in 'The Imagination of Charles Dickens: Some Preliminary Discriminations' (*NCF*), is also concerned with the uniqueness of Dickens's vision, discovering distinctions in his methods of description which enable one to understand better the relation between the presentational and the symbolic in his descriptions. Two articles examine Dickens's relation to his predecessors: Larry Kirkpatrick's 'The Gothic Flame of Charles Dickens' (*VN*) examines the use made of Gothic elements in *The Old Curiosity Shop, Little Dorrit,* and *Our Mutual Friend,* and Alexander Welsh discovers in the similarities between 'Waverley, Pickwick, and Don Quixote' (*NCF*), universal themes which account for their broad appeal.

Other articles of a general nature include: 'Dickens and Punch' (*DS*), by Philip Collins; 'Disraeli and Dickens on Young England' (*D*), by Beth R. Arnold; 'Ignorance and its Victims; Another New Article by Dickens' (*D*), by Alec W. Brice; 'W. C. Macready and Dickens: Some Family Recollections' (*DS*), by Philip Collins; 'Manchester Men and their Books' (*D*), by R. Gilmour; 'An Omission Unnoticed: *Nickleby* Forgotten' (*D*), by H. M. Levy Jr.; 'Boz and the American Phrenomesmerists' (*DS*), by N. C. Peyrouton; 'The Dickens of a Drink' (*D*), by Ross Wilson; and 'The Death of Mary Hogarth—Before and After' (*D*), and 'Dickens and the Royal Society of Arts' (*D*), both by William J. Carlton.

With the exception of *Hard Times, Oliver Twist, A Tale of Two Cities,* and *Martin Chuzzlewit,* articles have been published on all Dickens's novels. There are three essays on *Pickwick Papers,* all of them devoted to examining the book's structural organization. Two of them, indeed, cover exactly the same ground, and

elaborate upon Robert Patten's research: Patten himself writes a further article on 'The Art of *Pickwick's* Interpolated Tales' (*ELH*), in which he shows that all the tales have some thematic relationship to the main plot; and H. M. Levy, Jr. and William Ruff use the Pilgrim edition of the letters in 'The Interpolated Tales in Pickwick Papers, a further Note' (*DS*), to prove that two other stories were composed at the same time as the main narrative, and thus are not, strictly speaking, interpolations at all. Mary Colwell studies the wider problem of 'Organization in *Pickwick Papers*' (*DS*), and discovers a break away from the imposed, mechanical organization of the novel's first half, when he comes to write the Fleet Prison sequence and, for the first time, begins to internalize the organization by excluding the consciousness of the reader altogether. John R. Reid's essay examines 'Some Indefinable Resemblance: Moral Form in Dickens's *Nicholas Nickleby*' (*PLL*). A. E. Dyson contributes an essay on '*Barnaby Rudge*: The Genesis of Violence' (*CQ*), in which he seeks to show that the novel marks an advance in Dickens's artistry, 'and in exactly the respects where it is usually said to fall short. It is more coherently planned than his previous novels, with important connexions and ironies developing through both of its parts'. Joan Stevens demonstrates in her article, '"Woodcuts dropped into the Text": The Illustrations in *The Old Curiosity Shop* and *Barnaby Rudge*' (*SB*), that the exact placing of the original illustrations in the text of these two novels is vital if they are to function significantly in narrative, characterization, and theme, and that their function has been obliterated by a subsequent failure to honour Dickens's intentions. Reflections of some of the deep-seated neuroses of early Victorian England in *The Old Curiosity Shop* are the subject of Laurence Senelick's essay, 'Little Nell and the Prurience of Sentimentality' (*DS*), while Warrington Winters examines others in '*The Old Curiosity Shop*: A Consummation Devoutly to be Wished' (*D*).

Philip Collins examines sixteen of the original reviews of the novel in order to show how critical emphases have shifted in respect of '*Dombey and Son*—Then and Now' (*D*). In 'Mr. Micawber and the Redefinition of Experience' (*D*), William Oddie compares passages from Forster's *Life* with passages from *David Copperfield* in order to determine how far it is possible to relate Mr. Micawber's capacity for making us laugh to his capacity for redefining painful experience.

Ann Y. Wilkinson's essay, '*Bleak House*: From Faraday to Judgement Day' (*NCF*), explores some of the great scientific laws discovered in the nineteenth century, and shows how Dickens's intuitive apprehension of them is put to use in the novel. Trevor Blount discusses '*Bleak House* and the Sloane Scandal of 1850 Again' (*DS*), finding a parallel in Judy's treatment of Charley, and Stephen C. Gill considers the use of 'Allusion in *Bleak House*: A Narrative Device' (*NCF*).

The themes of pride, prisons, and irresponsibility are at the centre of *Little Dorrit*; Jerome Mackie analyses the variations on them in 'Dickens's *Little Dorrit*: "Sundry Curious Variations on the same Tune"' (*DS*).

Richard J. Dunn examines a favourite topic of Dickens critics: the use of doubles to portray man's dual nature. He chooses to discuss the minor figures 'Drummle and Startop: Doubling in *Great Expectations*' (*D*). Imagistic criticism is also fashionable among Dickens's critics and William H. New explores 'The Four Elements in *Great Expectations*' (*DS*), and relates them to the 'intangible alchemy that allows human development'. Annabel Endicott makes out a tenuous case for believing that Dickens owed something to *Astrophel and Stella* in 'Pip, Philip and Astrophel: Dickens's Debt to Sidney?' (*D*).

Fr. F. X. Shea, S. J. makes out a good case against Chesterton's contention that Boffin's corruption in *Our Mutual Friend* was first conceived as genuine. Reference to the holograph MS. proves that there was 'No Change of Intention in *Our Mutual Friend*' (*D*).

Finally there are two essays on *Edwin Drood*: Jane Rabb Cohen argues in 'Dickens's Artists and Artistry in *The Mystery of Edwin Drood*' (*DS*), that Dickens endows all his characters in the novel with artistic gifts in order to delineate them more clearly, and which also prove essential to the plot; and Arthur J. Cox, in '"If I Hide my Watch"' (*DS*), takes issue with the Aubrey Boyd/Edmund Wilson speculation, and makes some of his own.

William Lane's biography of Richard Harris Barham[94] will be welcomed by students of Victorian letters. Since the publication of his son's biography in 1870, the author of *The Ingoldsby Legends* has been virtually ignored, though the *Legends* continue to be reprinted. Barham's many friendships in the Victorian literary world make him an admirable focus for this kind of socio-literary study, and in the absence of any biography of Richard Bentley, Lane's long account of Barham's connexion with the famous publisher is invaluable. In an appendix Lane

[94] *Richard Harris Barham*, by William G. Lane. Missouri U.P. pp. xv+271. $7.

also publishes an excellent biblio-graphy.

J. A. V. Chapple writes on Mrs. Gaskell's 'North and South: A Re-assessment' (EIC), and concludes that the union of North and South in the persons of Margaret Hale and John Thornton is not the main point of the novel; nor is it the gradually achieved harmony between masters and men in the Thornton works, but the inner progress of Margaret herself. Other articles and notes on Mrs. Gaskell include: 'Mrs. Gaskell on the Con-tinent' (NQ), by J. B. Ellis; 'Mrs. Gaskell's Reading—Some Notes on Echoes and Epigraphs in Mary Barton' (DUJ), by Graham Handley; and 'Mrs. Gaskell and Effie' (TLS 23 Mar.), by Mary Lutyens.

William H. Scheuerle has edited Henry Kingsley's best known novel[95] and written an introduction in which he defends the Victorian Romance, finding in it a charm lacking in most of Kingsley's work.

J. R. Dinwiddy contributes an interesting essay to NCF–in which he refutes A. O. Cockshut's argument that Trollope had no intention of portraying real personages, and goes on to outline 'Who's Who in Trol-lope's Political Novels'. Mary D. Smith has 'A Note on the Fluctuation of Fortune in Trollope's Barsetshire' (VN), in which she uncovers some of Trollope's inaccuracies and incon-sistencies in respect of money. Roger L. Slakey in 'Melmotte's Death: A Prism of Meaning in The Way We Live Now' (ELH), argues that this suicide helps to define a crucial theme in the novel: the question of what meaning a word should have. Other articles on Trollope include: 'The Relevance of Trollope' (English), by Kathleen E. Morgan; and 'Trollope, Carlyle, and Mill on the Negro: An

Episode in the History of Ideas' (Journal of Negro History), by Iva G. Jones.

The publishers of a new collection of critical essays on Middlemarch[96] speak of it as 'something of an innovation in organized criticism'. The multiplication of similar ventures may easily be predicted. Middlemarch itself, however, is a large enough work to justify a diverse number of 'approaches', and whilst the contri-butors do not come into open conflict with each other, a reading of all the essays makes one aware of the variety of methods employed by modern criticism. The individual essays are: 'The Structure of the Novel: Method, Metaphor and Mind', by Mark Schorer; 'The Intellectual Back-ground of the Novel: Casaubon and Lydgate', by W. J. Harvey; 'The Text of the Novel: A Study of the Proof', by Jerome Beaty; 'The Langu-age of the Novel: The Character of Dorothea', by Derek Oldfield; 'The Language of the Novel: Imagery', by Hilda M. Hulme; 'Criticism of the Novel: Contemporary Reception', by W. J. Harvey; 'The Surface of the Novel: Chapter 30', by Barbara Hardy; and 'A Plea for Ancient Lights', by J. M. S. Tompkins.

This collection almost exhausts the work published on Middlemarch this year, but not quite: Larry M. Robbins has an essay on 'Mill and Middlemarch: The Progress of Public Opinion' (VN), in which he shows how George Eliot applies some of the social theories set out in On Liberty. In a general essay on the fiction, Darrel Mansell Jr. concentrates upon 'George Eliot's Conception of Tra-gedy' (NCF), and relates her practice to Aristotelian precept. Edward T.

[95] Ravenshoe, ed. by William H. Scheuerle. Nebraska U.P. pp. xxix+453. $2.25.

[96] Middlemarch: Critical Approaches to the Novel, ed. by Barbara Hardy. Athlone Press. pp. 192. 35s.

Hurley also examines theoretical matters as they are broached in the fiction in 'Piero di Cosimo: An Alternate Analogy for George Eliot's Realism' (*VN*), and finds Piero di Cosimo, the Renaissance Classicist of *Romola*, a better analogy for describing George Eliot's art than the Dutch realist painters in Chapter XVII of *Adam Bede*. Other essays of general interest include: Daniel P. Deneau's 'The River and the Web in the Works of George Eliot' (*RS*); and William H. Marshal's first instalment of 'A Selective Bibliography of Writings about George Eliot to 1965' (*BB*). There are also two essays on individual works: Ian Milner writes about 'Structure and Quality in *Silas Marner*' (*VN*); and V. C. Knoepflmacher about 'George Eliot's Anti-Romantic Romance: "Mr. Gilfil's Love-Story"' (*VN*).

John Henry Smith's study of Meredith[97] is primarily concerned with a comparison of imagery in *The Ordeal of Richard Feverel*, published in 1859, and his sonnet sequence, *Modern Love*, published three years later. The two themes which the images illuminate are man's relationship to earth and nature, and the conflict of good and evil in man; and both are central to the philosophy Meredith was developing at this stage of his life, summarized in one of his letters of this period: 'Our great error has been (the error of all religion, as I fancy) to raise a spiritual system in antagonism to Nature.' Smith also finds similar character conception in the two works. Clare and the wife of *Modern Love* share traits, and Richard's ordeal is an earlier version of the husband's in the sonnets. The 1862 version of *Modern Love*, upon which the study is based, and which

is not easily accessible is also published as part of the volume.

Lionel Stevenson's biography of Meredith, which is now reissued,[98] was first published in 1953. It utilizes the findings of scholars and biographers made since the twenties, the period when interest in Meredith was at its height. Using the MS. of *The Amazing Marriage*, Judith Ann Sage discovers evidence for the view that its heroine is based upon Susannah Touchango in *Crotchet Castle*. She publishes her findings in 'George Meredith and Thomas Love Peacock: A Note on Literary Influence' (*ELN*). In 'Hands Around: Image and Theme in *The Egoist*' (*ELH*), Roger B. Wilkenfeld carefully analyses Meredith's use of an image to compress the verbal design of his novel. Taking for a starting point, Meredith's poem, 'The Two Muses', I. M. Williams discusses 'The Organic Structure of *The Ordeal of Richard Feverel*' (*RES*), and finds that if we follow Meredith's definition which relates not to the pattern of action, but to the motivation of characters, then *Feverel* is indeed a comedy. The same novel is the subject of Laurence Poston III's 'Dramatic Reference and Structure in *The Ordeal of Richard Feverel*' (*SEL*).

Harold Orel's collection of Hardy's shorter non-fictional writings is a most interesting compilation.[99] He divides the sixty-three pieces into four groups: 'Prefaces to Hardy's Writings'; 'Prefaces to the Works of Other Writers'; 'Literary Matters'; and 'Reminiscences and Personal Views'. This last section contains the most interesting writing; Hardy did not write really good prefaces to his

---

[97] *Hiding the Skeleton: Imagery in Feverel and Modern Love*, by John Henry Smith. Wesleyan U.P. 1966. pp. vii+134. $4.75.

[98] *The Ordeal of George Meredith*, by Lionel Stevenson. N.Y.: Russell & Russell. pp. 368. $12.50.

[99] *Hardy: Personal Writings*, ed. by Harold Orel. Kansas U.P. 1966. Macmillan. pp. xii+295. 50s.

own or to other people's work, but his reminiscences of Dorset life, ranging over the whole of his life, have the same appeal as parts of the novels themselves.

Another good collection—this time of short stories—is edited by John Wain.[100] As he writes in his introduction, the stories are selected to show Hardy's rough humour as well as his relentlessness, and as a whole they combine to exhibit Hardy's 'world'. In the same series Edmund Blunden's book, first published twenty-five years ago, is reprinted.[101]

Among general essays on Hardy's fiction, Roy Huss writes about 'Social Change and Moral Decay in the Novels of Thomas Hardy' (*DR*), and David J. de Laura about '"The Ache of Modernism" in Hardy's Later Novels' (*ELH*). De Laura believes that discussions of Hardy's intellectual life have been inadequate and in examining *The Return of the Native, Tess of the D'Urbervilles*, and *Jude the Obscure*, he seeks to remedy this deficiency by relating Hardy's anatomy of modern life to its intellectual background.

Perhaps the most important work on single novels is Dale Kramer's essay on 'Two "New" Texts of Thomas Hardy's *The Woodlanders*' (*SB*), in which he looks in detail at the separate stages of composition of the novel, and suggests some implications for criticism. The 'deadly war waged between flesh and the spirit' is the central theme of *Jude the Obscure*, according to Myron Taube, and he studies its expression in his essay '"The Atmosphere . . . from Cyprus": Hardy's Development of Theme in *Jude the Obscure*' (*VN*).

Other essays on the same novel include: Marion Montgomery's 'The Pursuit of the Worthy: Thomas Hardy's Greekness in *Jude the Obscure*' (*UDQ*); H. L. Weatherby's 'Jude the Victorian' (*SHR*); and Irving A. Yevish's 'The Attack on *Jude the Obscure*: A Reappraisal Some Seventy Years After' (*JGE*). Raymond O'Dea claims that critics have hitherto failed to understand the role played by Elizabeth-Jane, and more especially 'The "Haunting Shade" that Accompanies the Virtuous Elizabeth-Jane in *The Mayor of Casterbridge*' (*VN*). He examines her character and her adherence to a stoical philosophy, and its implications for the central characters in the novel.

There are a few other brief notes and articles on Hardy which deserve mention: 'Natural Settings and Natural Characters in Hardy's *Desperate Remedies* and *A Pair of Blue Eyes*' (*Thoth*); 'The Importance of Things Past: An Archetypal Reading of the Mayor of Casterbridge' (*MSE*), by John R. Cooley; 'Telling Time by the Stars in *Far From the Madding Crowd*' (*NQ*), by Edward C. Sampson; and 'William Cox and *The Trumpet-Major*' (*NQ*), by Peter D. Smith.

'It will no doubt come as a surprise to the reader to learn that "Jabberwocky" is the code name for the Baal Shem Tov of Medzhbish in the Province of Kamenetz Podolsk in the Ukraine, on the Bug River'. Not entirely; nor to discover that the subject under discussion in *Through the Looking Glass* is really Judaism! It is the fate of Lewis Carroll to inspire such decoding efforts as this.[102]

As John Gross writes in his introduction to a new edition of *New*

---

[100] *Selected Stories of Thomas Hardy*, chosen and introduced by John Wain. Macmillan, 1966. pp. xx+217. Paperback 6s.
[101] *Thomas Hardy*, by Edmund Blunden. Macmillan. pp. ix+286. Paperback 8s. 6d.

[102] *Lewis Carroll's 'Through the Looking Glass' Decoded*, by Abraham Ettleson. New York: Philosophical Library. pp. 84. $3.75.

Grub Street,[103] 'Gissing is one of the permanently odd men out of literature'. Most of his novels are out of print, and this admirably produced, though rather expensive edition, is welcome. Paul F. Mattheisen and Arthur C. Young contribute an article to *VN* on the subject of Gosse's work in obtaining a pension for Gissing's dependents; it is called 'Gissing, Gosse, and the Civil List'.

Bonamy Dobrée subtitles his new book on Kipling[104] 'Realist and Fabulist', and these terms are central to his understanding of the writer and the man. Just as his basic attitudes to life seem mysteriously paradoxical so, argues Dobrée, in his fiction he remains the Kipling it is impossible *wholly* to understand. This study is neither a biography nor, strictly, an analysis of the poetry and fiction, but an essay in appreciation by a critic responding directly to Kipling's voice.

Among a number of interesting essays in the *Kipling Journal* mention should be made of: '*Kim*—Novel, or Propaganda?', and 'Three Criticisms of The Jungle Books', both by Elliot L. Gilbert; and the third part of Andrew Rutherford's study of 'Carlyle and Kipling'.

Finally in an excellent essay on 'Francis Adams, 1862–1893: A Forgotten Child of his Age' (*E & S*), Edgar Jones argues that even if Adams's scheme to create a series of novels drawing types of all the social life of the day fails, 'in the novel *A Child of the Age*, Adams achieved a distillate of the spirit of the Age, a concentrate of the *Zeitgeist*'.

4. SELECTED PROSE WRITERS

The superb edition of Cobbett's autobiography edited by William Reitzel is now available in a paperback edition.[105] Reitzel used *The Political Register* mainly, but also *A Year's Residence, The Life and Adventures of Peter Porcupine, Advice to Young Men*, and *Rural Rides*, to compile a work of great fluidity, where the linking editorial commentary is scarcely ever necessary.

A new volume is published in the 'Landmarks in Rhetoric and Public Address' series.[106] It contains five of De Quincey's essays: 'Rhetoric'; 'Style'; 'Language'; 'Conversation'; and 'A Brief Appraisal of the Greek Literature in its Foremost Pretensions'. Burwick's long introduction to the volume is an important contribution to the study of De Quincey's prose style and his belletristic theory of rhetoric based upon paradox and informality.

Robert Hopkins also has a substantial essay on 'De Quincey on War and the Pastoral Design of *The English Mail-Coach*' (*SIR*). He complains of the dearth of critical interpretations of the work, which is, he believes 'a meaningful, coherent, imaginative prose work written by a conservative first-generation Romantic trying to sum up the profound significances, historical and cultural, of the Napoleonic Wars for himself *and* for the Victorian era'. There is also one relevant essay on Lamb, by G. D'Hangest, entitled 'Réflexions sur l'art des *Essais D'Elia*' (*EA*).

Edmund Blunden's excellent book on *The Examiner* is reprinted.[107] In it he traces volume by volume what

[103] *New Grub Street*, by George Gissing, with an Introduction by John Gross. Bodley Head. pp. viii+425. 35*s*.

[104] *Rudyard Kipling: Realist and Fabulist*, by Bonamy Dobrée. O.U.P. pp. x+244. 30*s*.

[105] *The Autobiography of William Cobbett*, ed. by William Reitzel. Faber & Faber. pp. 272. Paperback 9*s*. 6*d*.

[106] *Selected Essays on Rhetoric*, by Thomas de Quincey. Ed. by Frederick Burwick. S. Illinois U.P. pp. xlviii+352. $7.

[107] *Leigh Hunt's 'Examiner' Examined*, by Edmund Blunden. Archon Books. pp. xiii+263. $7. 50*s*.

he calls 'The writers' share of the "Examiner"', and then goes on to print a selection of contributions by Leigh Hunt, Robert Hunt, and Lamb.

Sydney Mendel in his essay 'Carlyle: Notes Towards a Revaluation' (*ESA*), takes up a theme of Hillis Miller's, the disappearance of God, and tries to show, by comparing *Sartor Resartus* with Sartre's *Nausea*, that Carlyle is a forerunner of twentieth-century existentialism.

Arthur A. Adrian publishes a letter in *VN* from a Miss Jewsbury to the publisher Bentley which contains some thoughts from 'Carlyle on Editing Letters'. Edwin W. Marrs Jr. has a note in *NQ* on the 'Dating and Writing of *Past and Present*'.

Donald R. Swanson discusses some of the influences of Carlyle upon Ruskin, in particular his espousal of 'righteous' causes, and the concept of superior men and hero worship, in 'Ruskin and his "Master"' (*VN*).

XIV

The Twentieth Century

MARGARET WILLY, H. C. CASTEIN and J. REDMOND

THE chapter has the following sub-divisions: 1. The Novel: books, noticed by Margaret Willy; 2. The Novel: articles, noticed by H. C. Castein; 3. Biography; 4. General Prose Works, and 5, Poetry, noticed by Margaret Willy; 6. Drama: books; 7. Drama: articles, noticed by J. Redmond.

1. THE NOVEL: BOOKS

Intended as 'a student's guide to contemporary fiction', aimed at directing the attention of those who 'want to organize their reading economically' towards what is best in the field, Anthony Burgess's *The Novel Now*[1] does not pretend to offer detailed critical analysis. After considering the nature of the novel and taking a backward look at some giants of the immediate past, Burgess proceeds to a characteristically stimulating and often provocative survey of contemporary novelists under such headings as 'Utopias and Dystopias' (Wells, Huxley, and Orwell), 'Good and Evil' (Greene, Golding, and others), 'A Sort of Rebels' (Amis, Braine, Wain), and so on. The very full booklists at the end of each chapter are particularly helpful.

Peter M. Axthelm sees the origins of the modern 'confessional' novel[2] in Dostoyevsky, to whom his opening chapter is devoted; while Gide, Sartre and Camus lead 'the confessional *genre* into a world which lacks even the fleeting and tentative approaches to purgation and perception that Dostoyevsky's heroes experience', portraying an existence 'in which no values are formed, no regeneration is anticipated, and even basic personal relationships have become futile'. Koestler and Golding are considered side by side in their recognition of disintegration—which is, however, approached in a spirit of hope that meaning and order can still be imposed upon the chaos of contemporary experience. Axthelm makes a detailed exploration of *Free Fall*, with its consistent religious themes and metaphor through which the hero, Sammy Mountjoy, examines the past in his search for a positive pattern amid disintegration. The book concludes with a chapter on the novels of Saul Bellow.

In his study of twentieth-century fiction[3] Robert Scholes's subject is the modern 'fable', and the extent of its departure, with the deliberate dislocations of time and space which blur the lines between actual and artificial, from the ordered realistic structures of nineteenth-century convention. To him 'the emergence of fabulation in recent fiction is not only an exciting development in itself; it also provides one answer to the

---

[1] *The Novel Now*, by Anthony Burgess. Faber. pp. 224. 25s.

[2] *The Modern Confessional Novel*, by Peter M. Axthelm. Yale U.P. pp. x + 189. 43s.

[3] *The Fabulators*, by Robert Scholes. O.U.P. pp. xxi + 180. 42s.

great question of where fiction could go after the realistic novel'. Apart from a scrutiny of the fable rooted in the satirical and picaresque traditions in some recent American fiction, and fabulation as the vehicle for epic vision in the American John Barth's *Giles Goat-Boy*, Scholes examines Lawrence Durrell's *Alexandria Quartet* as an example of 'fabulation as revival of romance'; and the fable as allegory in *The Unicorn*, Iris Murdoch's 'fantasy of the spiritual life' which poses so many unanswered questions and metaphysical possibilities for the reader's choice.

The 'fabulist' as well as the realist element in Kipling as a story-teller is considered by Bonamy Dobrée in his study[4] of an author who, he affirms, 'has been more grotesquely misunderstood, misrepresented, and in consequence denigrated, than any other known writer'. He sets out to dispel prejudice by presenting neither biography nor critical analysis, but 'an unbiased view of the totality of his work' against the historical background of the events and thought of his day. Dobrée discusses Kipling as a professional writer, his attitude to religion, and his basic intuitions about the human condition, especially the loneliness of man; his philosophy, views on the institutions of society, law and empire, and his much-publicized role of 'reactionary'; and the art of his fiction and his poetic craftsmanship, in which a distinction is drawn between poetry and verse.

A main concern of T. R. Henn's monograph[5] is also to defend Kipling from the 'vituperative condemnation' of his hostile critics, and he examines and largely refutes their charges of imperialism, violence, and even sadism. Opening with a biographical chapter, he proceeds to trace the writer's themes and style in his poems, short stories, novels—of which he regards *Kim* as the high point of Kipling's achievement—and travel writings. Useful bibliographies, an alphabetical list of Kipling's short stories and a chronological one of his collections, are also included.

K. Bhaskara Rao takes an opposite view from the two preceding writers in his scrutiny of Kipling's treatment of India[6] in his short stories, poems, and the two novels *Kim* and *Naulahka*. Here Kipling is uncompromisingly convicted in his early work of the chauvinism of one 'whose mind and spirit were dedicated to the glorification of the British Empire and the Anglo-Saxon race', who 'made a religion out of the imperial theme', and whose interpretation of Indian life succeeded in alienating the two races. The author does, however, except *Kim*, Kipling's last and most mature work on India, which to him reveals a genuine awareness of the spiritual realities of Indian life. On the strength of this novel he feels that Kipling's 'early writings may be pardoned as the somewhat irresponsible expressions of a self-confident young boy to whom success and fame came too soon'.

In his study of the imperial idea in some late nineteenth-century and early twentieth-century fiction[7] Alan Sandison corrects what he feels to be the conventional over-simplification of Kipling's political jingoism, as well as that of Conrad's use of the empire merely as an exotic backdrop for the action of his stories. Con-

[4] *Rudyard Kipling: Realist and Fabulist*, by Bonamy Dobrée. O.U.P. pp. x+244. 30s.

[5] *Kipling*, by T. R. Henn. Oliver & Boyd. pp. 141. 7s. 6d. Paperback.

[6] *Rudyard Kipling's India*, by K. Bhaskara Rao. Oklahoma U.P. pp. ix+190. 48s.

[7] *The Wheel of Empire*, by Alan Sandison. Macmillan. pp. viii+213. 30s.

centrating on the work of four writers, Rider Haggard, Kipling, Conrad and Buchan, he sets out to show how each was in fact deeply concerned with the cultural influence and moral significance of the British Empire. Working and writing within the context of empire in its heyday—Haggard as Master of the High Court of the Transvaal, Kipling as a journalist in India, Conrad as an officer of the Merchant Marine in the Far East, and Buchan as one of Lord Milner's 'young men' engaged in the work of reconstruction after the Boer War— they used it for primarily moral and artistic rather than political purposes, to explore the problems of man's integrity and identity.

Bernard C. Meyer is a practising psycho-analyst, who in his biography of Conrad[8] contends that such insights as his specialized knowledge provides are indispensable for a full understanding of what this complex creative artist himself once hoped might emerge from his books: 'a coherent justifiable personality both in its origin and its actions'. For Conrad's life Meyer has drawn upon a mass of material available in letters, the writer's quasi-autobiographical works, and the testimony of those who knew him. The skills of psycho-analytic methods are brought to his close examination of the 'multi-faceted journey' of Conrad's personal history—'at least five separate and distinct lives'; and to trace the complex interaction between fact and fiction in the novels and short stories, with their re-iterated themes of rescue, betrayal and self-destruction.

The 'dual heritage' of the title of Robert R. Hodges' study of Conrad[9]

refers to the two contrary influences which, affirms the author, so long as they existed in opposition or tension, gave rise to his best writings. A Polish exile in England and a sailor gone ashore, Conrad himself succinctly described the basic division in his mind in the phrase 'homo duplex'. Hodges's central aim has been to explore the nature of this dichotomy, originating in Conrad's early years in the contrast between the lives and values of his father and his uncle, who in turn were responsible for his education and upbringing. 'Conrad felt himself torn between his father's impractical idealism and his uncle's practical morality. . . . Out of these tensions between father and uncle, patriot and cosmopolitan, revolutionist and conservative, romantic and realist, dilettante and craftsman, real father and spiritual father, Conrad created some of his finest fiction.' This is the thesis of the first two chapters of the book, while in the concluding two Hodges discusses Conrad's apparent reconciliation of these contraries, demonstrating that 'when the homo duplex became the homo simplex, his writing suffered accordingly'.

From the same publisher comes another book on Conrad: Donald C. Yelton's 'inquiry into the genesis and scope of [his] symbolic imagery',[10] which makes a systematic and comprehensive investigation of the novelist's use of metaphor, both in his themes in eight of the novels and in his symbolic use of natural setting. Yelton traces certain parallels between Conrad's aesthetic goals and those of the French Symbolists, seeing his fiction as transitional work which explores new modes in the novel while remaining firmly based in the

[8] *Joseph Conrad: A Psycho-Analytic Biography*, by Bernard C. Meyer. O.U.P. and Princeton U.P. pp. x+396. 68s.

[9] *The Dual Heritage of Joseph Conrad*, by Robert R. Hodges. The Hague: Mouton. pp. 229. 27 Guilders.

[10] *Mimesis and Metaphor*, by Donald C. Yelton. The Hague: Mouton. pp. 336. 32 Guilders.

tradition of nineteenth-century realism and such masters as Dickens, Flaubert, and Turgenev. Two final chapters devote close analysis to symbol and metaphor in two of the shorter works, *The Secret Sharer* and *The Shadow Line*; and the author suggests that Conrad's richly suggestive use of metaphor is controlled by his instinctive adherence to the Aristotelian principle of *mimesis*, and that he is a symbolic writer in the classic sense as defined by Goethe, Coleridge and Baudelaire.

Jerry Allen's long work on Conrad[11] focuses attention on his experience at sea over some twenty years—a period which provided him with all the raw material for his later career as a novelist. The author set out to trace the people and events in Conrad's life and the places he knew during those seafaring years; and her book is the result of ten years' research among records in reference, law, marine and newspaper libraries, and among private collections of manuscripts and letters, in fifteen different countries. Some of her findings include identification of the originals for the characters of Tom Lingard and Lord Jim, and the part played by the latter (its first mate, A. P. Williams) in the episode of the British steamship *Jeddah*, on which Conrad's novel was based; of the Borneo village of Berau as the setting for *Almayer's Folly* and much of Conrad's Eastern fiction; and Conrad's use in *The Arrow of Gold* of his own love affair and duel in Marseilles, and in *Nostromo* of his contact with the 1876 revolution in Colombia. There are many unusual photographs —most of them, like so much of the biographical material, published for the first time—an appendix giving details of Conrad's voyages and

naming his shipmates, and a very full bibliography.

Conrad is one of the three novelists examined by James Guetti in *The Limits of Metaphor*,[12] whose central argument is that in the disintegration of conventional forms and techniques in much modern fiction the novelist is employing metaphor to express meanings impossible to communicate through traditional structures. Through exploring the linguistic techniques and various thematic conflicts in *Heart of Darkness* side by side with works by Melville and Faulkner, Guetti demonstrates the limitations of metaphor. While these methods have, he concludes, produced some of the most interesting and important modern fiction, they have at the same time resulted in a 'final failure of language to structure experience in an ultimate way' because they are 'fundamentally unstable and inevitably end, if extended, in imaginative collapse'.

In his short monograph on Conrad[13] Neville H. Newhouse attempts to communicate some simple lines of approach to the more important novels and stories of a writer he considers both difficult and uneven. Beginning with a sketch of Conrad's life, literary background, the inception of some of his work, and his commitment to the role of artist, Newhouse analyses his fictional technique—characterization, handling of narration and time, and his gift of impressionism—with concluding chapters on his attitude to the imagination and to man in society.

George H. Thomson's book on Forster[14] is a critical study of the

[11] *The Sea Years of Joseph Conrad*, by Jerry Allen. Methuen pp. xx+366. 63s.

[12] *The Limits of Metaphor: A Study of Melville, Conrad and Faulkner*, by James Guetti. O.U.P. and Cornell U.P. pp. 196. 52s.

[13] *Joseph Conrad*, by Neville H. Newhouse. Evans. pp. 143. 7s. 6d. Paperback.

[14] *The Fiction of E. M. Forster*, by George H. Thomson. Wayne State U.P. pp. 304. $9.95.

short stories, the Italian romances, *The Longest Journey, Howards End,* and *A Passage to India* in their use of symbolism and myth. He believes that Forster is a writer primarily of romance rather than realistic fiction, and that in this romance-form symbolism is central to his achievement. Differentiating Forster's myths from those of both Joyce and Eliot, who impose a pre-existing pattern of order on the chaos of contemporary experience, he affirms that the archetypal symbols in Forster's fiction constitute the substance and significance of his art, as objects of mystical vision and vehicles of ecstatic experience and perception. 'With splendid narrative and symbolic evocation,' concludes the author, 'he expressed the polarities of man's experience of the universe from his encounters with absolute negation to his entry into ultimate affirmation.'

In his 'Studies in English Literature' monograph on *A Passage to India*[15] John Colmer stresses that the novel is not, as often suggested, primarily concerned with questions of rule and race, but with man's quest for ultimate truth. Forster sees 'man's attempts to create unity dominated and diminished by forces he cannot control', and relates 'ideas of human harmony to the secrets of the inner life and the mystery of the whole universe'. Colmer's analysis of the novel, with its 'tensions between poetic vision and ironic comment' and in which form and meaning are organically related, falls under the three section-headings of Forster's own 'large-scale tripartite musical form'—'Mosque', 'Caves', 'Temple'. He concludes that what makes *A Passage to India* so profoundly satisfying is 'its perfect combination of symbolic suggestion,

[15] *E. M. Forster: A Passage to India,* by John Colmer. Arnold. pp. 64. 8s. 6d.

psychological insight, and social realism'.

The publication of Leslie Hancock's word-index to Joyce's *Portrait of the Artist*[16] now leaves only two works by this author, *Dubliners* and *Exiles,* to be similarly indexed. Based on the Viking Press edition of 1964, the index, made by a computer, lists alphabetically every word in the book, with its frequency and place of occurrence; and the editor in a brief prefatory essay explains the step-by-step process of computerized indexing, for the benefit of those contemplating the use of this technique.

In the introduction to his lexicon of the German in *Finnegans Wake*[17] Helmut Bonheim explains how the work grew out of a search for Joyce's guiding principle in the use of German, a language he spoke fluently. The compiler's aim is 'to supply non-German readers with a modest but indispensable aid which . . . when used in conjunction with *Finnegans Wake* will help penetrate the obscurities of that encyclopedic work'. Only a few of the words in the list— arranged according to their sequence in the book with page- and line-numbers referring to the English (Faber) editions of 1950 and after and the American Viking Press printings of 1958 and after—are German and nothing else. The majority are coinages which include German elements; for 'already fascinated by seemingly chance connexions between apparently unrelated words in English, Joyce extended his explorations of such connexions into other languages', which Bonheim hopes may in time be the subject of lists similar to his own.

[16] *Word Index to James Joyce's 'Portrait of the Artist',* by Leslie Hancock. Southern Illinois U.P. pp. ix + 145. $6.

[17] *A Lexicon of the German in 'Finnegans Wake',* by Helmut Bonheim. München: Max Hueber Verlag. DM 19.80. Paperback.

The subjects of Laurence Lerner's study[18] are an unexpectedly juxtaposed trio of novelists—Jane Austen, George Eliot, and D. H. Lawrence. Lerner contends that all three compel the reader to reconsider his view of man. In the first part he deals with what he considers the three writers share in common—principally their honesty and concern with telling the truth at all costs; and in the second points to the contrast between the views of man which emerge from their work. Lawrence's artistic success or failure corresponds, he believes, with what is pernicious in his message, and he illustrates this with a critique of *The Plumed Serpent*. The conflict between 'blood and mind' is exemplified by an examination of *St. Mawr*; and Lerner ends his discussion of Lawrence by considering what he rejects and what he accepts, concluding that 'What led Lawrence astray as an artist was a didactic passion.'

George Woodcock, in his comprehensive critical study of Orwell,[19] observes that 'to speak for a generation without being typical of it is one of the marks by which we can tell the exceptional writers of any time'; and he feels that Orwell stands out as different from his contemporaries while at the same time reflecting most clearly and poignantly the peculiar insights of his age. Here was a novelist preoccupied with the theme of the individual's alienation from all social classes but his own—against which he himself rebelled in his life as well as in his work—and his vision of the evils of a class-divided society reached its culmination in *1984*, the epitome of his earlier novels. Orwell as a revolutionary patriot, who loved his country while rejecting its imperialist policies, is examined in the elements of conservatism and rebellion which characterized his worldview. The concluding section considers him as critic and stylist, and his concern 'with the purity and intelligibility of the written language which in England has been the mark of the great literary reformer from John Dryden down to the present'.

B. T. Oxley's essay on Orwell[20] considers the author against the social and political background of his time, his basic attitudes towards its totalitarianism, struggles for power, and its violence, his involvement in and writing about the Spanish Civil War, and the activities of some of the individual characters in his five novels, of which *Animal Farm* and *1984* are treated in especial detail.

In the first full-length book on William Golding[21] to be published in this country, Mark Kinkead-Weekes and Ian Gregor set out to explore the aims and problems, and elucidate some of the alleged difficulties, of one of the most interesting and important novelists to emerge since the war. They present a detailed reading of each of his five novels, with particular emphasis on the first two because *Lord of the Flies* 'tends to be treated more simply than it deserves, and because *The Inheritors* is difficult and neglected'. *Pincher Martin* is seen as 'the most myth-like of Golding's fictions'; *Free Fall*, 'the most elusive and difficult', and *The Spire*, abounding in 'ambiguity, paradox, reversal', seek 'a path through irreconcilable kinds of vision'. In their final chapter the authors crystallize their view of the characteristics which constitute a Golding novel,

[18] *The Truth Tellers*, by Laurence Lerner. Chatto. pp. 291. 35s.
[19] *The Crystal Spirit*, by George Woodock. Cape. pp. 287. 50s.
[20] *George Orwell*, by B. T. Oxley. Evans pp. 144. 8s. 6d. Paperback.
[21] *William Golding*, by Mark Kinkead-Weekes and Ian Gregor. Faber. pp. 257. 35s

laying stress on his resourcefulness and imaginative vitality and power.

Australia's leading prose writer, Patrick White, is the subject of a monograph by Barry Argyle[22] in the 'Writers and Critics' series. Feeling that a mature and considerable artist has been critically neglected and frequently misunderstood, Argyle attempts to remedy this by a sympathetic consideration of White's 'prentice work, his major novels, his short stories and his plays.'

From Italy comes a large-scale and fully-documented study by Giuseppe Sertoli of the prose and the poetry of Durrell.[23]

2. THE NOVEL: ARTICLES

Conrad, as usual, is one of the very few modern novelists who attract much comment, and the articles devoted to him have been as much concerned with biographical information and possible sources of plots, as with interpretation or analysis.

In 'A Little More Light on Joseph Conrad' (*ABC*) H. F. West writes on the role played by Conrad's friend Chesson in encouraging him to persevere with his career as a novelist and in correcting the English of *Almayer's Folly*. A. G. H. Bachrach discusses the same novel under the title 'Joseph Conrad and the Dutch' (*REL*), seeing the protagonist—'an up-rooted, self-exiled, "fantastic" of doubtful lineage'—as an analogue of the author. Again in *REL*, V. Allen records some of her 'Memories of Joseph Conrad', which are of his family life during the final years. D. Hamer briefly recounts 'Conrad: Two Biographical Episodes' in *RES*, and to *NQ* C. T. Watts contributes

a note 'Joseph Conrad, Dr. Macintyre, and *The Inheritors*', explaining that in 1898 Conrad visited a Dr. Macintyre who was a pioneer radiologist and owned one of the earliest X-ray machines: Conrad and Ford Maddox Hueffer soon afterwards began to write *The Inheritors* and Watts suggests that, impressed by the great success of Wells's science fiction, they decided to exploit Conrad's recent encounter with the Röntgen machine.

In 'The Writer and His Use of Material: The Case of *The Secret Sharer*' (*MFS*) D. Curley writes on the incorporation into that novel of some of Conrad's experiences in 1888, during his first command, and also of what he had learned of the 1880 voyage of the 'Cutty Sark'. Curley argues that where Conrad changed his raw material, it was in the interest of defining the moral centre of the story. In *RES* N. Sherry discusses the relationship between 'The Greenwich Bomb Outrage and *The Secret Agent*', and in the same journal J. Raskin considers '*Heart of Darkness*: The Manuscript Revisions'. In *SSF* J. W. Canario writes on 'The Harlequin in *Heart of Darkness*'.

In '*The Power of Darkness*' (*PR*) F. Crews discusses the tension in Conrad's writing between inadmissable impulses from the subconscious and his Victorian sense of propriety. In *Pol R* J. H. Walton writes on 'Conrad and *The Secret Agent*: The Genealogy of Mr. Vladimir', arguing that this was the first, and perhaps only, novel which reflected the writer's preoccupation with his revolutionary heritage and the first to reveal his awareness of himself as a neglected English novelist. Sister Marian Francis in her study of 'Corruption as Agent in the "Narcissus"' (*EJ*) sees the ship, the crew,

[22] *Patrick White*, by Barry Argyle. Oliver & Boyd. pp. 109. 7s. 6d. Paperback.

[23] *Lawrence Durrell*, by Giuseppe Sertoli. Civiltà Letteraria del Novecento: Sezione Inglese-Amèricana. Mursia: Milano. pp. 231. L. 2.500. Paperback.

and the major characters in *The Nigger of the Narcissus* as corrupt: the ship is defective, the crew tainted with self-love, Singleton, Podmore, Donkin and Wait are morally unsound; Conrad has also 'corrupted' incidents and rhetoric from *The New Testament*, Jimmy's rescue, for example, being a distorted resurrection. In '*The Nigger of the "Narcissus"*: Myth, Mirror, and Metropolis' (*Wascana R*), D. T. Torchiana sees the dying Jim Wait as embodying the deadly metropolitan narcissism of London, while in the voyage of the 'Narcissus' Conrad represents the course being taken by the ship of England, warning that her 'progressive, liberal, and wealthy' culture is dying. In 'Mr. X's "Little Joke"': The Design of Conrad's *The Informer*' (*SSF*) J. H. Walton shows that *The Informer* successfully illustrates Conrad's attempt to reconcile his wish for popularity, and his contempt for the middle-class reading public; the story also explores the social themes that characterize the great novels of Conrad's middle period.

There are studies of various aspects of theme or style in the major novels. In *EIC* I. Vidan and J. McLauchlan write on 'The Politics of *Nostromo*', while A. Guidi contributes 'Struttura e linguaggio di *Nostromo*' to *Convivium*. J. W. Heimer has a detailed study of 'Betrayal, Confession, Attempted Redemption, and Punishment in *Nostromo*' (*TSLL*), and the same writer has a more general essay on 'Patterns of Betrayal in the Novels of Joseph Conrad' in *BSUF*. In *NQ* E. E. Duncan-Jones notices some passages in *Nostromo* Pt. III Ch. XI which seem to reflect passages in the third chapter of Thackeray's *The Rose and the Ring*.

S. B. Purdy writes 'On the Relevance of Conrad: Lord Jim Over Sverdlovsk' in *MQ*, and in *Ex* R. A. Sherrill has a piece entitled 'Conrad's *Lord Jim*'. There are two articles concerned with Conrad's interest in the theatre. In *ELT* J. Kilroy writes on Conrad's 'Succès de Curiosité': The Dramatic Version of '*The Secret Agent*', and T. Schultheiss contributes a note to *ANQ* on 'Conrad on Stage Censorship'.

In 'Joseph Conrad, William Faulkner, and The Nobel Prize Speech' (*NQ*) E. Solomon points out that much of the rhetoric and many of the key ideas that distinguish the famous final paragraph of Faulkner's speech appear in Joseph Conrad's 'Henry James: Appreciation' published in 1905.

Most of the work on Joyce appears in *JJQ*, with which all Joyce enthusiasts will be acquainted. There is neither room nor need to notice the contents of *JJQ* in much detail here: the issue for Spring 1967 is devoted to the problems met with in translating Joyce, and the Summer number is devoted to papers on various aspects of *The Portrait of the Artist as a Young Man*, ranging from short notes on people Joyce knew to essays that offer detailed explication and analysis of the novel. The other issues of *JJQ* have much of interest on *Ulysses, Finnegans Wake, Dubliners*, and Joyce's correspondence. *A Wake Newslitter* issued from Newcastle University College, N.S.W., is entirely devoted to short explanatory notes on cruxes in *Finnegans Wake*. In 'James Joyce und Joachim von Fiore' (*Ang*) W. Weiss argues that Joyce's interest in cyclical theories of history—usually attributed to his knowledge of Vico—cannot be independent of his knowledge of the theories of the twelfth-century monk Joachim, whose teaching was influential in the Middle Ages and known to Joyce before he came across the work of Vico;

Joyce first learned of Joachim from Yeats's *The Tables of the Law*, and Joachim is referred to in the first version of the *Portrait*, in *Stephen Hero*, and in *Ulysses*.

F. L. Walzl and R. Scholes write on 'The Epiphanies of Joyce' in *PMLA*, C. Hart on 'James Joyce's Sentimentality' in *PQ*, and D. C. Pittman on 'James Joyce: Critic of a Dead Society' in *SoQ*. The question of what the steady stream of what calls itself 'criticism' is *for* is raised very acutely by Joyce commentary: T. F. Staley in *DM* writes on 'James Joyce and the Dilemma of American Academic Criticism' and in *CQ* T. H. Gibbons writes sceptically about the various attempts to find a valid critical approach to the short stories, under the title '*Dubliners* and the Critics'.

R. P. apRoberts contributes '"Araby" and the Palimpsest of Criticism' to *AR* and W. Burto writes on the same story in *Ex*, while D. Madden considers 'James Joyce's "Clay"' in *UR*. In 'The Crucifixion in "The Boarding House"' (*SSF*) B. A. Rosenberg interprets Bob Doran as 'A diminished Jesus'—his age corresponds, he is questioned by a priest, and so on.

In *MFS* P. Manso offers 'The Metaphoric Style of Joyce's *Portrait*' which illustrates the ways in which the style changes and suggests reasons for these changes. In *So R* R. J. O'Dea writes on 'The Young Artist as Archangel', and W. French compares 'Two Portraits of the Artist: James Joyce's *Young Man*; Dylan Thomas's *Young Dog*' in *UR*. Some fairly substantial papers have been devoted to *Ulysses*. In 'Joyce and the Tragedy of Language' (*Forum H*) W. Weathers sees the handling of language in *Ulysses* as symbolic of the inadequacy of language as a means of communication. The novel

offers three main types of language —'aesthetically-oriented', 'socially-oriented', and 'sensually-oriented'— each being a mark of the tragic failure to communicate.

In 'Science in Ithaca' (*WSCL*) Avrom Fleishman looks at the astronomical material in the seventeenth section of *Ulysses* and shows that 'Joyce's vocabulary and the theory underlying even the most bizarre suggestions of his prose are drawn from long-established classical mechanics and astronomy.'

J. R. Bryer in 'Joyce, *Ulysses*, and *The Little Review*' (*SAQ*) discusses the obscenity charge brought against *The Little Review* as the publishers of *Ulysses* in 1920, and in 'The Last Adventures of Ulysses' (*PULC*). A. W. Litz gives an account of the publishing history of the novel 'focusing upon that day early in April 1921 when Sylvia Beach offered her services to Joyce as publisher'.

In *TCL* R. O. Richardson has a piece on 'Molly's Last Words' and in *Carrell* J. Novak compares 'Verisimilitude and Vision: Defoe and Blake as Influences on Joyce's Molly Bloom'. To *ELH* D. Hayman contributes 'Forms of Folly in Joyce: A Study of Clowning in *Ulysses*'.

In *PMLA* B. Benstock has an interesting paper on 'L. Bloom as Dreamer in *Finnegans Wake*', and in *YR* J. M. Morse writes on 'HCE's Chaste Ecstasy'.

There are only a handful of papers on Lawrence, some of which are biographical, and the critical essays are not always sympathetic.

In 'Who is Frieda Lawrence?' (*Sew*) R. Sale argues that Lawrence's three artistically successful novels— the revised *Sons and Lovers*, *Women in Love*, and *The Rainbow*—came out of Lawrence's relationship with Frieda. In 'Princess on a Rocking Horse' (*SSF*) G. R. Turner suggests that the child in 'The Rocking-Horse Winner' was based on Leonora, daughter of Sir Charles Brooke, the White Rajah of Sarawak, with whom Lawrence became well acquainted through Lady Brooke's sister, Miss Brett. Also in *SSF*, K. Sagar writes on 'A Modern Lover' and 'The Shades of Spring', and in 'D. H. Lawrence's "The Princess" as Ironic Romance' J. C. Cowan looks at the mythic element in the story, seeing the inversion of the usual myth-pattern as central to the 'brilliantly realized ironic romance'.

In '"Silence" in D. H. Lawrence' (*NQ*) W. T. Andrews examines Chapter 18 of *Lady Chatterley's Lover* and Chapter 15 of *Kangaroo* to demonstrate that Lawrence is a 'formal and mannered' novelist who employs set formulaic phrases in a way that cannot be reconciled with his reputation for 'spontaneity and vitality'—the qualities seen in his writing by 'romantic critics'. In '*Women in Love*' (*EIC*) F. H. Langman argues that Lawrence's rigorously schematic conception of the novel led him into passages of notoriously bad writing, and in *REL* D. Bickerton examines various mannerisms in 'The Language of *Women in Love*', finding too much repetition and loose phrasing: in *TSLL* R. D. Erlich has a paper entitled 'Catastrophism and Coition: Universal and Individual Development in *Women in Love*'. In 'Lawrence's Quarrel with Tenderness' (*CQ*) M. Spilka contributes a thoughtful—and the most sympathetic—paper, considering the implications of Lawrence's attitudes to the quality of tenderness in physical relationships: he discusses 'In Love', *Sons and Lovers, Women in Love, The Man Who Died*, and *Lady Chatterley's Lover*—which at one stage was intended to have the title *Tenderness*.

In 'A "Key" to Lawrence Durrell' (*WSCL*) A. W. Friedman attempts to define Durrell's value as a writer and his place in the development of twentieth-century fiction. He is concerned mainly with *The Alexandria Quartet* and for a starting-point uses some of the ideas and critical criteria expressed in Durrell's own critical book *A Key to Modern British Poetry*.

The Autumn number of *MFS* is devoted to Lawrence Durrell. M. P. Levitt writes on 'Art and Correspondences: Durrell, Miller and *The Alexandria Quartet*', considering the ways in which Henry Miller's influence on Durrell changed during the composition of the *Quartet*. S. L. Brown in '*The Black Book*: A Search for Method' considers the themes and techniques of the earlier work as leading towards those employed more consistently in the *Quartet*. A. W. Friedman in 'Place and Durrell's Island Books' writes mainly on *Bitter Lemons*, which he considers Durrell's greatest success in relating description to plot. M. L. Morcos writes on 'Elements of the Autobiographical in *The Alexandria Quartet*', concentrating on the aspects of Durrell that are attributed to Darley, Arnanti, Nessim, and Pursewarden, while Justine and Clea are related to Durrell's second and third wives. In 'Some Sources of Durrell's *Alexandria Quartet*' W. L. Godshalk cites Forster's *Alexandria*, Hartmann's *Life of Paracelsus*, MacPherson's *The Moulids of Egypt*, Leeder's *Modern Sons of the Pharaohs* and other books from which Durrell seems to have borrowed. In 'Durrell's Heraldic Universe' C. J. Burns argues that Durrell is indebted to Plotinus's discussion of the four faculties of the mind—sense, imagination, reason, and self-knowledge; the four parts of the *Quartet* represent these four faculties and the whole work shows Darley's ascent to the highest faculty. P. J. Read in 'The Illusion of Personality', writes on the concept of cyclical time in the *Quartet*. J. E. Kruppa contributes 'Durrell's *Alexandria Quartet* and the "Implosion" of the Modern Consciousness' and M. Beelze supplies a selected checklist of critical work on Durrell.

An issue of *UWR* is devoted to essays on various aspects of H. G. Wells's work. In 'Failure of Nerve: H. G. Wells' C. P. Crowley writes on the pessimism and frustration which increasingly characterize Wells's later work. M. W. Steinberg writes on 'H. G. Wells as a Social Critic'. V. Brome considers 'H. G. Wells as a Controversialist' and J. K. Farrell 'H. G. Wells as an Historian'. E. McNamara in 'H. G. Wells as Novelist' discusses *Tono-Bungay*, and in 'H. G. Wells and the World of Science Fiction' E. D. LeMire considers Wells's literary intentions in the early science fiction novels and especially with regard to *The Island of Dr. Moreau*. In *RQ* J. Williams has a piece on 'The Ideas of H. G. Wells' and in *ELT* R. H. Costa has a short review of recent studies of *Tono-Bungay*. In *NQ* K. C. Phillips in 'H. G. Wells: A Possible Debt to Trollope' points to similarities in the train journeys taken by Mr. Polly and Miriam in section eight of *The History of Mr. Polly*, and by Adolphus Crosbie and Lady Alexandrina in Trollope's *The Small House at Allington*.

Ford Madox Ford has been the subject of papers written from various viewpoints. There is a short superficial 'Profile' by P. Bartlett in *QQ*. C. G. Hoffman in *NQ* points to '*The Life and Times of Henry VIII*: An Original for Ford Madox Ford's Fifth Queen Trilogy'. R. H. Huntley relates Ford to Flaubert in 'The Fallacy of *le mot juste*' (*ELN*) and

the same writer considers Ford's possible debt to Goethe in '*The Good Soldier* and *Die Wahlverwandtschaften*' (*CL*). In *EC* G. Wagner in his 'Ford Madox Ford: the Honest Edwardian' writes on the conflict in Ford's work between his romantic impulse, his conservatism, and his attempt to achieve a detached irony. There are two papers on *The Good Soldier*: in *TCL* B. D. Bort considers the question of whether the novel is 'Comedy or Tragedy?' and in *Crit* J.-A. Baernstein has a lengthy analysis of 'Image, Identity, and Insight in *The Good Soldier*'.

J. Gindin in 'The Fable in Recent British Fiction' (*WSCL*) writes on the strain of fable-like novels, as distinct from the general run of novels which 'establish a greater verisimilitude to the conditions of actual experience'. He discusses the work of Durrell, Angus Wilson, Arthur Machen, David Storey, William Golding and other contemporary novelists, estimating their various successes and failures and discussing the uses and limitations of what he calls the 'fabulistic novel'. In the same issue of *WSCL* D. Roper writes on 'Allegory and Novel in Golding's *The Spire*' expressing admiration for the subtlety of character portrayal in the creation of Jocelin, but arguing that the allegorical method, employed so successfully in *The Lord of the Flies*, is in *The Spire* unsatisfactorily related to the realistic element in the book, and is not successfully brought 'to the test of concrete experience'. Mr. Roper concludes that the 'lesson of *The Spire* is that where this is not done . . . the work remains . . . the diagram of a novel'. D. W. Crompton contributes a detailed paper on '*The Spire*' to *CQ*. In *Cent R* B. A. Rosenberg has an essay called 'Lord of the Fire-Flies' in which he emphasizes Golding's use of fire as a recurring symbol in *The Lord of the Flies*. In 'Grendel's Point of View: *Beowulf* and William Golding' (*MFS*) J. R. Hurt suggests that in *The Inheritors* Golding has inverted the roles played by man and beast in *Beowulf*.

'Two Printed Texts of Somerset Maugham's *Mrs. Craddock*' (*ELN*) are studied by C. Heywood, who points out that passages cancelled by Maugham's publisher in the first edition of the novel (1902) were restored by Maugham himself for the 1937 edition.

The papers on Iris Murdoch's work concentrate on *The Bell* and are appropriately earnest in their approach to the treatment of ideas and passions. In *PMLA* S. Kaehele and H. German in their 'The Discovery of Reality in Iris Murdoch's *The Bell*' dwell on the great difficulties writers have encountered in their attempts to bring together the apparently complementary purposes of literature and philosophy, pointing out the general failure of such attempts, but maintaining that 'Iris Murdoch has succeeded in creating genuine fictitional worlds which are enriched but not dominated by her philosophical interests.' The article is concerned to clarify the philosophical, moral, and emotional richness of the novel by analysing its use of symbols. In 'Love and Morality in Iris Murdoch's *The Bell*' (*Meanjin*) Dorothy Jones brings to her appreciation of that novel her reading of Miss Murdoch's own theoretical and critical remarks on contemporary fiction in the essays 'The Sublime and the Good', 'The Sublime and the Beautiful', and 'Against Dryness'. Miss Jones discusses *The Bell* in terms of Miss Murdoch's maxim that 'the discovery of reality' is to be made through art where love is the essence of morality. In *MR* W. Berthoff has a paper on 'Fortunes of

the Novel', where he discusses work by Iris Murdoch and Muriel Spark.

George Orwell's character and his persona as a writer continue to absorb most of the attention paid to his work. In 'George Orwell: Our "Responsible Quixote"' (*WCR*) W. Burns considers Orwell's self-encouraged image as the champion of the ordinary values held by 'decent people', whereas in 'George Orwell: A Memoir' (*AM*) Anthony Powell maintains that in his life and in his books Orwell's 'interest in individuals was never great', his approaches and attitudes often being characterized by an 'extraordinary unreality'. W. Warncke contributes a short general piece on 'The Permanence of Orwell' (*UR*) and R. A. Fanald in *SAQ* has a paper on 'George Orwell and the Mad World: The Anti-Universe of 1984'. In *VQR* under the title 'Fantasy as Technique' R. B. Schmerl considers some of the roles played by fantasy in the work of Orwell and E. M. Forster.

In 'Ritual Aspects of E. M. Forster's *The Longest Journey*' (*MFS*) J. Magnus offers a reading of the novel which sees it as having some ritualistic features. Stephen Wonham's ablutions and Rickie's sacrifice are interpreted as ritual acts which make possible the rebirth of Demeter (Mrs. Elliott) and the salvation of the race. The other papers on Forster are devoted to *A Passage to India*. In *ELT* M. L. Raina offers 'Imagery of *A Passage to India*: A Further Note' in which he gives examples of Forster's use of imagery involving birds, insects, and animals in conformity with their significance in Indian mythology. V. M. Bell writes on 'Comic Seriousness in *A Passage to India*' in *SAQ* and W. R. McDonald has a piece on the same novel in *Ex.* F. P. McDowell has a bibliographical entry on Forster in *ELT*.

In 'Fiction and the Rising Industrial Classes' (*EIC*) David Craig discusses the general failure of the modern novel to present an adequate account of industrial society. Mr. Craig looks at *Women in Love, Howards End, A Passage to India* and other novels and finds that, since they work mainly through individually realized characters, they are concerned more with 'the purely moral' than with 'the merely social'. And in 'Some Observations on the novels of Raymond Williams' (*AWR*) W. Binding finds that *Second Generation*, in spite of the careful documentation of industrial work and the activities of trade unions, is less impressive than *Border Country*, where the traditional conflicts of the novel—classes, generations, town and country etc.—are handled with the intimacy that comes from authorial experience.

Three short notices on Evelyn Waugh appear in *EWN*: P. A. Doyle writes on '*Decline and Fall*: Two Versions'; W. A. English offers 'Some Irish and English Waugh Bibliography'; Charles E. Linck Jr. provides an annotated finding list of 'Waugh Letters at the Texas Academic Center'. R. M. Davis considers 'Some Textual Variants in *Scoop*' (*EWN*) and writes on 'The Mind and Art of Evelyn Waugh' in *PLL*. T. Churchill indicates 'The Trouble with *Brideshead Revisited*' (*MLQ*) and S. A. Jervis examines 'Evelyn Waugh, *Vile Bodies*, and the Younger Generation' (*SAQ*).

There are only three articles on Virginia Woolf to be noticed, and two of those express lack of enthusiasm about one of the major novels. In 'The Match in the Crocus: Obtrusive Art in Virginia Woolf's *Mrs. Dalloway*' (*MFS*), S. Rosenberg discusses some metaphors which seem inappropriate to the characters they are attributed to and suggests that they are the mark of unwarranted authorial intrusion. In 'Beyond the Lighthouse: *The Years*' (*Bu R*) H. Marder argues that *To the Lighthouse* is restricted unduly to an evocation of the inner lives of its characters and that the necessary balance of interest between society and the private experience of the individual is more successfully achieved in *The Years*. In 'The Symbol of Painting in Virginia Woolf's *To the Lighthouse*' (*REL*) K. M. May points out that Mrs. Woolf uses the art of painting as representative of all the arts. Lily Briscoe's attempt to achieve 'significant form' in her painting and her hope of making it suggest 'the multitudinous variety of interrelated perceptions' are analogous to Mrs. Woolf's own purpose and desire in writing the novel.

A. R. Penner in '"What are Yo' Looking So Bleddy Black for?": Survival and Bitters in "On Saturday Afternoon"' (*SSF*) discusses Alan Sillitoe's ability to look candidly upon the grossness and occasional cruelty of life, without despairing. The same story is considered in 'No Man in His Humour: A Note on Sillitoe' (*SSF*) where Neil D. Isaacs explains that the structure of 'On Saturday Afternoon' is based in part on an inversion of the traditional theory of 'humours', and that this causes an ironic juxtaposition of 'blood' (sanguinity) and 'blackness' (melancholy).

In 'Intuition and Concept: Joyce Carey and the Critics' (*TSLL*) E. L. Galligan suggests that criticism of Carey's work has been inadequate, because it has tended to adopt a 'fiercely conceptual' approach to a writer who worked by 'intuition'.

3. BIOGRAPHY

Michael Hasting's book,[24] its title

[24] *The Handsomest Young Man in England: Rupert Brooke*, by Michael Hastings. Michael Joseph. pp. 240. 50*s*.

adapted (or, in the light of its contents, more probably misquoted) from Yeats's description of Rupert Brooke, can best be described as a handsomely produced scrapbook with a biographical running commentary, whose aim is to present the man as he was, stripped of the idolatries, of the 'legend' and unrealities of the romantic myth, and likewise of the prejudice bred by those extravagances. Its main interest lies in the many hitherto unpublished photographs of Brooke and his circle, although the selection of these often seems disproportionate to the importance of the subjects and arbitrarily arranged in relation to the sequence of the text. The latter is chatty and discursive, and contains a number of factual inaccuracies; and what criticism there is is ill-considered, superficial and often naïve. What, for example, are we to make of such a statement as 'Whether or not the poems stand up as poetry, ceases to matter'? That, surely is in the last resort the only thing which does.

In his biography of Galsworthy[25] (first published in 1963 and reprinted during the current year) Dudley Barker stresses the important role played by his cousin's wife Ada, first as mistress and then as wife, in the encouragement of Galsworthy's literary talent and ambition. Much of his fiction was admittedly autobiographical; and Barker's account of it relates the personalities and events of the author's life to what he wrote. Ada, and the circumstances of her first marriage, inspired the portrait of Irene in *The Forsyte Saga*. Old Jolyon and the silly, tactless Aunt Juley originated in his own loved father and disliked mother.

The jilting of June Forsyte by Bosinney was suggested by a similar happening to one of his own sisters. Galsworthy emerges from this sober study as a man of scrupulous conscience and integrity, often 'humourlessly sincere'; a generous giver both of his material goods and of his time in campaigning for humane causes and social reform.

The autobiography of S. C. Roberts[26] is that of a bookman who, as a distinguished publisher (Secretary to the Syndics of the Cambridge University Press) and later as Master of Pembroke and Vice-Chancellor of the University, had the privilege of knowing some of the most interesting figures of his time. His book is full of memories and glimpses of, and good stories about, such personalities as Shaw, Beerbohm, Housman, De la Mare, his neighbour G. M. Trevelyan, the Dover Wilsons and the Granville-Barkers. This is a record of a full and busy life enjoyed in all its aspects, from soldiering to amateur dramatics, lecturing and writing on Dr. Johnson to the 'mock-solemnity of [Sherlock] Holmesian scholarship'; and it provides a detailed picture of the evolution of life at the university between the Edwardian era, when the writer was there as an undergraduate, and the period after the Second World War.

The fourth volume of Leonard Woolf's autobiography,[27] covering the period between the 'senseless savagery' of the two wars, is also an absorbing document of intellectual London society of the time, and in particular of the Bloomsbury group during the '20s and '30s. The pressure of events during these years forced the author into practical political

[25] *The Man of Principal: A View of John Galsworthy*, by Dudley Barker. Allen & Unwin. pp. 240. 28s.

[26] *Adventures with Authors*, by S. C. Roberts. C.U.P. (1966). pp. vii+276. 35s.

[27] *Downhill all the Way*, by Leonard Woolf. Hogarth. pp. 259. 35s.

activity with the Fabian Society and the Labour Party; but this is also the story of his literary editorship of *The Nation* and the contacts this brought him, and of his successful directorship of the Hogarth Press, with Gorki, Freud and Rilke among his distinguished authors and he published the first poems of Eliot and *The Waste Land*, Muir's first poems, Vita Sackville-West's *The Edwardians*, Isherwood's *Mr. Norris Changes Trains*, Roger Fry's *Cézanne*, and the novels of Virginia Woolf. There is an intimate portrait of her at work on these, and Woolf gives an interesting inside picture of the economics of publishing and authorship during this time, with details of his own and his wife's earnings from their writing.

The sixth volume of Compton Mackenzie's chatty, anecdotal reminiscences[28] covers part of the same period—the eight years after his fortieth birthday. With undiminished exuberance he recalls his activities in the pioneering days of radio and as co-editor of *The Gramophone*, his encounters with writers during the '20s, and how he continued to indulge his passion for acquiring islands—this time in the Outer Hebrides, whose wildlife he describes in delighted detail. He also became embroiled in Scottish Nationalist politics, and introduces the originals of some of the characters and incidents from these days used in his novel *Whisky Galore*. Extensive quotation from his own reviews, articles, broadcasts and letters makes these memoirs read at times more like a scrapbook of events for each individual year than a consecutive narrative; but there can be no disputing the zest and energy with which

the author sets down the detail of forty years ago as if it happened only yesterday.

Frances Donaldson's 'portrait of a country neighbour'[29] can be read as complementary to Evelyn Waugh's autobiography, which covered only the first twenty-five years of his life; for her acquaintance with him began in 1948, after he went to live in the Cotswolds, and ended only with his death in 1966. It was an achievement that she and her husband, as Socialists, became his friends, for she acknowledges that he was 'enormously prejudiced'. From her book full of revealing anecdotes, describing her meetings with him and reproducing all his letters and postcards to her, Waugh emerges as a many-sided personality: a man of wit and asperity, fond of gossip, suffering from boredom and 'a melancholia of Johnsonian proportions', whose social snobbery was matched only by his unpredictable bad manners and who alienated many of his friends through the acidity of his tongue and pen.

Elizabeth Salter also offers a portrait of an eccentric[30] observed at close quarters, with initial trepidation and a growing sympathy and affection. For the last eight years of Edith Sitwell's life she worked as her secretary and personal assistant and was immediately involved in all the crises and controversies which the celebrity of her employer seemed inevitably to attract. This informal biography is not only highly entertaining, but moving; for it depicts not only those aspects of the formidable public façade known through Edith Sitwell's spectacular appearances as

---

[28] *My Life and Times, Octave Six: 1923–30.* By Compton Mackenzie. Chatto. pp. 244. 35s.

[29] *Evelyn Waugh: Portrait of a Country Neighbour*, by Frances Donaldson. Weidenfeld & Nicolson. pp. xvii+124. 25s.

[30] *The Last Years of a Rebel*, by Elizabeth Salter. Bodley Head. pp. 208. 30s.

a performer and in her furious literary feuds—which in any case had begun to subside in her later years—but the human frailties and handicaps, generosities and courage of the woman she gradually came to respect and love.

4. GENERAL PROSE WORKS

The selection from the *Journals* of George Sturt[31] made by E. D. Mackerness is the most comprehensive so far; extending up to 1927, the year of the diarist's death, it presents for the first time a transcription from the later journals from the British Museum manuscripts. As the author of *Change in the Village* and *The Wheelwright's Shop*, Sturt is interesting for his reflection of contemporary social and political events from the standpoint of a humane socialist employer in a rural district. Deeply concerned with the lot of the craft worker and farm labourer since enclosure and the Industrial Revolution, he was influenced in youth by the philosophy of Morris, Ruskin and Thoreau, and also anticipated some of the attitudes in the writing of D. H. Lawrence.

The life of the farm labourer—this time in Dorset—is also the subject of one of the longer pieces in the collection of Hardy's miscellaneous occasional writings[32] assembled by Harold Orel from a variety of sources, including periodicals which have long ceased publication. All his prefaces to his own work, ranging from *Desperate Remedies* in 1871 to *Winter Words* in 1928, and to the work of other writers including that of William Barnes, are brought together for the first time. There are articles and

letters on literary matters, such as the use of dialect in the novel, aspects of the reading and writing of fiction, and a defence of *The Dynasts*; reminiscences of Stevenson and Meredith, and his views on topics which reflect his enduring interest in his native West Country—some Romano-British relics discovered at Max Gate, archaeological excavation at Maumbury Ring, the abuses of church restoration, and the preservation of Stonehenge.

Hardy, like Trollope and Kipling, was a Macmillan author. Founded in 1843, the firm also published poets from Tennyson and Arnold to Yeats and the Sitwells, and eminent writers in other fields like Gladstone, J. P. Green, T. H. Huxley, Bergson, Churchill and J. M. Keynes. The eighty-four distinguished writers who are represented in Simon Nowell-Smith's selection from letters to the firm[33] illustrate many interesting aspects of the author-publisher relationship—problems of copyright, royalties and advertising, and not least the humours of professional vanity.

A further volume of letters from the same publisher are those of Charles Morgan,[34] prefaced by a memoir by their editor, Eiluned Lewis, which gives a sympathetic portrait of a personality often thought of as chilly and remote. They have been chosen specifically to illustrate Morgan's attitude to his craft and to the position of the writer in society and offer many interesting glimpses of his habits of composition, techniques and views about writing. Chronologically arranged, the letters extend from the time of the writer's internment in Holland during the

---

[31] *The Journals of George Sturt, 1890–1927*, ed. by E. D. Mackerness. C.U.P. Vol. I: pp. viii+453. Vol. II: pp. v+455–915. £6.
[32] *Thomas Hardy's Personal Writings*, ed. by Harold Orel. Macmillan. pp. xii+295. 35s.
[33] *Letters to Macmillan*, ed. by Simon Nowell-Smith. Macmillan. pp. 384. 55s.
[34] *Selected Letters of Charles Morgan*, ed. by Eiluned Lewis. Macmillan. pp. 235. 42s.

First World War (his background for *The Fountain*) to the height of his international reputation at the time of his death. That reputation, both as stylist and thinker, has suffered a sharp decline; his letters nevertheless bear witness to the integrity of his purpose, the seriousness of his dedication as a creative artist, and of his concern with human personality and with questions of individual responsibility.

First published in 1949, C. M. Bowra's studies of seven poetic innovators[35] active in the first part of this century—Cavafy, Mayakowsky, Apollinaire, Pasternak, Eliot, Lorca and Alberti—has been reprinted. The essay on Eliot concentrates on an analysis of *The Waste Land*—its appeal to the spirit of its time in both style and subject, its symbolism and use of ironic juxtaposition, and as 'the last voice of a civilization which knows that it is doomed and struggles without hope to regain a splendour which is lost for ever'.

Although the most substantial item in F. R. Leavis's collection of essays[36] is on *Anna Karenina*, a number of others are concerned with twentieth-century English letters. There are pieces on Conrad's *The Shadow Line*—analogous in the body of his work to *Silas Marner* in George Eliot's—and *The Secret Sharer*; on D. H. Lawrence and the disservice done him, in Leavis's eyes, by his recent critics and editors of his letters, with some astringent comment on the court proceedings over *Lady Chatterley's Lover*; some thoughts about Pound and his 'painfully limited mind', and an analysis of Eliot's criticism which concludes that

for all its influence 'the trenchancy and vigour are illusory', there is 'abundant evidence of negative attitudes towards life', and that he evades 'the essential responsibility of a critic'.

In *The Backward Look*,[37] Frank O'Connor's last book based on a series of lectures delivered at Trinity College, Dublin, the distinguished Irish short-story writer and critic presents a comprehensive survey of Irish literature from its beginnings in the sixth century, through the medieval sagas, the Renaissance, and the eighteenth century to which Yeats owed such a debt, to the work of that poet and of Joyce and O'Casey in the twentieth. The recurring theme which O'Connor discerns in Irish literature as a whole is 'the backward look' to the ancient native traditions, folklore and superstitions which have always haunted the work of Irish writers. Other aspects he explores are the strong oral tradition in Irish verse, its struggle to eschew alien—especially English—influences, and the sometimes stultifying effect of the Irish Government and the Catholic Church on the country's literature.

The political history of modern Ireland which is the background for its literature is charted in Anne Marreco's life-story of Constance Markievicz.[38] This remarkable woman, beautiful, courageous and forcefully independent, was at the centre of her country's literary and political renaissance in the early years of this century, was closely associated with figures like AE and O'Casey, and was the object, with Maud Gonne, of Yeats's frequently expressed antagonism towards women

---

[35] *The Creative Experiment*, by C. M. Bowra. New edition. Macmillan. pp. vii + 255. 36s.

[36] *'Anna Karenina' and Other Essays*, by F. R. Leavis. Chatto. pp. 248. 30s.

[37] *The Backward Look*, by Frank O'Connor. Macmillan. pp. 264. 40s.

[38] *The Rebel Countess: The Life and Times of Constance Markievicz*, by Anne Marreco. Weidenfeld & Nicolson. pp. xiii + 330. 45s.

in politics. She was born into a well-known Anglo-Irish family; and her rebellion outraged not only the conventions of her day but the social traditions of her environment and upbringing. Her consistent championship of the less fortunate and oppressed, which earned her the love of the Dublin poor, culminated in her Sinn Feinist activities and enthusiastic part in the Easter Rising of 1916 for which she was condemned to death—a sentence later commuted to penal servitude for life. After her release from Aylesbury Jail in 1917 her struggle for her country's freedom continued undaunted until her death in the year of the General Strike.

William Irwin Thompson's 'study of an ideological movement'[39] sets out to demonstrate the relationship between artistic imagination and historical reality in the interaction of the Irish Literary Renaissance with the insurrection of Easter 1916 which gave Ireland its independence. He begins with a survey of 'the movement towards the event': the recapturing by eighteenth- and nineteenth-century historians and archaeologists of the history of ancient Ireland—a rediscovery of a nation's past which lit the fuse of both the Irish political and poetic imagination in the twentieth century. The second part of the book traces the workings of that imagination in the three poet-revolutionaries who were executed for their role in the rising—Pearse, MacDonagh and Plunkett, whose self-dramatization and romantic gesture of sacrifice was the culmination of their 'common desire to live a myth'. The final section examines the impact and survival of the event in the minds of three major literary figures intimately involved in it: through the tragic

image in Yeats, the mystic in AE, and the naturalistic drama of Sean O'Casey.

O'Casey's own characteristically-titled *Blasts and Benedictions*,[40] selected and introduced by Ronald Ayling, is a collection of articles, reviews, broadcasts and stories written between 1962, when the author came to England, and the year of his death in 1964. Reprinted from a variety of sources, the pieces represent O'Casey's views and style at their most exuberantly idiosyncratic. There are autobiographical fragments; essays on the theatre—Synge, Tchekov, Ibsen, and questions of such perennial interest as the playwright and the box office, the theatre and the politician, and the play of ideas; on books and writers including Shaw, Lady Gregory, and Lawrence, and a topical article on censorship; on people and places; and three short stories.

5. POETRY

The emphasis of T. R. Barnes's study of English verse from Wyatt to Yeats,[41] whose aim is to encourage the student to listen to poetry with a more finely attuned ear, is on the poet's characteristic tone of voice and individual 'movement'—the sound of his verbal patterns and the way their rhythms impose themselves upon ear and imagination. His final chapter on the twentieth century considers Hardy's ingenious exploitation of traditional rhythms, compared with Housman's neatly melodious but often monotonous treatment of similar themes; Kipling's 'crude minatory drum-beats', the 'skilfully modulated' tunes of De la Mare, and the

---

[39] *The Imagination of an Insurrection: Dublin, Easter 1916*, by William Irwin Thompson. O.U.P. pp. xiii + 262. 48s.

[40] *Blasts and Benedictions*, by Sean O'Casey, ed. by Ronald Ayling. Macmillan. pp. xx + 314. 30s.

[41] *English Verse: Voice and Movement from Wyatt to Yeats*, by T. R. Barnes. C.U.P. pp. ix + 324. 35s.

work of Edward Thomas and Owen in moving away from the 'stale rhythms' of the Georgians; Lawrence's free verse, the virtuosity of Eliot's rhythmic techniques, and Yeats's movement towards the powerful economy of his mature style.

Housman, and the imaginative stimulus of soldiering and war-like themes which produced some of his best poetry, is the subject of an essay by R. B. Pearsall in *PMLA*, which illustrates his use of the traditional qualities of public responsibility, comradeship and physical courage to depict his individual situations of contrast and irony.

Robert H. Ross's study of the Georgian poets[42] is the first full-scale survey of the movement which attempts to place it in the historical perspective of its time. His purpose is less to evaluate than to explain, and thus he does not essay any systematic critical assessment of the Georgian poetic achievement. Drawing freely upon the personal recollections of survivors of the movement, and on the collection of letters written by its members to its founder, Edward Marsh, he reconstructs in detail the conditions and circumstances of the genesis, heyday and decline of the six anthologies, describes and defines the Georgian poetic temper and the changes which occurred in poetry between 1912 and 1922, and examines the 'failure of imagination' which led to the death of the poetic ideal. Ross writes with sympathy yet discrimination, justly feeling that the major poets of the movement deserve to be rescued from the obloquy which nowadays attaches to the word 'Georgian', but facing squarely the characteristic weaknesses common to most of them.

[42] *The Georgian Revolt: Rise and Fall of a Poetic Ideal, 1910–1922*, by Robert H. Ross. Faber. pp. 296. 45s.

John D. Gordan's workmanlike guide to an exhibition recently on display in New York,[43] of letters written to Marsh by his contributors to *Georgian Poetry*, contains an introduction, and a postscript on the 'Imitators and Parodists' of *Georgian Poetry*. In between come chronologically presented biographical notes on Marsh and his 'mentors'—Bridges, Gosse, Maugham, Forster, Middleton Murry and Katherine Mansfield—and on the poets who contributed to his anthologies, ranging from Sturge Moore, Davies and De la Mare to some, like Graves and Blunden, who are still living.

Blunden's poetry is the subject of an essay by M. Thorpe (*ES*), who first considers his place in the tradition of Clare and Hardy as elegist of the forefathers and the old rustic order. After weighing Leavis's criticism of Blunden's later work as imitative and 'literary', Thorpe discusses his Wordsworthian themes, his valuation of nature, especially in relation to war, his religious sense, and his poems of human affection.

The work of another Georgian, Edward Thomas is examined by A. John (*AWR*) on the fiftieth anniversary of the poet's death. After reviewing the critical attention paid to Thomas's poetry and prose, John concentrates on refuting the view of him—expressed by Frost, De la Mare, and others—as a Welsh poet, even though Thomas came of Welsh stock and had a warm regard for Wales.

In his inaugural lecture[44] Francis Berry feels that Masefield's narrative poetry, in which he excelled, has been

[43] *Letters to an Editor: 'Georgian Poetry', 1912–22. An Exhibition from the Berg Collection*, ed. by John D. Gordan. New York Public Library. pp. 36. $1. Paperback.

[44] *John Masefield: The Narrative Poet*, by Francis Berry. Inaugural Lecture delivered 25 October 1967 in the University of Sheffield. pp. 18. Paperback.

generally neglected in favour of the shorter anthology pieces, and that his reputation has suffered accordingly. He stresses Masefield's debt to Chaucer in *The Widow in the Bye Street*, his ability, in *Reynard the Fox*, to enter sympathetically into the feelings and viewpoints of his characters, and his psychological accuracy in *The Everlasting Mercy*. His conclusion is that Eliot and his admirers, discrediting the Chaucer-*genre* of narrative poetry, effectively destroyed Masefield's reputation in the '20s and '30s.

In *Columbia University Forum* B. Deutsch sets the poetry of De la Mare beside that of Hardy, as the work of men 'who used to notice such things' as the sombreness of life but finally rejected despair and allowed room for the recording of joy.

The many short lyrics addressed in the first person to an anonymous lost love in a rural setting unspoiled by urban influence is T. Holmes's subject in 'Thomas Hardy's City of the Mind' (*Sew*). He believes they are not personal but symbolic of a conflict in Hardy of 'two divergent inclinations in the same life impossible of reconciliation': Hardy's passion for his native countryside, and the 'fashionable abstractions of modern conceptual science' which filled his mind—a polarity allegorically explored and elegized in his poems of mysterious severed love affairs and sexual misalliance.

The central preoccupation of Todd K. Bender's study of Hopkins[45] is the ideas which helped to form the intellectual context in which he wrote and in which, a generation later, his poetry was read. The opening chapter outlines the critical reception of

the first and second editions of the poems; and after considering Hopkins's prose and his unpublished notebooks Bender proceeds to examine the non-logical structure of *The Wreck of the Deutschland* in the light of Hopkins's understanding of the Greek odes and in particular Pindar's poetry and methods of composition. Hopkins's distortions of normal grammar and syntax are then discussed in the light of his study of the Greek and Latin poets who, it is convincingly demonstrated, influenced his techniques and produced that 'precocious development ahead of the trend in Victorian art' which anticipated many present-day critical assumptions. The final chapter compares Hopkins's metaphysical imagery and 'explosive meaning' with that of Crashaw, to whom he is so frequently likened, and the debt of both to the Latin epigrams of Martial.

From Munich comes a fully-documented study (in German)[46] of the work of Hopkins, of the Imagists under the main influences of Pound and Amy Lowell, and of Eliot in relation to other poets—the Metaphysicals, the French Symbolists, Hopkins, Pound and the Imagists, and German verse—with detailed attention paid in all three sections to verse techniques.

In 'Making Earnest of Game' (*MLQ*) D. Sonstroem 'draws some interesting parallels between Hopkins and Edward Lear. Both make use of 'portmanteau' words, forced rhymes and double meanings, and share a fondness for lists—especially of adjectives—and a quirkiness of thought. But whereas Lear employed these for the purpose of writing nonsense verse

[45] *Gerard Manley Hopkins: The Classical Background and Critical Reception of His Work*, by Todd K. Bender. O.U.P. and Johns Hopkins Press. 1966. pp. ix+172. 48s.

[46] *Die Versauffassung bei Gerard Manley Hopkins, den Imagisten und T. S. Eliot*, by Kurt R. Janhowsky. Max Hueber Verlag: München. pp. 338. DM 19.80. Paperback.

—whose nature the writer considers—Hopkins's verbal play and emphasis on sound served him 'as the means that permitted him to move from quandary to Christian assurance'.

Hopkins considered *The Windhover* the best thing he ever wrote. In *PMLA* E. R. August traces through all its extant manuscripts, their revisions, and Hopkins's references in his letters, the growth of the poem from its first composition in May 1877 through the next ten or twelve years during which it was slowly brought to its finished form.

Attention is drawn by Sister M. Sharples in *Ren* to a point of similarity between Hopkins and Joyce. The former's favourite theory of 'inscape', borrowed from the philosophy of Duns Scotus, closely resembles the theory of the epiphany which Joyce derived from the same source. Both writers employed the concentrated concrete image 'to express the individuality of a thing rather than simply its general or universal aspects'.

A fresh, geological interpretation of Hopkins's image of the 'ooze of oil' in *God's Grandeur*, which heightens for the reader his sense of the 'immense source of power which is God', is offered by M. Taylor in *Ex*.

Allen Tate's symposium of appreciative essays on Eliot,[47] all reprinted from *The Sewanee Review*, covers the whole range and scope of his contribution to modern literature as poet, dramatist, critic, and major influence on contemporary thought. It also reveals many facets of the personality behind the work—a biographical aspect supplemented by sixteen pages of photographs of the poet at different stages in his life—in reminiscences by I. A. Richards, Herbert Read, Stephen Spender, Bonamy Dobrée,

and his fellow-publisher Frank Morley: 'A Director's Memories', by E. Martin Browne, of 'T. S. Eliot in the Theatre', and an actor's by Robert Speaight, on playing Becket in *Murder in the Cathedral*. Among many other distinguished critics Helen Gardner writes on the comedies, John Crowe Ransom on *Gerontion*, Leonard Unger on 'T. S. Eliot's Images of Awareness', Frank Kermode on *The Waste Land*, Cleanth Brooks on Eliot as thinker and artist, Mario Praz and Austin Warren on his criticism, and Wallace Fowlie on a comparison of Eliot and Baudelaire as interpreters of their age.

Leonard Unger's essay is also included in his volume of seven critical pieces[48] written over a period of nearly three decades. All but two, on *Ash Wednesday*—the early experience of which was the starting-point for his subsequent explorations—and Eliot's critics, are concerned with details selected from the larger body of the writer's poetry, plays and criticism, which yield an interweaving pattern throughout his work. 'T. S. Eliot's Magic Lantern', originally written as a general introduction to Eliot, traces his recurring themes of time, alienation, the isolation of the individual, and the impossibility of communication and understanding, showing how these compose a steadily developing pattern of inter-related images and symbols which contribute to the continuity of the whole. In other essays Unger focuses attention on the childhood experience in the rose-garden as a persistent theme throughout Eliot's poetry and plays; on Eliot's debt to Laforgue and Conrad's *Heart of Darkness*, particularly in *The Waste Land* and *The Hollow Men*, in many rhythmical

[47] *T. S. Eliot: The Man and His Work*, ed. by Allen Tate. Chatto. pp. vi+400. 36s.

[48] *T. S. Eliot: Moments and Patterns*, by Leonard Unger. O.U.P. and Minnesota U.P. pp. 196. 1966. 40s.

devices, themes, and correspondences of diction as well as meaning; and on Eliot's recurring use of certain images, such as those of flowers, water and stairs.

Audrey F. Cahill's study of Eliot's poetry[49] sees its central concern as 'the human predicament': his sense 'that human existence is a challenging and perplexing and often painful experience; that it is fraught with contradictions and tensions; and that to live with any degree of consciousness is to be aware of unreconciled conflicts clamouring to be resolved'. Taking this as a common point of departure in each of the poems, she traces its development as much in form and manner as in meaning. Eliot presented a single, coherent view of life, and 'the glimpses given in the early poems of man's relationship to his social and spiritual environment contribute to the integrated picture of that relationship given in *Four Quartets*. The difference between them derives not from a changed view of human nature, but from an extended vision of the environment of human life.' *Prufrock* and *Portrait of a Lady* express a failure to transcend individual isolation and establish contact, the group of poems from *Preludes* to *Gerontion*, spiritual inertia and absence of an integrating purpose in life, *The Waste Land* the futility of uncommitted lives, and *The Hollow Men* the despair of those who refuse the possibility of redemption. The death-and-renewal experience of the 'Ariel' poems leads to the acceptance in *Ash Wednesday* of the Christian who has made the initial submission but is still aware of the conflict of wills between himself and God. The reconciliation of these tensions is reached in *Four Quartets*, in which

the poet attempts to synthesize experience and see life as a whole. The change between the world of the last and the earlier poems is, concludes Miss Cahill, 'comparable to the change in outlook of a scientist who, looking again at the data that have confronted him for many months, perceives the relationship between them that will enable him to complete his work'.

T. S. Pearce's short monograph on Eliot[50] provides a useful introduction to the poet. Beginning with an outline of Eliot's life and literary and historical background, he proceeds to an analysis of his poetic form, including his use of metre, imagery and symbolism, and to a consideration of the individual poems and plays.

Collected by John Hayward and originally printed privately in Sweden, the small volume of Eliot's poems written in early youth [51] has now been reissued, as a corrective to certain inaccurate pirated editions and in response to the interest expressed in the collection. It contains all the surviving poems written between the winter of 1904 and the spring of 1910, between the ages of sixteen and twenty-two when Eliot was still a schoolboy and undergraduate in America, and carries a short biographical note by his widow.

Writing on 'Eliot and the Tradition of the Anonymous' (*CE*), H. Kenner compares the mature Eliot with Pope and the great Augustans in their common impersonal care for the language itself and their 'habits of imitation, allusion and quotation'. *The Waste Land*, however, is written on a different principle and in a different *genre* from Eliot's later

[49] *T. S. Eliot and the Human Predicament*, by Audrey F. Cahill. Natal U.P. x+222.

[50] *T. S. Eliot*, by T. S. Pearce. Evans. pp. 160. 8s. 6d. Paperback.

[51] *T. S. Eliot: Poems Written in Early Youth*, ed. by John Hayward. Faber. pp. 43. 12s. 6d. Paperback.

Y

poems—'a *genre* less close to the vatic than to the grotesque'—and the writer has some astringent things to say about the confusions of some critics' approaches to its perplexities and to Eliot's intentions.

Eliot's 'Cult of Impersonality' is also examined by D. E. Ward in *EC*. Some of his critical dicta are related to their translation into verse in *Gerontion*. Their 'complex fusion of thought and feeling derives' in part from the imagery and ideas of St. Augustine, Joyce's theory of impersonality expanded in *Portrait of the Artist*, and from the critical theory of Rémy de Gourmont, leading back to the aesthetic of Flaubert, with whom Eliot expressed his sense of affinity.

Several articles have appeared which explore parallels between Eliot and other writers. In *Criticism* P. L. Marcus writes on 'T. S. Eliot and Shakespeare', R. Tamplin on '*The Tempest* and *The Waste Land*' (*AL*), while in *TQ* M.C. Weirick examines 'Myth and Water Symbolism in T. S. Eliot's *The Waste Land*'. J. Clendennings' 'Time, Doubt and Vision' (*A Sch*) offers notes on Eliot and Emerson, and G. M. Reeves a brief one on 'Mr. Eliot and Thomas Wolfe' (*South Atlantic Bulletin*). In *RES* a two-part article by P. Le Brun demonstrates the influence on Eliot—despite his avowed hostility—of Bergson, in particular his theories of time, change, and the individual consciousness. Some of the difficulties encountered in Eliot's statements about the relation of the artist to the tradition and artistic impersonality are, the writer contends, clarified by a recognition of Bergson's influence. F. N. Lees notes (*NQ*) that Eliot's familiar pronouncement on the 'dissociation of sensibility' was in fact anticipated in 1831 by Arthur Hallam, whose diagnosis of this characteristic in modern poetry is essentially similar.

Other articles on Eliot relate to individual poems. G. Fortenberry in *Ball State University Forum* writes on 'Prufrock and the Fool Song'; R. Walz in *Die Neueren Sprachen* on 'T. S. Eliot: *The Love Song of J. Alfred Prufrock*, behandelt an einer Prima'; B. K. Martin contributes a note to *NQ* on the sources of two of the exotic personal names of the kind Eliot often uses in his earlier writing —Prufrock and Bleistein; and P. J. Dolan writes on *Ash Wednesday* (*Ren*). R. Germer writes on *Journey of the Magi* in *Die moderne englische Lyrik: Interpretationen*,[52] which contains interpretations by different German writers of work by many other poets, including Auden, Brooke, De la Mare, Empson, Graves, Larkin, Lawrence, Owen, Dylan Thomas, and Yeats. M. O'Nan (*Symposium*) writes about a poem not closely studied by the critics—*Le Directeur*, which Eliot wrote in French and which appeared in *The Little Review* in 1917. Eliot spoke once of 'poetry so transparent that we should not see the poetry, but that which we are meant to see through the poetry'; and the writer sees this poem as 'an experiment in transparency'.

In *Universitas* (Stuttgart) R. Stamm considers 'Rebellion und Tradition im Werke T. S. Eliots'; and B. Y. Malawsky has compiled an Eliot check-list from 1952 to 1964 (*BB*).

In *NQ* O. Øverland identifies and enlarges upon two sonnets by W. S. Blunt which are the subject of Pound's allusion in Canto 81, and upon Pound's regard for Blunt as a poet and a man.

During the year articles on Yeats

---

[52] *Die moderne englische Lyrik: Interpretationen*, ed. by Horst Oppel. E. Schmidt Verlag: Berlin.

have outnumbered those on any other single poet. M. Perloff, attempting to define the stylistic characteristics of his later poetry (*PMLA*), isolates the poetic structure itself, which she calls 'spatial form', as the distinctively 'new' note in his work of the mid-'20s and early '30s. This is illustrated by a scrutiny of the disparity of structure in two closely related poems dealing with the effects of political engagement on the Gore-Booth sisters at Lissadell, *On a Political Prisoner* (1920) and *In Memory of Eva Gore-Booth and Con Markiewicz* (1927).

In the same journal T. McAlindon shows that Yeats's commitment to aristocratic values, which became evident with the publication of *The Green Helmet* in 1910 and *Responsibilities* in 1914, is attributable not only to his reading in 1907 of Castiglione's *The Courtier* and the cultural stimulus of his visit in that year to Italy, but to his continuous study in the first six years of the century of Spenser, Shakespeare and Jonson. Preoccupied with the relationship which should exist between poets and great men, they 'expected from the nobility not only enlightened support but boldly developed patterns of human excellence'.

P. Cosgrave in *LM* offers a detailed rebuttal of Conor Cruise O'Brien's view of Yeats as a political time-server, a hypocrite, a snob and a Fascist. Cosgrave contests the historical accuracy of many of O'Brien's facts about Yeats's involvement with the leading figures and events of the crucial years in the Irish struggle for independence, and accuses him of selecting only those which support his case while ignoring other important facts and implications, thus doing considerable disservice not only to the poet's integrity but to O'Brien's own reputation and achievement.

The political Yeats is also the subject of G. M. Harper writing on 'Art and Propaganda in the Nationalism of William Butler Yeats', in a volume which also contains an article by H. Reiss on 'Tradition in Modern Poetry' which compares Eliot with Rilke.[53] Yeats's ambivalent attitude towards his Irish identity is examined by J. D. Boulger in *Thought*. The tension revealed by a number of the Irish poems, beginning with *Easter 1916*, between Yeats's aesthetic and his ethical attitude towards his countrymen, resulted in a 'crisis of conscience' finally resolved in an identification with the Irish in a poetry of 'delicate ironic poise and complexity'. Yeats's debt to his native background is traced in an article by Sister M. B. Quinn on 'Symbolic Landscape in Yeats: County Galway'.[54]

In *REL* W. M. Murphy writes about Yeats's early education, and especially his debt to his father to whom he acknowledged 'how fully my philosophy of life has been inherited from you in all but its details and applications'. The article is based on three unpublished manuscript volumes of John Butler Yeats's memoirs to which Murphy has had access, and which provide first-hand biographical material about this unusual personality whose views and advice so strongly influenced the poet.

L. Conversi in *YR* sets out to explore 'the truth of art' as exemplified in the poetry of Yeats and the novels of Thomas Mann. His theme is 'their incapacity as men and artists to take anything but a warped view'. Contesting the 'prevailing estimate'

[53] *Proceedings of the IVth Congress of the International Comparative Literature Association, Fribourg, 1964,* 2 vols. The Hague: Mouton. (1966).
[54] In *The Hidden Harmony: Essays in Honor of Philip Wheelwright.* Odyssey. N.Y. (1966).

of Yeats as 'the greatest modern poet and one of the greatest poets in the language', his attitude is unremittingly unsympathetic.

A different view of Yeats is taken by D. Marsh (*QQ*) in 'The Artist and the Tragic Vision', an examination of themes in the later poetry. J. H. O'Brien in *Person* explores 'Yeats's Search for Unity of Being', D. C. Agarwala his concept of image in *Triveni* (Machilipatnam, India), R. V. Adkinson writes on 'Criticizing Yeats' in *RLV*, and there is an essay on Yeats by P. P. Rohde in *Fremmede digtere i det. 20. århundrede.*[55]

Among studies of individual poems by Yeats, those on the Byzantium group preponderate. In 'Miraculous Birds, Another and the Same' (*ES*) J. L. Allen, Jr. examines the artificial golden bird which is their central image. A bird as symbol of the human spirit after death recurs before and after the Byzantium poems, and Yeats also thought of it in terms of the fabulous phoenix of ancient legend and tradition symbolizing rebirth. Allen compares this myth with Yeats's golden bird of Byzantium, establishing that in the poet's mind the two 'were conscious analogues, with meanings devolving from one to the other'.

In *MP* T. McAlindon considers side by side 'The Idea of Byzantium in William Morris and W. B. Yeats', tracing Yeats's debt to the view of Byzantium held by Morris, 'who of all Yeats's early acquaintances exercised the most profound and lasting influence on his mind'. The writer shows how many of Yeats's ideas were derived from Morris's teaching, in particular that 'the unity of being which his father had taught him to exalt was dependent on unity of culture', with Byzantine art, 'enriched

[55] Ed. by S. M. Kristensen. Vol. I. G.E.C. Gad: Copenhagen.

by a multiplicity of traditions, all of which had root in a perfect unity of being', as the archetypal pattern.

J. A. Venter contends (*ESA*) that the sound structure which contributes to the richness and complexity of a poem and its ultimate significance is all too often neglected in favour of linguistic and prosodic elements. He subjects *Sailing to Byzantium* to a close analysis in terms of its 'phonic patterning'—the 'audible shape' of the poem and its harmonies of sound.

In *CE* S. O. Lesser challenges the accepted interpretation of the poem, based on Elder Olson's influential essay of 1942, as a happy one in which all the old man's problems are resolved. He offers his own reading of it as 'a cry of agony' with at best only a negative resolution, and justifies this contention in a stanza-by-stanza analysis. 'Backward to Byzantium' is the subject of an article by R. E. Sullivan in *L & P*.

In *Wascana Review* D. R. Clark considers the parallels between Yeats's poem *News for the Delphic Oracle* and the painting by Poussin 'The Marriage of Peleus and Thetis', whose 'startlingly exact correspondences' were noted by T. R. Henn. Clark examines in detail the familiar story as Yeats adapted Poussin's rendering of it for his own poetic purposes.

B. A. Rosenberg discusses 'Irish Folklore and *The Song of Wandering Aengus*' (*PQ*), whose theme he sees as the search for poetic inspiration and an ideal beauty which later came to fruition in *Sailing to Byzantium*. He relates its sources and imagery to the ceremonies of a new mystic brotherhood of Celts which Yeats planned to revive as part of his work for an Irish renaissance, and to the folk tales and ancient myths which he believed held significance for the modern reader. In *Massachusetts*

Studies in English V. J. Goldzung also examines *The Song of Wandering Aengus*, in relation to 'Yeats's tradition'.

In *ELN* W. J. Keith discusses *The Empty Cup*, especially in its biographical overtones: both in the poem's usual erotic interpretation and on a more spiritual level of meaning in the image of the cup as a grail-symbol suggesting immortality.

Three notes on individual poems by Yeats are contributed to different issues of *Ex*. P. Sanders explores the nature of the search of the Magi for a 'second coming' ('Being by Calvary's turbulence unsatisfied') which anticipates one of Yeats's later themes. R. W. Caswell considers the reasons for the shift in tone of the faery speaker in *The Stolen Child* from the first three to the final stanza, posing the tension between 'man's desire for the timeless and irresponsible world of faery and the mortal world of responsibility'. J. H. Natterstad offers an interpretation contrary to R. Ellmann's of *The Cap and Bells*, reading it as 'a symbolic rendering of Yeats's own aesthetic position, which holds that beauty is a product of the integrative function of art'.

'Yeats's Dark Night of Self and *The Tower*' is the subject of an article by J. H. O'Brien in *Bu R*.

In *NQ* P. L. Marcus finds possible sources for Yeats's early story *Dhoya*, which he finished in 1887, in the story which had already appeared in at least four versions, two of which there is evidence he may well have used.

In 'Grammar and Meaning in Poetry' (*PMLA*) S. B. Greenfield uses Yeats and Larkin, as well as *Beowulf* and Shakespeare, to demonstrate his point that a grammatical and syntax-orientated interpretation of poetry cannot be accepted as entirely valid, for the linguistic approach tends to ignore 'lexical and contextual meanings'.

In *RES* C. T. Watts offers, with a commentary, a hitherto unpublished letter of Yeats to the Scottish writer and orator R. B. Cunninghame Graham, courteously rejecting a Spanish play which the latter had submitted for performance at the Abbey Theatre.

AE, one of Yeats's leading compatriots active in the Irish Renaissance, is the subject of an article by W. Daniels in *UR*.

Daniel Hoffman makes a detailed exploration of the use in their poetry by Yeats, Muir and Graves of the material of myth, folklore and dream.[56] All three, identified with the primitive cultures of these islands—Celtic Ireland, the Orkneys and Wales—experienced the need to root their work in archetype or myth, and began their careers as ballad poets. Hoffman examines how Yeats employed Irish folklore and legend in his ballads, in his creation in *The Tower* of the peasant poet as hero, and his embodiment of an epic theme in his five plays about the legendary Cuchulain. He traces the predominant themes in Graves's poetry of his romantic conviction of the supremacy of intuition over intellect and reason, and of the submission of the poet to his muse. In Muir certain universal fables of the human condition—in particular the Fall and loss of Eden, and the tale of Troy—are shown to have been used as the vehicle of an individual man's spiritual journey towards understanding and significant meaning.

In 'Graves: Echoes and a Skeleton Key' (*Poetry*) the same writer comments upon Graves's drastic editing

[56] *Barbarous Knowledge: Myth in the Poetry of Yeats, Graves and Muir*, by Daniel Hoffman. O.U.P. pp. xvi+266. 42s.

of the ninth edition of his *Collected Poems*, which has resulted in the loss of some excellent early work on other themes in order to make room for nearly all his poems of the last four years which reflect his preoccupation with love between men and women. The writer suggests the use of Higginson's bibliography by those who wish to retrace the sacrificed material.

Graves himself is the author of a collection of lectures and talks[57] given while he occupied the Oxford Chair of Poetry in 1964–5, but completely rewritten for publication. He reiterates some of his familiar beliefs: that poetry is a vocation, a way of life—'the profession of private truth supported by craftsmanship in the use of words', and a definition of poetic principle as 'a simple, obstinate belief in miracle: an asseveration of personal independence against all collective codifications of thought and behaviour'; and the role of the Muse Goddess, 'guardian of the love magic which all religious leaders, philosophers and legalists in turn officiously attempt to define for her but which always eludes them'. In the first lecture he considers various editorial shortcomings of selection and annotation in *The Oxford Book of English Verse*, and castigates the artificiality of the pastoral tradition, and in the second and third is astringent about some of the inclusions— Milton, Herrick, Gray, Longfellow, Poe, Landor and Lamb. The concluding lecture, delivered at Yale, elaborates his conception of the meaning of the word 'romantic'.

T. Merton (*Sew*) considers the poetry and criticism of Edwin Muir under the heading 'The True Legendary Sound'. His poetry shows a 'profound metaphysical concern' which

seeks the reconciliation of the inner and the outer man, of the world of the present with its roots in the past'. Merton illustrates Muir's 'in-seeing' —his capacity for complete identification with the existence he sees—by his poems about the horses which awed and fascinated him from early childhood.

I. Jack also writes on Muir in *Filologia Moderna* (Madrid); and he is the subject of one of the essays in Kathleen Raine's collection,[58] seen as 'spectator and participator of a great cosmic drama', speaking 'with the voice of the ancestors', and expressing through the personal the immediacy of the universal. Other essays are on the influence of the bardic tradition on the Welsh poet Vernon Watkins; on Yeats's debt to Blake both in his thought and use of symbolism; and on the 'prophetic role' of David Gascoyne and the part played by surrealism in his inspiration and work (an essay reprinted from *Sew*, in which it also appeared during the current year). There is a general essay on the traditional use of symbolic analogy and myth in poetry, and of the 'idea of the beautiful', which 'cannot be achieved by the poet writing from his mundane consciousness, but only in that divine madness in which he is possessed by the "other" mind'.

P. Gardner in *HAB* makes a detailed reappraisal, founded on a study of his 'meaning', of the poetry of William Empson, whose concern for solving problems of technique and refusal to make extravagant gestures reawakened interest, after a decade of neglect, among young poets in the '50s. After examining various critical approaches to his work, which stress its difficulties of ambiguity, extreme compression, use

---

[57] *Poetic Craft and Principle*, by Robert Graves. Cassell. pp. viii+195. 30s.

[58] *Defending Ancient Springs*, by Kathleen Raine. O.U.P. pp. 198. 30s.

of scientific facts and terminology, and esoteric literary allusions, he concludes by analysing a poem neglected by most commentators, *Part of Mandevil's Travels*. In an article called 'Finite, but Unbounded' (*University of Windsor Review*, Ontario) S. Pinsker discusses Empson's poetic world.

In *PMLA* W. H. Sellers sheds 'New Light on Auden's *The Orators*', the poet's second book which has been found by most critics to be his 'most puzzling work'. Admitting the obscurity of the allusions, 'bewildering variety of tone and style', and of its informing ideas—primarily dependent on D. H. Lawrence—Sellers seeks through close analysis of the text to clarify its thematic coherence. As a diagnosis of 'the contemporary human condition in a series of discontinuous but not disconnected parables', it remains 'the key to the Auden of the '30s'.

A special issue of *Shenandoah* (18: ii) is devoted to articles on Auden by B. Dobrée, E. R. Dodds, M. K. Spears, and many other critics. In *Dublin Magazine* D. Fitzgerald writes on 'Auden's City', and D. E. Morse (*Ren*) a two-part article on *For the Time Being*, the first exploring 'The Nature of Man' in the poem and the second 'Man's Response to the Incarnation'. Auden's poetry as a whole is the subject of a detailed monograph from Milan by Francesco Binni.[58a]

Spender's poem *Vienna* (1934), the longest and perhaps the most ambitious he has written, yet never reprinted or collected and dismissed by its author as a failure, is the starting-point of an essay by W. H. Sellers in *HAB*. 'What he thought,

what he felt and particularly what he learned about himself during that fateful year remained so deeply significant to Spender' that he re-explored his Viennese experience thirteen years later in *Returning to Vienna 1947*, 'an elegiac statement of personal and political failure'. Sellers examines in detail these two poems, which span the most critical years of Spender's career, as 'a revealing index to his development as a poet'.

The aim of A. T. Tolley's chronology of Spender's seventy-three early short poems published in books and periodicals up to 1934[59] is to give the necessary information for tracing the poet's development over the first six years of his publication. This is not a bibliography in the usual sense, for it gives no physical description of the books mentioned, but it is intended as more than a checklist, as the poems are arranged in chronological order of composition, details given of the evidence for this arrangement, and variants between the original published form and subsequent versions are noted.

In 'The Black Clock' (*Hollins Critic*) W. J. Smith examines the poetic achievement of Louis Mac-Neice with particular emphasis on his preoccupation with death: from the sparkling satire of his early work, through the recognition in *Prayer in Mid-Passage* that death is the compulsive force behind his work, to the fine late volume *The Burning Perch*, in which he confronts death in many guises and in the process achieves some of his most mature and memorable work. There is also an article on MacNeice in *Dublin Magazine* in which M. Longley sees him as 'A Misrepresented Poet'.

[58a] *Saggio su Auden*, by Francesco Binni. Civiltà Letteraria del Novecento: Sezione Inglese-Americana. Mursia: Milano. pp. 203. Lire 2.400. Paperback.

[59] *The Early Published Poems of Stephen Spender: A Chronology*, by A. T. Tolley. Carleton University, Ottawa. pp. 19. Paperback.

In *Sew* J. R. Doyle, Jr., begins his discussion of William Plomer by looking at a poem written in the mid-'50s, *A Transvaal Morning*, as a starting-point for demonstrating the potency in the poet's imagination of his early years in South Africa, which lay for thirty years in his subconscious before re-emerging in his poems. He examines the other three poems in the sequence, some early South African poems and the work of his Japanese and Greek periods, and his veins of comedy and pathos, and concludes that the poems of the middle years 'resulted from detachment rather than involvement'.

A special David Jones issue of *Agenda* contains articles by R. Hague, S. Piggott, P. Levi, N. K. Sandars, D. Blamires, S. Lewis, M. Alexander, L. Bonnerot, T. Stoneburner, N. Grey and A. T. Davies. Considering the contributions in this issue (*Sew*), K. Raine writes on the aspect which emerges from them of Jones as 'Solitary Perfectionist'. She notes that his poetic individuality is more fundamentally shaped by his Catholicism than is Eliot's by his Anglicanism, and that we can more easily detach Eliot's learned allusions and quotations from the text than we can those of David Jones because 'the poetry of Eliot is in the nature of a structure; David Jones's work, intrinsically organic'.

In *UTQ* W. Blissett investigates the idiosyncratic world of David Jones in the image of 'Himself at the Cave-Mouth', with his 'accumulation . . . of things worth shaping and signing, after threading a labyrinth'. Through this unifying metaphor the techniques and meanings are explored of the two great Christian poems *In Parenthesis* and *Anathemata*, 'both deeply involved in the paradox of joy and suffering', and 'the luxuriance

of his word-hoard, the profusion and plenitude of things in his locker'.

P. Gardner in the same journal contributes a long appreciation of 'The Provincial Poetry of Norman Nicholson', whose many years of patient effort to understand the area in which he was born have made him into 'a poet of more than merely local interest: in getting under the skin of one particular region he discovered the world to which all men belong'. Stressing how the image of 'the rock' stands for both Christian belief and for Cumberland, the writer concentrates on the second aspect of Nicholson's work, and his 'interest in the fusion of geology and humanity', in a detailed analysis of poems from each of his volumes.

In his article 'Shall These Bones Live?' (*Poetry Review*) J. Smith writes about the poetry of Sacheverell Sitwell, whom he considers in many ways a more interesting writer than either Osbert or Edith. Smith compares his gift, methods and themes with various of his contemporaries, and shows how Sitwell's inspiration has been drawn mainly from the world of art rather than that of immediate experience. In *Criticism* (Wayne State) D. V. Harrington writes on 'The "Metamorphosis" of Edith Sitwell'.

In his concordance of the collected poems of Dylan Thomas[60] Robert Coleman Williams uses the text of the 1954 Dent reprint of *Collected Poems* and the eighteenth printing of the American edition. Each indexed word, alphabetically arranged, is followed by each line of poetry in which it occurs, citing page and line numbers of the English and American editions, and the textual divergences

[60] *A Concordance of the Collected Poems of Dylan Thomas*, ed. by Robert Coleman Williams. Nebraska U.P. pp. xiii+579. $13.95.

between these are noted in the introduction.

In *Ex* O. D. Harvill examines Dylan Thomas's poem *O Make Me a Mask*.

G. S. Singh devotes a long article to 'The Poetry of John Betjeman' in the same volume as S. Cattaneo writes on 'La Poesia di Michael Roberts'.[61]

A. Denson contributes to *Dublin Magazine* an appreciation of the Irish poet Padraic Colum, with a check-list of his publications.

The doyen of Scottish poetry, Hugh MacDiarmid, is the subject of a special number of *Agenda* devoted to different aspects of his work. Contributors include A. Scott on his plays in the Scots tradition, J. Montague on the unity of his preoccupations, D. Glen on his use of his nationalistic and linguistic theories in his verse, H. More on his role in politics, K. Cox on his Neo-Platonism, and M. P. McDiarmid on his efforts to free the Scots poet from his folk *persona* in a language 'neither obtrusively colloquial nor obtrusively literary'.

An article on MacDiarmid and the Scottish Renaissance by W. A. S. Keir appears in a special Scottish number of *English*, with a detailed assessment by P. Butter of Muir's long poem *The Journey Back* and a survey by R. Fulton of contemporary Scottish poetry.

In the same journal Y. Gooneratne writes about the development of the creative writer in Ceylon, showing how subject, theme and diction have reflected the Romantic tradition of English nineteenth-century poetry. M. Morris touches in the same issue on some problems of the West Indian poet today.

M. L. Rosenthal's study of *The New Poets*[62] examines in detail the whole range of British and American poetry since the Second World War. An introductory chapter considers the 'new' poetry in its context of the modern tradition by relating it to the attitudes, preoccupations and formal characteristics of twentieth-century poetry as a whole. In the second half of the book the author surveys the contemporary British poetic scene in general, including the 'wars of the anthologies' and such trends as the Movement, the Group, and Concrete and Confessional poetry. Through a close scrutiny of poems and passages he then evaluates the work of individual writers—Larkin, Hughes, Gunn, Tomlinson, Redgrove and others (the misprint referring throughout to Edwin Brock as 'Bronk' needs to be rectified). A final chapter deals with leading contemporary Irish poets such as Austin Clarke, Patrick Kavanagh and Thomas Kinsella.

Ted Hughes is the subject of an article by B. John (*Ar Q*) in his aspect of a 'Poet at the Master-Fulcrum of Violence'.

In an article on Dannie Abse (*AWR*) R. Mathias discusses some characteristics of his later poetry, including his search for new poetic experience, his use of symbols, 'honest closeness of observation', particularly in the context of poems of personal relationship, and his continuously developing technical skill and individuality.

6. DRAMA: BOOKS

In writing about twentieth-century drama, many critics feel obliged to relate their subject to earlier ages of European, or even non-European, theatre; there is an increasing flow of books where the primary interest is

---

[61] *Studi e ricerche di letteratura: inglese e americana, I*, ed. by A. Lombardo. 1st editoriale Cisalpino: Milano.

[62] *The New Poets*, by M. L. Rosenthal. O.U.P. pp. xiv+350. 45s. (Paperback, 13s.).

in what is happening in contemporary drama, but where the approach is not one of direct analysis of modern texts.

Louis Kampf[63] confronts some problems that arise in modern art and philosophy, making special reference to the drama. He defines what he calls 'the discouraging confusions of our time', and asks how these may 'be related to what is left of our traditional artistic objectives'. Professor Kampf ranges wide, and is concerned as much with epistemology as with critical analysis, but the book raises questions relevant to any approach to twentieth-century drama, and there are perceptive passages on Beckett, Gelber, Büchner and other pioneers of 'modernism' in the theatre.

Raymond Williams[64] approaches the problems of modern tragic drama in a book which he admits is 'unconventional and mixed': he wished to achieve a unity of response unusual in academic criticism, to create within the book 'a whole structure of feeling and thinking'. There are three distinct sections, each allowing for the fact that 'we come to tragedy by many roads' but nevertheless remaining discrete. The first section is a critical history of the idea and development of tragedy, the second section offers critical analyses of the main practitioners of 'modern tragic literature', and the third section is taken up with Mr. Williams's own contribution to modern tragic drama. The book has a welcome combination of intelligence, erudition and sensitivity, and it asks questions about the personal response to tragedy that are too often ignored in academic criticism. The style is often

cumbersome but, as is the case with Mr. Williams's earlier books, the reader is well rewarded for perseverance.

Walter Kerr[65] surveys the development of European drama mainly with the purpose of clarifying the nature of some contemporary plays. He writes with the panache regarded as appropriate to 'superior journalism', and his book has the qualities relevant to his purpose of engaging a general audience. The discussion has many lively moments, and there are some interesting remarks on Osborne and Beckett.

Leonard C. Pronko[66] offers 'perspective towards a total theatre', by surveying various aspects of Eastern drama that might be of value to Western playwrights and producers anxious to regain something of 'the healthy, complete, vigorous theatrical experience' which has been excluded from modern bourgeois drama. Mr. Pronko is convincing in his argument that Yeats failed to comprehend the essence of Noh drama and wrote plays which were 'diametrically opposed' to the spirit of his models, and convincing too in his claim that various forms of oriental drama have much to offer our own theatre.

G. G. Sedgewick's[67] study, first published in 1935, is re-issued by Toronto U.P. The first two of his four chapters have a good deal of relevance to the different kinds of black comedy in the twentieth-century theatre.

B. N. Chaturvedi[68] offers a short,

[63] *On Modernism*, by Louis Kampf, M.I.T. Press, pp. viii+338, no stated price.
[64] *Modern Tragedy*, by Raymond Williams. Chatto & Windus. pp. 288, Paperback, 15s.

[65] *Tragedy and Comedy*, by Walter Kerr. Bodley Head, pp. 341, 30s.
[66] *Theater, East and West*, by Leonard C. Pronko. California U.P. pp. x+230. 71s. 6d.
[67] *Of Irony, Especially in the Drama*, by G. G. Sedgewick. Toronto U.P. pp. 127. $1.75.
[68] *English Poetic Drama of the Twentieth Century*, by B. N. Chaturvedi. Kitab Ghar, Gwalior. pp. 114. Rs. 10.

superficial survey of English verse drama in the twentieth-century. He has chapters on Yeats, Eliot, and Christopher Fry, and mentions plays by Hardy, Masefield, Drinkwater, Flecker, Philips, Auden, Spender, and MacNeice.

Frederick Lumley's[69] *New Trends in Twentieth-Century Drama* is a new and enlarged edition of the study he first published in 1956. He ranges over the drama of America and Western Europe, but has some useful things to say in the pages devoted to British dramatists. Among those discussed for the first time in this edition of the book are Osborne, Pinter, Arden, and Schaffer.

There are a few books which deal with aspects of the English theatre, as distinct from English drama.

Richard Findlater[70] makes a devastating attack on the role censorship has played in the British theatre for the past four centuries. As he promises in his introductory chapter, the story 'is one of corruption, injustice, petty tyranny, humbug, waste, ignorance, bigotry, and superstition'. The book is intelligent, witty, and widely informed; the index is full and the book-list useful. The argument for abolition of stage censorship could not have been put more forcefully.

Stephen Joseph[71] offers a lively, well-illustrated account of 'theatre in the round', defining the scope of this method of presentation, and giving much practical advice which ought to benefit school or university drama groups who do not have access to a theatre.

Brian Way[72] writes of his practical experience of teaching drama to young people, and directs his book to those who are interested in dramatic practice as a means of education.

St. Vincent Troubridge[73] supplies a full and very readable account of the different forms of benefit system that have operated in the English theatre since the 1680s. The subject is peripheral to an interest in dramatic literature, but the book conveys many facts and insights that are relevant to theatrical history.

Robin May's[74] two books are personal records of an experienced actor and inveterate play-goer: the author's enthusiasm never flags, the illustrations are apt, and the books are very nicely designed.

Robert Hogan and Michael J. O'Neill[75] present a selection from 221 manuscript volumes in the National Library of Ireland. Joseph Holloway recorded the cultural life of Dublin for half a century, and this one-volume selection makes a fascinating first-hand account of activity in the Dublin theatre at its most lively. Holloway records conversations with Yeats, Lady Gregory, AE, Synge, Joyce, Moore, O'Casey, and the greatest actors of the day, and he gives long appreciative accounts of Shaw as a public orator. As the editors remark, the original diary may claim to be 'one of the worst books ever written', but the editors have earned our gratitude for producing a book that is amusing as well

[72] *Development Through Drama*, by Brian Way. Longmans. pp. x+308. Paperback 16s.
[73] *The Benefit System in the British Theatre*, by St. Vincent Troubridge. The Society for Theatre Research. pp. 172. 50s.
[74] *Theatremania* and *Operamania*, by Robin May. Vernon & Yates. pp. 147, and 96. 35s. each.
[75] *Joseph Holloway's Abbey Theatre*, ed. by Robert Hogan and Michael J. O'Neill. Preface by Harry T. Moore. Southern Illinois U.P. pp. xxiii+296. $6.95.

[69] *New Trends in Twentieth-Century Drama*, by Frederick Lumley. Barrie & Rockliff. pp. 398. 42s.
[70] *Theatrical Censorship in Britain*, by Richard Findlater, MacGibbon & Kee, Panther Paperback. pp. 6s.
[71] *Theatre in the Round*, by Stephen Joseph. Barrie & Rockliff. pp. 179. 30s.

as essential reading for all students of the Irish Renaissance.

Only a handful of books are devoted to individual dramatists, and as usual Shaw gets most attention.

Harold Fromm[76] is concerned with Shaw as critic and theorist of the drama, arguing that 'the principles and standards which Shaw believed in during the nineties were those he was to maintain throughout his lifetime, his career as a dramatic critic is the very seed from which everything that is characteristically Shavian emerged'. Fromm relies heavily on lengthy quotations from Shaw, and Fred Mayre[77] extends this practice so much that his book becomes an annotated anthology of Shaw quotations, with some of the annotations superficial, some uninformative, and some rather bored. Warren Sylvester Smith[78] offers a much more useful book, in his edition of various pieces which Shaw brought together for a volume in the Standard Edition of his collected works: three of the entries were previously unpublished and, although it is odd that *Back to Methuselah* and its preface should be included, the volume is a useful contribution to the Shavian library.

There are two relevant volumes in the series entitled 'The Cooper Monographs'. Erika Meier[79] has a comprehensive and detailed discussion of the various functions of stage directions in English plays from Tom Robertson to Shaw. Anne Dedio[80]

offers a painstaking analysis of Lady Gregory's plays, finding three main themes or motifs which may be classified as 'myths', 'dreams', and 'visions'. Dr. Dedio, whose main text is in German, adds an appendix which contains extracts from interesting interviews, reviews, and previously unpublished letters.

In the series 'Writers and Their Work', W. A. Armstrong[81] offers a short introduction to the work of Sean O'Casey, explaining the general biographical, cultural, and political contexts. Professor Armstrong points briefly to the comedy, the symbolism, and 'the archetypal quality' which raises O'Casey's early plays 'above the level of topical realism'. He discusses the expressionism of the middle period, the satirical fantasy of the last plays, and includes a select bibliography.

To the series *Civiltà Letteraria del Novecento* Renato Oliva[82] contributes a perceptive study of Beckett's dramatic work, relating it to other aspects of modern European literature, and especially to the work of Franz Kafka.

Johannes Fabricius[83] attempts to demonstrate that the 'unconscious background' to T. S. Eliot's work becomes explicit in his critical concepts, and to analyse the poems and plays in the light of the European-wide Expressionist movement. *Sweeney Agonistes, Murder in the Cathedral, The Family Reunion, The Cocktail Party, The Confidential Clerk*, and *The Elder Statesman*, are all interpreted as Expressionist plays which operate 'on two different levels,

[76] *Bernard Shaw and the Theatre in the Nineties*, by Harold Fromm. Kansas U.P. pp. viii+234. 47s. 6d.

[77] *The Wit and Satire of Bernard Shaw*, by Fred Mayre. Arnold. pp. x+154. 30s.

[78] *Shaw on Religion*, ed. with Introduction and Notes by Warren Sylvester Smith. N.Y.: Dodd, Mead. pp. 240. $5.

[79] *Realism and Reality*, by Erika Meier. Bern: Francke. pp. 334. S.Fr. 38.

[80] *Das dramatische Werk von Lady Gregory*, by Anne Dedio. Bern: Francke. pp. 135. S.Fr. 16.80.

[81] *Sean O'Casey*, by William A. Armstrong. Longmans, Green. pp. 39. 3s. 6d.

[82] *Samuel Beckett: Prima del Silenzio*, by Renato Oliva. U. Mursia. pp. 207. Lire 2,500.

[83] *The Unconscious and Mr. Eliot*, by Johannes Fabricius. Copenhagen: Nyt Nordisk Forlag Arnold Busk. pp. 160, no price stated.

with a realistic and "conscious" plot running side by side with a psychological and "unconscious" subplot'.

7. DRAMA: ARTICLES

Shaw's plays have attracted more attention than those of any other single dramatist. Three journals are devoted entirely to Shaw—*The Shaw Review*, *The Shavian*, and *The Independent Shavian*; the enthusiast will be familiar with these publications, and not every paper in them will be individually mentioned. In 'Vivie Warren's Profession' (*Shaw Review*) S. Grecco looks for autobiographical aspects of *Mrs. Warren's Profession*, and suggests that Mrs. Warren herself is based on Shaw's mother. In 'Shaw and Chesterton: The Link was "Magic"' (*Shaw Review*) W. B. Furlong describes how Shaw eventually forced Chesterton to write *Magic*, his only successful play. Again in *Shaw Review*, H. J. Donaghy has a paper on 'Chesterton on Shaw's Views of Catholicism'.

In 'Two Anti-Puritans' (*YR*) D. J. Gordon offers a 'psychological approach' to Shaw and D. H. Lawrence, seeing both as 'contending with the dominant ethic of their day, with Puritanism as it merged into Victorianism and popular Christianity in general'. Both loathed the unconscious hypocrisy that lay behind popular 'Idealism', and both were opposed to libertinism and materialism. For both writers 'the real alternative . . . is to smash the whole complex and to establish a new moral centre beyond good and evil. The new center in its transvaluation of values is vital energy itself, whatever possesses it or promotes its flow: evil is redefined as whatever lacks vital energy or obstructs its flow; mechanism, fear, boredom, obsolete ideals and institutions.' Mr. Gordon argues

that by both writers the 'renunciation of the ordinary world is presented with too much intensity to be *sufficiently* explained with reference to the real plight of man in modern society, or even with reference to the real plight of genius', and that in each case the renunciation 'points to unadmitted guilt connected with the normal social roles of the male adult'.

Shaw and Lawrence are also discussed, together with Yeats, by W. H. G. Armytage in 'Superman and the System' (*Riverside Quarterly*) where the influence of Nietzsche on these writers is discussed: Mr. Armytage is especially concerned with the Nietzschean influence on *Man and Superman*, the Don Juan aspect of which is handled by R. L. Blanch in *RLV* and by C. H. Mills in *CL*. In *Shaw Review*, A. Andrews points to a possible influence in 'Mendoza and Sir Arthur Conan Doyle', and C. Levine discusses 'Social Criticism in Shaw and Nietzsche'. In *Komos* R. J. Kaufmann discusses Shaw's first decade as a dramatist in 'Shaw's Elitist Vision', and M. M. Morgan writes on 'Shaw, Yeats, Nietzsche, and the Religion of Art'. In *Kunst und Literatur*, J. A. Sawadski discusses 'Die philosophischen Dramen Shaws und die moderne Theaterästhetik'.

In 'Fun and Games: Two Pictures of *Heartbreak House*' (*Dram S*) D. C. Coleman compares the structures and quality of black comedy in Shaw's play and in Albee's *Who's Afraid of Virginia Woolf?* Again in *Dram S*, A. H. Silverman in 'Bernard Shaw's Political Extravaganzas' discusses *The Apple Cart*, *Too True to be Good*, *On the Rocks*, *Geneva*, and *The Simpleton of the Expected Isles*, seeing them as coming from different aspects of the generalized disillusion in Shaw's later work. In 'Shaw's Doomsday' (*ETJ*)

B. F. Dukore discusses the unifying force of the doomsday motif in *The Simpleton of the Unexpected Isles*, and in the October number of *ETJ* Mr. Dukore presents the first publication of Shaw's skit on Macbeth, written for Gerald Du Maurier and Lillah McCarthy in 1916, but never performed.

In 'Politics, Comedy, Character, and Dialectic' (*PMLA*) F. P. McDowell writes in praise of *John Bull's Other Island* as 'one of the pinnacles of Shaw's dramaturgy', highly valued by Shaw himself but little esteemed by his critics today. Russian criticism of the social relevance of *Heartbreak House, Arms and the Man, Caesar and Cleopatra* and other plays is reviewed by D. C. Gerould in 'Soviet Shaw: Slavic Shaw' (*Shaw Review*).

In 'One Man and His Dog' (*MD*) B. Tyson discusses the deleted draft of *The Philanderer,* seeing the rejected, well-made play about antivivisectionism as the kind of work to be expected from a 'disciple of W. S. Gilbert'. In *REL* D. Roll-Hansen compares 'Shaw's *Pygmalion*: The Two Versions of 1916 and 1941'. In *Th R* G. Staud writes on 'G. B. Shaw's Letters to Sándor Heresi', and in the *Bulletin of the New York Public Library* P. A. Doyle presents two previously unpublished Shaw letters under the title 'Shaw on Immorality and on Illustrating His Dramatis Personae'.

A few interesting papers have appeared on Yeats's plays, and his influence on other Irish dramatists. In *Aryan Path* R. M. Fox looks at 'Social Criticism in the Irish Theatre', considering the lasting effects of Yeats's dislike of plays that were socially polemical. Because of Yeats's influence, the Abbey continued to favour rhetorical verse drama, although the plays by Keanes now

being performed are praised as both good drama and good social criticism. In *Col Q* R. H. Hethmon writes on 'Total Theatre and Yeats' discussing the effects of Yeats's obsession with the idea that the Irish National Theatre could bring about a unification of culture and theatre, unachieved since the Middle Ages. Yeats's optimism was dispelled by the Theatre's commercial success.

In 'Action and Reaction at the Dublin Theatre' (*ETJ*) J. W. Flannery writes on the 1965 Dublin Theatre Festival experimental productions of *Calvary* and *The Resurrection*. In 'A Play on the Death of God' (*MD*) M. J. Baird writes on Yeats's employment of dramatic irony in *The Resurrection,* reading the play as a celebration not of Christ's triumph but of the 'impending death of Christianity'.

In *The London Magazine* Gaddis considers 'The Purgatory Metaphor of Yeats and Beckett', showing that both dramatists represent human existence as a purgatory from which there is no escape; and each presents stage action which is to be taken as indicative of processes within the reflective mind. On the other hand, R. E. Todd in 'Proust and Redemption in *Waiting for Godot*' (*MD*) reads the play as 'a Proustian version of salvation'. In 'Modes of Being and Time in the World of *Godot*' (*MLQ*) R. M. Torrance uses Beckett's essay on Proust to elucidate the two groups of characters in the play; Didi and Gogo represent the mode of habit-waiting-boredom, i.e. timelessness, while Pozzo and Lucky represent the mode of man's retrogression and meaningless suffering, i.e. history. In 'Religious Language in *Waiting for Godot*' (*Cent R*) V. A. Kolve notices some of the effects which Beckett achieves by using Christian vocabulary with agnostic irony. K. Schwarz has a piece on 'Zeitproble-matik in Samuel Beckett's *En attend-ant Godot*' (*NS*), and in *ETJ* A. Atkins under the title 'Lucky's Speech in Beckett's *Waiting for Godot*' provides what he calls 'a punctuated sense-line arrangement' together with a commentary which is intended to reveal 'some of the latent intelligibility of the speech'. In *French Review* N. Berlin writes on 'Beckett and Shakespeare', and J. O'Brien briefly on a possible connexion be-tween 'Samuel Beckett and André Gide'. In 'Politics in the Theatre' (*Wascana Review*) H. Blau looks at some plays which are not regarded as primarily political: *Waiting for Godot*, and Pinter's *The Homecoming*, are seen as defining an experienced political condition. In '"Theatrum Mundi" and Contemporary Theater' (*ComD*) R. Cohn argues that Beckett and several other contem-porary dramatists work with an attitude to their audience in some ways reminiscent of 'theatrum mundi'.

In 'Satire in O'Casey's Cock-a-Doodle Dandy' (*Ren*) B. L. Smith writes on farcical satire where the forces of 'good' are courage, exu-berance, and gaiety, and the forces of 'evil' are materialism, com-placency, hypocrisy, and lethargy. In *Wascana Review* S. Cowasjee writes on 'The Juxtaposition of Tragedy and Comedy in the Plays of Sean O'Casey'. In *WVB* B. J. Harman and R. G. Rollins consider some 'Mythical Dimensions in O'Casey's *Within the Gates*', suggesting that the play employs mythic prototypes to interpret contemporary history. The scenes move through the seasons, and times of day, suggesting the life cycle, and O'Casey uses music and dance motifs from Elizabethan and Greek drama.

R. G. Rollins writes on 'O'Casey's *Purple Dust*' in *Ex*, and the same writer contributes 'Shaw and O'Casey: John Bull and His Other Island' to *Shaw Review*. In *MD* C. A. Carpenter offers a selected list of 'Sean O'Casey Studies through 1964'.

In 'J. M. Synge and the Drama of Art' (*MD*) A. Ganz argues that Synge's main impulse was not to portray the lives of the Irish peasants, but 'to create an image of beauty that would stand against the sense of the absoluteness of death', and in her paper on Synge's dramatic art in *Komos* A. Saddlemeyer sees it as involving the conflict 'Rabelais *versus* a Kempis'. In 'The Pagan Setting of Synge's *Playboy*' (*Ren*) W. H. Johnson reads the play in the light of Synge's *The Aran Islands*, where attention is drawn to the traces of pagan belief still important in the islanders' credulousness; in the *Play-boy of the Western World* Synge combines his satire of hero-worship with his presentation of a community predisposed to believe some kinds of improbable stories. In *ELT* P. Barnett has an analysis of some aspects of 'The Nature of Synge's Dialogue'.

In 'Two Notes on *Murder in the Cathedral*' (*NQ*) H. Z. Maccoby argues that the function of the Fourth Tempter 'is not taunting but teaching, not sneering but comfort-ing . . . Eliot has hit on a conception of the tempter as the servant of God. This is a Jewish rather than a Chris-tian notion.' Mr. Maccoby's second note offers a reading of the lines of the Chorus beginning 'I have smelt them the death bringers; now is too late/ For action, too soon for contri-tion.'

In 'A Source for Eliot in Shaw' (*NQ*) J. H. Adler notices the possi-bility that Eliot in examining 'the difference between martyrdoms true and false' in *Murder in the Cathedral* and in handling the report of Celia's martyrdom in *The Cocktail Party*, may have been influenced by Shaw's treatment of martyrdom in *St. Joan, Androcles and the Lion*, and *Arms and the Man*.

In 'The Rhetoric of Repetition in *Murder in the Cathedral*' (*Ren*) Sister M. Geraldine notices three kinds of repetition in the play—of metaphors, of words and phrases, and of concepts connected with denial, fire, and animal life.

Other English dramatists have together inspired only a handful of papers. In *Dram S* M. Page examines 'The Motives of Pacifists: John Arden's *Sergeant Musgrave's Dance*' suggesting that the play presents characters who in their pacifism 'are not sure enough what they are trying to do, and have not understood the complexities of the world'. In 'Robert Bolt: Self, Shadow, and the Theater of Recognition' (*MD*) A. Atkins argues that in *A Man for All Seasons* Bolt is aiming at 'a triple recognition: of ourselves as the Common Man, of the Common Man as More, and (therefore) of ourselves as More'. In 'A Meeting with Somerset Maugham' (*Meanjin*) L. Rees recounts a conversation of 1933 where Maugham spoke of his decision to stop writing plays after *Sheppey*, because of the writer's lack of freedom in the theatre. In 'The Theatre of John Osborne' (*MD*) G. Gersh points out that Osborne has had no imitators in spite of the importance of his contribution to modern British drama; Mr. Gersh sees the reason in Osborne's refusal to adopt a definite imitable style, and looks at the paradox in Osborne's deeply personal plays that seem nevertheless to be 'speaking for a whole generation'.

In 'Messages from Pinter' (*MD*) A. Walker distinguishes two kinds of play in the Pinter canon; there are plays of dark allegory, such as *The Dumb Waiter* and *The Room*, where the subject is man's absurd and 'aimless clinging to a totally unaccounted-for term of exile'—and there are plays such as *The Collection* and *The Caretaker*, which are concerned with the violence and destructiveness that emerge from the failure of individuals to maintain creative associations with each other.

In 'Pinter's Usurpers' (*Dram S*) J. Pesta writes on the theme of what he calls the 'usurper' in Pinter's plays, 'a menacing figure who . . . undermines the existence of other characters'. In the early plays—*The Room, The Dumb Waiter*, and *The Birthday Party*—the usurper appears 'as a mysterious agent in direct conflict with a gradually disintegrating victim'. Later works, such as *The Caretaker, The Servant*, and *The Homecoming*, 'explore more complicated relationships between the usurpers and their victims; the plays become subtle psychological studies of characters who are at once aggressive, yet in need of personal relationships to supply the security which they desperately require'.

In 'Harold Pinter—Some Credits and Debits' (*MD*) V. E. Amend, while granting that Pinter is the most skilful English playwright in the Absurd school, discusses some unsatisfactory elements in his handling of symbol, ambiguity, problem of communication, characterization and approach to values. In 'An Interview with Harold Pinter' (*First Stage*) W. Packard reports Pinter as having insisted that he has never read Freud, and that his 'plays are about what the titles are about'. In 'A Room with Three Views' (*Komos*) D. Cook and H. F. Brooks write on *The Caretaker*.

In 'The House: A Lecture in Birmingham' (*Encounter*) Arnold Wesker considers the rôle of the politically oriented artist in a society where the politicians have failed to construct a sane 'house'. A. Rothberg writes on Wesker under the title 'East End, West End' in *SWR*.

In 'Three Modern English Plays' (*PP*) S. Prickett writes on *The Caretaker*, *Serjeant Musgrave's Dance* and Anne Jellicoe's *The Knack*, seeing these plays as representative of the contemporary English theatre in that they employ themes and styles that derive from Brecht and Beckett mixed with a basic convention of stage action which is a mirror of ordinary life.

In 'Die rücksichtsvollen Rebellen: Politisches Kabarett und Theater in England' (*Forum, Wien*) F. Thorn writes on the decline of the so-called 'satirical' movement on the English stage and television in the 'sixties and decides that the impulse was dispersed into journalism and the entertainment industry.

The June number of *ETJ* is devoted to papers on general aspects of drama and theatre read at the Conference on Theatre Research, and in *The London Magazine* Frank Marcus in 'Comedy or Farce' attempts to separate the terms with regard not to form but to attitude, comedy having a moral purpose and seeking to improve the quality of life. Joe Orton's *Loot* is examined as an example of farce, which treats people as things and is amoral.

XV

American Literature

GEOFFREY MOORE and R. W. WILLETT

BOOKS

Sections 1 and 2 are by R. W. Willett; sections 3, 4, and 5 by Geoffrey Moore.

1. GENERAL

America in Fiction[1] appears in a fifth edition, enlarged and revised, but this guide to narratives depicting various aspects of life in North America continues to ignore a number of important contemporary novelists. Although the editorial comments on particular novels are often perfunctory or naïve, the division of the book into sections, such as Industrial America, Farm and Village Life, Politics and Institutions, is useful, especially to students groping for a thesis topic.

A more specialized bibliography by Helen H. Palmer and A. J. Dyson[2] is comparable in its intention to James Salem's *A Guide to Critical Reviews (Part I—American Drama)* (*YW* xlvii. 370–1), but the work under discussion includes references to books, scholarly articles and European commentaries, as well as newspaper reviews. Unfortunately, many of the items listed are not readily available in Britain. Also, the book is not

without errors and omissions: there is no such play as *Babbitt* by Arthur Miller, and Rabkin's solid book on the drama of the thirties goes unmentioned.

From Louisana State U.P. comes a handsomely produced volume[3] containing twenty authentic narratives and descriptions of hunting in the antebellum South. The authors of these pieces, which are taken from a variety of sources, range from professional journalists to ordinary sportsmen. The introduction places hunting in its social and historical context, although comments such as: 'hunting was a factor which promoted integration' are of little value, since the same might be said of white sexual exploitation of Negresses. Of special interest to the scholar are two reports by South-western humorists, Davy Crockett's account of shooting bears and Thomas Bangs Thorpe's 'Woodcock Fire Hunting'.

The core of Marston La France's collection of essays by different critics[4] is a series of lectures given in 1965 at Carleton University. The lectures show how difficult it is to make new and exciting points about Whitman, Melville and Hawthorne by means of traditional techniques, but at least the organizers' request for 'commonsense criticism' has been

---

[1] *America in Fiction: An annotated List of Novels that Interpret Aspects of Life in the United States, Canada and Mexico,* by Otis Coan and Richard G. Lillard. 5th ed. Palo Alto, Calif.: Pacific Books. pp. viii+232. $5.50.

[2] *American Drama Criticism,* by Helen H. Palmer and Anne J. Dyson. Hamden, Conn.: Shoe String Press. pp. 239. 52s. 6d.

[3] *Hunting in the Old South,* ed. by Clarence Gohdes. Baton Rouge: Louisiana State U.P. pp. xviii+176. $7.50.

[4] *Patterns of Commitment in American Literature,* ed. by Marston La France. Toronto U.P. pp. 210. $2.95. Paperback.

met. Also, as La France points out, a pattern did emerge—'commitments to action, based upon the individual's perception of reality'—and this is established in the first essay (by William Gilman) which employs Fergusson's tripartite scheme of purpose, passion and perception. The freshest writing appears in Roger B. Salomon's 'Mark Twain and Victorian Nostalgia', an article which places Twain in the context of Western rather than American literature. Salomon describes the author as a practitioner of 'nostalgic irony', a strategy which asserts the 'absurdity' of what is 'emotionally compelling'.

The essays in the Hubbell *Festschrift*[5] are also published for the first time, but they have no unifying theme. The majority of the articles are concerned with a single author, sometimes a single work, and over half of them focus on nineteenth-century writers. In general, it is the minor figures of American literature who have inspired the most worthwhile contributions: Theodore Hornberger describes the joyful sermons of Thomas Prince, Russell B. Nye examines Parkman's complex attitude towards the Indian and his fate, and Walter Blair puts the case for seriously studying the novels of Dashiel Hammett. In addition, Walker Franklin resuscitates some lesser known works by Jack London, and Lewis Leary writes with his customary ease and objectivity about Lafcadio Hearn.

The 'newness' of the perspectives on American literature in *Topic: 12*[6] is debatable. It is hardly original to

report Hemingway was an early existentialist, sceptical towards religion, and John V. Hagopian's 'Literary Criticism as Science' would appear to owe a debt to the concept of the 'affective fallacy'. However, the literary evidence in C. N. Stavrou's article on Hemingway is carefully ordered and Richard G. Landini's 'Confucianism and *The Cantos of Ezra Pound*' is a brief but thorough piece of research. Landini argues persuasively that the Confucian ethic appealed to Pound as a perfect context for his economic theories.

Explorations of Literature[7] includes three articles of interest to scholars of American literature. William E. Doherty analyses Fitzgerald's disillusioned treatment of the Romantic dream in '*Tender is the Night* and the "Ode to a Nightingale"' and Kenneth Holditch comments on the use of the continuing symbol and, more particularly, the symbolic act in '*One Man's Initiation*: The Origin of Technique in the Novels of John Dos Passos'. However, the best of the three is Malcolm O. Magaw's '*The Confidence-Man* and Christian Deity: Melville's Imagery of Ambiguity'. Magaw finds in the novel a comprehensive ambiguity of tone and meaning, and argues that the Confidence-Man is not a Christian deity but a symbolic God in his own right.

The Sunny Slopes of Long Ago[8] takes its title from the favourite toast of John A. Lomax, founder of the Texas Folklore Society, and is a collection of local folklore with the theme of the Western Cowboy being prominent. The separate items vary widely in importance, but three of

---

[5] *Essays on American Literature in Honor of Jay B. Hubbell*, ed. by Clarence Gohdes, Durham, N.C.: Duke U.P. pp. viii+350. $8.50.

[6] *Topic: 12. New Perspectives in American Literature*. Washington and Jefferson College, Penn. pp. 66. $2.

[7] *Explorations of Literature*, ed. by Rima Drell Reck. Baton Rouge: Louisiana State U.P. pp. viii+179. $3.50.

[8] *The Sunny Slopes of Long Ago*, ed. by Wilson M. Hudson and Allen Maxwell. Dallas, Texas: Southern Methodist U.P. pp. viii+204. $5.95.

them should interest students of literature and popular culture: Everett A. Giles's study of Cowboy ballads, James T. Bratcher's essay on the origins and tradition of 'The Baby-Switching Story' (used in Wister's *The Virginian*) and James Ward Lee's 'The Penny Dreadful as a Folksong'.

A valuable contribution to intellectual history is the four long essays (originally lectures) collected by Robert H. Bremner,[9] essays which deal, in Bremner's words, with 'the analysis, evaluation, organization and presentation of historical evidence'. Daniel Aaron exposes the problems involved in writing about the recent past—in this case the American Literary Left in the '30s—when many of those involved are still alive. Edward Lurie attempts to undermine the modern view of the late nineteenth century as a period of barren materialism by emphasizing the persistent alliances of intellectuals with businessmen and politicians. Finally, Stow Persons examines the social origins of the genteel tradition and Russell Nye explores the similarities and differences between history and literature. Books and articles dealing with the relationship of the two disciplines are listed in a selected bibliography.

The first of three volumes of essays, each written by a single critic, also denies the belief that history and literature are separate entities. David Levin[10] holds the opinion that critics of fiction and drama should have an interest in historical theory and fact; he also considers that literary criticism can be applied to history and

biography, in the manner of his own *History As Romantic Art*. Levin is particularly drawn to the eighteenth century, and the reprinting of his essays on Mather, Franklin, and what might be termed 'Salem witchcraft trials' literature is most welcome. His efforts to achieve clarity of meaning are consistently successful without suggesting condescension and he never allows his interest in history to inhibit the expression of exclusively literary perceptions.

Louis D. Rubin Jr. has an established reputation as a critic of Southern literature, and the essays in *The Curious Death of the Novel*[11] justify that reputation. As a Jewish Southerner, Rubin is principally concerned with the writer's awareness of being alienated from the society around him, and with social and cultural change. But the importance of the past, both historical and literary, also engages him, particularly in the second section which is devoted entirely to Southern literature. The author has an alert, lively mind, so that his judgements are frequently interesting and his subject matter (e.g. novels about Huey Long) often fresh.

The fifteen essays in Volume I of Carlo Izzo's *Civiltà Americana*[12] consist of reports on particular writers, ranging from Henry James to E. E. Cummings, and studies of a more general nature on such topics as American Negro poetry and American poetry in the early part of this century. As one would expect, Izzo comments on the interaction of cultures, notably in the long essay *Echoes of Italian literature beyond the Atlantic*.

[9] *Essays on History and Literature*, ed. by Robert H. Bremner. Columbus: Ohio State U.P. pp. xi+190. $5.
[10] *In Defense of Historical Literature: Essays on American History, Autobiography, Drama and Fiction*, by David Levin. N.Y.: Hill & Wang. pp. x+144. $3.95.

[11] *The Curious Death of the Novel: Essays in American Literature*, by Louis D. Rubin, Jr. Baton Rouge: Louisiana State U.P. pp. vii+302. $6.95.
[12] *Civiltà Americana*, Vol. I, *Saggi*, Vol. II, *Impressioni e note*, by Carlo Izzo. Rome: Edizioni di storia e letteratura. pp. 300.

The subject matter of the reprinted newspaper and magazine articles in Volume II is less confined to literary matters, though it does close with a collection of Pound's *inedita*, particularly the correspondence between Izzo and Pound. In both volumes, Professor Izzo's scholarship is enlivened, where appropriate, by wit and humour.

Jeffersonianism in Howard Mumford Jones's polemical pamphlet[13] is a mixture of human rationality, the moral sense, and a sense of social obligation. Professor Jones regrets that the novelist in America has so often denied the relevance of these values to the contemporary human condition. So, as Martin Dworkin observes, this short book 'recalls fiction to civic responsibility'. Novelists are at fault, in Jones's opinion, because they disseminate propaganda for irrationalism and alienation, and he laments the American fascination with Dostoievsky, Kierkegaard, Kafka and others. Jones allows it would be 'fatuous and immoral' to make artists be cheerful and write about 'nice people', but that is the conclusion towards which his criticism tends.

James Guetti, in his analysis of *Moby-Dick*, 'Heart of Darkness' and *Absalom, Absalom!*[14] argues that the disintegration of traditional narrative forms is a consequence of instability in the nature of language itself. In modern fiction, therefore, the emphasis is on the inexpressible nature of reality and the 'unreality of imaginative structures'. It follows that to insist on the 'ordering, cognitive function' of metaphor is a mistake (a destructive one in Captain Ahab's case). Ideal or true metaphors, used by Melville, Conrad, and Faulkner are the extended simile and the oxymoron, which remain complex and vital, suggesting order yet also presenting 'the richness of the imaginative experience'.

A bilingual anthology of Negro poetry, chosen by Langston Hughes,[15] contains work by forty-four poets. Ten poems by the editor are included, but the only other poets to be substantially represented are Claude McKay, Countee Cullen and Leroi Jones. It is a pity that A. B. Spellman has been omitted altogether, but a number of fine poems from Hughes's *New Negro Poets: U.S.A.* reappear, notably Ted Joans's 'It is Time', Leroi Jones's 'Epistrophe' and Mari Evans's 'Where have you gone?'.

Emily Hahn sets out, in *Romantic Rebels*,[16] to trace the development of the cult of Bohemia from Poe and Whitman to Kerouac and Ginsberg by means of a series of profiles. The result is Bohemia as showbiz and often as Miss Hahn's autobiography. She writes for the *New Yorker* but the freewheeling, informal style resembles the colour supplements rather more closely. The book covers the same ground as *Garrets and Pretenders* which is generously commended, but it lacks the drawings and cartoons which gave Albert Parry's book another, less subjective dimension.

Stratford-upon-Avon Studies have followed up their earlier venture into the area of American literature (*American Poetry*) with a volume of essays on aspects of modern American theatre.[17] Of the ten essays, four

[13] *Jeffersonianism and the American Novel*, by Howard Mumford Jones. N.Y.: Teacher's College Press (Columbia U.) pp. x+77.

[14] *The Limits of Metaphor: A Study of Melville, Conrad and Faulkner*, by James Guetti Ithaca, N.Y.: Cornell U.P. pp. vii+196.

[15] *La Poésie Negro-Américaine*, ed. by Langston Hughes. Paris: Editions Seghers. pp. 303.

[16] *Romantic Rebels: An Informal History of Bohemianism in America*, by Emily Hahn. Boston: Houghton Mifflin. pp. xiv+318. $5.95.

[17] *American Theatre* (Stratford-upon-Avon Studies 10). London: Arnold. pp. 258. 25s.

discuss individual playwrights: O'Neill, Williams, Miller and Albee, and among the general topics are realism, European influences and poetic drama. The level of critical intelligence is consistently high, but Gerald Weales's excellent 'The Group Theatre and its plays', an examination of ideological and stylistic similarities, deserves to be singled out. Two other notable pieces are Eric Mottram's study of Arthur Miller as a bewildered liberal unable to conceive of social change, and Morris Freedman's 'Success and the American Dramatist'.

Black Drama[18] by Loften Mitchell, a Negro dramatist and lecturer, is a welcome contribution to American studies. The structure is particularly important: Part Two, which describes in detail the history of the Harlem theatre movement acquires extra meaning by coming after Mitchell's revelation of the way false images, created by white theatre, contributed to the dehumanization of the Negro in the eighteenth and nineteenth centuries. But the third section, 'Today', is disappointing; a sense of distance is wanting, and the sentimental eulogy of Sidney Poitier is disastrous. The material on the Black Drama conferences of the sixties, however, is informative.

2. COLONIAL

Norman Pettit's prize-winning study[19] (Egleston History Prize 1963) is concerned with a particular theological issue: the concept of preparation for grace. The author focuses on Puritan discussions of the extent to which a man could prepare himself for grace and the efficacy, however limited, of such a process. After rehearsing the arguments of Preparationists such as Hooker and Bulkeley, Pettit devotes a chapter to the Antinomian Controversy in Massachusetts and demonstrates the growth of 'innate antinomianism' stimulated by the views of Giles Firmin. In the book's epilogue, the *conscious* ambivalence of covenant theology is emphasized: while it regarded the inner reformation of the heart as the basis of salvation, it also maintained that God was arbitrary and omnipotent. On the same subject, Professor Pettit takes issue with the late Perry Miller as he finds it hard to see 'how covenant theology was intended to supply a bargaining basis for man's relationship with God'.

Scholars' Facsimiles and Reprints have published Cotton Mather's *Bonifacius*,[20] but this reproduction of a copy in the Howard Library does not constitute a serious challenge to the Belknap Press edition of 1966 (*YW* xlvii. 337–8) with its well-argued defence of Mather by David Levin. In her introduction, Josephine K. Piercy draws attention to the persistence of 'doing good' in Mather's life and work, and she notes that shortly before the appearance of *Bonifacius* the phrases 'doing good' and 'Good Devices' appeared more frequently in his diary. The modernity of the work is often stressed; Mather's 'broad social and humanitarian vision' was, in Piercy's view, far ahead of his time.

Edwin Sponseller's short pamphlet on Edwards[21] is nothing more or less

---

[18] *Black Drama: The Story of the American Negro in the Theatre*, by Loften Mitchell. N.Y.: Hawthorn Books. pp. 248. $5.95.

[19] *The Heart Prepared: Grace and Conversion in Puritan Spiritual Life*, by Norman Pettit. New Haven and London: Yale U.P. pp. ix+252. $5.75.

[20] *Bonifacius: An Essay . . . To Do Good (1710)*, by Cotton Mather, with an introduction by Josephine K. Piercy. Gainesville, Fla.: Scholars' Facsimiles and Reprints. pp. xii+206. $7.50.

[21] *Northampton and Jonathan Edwards*, by Edwin Sponseller. Shippensburg State College P. pp. 32.

than a potted biography of America's great eighteenth century clergyman. There is little discussion of ideas, but Edwards's Puritan heritage is clearly and economically expounded and the quality of his day-to-day life is successfully evoked. Occasionally the style is banal, but this unpretentious work would be useful to anyone encountering Edwards for the first time.

Students of the early national period in America will welcome the resuscitation of the Connecticut Wits' mock-epic collaboration *The Anarchiad* (1786–1787), a popular satire designed to counteract the anarchic tendencies of the post-war period.[22] In his introduction, William K. Bottorff comes to the conclusion that this Federalist poem did affect public opinion in 1787 and that the Connecticut Compromise may, to some extent, have been prompted by the satire. Of particular interest in this reprint of Luther G. Riggs's 1861 edition is the preface by Riggs which explicitly draws the attention of the ante-bellum reader to the nationalistic sentiments of the poem. As Bottorff points out, it was Riggs's strong Union sympathy that led him to edit *The Anarchiad* and put it for the first time into book form.

While it is desirable to have in print an authoritative account of the essays, narratives and dramas of Hugh Henry Brackenridge, the prospective reader of Daniel Marder's new study[23] will probably turn initially to the chapter on Brackenridge's best-known work, the novel *Modern Chivalry*. Professor Marder

does not, in his examination of the book, emulate the comprehensiveness of Claude M. Newlin or the critical shrewdness of Lewis Leary. But he begins well with a comment on the limitations of Brackenridge's form of satire, and his cool determination to be objective in his assessment is to his credit. Indeed, he is doubtful whether *Modern Chivalry* can really be classed as a novel, either a didactic or a picaresque one.

Rodney M. Baine's book on Robert Munford[24] may help to alter the view that Royall Tyler was America's only noteworthy eighteenth century playwright. Professor Baine's principal object, however, has been to correct the errors about Munford and his plays that literary 'scholarship' has perpetuated (notably the date of his birth), and to provide hitherto unavailable information about Munford's early life and his career as a Virginia politician and planter. The evidence of thorough research is impressive and the chapters on Munford's two dramas *The Candidates* and *The Patriots* achieve a nice balance of contextual information and literary criticism. In this way Professor Baine is able to support his claim that the two plays dramatize 'basically native characters and themes'.

Early American drama is also the area chosen by Kent G. Gallagher,[25] whose interest lies in the dramatic utterance of cultural ideas. His investigation of attitudes towards foreigners in particular plays is confined to a period (1770–1830) when foreign relations were important to American government and culture. In the Revolutionary period 'patriot

[22] *The Anarchiad: A New England Poem (1786–1787)*, by David Humphreys, Joe Barlow, John Trumbull, Lemuel Hopkins, with an introduction by William K. Bottorff. Gainesville, Fla.: Scholars' Facsimiles and Reprints. pp. xii+124. $6.

[23] *Hugh Henry Brackenridge*, by Daniel Marder. New York: Twayne Publishers. pp. 159. $3.95.

[24] *Robert Munford: America's First Comic Dramatist*, by Rodney M. Baine. Athens, Ga.: Georgia U.P. pp. ix+132. $5.

[25] *The Foreigner in Early American Drama*, by Kent G. Gallagher. The Hague & Paris: Mouton. pp. 206.

playwrights' offered stereotypes of wicked Englishmen, and post-revolutionary drama attacked European systems as 'effete', 'decadent' and 'monarchical'. But at the beginning of the nineteenth century foreigners who were prepared to accept American manners and mores were presented sympathetically, and gradually America began to welcome European taste and culture once more. Romanticism stimulated a curiosity about the exotic foreigner which was satisfied by melodrama, tragedy and opera, but later it encouraged the dramatic treatment of the aboriginal American, the free and courageous Indian.

Thomas Jefferson was an indefatigable letter writer and his letters to his family have recently been edited.[26] Addressed principally to his two daughters, Martha and Mary, they reveal him as a loving, affectionate father, very conscious of his paternal obligations. Aware that his political career often made him a 'vagrant' father, he often used the family letter as a means of imparting moralistic advice. The picture one has of Jefferson is amplified by such admonitions and by his comments on farming, local affairs, the fine arts and the building of Monticello.

The eleventh volume[27] of the Franklin Papers has appeared and covers the year 1764, an important one for Franklin as it marked the termination of his direct involvement in Pennsylvania politics for just over a decade. The first major item in the volume is *A Narrative of the Late*

Massacres, written to arouse public feeling against the Paxton boys who had murdered a number of friendly Indians living near by. The political crisis resulting from the dispute between Penn and the Assembly was the occasion for Franklin's *Cool Thoughts* which supported a change in government. Later in the year, Franklin, after an election defeat, was appointed as agent for the province in England and was obliged to defend his appointment in the pamphlet *Remarks on a Late Protest*.

3. EARLY NINETEENTH CENTURY

Two general collections include essays on early nineteenth-century American novels. *Tradition and Tolerance in Nineteenth-Century Fiction*[28] contains, amongst its six essays, two by David Howard, one entitled 'James Fenimore Cooper's *Leatherstocking Tales*: "without a cross"' and the other '*The Blithedale Romance* and a Sense of Revolution'. Howard points out, rather gratuitously, that Cooper can no longer be regarded as a 'mere adventure writer', since he was one of the first to deal with the confrontation of America and Europe and to explain the meaning of 'the American myth'. He finds Cooper much more of an artist than he has been considered in the past; 'a controlling ironic vision' informs *The Leatherstocking Tales*. In his contribution on *The Blithedale Romance* Howard confesses that he finds this novel 'a great relief' after *The House of the Seven Gables*. It is difficult, in fact, for him to understand how the latter was ever highly thought of—a salutory shake-up for Hawthorne criticism.

[26] *The Family Letters of Thomas Jefferson*, ed. by Edwin Morris Betts and James Adam Bear, Jr., Columbia: Missouri U.P. pp. 506. $9.

[27] *The Papers of Benjamin Franklin*, ed. by Leonard W. Larabee, Helen C. Boatfield, and James H. Hutson. Vol. XI, January–December 1764. New Haven and London: Yale U.P. pp. xxviii+593. 135s.

[28] *Tradition and Tolerance in Nineteenth-Century Fiction: Critical Essays on Some English and American Novels*, ed. by David Howard, John Lucas and John Goode. London: Routledge. 1966. pp. 281. 42s.

Howard also contributes a piece entitled 'The Fortunate Fall and Hawthorne's "The Marble Faun"' to *Romantic Mythologies*,[29] edited by Ian Fletcher. If there is one general lesson that *The Marble Faun* teaches us, he maintains, it is that permanence inevitably involves decay. As in his piece on Cooper, Howard makes a great point (*pace* R. W. B. Lewis) of irony. The keynote of *The Marble Faun* is for him one of fear, the thrusting off of that final mockery, the idea of the fortunate fall.

Historians are often denigrated for their treatment of literature but in *The American Mind in the Mid-Nineteenth Century*[30] Irving H. Bartlett deals sympathetically with Whitman, Hawthorne and Melville ('The Democrat as Poet', 'The Democrat as Puritan' and 'The Democrat as Skeptic'). Though, from a literary point of view, this treatment of the authors is the wrong way round, Bartlett is no Philistine. His discussion of the state of religion, philosophy and science at mid-century, of political and social thought and of the situation of the South, although necessarily brief, is equally perspicacious.

Letters from the West[31] is a Scholars' Facsimiles and Reprints edition introduced by John T. Flanagan. This book, by James Hall, was first published by the English firm of Henry Colburn in 1828. The twenty-two letters it contains divide themselves naturally into two sections. The first twelve deal with Hall's experiences before he reached Shawneetown, Illinois, on 6 May, 1820, and include descriptions of the scenery along the Ohio, characterizations of immigrants and boatmen, and anecdotes and fragments of balladry. The rest describe Shawneetown and whatever the writer found of interest in the western countryside, its history, its legends and the character of its people. Though Hall was no Doughty or Burton, he makes the Ohio valley of the 1820s come alive by the acuteness of his observation.

The material printed in *With the Bark On*[32] appeared in newspapers and magazines between 1835 and 1860. John Q. Anderson has collated it under eight headings: 'The River', 'The Backcountry', 'Varmints and Hunters', 'Fun and Frolic', 'The Professions', 'Jokes and Jokers', 'Masculine Amusements' and 'Politicians, Actors, Yokels in the City'. The Southern and Western writers of the ante-bellum period printed here combine, in a curiously attractive way, the genteel and the colloquial. Such examples of early 'local colour' tell us a good deal about the conditions and prejudices of the time, even if their value as literature is not particularly high.

In *Gli Umoristi della Frontiera*[33] Claudio Gorlier asks 'Che cos'è l'umorismo americano?' He answers his own question, first of all, with a series of extracts, translated from

---

[29] *Romantic Mythologies*, ed. by Ian Fletcher. London: Routledge. pp. xiii+297. 50s.

[30] *The American Mind in the Mid-Nineteenth Century*, by Irving H. Bartlett. (The Crowell American History Series.) New York: Thomas Y. Crowell. pp. vi+133.

[31] *Letters from the West: Containing Sketches of Scenery, Manners and Customs: and Anecdotes connected with the First Settlements of the Western Sections of the United States (1828)*, by James Hall, with an introduction by John T. Flanagan. Gainesville, Fla.: Scholars' Facsimiles and Reprints. pp. xv+vi+385. $10.

[32] *With the Bark On: Popular Humor of the Old South*, ed. and with an introduction and notes by John Q. Anderson. Nashville, Tennessee: Vanderbilt U.P. pp. xi+337. $7.50.

[33] *Gli Umoristi della Frontiera*, ed. by Claudio Gorlier. (Tradizione Americana, No. 13.) Vicenza, Italy: Neri Pozza. pp. lxxvii+626.

'The Humour of the East', from which source he considers frontier humour to be derived (i.e. the stories of 'Jack Downing' and 'Sam Slick'). He then proceeds to consider 'The World of Davy Crockett', 'The Heroes and Adventurers of the South and South-West' (e.g. A. B. Longstreet, Joseph G. Baldwin, T. B. Thorpe, George Washington Harris etc.), 'The Whites, the Negroes, and the Indians of The West' (Joel Chandler Harris, David Ross Locke and others), 'The Humorist as Actor' (Bill Nye and Artemus Ward) and 'The Reality and Paradise of the American Dream' (F. P. Dunne). This book is the thirteenth in the series entitled *Tradizione Americana*, edited under the chairmanship of Agnostino Lombardo, and presents one more indication of the strides which Italian scholars are making in the field of American Studies.

Yet another Scholars' Facsimiles and Reprints edition is entitled *The Home Book of the Picturesque: or American Scenery, Art, and Literature. Comprising A Series of Essays by Washington Irving, W. C. Bryant, Fenimore Cooper, and others (1852)*[34]. Fenimore Cooper compares American and European scenery, Washington Irving describes the Catskill Mountains and Bayard Taylor Pennsylvania, H. T. Tuckerman writes on the Western pioneer, William Cullen Bryant on the valley of the Housatonic, and G. W. Bethune on art in the United States. Motley F. Deakin, who edits the volume, suggests that *The Home Book of the Picturesque* would make a good start for the study of the significance of sight in nineteenth-century literature which was suggested by F. O. Matthiessen in *American Renaissance*. Henry Nash Smith also notes how responsive nineteenth-century Americans were to their environment.

Washington Allston's *Lectures on Art and Poems (1850)* and *Monaldi (1841)*[35] are reproduced with an introduction by Nathalia Wright. These facsimile editions also include eight paintings. Allston was the first modern American painter to emerge after the Revolution. Unlike his predecessors, he ventured into landscape and dramatic scenes, although much of his inspiration was literary. His significance in American art lies partly in the fact that he sought—presumably inspired by Blake—to paint visions. *Lectures on Art* constitutes a statement of his theory of art, apparently based on German idealist philosophy, since Allston defines a work of art as the 'form' in which an 'Idea' of the artist is manifested. This 'Idea' is called into çonsciousness by some physical phenomenon which has 'a predetermined correspondence or correlation' (a forerunner of the 'objective correlative'?) The volume also contains a collection of aphorisms, an essay entitled 'The Hypochondriac' and a collection of poems, more distinguished for their Romantic sentiments than for their originality. *Monaldi* is a tale of Italy, Gothic in character.

Emerson's Library[36] by Walter Harding is a companion volume to his *Thoreau's Library* published in 1957, and is the first catalogue of Emerson's collection to be published,

---

[34] *The Home Book of the Picturesque: or American Scenery, Art, and Literature*, comprising a series of essays by Washington Irving, W. C. Bryant, Fenimore Cooper, and others, with an introduction by Motley F. Deakin. Gainesville, Fla.: Scholars' Facsimiles and Reprints. pp. 8+188. $7.50.

[35] *Lectures on Art and Poems* (1850) and *Monaldi* (1841), by Washington Allston, with an introduction by Nathalia Wright. Gainesville, Fla.: Scholars' Facsimiles and Reprints. pp. xx+xi+253. $15.

[36] *Emerson's Library*, by Walter Harding. Charlottesville: Va. Virginia U.P. pp. xi+338. $10.

despite the fact that unlike Thoreau's, it was found almost intact. The book, based on a card catalogue prepared by Morrison C. Haviland of Harvard, includes volumes now in the Concord Antiquarian Society's collection which were owned by members of the Emerson family other than Ralph Waldo. Harding says that he has left them in since they were taken directly from Emerson's home and there is therefore a good possibility that he used them himself. Although only first-hand acquaintance with the books themselves (sets of pages, annotations, personal footnotes etc.) could give any real idea as to Emerson's sources, the list which Harding provides does at least give us some sort of evidence about Emerson's sources. One notices, for example, that he possessed two volumes of Hafiz, one in German and the other (of selections) in English. Although this is not conclusive evidence that Emerson did not read the Persian poets in the original, we may suspect that this was the case.

City of the West[37] is a study of 'the important role played by urban metaphors in Emerson's dialectical strategy'. Michael H. Cowan sees the 'City of the West' as a master metaphor which includes the idea both of the City of God and of the City of Man. He also deals with what he calls 'the organic city' and the 'freedom of the city', analysing in the process, Emerson's 'role' as a poetic experimenter who worked in an atmosphere of intellectual conflict and romantic haze. This is a compact and, within its limits, helpful book.

Scholars' Facsimiles and Reprints have produced *Two Brahman Sources*

of Emerson and Thoreau,[38] one, the *Translation of Several Principal Books, Passages, and Texts of the Veds (1832)* and the other, *A View of the History, Literature, and Mythology of the Hindoos. Part III, Section XIII: Of the Six Darshanas (1822)*, edited, with an introduction, by William Bysshe Stein. Stein believes that Rajah Rammohun Roy, the writer of the first book, was 'a silent but powerful force in the shaping of the Transcendental Movement in New England', and finds much in the creed of the Atmiya Sabha or Spiritual Society which Roy established in 1816 to support the views of Emerson and Thoreau. The second reprint, by William Ward, an Englishman born in 1769, provided Emerson and Thoreau with an epitome of the Upanishads. This little book is valuable in giving us evidence of some of the possible sources of Transcendental ideas.

The second edition of Reginald L. Cook's *Passage to Walden*[39] contains a 'Key to References and Citations'. This pleasant and sympathetic study written by one New Englander about another is a welcome reminder that American scholars can write well and do not necessarily have to focus their attention upon purely clinical and allegorical details in order to produce worthwhile critical studies.

Charles Crowe's *George Ripley*[40] records Ripley's friendships with Emerson, Thoreau, William Henry Channing, Horace Greeley, Andrew

[37] *City of the West: Emerson, America and Urban Metaphor*, by Michael H. Cowan (Yale Publications in American Studies, No. 13). New Haven and London: Yale U.P. pp. xiv+284. $6.50. 58s.

[38] *Two Brahman Sources of Emerson and Thoreau*, ed. with an introduction by William Bysshe Stein. Gainesville, Fla.: Scholars' Facsimiles and Reprints. pp. xx+viii+292. $8.

[39] *Passage to Walden*, by Reginald L. Cook. Second Edition. Containing a Key to References and Citations. New York: Russell & Russell, 1966. pp. xvi+253. $7.50.

[40] *George Ripley: Transcendentalist and Utopian Socialist*, by Charles Crowe. Athens: Georgia U.P. pp. x+316. $7.95.

Norton, John Sullivan Dwight, Margaret Fuller and Theodore Parker. When Ripley died, in 1880, he had had several careers. Prior to 1841, he had been preoccupied for twenty years with the debate between Transcendentalism and Unitarianism. In that year, he left his position as a Unitarian minister to become one of the founders of the Brook Farm experiment. There, he was a sort of 'prime minister of Utopia' and a leading American disciple of Fourier. The opening chapters of Crowe's book are concerned with Ripley's background in Greenfield, Massachusetts, his years at Harvard, and his Unitarian ministry. Subsequently, he describes the emergence of Ripley's Transcendental ideas, the famous Ripley-Norton controversy and the idealism of the Brook Farm period. The final section concerns Ripley's Fourierist views and his last years in New York, when he wrote reviews, articles and essays for the *Tribune*.

Walter Harding introduces a facsimile reproduction of *The Collected Poems of William Ellery Channing The Younger, 1817–1901*.[41] This Channing must be distinguished from his paternal uncle, the Unitarian minister, who was also a great figure of the early part of the nineteenth century. (Yet another Channing, Edward T., was Boylston Professor of Rhetoric at Harvard at the same time). During the 1840s—having married Margaret Fuller's sister, Ellen—he settled down in Concord in order to be near Emerson. There, he became so interested in Transcendentalism that he neglected his family and, after Thoreau's death in 1862, lived alone in Concord. His verse was not highly regarded at the time, the most devastating criti-

cism, of course, being by Poe in his review of Channing's volume of 1843. However, the best of it has an historical interest in its revelation of Transcendental thought. Harding has reproduced Channing's seven volumes in chronological order and appended the texts of his uncollected poems.

Channing of Concord[42] is a biography of the same William Ellery Channing. Frederick T. McGill, Jr. points out that, although he was a failure in the world's eyes, he could write well. It is true ('Dull I came upon the planet, untalented, the one talent still in that tremendous napkin, out of which I have never been able to unwrap it and where it is still like to be for all I can discern thro its folds'). McGill became interested because Channing was 'a part of the Concord environment', an integral member of the Transcendental circle and an intimate of Emerson, Alcott and Hawthorne. He was also a prolific contributor to *The Dial*, and 'made tracks in the snow for others to follow in'. In fifteen chapters he follows Channing's career from 'Childhood (1817–1834)' to '"Come My Little Skipjack" (1891–1901)'.

Baudelaire's translation of Poe's 'Tales Grotesque and Arabesque' is reprinted under the title of *Histoires Grotesques et Sérieuses*.[43] Roger Asselineau, who supplies a chronology and introduction, quotes Baudelaire's remark 'Do you know why I have translated Poe so patiently? Because he is like me. The first time that I opened one of his books I saw with

---

[41] *The Collected Poems of William Ellery Channing The Younger, 1817–1901*, ed. with an introduction by Walter Harding, Gainesville, Fla.: Scholars' Facsimiles and Reprints. pp. xxii + viii + 1026. $20.

[42] *Channing of Concord: A Life of William Ellery Channing II*, by Frederick T. McGill, Jr. New Brunswick, N.J.: Rutgers U.P. pp. xiii + 219. $7.50.

[43] *Histoires Grotesques et Sérieuses*, by Edgar Allan Poe, translated by Charles Baudelaire and with an introduction by Roger Asselineau. Paris: Garnier-Flammarion, 1966. pp. 189.

astonishment and ecstacy not only subjects dreamed by me but phrases thought by me and imitated by him twenty years before'. These remarks help to show why Poe is still so attractive to French taste.

A collection of critical essays[44] on Poe in the Prentice-Hall Twentieth Century Views Series is edited by Robert Regan. It includes, among other essays, Allen Tate's well-known 'Our Cousin, Mr. Poe', 'The French Response to Poe' by Patrick F. Quinn and 'The Conscious Art of Edgar Allan Poe' by Floyd Stovall. There are also useful interpretations of individual stories—for example, 'Ligeia' by Roy P. Basler, 'The Fall of the House of Usher' by Maurice Beebe, 'The Masque of the Red Death' by J. P. Roppolo and 'Arthur Gordon Pym' by Sidney Kaplan.

Eric W. Carlson's *Introduction to Poe*[45] is sub-titled 'A Thematic Reader'. This means, in effect, that Carlson, apart from dividing his collection into three sections entitled 'Poems', 'Tales', and 'Essays, Criticism and Marginalia', has sub-divided each section with such abominations as 'The Ideal', 'The Human Condition', 'The Haunted Mind' and 'Revelations'. A third, even more annoying, stage of categorization consists of a series of sub-sub-titles— for example, under 'The Ideal': 'The Dream of Reality' and 'The Hunger for Supernal Beauty' and, under 'The Human Condition': 'The Lost Eden', 'The Dark Powers' and 'Man's Fate: Death in Life'. It is possible that there are some who are helped by this kind of editorializing, but for the reader

with any degree of sensibility such interference with Poe's text cannot but be frustrating. Is it too obvious to be said? The basic essentials of any reproduction of an author's work are (a) chronological printing, and (b) accuracy of text. Given these, we may work out for ourselves what themes we think Poe wrote about.

J. Lasley Dameron has produced a checklist[46] of Edgar Allan Poe criticism published between 1942– 1960. Originally a part of Dameron's dissertation entitled 'Edgar Allan Poe in the Mid-Twentieth Century: His Literary Reputation in England and America 1928–1960 and a Bibliography of Poe Criticism 1942–1960', this little volume is published by the Bibliographical Society of the University of Virginia as a preliminary step in the compilation of a complete bibliography of Poe criticism.

Edwin Gittleman has undertaken a study of Jones Very[47] during his 'effective years', 1833–1840. His book is divided into three sections— 'Preparations' in which he explores Very's early life in Cambridge and Salem, 'Performances' which deals with the years from 1836–1838 and 'Visions and Revisions' (1838–1840). Very was a possessed, gifted and, in many ways, infuriating man whose eccentricity and religious fervour set him at odds with his College authorities and his neighbours in Salem. Gittleman analyses Very's poems both from the point of view of their literary contribution and as expressions of a remarkable personality. After the first twenty-seven years his life was an anti-climax. When his

---

[44] *Poe: A Collection of Critical Essays*, ed. by Robert Regan. (Twentieth Century Views) (A Spectrum Book). Englewood Cliffs, N.J.: Prentice Hall. pp. 183. Paperback $1.95. 18s. 6d., Cloth 46s. 6d.
[45] *Introduction to Poe: A Thematic Reader*, ed. by Eric W. Carlson. (Key Editions). Glenview, Ill.: Scott, Foresman. pp. xxxix+601.

[46] *Edgar Allan Poe: A Checklist of Criticism 1942–1960*, by J. Lasley Dameron. Charlottesville, Va.: The Bibliographical Society of the University of Virginia, 1966. pp. xii+15–159.
[47] *Jones Very: The Effective Years, 1833– 1840*, by Edwin Gittleman. New York and London: Columbia U.P. pp. xx+436. 90s.

mother died, he lived out the rest of his days in a bachelor establishment with two spinster sisters and mulled interminably over the events and ideals of his productive years.

In *Hawthorne and the Modern Short Story*[48] Mary Rohrberger gives an account both of the short story as a literary form and of the relationship of Hawthorne's literary theory to his own short stories. After an analysis of 'Roger Malvin's Burial', 'My Kinsman, Major Molineux' and 'Young Goodman Brown', she examines the 'literary theories' of representative modern short-story writers and provides detailed comments on stories by Conrad, Katherine Mansfield, D. H. Lawrence, Faulkner, Hemingway, Sherwood Anderson and Eudora Welty. Three concluding chapters deal with the short story and the simple narrative, the short story and the novel, and a proposed definition of the short story.

Perhaps the fact that Jac Tharpe has dedicated his book[49] on Hawthorne to 'Prince Hal' ought not to be held against him. Apart from a slight whimsicality of approach, Tharpe's approach is sensible. He believes that Hawthorne's work needs to be placed in the context of Western rather than specifically American literature and suggests stimulating lines of investigation, such as Hawthorne's relationship to the 'neo-Gothicists of the South' and to German literature. His own approach is by way, first, of 'The Narrative

Masks' and 'The Man Behind the Masks'. He is particularly good on Hawthorne's 'Search for Awareness', says a little about his subject's devotion to allegorical types and devotes a chapter to 'Rappaccini's Daughter'. The book ends with short sections on the *Blithedale Romance* and *The Marble Faun*. It is a slight book for such large themes and, although Tharpe is perceptive, he would have done better to have devoted more time to fewer lines of investigation.

Claire McGlinchee's book on James Russell Lowell[50] follows the usual pattern of the Twayne's United States Authors Series—that is, an account of his life (from 1819–1853 and from 1854–1860), a statement about the early poems and his work as a critic, his professorship at Harvard and his political and diplomatic contribution, and a consideration of the poems of his later years—in other words, a workmanlike and unfussy account. Martin Duberman is much more ambitious. His biography[51] runs to 516 pages and seeks to re-establish Lowell as one of the great representative figures of mid-nineteenth-century America. It will warm the hearts of those who, like George Arms, have long wished to restore the fortunes of 'the fire-side poets'. The book is based on manuscript material and is copiously documented; in fact, the bibliography and index alone take up 144 pages. This is a useful and welcome addition to Lowell scholarship and, although it bears the marks of having been written by a professor of history, it is nevertheless of interest to the literary-minded.

Volume 1 of *The Papers of Ulysses*

[48] *Hawthorne and the Modern Short Story: A Study in Genre*, by Mary Rohrberger. (Studies in General and Comparative Literature, Vol. II). The Hague and Paris: Mouton. 1966. pp. 148.

[49] *Nathaniel Hawthorne: Identity and Knowledge*, by Jac Tharpe, with a preface by Harry T. Moore. (Crosscurrents Modern Critiques.) Carbondale and Edwardsville: Southern Illinois U.P. London and Amsterdam: Feffer and Simons. pp. viii+180. $4.95.

[50] *James Russell Lowell*, by Claire McGlinchee. (Twayne's United States Authors Series, No. 120.) New York: Twayne. pp. 143. $3.95.

[51] *James Russell Lowell*, by Martin Duberman. (The Riverside Press.) Boston, Mass.: Houghton Mifflin. 1966. pp. xxii+516. $8.

S. Grant[52] covers the years from 1837 to 1861 and begins with Grant's impressions of West Point. Most of the letters in this pre-Civil War period are to Julia Dent, from whom he was separated during his four years of service in Louisiana, Texas and Mexico. Others, addressed to his father from St. Louis between 1856–58, speak not only of loneliness but of the kind of determination which led him to his later success. In fact, Grant's earlier years were not, as they have often been called, 'forty years of failure'; they were, according to his editor, John Y. Simon, necessary experiences in the shaping of a complex personality. This volume provides a useful and welcome complement to the creative literature of the period, revealing as it does the life of a professional man during the years of the 'American Renaissance'.

Harrison Hayford and Hershel Parker have edited 'An Authoritative Text' of Moby-Dick[53] together with reviews and letters by Melville and a selection of 'Analogues and Sources' of criticism. The latter section contains contemporary reviews, 'Interim Appraisals' written between 1893 and 1913, and criticism under the heading of 'Revival and Reaction' from the period 1917–1936. The final section ('Academic Criticism') includes essays written during the thirty years ending in 1962 (for example, Charles Feidelson Jr.'s 'Moby-Dick as Symbolic Voyage', R. W. B. Lewis's 'The Try-Works' and Warner Berthoff's 'Characterization in Moby-

Dick'). This valuable book, one of a series of Norton Critical Editions, contains a detailed section on the history, variants and emendations of the Moby-Dick text, and the reasons for various textual decisions. There are also maps of Melville's voyages, of the route of the Pequod, and of the principal ports of south-eastern New England in the mid-1800's.

In Melvilles Erzählungen[54] Klaus Ensslen contributes a stylistic and constructive analysis of 'Bartleby the Scrivener', 'The Encantadas or Enchanted Isles', 'Benito Cereno', 'The Bell-Tower', 'Cock-A-Doodle-Doo! or The Crowing of the Noble Cock Beneventano and The Piazza', 'I and My Chimney, The Apple-Tree Table, or, Original Spiritual Manifestations and The Lightning-Rod Man', 'The Two Temples; Poor Man's Pudding, Rich Man's Crumbs; The Paradise of Bachelors, The Tartarus of Maids', 'The Happy Failure, The Fiddler and Jimmy Rose' and 'Billy Budd, Sailor'. This, the fourteenth volume in the American Studies Library, generally edited by Ernst Fraenkel, Hans Galinsky, Dietrich Gerhard and H. J. Lang, is a typically thorough piece of German scholarship.

Hershel Parker's The Recognition of Herman Melville[55] is a selection of criticism since 1846. In 'Reviews and Early Appraisals: 1846–76' Parker prints forty-four reviews of the period, ranging from Margaret Fuller's notice on Typee to the anonymous review of Clarel in the London Academy in 1876. 'Academic Neglect and Prophecies of Renown: 1884–

[52] The Papers of Ulysses S. Grant, Volume I: 1837–1861, ed. by John Y. Simon. Carbondale and Edwardsville: Southern Illinois U.P. London and Amsterdam: Feffer & Simons pp. xxxix+458. $15.
[53] Moby-Dick, by Herman Melville, an authoritative text, reviews and letters by Melville, analogues and sources criticism, ed. by Harrison Hayford and Hershel Parker. (Norton Critical Editions.) New York: W. W. Norton. pp. xviii+728. $1.95.
[54] Melvilles Erzählungen: Stil- und strukturanalytische Untersuchungen, by Klaus Ensslen. (Beihefte zum Jahrbuch für Amerikastudien, No. 14). Heidelberg: Carl Winter. 1966. pp. 220.
[55] The Recognition of Herman Melville: Selected Criticism 1846, ed. by Hershel Parker. Ann Arbor: Michigan U.P. xvii+364. $7.50.

1912' contains, among other essays, W. P. Trent and John Erskine's contribution to the *Great American Writers* series published in 1912 and H. S. Salt's 'Herman Melville' which appeared in *The Scottish Art Review* between June and December 1889. In 'The Melville Revival' we find Raymond M. Weaver's essay from *Herman Melville: Mariner and Mystic*, Arnold Bennett's essay on *Pierre* and Lewis Mumford's chapter on *Moby-Dick* from *Herman Melville*, published in 1939. 'Academic Recognition: 1938–67' contains, among other essays, F. O. Matthiessen's 'A Bold and Nervous Lofty Language' from *American Renaissance*, and Walker Cowen's 'Melville's "Discoveries": A Dialogue of the Mind with Itself', taken from *Melville's Marginalia*, published in 1965. This is a comprehensive and important collection, presenting as it does, in chronological order, the stages of Melville's gradual acceptance by the serious literary world.

4. LATER NINETEENTH CENTURY

Marilyn Austin Baldwin edits and introduces William Dean Howells's *My Mark Twain*[56] originally printed in 1910. It is refreshing to read the comments of a born writer among so many indifferent or heavily-written scholarly accounts. In fact, it is tempting to say that there is more value in Howells's book than in a great deal of the criticism on Twain which has emerged during the past half century. He manages to convey that sympathy which Coleridge says is necessary for criticism.

Three books on Mark Twain 'material' are part of a University of California Press Twain Library, the general purpose of which is to present new and accurate texts. First, John S. Tuckey edits and introduces *Which Was The Dream? and Other Symbolic Writings of the Later Years*.[57] Under the heading of 'other symbolic writings' Tuckey prints such stories as 'The Great Dark', 'Which Was It?' and 'Three Thousand Years Among the Microbes'. These later stories are bizarre and even bitter, coming as they do from Twain's 'dark night of the soul'; like *The Mysterious Stranger*, they make painful reading. Second on the list is Hamlin Hill's edition of Twain's *Letters to His Publishers: 1867–1894*[58] and, third, Franklin R. Rogers's edition of *Satires & Burlesques*.[59] Many of the 290 letters printed in Hill's volume have never been published before; they cover the period from the publication of 'The Celebrated Jumping Frog of Calaveras County' in 1867 to *Pudd'nhead Wilson* in 1894. Hill has supplemented the letters with copious annotations, and the result is a full and fascinating history of the period covered. The 'satires and burlesques' chosen by Rogers include one of 'Il Trovatore', 'The Story of Mamie Grant', 'The Child-Missionary', 'L'Homme Qui Rit', a burlesque of *Hamlet* (reminiscent of a section of *Huckleberry Finn*), '1,002^d Arabian Night', 'The Hellfire Hotchkiss Sequence' and 'The Simon Wheeler Sequence'. The publication of these

[57] *Mark Twain's 'Which was the Dream?' and Other Symbolic Writings of the Later Years*, ed. with an introduction by John S. Tuckey. Berkeley and Los Angeles: California U.P. xi+588. $10. 80s.
[58] *Mark Twain's Letters to his Publishers 1867–1894*, ed. with an introduction by Hamlin Hill. Berkeley & Los Angeles: California U.P. pp. xiv+388. $10. 80s.
[59] *Mark Twain's Satires & Burlesques*, ed. with an introduction by Franklin R. Rogers. Berkeley & Los Angeles: California U.P. pp. viii+485. $10. 80s.

[56] *My Mark Twain: Reminiscences and Criticisms*, by William Dean Howells. Ed. with an introduction by Marilyn Austin Baldwin. Baton Rouge: Louisiana State U.P. pp. xviii+189. $7.50.

pieces provides an interesting background to a study of Twain as a satirist. The material is in the vein of *Innocents Abroad* and, as the editor has suggested, is probably nearer to burlesque than to true satire. Rogers provides interesting notes on the relationship between the pieces he has chosen and Twain's previously published work.

The third edition of *Mark Twain: The Man and His Work*[60] reminds us of the breadth of Edward Wagenknecht's contribution to American literary criticism. Originally published in 1935, Wagenknecht's biography is sound and sympathetic. The original version was considerably re-written in 1961, when it was taken over by the present publishers. The author has added a chapter of commentary on Mark Twain criticism since 1960. *Mark Twain and The Backwoods Angel*[61] deals with the theme of innocence in Twain's work. William C. Spengemann suggests that this theme was a symbolic one—in fact, a sense of American innocence which Twain could 'neither abjure nor accept uncritically'. The moral dilemma in which he was thrown by this awareness was, Spengemann suggests, a major element in his work. He finds the genesis of the innocent hero in 'The Backwoodsman and the Pilgrim'. Other chapters are devoted to *Roughing It* ('The Greenhorn and the Captain'), *The Gilded Age* and *Tom Sawyer* ('The Fallen Woman and the Bad Boy'), *The Prince and the Pauper* ('The Cub, the Changeling and the Recruit'), *Huckleberry Finn* ('The Backwoods

Angel'), *Connecticut Yankee* ('The Yankee Pirate'), *Joan of Arc* ('The Saint') and *The Mysterious Stranger* ('The Angel'). There is no doubt of the importance in Twain's work of the theme which Spengemann has selected.

In his introduction to Emily Dickinson's *Poems, 1890, Poems, Second Series, 1891* and *Poems, Third Series, 1896*,[62] George Monteiro considers Thomas H. Johnson's variorum edition of 1955 in comparison with the texts he has reprinted, pointing out some errors, and offering a number of other versions. In *The Editing of Emily Dickinson*[63] R. W. Franklin examines in detail the editorializing work of Mabel Loomis Todd and Thomas H. Higginson. In his hunt for variants, he has gone to manuscripts and transcripts, and his detective work is keen and assiduous. The result is to leave no doubt in anyone's mind that Thomas H. Johnson had not considered all the problems when he produced the 1955 edition. David Higgins turns to Emily Dickinson's prose[64] as a guide to her poetry and character. He has, in fact, written a biography based on the evidence of her letters, revealing a 'precocious child' and 'sentimental adolescent' who wrote letters of great length to various relatives and friends; Mary Lyon and Mount Holyoke were, he believes, major influences on her writing. Higgins also finds in Miss Dickinson's prose of the early eighteen-fifties a marked rhythmic pattern which suggests to him that she

[60] *Mark Twain: The Man and his Work*, by Edward Wagenknecht. Third edition. Norman: Oklahoma U.P. pp. xiii+302. $4.95.

[61] *Mark Twain and The Backwoods Angel: The Matter of Innocence in the Works of Samuel L. Clemens*, by William C. Spengemann. (Kent Studies in English.) Kent State U.P. 1966. pp. xvi+144. $5.75..

[62] *Poems (1890–1896)*, by Emily Dickinson with an introduction by George Monteiro, Gainesville, Fla.: Scholars' Facsimiles and Reprints. pp. xxii+xii+13–200. $15.

[63] *The Editing of Emily Dickinson: A Reconsideration*, by R. W. Franklin. Madison, Milwaukee and London: Wisconsin U.P. pp. xvii+187. $7.

[64] *Portrait of Emily Dickinson: The Poet and Her Prose*, by David Higgins. New Brunswick, N.J.: Rutgers U.P. pp. 266. $7.50.

was already writing poetry at that time. He devotes considerable space to her relationship with Samuel Bowles, the editor of the *Springfield* (Mass.) *Republican*, to whom Higgins maintains that Emily sent a number of love poems in the mistaken impression that he was in love with her. He does not believe that she loved the Rev. Charles Wadsworth but rather—as has already been suggested—Judge Otis Lord. Although this rather gossipy book does not tell us anything of Emily Dickinson's quality as a poet, it provides a new and interesting account of her many possible relationships.

Although Carey McWilliams's biography of Ambrose Bierce[65] was published as long ago as 1929, it has remained a standard work. In a new introduction, in which he details the circumstances in which his book was written and comments on some of the major studies and articles which have appeared since the late twenties, McWilliams reminds us that in the twenties it was more common to say 'Who was Ambrose Bierce?' than 'Whatever happened to Ambrose Bierce?' All that is needed to insure Bierce's place in world literature, he maintains, is a one- or two-volume edition of the best of his writing, rigorously selected, 'with all marginal items eliminated'.

Frieder Busch contributed the eighth volume in the *Mainzer Amerikanistische Beiträge* series.[66] His subject is the storyteller and the point of view of both author and reader in *The Ambassadors*. The first section is

devoted to the perspective of the storyteller, with a sub-section on James's humour and irony; the second to James's 'viewpoint' theory, his impressionism and 'foreshortening' of scenes; the third to the dimension of time, and the fourth to the point of view of the reader (the 'theory of identification') together with a general summary.

It may be mentioned that Michael Swan's essay on Henry James,[67] published in the British Writers and Their Work series along with pieces on Joseph Conrad and D. H. Lawrence, has been reprinted. It is good to see Dorothea Krook's *The Ordeal of Consciousness in Henry James*[68] published in paperback format at a reasonable price. This book was reviewed when it appeared (*YW* xliii. 317).

In his foreword to David Galloway's contribution to *Studies in English Literature*,[69] David Daiches informs us that what both 'the advanced sixth-former and the university student need most . . . are close critical analyses and evaluations of individual works'. In his limited space Galloway does a good job on *Portrait of a Lady*, but one cannot help comparing this slim eight-and-sixpenny volume with the comprehensive and scholarly paperback *compendia* produced by our American colleagues at little more than that price.

Underlying *Soliloquies in England*

---

[65] *Ambrose Bierce: A Biography*, by Carey McWilliams (and with a new introduction). Hamden, Connecticut: Archon Books. pp. xxxi+358. $12.

[66] *Erzähler-, Figuren- und Leserperspektive in Henry James's Roman 'The Ambassadors'*, by Frieder Busch. (Mainzer Amerikanistische Beiträge, No. 8.) Munich: Max Hueber. pp. 205. DM.16.80.

[67] *Henry James*, by Michael Swan, *Joseph Conrad*, by Oliver Warner, *D. H. Lawrence*, by Kenneth Young. Ed. by J. W. Robinson. (British Writers and Their Work, No. 10.) Lincoln: Nebraska U.P. pp. 138. $1.60.

[68] *The Ordeal of Consciousness in Henry James*, by Dorothea Krook. New York and London: C.U.P. pp. xiii+422. $2.75. 15s. Paperback.

[69] *Henry James: The Portrait of a Lady*, by David Galloway. (Studies in English Literature, No. 32.) London: Arnold. pp. 64 8s. 6d. (hardback) 5s. (paperback).

and Later Soliloquies,[70] says Ralph Ross, is 'the philosophy of civilization that Santayana published in 1905 in five volumes as *The Life of Reason*'. This reprint makes interesting reading when compared with the accounts by other Americans (Irving, Emerson, Melville) of their journeys through England. Unlike these earlier authors, however, Santayana conveys little of the details of the English scene. Though he wrote *Soliloquies in England* between 1914–18 he says almost nothing of the First World War. His essays are for the most part on general topics (e.g. 'Atmosphere', 'Praises of Water', 'Seafaring', 'Privacy'). Even when he chooses such subjects as 'The British Character', 'Dickens' and 'Tipperary', he shows a tendency to philosophize; the manner striking one as a cross between Hazlitt and Alpha-of-the-Plough. However, these essays provide considerable insight into Santayana's own attitudes of mind, and the book is perhaps rather more valuable for this quality than for its information about the English character.

A brief account of William Dean Howells[71] in the University of Minnesota Pamphlets on American Writers series follows the usual pattern of biography, review of work, and critical assessment. William M. Gibson is particularly interested in Howells's use of the term 'symmetry' to describe his approach to the novel. He applauds Howells's dictum that the business of the novel is to picture life 'with an absolute and clear sense of proportion' and his belief that the novel can affect readers only in so far as it can 'charm their minds and win their hearts'.

In *The Literary Realism of William Dean Howells*,[72] William McMurray discusses twelve of what he considers to be Howells's best novels, from *A Foregone Conclusion* (1875) to *The Vacation of the Kelwyns* (1920), devoting a chapter to each book. His general theme is that there is a parallel between Howells and William James; realism in literature he sees to be the counterpart of pragmatism in philosophy. Both Howells and James saw a world where ultimate freedom was impossible because man cannot reconcile his ideals and his practice. This conflict is portrayed in each of Howells's groups of characters, and is only resolved when they accept the imperfection of the human situation. It is a stimulating study, the more valuable since, although each volume is dealt with as a separate entity, the themes which emerge are traced from one book to the next.

John Adam Moreau believes that his biography of Randolph Bourne[73] is timely, since many of Bourne's ideas about war and the nature of the state would seem to be applicable to the 1960s. He even, according to Moreau, suggested the idea of a Peace Corps. Although Moreau tells us that he was born in the same place as Bourne (Bloomington, New Jersey), the sympathy which is evident in this badly printed, but not un-

[70] *Soliloquies in England and Later Soliloquies*, by George Santayana, with a new introduction by Ralph Ross. (Ann Arbor Paperbacks, No. 123.) Michigan U.P. pp. viii+264. $2.25. 15s.

[71] *William D. Howells*, by William M. Gibson. (University of Minnesota Pamphlets on American Writers, No. 63.) Minneapolis: Minnesota U.P. pp. 48. 95c.

[72] *The Literary Realism of William Dean Howells*, by William McMurray, with a preface by Harry T. Moore. (Crosscurrents Modern Critiques). Carbondale and Edwardsville: Southern Illinois U.P. London and Amsterdam: Feffer & Simons. pp. x+147. $4.95.

[73] *Randolph Bourne: Legend and Reality*, by John Adam Moreau. Washington, D.C.: Public Affairs Press, 1966. pp. viii+227. $5.

interesting, book, seems not entirely chauvinistic.

Harold P. Simonson objects to the canonization of certain 'major figures' in American literature and the virtual ignoring of other writers. However, his subject, Francis Grierson[74] (No. 97 in the Twayne's United States Authors list) is hardly outstanding enough to make up for our sense of relief on being spared yet another book about Melville, Hawthorne or Faulkner. Grierson, the pseudonym, after 1899, of one Benjamin Henry Jesse Francis Shepard, is said to be a significant historian of the pre-Civil War period. In so far as Victorian romantic sentiments have documentary value, Simonson's study was worth writing.

The fact that John Donald Wade was both a Georgian and a friend of Donald Davidson would seem to be part of the reason for the University of Georgia Press's lavish edition of Wade's *Selected Essays and Other Writings*.[75] John O. Edison, who is also connected with the University of Georgia, writes a biographical sketch. Wade's writings present the perfect portrait of an old-world Southern gentleman and scholar; even the 'poems' printed at the end have a charm which shines through the banality of the lines ('Last night when tea was done at Cousin Pearl's/We all played cards, but Claude, her better half . . .)

Four books in the Twayne's United States Authors Series deal, respectively, with Mary N. Murfree[76]

Joaquin Miller[77] Thomas Nelson Page[78] and Mary Wilkins Freeman.[79] Miss Murfree, who sometimes used the engaging pseudonym of Charles Egbert Craddock, is well known as one of the main figures of the 'local colour movement'. Although she published twenty-five books, her biographer, Richard Cary, rather sadly points out that not one of them is in print today. After a workman-like biographical and critical account, he comes to the resounding conclusion that it is on Mary Murfree's 'vivid and authentic use of local colour that final judgment of her artistry will rest'. Whereas most English readers—apart from that rare band who actually teach American literature in the United Kingdom —will scarcely have heard of Mary Murfree, Joaquin Miller is less buried in obscurity. Not that Miller was any better in his way than Mary Murfree in hers; in fact, he was probably of lesser stature, since Miss Murfree could, as her biographer attests, write vividly. Miller, on the other hand, was a cross between McGonigall and Edgar Guest ('He turned, he caught her suddenly/And instant wrapped her close within;/Then down the stairs and back and out/Beneath the blossomed Nippon tree—' etc.). However, as O. W. Frost points out, there has developed a 'Miller legend', and the fact that the *Times Literary Supplement* actually noticed Miller's work on publication probably helped its growth. There is, at least, no disputing his great popular appeal,

[74] *Francis Grierson*, by Harold P. Simonson. (Twayne's United States Authors Series, No. 97.) New York: Twayne, 1966. pp. 158. $3.95.

[75] *Selected Essays and Other Writings of John Donald Wade*, ed. with an introduction by Donald Davidson. Athens, Georgia U.P. 1966. pp. ix+237. $7.50.

[76] *Mary N. Murfree*, by Richard Cary (Twayne's United States Authors Series, No. 121.) New York: Twayne. pp. 192. $3.95.

[77] *Joaquin Miller*, by O. W. Frost. (Twayne's United States Authors Series, No. 119.) New York: Twayne. pp. 140. $3.95.

[78] *Thomas Nelson Page*, by Theodore L. Gross. (Twayne's United States Authors Series, No. 111.) New York: Twayne pp. 175. $3.95.

[79] *Mary Wilkins Freeman*, by Perry D. Westbrook. (Twayne's United States Authors Series, No. 122.) New York: Twayne. pp. 191. $3.95.

although whether he can, as Frost says, be accounted a contributor to 'American folk literature' is debatable. Theodore L. Gross believes that nowhere else in late-nineteenth-century American literature is the antebellum South so elaborately or memorably described as in the work of Thomas Nelson Page. Yet Page is usually accounted to be no more than a 'local colourist'. Gross's contribution to the Twayne series seeks to document Page's importance both as a writer of the first rank and as a chronicler of the Southern 'myth of heroism'. Although his first objective is not achieved, the book makes a useful comment on Southern styles and *mores*. Mary Wilkins Freeman was one of the most successful of the 'local colourists'. In a sense, she might be said to have been helped by the nature of her subject—the grainy quality of New England village life. F. O. Matthiessen even wrote, in 1930, that she was 'unsurpassed among all American writers in her ability to give the breathless intensity of a moment'. Perry D. Westbrook provides a sympathetic and well-written account both of her life and her major works.

Joseph Katz introduces, with textual notes, a facsimile reproduction of the Philadelphia Press's printing of *The Red Badge of Courage*[80] between December 3rd and 8th, 1894. There are also eight illustrations, including photographs of Crane as a child and in uniform. Katz's introduction is full of interesting material. The organization which released the story was a newspaper syndicate which had a 'Six Day Serial Service' and provided its customers (estimated at 750 newspapers across the country) with proof sheets. There are eleven pages of textual variants.

Maurice Bassan's collection of critical essays on Stephen Crane[81] is divided into three sections. In the first, Willa Cather and A. J. Liebling provide 'portraits' and, in the second, there are 'general discussions' by, among others, John Berryman, Philip Young and Daniel Hoffman. The third section is devoted to analyses of individual works. Larzer Ziff, Donald Pizer, and Bassan himself write on *Maggie*. Conrad's personal anecdote on his discovery of *The Red Badge of Courage* is balanced by R. W. Stallman's ingenious analysis—to which are appended also pieces by Olov Fryckstedt and W. D. Anderson. William Bysshe Stein examines 'The Open Boat', Daniel Weiss 'The Blue Hotel' and Eric Solomon 'Whilomville Stories'. It is a pity that the *Twentieth Century Views* series cost 16s.; $1.95, their American price, represents nothing like the same outlay of cash in the United States, whatever the exchange equivalent.

5. TWENTIETH CENTURY

Reading Nicholas Joost's account of *The Dial* between 1912 and 1920,[82] one cannot help feeling that the money spent on the production of this excellently-printed book might have been better devoted to reproducing *The Dial* itself. Although it is true that back numbers can be obtained (at some cost) it is not so easily available that every reader, even the specialist, can gain much from the

---

[80] *The Red Badge of Courage*, by Stephen Crane, with an introduction and textual notes by Joseph Katz. Gainesville, Fla.: Scholars' Facsimiles and Reprints. pp. 117. $6.

[81] *Stephen Crane: A Collection of Critical Essays*, ed. by Maurice Bassan. (Twentieth Century Views.) (A Spectrum Book.) Englewood Cliffs, N.J.: Prentice-Hall. pp. 184. $1.95. 16s. (Paperback). 40s. (Cloth).

[82] *Years of Transition, 1912–1920: The Dial*, by Nicholas Joost. Barre, Massachusetts: Barre Publishing Co. pp. xxvii + 321. $8.50.

commentary which Joost supplies. This said, however, it may be stated that his account is full of fascinating details and contains some enlivening illustrations.

Write and Rewrite[83] by John Kuehl is sub-titled 'A Study of the Creative Process'. It is divided into nine sections, to which are appended a facsimile of a draft of *The Long March* by William Styron. The book, says Kuehl, came into being as a result of his experiences as a teacher of creative writing at Princeton. Finding among the Fitzgerald papers at that University a pencil draft of *The Great Gatsby*, he set his class to consider the changes which Fitzgerald had made on the manuscript itself and, after that, those he had made between the composition of the holograph and the publication of the novel. Following the same process, Kuehl has provided drafts and final versions of writings by Eudora Welty, Kay Boyle, James Jones, Bernard Malamud, Wright Morris, Fitzgerald, Philip Roth, Robert Penn Warren and John Hawkes. This is a valuable contribution not only to our knowledge of the creative process in a number of modern American writers, but also to our awareness of the ways in which 'creative writing' can be taught.

It is good to have a selection of William Troy's essays.[84] Although he did not write much, he was one of the most intelligent and well-informed critics of the forties and fifties, and his contributions to *Partisan Review* and *The New Republic* remain vividly in the mind. Troy was an Irish-American—in Allen Tate's words 'a

Catholic puritan who had left the Church'. This gives great interest to his writings on Joyce, but his range was wide and his understanding of James, Virginia Woolf, Lawrence, Gertrude Stein and Fitzgerald was as profound as his appreciation of Stendhal, Balzac, Proust, André Malraux, Paul Valéry and Thomas Mann. These individual studies plus three essays on general critical principles and two on tragedy make one feel that Stanley Edgar Hyman—who provides an appreciative introduction—has indeed picked the best of Troy.

Nicholas J. Karolides's *The Pioneer in the American Novel 1900–1950*[85] is an over-written and 'thematic' study. However, although Karolides organizes his work under such distressing headings as 'He Towered Above Them' and 'Silks and Calico', it must be admitted that the chapters on 'Class on the Frontier' and 'The Image of the Pioneer' are rewarding and informative.

After *The Machine in the Garden, Literature and the Machine in American Culture*.[86] Thomas Reed West is no Leo Marx, but his subject, like Marx's, seeks to combine literature and history in an American Studies approach. Unlike Marx, West is an historian and he analyses the works he has chosen not for their literary quality but for the degree to which they illustrate his themes. For example, Sherwood Anderson's work is said to represent 'The Machine and the Craftsman's Sensibility' and Waldo Frank's 'The Machine in Cultural Ferment'. There are also chapters on John Dos Passos ('The Libertarian Cause'), Veblen and

[83] *Write and Rewrite: A Study of the Creative Process*, ed. by John Kuehl. New York: Meredith Press. pp. xii+308. $6.95.

[84] *William Troy: Selected Essays*, ed. with an introduction by Stanley Edgar Hyman, and with a memoir by Allen Tate. New Brunswick, N.J.: Rutgers U.P. pp. xi+300. $9.

[85] *The Pioneer in the American Novel 1900–1950*, by Nicholas J. Karolides. Norman: Oklahoma U.P. pp. xii+324. $5.95.

[86] *Flesh of Steel: Literature and the Machine in American Culture*, by Thomas Reed West. Nashville, Tennessee: Vanderbilt U.P. pp. xv+155. $4.50.

Sandburg, Harold Stearns and Lewis Mumford ('In Affirmation of the Machine'), and Sinclair Lewis ('In Affirmation of Main Street'). The rather curious sub-title of the last chapter in conjunction with the name of Sinclair Lewis indicates that West has perhaps not quite grasped every nuance of the works that he has analysed.

Seven Modern American Poets[87] is a reprinting of pamphlets in the University of Minnesota American Writers series. Lawrance Thompson writes on Robert Frost, William York Tindall on Wallace Stevens, John Malcolm Brinnin on William Carlos Williams, William Van O'Connor on Ezra Pound, John L. Stewart on John Crowe Ransom, Leonard Unger on T. S. Eliot and George Hemphill on Allen Tate. Unger, who edits the volume, also provides an introduction explaining that he has selected these particular volumes because they provide a 'representative survey' of modern American poetry. Although this remark is challengeable—Hart Crane, for example, is omitted and John Crowe Ransom and Allen Tate are not of the same stature as Frost and Stevens—the selection is judicious from the point of view of quality. It also underlines the fact that the compendious form would have been better than single pamphlets in the first place.

Poets in Progress[88] is a reprint of a book originally published in 1962. Edward Hungerford has 'augmented' what he originally described as 'Critical Prefaces to Ten Modern American Poets' by three more—on Louis Simpson, Anne Sexton and

Denise Levertov. The original ten 'prefaces' first appeared in *The Tri-Quarterly*, a review published by Northwestern University. The book provides a useful survey but, given the length of the essays, leaves one with a sense of superficiality.

Quintet[89] is the title given to essays on five American woman poets by George Brandon Saul. Reading these delicate discourses on the verse of Sara Teasdale, Elinor Wylie, Hazel Hall, Abbie Huston Evans and Winifred Welles, one wonders why the author bothered.

Jean Burden begins *Journey Toward Poetry*[90] with a 'personal statement' about her attitude towards verse entitled 'Woman as Artist' and proceeds to give us an account of how she started to write poems and get her book published. The calibre of Miss Burden's literary comment can perhaps be indicated by quoting the title of one of the chapters: 'They Get Madder in Maine'. *Poets Laureate of Texas, 1932–1966*[91] is an equally boring collection. It opens with pictures of the 'Poets Laureate' from Judd Mortimer Lewis (1932–34) to Bessie Maas Rowe (1966). One name, however, may be rescued from the list of nonentities enshrined here and that is Vassar Miller's. How she got into the collection it is difficult to imagine when one considers that the quality of verse here described is of the order of 'A fairy walked among the hills/ And over the Texas plains'.

Edna B. Stephens's book on John

[87] *Seven Modern American Poets: An Introduction*, ed. by Leonard Unger. Minneapolis: Minnesota U.P. pp. 303. $6.50.

[88] *Poets in Progress: A Reprint, Augmented Critical Prefaces to Thirteen Modern American Poets*, ed. by Edward Hungerford. Evanston, Ill.: Northwestern U.P. pp. xii+298.

[89] *Quintet: Essays on Five American Woman Poets*, by George Brandon Saul. (Studies in American Literature, vol. XVII). The Hague and Paris: Mouton. pp. 50.

[90] *Journey Toward Poetry*, by Jean Burden. New York: October House, 1966. pp. vii + 112. $2.95.

[91] *Poets Laureate of Texas—1932–1966*, by Margaret Royalty Edwards. San Antonia, Texas: Naylor. 1966. pp. xiii+140. $4.95.

Gould Fletcher,[92] No. 118 in the Twayne's United States Authors Series, is a very worthwhile enterprise. Fletcher's reputation has suffered since the twenties because of the fashion for hard, clear and, lately, 'projective' verse. However, although by no means a major poet, he had a clear lyric gift. He was also interested in oriental imagery and symbolism, and used the Haiku form long before its modern Western exponents. Although Miss Stephens is a little weak on evaluation, her survey is informative and useful.

Wallace L. Anderson contributes a critical introduction to Edwin Arlington Robinson[93] in the Riverside Studies in Literature series. These studies allow more space than the Minnesota Pamphlets and are comparable to those in the Writers and Critics series, published by Oliver and Boyd. Anderson has drawn on the work of previous critics and biographers of Robinson, although, oddly, he singles out only the very early and brief study by Charles Cestre for special mention. He has, however, done original work on Robinson's relation to Swedenborgianism and other biographical material. In fact this is a much more worthwhile contribution to Robinson scholarship than might have been expected in such a small space. W. R. Robinson's *Edwin Arlington Robinson: A Poetry of the Act* is more ambitious. The author sees his subject essentially as a modern rather than

a nineteenth-century poet. He believes that critics have been misled by the classic felicity and conventional rhyme scheme of Robinson's verse and have not paid sufficient attention to his revolutionary sentiments. Robinson participated fervently in the mood of discontent against early nineteenth-century American materialism and his poetry, the author argues, was an attempt to reflect 'the contours of a new reality then being unveiled'. He places the poet in the context of American thought, with particular attention to William James, Whitehead, Mead, Santayana, and Dewey. His most interesting contributions, however, are his analyses of the poetry and his comments on the lengthier later works. Robinson's contribution, *pace* Robinson, was to provide a bridge between the old order and the new; understanding Robinson therefore becomes a means of understanding Frost and Stevens, with whom he has more in common, the author believes, than had previously been supposed.

Walter Baumann's *The Rose in the Steel Dust*[95] is a close examination of Pound's *Cantos*. This, the fifty-eighth book in the Swiss Studies in English series, was written under the supervision of Heinrich Straumann. Baumann divides his study into three main parts: 'Towards the Ideal City', 'In the Wake of Odysseus' and 'The Point of Crisis'. An epilogue, 'Amo Ergo Sum', includes plans of Cantos IV and LXXXII, together with a bibliography. This kind of detailed study on Pound is precisely what is needed, and Baumann is to be congratulated on a thorough piece of work. Noel Stock sub-titles his

[92] *John Gould Fletcher*, by Edna B. Stephens (Twayne's United States Authors Series, No. 118.) New York: Twayne. pp. 160. $3.95.

[93] *Edwin Arlington Robinson: A Critical Introduction*, by Wallace L. Anderson. (Riverside Studies in Literature). Boston: Houghton Mifflin. pp. xvi+175. $5.95.

[94] *Edwin Arlington Robinson: A Poetry of the Act*, by W. R. Robinson. Cleveland, Ohio: Western Reserve U.P. pp. 183. $5.95.

[95] *The Rose in the Steel Dust: An Examination of the Cantos of Ezra Pound*, by Walter Baumann. (Swiss Studies in English, No. 58.) Bern: Francke. pp. 211. Sw.Fr.25.

Reading the Cantos,[96] 'A Study of Meaning in Ezra Pound'. He has tried, he says, to show what Ezra Pound actually wrote and insists that too much has been read into *The Cantos* which is simply not there. Both Hugh Kenner and Donald Davie, he believes, have erred in this respect. They have refused to concentrate on the words on the page and have, therefore, commented on a poem which exists only in their own imaginations. Stock's short book is lucid and workmanlike. He considers, first of all, a draft of XXX Cantos and devotes subsequent chapters to 'Nuevo Mundo 1834', 'The Fifth Decad 1937', 'China and Adams 1940,' 'The Pisan Cantos 1948', 'Rock-Drill 1955' and 'Thrones 1959'. With his conclusion—that the Cantos do not constitute a poem, but a disjointed series of fragments, often of exceptional beauty or interest, but uninformed, poetically or otherwise, by a larger purpose—one may feel substantially in agreement.

The Seed is Man[97] is a collection of poems by Edward L. Meyerson, together with an essay on Ezra Pound. Both poems and essay are slight pieces of work. In *Rosen aus Feilstaub*[98] Lore Lenberg has hit upon the same title as Walter Baumann, although her subject is Pound's lyricism rather than a close examination of the *Cantos*. She devotes a chapter to one of Pound's *personae*, 'The Mask of Death', and proceeds to consider 'Image and Ideogram', 'Logopoeia', 'The Theme of Fugue:

Canto I and Canto II' and the 'Odysseus Symbol'. Among the later chapters, one on Pound's use of usury is of particular interest. Eva Hesse has collected twenty-two essays on Ezra Pound[99] for circulation in Germany. These essays, mostly by English and Americans, have all been translated into German. Among them may be found Richard Ellman's 'Ez and Old Billyum', Earl Miner's 'From Image to Ideogram', Hugh Kenner's 'Ezra Pound and the Enlightenment', George Dekker's 'Myth and Metamorphosis', Noel Stock's 'Pound the Historian', Iris Barry's 'Ezra Pound in London' and Ernest Hemingway's 'Homage to Ezra'.

Edward Connery Lathem and Lawrance Thompson have compiled, for the Grolier Club, a fascinating and lavish book,[100] with facsimiles, around Robert Frost's contributions to the Lawrence, Massachusetts, *High School Bulletin*. Frost entered Lawrence High School in 1888 and wrote for the *Bulletin* from 1890 on. Although the poetry is naturally not of a high calibre, it is interesting to see the poet's early work and, even more, to be presented with reproductions of publications of the 1890s.

Lord Snow has written accounts[101] of nine men who have affected the shape and spirit of the twentieth century and, together with Rutherford, G. H. Hardy, H. G. Wells, Einstein, Lloyd George, Winston Churchill, Dag Hammarskjöld and

[96] *Reading the Cantos: A Study of Meaning in Ezra Pound*, by Noel Stock. London: Routledge. pp. viii+120. 28*s*.

[97] *The Seed is Man: A Collection of Poetry and an Essay on Ezra Pound*, by Edward L. Meyerson. (The William-Frederick Poets: 145.) New York: William-Frederick. pp. 55. $3.50.

[98] *Rosen aus Feilstaub: Studien zu den Cantos von Ezra Pound*, by Lore Lenberg. Wiesbaden: Limes. 1966. pp. 272.

[99] *Ezra Pound: 22 Versuche über einen Dichter*, ed. and introduced by Eva Hesse. Frankfurt am Main and Bonn: Athenäum. pp. 456. DM.48.

[100] *Robert Frost and the Lawrence, Massachusetts, 'High School Bulletin': The Beginning of a Literary Career*, by Edward Connery Lathem and Lawrance Thompson. New York: Grolier. 1966. pp. 94.

[101] *Variety of Men*, by C. P. Snow. London, Melbourne. Toronto: Macmillan. pp. x+204. 30*s*.

Stalin, he has included Robert Frost. Like the other essays, the one on the poet is personal. Snow describes how he noticed an advertisement for a memorial lecture in the Foreign Languages Library in Moscow and went in to listen; he found the lecture, given by a Lithuanian poet, 'curiously moving'. Analysing Frost's character, he notes that he was an obsessive letter writer, particularly to Louis Untermeyer; he was also capable of lying. Snow makes fun of Frost's *persona* of the dedicated farmer, but admits that although the 'Thoreau-inspired years were not professional', they meant hardship. The last personal reminiscence is of Frost in Berkeley, in November 1960, just after he had suffered his 'annual disappointment over the Nobel Prize'. It was a couple of months after that he appeared as 'America's national poet' at the inauguration of President Kennedy. Although Snow's essay does not set out to be a literary assessment of Frost's value as a poet, it is full of shrewd insights.

James Gray has written an account of Edna St. Vincent Millay[102] in the University of Minnesota Pamphlets on American Writers series. He believes that she should be seen not so much as the 'nymph of Greenwich Village' but as a tragic writer, 'an artist born mature and burdened with a scrupulous sense of responsibility toward her gift'. Of this he almost convinces us. However, despite the persuasiveness of Gray's arguments, Millay will remain for many readers rather too much of a poetic attitudinizer to be completely convincing.

In his study of Langston Hughes,[103]

James A. Emanuel explores Hughes's attempt to 'explain and illuminate the Negro condition in America'. Although the book is marred by the chapter headings—for example, 'The Christ and the Killers' and 'A Wheel in Harlem'—Emanuel has written a full and interesting account of one of the best known of Negro poets. It is a pity, however, that so little of Hughes's work really succeeds on the page.

Il Ponte di Brooklyn[104] is a close study of Hart Crane's major work by an Italian critic. Pietro Spinucci devotes a chapter to '"The Bridge" and the Critics', considers whether the poem is an epic or a 'quest', and proceeds to discuss Crane's themes and poetics. He concludes with a chapter of interpretation and comment on the poem, an account of its structure, symbolism and language, and a discussion of its relation to American poetry of the eighteenth and nineteenth centuries.

A book on Allen Tate was no doubt needed and Ferman Bishop[105] has supplied it. He begins with the *Fugitive* poems, written when Tate was at Vanderbilt, and then devotes some time to *Mr. Pope and Other Poems*. He then considers Tate's biographies of Stonewall Jackson and Jefferson Davis, and his 'digressions' into 'the polemics of economic and political writing' as an Agrarian. Bishop's analysis of *The Fathers* is keen, but not perhaps as judicious as it might be—for example, he recognizes the intellectual force and technical skill of the novel, but does not account for

[102] *Edna St. Vincent Millay*, by James Gray. (University of Minnesota Pamphlets on American Writers, No. 64.) Minneapolis: Minnesota U.P. pp. 48. 95c.

[103] *Langston Hughes*, by James A. Emanuel. (Twayne's United States Authors Series, No. 123.) New York: Twayne. pp. 192. $3.95.

[104] *Il Ponte di Brooklyn: 'The Bridge' di Hart Crane e la Poesia Americana degli Anni Venti*, by Pietro Spinucci. (Contributi Serie Terza, Scienze Filologiche e Letteratura – 11.) Milano: Società Editrice Vita e Pensiero, 1966. pp. 277.

[105] *Allen Tate*, by Ferman Bishop. (Twayne's United States Authors Series, No. 124.) New York: Twayne. pp. 172. $3.95.

the deadness of its effect upon some readers. In addition to examining Tate's most important critical ideas, Bishop analyses the 'representative poems of each phase of Tate's career', the most important being 'Ode to the Confederate Dead' and 'Seasons of the Soul'.

Robert Lowell, Peter Taylor and Robert Penn Warren have edited a series of essays on Randall Jarrell.[106] Hannah Arendt provides a personal reminiscence, John Berryman an account of *Poetry and the Age* and Cleanth Brooks writes on 'Jarrell's "Eighth Air Force"'. Among the other contributors are James Dickey, Denis Donoghue, Leslie Fiedler, Robert Fitzgerald, Alfred Kazin, Lowell himself, Marianne Moore, John Crowe Ransom, Delmore Schwartz, Karl Shapiro, Allen Tate and Peter Taylor. As a gesture, the contributors agreed to donate all royalties to the Randall Jarrell Writing Scholarship at the University of North Carolina. The general impression conveyed is of the extraordinary luminosity and charm of Jarrell's character. All the contributors, including those who—like James Dickey—do not like his type of verse, testify to the brilliance and range of his art. Jarrell's high point was the fifties, after the success of his poems and *Pictures from an Institution*. As well as being a poet and satirist he was, together with R. P. Blackmur and Yvor Winters, one of the most attractive and original American critics of the twentieth century; *Poetry and the Age* is a major book.

In his book on Richard Wilbur,[107] Donald Hill concentrates on *The*

Beautiful Changes (1947), *Ceremony* (1950), *Things of This World* (1956) and *Advice to a Prophet* (1961), devoting a final chapter to 'Studies and Aversions'. Hill acknowledges that his study is not an impartial one; he had long been convinced that Wilbur was one of the most accomplished and rewarding of contemporary poets. With this we may well agree. But it is not merely a eulogy which Hill provides; his analyses are always penetrating, even if one could have anticipated that they would be sympathetic.

Although it is not customary to include original works in this account, Robert Lowell is such a major figure on the American landscape that one cannot forbear to note the publication of his latest book of verse, *Near the Ocean*.[108] In particular, one poem may be singled out. 'Waking Early Sunday Morning' is one of the best that Lowell has written; it has the looseness and careful grace of his later manner but combines with it the deep thought and symbolic implication of the earlier poems. There can be no better example of the mood of the dedicated American intellectual at a time when most of the news from the United States is to do with anything but dedication and intellectuality.

William J. Martz's *The Achievement of Robert Lowell*[109] is published in a new Modern Poets Series, produced by Scott, Foresman and Company. The aim is to provide a 'comprehensive selection of his poems with a critical introduction'. The selection is reasonable but the introduction is so short as to be of little

---

[106] *Randall Jarrell, 1914–1965*, ed. by Robert Lowell, Peter Taylor and Robert Penn Warren. New York: Farrar, Straus & Giroux. pp. xii+308. $6.50.

[107] *Richard Wilbur*, by Donald Hill. (Twayne's United States Authors Series, No. 117.) New York: Twayne. pp. 192. $3.95.

[108] *Near the Ocean*, by Robert Lowell. London: Faber & Faber. pp. 55. 18s.

[109] *The Achievement of Robert Lowell: A Comprehensive Selection of his Poems with a Critical Introduction*, by William J. Martz. (The Modern Poets Series.) Glenview, Ill.: Scott, Foresman. 1966. pp. 86.

value. The idea of the series is probably a good one, but these slim volumes would be more useful if there were specific comments on each poem. The same comments apply to *The Achievement of Theodore Roethke*[110] also edited by Martz.

Two bibliographies, published by the Phoenix Book Shop of New York, are worth mentioning, one of Gregory Corso[111] and the other of Michael McClure.[112] The first covers the period from 1954 to 1965 and the second from 1956 to 1965; the former was compiled by Robert Wilson and the second by Marshall Clements.

It is strange to think that Denise Levertov has now attained 'classic' stature by being included in the Twayne's United States Authors Series.[113] Miss Levertov, who was born in London of Russian-Jewish and Welsh parents, became known during the war through her poems in *Poetry Quarterly* and other small magazines. Since 1948, however, when she went to New York with her husband, American critics have annexed her for their own. Whatever her nationality, however, Miss Levertov writes well—although perhaps not as well as a full-length study of this kind would imply. Linda Welshimer Wagner, whose critical study

of the poems of William Carlos Williams was reviewed in an earlier *YW*, has done a thorough job on what some would regard as rather less than adequate material.

In *The Modern American Novel*,[114] Max Westbrook has published essays on eleven American novelists. The choice is interesting: Theodore Dreiser, Sherwood Anderson, Sinclair Lewis, F. Scott Fitzgerald, Thomas Wolfe, Ernest Hemingway, William Faulkner, John Steinbeck, Robert Penn Warren, J. D. Salinger and Saul Bellow. It is an adequate collection, although one wonders why Dos Passos was omitted; there would also be a case for including Willa Cather and Nathanael West. There are some old favourites here—such as Lawrance Thompson's 'Mirror Analogues in *The Sound and the Fury*' and Irving Howe's 'The Book of the Grotesque'. Among the most interesting of the less well known essays are those by Richard Lehan on *An American Tragedy* and Ihab Hassan on *Henderson the Rain King*.

According to the late Frederick J. Hoffman, there are at least four categories of contemporary American fiction: the Southern novel, the Negro novel, the Jewish novel, and the War novel. Of these, he has undertaken to explore the characteristics of Southern literature.[115] He feels that although the Civil War obviously had a shattering effect on the South, it also provided a 'literary opportunity'. Southerners became closer-knit

[110] *The Achievement of Theodore Roethke: A Comprehensive Selection of his Poems with a Critical Introduction*, by William J. Martz. (The Modern Poets Series). Glenview, Ill.: Scott, Foresman. 1966. pp. 86.

[111] *A Bibliography of Works by Gregory Corso, 1954–1965*, compiled by Robert A. Wilson. (The Phoenix Bibliographies.) New York: The Phoenix Book Shop, 1966. pp. v+40. $1.50.

[112] *A Catalog of Works by Michael McClure, 1956–1965*, compiled by Marshall Clements. (The Phoenix Bibliographies.) New York: The Phoenix Book Shop. 1965. pp. v+36. $1.50.

[113] *Denise Levertov*, by Linda Welshimer Wagner. (Twayne's United States Authors Series, No. 113.) New York: Twayne. pp. 159. $3.95.

[114] *The Modern American Novel: Essays in Criticism*, ed. with an introduction by Max Westbrook. (Studies in Language and Literature, No. 6.) New York: Random House. 1966 (pp. x+243. $2.25.

[115] *The Art of Southern Fiction: A Study of Some Modern Novelists*, by Frederick J. Hoffman, with a preface by Harry T. Moore. (Crosscurrents Modern Critiques.) Carbondale and Edwardsville: Southern Illinois U.P. London and Amsterdam: Feffer & Simons. pp. x+198. $4.95.

as a group and, like the Jews, developed a culture impregnated with a wit and humour which arose, at least partially, from their troubles. The only difficulty about accepting Hoffman's theory is that there was a good deal of wit and humour in Southern local-colour writing before the Civil War and it could be argued that the South was as closely-knit (although in a different way) in the ante- as in the post-bellum period. At all events, Hoffman explores Southern fiction in terms of time and place, with particular reference to the work of Eudora Welty, Carson McCullers, James Agee and Flannery O'Connor. He also discusses the relationship of society and history in the work of Allen Tate, Andrew Lytle, William Humphrey, Shirley Ann Grau and Walter Sullivan. Finally, he turns his attention to the later writers— Truman Capote, William Goyen, Walker Percy and Reynolds Price— and devotes a chapter to the work of William Styron.

Vito J. Brenni has compiled a bibliography[116] of the works of Edith Wharton and supplied a brief introduction. This supplants the bibliographies of Mrs. Lawson M. Melish, published in 1927, of Lavinia R. Davis in 1934, and of Nancy R. Leach and Patricia R. Plante, which were parts of dissertations. The compiler notes that he himself owns a collection of 150 Wharton volumes.

William A. Sutton has published a monograph on Sherwood Anderson,[117] entitled *Exit to Elsinore*, dealing with Anderson's life between 1907 and 1913. Sutton's theory is that Anderson began writing as a therapy for psychological illness and in sup-

port of this he publishes two Anderson letters for the first time: one from the author to his wife while he was staying in Cleveland, and the other, dated 1916, which comments on the 'attack' which he was having when he wrote the first letter.

In *The Art of Sinclair Lewis*,[118] D. J. Dooley says that although many critics would agree with Mark Schorer that Lewis was 'one of the worst writers in modern American literature', they would also have to agree that it is impossible to imagine American literature without him. Dooley considers a variety of critical opinions on Lewis since *Main Street* appeared in 1920, including those of Vernon L. Parrington, T. K. Whipple, Henry Seidel Canby, Constance Rourke, Robert Spiller and Maxwell Deismar. His contention is that if Lewis's reputation was once too high, it is probably now too low. This is a well-argued book and worth the writing in spite of the existence of Schorer's monumental study, Dooley's emphasis being critical rather than biographical.

In his book on James Branch Cabell,[119] Desmond Tarrant maintains that the wide current interest in Tolkien's 'adult fairy tales' suggests that 'the world is ready for a more just appraisal' of Cabell's work. This, however, is to set up an unreal affinity between Cabell and Tolkien; in the latter's world there is little, if any, of the genteel whimsicality which mars so many of Cabell's writings. In fact, Cabell's work is dated by its style and it is the lack of perception of this which makes Tarrant's book less valuable than it might have been. Although his study is thorough and

[116] *Edith Wharton: A Bibliography*, by Vito J. Brenni. Morgantown; West Virginia University Library. 1966. pp. xvi+99.

[117] *Exit to Elsinore*, by William A. Sutton. (Ball State Monograph No. 7.) Muncie, Indiana: Ball State University. pp. v+45.

[118] *The Art of Sinclair Lewis*, by D. J. Dooley. Lincoln: Nebraska U.P. pp. xvi+286. $2.25 Paperback. $5.50 Cloth.

[119] *James Branch Cabell: The Dream and the Reality*, by Desmond Tarrant. Norman: Oklahoma U.P. pp. xii+292. $5.95.

detailed, it shows little sense of humour in dealing with the mock-Rabelaisian work of that gentlemanly Southerner.

Waldo Frank, says Paul J. Carter, was a 'man of letters' in the old sense of the phrase. As one of the bright young men of the 1920s, he became an editor of *Seven Arts* magazine and what Gorham Munson called 'the most exciting figure in contemporary American letters'. Although, after that, Frank wrote 'better novels and more significant cultural histories than those Munson praised' he lost his audience. Carter's study [120] deals chronologically with Frank's work. His writing is sympathetic and detailed, but without having available most of the texts on which the book is based, some of its value is taken away. One cannot but feel that Frank's work has more of an historical than a literary interest at the present time, and therefore react unfavourably when Carter tells us that Frank was a member of an 'ancient priesthood' dedicated to the preservation of the 'values that underlie the organic sense of life and of man's individual and holy share in it'.

An interesting collection appears under the title of *The Edward Dahlberg Reader*.[121] In 'a Note to the Reader' the editor, Paul Carroll, provides a sketch of Dahlberg's career. Three major themes, he maintains, distinguished Dahlberg's writings: 'his dialogue with the body; his criticism of other writers; and his condemnation of the modern world'. The first three sections of Carroll's book contain a selection embodying

one or other of these themes; the fourth consists of letters written between 1939 and 1946. A cross between H. L. Mencken and Scott Fitzgerald, Dahlberg is too often neglected by the literary historians of the between-wars period, and this collection provides ample evidence of his liveliness and versatility.

There may be found in *Willa Cather and her Critics*[122] some of the best essays that have been published on this somewhat neglected writer—among them—H. L. Mencken's reviews of *Song of the Lark*, *My Antonia*, *Youth and the Bright Medusa* and *One of Ours*, Edmund Wilson's 'Two Novels of Willa Cather', Sinclair Lewis's 'A Hamlet of the Plains', Rebecca West's 'The Classic Artist' and pieces by Alfred Kazin, Maxwell Geismar, Morton D. Zabel and Leon Edel. James Schroeter organizes his selection under the headings of '"America's Coming-of-Age" Criticism: Early Views', 'Distance, Tone, and Point of View: The Artistic Problem', 'Personal Views, Impressions and Reminiscences', 'Criticism on the Barricades: The Social Temper of the 1930s', 'The Search for Historical Perspective' and 'Thematic and Mythic Criticism: Recent Views'.

Edwin M. Moseley's essay on F. Scott Fitzgerald[123] is one in the series entitled 'Contemporary Writers in Christian Perspective'. Moseley writes briefly on *This Side of Paradise* ('Ordination, Mystery, and Sacrifice'), *The Beautiful and Damned* ('The Lack of Vocation and the Loss of Mystery'), *The Great Gatsby* ('Initiation and the Quest for the Grail'), *Tender is the Night* ('Healer

---

[120] *Waldo Frank*, by Paul J. Carter. (Twayne's United States Authors Series, No. 125.) New York: Twayne. pp. 191. $3.95.

[121] *The Edward Dahlberg Reader*, ed. with an Introduction by Paul Carroll (A New Directions Paperback.) New York: New Directions. pp. xxii+330. $3.25.

[122] *Willa Cather and Her Critics*, ed. by James Schroeter. Ithaca, New York: Cornell U.P. pp. xiii+392.

[123] *F. Scott Fitzgerald: A Critical Essay*, by Edwin M. Moseley. (Contemporary Writers in Christian Perspective.) Grand Rapids, Michigan: William B. Eerdmans. pp. 47. 85c.

and Scapegoat') and *The Last Tycoon* ('Christ on Earth'). *The Critical Reputation of F. Scott Fitzgerald*[124] is the title of a bibliography by Jackson R. Bryer, who reminds us that Fitzgerald's writings have been extremely carefully scrutinized since his death in 1940, and that, by 1965, there were many more books about Fitzgerald than by him. There is even a small journal devoted to Fitzgeraldiana. Bryer documents the full extent of this posthumous recognition, his bibliography being arranged chronologically and including reviews and periodical essays as well as books about Fitzgerald. It supplies, Bryer maintains, a continuous history of Fitzgerald's literary reputation as well as a catalogue of his works.

Egri Péter's *Hemingway*[125] is a paperback Hungarian study in a series which includes Pushkin, Stendahl, Ivan Olbracht and Tóth Arpád.

In *The Falkners of Mississippi*[126] Murray C. Falkner gives us his account of his early years in Oxford, Mississippi, where he grew up with his brothers, William, John and Dean. Most of the familiar details of the twenties are here—the first motion pictures and automobiles, as well as incidents of small-town Southern life. The book may be used as an adjunct to the author's *William Faulkner of Oxford*, which appeared in 1965 and, taken together with it, provides a fascinating insight into one aspect of Faulkner's background. Among the photographs there is one of Colonel (*White Rose of Memphis*) Falkner

and his 1910 Buick trapped in a mud-hole near Oxford.

Faulkner once said that if he could rewrite all his work, he believed he would do it better. In *Faulkner's Twice-Told Tales*,[127] Edward M. Holmes attempts to show how much he re-used material, to give examples of the sort of changes which he made, and to assess the effect of 're-use' on Faulkner's 'art'. This is a rewarding approach and deserves longer and more detailed treatment. In yet another analysis of Faulkner's works,[128] Kenneth E. Richardson considers the question of 'what dooms and saves' Faulkner's characters in an attempt to make some parallel between their situation and that of contemporary Americans. The destructive force, according to Richardson, is men's inflexibility; the wilderness teaches us flexibility. A 'second destructive force' is sexual irresponsibility, generally pictured in a female; women like Mrs. Compson, Addie Bundren, Temple Drake and Charlotte Rittenmeyer 'forsake the responsibilities of motherhood in favor of a selfish and a carnal gratification'. The third destructive force is Snopesism, or a soulless, predatory amorality. This earnest and rather laboured book is not without merit.

The Twentieth Century Views selection of Faulkner[129] includes, among

[124] *The Critical Reputation of F. Scott Fitzgerald: A Bibliographical Study*, by Jackson R. Bryer. Hamden, Conn.: Archon Books. pp. xvii+434. $15. £5 10s.

[125] *Hemingway*, by Egri Péter. (Irodalomtörténeti Kiskönyvtar, No. 32.) Budapest: Gondolat. pp. 170.

[126] *The Falkners of Mississippi: A Memoir*, by Murray C. Falkner. Baton Rouge: Louisiana State U.P. pp. xxv+205. $5.95.

[127] *Faulkner's Twice-Told Tales: His Re-Use of his Material*, by Edward M. Holmes. (Studies in American Literature, Volume X.) The Hague and Paris: Mouton. 1966. pp. 118.

[128] *Force and Faith in the Novels of William Faulkner*, by Kenneth E. Richardson. (Studies in American Literature, Volume VII.) The Hague & Paris: Mouton. pp. 187. Fr.23.

[129] *Faulkner: A Collection of Critical Essays*, ed. by Robert Penn Warren. (Twentieth Century Views.) (A Spectrum Book.) Englewood Cliffs, N.J.: Prentice-Hall. pp. 311. $2.45. 20s. Paperback. 40s. Hardback.

others, the well-known essays by Robert Penn Warren, George Marion O'Donnell, Malcolm Cowley and Jean-Paul Sartre. Almost equally well known—and just as welcome— are 'Mirror Analogues in *The Sound and the Fury*' by Lawrance Thompson, 'The Stillness of *Light in August*' by Alfred Kazin, 'History and the Sense of the Tragic: *Absalom, Absalom!*' by Cleanth Brooks and 'William Faulkner: The Hero in the New World' by R. W. B. Lewis. V. S. Pritchett and Norman Podhoretz write on the rather unrewarding subject of *A Fable*, and the book concludes with a recent piece by Warren on 'Faulkner: The South, the Negro, and Time'.

Henry Dan Piper has edited what he calls a 'Contemporary Chronicle of the 1930s', entitled *Think Back on Us*.[130] This collection of essays by Malcolm Cowley is organized under the headings of 'The Social Record' and 'The Literary Record'. The essays and reviews in the former have been chosen to 'illuminate the issues, problems, and ideas of the period'; among them are several general pieces which consider the familiar themes of the thirties—communism, pacifism and the Depression. In Part II, Piper maintains, 'the quality of Mr. Cowley's discernment is seen in the fact that almost no major American or European writer of the thirties has been overlooked'. One is inclined to agree; this is not only a valuable contribution to the study of a decade, but also an insight into the mind of a critic who has been neglected of late. It is a wonder that Cowley did not do the job himself a number of years ago.

Years of Protest[131] also deals with the 1930s, and is a collection of writings published during the decade. Jack Salzman and Barry Wallenstein have organized the material in Part I of their book under the headings of 'No One Has Starved', 'A Lack of Confidence' and 'Let us Have Madness', in which we find pieces by, among others, Erskine Caldwell, John Steinbeck, James Agee, Dos Passos, Clifford Odets, Hemingway, Edna St. Vincent Millay and Thomas Wolfe. In Part II, the authors' interest may be judged by such titles as 'Archibald MacLeish and the Social Muse', 'The Writer on Middle Ground' (a discussion of Stanley Burnshaw and Wallace Stevens), 'James T. Farrell and the Literary Left' and 'Four Martyrs'. Finally, a hopeful section entitled 'A Blazing Sun', includes pieces by Henry Miller, e. e. cummings, Robinson Jeffers and Nathanael West. Harvey Swado's collection[132] of pieces from the same period concentrates on the end of the era. He has sought to convey the impact of the Depression on America as well as to provide 'a cross section of good writing of the period'. In this case, his material is gathered under the headings of 'Miners, Millhands, Factory Workers', 'Farmers: Share-croppers, Tenants, Migrants', 'Hungry Women and Faltering Homes', 'Jobhunting', 'Hitting Bottom', 'Concern and Hope' and 'Organizers, Capitalists, Fascists, Communists'. In a final section, Swados prints three of the more hopeful 'grand' views of what America could be: 'Speech to

[130] *Think Back On Us . . . A Contemporary Chronicle of the 1930's*, by Malcolm Cowley, ed. with an introduction by Henry Dan Piper. Carbondale and Edwardsville Southern Illinois U.P. London and Amsterdam: Feffer & Simons. pp. xv+400. $10.

[131] *Years of Protest: A Collection of American Writings of the 1930's*, ed. by Jack Salzman with Barry Wallenstein. New York: Pegasus. pp. 448. $2.50 Paperback. $7.50. Hardback.

[132] *The American Writer and the Great Depression*, ed. by Harvey Swados. (The American Heritage Series. No. 63.) Indianapolis, New York and Kansas City: Bobs-Merrill. 1966. pp. xli+521. $2.75.

Those Who Say Comrade' by Archibald MacLeish, 'Let America Be America Again' by Langston Hughes and a section from *You Can't Go Home Again* by Thomas Wolfe. The final volume in this plethora of books about the thirties is a collection edited by Warren French.[133] Under 'Fiction' he includes pieces by, among others, Sheldon Grebstein, Richard Walser, Frederick J. Hoffman and Pascal Covici, Jr. In the 'Poetry' section Donald Sheehan writes on Wallace Stevens, and Guy Owen on 'Southern Poetry During the 30s' and under 'Drama' Patrick Hazard contributes a piece mainly on radio drama and Robert A. Griffin writes on the love songs of Clifford Odets.

Renate Schmidt-von Bardeleben's volume[134] in the Mainzer Amerikanistische Beiträge series concerns the 'image' of New York in the work of Dreiser and Dos Passos. In her first two chapters she concentrates on *Sister Carrie* and *Manhattan Transfer*, then proceeds to consider Dreiser's short stories and Dos Passos's *District of Columbia, Chosen Country* and *Midcentury*. The result is a thorough and systematic study in a series which already includes some outstanding contributions.

Everetta Love Blair has written an account of the life and works of Jesse Stuart[135] who, thirty years ago, was labelled by Mark Van Doren as 'an American Robert Burns'. Mrs. Blair tells Stuart's story from the traditional log cabin in Kentucky to the present, when he is honoured, according to her, as 'the Poet Laureate of his state, as the Bard of the Hills'.

An only slightly more important writer, Marjorie Kinnan Rawlings, is the subject of a study by Gordon E. Bigelow. In *Frontier Eden*[136] we have an account of Mrs. Rawlings's background and an attempt to 'assess Marjorie's strengths and weaknesses as a literary artist'. Bigelow apparently shares Mrs Rawlings's passion for Florida; there are pen-and-ink sketches by Robert E. Carson, also of Florida.

The Mind and Art of Henry Miller[137] has the advantage of a foreword by Lawrence Durrell and a preface by Richard Harter Fogle. Durrell prints an interesting letter from Bernard Shaw, admitting that Miller could write but maintaining that he had 'totally failed to give any artistic value to his verbatim reports of bad language'. In a balanced and penetrating study, Gordon follows Miller's work from the early Brooklyn days to life at Big Sur. One can agree with Durrell that 'there is no other treatment of Miller as serious, not even an essay, much less a book'.

Randall Reid acknowledges his indebtedness to James F. Light for the biographical material provided in Light's *Nathanael West: An Interpretative Study*. He also makes acknowledgement to John Sanford, Josephine Herbst, Daniel Aaron and Thomas Moser. Despite this modesty, there is much that is original in Reid's *The Fiction of Nathanael West*.[138] He concentrates simply (and helpfully)

[133] *The Thirties: Fiction, Poetry, Drama*, ed. by Warren French. Deland, Fla.: Everett Edwards. pp. ix+253.
[134] *Das Bild New Yorks im Erzählwerk von Dreiser und Dos Passos*, by Renate Schmidt-von Bardeleben. (Mainzer Amerikanistische Beiträge, No. 9.) Munich: Max Hueber. pp. 206. DM.16.80.
[135] *Jesse Stuart: His Life and Works*, by Everetta Love Blair. Columbia: South Carolina U.P. pp. xxiv+288. $8.95.
[136] *Frontier Eden: The Literary Career of Marjorie Kinnan Rawlings*, by Gordon E. Bigelow. Gainesville, Fla.: Florida U.P. 1966 pp. xvii+162. $6.50.
[137] *The Mind and Art of Henry Miller*, by William A. Gordon, with a foreword by Lawrence Durrell and preface by Richard Harter Fogle. Baton Rouge: Louisiana State U.P. pp. xxxii+232. $5.
[138] *The Fiction of Nathanael West: No Redeemer, No Promised Land*, by Randall Reid. Chicago U.P. pp. viii+174. $4.50. 40s.

on West's four novels: *The Dream Life of Balso Snell, Miss Lonelyhearts, A Cool Million* and *The Day of the Locust*. Victor Comerchero also devotes chapters to each of Nathanael West's books, but precedes them with two general sections on the ways in which the author reveals himself and shows qualities of 'tension'. The last sections are entitled 'Westian Man' and 'He Charts Our World'. Comerchero believes in West's greatness and analyses the novels with this belief firmly in mind. His study[139] is acceptable within its own terms—that is, as a consideration of West's protagonist as 'the dramatized victim of a declining Western culture'— but one would wish for rather more objective analysis and comparison.

John Hersey is the subject of a volume[140] by David Sanders in the Twayne's United States Authors Series. Sanders follows the usual pattern, opening with a biographical sketch (Hersey was born in Tientsin, in 1914) and proceeding to an analysis of *Hiroshima, The Wall, The Marmot Drive, A Single Pebble, The War Lover, The Child Buyer* and *White Lotus*. Of Hersey 'in mid-career' Sanders says that he is both blessed and cursed by the compulsion to deal with a wide variety of subjects and to attempt as great a diversity of fictional forms. One would not wish to quarrel with this judgement.

Of the three studies on Saul Bellow this year, two are short paperback essays and one a full-length account. In his contribution[141] to the Contemporary Writers in Christian Perspec-

tive series, Robert Detweiler analyses Saul Bellow's work from a Christian point of view. This is ironical, as Detweiler admits, since Bellow is a Jew. However, he manages to find hope for Bellow, giving him what he himself calls 'the theological signature of approval'. One would have thought that the similarity between the Judaic and Christian ethics would have led to this conclusion without much argument—particularly with such themes as Redemption. Irving Malin's collection of criticism on the fiction of Saul Bellow[142] includes essays by, among others, Leslie A. Fiedler, Maxwell Geismar, Richard Chase, J. C. Levenson, Marcus Klein, Malin himself, Earl Rovit and John W. Aldridge. A final piece by Bellow is entitled 'Where Do We Go From Here: The Future of Fiction'. This is a well-chosen collection on one of the most important of twentieth-century novelists; of particular note are the insights provided by Fiedler, Chase and Rovit. Earl Rovit's pamphlet on Bellow in the Minnesota series[143] is, in its small space, an extremely good account. One would wish Rovit to have written at greater length on an author whom he understands so well. He recognizes Bellow's narrowness of scope but believes that his style is 'triumphantly a record of his remarkable strengths as well'.

Keith Opdahl's study[144] follows the historical sequence of Bellow's novels but is marred by such chapter

[139] *Nathanael West: The Ironic Prophet*, by Victor Comerchero. (Washington Paperbacks, No. 30.) Seattle & London: Washington U.P. pp. xii+189. $2.95. 25s.

[140] *John Hersey*, by David Sanders. (Twayne's United States Authors Series, No. 112.) New York: Twayne. pp. 159. $3.95.

[141] *Saul Bellow: A Critical Essay*, by Robert Detweiler. (Contemporary Writers in Christian Perspective.) Grand Rapids, Michigan: William B. Eerdmans. pp. 48. 85c.

[142] *Saul Bellow and the Critcs*, ed. with an introduction by Irving Malin. New York: New York U.P. and London: London U.P. Ltd., pp. xvi+227. $6.50 Hardback. $1.95 Paperback.

[143] *Saul Bellow*, by Earl Rovit. (University of Minnesota Pamphlets on American Writers, No. 65.) Minneapolis: Minnesota U.P. pp. 46. 95c.

[144] *The Novels of Saul Bellow: An Introduction*, by Keith Michael Opdahl. University Park and London: Pennsylvania State U.P. pp. 200. $7.50.

headings as 'The Ifrit and the Fellahin', 'Come then, Sorrow' and 'The Dream and the Jest'. Opdahl attempts to place Bellow in the current intellectual scene and show how the basic conflicts of his novels reflect current issues. He believes that Bellow's ultimate purpose is religious; of all modern novelists he offers the most searching fictional account of the problems and attitudes of our time.

Two more pamphlets in the Contemporary Writers in Christian Perspective series deal respectively with J. D. Salinger[145] and John Updike[146]. Both are interesting general accounts but lack penetration owing to their having to be contained within forty-six pages.

The Furious Passage of James Baldwin[147] is the title which Fern Marja Eckman has given to her book on the writer. Basing her account on taped interviews with Baldwin, she has presented what is essentially a journalist's view of him. She has, in other words, worked the other way round from the literary critic who takes as his text the words on the page. Using Baldwin's own autobiographical reminiscences, she tends to read into his work some of the things of which he has spoken. As instant-biography, her book makes compulsive reading.

In *Seven Contemporary Authors*[148] R. W. Lewis writes on 'The Conflicts

of Reality: Cozzens' *The Last Adam*', Alan Friedman on 'The Pitching of Love's Mansion in the *Tropics* of Henry Miller', Roger D. Abrahams on 'Androgynes Bound: Nathanael West's *Miss Lonelyhearts*', George Clark on 'An Illiberal Education: William Golding's *Pedagogy*', Vance Ramsey on 'From Here to Absurdity: Heller's *Catch-22*', Anthony Channell Hilfer on 'George and Martha: Sad, Sad, Sad' and Robert G. Twombly on 'Hubris, Health, and Holiness: The Despair of J. F. Powers'. The reason for collecting these essays is that all the writers are members of the English Department of the University of Texas and gave them as public lectures during the session 1964–65. (N.B. Despite the fact that the title of his essay contains the word 'Adam', R. W. Lewis is *not* R. W. B. Lewis.)

The Death of Tinker Bell[149] is the title which Joseph Golden has given to his book on the American theatre in the twentieth century. The American theatre has failed society, he maintains, because Americans have 'failed to provide a favourable environment for its growth'. Golden analyses selections from O'Neill, MacLeish, Wilder, Williams and Arthur Miller, in an attempt to answer such questions as why the theatre has falsified reality and why poetic drama has not achieved excellence. The result is an interesting rather than a deep study.

In the Prentice-Hall Twentieth Century Views series Alvin B. Kernan collects a number of essays under the title of *The Modern American Theater*.[150] Kernan himself contri-

[145] *J. D. Salinger: A Critical Essay*, by Kenneth Hamilton. (Contemporary Writers in Christian Perspective). Grand Rapids, Michigan: William B. Eerdmans. pp. 47. 85c.

[146] *John Updike: A Critical Essay*, by Alice and Kenneth Hamilton. (Contemporary Writers in Christian Perspective.) Grand Rapids, Michigan: William B. Eerdmans. pp. 48. 85c.

[147] *The Furious Passage of James Baldwin*, by Fern Marja Eckman. New York: M. Evans. 1966. pp. 254. $4.50.

[148] *Seven Contemporary Authors: Essays on Cozzens, Miller, West, Golding, Heller, Albee, and Powers*, ed. with an introduction by Thomas B. Whitbread. Austin and London: Texas U.P. 1966. pp. xv+175. $5. 47s. 6d.

[149] *The Death of Tinker Bell: The American Theatre in the 20th Century*, by Joseph Golden. Syracuse U.P. pp. ix+181. $5.

[150] *The Modern American Theater: A Collection of Critical Essays*, ed. by Alvin B. Kernan. (Twentieth Century Views.) (A Spectrum Book.) Englewood Cliffs. N.J.: Prentice-Hall. pp. 183. $1.95. 18s. 6d. Paperback. 46s. 6d Cloth.

butes an essay on the modern theatre in general, there is a section on the playwrights (Miller, Williams, Wilder, Inge and Albee), one on the theatres, and a final one on the problems of modern American drama. Edward Albee's essay, 'Which Theater is the Absurd one?', is of particular note.

In another series of essays—entitled *The American Theater Today*[151]— Alan S. Downer divides his material under the headings of 'Background', 'The Big Time', 'The Makers' and 'Off-Broadway'. He himself provides an epilogue on 'The Future of the American Theater'. Outstanding among the contributions are those of John Gassner on 'Pioneers of the New Theater Movement', on 'Comedy and the Comic Spirit in America' by Eric Bentley and on 'Arthur Miller' by Gerald Weales.

Walter J. Meserve has edited an American drama volume[152] in the Discussions of Literature series published by D. C. Heath. Among other contributors, Arthur Hobson Quinn, Lionel Trilling and Edd Winfield Parks write on Eugene O'Neill; Harold Clurman 'introduces' the plays of the 1930s; Joseph Wood Krutch considers the post-war scene; Robert Brustein writes on 'Why American Plays Are Not Literature', and Mary McCarthy examines 'The American Realist Playwrights'. Among the seven concluding essays by playwrights themselves, those by O'Neill, Maxwell Anderson, Tennessee Williams, Arthur Miller and Edward Albee are of special interest.

Robert Brustein, the drama critic of the *New Republic*, has collected his reviews under the headings of 'Off Broadway', 'Broadway', 'From Abroad', 'Companies' and 'General'. *Seasons of Discontent*[153] is the work of a dedicated and highly literate critic of the theatre. Brustein sees his subject not so much as an activity in itself as part of contemporary cultural life. He is 'the implacable enemy of pseudo art', waging war on 'all the conditions which produce it'. It is unusual to have such an elegantly-written account from an American writer. Of especial interest are Brustein's reviews of Albee's various plays, and his articles on the Lincoln theatre.

James Albert Miller has undertaken to write an account of the Detroit Yiddish theatre,[154] which flourished from 1924 to 1937. As a preamble, he goes back to the beginnings of the Yiddish theatre in Roumania in 1876. This book, written essentially from the inside, is full of valuable information, not only about the Yiddish theatre itself, but about the situation of the Jewish community in Detroit. It ends with biographical sketches of thirteen members of the original (Littman) company.

Love as Death in The 'Iceman Cometh'[155] is Winifred Dusenbury Frazer's title for a monograph on what she calls 'an ancient theme'. *The Iceman Cometh*, she believes, speaks with 'psychic universality'. O'Neill has imposed the rhythm of life upon the world of action; his theme is that 'love is death' is the chief irony—'for man nourishes and lives by the illusion that love is life'.

[151] *The American Theater Today*, ed. by Alan S. Downer. New York and London: Basic Books. pp. ix+212. $5.95.

[152] *Discussions of Modern American Drama*, ed. with an introduction. by Walter J. Meserve. (Discussions of Literature.) Boston: D. C. Heath. 1966. pp. x+150.

[153] *Seasons of Discontent: Dramatic Opinions, 1959–1965*, by Robert Brustein. London: Cape. 1966. pp. 322. 35s.

[154] *The Detroit Yiddish Theater: 1920–1937*, by James Albert Miller. Detroit: Wayne State U.P. pp. 195. $7.95.

[155] *Love as Death in 'The Iceman Cometh': A Modern Treatment of an Ancient Theme*, by Winifred Dusenbury Frazer. (University of Florida Monographs: Humanities – No. 27.) Gainesville, Fla.: Florida U.P. pp. 63.

Eberhard Brüning's *Das Amerikanische Drama der Dreissiger Jahre*[156] is an account of the theatre of the thirties. Brüning deals with the theatre on Broadway, the thirties scene, the socially conscious drama of the thirties, Hollywood and its influence and, finally, the effect of the radical movement, the development of anti-fascist drama, and the influence of the Spanish Civil War. Although this production from East Germany is, as might be expected, slanted in its approach, the study is a thorough one.

In his study of Arthur Miller,[157] in the Twayne's United States Authors Series, Leonard Moss concentrates his attention on Miller's technical resources—his dialogue, his symbolism, and what Moss calls his 'structural principles', concluding that Miller has often been led into enlarging the 'interior psychological question' with 'codes of social and ethical importance'. These somewhat barbarous phrases are, surprisingly, Miller's own. Moss believes that Miller's moral insight focuses most clearly upon psychological processes, that his characters defend egocentric attitudes and 'their futility evokes a genuine sense of terror and pathos'. All in all, Moss seems to approve, albeit with some reservations. Edward Murray's study of Arthur Miller[158] is an extremely helpful analysis of seven plays; *All My Sons, Death of a Salesman, The Crucible, A Memory of Two Mondays, A View from the Bridge, After the Fall* and *Incident at Vichy*. The book is more useful than most of those by other critics, who have tended to treat Miller's 'ideas' as things separate from his expression of those ideas. In emphasizing that the creative writer does not work in this way, Murray has done a great service to criticism. He does not even mention Marilyn Monroe and forbears to discuss once more the hackneyed question of whether *Death of a Salesman* is a 'true' tragedy.

[156] *Das Amerikanische Drama der Dreissiger Jahre*, by Eberhard Brüning. (Neue Beiträge zur Literaturwissenschaft, No. 23.) Berlin: Rutten & Loening. 1966. pp. 405. DM.19.80.

[157] *Arthur Miller*, by Leonard Moss. (Twayne's United States Authors Series, No. 115.) New York: Twayne. pp. 160. $3.95.

[158] *Arthur Miller, Dramatist*, by Edward Murray. New York: Frederick Ungar. pp. ix+186. $1.95.

ARTICLES

Articles are noticed by R. W. Willett.

1. GENERAL

John R. Milton begins his 'The American West: A Challenge to the Literary Imagination' (*WAL*) by describing how the earliest American writers responded to the Western landscape and how the expression of that response was inhibited by the influence of English Romantic terminology. But he soon turns to the dilemma of the contemporary Western author, beset by legends, myths and stereotypes. Surveying Guthrie's realism, Clark's symbolism, Water's mysticism and Fisher's rationalism, Milton suggests that for novelists understatement may be 'the only solution in the West'. Irving Howe is also interested in the literary reaction to landscape in 'Anarchy and Authority in American Literature' (*UDQ*). He notes how the wish to burst the limits of the human condition gives rise to images of space and possibility. The political counterpart to these images, especially in nineteenth-century American literature, is 'a vision of a human community . . . beyond the constraints of authority'. However 'anarchic yearning' in the modern world can only produce a 'ferocious impasse'. On the other hand, C. W. Bush's 'This Stupendous Fabric: the Metaphysics of Order in Melville's *Pierre*, and Nathanael West's *Miss Lonelyhearts*' (*J Am S*) deals with visualization in America as a more personal process, an attempt 'to order all experience in terms of the work of art', to join reality and ideality. But the novels chosen are satires on such attempts; 'dreams of ideality end only in nightmare and disorder'.

J. J. Boies seems to want to exorcize 'The Calvinist Obsession in American Letters' (*JGE*). From the twenties onwards, he complains, the Puritan has been a scapegoat for liberal and Marxist critics who have assumed that Puritanism, like Federalism, was 'anti-creative, antihumanistic'. Boies takes issue with the different 'Calvinist obsessions' of Thompson, the Melville scholar, and Perry Miller.

'Literary Revivalism in America: Some Notes towards a Hypothesis' (*AQ*) by Michael Zimmerman maintains that American writing 'vibrates between highbrow and lowbrow experience'. It follows that the finest writers have often been neglected because of the persistence of middlebrow criticism. The main substance of the article is devoted to tracing the fluctuating reputations of Melville, Dickinson, James and Faulkner.

2.COLONIAL

Edward Taylor's poetry continues to attract scholarly attention, particularly in *AL* which has published Robert M. Benton's 'Edward Taylor's Use of His Text', Allen Richard Penner's study of 'Edward Taylor's Meditation One' and Michael J. Colacurcio's '*God's Determination*: *Touching Half-Way Memberships*: Occasion and Audience in Edward Taylor'. Benton claims that the Preparatory Meditations reveal 'a direct dependence on the text and its context for their images, unity and motivation' and relates his method of composition to the tradition of meditating on the scriptures. Analyses of Meditations 47 and 43 are used to support his argument. Penner believes that in Meditation One, Taylor wanted to demonstrate the relationship between God, Christ and The Elect. The poem, like the other Preparatory Meditations, is 'an acknowledgement of man's spiritual inadequacy and his utter dependence upon the Grace of God'. Colacurcio puts Taylor's morality *God's Determinations* in the context of the religious issues of the 1680s, notably the unsuccessful efforts of New England's congregational churches to replenish themselves with 'saints'. He believes the work to be directed at 'half-way members', thus the theme is the 'desirability of a more complete and active participation than that provided for by the Half-Way Covenant of 1662'.

'Edward Taylor's Poetry' (*NEQ*) by Evan Prosser is notable for its attention to Taylor's imagery. In particular, Prosser focuses on the figurative use of gardens, homely containers (to suggest being enclosed by God) and conduits.

The other major Puritan poet of the period is scrutinized by Robert D. Richardson Jr. in 'The Puritan Poetry of Anne Bradstreet' (*TSLL*). The pattern of theological acceptance and rejection in Miss Bradstreet's poetry is once again demonstrated;

more valuable is the detailed discussion of 'Contemplations'.

J. A. Leo LeMay does not allow his title 'Franklin and the Autobiography: An Essay on Recent Scholarship' (*ECS*) to restrict the subject matter on which he is prepared to comment. Indeed, the most important part of his article is his detailed remarks on the Yale U.P. editing of Franklin's papers.

Two works of self-revelation less well-known to students of American literature engage Earl N. Harbert in 'John Adams' Private Voice: The *Diary* and *Autobiography*' (*TSE*). Harbert claims that whereas Adams manipulated his public offerings to suit popular taste, his private literature reveals 'human doubts and uncertainties'. These are prominent in the *Diary*, the major themes of which are ambition and failure.

The study of the eighteenth-century novel is usually confined to the writings of Brown and Brackenridge, while it is rare to find any dramatist but Tyler stimulating critical activity. Arthur G. Kimball, in 'Savages and Savagism: Brockden Brown's Dramatic Irony' (*SIR*) shows how the Philadelphia novelist uses Indian 'savagery' in *Edgar Huntly* to expose the savage potential of the white man. Brown's novels are ironic studies in violence which undermine Enlightenment optimism. The 'Satiric Elements in Brackenridge's *Modern Chivalry*' (*TSLL*) are principally irony and burlesque, in the opinion of William L. Nance. Both verbal irony and an authorial irony of manner are employed, and although the irony is 'often crude and irregular' it heightens the burlesque and provides a unity of tone to counter the book's structural disunity. Marius B. Péladeau in 'Royall Tyler's *Other* Plays' (*NEQ*) can offer nothing to compare in quality with *The Contrast*, though he does regard the blank verse of Tyler's sacred dramas as being occasionally lyrical and distinguished.

An examination of *Letters from an American Farmer* and *Journey into Northern Pennsylvania and the State of New York* has been undertaken by Elayne Antler Rapping; the result is entitled 'Theory and Experience in Crèvecoeur's America' (*AQ*). 'Theory' is the eighteenth-century belief that man could govern himself and his environment by rational action based on the laws of nature; 'experience' reveals the savagery and irrationality that make the ideal of an agrarian civilization unrealizable. In both books it is the Indian who emerges as the 'more truly civilized man'.

3. EARLY NINETEENTH CENTURY

E. Arthur Robinson wants to demonstrate 'that *The Pioneers* is structured with considerable unity about the manner in which man regards his natural environment'. In 'Conservation in Cooper's *The Pioneers*' (*PMLA*), he groups the characters of the novel according to their responses to this frontier problem.

The most original piece of work on Emerson's prose writings is 'The Architectonics of Emerson's *Nature*' (*AQ*). Because of its sense of exultation and its cantata-like construction, R. Lee Francis defines this seminal nineteenth-century work as baroque. Above all, *Nature* is baroque for its combination of the scientific and the imaginative; the pattern achieved is of simple substantive definitions giving way to 'highly poetic assertions'. John M. Reilly looks at Emerson's use of poetic convention in '"Threnody" and the Traditional Funeral Elegy' (*ESQ*). Reilly's idea is that Emerson presents the deceased boy traditionally as a demi-god, close to the 'divine and transcendent', in order to express appropriately his feelings of loss. Hugh H. Witemeyer is more interested in meaning than genre; in '"Line" and "Round" in Emerson's "Uriel"' (*PMLA*) he explicates the poem in terms of a central antithesis. Emerson is criticizing the 'angelic doctrine' of 'line' (hypertrophied aesthetics, poetry and epistemology) and offering in its place, the transcendental doctrine of 'round' which imposes no arbitrary limits to 'the life's circulation, radiation and generation'. Carl F. Strauch uses Emerson's poetry to show how the New England writer oscillated between affirmation and scepticism when considering man's possible harmony with Nature. Strauch's 'Emerson and the Doctrine of Sympathy' (*SIR*) is recommended for its thorough examination of 'Woodnotes'.

Like Cooper, Washington Irving affirms in his fiction 'a stable society that places its emphasis on order, tradition, and the family values that accompany social stability'. Such a society is that of New York State, but it is threatened by the 'restlessness and desire for change' of ungainly, acquisitive Yankees. This is the thesis of Donald Ringe's 'New York and New England: Irving's Criticism of American Society' (*AL*), a thesis he supports convincingly with analyses of 'Rip Van Winkle' and 'The Legend of Sleepy Hollow'.

Nina Baym can find no instances of a 'purely intellectual mania' in Hawthorne's fiction. In 'The Head, the Heart, and the Unpardonable Sin' (*NEQ*) she insists that the focus of his novels and tales is the heart which is capable of both good and evil. His so-called intellectual sinners are not in the least cold; 'all are motivated by passion which turns them into monomaniacs'. In the opinion of Christoph Lohmann, sin is 'The Burden of the Past in Hawthorne's American Romances' (*SAQ*), a burden which Hawthorne believes is inescapable. Consequently Lohmann has to claim that the ending of *The House of the Seven Gables* is an unhappy one. More convincing is a study by Francis Joseph Battaglia 'The House of the Seven Gables: New Light on Old Problems' (*PMLA*), which points out that the Preface 'admits the possibility of escape from hereditary evils'. Battaglia concludes: 'The world of *The House of the Seven Gables* is optimistic, though Hawthorne's is a careful optimism.' Also in *PMLA*, Joseph C. Pattison contends that the 'Point of View in Hawthorne' is 'one of dream'. Hawthorne is the artist as conscious dreamer revealing 'the hidden life of the self'.

'The *Faery Land* of Hawthorne's Romances' (*ESQ*) is Spenserian, and Buford Jones's article concentrates on 'the accretion of Spenserian details' in *The Threefold Destiny, The House of the Seven Gables, Egotism: or the Bosom Serpent* and *The Blithedale Romance*. Of particular value is Jones's examination of the use Hawthorne makes of Spenser's sixth Mutability Canto (the legend of Faunus and Diana) in *The Blithedale Romance*.

In *NEQ*, Hawthorne's greatest novel is interpreted as wholly in accord with Puritanism in its approach to the problems of Hester and Dimmesdale. As his chosen title 'Public Confession and *The Scarlet Letter*' implies, Ernest W. Baughman believes the tradition of public confession, 'an essential of church discipline and civil law' is basic to the novel's structure and meaning. 'The Design of Hawthorne's "Custom-House"' (*NCF*) by Dan McCall is really about the relationship of this introductory essay to the rest of *The Scarlet Letter*. Hawthorne's own sense of alienation anticipates Hester's; in both 'The Custom-House' and *The Scarlet Letter*, an American community frustrates the impulses of creative people and intensifies their solitude.

Sheldon W. Liebman is preoccupied with structure rather than purpose in 'The Design of *The Marble Faun*' (*NEQ*). Liebman detects two motifs, those of 'The Fall' and 'transformation', both of which are ambivalent; then he notices how chapters are patterned to dramatize the ascent and descent of characters; and concludes that the novel presents life as 'absurd' and 'pathetic'.

'Melville's Use of Interpolations' (*UR*) is the starting point for Joan Joffe Hall's panoramic survey of Melville's novels: what started out as a way of writing travel books became a characteristic novel device and in the later novels anecdotes are used as parables. *Omoo* is preferred to *Typee* for its superior integration of facts, and a lengthier plea on behalf of the novel, 'The Romantic Unity of Melville's *Omoo*' (*PQ*) is made by Edwin M. Eigner. The pervasiveness of alienation is emphasized and consequently Eigner finds the ending is contrived; Melville fails to convince the reader that despair has been defeated.

Another early novel of Melville's that is infrequently analysed is the subject of James Schroeter's '*Redburn* and the Failure of Mythic Criticism' (*AL*). To stress the 'initiation into evil' theme, maintains Schroeter, is to ignore the ironic tone by means of which Melville separates himself from Redburn's absurdly naïve morality. But though Melville rejects Redburn's 'narrow gentility' he does not romanticize 'the crudities of shipboard life'.

'Ahab's Other Leg: Notes on Melville's Symbolic Method' (*ESQ*) is the attempt of Allan and Barbara Lefcowitz to chart the phases of Melville's methodology in *Moby-Dick*. In their opinion, it is not until the end of the book that the leg becomes a sign of the painful condition of 'limitation', 'dependence' and 'death'. It is the scene between Ahab and the carpenter that initiates the process of symbolic discovery. Herbert G. Eldridge's article on the same novel, '"Careful Disorder": The Structure of *Moby-Dick*' (*AL*) assumes that its shape is loosely dictated by stages in the journey from New England to the Pacific. The chapter in which the voyage begins ('Merry Christmas') is an important juncture; so too are 'The Spirit-Spout', 'The Grand Armada', 'The Pacific', and 'The Hat', which not only provide the main geographical details, but re-affirm Ahab's dedication to the quest.

R. K. Gupta considers 'Melville's Use of Non-Novelistic Conventions in *Pierre*' (*ESQ*), chiefly those of epic and the drama, while John Logan picks out 'Psychological Motifs in Melville's *Pierre*' (*Minn R*). Logan concentrates on Pierre's 'terrific need for punishment' and the process of self-destruction which begins when Pierre transfers his feelings for his mother to his sister.

In 'Herman Melville's Benito Cereno: An Anatomy' (*TSLL*) David D. Galloway describes Melville's fall as 'a chiaroscuro of insinuation and reflection on the persistent intermingling of good and evil and a paradigm of the dangers of warped consciousness'. Good and evil are mixed in the slaves, whose desire for freedom is natural; their complexity lies beyond the range of Delano's 'commonplace, provincial mind'.

Leon F. Seltzer draws profitably on modern philosophical ideas in 'Camus's Absurd and the World of Melville's *Confidence-Man*' (*PMLA*).

Since he could find no way of ascertaining what was genuine, no norms on which to base judgements, Melville, claims Seltzer, wrote a nihilistic novel, exposing the 'utter groundlessness and therefore absurdity of confidence'. Robert Penn Warren, however, finds tragedy and stoicism in 'Melville's Poems' (*SoR*) particularly in *Battle-Pieces* where Melville recognizes 'the necessity for action in the face of the difficulty of knowing truth'. Warren's exhaustive commentary includes a deft comparison of the war poetry of Whitman and Melville, and some original thoughts on *Clarel*, 'an important document of our modernity'.

The recent edition of *Billy Budd, Sailor* has certainly encouraged re-valuations of Melville's novella. Paul Brodtkorb, Jr., in his excellent 'The Definitive *Billy Budd*: "But Aren't It All Sham?"' (*PMLA*) postulates an Ur-Billy Budd that now 'co-exists with various more or less incompatible descendants'. Thus the story is not wholly unified, its narrator is inconsistent and 'each character ends up as merely *given*, never solved'. Both Charles A. Reich in *YR* and Ralph Willett in *PMLA* focus upon Captain Vere. In 'The Tragedy of Justice in *Billy Budd*', Reich describes Vere as 'a very superior man' who grows in humanity as he learns what is sacrificed by obeying the law. Willett puts Vere in a reductive context by comparing him with Nelson, the 'ideal version of the governing principle', but he regards him as an illustration of Melville's contention that man is usually a 'victim of his own ambiguities and inconsistencies, and of history'.

'Poe and the Literary Ladies' (*TSLL*) is Richard Cary's examination of Poe's infractions of his critical precepts. These usually occur, in the form of exaggerated praise, when he is reviewing work by 'contemporary sentimental poetesses'. James L. Allen, Jr. studies the operation of 'variety within uniformity' in Poe's verse. 'Stanza Pattern in the Poetry of Poe' (*TSL*) includes discussions of 'To Helen' (1831) and 'Annabel Lee' and asserts that 'the integral pattern in each unit of a poem shares a significant number of common or analogous features with the patterns of other units in the same poem'. 'From Fancy to Failure: A Study of the Narrators in the Tales of Edgar Allan Poe' (*UR*) by Marvin and Frances Mengeling discriminates between the methods of Dupin and other narrators. Dupin solves problems by a combination of reason and imagination ('analysis'), but the protagonists in the 'tales of lost love' are unsuccessful since they rely on 'fancy'. Sydney P. Moss, also in *UR*, discovers a disabling split in Poe's only completed novel. In '*Arthur Gordon Pym*, or the Fallacy of Thematic Interpretation', he argues that Poe added the 'pseudo-voyage' of the alleged Antarctic adventures to the original 'imaginary voyage', of initiation in order to satisfy Harper's and get his collection of tales published.

Lauriat Lane, Jr. has scrutinized all three accounts in order to describe 'Thoreau's Response to the Maine Woods' (*ESQ*). As one would expect, Lane finds an abundance of natural details, but he shows that Thoreau used his Maine experiences for direct social criticism by praising the superiority of life on the edge of the wilderness. The theme of *Walden* in the opinion of Melvin E. Lyon (*PMLA*), is the 'desire for redemption and the achievement of it through identification with the pond, the physical attributes of which are made to stand for moral values. Lyon believes the book is positive in tone, its main concern being to praise nature and solitude rather than criticize modern society.

Two 'Natures' are identified by Anthony Herbold in 'Nature as Concept and Technique in the Poetry of Jones Very' (*NEQ*). The first of these, a Calvinist position, looks on nature as 'finite, contingent, imperfect'; the second, formed under the influence of Emerson's *Nature*, regards it as 'infinite, self-generating, perfect'. Herbold maintains that Very was a better artist when he subordinated the nature poet in him to the Calvinist.

4. LATE NINETEENTH CENTURY

A sudden spate of articles on Henry Adams is welcome. In one of his pieces Charles Vandersee makes it clear that Adams was one of the large body of Northern intellectuals who neither knew nor intelligently considered the situation of Negroes in the U.S. Hence the title 'Henry Adams and the Invisible Negro' (*SAQ*). Elsewhere, in *AQ*, Vandersee looks at one aspect of an Adams novel in 'The Pursuit of Culture in Adams' *Democracy*'. Vandersee traces Madeleine's (and Adams's) shift from the avid pursuit of culture to criticism of the process, criticism which grew out of Adams's disgust with an uncritical worship of European culture and with a fanatical but superficial lust for education.

Michael Colacurcio, discussing the same novel affirms that Madeleine is never fully undeceived about Ratcliffe. She grants his position as an 'exponent of the whatever-*must*-be-done theory of politics', and merely denies its adequacy for *her*, so Adams fails to answer the argument for pragmatism. Elsewhere in '*Democracy* and *Esther*: Henry Adams' Flirtation with Pragmatism' (*AQ*), Colacurcio discusses Adams's other novel as a story of the problem of what William James

called the 'Will to Believe', which Esther resolves by a 'pragmatism' of her own.

Peter Shaw has interpreted Adams's *History of the United States During the Administrations of Jefferson and Madison* as an attempt 'to vindicate the Adams family by exposing the failure of an administration that had rested on a repudiation of John Adams'. 'Blood is Thicker than Irony: Henry Adams's *History*' (*NEQ*) concludes with the observation that Adams's negative portrait of Jefferson is but one in a series of justifications of Adams fathers by Adams sons.

'Stephen Crane: Some New Sketches' (*BNYPL*) is three Mexican sketches of the capital city presented by R. W. Stallman. John Fraser takes issue with the naïve liberalism of critics who regard Henry Fleming's adjustment to the war situation as ethically undesirable. In 'Crime and Forgiveness: '"The Red Badge" in Time of War' (*Criticism*), he maintains that the change in Fleming is a psychological improvement, creating in him a unified state of consciousness and removing his feelings of guilt and worthlessness.

Roy B. Meyer comments on *The Captain of the Gray-Horse Troop* (1902) and some short stories in 'Hamlin Garland and the American Indian' (*WAL*). Garland's sympathy for the Indian is satisfactorily documented, but Meyer is also aware of the writer's paternalism. Particularly damaging in Meyer's eyes is Garland's failure to create 'one memorable character' in his Indian fiction.

Frank Turaj considers Howells's social and religious views to be 'inextricably connected'. In 'The Social Gospel in Howells's Novels' (*SAQ*), he points to Howells's concern with how far 'good measures' can succeed in a society 'invidiously ordered at the base'. It is highly unlikely that Arthur Boardman would subscribe to Turaj's evaluation of *A Hazard of New Fortunes* as 'a reasonable picture of proletarian life'. Boardman's 'Social Point of View in the Novels of William Dean Howells' (*AL*) is an attack on Howells's middle class stance which 'belittles' the lower classes of society and 'romanticizes' the upper classes. The world of Howells, Boardman insists, is 'one in which the values of the highest social level are dominant'. Patricia Kane tries to link Howells with James in 'Mutual Perspective: James and Howells as Critics of Each Other's Fiction' (*Minn R*), but, despite the wealth of detail, reaches no definite conclusions.

'Henry James and the Morality of Fiction' (*AL*) is Robert J. Reilly's thoughtful meditation on the 'moral character' of James's work. The typical Jamesian character has no fixed moral code, concludes Reilly, and he is graded according to the refinement of his consciousness.

James W. Gargano analyses *The Awkward Age* in terms of Mr. Longdon's plan to 'save Vanderbank from Mrs. Brook and a corrupt society by means of marriage with Nanda', hence his title is 'The Theme of Salvation in *The Awkward Age*' (*TSLL*). Gargano focuses on Vanderbank's confusion and lack of self-knowledge: '. . . in jealously preserving the purity of his freedom, he ultimately loses identity and integrity'. Confusion is also a central occupation in John L. Kimmey's article, '*The Princess Casamassima* and the Quality of Bewilderment' (*NCF*). Hyacinth's bewilderment results from the 'pattern of contradictions' that are at the heart of his character, claims Kimmey. These contradictions are reflected in the structure of the novel, 'a system of

ironies and paradoxes' based on the dualism of opposing social classes.

In 'Point of View in *The Spoils of Poynton*' (*NCF*) Philip L. Greene believes that the implied author is totally committed to the reliability of Fleda Vetch and that the theme of the novel is the 'heroics of concealment'. He concludes that Fleda's love for Owen becomes a flaw because she has to assure herself that her love is 'cleansed of moral imperfection'. Caroline G. Mercer chooses to apply Constance Rourke's definition of 'Yankee' humour to clarify the character of 'Adam Verver, Yankee Businessman' (*NCF*). Mercer maintains that Verver deliberately appears simpler than he is; his speech is like the 'allusive, self-protective' talk of the inhabitants of Faulkner's Frenchman's Bend.

'Another Twist to *The Turn of the Screw*' (*MFS*) is provided by C. Knight Aldrich, M.D. who subscribes to the theory that the governess (analysable in terms of paranoid psychopathology) was hallucinating. He suggests that Mrs. Gross hates the governess and therefore encourages the belief that the 'casual relationship' between the children and the two employees was somehow 'sinister'. Courtney Johnson in 'Henry James's "The Jolly Corner": A Study in Integration' (*American Imago*) stresses the duality of imagery which reflects Brydon's psychological ambivalence. Johnson's conclusion is that the story 'exhibits a benign development': Brydon rediscovers both his conscience and his ability to love.

A neglected authoress is the subject of Paul John Eakin's article in *AL*. The discussion in 'Sarah Orne Jewett and the Meaning of Country Life' is not confined to theme and meaning. Eakin notes that Jewett never mastered the art of character development and that her fiction

tends to become false and sentimental. His main point is that the
aristocratic Jewett dedicated her art
to 'the conservation of traditional
community values'.

In 'Olivia Clemens's "Editing"
Reviewed' (*AL*), Sydney J. Krause is
supplementing Paul Carter Jr.'s
article on Mrs. Clemens's editing of
Following the Equator by examining
the manuscript of the British edition
(*More Tramps Abroad*) in the New
York Public Library. His findings are
most important: Mrs. Clemens was
more worried about accuracy of
detail than impropriety; her 'blue
pencil' alterations were innocuous.

M. J. Sidnell contends that it is
wrong to accuse Twain of 'a lapse of
moral vision' at the end of *The
Adventures of Huckleberry Finn*; on
the contrary, he asserts in 'Huck Finn
and Jim; Their Abortive Freedom
Ride' (*CQ*), the irony of the ending is
true to American reality. 'Huck is
finally dominated by an illiberal
imagination, by a genteel tradition
and by the stereotype of the nigger'.

Irony and disenchantment are also
present in the work analysed by
Clyde L. Grimm in '*The American
Claimant*: Reclamation of a Farce'
(*AQ*). Grimm considers the story
important; in the form of 'meaningful satire' it reiterates political and
social themes which recur elsewhere
in Twain's writings.

Ernest Sandeen is interested in a
batch of about twenty poems by
America's greatest woman poet. The
mood of these 'late summer' poems
(that is the common metaphor) is, for
Sandeen, one of 'religious drive and
prophetic mystery'. The pleasures of
summer are reviewed before they are
lost 'n the 'non-being of winter'.
Sandeen concludes 'Delight Deferred
by Retrospect: Emily Dickinson's
Late-Summer Poems' (*NEQ*) by
pointing to the poems' two-part

process: intuitive response followed
by analytic scrutiny. 'My Life had
stood—a Loaded Gun' is explicated
in Cody's 'Emily Dickinson's Vesu-
vian Fire' (*American Imago*). Among
themes Cody discovers are the fusion
of sexuality and destructiveness, and
the poet's acceptance of the masculine
components of her personality. The
poem is a sadistic fantasy, according
to Cody, a vehicle for releasing pent-
up hostile feelings.

The Whitman scholar need not
range beyond the covers of *WWR*
for this year's articles. J. R. Le
Master's 'Some Traditional Poems
from *Leaves of Grass*' is mainly
devoted to comments on 'Ethiopia
Saluting the Colors'. The traditional
prosody of the song from 'The Singer
in the Prison' is also mentioned.
Quite different in approach is Ray
Benoit's 'The Mind's Return: Whitman, Teilhard, and Jung' which
suggests that de Chardin's geo-
biology and Jung's psychology clarify
Whitman's future vision of Democracy as Spiritualized Matter. Benoit
uses 'Passage to India' to show
similarities of thought between Whitman and de Chardin. T. J. Kallsen
seeks to explain 'The Improbabilities
in Section 11 of "Song of Myself".'
Although he gives a meaning to the
woman in this section by making her
the 'agent of spiritual completion',
he does not resolve all the difficulties.
'The Function of Whitman's Imagery
in "Song of Myself" (1855)' is
reconciling the paradoxical nature of
the poem. This is the view of Griffith
Dudding who discriminates between
sensory and metaphysical levels of
imagery. The former attempts 'to
evoke in them [the audience] the
enthusiasm which the American scene
had awakened in him'; the latter is
intended to carry the reader from the
world of sensory perception to the
world of thought.

5. TWENTIETH CENTURY

Lewis A. Lawson in *TQ*, traces the growth of a sense of personal and regional defeat in Southern writing. He also perceives in 'Portrait of a Culture in Crisis: Modern Southern Literature' a new willingness to depict the Negro as a man rather than as an abstraction. Negro literature is the chosen subject of Nathan A. Scott, Jr., in 'Judgment Marked by a Cellar: the American Negro Writer and the Dialectic of Despair' (*Denver*). Scott insists that Negro literature is inseparably part of American culture: it is 'as devious and duplicitous and just as riddled with ambiguity' as white American literature.

Two other articles offer responses to contemporary poetry and prose. In 'The Emotive Imagination: A New Departure in American Poetry' (*So R*), Ronald Moran and George Lensing discuss the poetry of Stafford, Wright, Simpson and Bly, 'a displaced generation alienated in a land they love immensely'. Their poems lead the reader to 'understanding through feeling', using the techniques of 'timing, leaps and muted shock'. This 'new romanticism' is described by Moran and Lensing as tough and matter-of-fact, but also compassionate. Richard Kostelanitz inveighs against the failure of most contemporary fiction writers to create works as significant as Cage's 'Variations V' and Rauschenberg's 'Oracle', or to achieve the insights into contemporary life produced by Kahn, McLuhan and Brown. However, '"New American Fiction" Reconsidered' (*Tri-Q*) does praise Mathews's *Tlooth* and Faust's *The Steagle*.

George D. Murphy has observed a 'hesitant, almost puritanical attitude towards physical sexuality' in Sherwood Anderson's best known work.

'The Theme of Sublimation in Anderson's *Winesburg, Ohio*' (*MFS*) suggests Anderson's attitude was more Platonic than Freudian: any sexual feelings not sublimated into 'a diffuse, transcendental mode of expression' were, in Murphy's opinion, repulsive to him.

American literary themes such as the loss of innocence and rugged individualism are extracted from Anderson's writings by Rosemary M. Laughlin in '"Godliness" and the American Dream in *Winesburg, Ohio*' (*TCL*). The symbolism in the story 'Godliness' is 'a weird and bizarre hodge-podge', but at least the tale lends the rest of *Winesburg, Ohio* an historical and sociological reality.

Tony Tanner has reviewed John Barth's *Giles Goat-Boy* at some length in *PR*. He relates Giles to earlier Barth heroes and decides that the novel is more about Barth's own mental processes than anything else. At the end of 'The Hoax that Joke Bilked', Tanner refers approvingly to the novel's farcical anarchic tone and its 'atmosphere of brilliant frivolity'.

'The Novels of Saul Bellow' (*So R*) express for Irvin Stock a vision of human life that is 'on the side of joy'. Bellow's work is 'one passionate retaliation against all those forces in our culture that inhibit or pervert our power to feel'. Stanley Trachtenberg's response is less elated; in 'Saul Bellow's *Luftmenschen*: The Compromise with Reality' (*Crit*), he describes Bellow's heroes as 'shabby, marginal' men whose activities are geared to surviving in a fluid social environment. Ironically, their 'self-effacement' is the very extinction of being they wish to avoid. Albert J. Guerard's 'Saul Bellow and the Activists: On *The Adventures of Augie March*' (*So R*) adopts a view of the novel close to Stock's interpretation of all Bellow's fiicion. Applauding

Bellow's 'rich, crowded observation of life', Guerard considers this activist belief in energy and vitality to be a response to the dull conformity of the Eisenhower era. His one reservation is that when the educated author intervenes, the narrator suddenly seems to fit neither his adventures nor his language.

Yoshinobu Hakutani's thesis in '*Sister Carrie* and the Problem of Literary Naturalism' (*TCL*) is that Dreiser was only half-heartedly a naturalist in that particular novel. Man is not entirely the victim of forces in *Sister Carrie*, argues Hakutani: instinct and reason are at war in Carrie herself, while Hurstwood is the victim of his own psychology.

However, Strother B. Purdy identifies naturalistic (and existential) elements in both *An American Tragedy* and *L'Etranger* (*CL*). Purdy contends that the novels reach the same conclusions: man is alone in an indifferent universe and crime is the invention of a wicked society.

MFS has produced a special issue of articles on Faulkner. In 'What Happens in *Absalom, Absalom!*'? Floyd C. Watkins suggests that the errors and inconsistencies in the novel are a deliberate part of Faulkner's design. The errors of the narrators are 'planted' in order to invalidate his or her opinions, and the novel demonstrates that 'the search for fact and the speculation about meaning can never arrive at the *truth*'. Frank Baldanza explains 'The Structure of *Light in August*' in terms of 'theme clusters' (or variations on themes). The most pervasive of these clusters is that of 'the outcast'; others include pursuit and flight, religious and racial dogma, and peace, the most ironic of them all. R. W. Franklin's argument in 'Narrative Management in *As I lay Dying*' is that Faulkner used the 'fictive present' in the novel in

order to make 'the point of narration' and 'the point of action' simultaneous. However, since the 'flow of the present is irreversibly sequential', Faulkner was obliged to use 'past narration' in the latter part of the novel. Franklin locates the beginning of Faulkner's failure to control the temporal structure in the sixth section. '"The Beautiful One": Caddy Campson as Heroine of *The Sound and the Fury*' is Catherine B. Baum's exaltation of Caddy as the central tragic figure of Faulkner's novel. The structure of *The Sound and the Fury* is based on the chronology of her life, which represents 'love, compassion, pity and sacrifice'. The meaning of the novel for John V. Hagopian is contained in his title: 'Nihilism in *The Sound and the Fury*'. Dilsey's version of Christianity is refuted by the structure, particularly that of the final section. Hagopian maintains that it is Mr. Campson's nihilistic values and sense of futility which finally prevail. Elizabeth M. Kerr announces that '*The Reivers*: The Golden Book of Yoknapatawpha County' is 'a suitable finale' to the saga, recalling other works, supplying needed information, and describing the changes that result from the coming of the automobile. Kerr stresses the parallels with chivalric romance and frequently compares the novel with *Go Down, Moses*. A general approach to Faulkner is tried by Eric Larsen, but he does use *Absalom, Absalom!* to demonstrate his argument in 'The Barrier of Language; the Irony of Language in Faulkner'. His main point is that, for Faulkner, words are 'inadequate for the expression of truth'; they are insufficient 'in the face of intense experience'. Thus, Faulkner places a burden on the reader who has to create 'experiental' truth out of the faulty medium of language. In another general article David M. Miller defines 'Faulkner's Women' as 'earthmothers or ghosts' whose characters are formed by their fertility or lack of it.

Elsewhere, *Soldiers' Pay* has been re-examined in two articles. Addison C. Bross in '*Soldiers' Pay* and the Art of Aubrey Beardsley' (*AQ*) brings evidence to show that Faulkner's characters share 'personalities, physiognomies, dress and gestures' with the creatures in Beardsley's drawings. John T. Frederick uses the title 'Anticipation and Achievement in Faulkner's *Soldiers' Pay*' (*Ar Q*) since he considers that the novel anticipates important elements in later work. For Frederick, the special achievement of *Soldiers' Pay* is the 'unique characterizations of Gilligan and Mrs. Powers'. Glenn Sandstrom's 'Identity Diffusion: Joe Christmas and Quentin Compson' (*AQ*) is an examination of two Faulknerian characters in relation to Erik Erikson's theories as expressed in 'The Problem of Ego Identity'. Sandstrom's conclusion is that their inability to achieve stable, intimate relationships with others is central to the tragedies of Christmas and Compson.

In 'F. Scott Fitzgerald's Types and Narrators' (*RLV*), William V. Nestrick concentrates on *The Great Gatsby* and *Tender is the Night*, novels which 'both deal with the problem of plucking the essential from the mass of individual idiosyncrasies'. In *Gatsby* Fitzgerald manipulates the narrator's sympathy to turn the individual Gatsby into the type of 'American imagination in quest of the ideal'. In the other novel 'the narrator's combination of critical sense and intense feeling helps define the "typical" experience in the novel: grotesquerie'. Peter Lisca sees Nick Carraway as a paradigm of order and

decorum contrasted to the disorder embodied in those around him. Consequently, as Lisca suggests in 'Nick Carraway and the Imagery of Disorder' (*TCL*), Nick's sensibility obliges him to describe characters and actions in terms of 'instability, dislocation and metamorphosis'. Richard Foster in *Minn R* is concerned with the power of Fitzgerald's imagination which was inclined to be at odds with 'method' and 'form'. However, 'in his formally most perfect works', states Foster, 'his "romantic" sensibility was neither overwhelmed nor falsified'. He concludes 'Fitzgerald's Imagination: A Parable for Criticism' by praising the 'extraordinary integrity' of Fitzgerald's 'artistic enterprise'.

In Part I of '*A Farewell to Arms*: Hemingway's Liebestod' (*UR*), Richard B. Hovey emphasizes Frederick Henry's 'self-absorption' and describes Catherine as a narcissistic fantasy: the perceptive Part II contains the observation that Hemingway's liveliest chapters are about death and war. Hovey finds Hemingway's concept of love inadequate for the author 'sees in sexual love only brief joys', and links love too insistently with sadism and the deathwish. Carlos Baker uses the information that the dying writer in *The Snows of Kilimanjaro* was originally named Henry Walden. The Purpose of 'The Slopes of Kilimanjaro: A Biographical Perspective' (*Novel*) is to tell the reader that just as Harry, the writer in the story, lamented his failure to set down his experience of life, so Hemingway feared he would die without fulfilling his talents and, in Thoreau's words, without managing to 'front only the essential facts of life'.

'Malamud's Novels: Four Versions of Pastoral' (*Crit*) looks at Malamud's work up to *The Fixer*, a novel both tragic and affirmative which insists on 'the cyclicality of life, the necessity for endurance and hope, and the value of suffering as well as its needlessness'. For James M. Mellard, the pastoral elements are to be found in Malamud's simplification of the complex and his use of seasonal rhythms and vegetation myths.

A special number of *WSCL* is devoted to Nabokov. Of the two bibliographies one lists the writings of Nabokov; the other is a checklist of criticism by Jackson R. Bryer and Thomas J. Bergin, Jr. The issue contains studies of *Pale Fire, Lolita, Blind Sinister, Despair* and, in an article on 'Nabokov's Treatment of the Artist', *The Eye*. Especially worthy of note is a study of his plays by Simon Karlinsky ('Illusion, Reality and Parody in Nabokov's Plays') which relates Nabokov's dramatic writings to the Russian tradition of Gogol and Chekhov and to his own novels.

In 'Robert Penn Warren: *All the King's Men*' (*So R*), Arthur Mizener articulates the problem with which Warren is occupied in that novel, the conflict between 'the conception of life that gives action meaning and value and the act of living in the world in which meaning and value have to be realized'.

'Thomas Wolfe, Max Perkins and Politics' (*MFS*) is Francis E. Skipp's scrutiny of Wolfe's claim that his achievement was limited by Perkins's political conservatism. Skipp's findings are that Wolfe exaggerated Perkins's conservatism. Moreover, Wolfe himself was no militant liberal, so there was 'no really wide divergence' between their 'basic social views'.

'Hart Crane's "Reflexes"' (*TCL*) are 'two essential motions of mind' in the early poems. Maurice Kramer considers Crane's basic reflex to be the 'change from suffering alienation to transcendent wholeness'; among the lesser reflexes is the alternation between hope and despair. Joseph J. Arpad's theory is that Crane's definition of the poet's way of acquiring knowledge came to resemble 'Plato's philosophic method of perceiving universal Forms or Ideas'. So, in 'Hart Crane's Platonic Myth: The Brooklyn Bridge' (*AL*), he claims that *The Bridge* is an attempt to expose the metaphysical form or idea of Brooklyn Bridge's physical form.

Marylyn Gaull observes that e. e. cummings shares with semanticists such as Sapir and Hayakawa the assumption that symbols are only of value if they can be translated into actual experience. Her article 'Language and Identity: A study of e. e. cumming's *The Enormous Room*' (*AQ*) points to cummings's concentration on the violation of liberty and religion that occurs when they are 'institutionalized within an outmoded symbolic structure'.

Reginald L. Cook assembles three artistic processes that justify his title 'Frost the Diversionist' (*NEQ*); these are (i) 'imaginative play' with variations inside the metre, (ii) diversion through humour and wit, and (iii) the 'diversionary art' of paradoxes and ambiguities. Cook analyses 'Neither Out Far Nor In Deep' in which Frost's 'deceptive simplicity' is a diversion.

'Death by Water: The Winslow Elegies of Robert Lowell' (*ELH*) by Marjorie Perloff compares 'In Memory of Arthur Winslow' and 'The Quaker Graveyard in Nantucket' with such later elegies as 'My Last Afternoon with Uncle Devereux Winslow' and 'Soft Wood'. Perloff perceives how the disdainful bitterness of the earlier poems is replaced by a humble, meditative tone, 'a new delicate balance between sympathy and judgment'. John Simon takes Lowell to task for his clumsy and distorted versions of such poems as Baudelaire's 'Receuillement' and Leopardi's 'L'infinito'. He concludes 'Abuse of Privilege: Lowell as Translator' (*HR*) with an attack on Lowell's *Prometheus Bound*. Simon considers the play inconsistent, and dislikes its dense, 'clotted' prose.

A more favourable report on an American translator appears in *TQ* which publishes a symposium 'Make It New; Translation and Metrical Innovation, Aspects of Ezra Pound's Work'. More than once the point is made that the value of Pound's translations lies not in his accuracy but in his choice of language which brings the original to life. In 'Allusion as Irony: Pound's Use of Dante in "Hugh Selwyn Mauberley"' (*Minn R*) Karl Malkoff's contention is that it is possible to read the poem as a parody of Dante's *Commedia*; the greatness of Dante, who discovered order in the universe, contrasts with the futility of Mauberley, who is out of touch with reality. *Mauberley* and the *Commedia* are for Malkoff 'personal, poetic and moral journeys that move in diametrically opposed directions'.

'The Meaning of Tilbury Town: Robinson as a Regional Poet' (*NEQ*) is Paul Zietlow's study of the values and fate of Robinson's characters. 'Tilbury Town itself is socially and spiritually ruined and decayed', but its inhabitants do not know where to look for 'valid alternatives'. Zietlow believes that Robinson discovers examples of the real and enduring in myths, and that he values the city since it allows men to become themselves.

Barton L. St. Armand's notion in 'The Power of Sympathy in the Poetry of Robinson and Frost: The "Inside" vs. the "Outside" Narrative' (*AQ*) is that whereas we can only gain knowledge of Frost's characters through their actions, the sympathetic Robinson gets inside his subjects. St. Armand anatomizes Robinson's 'Captain Craig' to support his argument. 'The *Gestalt* Configurations of Wallace Stevens' (*MLQ*) are the result of his intensive perception of a 'togetherness' of elements and forms; the part is experienced with a larger entity or, in other words, is 'whole-determined'. This is the thesis of Steven Foster who analyses 'Sea Surface Full of Clouds', 'Anecdote of the Jar', 'Domination of Black' and 'The Bouquet' ('the most perfect' of Stevens's 'still-lifes') in terms of *Gestalt* beliefs.

Frank Lentricchia Jr. is interested in the 'unresolved dialectic' discernible in Stevens's poems. He maintains in 'Wallace Stevens: The Ironic Eye' (*YR*) that Stevens wavers between subjectivism and naturalism, between mind and matter. Unlike Whitman, Stevens was unable to synthesize opposed values, and in *Notes Towards a Supreme Fiction* the resolutions offered are ironic, even desperate. Michael Zimmerman, in 'The Pursuit of Pleasure and the Uses of Death: Wallace Stevens's "Sunday Morning"' (*UR*) takes the real subject of Stevens's poem to be the 'problematic nature of pleasure'. After the woman in 'Sunday Morning' represses her instinct for pleasure 'death begins to dominate her existence'. Drawing on Norman O. Brown, Zimmerman speculates that because she will not affirm or celebrate death, her unconscious death instinct becomes a force that denies life, 'a principle of restless negativity'.

1902–14 and 1950–63 are periods of William Carlos Williams's career discussed by James E. Breslin and Linda Wagner respectively. Breslin's theory in 'Whitman and the Early Development of William Carlos Williams' (*PMLA*) is that through a new reading of *Leaves of Grass* in 1913, Williams was able to release the creative energies repressed by society and his family. Breslin affirms that the central theme of his poetry after 1913 became the power of the self to 'generate new growth'. Linda Wagner's 'A Bunch of Marigolds' (*KR*) acknowledges the 'technical accomplishment' of Williams's later poems and their tone of 'surety' and 'contentment'. She denies that Williams's more pronounced interest in culture and art during this period meant he was abandoning 'the local'.

Alan Holder's 'In the American Grain: William Carlos Williams on the American Past' (*AQ*) identifies a number of central concerns: concentration on the *tragic* element in human endeavour; selection of certain heroes as models; anti-Puritanism; and the celebration of the Indian whom Williams associates with the earth. Holder observes that for Williams, history is a matter of individuals, men influenced by the place in which they found themselves.

'Muckraking and the American Stage: The Emergence of Realism, 1905–1917' (*SAQ*) by Maxwell Bloomfield shows how the middle-class moralism of the muckrakers, who were 'less concerned with the passage of new laws than with the just administration of all law', was paralleled in the drama of the period. The plays were optimistic in tone; no problem was too serious or complex to admit of a remedy. Gerald Weales informs his readers that the thirties was also a decade of 'positive curtains', but his principal intention in 'Popular Theatre of the Thirties' (*TDR*) is to dispel the myth that the period 1924–41 was the great age of

radical theatre in America. In a series of shrewd commentaries, Weales discloses the ways in which 'Depression material' was softened and audiences reassured. David Madden's 'Happenings-Off-Off-Broadway' (*Shenandoah*) betrays his apprehensiveness as he surveys the new theatrical freedom. Madden laments the enslavement of the playwright, the dehumanization of the actor and the 'corporate narcissism' he observes off-off-Broadway. But he does place the phenomenon in its general artistic context.

'The Language of Movement in Albee's "The Death of Bessie Smith"' (*TCL*) is accompanied by imagery of inertia which, contends Paul Hetherington, creates 'an atmosphere of stasis and misdirected action'. All the characters are just '*going* to do something', but either escape into the past or turn to directing the affairs of others.

Stephen Fender in *JAm S* questions the belief that Arthur Miller's Puritans have a consistent moral outlook. 'Precision and Pseudo-Precision in *The Crucible*' exposes their language as 'the speech of a society totally without moral referents'; Proctor's achievement is to give Salem a 'viable language' and thus restore 'normal human values'.

In 'The Bitter Harvest of O'Neill's Projected Cycle' (*NEQ*), John J. Fitzgerald has assembled the relevant information about O'Neill's group of plays *A Tale of Possessors Self-Possessed*. Robert C. Lee charts O'Neill's changing attitude to the past in 'Eugene O'Neill's Remembrance: The Past is the Present' (*Ar Q*). Having attempted to 'subdue the past' in earlier plays, O'Neill, in the final non-cycle works, can 'deal more directly with that unsettled past'.

Index I. Authors

Index II. Authors and Subjects Treated